Karen Armstrong is one of the world's leading commentators on religious affairs. She spent seven years as a Roman Catholic nun, but left her teaching order in 1969 to read English at St Anne's College, Oxford. In 1982 she became a full-time writer and broadcaster.

She is the bestselling author of over a dozen books, including *A History of God*, *The Case for God*, *Twelve Steps to a Compassionate Life* and, most recently, *Fields of Blood: Religion and the History of Violence*. A passionate campaigner for religious liberty, Armstrong has addressed members of the US Congress and participated in the World Economic Forum. In 2013 she received the British Academy's inaugural Nayef Al-Rodhan Prize for improving transcultural understanding.

ALSO BY KAREN ARMSTRONG

KAREN ARMSTRONG

The Lost Art of Scripture

Rescuing the Sacred Texts

VINTAGE

1 3 5 7 9 10 8 6 4 2

Vintage
20 Vauxhall Bridge Road,
London SW1V 2SA

Vintage is part of the Penguin Random House
group of companies whose addresses can be found
at global.penguinrandomhouse.com

Cover images: Seljuk style Koran, Islamic School, 13th century
(Museum of the Holy Ma'sumeh Shrine, Qom, Iran); Chinese
Buddhist calligraphy from Mahaparinirvana-Sutra, 506,
China (© British Library Board); Bhagavad Gita engraved on a
Hindu temple (Godong/UIG); page from a Hebrew Bible by
Joseph Ha-Zarefati, 1299 (Instituto da Biblioteca Nacional,
Lisbon, Portugal). All photos © Bridgeman Images.

First published in Vintage in 2020
First published in hardback by The Bodley Head in 2019

penguin.co.uk/vintage

A CIP catalogue record for this book is available from the
British Library

ISBN 9781784705329

Printed and bound in Great Britain by Clays Ltd, Elcograf S.p.A.

Penguin Random House is committed to a sustainable future
for our business, our readers and our planet. This book is
made from Forest Stewardship Council® certified paper.

For Felicity Bryan

Shimshon went down along with his father and mother to Timna
when here, a full-maned roaring lion [coming] to meet him!
YHWH's spirit advanced upon him
and he tore it apart as one tears apart a kid,
without a thing in his hand.
But he did not tell his father and mother what he had done ...
He returned after a year ...
he turned aside to see the fallen lion,
and here: a swarm of bees in the lion's corpse, and honey!
He broke it off into his hands,
and went along, going and eating.
Then he went back to his father and mother,
and gave some to them, and they ate
But he did not tell them that it was from the lion's corpse
that he had broken off the honey.

Judges 14:5–9 (translated by Everett Fox)

To see a World in a Grain of Sand
And Heaven in a Wild Flower,
Hold Infinity in the palm of your hand
And Eternity in an hour.

William Blake, 'Auguries of Innocence' (1803)

Conclusion: If it were not for the Poetic or Prophetic Character the
Philosophic & Experimental would soon be the Ratio of
all things, and stand still, unable to do other than repeat
the same dull round over again.
Application: He who sees the Infinite in all things sees God. He who
sees the Ratio only sees himself only.
Therefore: God becomes as we are, that we may be as he is.

William Blake, *There Is No Natural Religion* (1788)

CONTENTS

A small ivory figurine in the Ulm Museum may be the earliest evidence of human religious activity. Lion Man is 40,000 years old. He has a partly human body and the head of a cave-lion; standing thirty-one centimetres tall, he gazes calmly and attentively at the viewer. Fragments of this statue, carefully stored in an inner chamber, were discovered in the Stadel Cave in southern Germany a few days before the outbreak of the Second World War. We know that groups of *Homo sapiens* hunted mammoth, reindeer, bison, wild horses and other animals in the region but they do not seem to have lived in the Stadel Cave. Like the Lascaux Caves in southern France, it may have been set aside for communal ritual where people gathered to enact the myths that gave meaning and purpose to their hard and often frightening lives: Lion Man's body is worn, as if he had been repeatedly stroked and caressed while worshippers told his story. He also shows that human beings were now able to think of something that does not exist. The person who crafted him had become fully human, since *Homo sapiens* is the only animal with the ability to envisage something that is not imme-diately apparent or has not yet come to be. Lion Man is, therefore, a product of the imagination, which Jean-Paul Sartre defined as *the ability to think of what is not.*[1] Men and women at this time lived in a reality that transcended the empirical and the factual, and throughout their history human beings would go to great lengths to do this.

The imagination has been the cause of our major achievements in science and technology as well as in art and religion. From a strictly rational perspective, Lion Man could be dismissed as a delusion. But neurologists tell us that in fact we have no direct contact with the world we inhabit. We have only perspectives that come to us through the intricate circuits of our nervous system, so that we all – scientists as well as mystics – know only representations of reality, not reality itself. We deal with the world as it appears to us, not as it intrinsically is, so some of our interpretations may be more accurate than others. This somewhat disturbing news means that the 'objective truths' on which we rely are inherently illusive.[2] The world is *there*; its energy and form exist. But our apprehension of it is only a mental projection. The world is outside our bodies, but not outside our minds. 'We *are* this little universe,' the Benedictine mystic Bede Griffiths (1906–93) explained, 'a microcosm in which the macrocosm is present as a hologram.'[3] We are surrounded by a reality that transcends – or 'goes beyond' – our conceptual grasp.

What we regard as truth, therefore, is inescapably bound up with a world that we construct for ourselves. As soon as the first humans learned to manipulate tools, they created works of art to make sense of the terror, wonder and mystery of their existence. From the very beginning, art was inextricably bound up with what we call 'religion', which is itself an art form. The Lascaux Caves, a cultic site since 17,000 BCE, are decorated with numinous paintings of local wildlife, and nearby, in the underground labyrinth of Trois Frères at Ariège, there are spectacular engravings of mammoths, bison, wolverines and musk-oxen. Dominating the scene is a massive painted figure, half man, half beast, who fixes his huge, penetrating eyes on visitors as they stumble out of the underground tunnel that provides the only route to this prehistoric temple. Like Lion Man, this hybrid creature transcends anything in our empirical experience but seems to reflect a sense of the underlying unity of animal, human and divine.

Lion Man introduces us to several themes that will be important in our discussion of scripture. He shows that from the very beginning, men and women were deliberately cultivating a perception of existence that differed from the empirical and had an instinctive appetite for a more enhanced state of being, sometimes called the Sacred. In what has been called the 'perennial philosophy', because it was present in all cultures until the modern period, it was taken for granted that the world was pervaded by and found its explanation in a reality that exceeded the reach of the intellect. This is not surprising, since, as we have seen, we are indeed surrounded by transcendence – a reality that we cannot know objectively. In the modern world, we may not cultivate this sense of the transcendent as assiduously as our forebears, but we have all known moments when we are touched deeply within, seem lifted momentarily beyond our everyday selves, and inhabit our humanity more fully than usual – in dance, music, poetry, nature, love, sex or sport as well as in what we call 'religion'.

There is no specific 'God-spot' in the human brain that yields a sense of the sacred. But in recent decades, neurologists have discovered that the right hemisphere of the brain is essential to the creation of poetry, music and religion. It is involved with the formation of our sense of self and has a broader, less focused mode of attention than the left hemisphere which is more pragmatic and selective. Above all, it sees itself as connected to the outside world, whereas the left hemisphere holds aloof from it. Specialising in language, analysis and problem-solving, the left side of our brain suppresses information that it cannot grasp conceptually. The right hemisphere, however, whose functions tended in the past to be overlooked by scientists, has a holistic rather than an analytical vision; it sees each thing in relation to the whole and perceives the interconnectedness of reality. It is, therefore, at home with metaphor, in which disparate entities become one while the left hemisphere tends to be literal and to wrest things from their context so that it can categorise and make use of them. News reaches the right hemisphere first, where it appears as part of an interlocking unity; it then passes to the left hemisphere, where it is defined, analysed and its use assessed. But the left can produce only a reductive version of complex reality, and once processed, this information is passed back to the right hemisphere, where we see it – insofar as we can – in the context of the whole.[4]

Our modern focus on the empirical and objective insights provided by the left hemisphere has unquestionably been of immense benefit to humanity. It has expanded our mental and physical horizons, dramatically enhanced our understanding of the world, has greatly reduced human suffering, and enabled more people than ever before to experience physical and emotional well-being. Hence, modern education tends increasingly to privilege the scientific endeavour and marginalise what we call the humanities. This, however, is regrettable because it means that we are in danger of cultivating only half of our mental capacities fully. Just as it would be insane to ignore the logic, analysis and rationality produced by the left hemisphere, psychologists and neurologists tell us that to function creatively and safely in the world, its activities must be integrated with those of the right.

The left brain is by nature competitive; largely ignorant of the work of the right, it tends to be overconfident. The right hemisphere, however, has a more comprehensive vision of reality, which, as we have seen, we can never grasp fully; it is more at home with embodiment and the physical than the left. The left brain is essential to our survival and enables us to investigate and master our environment, but it can offer us only an abstract representation of the complex information it receives from the right. Because the right hemisphere is less self-centred, it is more realistic than the left hemisphere. Its wide-ranging vision enables it to hold different views of reality simultaneously and, unlike the left, it does not form certainties based on abstraction. Profoundly attuned to the Other – to everything that is not ourselves – the right hemisphere is alert to relationships. It is the seat of empathy, pathos and our sense of justice. Because it can see an-other point of view, it inhibits our natural selfishness.[5]

The two sides of our brain normally work in tandem and their functions are closely intertwined, but in some periods of history, people have tended to cultivate one more than the other. Until recently, for example, neuroscientists referred to the right hemisphere as the 'minor' hemisphere, betraying our modern preference for analytic and propositional thought. But throughout history, artists, poets and mystics have carefully cultivated the insights of the right hemisphere. Long before the activities of the two sides of the brain had been fully explored, the American philosopher William James (1842– 1910) argued that our everyday rational awareness was only one kind of consciousness. There were other modes of perception, separated from it by the flimsiest of screens, where the laws governing our more mundane habits of thought seem to be suspended. James was convinced that to know ourselves fully required the nurturing of the 'peak' experiences that occur when ordinary – or, as we would say now, left-brain – consciousness was in abeyance.[6] We will see that from a very early period, certain gifted individuals have deliberately cultivated what we would now call a right-hemispheric awareness and have had apprehensions of the ineffable unity of reality. Some of these prophets, poets and seers expressed their insights in scripture; others were inspired by scripture to cultivate this awareness. But they were usually careful to integrate these right-brain intuitions with the practical imperatives of the left brain. These people were not freaks, nor were they deluded. They were exercising a natural faculty which brought them important insights that, as we shall see, are essential to humanity.

It was the right hemisphere of his brain that inspired the sculptor to create Lion Man, because its vision of the underlying unity of all things gave him intimations of the mysterious connection that somehow fused the ferocious cave-lion with vulnerable *Homo sapiens*. In hunting societies throughout human history, people have not regarded species as distinct and permanent categories: men, it is thought, can become animals, animals assume human form, and beasts are revered by shamans as emissaries of higher powers.[7] Carved from the tusk of a mammoth, the largest animal in the region, Lion Man's watching, listening gaze suggested that he was somehow akin to his human worshippers. In the Stadel Cave, the community saw two seemingly inimical species blended creatively and affectionately and revered this confluence as divine. These hunters were not worshipping a 'supernatural' deity. Rather, in Lion Man – as in the mysterious figure in the labyrinth of Trois Frères – two mundane and mortal creatures were revered as mysteriously one and as godlike.

Lion Man challenges some of our modern notions of the sacred, which is often envisaged as a distant, distinct and all-powerful Creator God. But if the transcendent were simply a remote reality 'out there' that one glimpsed only momentarily, if ever, and from afar, 'religion' would never have caught on. We shall see that nearly all the scriptures we will consider insist that men and women must also discover the divine within themselves and the world in which they live; they claim that every single person participates in the ultimate and has, therefore, unbounded potential. Over the centuries, people have talked about being 'deified', 'enlightened' or 'God-realised' – an insight derived from the holistic vision of the right hemisphere of our brain, in which the sacred and mundane interpenetrate. This does not mean, however, that what we call the Sacred or God is simply a mental experience or a 'delusion'. We will see that the prophets, mystics and seers who deliberately cultivated these experiences insisted that these were only intimations of a Reality that lay unknowably beyond. But without a careful cultivation of the holistic vision of the right brain, that transcendent insight would have been impossible.

Lion Man, therefore, also expresses a deep-seated human yearning for transformation. People did not merely seek an experience of transcendence; rather, they wanted to embody and somehow become one with it. They didn't want a distant deity but sought an enhanced humanity. This, we shall see, is a major theme of scripture: people want to 'get beyond' suffering and mortality and devise ways of achieving this. Today we are less ambitious; we want to be slimmer, healthier, younger and more attractive than we really are. We feel that a 'better self' lurks beneath our lamentably imperfect one: we want to be kinder, braver, more brilliant and charismatic. But the scriptures go further, insisting that each one of us can become a Buddha, a sage, a Christ or even a god. The American scholar Frederick Streng has this working definition of religion:

> Religion is a *means of ultimate transformation* ... An ultimate transformation is a fundamental change from being caught up in the troubles of common existence (sin, ignorance) to living in such a way that one can cope at the deepest level with these troubles. That capacity for living allows one to experience the most authentic or deepest reality – the ultimate.[8]

The myths, rituals, sacred texts and ethical practices of religion develop a plan of action 'whereby people reach beyond themselves to connect with the true and ultimate reality that will save them from the destructive forces of everyday existence'.[9] Living with what is ultimately real and true, people have found that they are not only better able to bear these destructive tensions, but that life itself acquires new depth and purpose.

But what is this 'true and ultimate reality'? We will see that the scriptures have given it various names – *rta*, Brahman, Dao, nirvana, Elohim or God – but in the modern West we have developed an inadequate and ultimately unworkable idea of the divine, which previous generations would have found naïve and immature. As a child, I learned this response to the question 'What is God?' in the Catholic catechism: 'God is the Supreme Spirit, who alone exists of himself, and is infinite in all perfections.' This is not only arid and uninspiring but fundamentally incorrect because it attempts to *define*, a word whose literal meaning is 'to set limits upon', an essentially illimitable reality. We shall see that when the left hemisphere was less cultivated than it is today, what we call 'God' was neither *a* 'spirit' nor *a* 'being'. God was, rather, Reality itself. Not only did God have no gender, but leading theologians and mystics insisted that God did not 'exist' in any way that we can understand. Before the modern period, the 'ultimate reality' came closer to what the German philosopher Martin Heidegger (1899–1976) called 'Being', a fundamental energy that supports and pervades everything that exists. You cannot see, touch or hear it, but can only watch it mysteriously at work in the people, objects and natural forces that it informs. It is essentially indefinable because it is impossible to get outside it and view it objectively.

Traditionally, the sacred was experienced as a presence that permeates the whole of reality – humans, animals, plants, stars, wind and rain. The Romantic poet William Wordsworth (1770–1850) carefully referred to it as 'something' because it was indefinable and, therefore, transcended propositional thought. He had experienced

> a sense sublime
> Of something far more deeply interfused
> Whose dwelling is the light of setting suns
> And the round ocean and the living air,
> And the blue sky and in the mind of man.[10]

He had, he says, 'learned' to acquire this insight.[11] We might say he achieved it by deliberately cultivating a right-hemispheric awareness by – for a limited time – suppressing the analytical activities of the left. When people tried to access the 'ultimate', therefore, they were not submitting to an alien, omnipotent and distant 'being' but were attempting to achieve a more authentic mode of existence. We shall see that right up to the early modern period, sages, poets and theologians insisted that what we call 'God', 'Brahman' or 'Dao' was ineffable, indescribable and unknowable – and yet was within them: a constant source of life, energy and inspiration. Religion – and scripture – were, therefore, art forms that helped them to live in relation to this transcendent reality and somehow embody it.

Lion Man was, of course, crafted long before the invention of scripture, which emerged when human beings started to live in larger and more complex societies and needed a common ethos that bound them together. The earliest civilisations were founded in the Middle East in the mid-fourth millennium BCE. Before the development of our modern industrialised economy, all states and empires were based economically on agriculture and were maintained only by ruthless exploitation. We shall see that in every agrarian society, a small aristocracy, together with its retainers, seized the surplus grown by their peasants and used it to fund their cultural projects, forcing ninety per cent of the population to live at subsistence level. No premodern civilisation ever found an alternative to this pattern. Yet, historians tell us, without this iniquitous system we would probably never have advanced beyond a primitive level, because it created a privileged class with the leisure to create the arts and sciences on which our progress depended.[12]

One of these civilised *arts* was scripture, and it depended on the civilised *science* of ritual. In the premodern world, a 'science' was a body of know-ledge that required specialised skill and training. We shall see that the care-fully crafted physical disciplines of ritual helped participants to cultivate the holistic vision of the right hemisphere, which is attuned to embodiment. Nearly all the sages, prophets and philosophers that we shall consider belonged to the elite classes, who alone had the time to engage in intensive contemplation and ritualised practice. It is true that the scriptures of Israel were initially developed and transmitted by marginal groups, but their descendants later developed regular agrarian states. Jesus and his disciples came from the peasant classes, but the texts of the New Testament were composed after his death by members of the educated Jewish elite. Yet nearly all these scriptures express a divine discontent with the inequity of their societies and insist that even the humblest human being was not only worthy of respect but potentially divine.

Scripture, therefore, began as an aristocratic art form. A 'scripture' can be defined as a text that is regarded as sacred, often – but not always – because it was divinely revealed, and forms part of an authoritative canon. Our English word 'scripture' implies a written text, but most scriptures began as texts that were composed and transmitted orally. Indeed, in some traditions, the sound of the inspired words would always be more important than their semantic meaning. Scripture was usually sung, chanted or declaimed in a way that separated it from mundane speech, so that words – a product of the brain's left hemisphere – were fused with the more indefinable emotions of the right. Music, born of the right hemisphere, does not 'mean' anything but is, rather, meaning itself. Even after a scripture became a written text, people often regarded it as inert until it was ignited by a living voice, just as a musical score comes fully alive only when interpreted by an instrument. Scripture was, therefore, essentially a performative art and until the modern period, it was nearly always acted out in the drama of ritual and belonged to the world of myth.

Today, in popular parlance, a 'myth' is something that is not true. If accused of a peccadillo in his past life, a politician may say that it is a myth – it did not happen. But traditionally, a myth expressed a timeless truth *that in some sense happened once but which also happens all the time*. It enabled people to make sense of their lives by setting their dilemmas in a timeless context. Myth has been called an early form of psychology: the tales of heroes struggling through labyrinths or fighting with monsters brought to light impulses in obscure regions of the psyche that are not easily accessible to rational investigation. Myth is essentially a programme of action: its meaning remains obscure unless it is acted out, either ritually or ethically. The mythical story can only place you in the correct spiritual or psychological attitude; you must take the next step yourself. The myths of scripture are not designed to confirm your beliefs or endorse your current way of life; rather, they are calling for a radical transformation of mind and heart. Myth could not be demonstrated by logical proof, since its insights, like those of art, depended on the right hemisphere of the brain. It was a way of envisaging the mysterious reality of the world that we cannot grasp conceptually; it came alive only when enacted in ritual, without which it could seem abstract and even alien. Myth and ritual are so intertwined that it is a matter of scholarly debate as to which came first: the mythical story or the rites attached to it.

In the Protestant West, ritual is often regarded as secondary to scripture or even dismissed as 'popish' superstition. But before the early modern period, reading scripture outside its ritualised context would have felt as unsatisfactory and unnatural as reading the libretto of an opera. Sometimes, as we shall see, ritual was regarded as far more important than scripture. Some essential teachings, such as the Christian belief that Jesus was the incarnate Son of God, are rooted in ritual practice and have little valence in scripture. Other traditions, such as Chan (or Zen) Buddhism, find scripture entirely dispensable. But ritual was rarely discarded: in the past, those reformers who rejected the ceremonial rituals of their day nearly always replaced them with new rites. The Buddha, for example, had no time for the Brahmins' elaborate Vedic sacrifices but required his monks to so ritualise their everyday physical actions that the way they walked, spoke or washed expressed the beauty and grace of nirvana. Ritual was important because it involved the body. Today neurophysicists tell us that we receive a considerable amount of information through our senses and physical gestures.[13]

Our modern society, however, is rooted in 'logos' or 'reason', which must relate precisely to factual, objective and empirical reality if it is to function efficiently in the world: logos is the mode of thought characteristic of the brain's left hemisphere. But just as both hemispheres are necessary for our full functioning, both mythos and logos are essential to human beings – and both have limitations. Myth cannot bring something entirely new into existence, as logos can. A scientist can cure hitherto incurable diseases, but this cannot prevent him from succumbing occasionally to despair when confronted with the mortality, tragedy and apparent pointlessness of our existence.[14]

The prevalence of logos in modern society and education has made scripture problematic. In the early modern West, people began to read the narratives of the Bible as though they were logoi, factual accounts of what happened. But we will see that scriptural narratives never claimed to be accurate descriptions of the creation of the world or the evolution of species. Nor did they attempt to provide historically exact biographies of the sages, prophets and patriarchs of antiquity. Precise historical writing is a recent phenomenon. It became possible only when archaeological methodology and improved knowledge of ancient languages radically enhanced our understanding of the past. Because it does not conform to modern scientific and historical norms, many people dismiss scripture as incredible and patently 'untrue' but they do not apply the same criteria to a novel, which yields profound and valuable insights by means of fiction. Nor do they dismiss the poetic genius of Milton's *Paradise Lost* because its account of the creation of Adam does not accord with the evolutionary hypothesis. A work of art, be it a novel, a poem or a scripture, must be read according to the laws of its genre and, like any artwork, scripture requires the disciplined cultivation of an appropriate mode of consciousness. We will see that when reading scripture, people would often sit, move or breathe in a way that enabled them to incorporate it physically.

*

We cannot examine every single one of the world's scriptures in this book; some scriptural canons are so huge that even the faithful do not attempt to read all the texts that they contain. But I will trace the chronological development of major scriptural canons in India and China, as well as in the monotheistic traditions of Judaism, Christianity and Islam, to throw light on the scriptural genre. These scriptures prescribe different ways of living in harmony with the transcendent, but on one thing they all agree. To live in genuine relation with what Streng called the unknowable 'ultimate', men and women must divest themselves of egotism. What the Greeks called *kenosis* (the 'emptying' of self) is a central scriptural theme. Furthermore, the scriptures all insist that the best way of achieving this transcendence of self is to cultivate habits of empathy and compassion, which are products of the right hemisphere. We hear a great deal today about the violence and hatred that scripture supposedly inspires and we will examine some of these intransigent passages. But, in different ways, the scriptures concur that you cannot confine your benevolence to your own people but must honour the stranger and even the enemy. It is hard to imagine an ethic that is more urgently needed in our perilously divided world.

Kenosis requires a transcendence of self that is extremely difficult to attain. That is why some traditions insist that you cannot read scripture by yourself. You need a teacher who trains his or her disciples to adopt a way of life that systematically 'goes beyond' the ego, dismantling our instinctive tendency to place ourselves at the centre of the world. Without such a teacher, one Chinese sage insisted, scripture remains impenetrable. But nearly all the scriptures present us with the final product – the human being who has achieved this transformation and become divine. These people have not been possessed by an alien force; rather, they have aligned their lives fully with the ultimate 'something' that pervades all things, and achieved a more authentic mode of being. The scriptures insist that this is not the attainment of a few exceptional people but is possible for anybody, even the man in the street, because you cannot think 'human' without also thinking 'divine'. In some traditions, divinity is presented as a third dimension of humanity, that mysterious element that we encounter within ourselves and in others that constantly eludes our grasp.

There are differences in emphasis, however. In some traditions, the focus is the cosmos; in others, it is society. The scriptures of India and China insisted from the very beginning that human beings must align themselves with the rhythms of nature. In India particularly, the universe was presented as chronically fragile, so it was essential to give something back to support our frail world. Again, at a time when scientists tell us that climate change is becoming irreversible, it is difficult to imagine a more relevant message. But the monotheistic traditions, which have emphasised the importance of justice and equity, also speak directly to our current predicament. Despite our modern emphasis on equality and human rights, these prophetic pronouncements are needed. As I write this, unacceptable numbers of people in Britain, one of the richest countries in the world, are sleeping in the streets during a particularly cold winter. We humans are 'wired' for transcendence, and in recent decades there has been a swing back to religion – even in the former Soviet Union and China where it was suppressed for decades. The aggressive scepticism of northern Europe is beginning to look endearingly old-fashioned. But to be authentic, this religious revival cannot simply be a private quest; it must revisit these scriptures and make them speak directly to the suffering, rage and hatred that is rife in today's world and imperils us all.

Before the early modern period, when the Renaissance humanists and Protestant reformers sought to return 'to the wellsprings' (*ad fontes*) of Christianity, scriptures were routinely revised, updated, and their message dramatically reinterpreted to meet the demands of the present. The art of scripture did not mean a return to an imagined perfection in the past, because the sacred text was always a work in progress. The art of scriptural exegesis was, therefore, inventive, imaginative and creative. So, to read the scriptures correctly and authentically, we must make them speak directly to our modern predicament. Instead, some Christian fundamentalists today aim to revive the Bronze Age legislation of the Hebrew Bible, while Muslim reformers are slavishly attempting to return to the *mores* of seventh-century Arabia.

Given our current problems, the scriptures' faith in the divine potential of all human beings seems particularly relevant. It is, perhaps, significant that Lion Man was discovered in the Stadel Cave on the eve of the Second World War, when we learned what can happen when a sense of the sacrality of every single human being has been lost.

PART ONE

Cosmos and Society

I

ISRAEL: REMEMBERING IN
ORDER TO BELONG

The Fall of Adam and Eve is one of the most famous stories of the Hebrew Bible. Yahweh, the divine creator, placed the first human beings in Eden, where there was 'every kind of tree, enticing to look at and good to eat, with the tree of life and the tree of the knowledge of good and evil in the middle of the garden'.[1] But Yahweh gave Adam a stern warning: he could eat the fruit of all these trees except the fruit of the tree of knowledge, 'for on the day you eat of it, you shall most surely die'.[2] But, alas, Eve succumbed to the temptation of the serpent and she and Adam were condemned to a life of hard labour and suffering that could end only in death.

This story is so deeply embedded in the Judaeo-Christian consciousness that it is, perhaps, surprising to learn that in fact it is steeped in the Mesopotamian Wisdom traditions that embodied the ethical ideals that bound the ruling aristocracy together.[3] Civilisation began in Sumer in what is now Iraq in about 3500 BCE. The Sumerians were the first to commandeer the agricultural surplus grown by the community in the fertile plain that lay between the rivers Tigris and Euphrates and create a privileged ruling class. By about 3000 BCE, there were twelve cities in the Mesopotamian plain, each supported by produce grown by peasants in the surrounding countryside. The Sumerian aristocrats and their retainers – bureaucrats, soldiers, scribes, merchants and household servants – appropriated between half and two-thirds of the crop grown by the peasants, who were reduced to serfdom.[4] They left fragmentary records of their misery: 'The poor man is better dead than alive,' one lamented.[5] Sumer had devised the system of structural inequity that would prevail in every single state until the modern period, when agriculture ceased to be the economic basis of civilisation.[6]

Adam and Eve, however, lived at the beginning of time, before the earth yielded brambles and thistles and humans had to wrest their food from the recalcitrant soil with sweat on their brow. Their life in Eden was idyllic until Eve met the serpent, who is described as *arum*, the most 'subtle', 'shrewd' and 'wise' of the animals. 'Did God really say you were not to eat from any of the trees in the garden?' the serpent asked her. Eve replied that only the tree of knowledge was prohibited on pain of instant death. The *arum* serpent's prediction of what would happen to Adam and Eve drew heavily on the terminology of Sumerian Wisdom: 'No! You will not die! God knows in fact that on the day you eat it your eyes will be opened and you will be like gods, knowing good and evil.' Of course, Eve succumbed: she wanted to transcend her humanity and become godlike. The couple did not, in fact, die as soon as they ate the forbidden fruit, as Yahweh had threatened. Instead, as the serpent promised, 'the eyes of both were opened'[7] – words that recall the exclamation of a Mesopotamian student to his teacher:

> Master-god, who [shapes] humanity, you are my god!
> You have opened my eyes as if I were a puppy;
> You have formed humanity within me![8]

For this student, 'divinity' was not 'supernatural' but an enhancement of his uncivilised and, therefore, subhuman nature. But their knowledge of good and evil made Adam and Eve ashamed of their naked, raw humanity, so 'Yahweh God made clothes of skins for the man and his wife, and they put them on'[9] – a reversal of an incident in the Mesopotamian *Epic of Gilgamesh*, when Enkidu, primal man, attains full humanity only when he dons the clothes required by civilised life.

The biblical author is drawing on these Mesopotamian motifs in a distinctive, perhaps ironic way but this narrative, placed at the very beginning of the Bible, makes it clear that scripture does not fall directly from heaven but is a human artefact, rooted in the presuppositions of a culture shared with people who are not blessed with divine revelation. This enigmatic tale also shows that scripture does not always yield clear, unequivocal teaching, but often leaves us puzzled and unmoored. In the first chapter of the Bible, God had repeatedly pronounced the whole of creation to be 'good', yet we are specifically told that the serpent, who urges Eve to disobey, is part of God's creation.[10] Did the potential for lawlessness and rebellion lie at the root of being – and is it, therefore, 'good'? And why was Yahweh economical with the truth, telling Adam that he would die on the very day he ate the forbidden fruit? The biblical author does not answer these questions and we will see that Jews and Christians would interpret this puzzling story in strikingly different ways.

This is not an isolated instance of Mesopotamian influence in Hebrew scripture. There are, for example, obvious parallels between Mesopotamian and Israelite legal and treaty traditions.[11] The epic literature of both peoples refers to a Great Flood that inundated the entire world in primordial times; and the story of Moses, whose mother hid him from Pharaoh's officials in the bulrushes, closely resembles the legend of Sargon, who, in the third millennium BCE, ruled the first agrarian empire, in what is now Iraq, Iran, Syria and Lebanon. More importantly, the preoccupation with social justice and equity, which would be essential to the monotheistic scriptures of Judaism, Christianity and Islam, was neither peculiar to Israel nor the result of a special divine revelation. Even though the agrarian economy depended upon the suppression of ninety per cent of the population, the protection of the weak and vulnerable was a common preoccupation in the ancient Near East.[12] The Sumerian kings had insisted that justice for the poor, the orphan and the widow was a sacred duty decreed by the sun god Shamash, who listened attentively to their cries for help. Later, the Code of King Hammurabi (r.1728–1686 BCE), who founded the Babylonian empire in Mesopotamia, decreed that the sun would shine over the people only if the king and his aristocracy did not oppress their subjects; in Egypt, Pharaoh must be just to his subjects because Re, the sun god, was the 'vizier of the poor'.[13] This reflected a nagging discomfort with the inherent injustice of the agrarian state and was also, perhaps, an attempt to distinguish the 'merciful' king from the officials who implemented it. There seemed to be no solution to the moral dilemma of civilisation. In the *Epic of Gilgamesh*, the common people complain of their king's cruelty, but when the gods put their case to Anu, the high god, he shakes his head sadly yet cannot change this chronically inequitable system.

Adam and Eve had violated a formal agreement with Yahweh; this too was an expression of a widespread Middle Eastern fear of breaking a sacred contract. It was the 'original sin'. The theme of a divine covenant, which would dominate the Hebrew Bible, pervaded the ancient Near East from the second half of the second millennium BCE.[14] The scribes of Egypt had also created a curriculum to enculturate elite youth in the ideology that would bind their society together and give it a distinctive ethos. Egyptians called this 'Maat', meaning 'truth, fairness, justice'. It required an individual to think of others and adhere to what is often called the Golden Rule, which demands that we treat others as we wish to be treated ourselves – though this, of course, did not apply to the peasants toiling in the fields.

But Maat did not come naturally to human beings. It had to be cultivated by what has been called 'cultural memory', which consisted of a body of recollections, stories of the past and visions for the future that created a communal consciousness. To form a cohesive society, individuals deliberately cultivated this memory, designing rituals that enabled them to keep it constantly in mind.[15] In the ancient world, ideal norms were usually traced back to the very distant past and embodied in such outstanding individuals as Gilgamesh, the ancient Sumerian king whose deeds were celebrated in the great Mesopotamian epic. This was not an exercise in nostalgia but a call to action: an ideal that had been realised once could be achieved again. The past was, therefore, a realisable 'present', a project for each generation.[16] In Mesopotamia, Phoenicia and Egypt, aristocratic youths were enculturated in an educative process that inscribed core texts, such as the *Epic of Gilgamesh*, together with proverbs, hymns, important historical treaties and tales of the beginning of time, in their minds and hearts.

Although these key texts were written down, they had first to be deeply etched into the psyche of the ruling class, who were in charge of the precarious agrarian economy. Our word 'scripture' implies a written text, and since the invention of printing, literacy has become widespread, even common, and reading a silent, solitary activity. But in the ancient world, manuscripts were often heavy, unwieldy and almost illegible; the oldest Greek manuscripts, for example, were all written in capitals with no spaces between the words.[17] In Mesopotamia, cuneiform clay tablets were often so small that they would have been extremely difficult to decipher. They were not designed to provide an initial reading, but functioned like a musical score for a performer who already knows the piece. It was taken for granted that a reader perusing the text of the *Epic of Gilgamesh* or Homer's *Iliad* already knew it by heart. A written version could only provide a permanent point of reference for the memorisation and transmission of those texts that were integral to society.[18] Students did not memorise a text from a manuscript, therefore; instead it was recited, chanted or sung to them until they could recite it verbatim.

In Mesopotamia and Egypt, the cultural tradition was preserved in the minds and hearts of the scribes who held society together and had 'libraries in their heads'. As students, they had been required to recite these key texts with impeccable accuracy so that they could convey them punctiliously to the next generation: 'You are of course a skilled scribe at the head of your fellows,' we read in an ancient Egyptian satire, 'and the teaching of every book is inscribed in your head.'[19] Scribal schools were usually small and family-based. A father would instruct his son in the Wisdom traditions but, because of the high level of mortality, he also took other pupils. The aim was not to impart facts, but rather to drill the values of the ruling class into the student's mind until he embodied the ethos that permeated society. He then became a 'civilised' human being. A Mesopotamian riddle describes the function of the scribal school:

> With closed eyes one enters it,
> With opened eyes one comes out.[20]

Students, as we have seen, regarded their teachers as 'gods', who had enabled them to gain 'humanity'. This did not imply that their education had made them compassionate and humane. Unlike the peasant masses who were regarded as an inferior species, only those students who had been fully enculturated in the Sumerian aristocratic ethos were regarded as fully human. Students were not educated to think for themselves; the survival of the precarious Sumerian civilisation demanded total and unquestioning conformity with the mores of the ruling class, which had to become second nature to each young aristocrat and scribal retainer. This so-called 'humanity' was embodied most fully in the person of the king, who was revered as the pre-eminent sage.

Writing was, therefore, associated with power and coercion. The cuneiform script was initially developed to record the taxes extorted from the peasantry. It furthered the project of political subjugation and centralisation. Writing enabled a government to communicate at a distance; it was useful in commerce, state transactions and legal affairs. But no state had either the resources or, indeed, the incentive to make the public literate. For centuries, long after the invention of writing, the oral transmission of tradition remained the norm.[21] Scribes were required to transform the unschooled student into an 'insider' in a numbing indoctrination that turned him into a docile, obedient subject.[22] Learning was usually enforced by corporal punishment and the students' minds were broken by the stultifying experience of memorising texts that imparted obsolete, boring and seemingly irrelevant information in ancient Sumerian, a language which over time became so arcane that it was well-nigh incomprehensible.[23]

But this gruelling regime did not always stunt creativity. An especially gifted scribe would sometimes be required to address current preoccupations by transforming and adapting the ancient traditions. He was even allowed to insert new material into the stories and Wisdom literature of the past. This introduces us to an important theme in the history of scripture. Today we tend to regard a scriptural canon as irrevocably closed and its texts sacrosanct, but we shall find that in all cultures, scripture was essentially a work in progress, constantly changing to meet new conditions. This was certainly the case in ancient Mesopotamia. An exceptionally advanced scribe was allowed – indeed expected – to improvise, and this enabled Mesopotamian culture to survive the demise of the original Sumerian dynasties and inform the later Akkadian and Babylonian regimes by grafting the new onto the old. The *Enuma Elish*, an ancient Sumerian creation hymn, was adapted to culminate in the founding of Babylon by Hammurabi. Later, scribes composed a version of the hymn that climaxed in Akkad, Sargon's capital. They also added material that transformed the Gilgamesh epic into an Akkadian text, while the Akkadian epic celebrating Sargon's career drew freely on ancient Sumerian tales. The scribes were not merely 'citing' earlier works, nor was this a 'cut and paste' operation. They had memorised these texts so thoroughly that they had become building blocks of their thinking process; like a jazz musician, they were improvising with material that had become integral to their very being and devising new texts that spoke directly to the present.[24]

Egypt tended to specialise in Wisdom texts that promoted Maat. Here too, the aim was to create a cohesive society by preventing the ruling class from advancing their own interests at the expense of others. Egyptian Wisdom linked success to virtuous conduct, and punishment to transgression. As in Mesopotamia, the education of the elite involved the memorisation and recitation of texts, which seem to have been set to music, and were chanted or sung. Constantly, the scribe urged his students to 'listen' to these beautifully composed maxims, to take them 'to heart' and experience them viscerally. The 'Instructions of Amenemope', which were reproduced in the Hebrew Bible, gives us the flavour of these oral teachings that insistently promoted Maat:

> Give ear to my words
>> and apply your heart to knowing them;
> For it will be a delight to keep them deep within you
>> to have them all ready on your lips.
> So that your trust may be in Yahweh,
>> today I propose to make your way known to you ...

> Because a man is poor, do not therefore cheat him,
>> nor at the city gate, oppress anybody in affliction;
> For Yahweh takes up their cause,
>> and extorts the life of their extortioners.
> Make friends with no man who gives way to anger,
>> make no hasty-tempered man a companion of yours.[25]

During the sixteenth century BCE, Bedouin tribesmen, whom the Egyptians called Hyksos ('chieftains from foreign lands'), managed to establish their own dynasty in the delta area. The Egyptians eventually expelled them but after this experience, Egypt, hitherto a relatively peaceable agrarian state, became more militant. Imperial conquest seemed the best mode of defence, so Egypt secured its frontier by subjugating Nubia in the south and coastal Canaan, which would become the land of Israel, in the north. The rulers of the city states of southern Canaan were therefore ruled by Egyptian officials who may have enculturated the Canaanite ruling class into their curriculum. But by the middle of the second millennium BCE, the Near East was dominated by foreign invaders. Kassite tribes from the Caucasus took over the Babylonian empire (c.1600–1155 BCE); an Indo-European aristocracy created the Hittite empire in Anatolia (1420 BCE); and the Mitanni, another Aryan tribe, controlled Greater Mesopotamia from about 1500 BCE until they were conquered in their turn by the Hittites from the eastern Tigris region. Finally, the Assyrians, emerging in the same region, conquered the old Mitanni territories from the Hittites and became the most formidable military and economic power in the Near East.

But then, in about 1200 BCE, the civilisations of the Near East succumbed to a Dark Age, during which the people known as Israel emerged in Canaan. We do not know exactly what happened – sudden climate change may have ruined local agrarian economies – but whatever the cause, the Canaanite ports of Ugarit and the cities of Megiddo and Hazor were destroyed, and Egypt was forced to relinquish control of the city states in the coastal plain of Canaan. After the departure of the Egyptian governors, one Canaanite city after another collapsed and desperate, displaced people roamed through the region.[26] As the city states disintegrated, there could have been conflict between the aristocrats and the peasants on whose crops the economy depended, and local aristocracies may have fought one another to fill the power gap left by the departing Egyptians.

Significantly, however, during this upheaval new settlements appeared in the Canaanite highlands. Hitherto, this barren terrain had been unsuited for farming, but recent technological advance had made settlement and water storage feasible. There is no evidence that these highland settlers were foreigners: the material culture of these villages is substantially the same as that of the coastal plain, so archaeologists have concluded that they were probably established by native Canaanites who had fled the failing cities.²⁷ One of the very few ways in which peasants could better their lot was to decamp when circumstances were insupportable and become economic fugitives.²⁸ The political chaos of the Dark Age may have enabled Canaanite peasants to make an exodus from the disintegrating cities and establish an independent society, without fear of aristocratic retaliation. As early as 1201 BCE, when the Egyptian governors of the Canaanite city states were obliged to ask for military reinforcements from Egypt, the highlands were already home to some 80,000 people and an Egyptian stele mentions 'Israel' as one of the rebellious peoples defeated by Pharaoh Mernepteh there. The biblical texts indicate that 'Israel' consisted of many local groups, who banded together for self-defence.²⁹ Those who came from the southern regions of Canaan brought their god Yahweh with them and their traditions would eventually become dominant in Israel.³⁰ But, like the Canaanite peasants who had fled the Egyptian-ruled city states on the Mediterranean coast, they felt that in a very real sense they had 'come out of Egypt'.

The Bible suggests that Israel held the agrarian city state in low esteem. After Adam and Eve were expelled from the Garden of Eden, their son Cain became the first farmer, built the first city state and was the first murderer.³¹ The Pentateuch, the first five books of the Hebrew Bible, would not be completed until the second century BCE. In its final form, however, the story of Israel begins in about 1750 BCE, when, it was said, Yahweh ordered Abraham, Israel's ancestor, to leave the city state of Ur in Mesopotamia and settle in Canaan, where he, his son Isaac and his grandson Jacob (also called 'Israel') could live free of agrarian imperialism. Yahweh promised that their descendants would one day own the land of Canaan, but Jacob and his twelve sons, founders of the twelve tribes of Israel, were forced by famine to migrate to Egypt, where they were enslaved. Finally, in about 1250 BCE, Yahweh brought them out of Egypt under the leadership of Moses. Pharaoh and his army pursued the departing Israelites and when they reached the Sea of Reeds, the waters parted miraculously and they crossed dry-shod, but all the Egyptians that were chasing them drowned. For forty years, the Israelites wandered in the wilderness and on Mount Sinai Yahweh gave them the *torah*, the law on which they must base their lives. Moses died before his people entered Canaan, but his lieutenant

Joshua led the Israelites to victory, destroying all the Canaanite cities and slaughtering their inhabitants.

The archaeological record, however, does not confirm this story. There is no evidence of the mass destruction described in the book of Joshua and no sign of a major foreign invasion.[32] But scriptural narrative does not pretend to be an accurate record of the past. The Israelites clearly saw a divine force at work in their history. In their declaration of independence, they had done something extraordinary. Peasants were usually doomed to lifelong serfdom, but Israel had defied the laws of probability and, against all odds, had not only survived but prospered. They may have concluded that this success could only be attributed to a superhuman power – *something* had marked them out for an exceptional destiny.

The Israelites personified this sacred force that had propelled their astonishing bid for freedom. They were not yet monotheists but shared many of their neighbours' traditions, regarding Yahweh as one of the 'holy ones' or 'sons' of El, the High God of Canaan, and a member of El's divine assembly. In one of the earliest texts of the Hebrew Bible, we read that at the beginning of time, El had assigned a 'holy one' to each of the seventy nations of the world and appointed Yahweh to be the 'holy one' of Israel:

> When the Most High gave the nations their inheritance
> He fixed their bounds according to the sons of El;
> But Yahweh's portion was his people,
> Jacob [i.e. Israel] his share of the inheritance.[33]

The idea of a divine council of equal gods made sense after the collapse of the Near Eastern empires, because they reflected the small kingdoms – Israel, Edom, Moab, Aram and Amman – that had emerged in their wake, all on a par and all competing for arable territory. The Hebrew term Elohim, usually translated as 'God', expressed everything that the divine could mean for human beings. The 'holy ones' of the Near East participated in and reflected the luminosity and brilliance of a power that transcended the 'gods' and could not be tied to a single, distinct form.[34] This was a right-hemispheric intuition of the numinous forces that pervaded the whole of reality: a perception of the relatedness of all things that inspired the empathic passion for justice that Israel shared with the other societies in the region. At a later point, Yahweh would merge with El, but in Psalm 82, he is still one of El's 'sons'. Here he is already beginning to rebel, because, unlike the other 'sons of El' who served richer and more powerful states, he is portrayed as the champion of the oppressed peasants, who denounces his fellow gods in the council:

> No more mockery of justice
> No more favouring of the wicked!
> Let the weak and orphan have justice,
> Be fair to the wretched and the destitute;
> Rescue the weak and needy,
> Save them from the clutches of the wicked.[35]

From the start, the religion of Israel was focused on the state of society, with a mandate of care for the weak and needy.

Hence Israel and the monotheistic traditions to which it gave birth would emphasise social justice but, unlike the Wisdom traditions of Egypt and Mesopotamia, its scriptures originally opposed the agrarian economy. The Hebrew Bible includes some early legislation that seems to have envisaged a different kind of society. Instead of being appropriated by an aristocracy, land must remain in the possession of the extended family; interest-free loans to Israelites in need were obligatory; wages should be paid promptly, contract servitude restricted, and there must be special provision for the socially vulnerable – orphans, widows and foreigners.[36]

In the highlands of Canaan, the *am Yahweh* ('the people of Yahweh') seem to have formed a confederacy, bound together in a covenant agreement. As the crisis of the Dark Age diminished, they had to compete with their neighbours for arable land, so Yahweh shared the martial qualities of other gods in the region that epitomised natural forces, such as Baal, a storm-god who was the source of rain and thus fertility; Mot, god of death, sterility and drought; and Yam-Nahar, representing the primal sea that threatened to inundate the settled lands.[37] But unlike Baal, Yahweh also intervened directly in human affairs. Some of the earliest texts in the Bible describe him leaving his sanctuary in the Sinai region and marching through southern Canaan to come to the aid of his people in the highlands:

> Yahweh came from Sinai
> For them, after Seir, he rose on the horizon,
> After Mount Paran he shone forth.
> For them he came, after the mustering at Kadosh,
> From his zenith, as far as the foothills.[38]

Such poems, recited during the festivals of the *am Yahweh*, depict perhaps Israel's early experience of being propelled forward by a providential force that was more than human as they struggled, against all odds, for independence.[39]

An ancient battle hymn describes Yahweh drowning the pursuing Egyptians in the Sea of Reeds. The enemy had given chase, intent on slaughtering their absconding slaves, but Yahweh had simply stretched out his hand and rescued his people:

> A blast from your nostrils and the waters piled high;
> The waters stood upright like a dyke,
> In the heart of the Sea the deeps came together ...
> One breath of yours you blew, and the Sea closed over them
> They sank like lead in the terrible waters.[40]

Yahweh, the hymn continues, then led Israel to safety, while the surrounding peoples, dumbstruck, had to watch them go:

> You will bring them and plant them on the
> mountain that is your own,
> the place you have made your dwelling, Yahweh,
> the sanctuary, Yahweh, prepared by your own hands.
> Yahweh will be king forever.[41]

In throwing off the imperial rule of Pharaonic Egypt and taking Yahweh as their king, the Israelites had overturned the fundamental political structures of the agrarian age. No wonder their neighbours lived in fear of Israel: the fact that hordes of runaway serfs had managed to establish an independent community in the highlands, while powerful Near Eastern empires crumbled, turned their conceptual world upside down. However, the fearful local peoples, described in the hymn as 'unmanned', 'dismayed' and 'trembling', are not Egyptians. Rather they are Israel's neighbours in Canaan, Philistia, Edom and Moab.[42]

Yet in this story of an exodus from one part of Canaan to another, we have the germ of a powerful mythos that would eventually hold the Hebrew Bible together. In these early days, however, the Exodus had not yet become Israel's national myth, so the Song of the Sea was probably performed only in those sanctuaries in the northern highlands where Moses was revered as the great hero of Israel.[43] But the *amYahweh*, a collection of disparate peoples, had to become a nation in the struggle for resources in the region so they needed a common history that bound them together. Originally, each of these unconnected peoples probably celebrated the stories of their own ancestors, who would eventually be honoured by the whole people of Israel. But this was not history as we know it. Until the invention of modern, scientific methods of dating and archaeological and linguistic research, it was impossible to record past events with the accuracy we now take for granted and there was no point in trying to do so. Instead of attempting a factual account of the past, 'history' described the meaning of an event.

The people of Yahweh, who had merged with El, celebrated momentous and formative events that had occurred in various parts of the Canaanite highlands in rituals that tied them to their new land and sacralised it. El seems to have been a sacred force that manifested itself in various forms on different occasions. Some tribes in the northern highlands honoured Jacob. It was said that at Bethel, Jacob had a numinous dream of a ladder linking earth with heaven, and when he woke, he said, 'Truly Yahweh is in this place and I never knew it! This is nothing less than "a house of God" [*beth-el*], this is the gate of Heaven.'⁴⁴ At this point El could sometimes manifest itself in human form. At Peniel beside the Ford of Jabbok, Jacob had wrestled all night with a mysterious stranger, only later realising that he had – somehow – seen 'the face of God' (*peni-el*). It was on this occasion that Jacob received the title *Isra-el* ('one who struggles with God'), which would eventually be adopted by all the tribes of northern Canaan.⁴⁵ Jacob's favourite son, Joseph, whose tomb was in Schechem, was another northern hero. But the tribes who settled in the southern highlands, near the Hittite-controlled city state of Jerusalem, revered Abraham, who had lived at Mamre and was buried in Hebron. These were not rival cults; they would, as we shall see, meld into a common history that bound the league together.

But towards the end of the eleventh century BCE, the league was unable to defend their settlements from the powerful armies of the Philistines, an Indo-European people – probably from the Aegean – who had settled in southern Canaan during the Bronze Age crisis in about 1175 BCE. There they ruled five city states – Gaza, Ashkelon, Ashdod, Ekron and Gath – and were intent on further expansion. In the face of this military threat, the Israelites reluctantly abandoned their exceptional status and established a kingdom. David – who, tradition had it, had decapitated the Philistine giant Goliath – would always be remembered as Israel's ideal king, not least for capturing the ancient city state of Jerusalem from the Hittite Jebusites, and making it the capital of a kingdom that united the northern and southern tribes in a single polity.[46] But his son Solomon is said to have created a typical empire: he had a chariot army, engaged in lucrative arms deals with neighbouring kings, and not only taxed his Israelite subjects but forced them into a corvée for his massive building programme. His most famous project was the temple he built in Jerusalem on the regional model, its rituals deeply influenced by the cult of Baal in neighbouring Ugarit.[47]

In a strange reversal, Yahweh, once the champion of uprooted, despised peasants, had become the patron of yet another oppressive agrarian state. Some scholars have argued that, because it left no archaeological trace, Solomon's empire never existed but there is now a general agreement that, by about 1000 BCE, the highland village culture was rapidly becoming a 'proto-urban' society that was more centralised, was enlarging its borders and was engaging in international trade.[48] Like other nations, Israel's new aristocracy had to develop a scribal class and an educational curriculum to initiate elite Israelite youth into its distinctive ethos. These scribes would create the first official canon of Israel but it was very different from the Hebrew Bible we have today.

We know very little about scribal schools in the kingdoms of David and Solomon, but later scribal culture in Israel – preserved in the Wisdom books of the Bible – shows a distinct similarity to other imperial systems in the region. David's entourage included the 'scribe of the king'.[49] This seems to have been a hereditary post, since his sons became Solomon's scribes.[50] Like the Sumerian and Egyptian kings, Solomon was regarded as the quintessential sage and the proverbs included in the curriculum were attributed to him:

> Give ear to my words
> And apply your heart [*leb*] to knowing them;
> For it will be a delight to keep them in your belly
> To have them all ready on your lips.
> So that your trust may be in Yahweh
> Today I propose to make your way known to you.[51]

Instruction was still oral – the student had to 'give ear' – and, as always in the ancient world, this Wisdom had to be deeply implanted in the student's *leb*, meaning both 'heart' and 'mind', by constant repetition. As an aide memoire, these maxims may have been set to music, the most physical of the arts; as they chanted and sang them, the sacred words would thus reverberate through the students' bodies as well as their minds, so that they

were imbibed almost viscerally – in the belly. In other proverbs, the pupil
is told to have a 'hearing heart' and an 'open ear', and to inscribe Solomon's
words of wisdom 'on the tablet of [his] heart'.[52] The short, rhythmical
aphorisms of the book of Proverbs in the Hebrew Bible seem designed to
aid memorisation. As in Mesopotamia and Egypt, beatings were part of the
educative process.[53] One pupil lamented his humiliation before the entire
scribal community:

> Alas, I hated discipline,
> My heart spurned all correction;
> I would not hear the voice of my masters,
> I would not listen to those who tried to teach me.
> Now I am all but reduced to the depths of misery
> In the presence of the whole community.[54]

The constant use of the terms 'father' and 'son' in Proverbs suggests that
in Israel too these schools were family-based. The teacher aimed to reproduce himself in his pupil so that he too would acquire the distinctive virtues
of a scribal retainer or a reliable aristocrat: fear of Yahweh, a disciplined
tongue, and respect for the powerful.[55]

Almost certainly, parts of the book of Proverbs were included in the
curriculum. Hymns and songs were regularly used in ancient scribal schools
and several of the Hebrew psalms also use acrostics or an alphabetical system
as an aide-memoire. The royal psalms of the Davidic monarchy, for example,
would implant reverence for the king. At his coronation, it was said that
Yahweh made the new king a member of the Divine Council, placed him
in a seat of honour, and promised to subdue his enemies:

> Yahweh said to you, my lord, 'Sit at my right hand
> And I will make your enemies a footstool for you!'[56]

Near Eastern monarchs were elevated to divine status, so this psalm has
Yahweh formally adopt the king: 'You are my son, today I have become
your father.'[57] The Song of the Sea describing Israel's triumphant crossing
of the River Jordan may have been included in the syllabus, as well as the
ancient poem, quoted earlier, that described El appointing Yahweh to be
the patronal god of Israel. The word *torah*, often translated as 'law', means
'teaching' – instruction that must be taken to heart, recited as a 'memorial'
or 'reminder' (*zikkaron*) and placed 'in the ears' of each generation.[58]

We can only speculate about the early curriculum for the elites' young, but all Israelites knew that on Mount Sinai, Yahweh had imparted a written *torah* to his people. First, he had instructed Moses orally and 'when he had finished speaking with Moses on the mountain, Yahweh gave him the two tablets of the Testimony, inscribed with the finger of Elohim', which imbued them with divine power so that they became a permanent assurance of a sacred presence.[59] For the unschooled, writing had numinous power and the phrase 'it is written' made a dictum divinely authoritative.[60] Writing, as we have seen, was probably invented for accountancy purposes, and, according to popular belief, Yahweh kept a 'book' (*sefer*) – or, more accurately, a 'scroll' – in heaven, in which he had recorded each person's fate and kept a record of their deeds, just like one of the scribes.[61]

But there had been a strange reversal. Yahweh had called Israel 'out of Egypt' because he was the champion of the oppressed peasant class. Yet these scriptures were designed to create scribal retainers and an aristocracy that were wholly subservient to the royal tyranny that Israel had tried to escape. While the early songs and poems had celebrated the *am Yahweh*'s exodus from oppression, the Wisdom proverbs presupposed a hereditary ruling class. But the intensity of this teaching method tells us something that would become essential to all scripture: it could not be read superficially, with eyes passing swiftly over a written page. Its message had somehow to be ingested, inscribed on the heart and mind, and fused with the depths of one's being.

After the death of King Solomon in about 928 BCE, the southern and northern tribes of Israel parted company and established separate kingdoms. Like other small states in the Near East, they could develop independently as long as there was no imperial power in the region. But before long, the Assyrians were once again in the ascendant, their massive military power forcing weaker kings to accept vassal status. This could be advantageous: when King Jeroboam of Israel (r. 786–746 BCE) became a trusted Assyrian ally, his kingdom enjoyed an economic boom. In any case, the northern kingdom of Israel, which was close to the major trade routes, was larger and wealthier than the kingdom of Judah in the south, which was isolated and, consisting almost entirely of unproductive steppe and mountainous land, lacking in resources. Its advantage was that for nearly a century the great powers left Judah alone.

As we have seen, some of the northern tribes had always seen the Exodus from 'Egypt' as the defining moment of Israel's history, but after the creation of the Davidic monarchy, the southern tribes, whose hero had formerly been Abraham, focused on the covenant that Yahweh had made with King David, and their holy place became the former Hittite city of Jerusalem:

> I will give you fame as great as the fame of the greatest on earth. I will provide a place for my people Israel; I will plant them there and they shall dwell in that place and never be disturbed again; nor shall the wicked continue to oppress them ... Your house and your sovereignty will always stand secure before me and your throne be established for ever.[62]

In the Near East, a temple was a locus of sacrality and Yahweh's cult in Jerusalem adopted aspects of the Baal-worship that had preceded it there. After Baal had killed his cosmic enemies, Mot and Yam-Nahar, El had permitted him to build a splendid palace near Mount Zaphon in the kingdom of Ugarit. Baal called Zaphon 'the holy place, the mountain of my heritage ... the chosen spot ... the hill of victory'.[63] Zaphon would be an earthly paradise of peace, fertility and harmony.[64] When the people of Ugarit entered his temple they felt that they were once again in communion with the sacred rhythms of life that were obscured in the everyday world. During the autumn festival that marked the start of the New Year, Baal's victories were ritually re-enacted to ensure that life-giving rain would fall and that Baal would save the city from the lawless forces of destruction. The Jerusalem cult of Yahweh in Solomon's temple closely mirrored that of Ugarit, with psalms celebrating Yahweh's enthronement on Mount Zion,[65] and Yahweh had also made Jerusalem a city of peace or *shalom*, a word that also signifies wholeness, harmony and security.[66] Some of the psalms even claimed that Jerusalem could never fall because Yahweh, the divine warrior, was the citadel of his people; they instructed pilgrims to admire Jerusalem's indomitable fortifications which proved that 'God is here.'[67] But how would Yahweh fare against Ashur, the patronal god of Assyria?

Assyrian imperial policy aimed to unite peoples of 'divergent speech' into a nation of 'one language'. As King Sargon (r. 722–705 BCE) announced:

> People of the four regions of the world, of foreign tongues and divergent speech, dwellers of mountain and lowland, all that were ruled by the light of the gods, the lord of all, I carried it off at my lord Ashur's command, by the might of my sceptre. I made them of one mouth, and settled them therein.[68]

Writing acquired a new importance in the Assyrian administration: scribes and overseers were dispatched to administer the vassal states, but instead of using their own Akkadian language as the imperial tongue, they chose Aramaic, because its alphabetical script was easier to master than their own complex cuneiform system. As a result, the art of writing spread from the Assyrian bureaucracy to other social groups.[69] But it would be a mistake to assume that literacy became widespread among the general population or that the influx of writing replaced habits of orality. There is no evidence that, as some have claimed, the kings of Israel and Judah established royal archives and libraries, though individual scrolls inscribed with a narrative, an ancient law or a psalm may well have existed in the palace. The old traditions were still memorised and performed orally as before.[70] The Levites, junior priests, are specifically named as keepers of the texts and the teachers of Israel.[71] They were also musicians and singers, so these texts too were probably sung as well as recited as an aide-memoire.[72] As one of the psalms suggests, a wise man – a sage – was one who 'finds pleasure in the *torah* ["teaching"] of Yahweh and murmurs his *torah* night and day', internalising it by constant repetition so that it never left his mouth or heart.[73]

But an entirely new curriculum had developed in Israel. During the ninth century BCE, we begin to hear of 'prophets' and the 'sons of prophets' in the northern kingdom – though, at this point, we know very little about them.[74] Prophecy was an established institution in the Middle East. From Canaan to Mari in the middle Euphrates, prophets 'spoke for' their gods, and in Israel and Judah they were usually associated with the royal court. Yet during the eighth century BCE, prophets began to create 'schools' in Judah which educated pupils in a 'counter-curriculum' that was highly critical of the official Wisdom traditions. Isaiah, for example, declared that these poems and proverbs of foreign origin were simply a 'human command- ment, a lesson memorised'.[75] The Judahite prophets claimed that because their contemporaries did not listen to them, Yahweh had commanded them to commit their teachings to writing for the benefit of future generations.[76] It seems that the prophets' oracles were indeed preserved by their pupils and that some of these prophetic texts were eventually included in the regular aristocratic curriculum, thus finding a place in the Hebrew Bible. This was a very unusual development in the Middle East: it seems that the prophets' warnings were used to teach students to understand the lessons of history. By avoiding the mistakes of the past, they could map a more successful future.[77]

The first prophet whose words were preserved in this way, however, had not attended a prophetic school. 'I was no prophet, neither did I belong to any of the prophetic guilds,' he insisted.[78] Amos was a shepherd from Tekoa in the kingdom of Judah, who, in about 780, had been ordered by Yahweh to leave his flock and prophesy in the kingdom of Israel, where King Jeroboam II, the favoured vassal of Assyria, was ruling a prosperous – and, therefore, inequitable – agrarian state. Jeroboam had recently conquered new territory in Transjordan, had begun major building projects with forced labour bands in Megiddo, Hazor and Gezer, and had built up a sophisticated bureaucracy and professional army.[79] As we have seen, at the very beginning of Israel's history, Yahweh had championed the victims of agrarian oppression. Now, through Amos, Yahweh was recalling his people to their original mission to promote justice. He would punish the nobility of Samaria, who lived in splendid ebony houses, slept on ivory couches and neglected the poor,

> Because they have sold the virtuous man for silver
> and the poor man for a pair of sandals,
> because they trample the heads of ordinary people
> and push the poor out of their path.[80]

Amos had no time for ritual: Yahweh was sick of listening to the priests' noisy chanting and devout strumming of harps. True religion did not exist to satisfy the aesthetic appetites of the ruling class, but was a summons to practical compassion. Yahweh wanted justice 'to flow like water and integrity like an unfailing stream'.[81] Soon, Amos warned the Samarians, an enemy would invade their country and loot their palaces, and this enemy would be none other than their good friend Assyria. Yahweh, the divine warrior who had rescued the *am Yahweh* from 'Egypt', was back on the warpath. He was going to shatter the kingdoms of Damascus, Philistia, Tyre, Moab and Ammon – all of whom were guilty of heinous injustice and horrific war crimes – and this time he would not be on Israel's side. On the contrary, he was fighting a holy war *against* Israel and Judah, using Assyria as his favoured instrument.[82] Jeroboam, who had neglected his sacred duty to the poor, would be killed, his kingdom destroyed, and its people 'taken into exile, far distant from its own land'.[83]

This prophecy was preserved in writing and later generations would hear it with fear and trembling, because, some sixty years after Amos had uttered this prediction, the kingdom of Israel – which at that time was

riding so high – would indeed be destroyed by Assyria. Amos did not necessarily need divine inspiration to make this prognostication. The prophets
were rather like today's political commentators. For some time, Assyria,
based in what is now northern Iraq, had been conquering kingdoms to the
west, steadily gaining control of the plains that stood between them and
the Mediterranean and the lucrative trade routes. The kingdom of Israel,
with its extended borders, stood in its path. The military might of Assyria
was unparalleled and its rulers had carefully cultivated a fearsome reputation for brutal punishment.[84] Jeroboam only had to make one false move
and Yahweh would use Assyria to punish Israel for its blatant cruelty to the
common people. When later generations of Israelites consulted the prophetic
oracles of the past to predict the future, they were creating a political
science to prevent unnecessary calamity. Amos's predictions would remind
them that the pursuit of material success at the expense of morality could
have fearful consequences.

But Amos did not rely entirely on his own common political insights.
He felt impelled by the divine, which he experienced as an irresistible force
within himself: 'The lion roars: who can help feeling afraid?' Amos asked.
'The Lord Yahweh speaks: who can refuse to prophesy?'[85] It had been
Yahweh who drove him, against his own inclinations, from Tekoa to the
northern kingdom of Israel where he was an unwelcome stranger.[86] He says
that he had a vision of Yahweh 'standing at the side of the altar', but the
divine was also a force that he experienced within.[87] This will be an important theme in the story of scripture: Yahweh was not simply experienced
as a 'Being' external to the self; he was, rather, an omnipresent reality,
immanent in the human psyche as well as in the natural world and historical events. The Israelites were not an introspective people, but Jeremiah,
who prophesied in Jerusalem in the sixth century BCE, eloquently described
the seemingly involuntary nature of his prophetic revelations. Yahweh, he
insisted, put these divine words into his mouth so that they became his
own.[88] He experienced the revelations as a seduction, an irresistible force
that compelled him to speak out whether he intended it or not:

> I used to say, 'I will not think about him,
> I will not speak in his name any more.'
> Then there seemed to be a fire burning in my heart,
> imprisoned in my bones.
> The effort to restrain it wearied me,
> I could not bear it.[89]

Amos's contemporary Hosea, the only northern prophet, seemed compelled by Yahweh to commit perverse and abnormal actions: 'Yahweh said this to him, "Go, marry a whore, and get children with a whore, for the country itself has become nothing but a whore by abandoning Yahweh."'[90] He thus became an embodiment of what he regarded as the kingdom of Israel's infidelity to Yahweh. As we have seen, the people of Judah and Israel were not yet monotheists. Yahweh was a god of war but he had no known expertise in the agriculture on which the economy depended. Like other peoples, Israelites experienced the forces of nature as sacred, so it was natural for them to celebrate the union of Baal and Anat. Had not the sexual congress of these two divinities made the earth fruitful after Mot, god of sterility, had reduced it to a barren desert? To ignore such a well-tried-and-tested resource would seem not only unnatural but, indeed, criminal folly, since a bad harvest could wreak appalling disaster. The Baal cult included ritualised sex and when Hosea's wife Gomer became a sacred prostitute in the cult, he came to believe that the jealousy he felt was identical to Yahweh's when his people went whoring after foreign gods. He experienced his longing to win back Gomer as Yahweh's yearning for the fidelity of faithless Israel.[91] Most of Hosea's contemporaries, however, would have regarded his condemnation of Baal-worship as eccentric, perverse and even blasphemous.

Hosea spoke of a time when the people of Israel had worshipped Yahweh alone, though it is most unlikely that this was ever the case. He was not preaching monotheism, however, but rather monolatry, which insisted that while other gods might exist, only one god – Yahweh – should be worshipped in Israel. Hosea depicted Yahweh as a ruthless monarch who, like the Assyrian kings, would mercilessly quash a disobedient ally:

> Samaria must atone for rebelling against her God,
> They shall fall by the sword; their little children dashed to pieces
> and their pregnant women disembowelled.[92]

Again, when later generations read these oracles and remembered that Assyria had indeed destroyed the kingdom of Israel, some would begin to see cultic infidelity to Yahweh as politically dangerous.

Hosea painted an appalling picture of the divine. Scriptures often reflect contemporary violence and brutality: Assyria had maintained its power in the region by committing exactly the kind of atrocities that Hosea now attributed to Yahweh as a matter of course. A rebellious vassal state invariably suffered a brutal military riposte, was forced to pay heavy tribute and – in a solemn covenant-ceremony – swear an oath to be faithful to Assyria alone. The Assyrians insisted that everybody – aristocrats and commoners alike – must show 'loyalty' (*hesed*) to the Assyrian king. *Hesed* is often translated as 'love' but 'loyalty' is a more accurate rendering. Vassals were not required to feel tender affection for their brutal overlord but rather to reject any alliance with a rival foreign power.[93] Hosea's prophecies would be edited long after Israel had indeed been annihilated by Assyria in 722 BCE. By then, the editors knew that the kingdom had participated in rebellious coalitions against Assyria and that the Assyrian armies had retaliated by slaughtering men, women and children. These later generations concluded that they too might pay a heavy price if they allied themselves with other deities, since Yahweh had warned Hosea that it was no use trying to appease him with the old sacrificial rituals, because 'what I want is loyalty [*hesed*], not sacrifice'.[94] It may have been Hosea who introduced the idea of a covenant between Yahweh and Israel; while the concept is expressed in stories set in a period long before Hosea's time, we do not know when and how those narratives achieved their final form.[95]

We shall see that the prophets of Judah would respond to political danger quite differently. When they were threatened by a great power, they never mentioned Israel's Exodus from 'Egypt'. Instead, they relied on God's covenant with David. But Hosea drew on the story of Jacob, Israel's eponymous northern hero, who was said to have 'fought with God' at Bethel. Jacob had betrayed his brother Esau – as Israel was currently betraying Yahweh – so to regain Yahweh's favour, Israel, like Jacob, would have to struggle with both Yahweh and itself:

> In the very womb [Jacob] supplanted his brother,
> in maturity he wrestled with God.
> He wrestled with the angel and beat him,
> he wept and pleaded with him.
> He met him at Bethel
> and there God spoke to him.[96]

Hosea also drew on the memory of the Exodus when Yahweh had brought Israel 'out of Egypt' and lived with the infant nation in the wilderness – a time of intimacy and innocence.[97] These are the earliest explicit biblical references to the 'wilderness years' that followed the Exodus, when Israel had escaped from imperial power and, guided by Yahweh, had lived beyond the reach of civilisation:

> I led them with reins of kindness,
> with leading-strings of love.
> I was like someone who lifts an infant close to his chest.[98]

But because Israel had sacrificed to Baal, they would fall prey to imperial might yet again: 'they will have to go back to Egypt, Assyria must be their king'.[99]

In 745 BCE, Tigleth-Pileser III abolished the system of vassalage and incorporated all subject peoples directly into the Assyrian state. At the merest hint of dissent, the entire ruling class of a rebellious people was deported and replaced by people from other parts of the empire. This was the political context of the vision of the southern prophet Isaiah.[100] Isaiah was a member of the royal family and probably a priest. Neither he nor Micah, the other contemporary southern prophet, ever mentions the Exodus; instead, Isaiah was inspired by the cult of Jerusalem, the City of David. Isaiah looked forward to the day when 'all the nations' would stream to worship Yahweh in his temple on Mount Zion, which replicated the Garden of Eden. This would be a return to the primal paradise, when all creatures would live together harmoniously, the wolf with the lion, the panther with the kid.[101]

Until this point, the kingdom of Judah had not been affected by the Assyrian threat, but it was drawn into the struggle when the Judahite king Ahaz (r.736–716 BCE) refused to join the anti-Assyrian coalition of Damascus and Israel, whose armies promptly marched south to besiege Jerusalem. Convinced that Jerusalem, the City of Yahweh, was impregnable, Isaiah tried to persuade Ahaz to stand firm. Yahweh himself had given Ahaz a sign. His queen was pregnant and the son she bore would restore the glory of the House of David: 'The young woman [alma] is with child and will soon give birth to a son, whom she will call Immanu-El [God-with-us]'.[102] But before the child had reached the age of reason, the kingdoms of Israel and Damascus would be devastated, so Ahaz should put his trust in Yahweh alone. Yet to Isaiah's disgust, Ahaz submitted to the Assyrian king, who promptly invaded the territories of Israel and Damascus, deporting large numbers of their inhabitants. By 733 BCE, the once-prosperous kingdom of Israel had been reduced to a mere city state, with a puppet king on the throne. As a gesture to his new overlord, Ahaz

built an Assyrian-style altar to replace the Altar of Sacrifice in the courtyard of Solomon's temple.

Isaiah deplored this lack of faith in the God-given security of Jerusalem.
Even though the fall of the kingdom of Israel was a temporary setback,
Yahweh was about to make good his covenant with David, he insisted; and
the birth of the royal baby, Hezekiah, whom Isaiah had honoured with the
title of Immanu-El, was a sign that God was indeed with his people. It was
also a beacon of hope to Judah's fallen neighbour: 'The people who walked
in darkness has seen a great light; on those who live in a land of deep
shadow a light has shone!'[103] Isaiah imagined the Divine Council bursting
into song to celebrate the royal birth:

> For there is a child born for us,
> a son, given to us
> and dominion is laid upon his shoulders.[104]

On his coronation day, Hezekiah would become a member of that Heavenly
Council, receiving the customary titles of the kings of Judah: 'Wonder-
Counsellor, Mighty God, Eternal-Father, Prince of Peace'.[105] Unfortunately,
when the Prince of Peace finally became king of Judah in 716 BCE, he
brought his kingdom to the brink of ruin. In 722 BCE, after a
futile rebellion, Samaria, the last remaining stronghold of the drastically
depleted kingdom of Israel, was destroyed by the Assyrian monarch
Shalmeneser V. Over 27,000 Israelites were deported to Assyria and were
never heard of again. They were replaced by colonists from all over the
Assyrian empire, who worshipped Yahweh, the local god, alongside their
own deities. Some of the undeported Israelites tried to rebuild their
shattered country, while others migrated to Judah, bringing their northern
traditions with them.

At first, Hezekiah tried to distance himself from his father's syncretising
policies and, perhaps buoyed up by Isaiah's conviction of Jerusalem's impreg-
nability, joined a coalition of kings during the disorder that broke out after
Shalmeneser's death in 705 BCE. But once Sennacherib, the new Assyrian
king, had quelled these revolts, he moved against Judah. Isaiah still insisted
that Yahweh would smite Sennacherib and usher in a reign of peace. And
against all odds, for reasons unknown to us, Sennacherib lifted the siege of
Jerusalem – but not before he had plundered forty-six villages and devastated the countryside, reducing Judah to a small city state. When Hezekiah's
son Manasseh came to the throne in 698 BCE, he wisely adopted a policy

of integration, setting up altars to Baal, re-establishing the country-shrines
to various deities, installing an effigy of Mother Goddess Asherah in the
temple, and building a house for sacred prostitutes in the temple courtyard.[106] Later biblical authors would condemn these policies, but Manasseh's
long reign gave Judah time to recuperate and when he died in 642 BCE, he
had recovered some of Judah's lost territory. Few of his subjects would
have been disturbed by his cultic innovations, since archaeologists have
discovered that many of them had similar 'graven images' in their own
homes.[107] But there was simmering discontent in the rural areas which had
borne the brunt of the Assyrian invasion, and after Manasseh's death, this
surfaced in a palace coup, which deposed Manasseh's son Amon and put
his eight-year-old son Josiah on the throne.

By this time, the northern traditions brought to Judah by the refugees
of 722 BCE had had time to percolate through the traditions of the south.
Some scholars believe that when literacy spread through the Near East in
the eighth century BCE, two documents had been composed – one in Judah,
known to modern scholars as 'J' (because its authors called Israel's god
'Jahwe' or 'Yahweh'); and a northern scripture known as 'E' because the
authors preferred the title Elohim – and that during the seventh century
BCE these manuscripts were merged in a 'cut and paste' editing job.[108] But
this theory reflects modern editorial methods which, given the unwieldiness
of scrolls, would have been impossible at this time. The northern refugees
would certainly have shared their stories with the Judahites, who, appalled
by Israel's fall and having so narrowly escaped a similar fate, were ready to
listen. There was therefore a strong northern input in the next stage of
scriptural development.

By this time, Assyria was in decline and Egypt in the ascendant. In
633 BCE, the Pharaoh had forced Assyrian troops to withdraw from the
Levant and as the great powers vied with one another, Judah was left to
its own devices. There was a new surge of national feeling and, perhaps, a
misplaced confidence. In 622 BCE, Josiah began repairs on Solomon's temple,
symbol of Judah's former greatness, and during the construction the high
priest Hilkiah claimed that he had found the 'torah scroll' (Sefer Torah) that
Yahweh had given Moses on Mount Sinai.[109] We do not know what this
scroll was. It may have been an early version of the book of Deuteronomy,
which describes Moses dictating a 'second law' (deuteronomion in Greek) to
the people shortly before his death; or perhaps the text of a short northern
law, ruling that all Israelite worship be centred in one shrine, on Mount
Gerizim or Mount Ebal.[110] And we have no idea what torah means in this

context. Was it a specific set of laws, such as the Ten Commandments (which appear for the first time in Deuteronomy), or, alternatively, a law prescribing the duties of an Israelite monarch?[111]

The scroll seems to have been difficult to decipher, so Josiah asked the prophetess Huldah to interpret it. She received an oracle from Yahweh declaring that the scroll had only one message: 'I am bringing disaster on this place and those who live in it, carrying out everything said in the scroll the King of Judah has read, because they have deserted me and sacrificed to other gods.'[112] Josiah now read the scroll aloud to the entire people and initiated reforms. The biblical account of this reform in the book of Kings indicates strong northern influence: it clearly endorsed Hosea's monolatry and was based on the Exodus rather than Davidic tradition. Josiah eradicated Manasseh's cultic innovations, burning the effigies of Baal and Asherah, abolished the rural shrines, and, finally, he invaded the territories of the former kingdom of Israel, demolishing Yahweh's ancient temples in Bethel and Samaria and slaughtering the priests of the country shrines.[113]

Whether the story of the 'lost book' was factually true or not, it was clearly inspired by a terror of extinction. The old piety had failed the Israelites and could be of no help to the Judahites in the new conditions of the late seventh century BCE. Scripture, as we have seen, tells us what we should remember; it also tells us what we must forget. The purging of the northern holy places was a violent attempt to forget, one that eradicated beloved sanctities that had failed and brutally extirpated once-cherished memories, forcing some traditions of the past into the background and focusing on those that would, hopefully, serve Judah better at this perilous moment.[114] The final version of the book of Deuteronomy, put together by the reformers, was a call to action. First, it outlawed all Canaanite symbols, such as the sacred pole (*asherah*) and 'standing stones' (*masseboth*) that had hitherto been perfectly acceptable and figured prominently in Solomon's temple.[115] To ensure its purity, worship was stringently centralised: sacrifice could be offered in only one shrine – the place 'where Yahweh had set his name'.[116] This now had to be the Jerusalem temple, the last surviving sanctuary. Finally, in an astonishing departure from Near Eastern tradition, the king was no longer a sacred figure with divine prerogatives; instead, like his people, he was subject to the law – his task was simply to study and diligently observe the *torah*.[117]

The reform had powerful supporters, who included the prophet Jeremiah, but events would render it obsolete. Yet the Deuteronomic scriptures would feature prominently in the Hebrew Bible and thus profoundly influence future generations. These scriptures were not yet prescribing 'monotheism'. The first of the Ten Commandments – 'Thou shalt not have strange gods before my presence' – clearly referred to Manasseh's introduction of 'strange gods' into the temple, where Yahweh's 'Presence' (Shekhinah) was enshrined; it did not yet deny the existence of these other gods. Thirty years later, Israelites still worshipped the Mesopotamian goddess Ishtar and Yahweh's temple remained full of foreign idols.[118]

Their iconoclastic theology was such a new development that the Deuteronomists had to rewrite the history of Israel and Judah to accommodate it, putting together a narrative of the two kingdoms that would later become the books of Joshua, Judges, Samuel and Kings. This history 'proved' that the destruction of the northern kingdom was caused by its idolatry. The Deuteronomists depicted Joshua slaughtering the Canaanite inhabitants of the Promised Land and destroying their cities like an Assyrian general. When a people are threatened by an external foe, they often attack an enemy within: the reformers had come to regard the Canaanite cults as 'detestable' and 'loathsome' and ruled that any Israelite who participated in them should be hunted down mercilessly.[119]

In this turbulent time, the old serene Wisdom curriculum seemed obsolete, so the Deuteronomists constructed a new one.[120] The young must study the northern traditions of the Exodus and the Mosaic torah instead, and education would no longer be confined to an elite but was obligatory for all male Israelites.[121] The aim was still to inscribe the 'teaching' (torah) on the tablets of their hearts, so Hosea's hesed – 'love' or, rather, 'covenantal loyalty' – would be instilled by constant recitation and repetition:[122]

> Listen, Israel. Yahweh, our Elohim, is the one Yahweh. You shall love Yahweh your Elohim with all your heart, with all your soul, with all your strength. Let these words I urge on you today be written on your heart. You shall repeat them to your children and say them over to them whether at rest in your houses or walking abroad, at your lying down or at your rising; you shall fasten them on your hand as a sign and on your forehead as a circlet; you shall write them on the doorposts of your house and on your gates.[123]

During this period of political uncertainty, the people of Judah must become 'Israelites', the Deuteronomists demanded; they must 'forget' their glorification of agrarian imperialism and their cult of Solomonic Wisdom and instead 'remember' the time when they were stateless outsiders, whom Yahweh had led 'out of Egypt'. They must study the *torah* day and night,[124] relying on the words of scripture alone, without the ritualised support of 'graven images'.[125]

In the book of Deuteronomy, Moses delivers a final address to the people just before they enter the Promised Land. He begs them to remember their time of marginality and homelessness in the wilderness. Yahweh had kept them in the desert for forty years 'to humble you ... to make you understand that man does not live by bread alone'.[126] They must not be seduced by the milk and honey of Canaanite civilisation, but remain spiritually separate from the security of a settled, agrarian life that was not of their making:

> When Yahweh brought you into the land which he swore to your fathers Abraham, Isaac and Jacob that he would give you, with great and prosperous cities not of your building, houses full of good things not furnished by you, wells you did not dig, vineyards and olives you did not plant, when you have eaten these and had your fill, then take care you do not forget Yahweh who brought you out of the land of Egypt, out of the house of slavery.[127]

An oppressed and marginalised people, they must cultivate their memory of the desert years as a form of resistance.[128] Behind the fearful intransigence of Deuteronomy lurks the horrifying memories of the annihilation of the kingdom of Israel, mass slaughter and brutal deportation.

Josiah's bid for national independence came to a tragic end in 609 BCE, when he was killed in a military skirmish with Pharaoh Neco. By now, the new Babylonian empire had replaced Assyria and competed with Egypt for control of the region. For a few years, Judah survived by dodging between the great powers, even though Jeremiah warned them that this was futile and dangerous. Yahweh commanded Jeremiah to prepare a written text of all his oracles so that future generations would remember that he had insisted again and again that Israel must submit to Babylon.[129] Jeremiah dictated his words to the scribe Baruch. King Jehoiakim, Josiah's son, had it burned. Jeremiah dictated a second copy, but the burned scroll would become a prophetic sign of the fate of Jerusalem.[130] In 597 BCE, Nebuchadnezzar II, king of Babylon, punished an uprising in Judah by deporting 8,000 Judahite aristocrats, soldiers and skilled artisans. In 586 BCE, after another futile rebellion, Nebuchadnezzar razed Solomon's temple to the ground. But some of the deportees heeded the Deuteronomists, and used their memories to resist the extinction of their nation. In exile, they found a substitute for the rituals of the lost temple in a new scripture, which would transform the disparate oral traditions of their people into the Pentateuch, the first five books of the Hebrew Bible. We now leave Israel, however, at this time of national calamity that would inaugurate a scriptural revolution.

2

INDIA: SOUND AND SILENCE

In about 1500 BCE, small bands of pastoralists left the Caucasian steppes and began to travel southwards through Afghanistan, settling finally in the Punjab in what is now Pakistan. This migration was neither a mass movement nor a military invasion but probably a continuous infiltration of various Aryan groups over centuries.[1] Other Aryans had already roamed further afield – to Greece, Italy, Scandinavia and Germany – taking their language and mythology with them. The Aryans were not a distinct ethnic group but a loose-knit confederation of tribes who shared a common culture and a language now known as 'Indo-European' because it became the basis of several European and Asiatic tongues. The Aryan settlers in the Punjab already spoke an early form of Sanskrit, the sacred language of one of the world's earliest scriptures.

About 300 years later, a priestly elite began to compile the massive anthology of Sanskrit hymns that would become the Rig Veda ('Knowledge in Verse'), the most prestigious text in the vast corpus of Indian scripture known as Veda ('knowledge'). The earliest of these hymns had been disclosed to seven great rishis ('seers') in the remote past and transmitted with impeccable accuracy by their descendants. In seven priestly families, each generation had memorised the hymns of their inspired ancestor and passed them on orally to their children.[2] Even today, when their ancient Sanskrit is well-nigh incomprehensible, these hymns are still recited with the precise tonal accents and inflections of the original, together with ritually prescribed gestures of the arms and fingers.[3] Sound had always been sacred to the Aryans – it was far more important to them than the meaning of these hymns – so when they intoned and memorised them, the priests felt possessed by a sacred presence.

The idea that the sound of a sacred text could be more important than the truths it conveys immediately challenges our modern notion of 'scripture', which, of course, implies a written text. But writing was unknown in India and, when it finally arrived in about 700 BCE, it was regarded as corrupt and polluting. One late-Vedic text ruled: 'A pupil should not recite the Veda after he has eaten meat, seen blood, had intercourse, or engaged in writing.'⁴ Like 'graven images' in Josiah's Israel, writing was regarded as a degrading and dangerous vehicle for the divine. Hence, even after the advent of writing, Vedic hymns continued to be learned by heart and transmitted orally. When the Europeans arrived in India during the eighteenth and nineteenth centuries, they wondered whether the Veda truly existed, because nobody could produce a copy. The Brahmin priests told them firmly: 'Veda is what pertains to religion; it is not in books.'⁵

In the West today, we tend to regard scripture as the Last Word, a canon sealed for all time, sacred, immutable and inviolable. But, as we have already seen, in the premodern world, scripture was always a work in progress. Ancient writings were revered but not fossilised; scriptures had to speak to ever-changing circumstances and, in the process, they were often radically transformed. This was certainly true of the Rig Veda. The earliest collections, known as the 'Family Books', are found in books Two to Seven in the extant Rig Veda; books Eight and Nine were composed by another generation of poet-priests and given the same status as the hymns of the seven original rishis, while the hymns in books One and Ten, created by rishis with a very different vision, were added later still.⁶ The American scholar Brian K. Smith has described the Veda as 'a peculiar kind of canon ... endlessly re-envisaged, and eternally unchanged'.⁷

The Aryans seem unlikely producers of a holy scripture, since their lives were not what we would call devout. They made a living by stealing the cattle of rival Aryan tribes and looting the settlements of the indigenous peoples, whom they contemptuously called *dasas* ('barbarians'). They saw nothing reprehensible in this: in their eyes, it was the only acceptable way for a 'noble' (*arya*) man to obtain goods – an attitude they shared with the aristocrats of agrarian civilisations who forcibly seized their peasants' produce.⁸ Aryans felt fully alive only when marauding and fighting. They were not peace-loving yogins but rough, hard-drinking cowboys, relentlessly pushing eastward in search of more cattle and new pastures.⁹

The Rig Veda celebrates this ethos. The hero of its earliest hymns was Indra, god of war and sworn enemy of the monstrous dragon Vritra, who symbolised everything that thwarted Aryan migration: his name was derived from 'VR', an Indo-European root that meant 'to obstruct, enclose, encircle'. The Aryans imagined Vritra as a huge snake, which at the beginning of time was coiled around the cosmic mountain so tightly that its life-giving waters could not escape and the earth was parched with drought. Indra made the world habitable by hurling his glittering thunderbolt at Vritra and then decapitating him. This violent myth spoke directly to the Aryans' predicament. They too felt compelled to fight their way through a ring of hostile enemies that seemed to box them in, thwarting their advance and preventing them from seizing the cattle, horses and food they needed for survival. Every scriptural tradition has a central theme or motif, which reflects its unique view of the human predicament. We shall see that a yearning for liberation (*moksha*) became entrenched in the Indian imagination: long after Vritra was all but forgotten, the people of India continued to feel cruelly trapped in the deadly impasse of their mortal condition. The opposite of *moksha* was *amhas* ('captivity'), an Indo-European word cognate with the English 'anxiety' and the German *Angst*, which evokes a profound unease and claustrophobic distress. Later generations developed meditative and ethical disciplines to help them transcend life's fateful coils; the early Aryans could only fight their way out.

The rishis took part in the raiding and contributed to each battle with gusto; we should not imagine them remaining piously on the sidelines.[10] In their hymns, these poet-priests depict themselves riding into the fray beside Indra,[11] and claimed that it was their ritualised chant that had empowered Indra to smash the mountain cave in which Vala, another demon, had imprisoned the sun and the cattle, depriving the earth of light, warmth and food.[12] Other hymns describe Indra's cohorts, the Maruts, strengthening Indra in battle with the sound of their hymns,[13] which not only supported Indra but could vanquish all other obstacles.[14] These poems were, therefore, deemed essential to the technology of warfare, the pastoral economy, the well-being of warriors and the survival of the Aryan people. Later Indian scriptures would develop a doctrine of *ahimsa* ('non-violence'), but at this point, the rishis' inspired words had lethal potential for the Aryans' enemies when they were intoned correctly.

If you had asked the Aryans whether these fierce cosmic battles had really happened or what evidence there was for the existence of Indra or Vritra, they would have struggled to understand the question. Indra, Vritra and Vala belong to the realm of mythos – the language of scripture – which looks back to primordial time to discover what is constant and essential to human life. For the beleaguered Aryans, Vritra and Vala were neither fantastic nor historical figures because they embodied an ever-present reality – the deadly, remorseless conflict that lay at the heart of existence. They saw Vritra and Vala in the *dasas* surrounding their encampments. They knew that animals preyed continuously on one another in a ceaseless struggle for survival. Terrifying storms, earthquakes and drought endangered all living things. Every evening, the sun was obliterated by the forces of darkness but somehow – wondrously – it always managed to rise again the following morning.

This was a community that felt constantly imperilled.[15] Even the names of the Aryans' more peaceable gods – Mitra ('compact', 'alliance') and Varuna ('covering', 'binding together') – not only sacralised the loyalty that held the tribes together but also presupposed an omnipresent foe.[16] Perpetually under threat, the Aryans projected their embattled situation onto the cosmos, where their own gods, the *devas*, were thought to be engaged in a constant battle with the *asuras*, older, primordial deities who had become demonic. Some hymns describe malign spirits roaming outside their encampments at night.[17] Others dwell on the ever-present spectre of famine and disease.[18] As Vedic thought progressed, it seemed that there could be no lasting transformation without prior danger and disintegration – that Vritra must first prevail before Varuna could bring peace and order.[19] Vedic mythology spoke of a primal unity broken into multiple parts: of a cosmos formed from a god's dismembered body; and of the divine Word falling from heaven and fragmenting into multiple syllables, which the rishis strove to put together again.[20]

Unlike other animals, human beings cannot take the world for granted. The Aryans relied on mythos to make sense of their lives but they also used practical logos to improve their circumstances. Raids had to be planned, fighting skills improved and the pastoral economy skilfully managed to ensure the welfare of the group. But like all warriors, they told themselves that their expeditions were setting the world to rights. Aryan mythology did not conflict with these logos-driven activities; rather, it embraced and enhanced them. Before a raid, priests chanted a hymn celebrating Indra's victories and, as Indra had done before his battles, the raiders all drank a draught of the hallucinogenic drug soma as they harnessed their horses to the war chariots. The numinous chanting of the Rig Veda gave dignity and significance to a way of life that could otherwise have seemed brutal, point-less and terrifying.

And it paid off. By the tenth century BCE, the Aryans were pushing steadily eastward and had settled in the Doab between the Yamuna and Ganges rivers – a region henceforth known as Arya Varta ('Land of the Arya'). Each year, during the cool season, teams of warriors were dispatched to subdue the locals and create a new settlement a little further east and new rituals were devised to sanctify this incremental progress.[21] Another *deva*, Agni, god of fire, now became the Aryans' hero, because the pioneers had to clear land for their encampments by setting fire to the dense forests. For the Aryans, the *devas* were not 'other' beings, but were experienced as a sacred dimension of themselves. Agni not only symbolised the settler's ability to conquer and control his new environment but was also his alter ego, his best and deepest 'self' (*atman*), which was also sacred and divine.[22]

We should not confuse a *deva* with our modern Western notion of 'God'. *Deva* means 'shining', 'exalted': qualities that could apply to anything – a hymn, an emotion, a river, a storm or a mountain – in which the Aryans glimpsed a transcendent potency.[23] Far from being sealed off in a metaphysical sphere of its own, the divine permeated the whole of reality, so the *devas* epitomised the natural forces as well as human passions, such as love or the ecstasy of battle, which seem momentarily to lift us to a more intense mode of existence. Modern Western science has separated the material from the psychological and spiritual, but inspired by the holistic vision of the brain's right hemisphere, for the Vedas nothing was ever merely material since everything was imbued with transcendent potential.[24]

Thus, Agni was identical with the sacred fire that was central to the Aryans' sacrificial cult: it was said that the sun, the fire that sustains life, had descended to our world and was buried beneath the earth's crust. But when sticks or stones were rubbed together or struck, Agni flared forth again and conveyed the gifts thrown into the sacred fire back to the heavenly world. Agni was also the 'fire' of the mind that rises from the mysterious depths of our being and is manifest in thought. Soma, the intoxicating plant, was also a *deva*, because it enhanced a warrior's courage; and it was a source of revelation that so sharpened a rishi's intuitive powers that he himself became momentarily divine.[25] One rishi described this sense of limitless expansion and freedom from the constriction of mundane existence:

> We have drunk the Soma; we have become immortal; we have gone to the light; we have found the gods. What can hatred and the malice of a mortal do to us now, O immortal one? ...
> Weakness and diseases have gone; the forces of darkness have fled in terror. Soma has climbed up in us, expanding. We have come to the place where they stretch out lifespans.[26]

Anything that enlarged the Aryans' vision and gave them intimations of the sacred was a *deva*: it helped them to feel at home in the world. In the Rig

Veda, both Agni and Soma were called the Aryans' 'compassionate friend';
Mitra, who ruled over the day, woke the Aryans at dawn: his name also
means 'friend'.[27] The rishi imagines him and Varuna, lord of the night, sitting
in the sacrificial arena beside the Aryans as beloved companions.[28]

The Aryans had no organised pantheon and there was no supreme deity
or 'High God', because all these *devas* participated in an all-pervasive,
ultimate, impersonal power. 'They call it Indra, Mitra, Varuna, Agni,' one
rishi explained. 'The wise speak of what is One in many ways.'[29] Each of
the *devas* is praised as the creator and sustainer of the cosmos because each
one is a lens through which the whole of reality can be glimpsed and offers
a different perspective of the Absolute. But that reality was not a supreme,
self-existent and omnipotent being: it does not 'exist' in the same way as
most things we know that are fallible, frail and mortal. This all-encompassing
and ultimately mysterious reality was, rather, Being itself.

When they surveyed the intricate working of the cosmos, the Aryans
marvelled at its coherence. The rising of the sun each morning seemed a
daily miracle: why did the sun, moon and stars not fall from the sky? Rivers
flowed continuously into the ocean, so why did it not inundate the land?
How did the seasons follow one another with such regularity? Modern
science has answered these questions, but the Aryans were cultivating sacred
mythos rather than *logos*. When they contemplated the functioning of the
cosmos, they became aware of a force that somehow pulled the potentially
warring elements of the universe together. This power was neither a *deva*
nor a modern Creator God. It was rather a transcendent impersonal force
which the Aryans called *rta*, the rhythm of the universe. They noticed that
the elements of the cosmos always seemed to return to their source, a
dynamic that they tried to imitate in their cult when Agni conveyed their
sacrificial offerings back to heaven. Any divisive action that tried to appropriate things for oneself was 'false' – a betrayal of *rta*. It was the ethos of
Vritra and Vala, who had constricted the expansive beauty of the natural
order and fractured the integrity of the cosmos, creating a world of darkness, sterility and death.[30]

Even though the ultimate reality is emphatically declared to be ineffable,
the rishis somehow 'saw' it in verbal form. In one of the late hymns of the
Rig Veda, Speech (Vac) presents herself as the transcendent reality that
encompasses the *devas* and all earthly things:

> I move with the Rudras, with the Vasus, with the Adityas and all the gods.
> I carry both Mitra and Varuna, both Indra and Agni, and both the Ashvins ...

I gave birth to the father on the head of this world. My womb is in the waters, within the ocean. From there I spread out over all creatures and touch the very sky with the crown of my head.

I am the one who blows like the wind, embracing all creatures. Beyond the sky, beyond this earth, so much have I become my greatness.[31]

In both the Hebrew Bible and the New Testament too, the 'Word' of God is a creative force: 'Through him all things came to be.'[32] The near-ubiquitous metaphor of the Word expresses a truth of the human condition. We create the world for ourselves by means of speech. A child is hungry for language and creates a 'cosmos' – an ordered world – for herself by playing with words; her understanding of her environment develops simultaneously with her mastery of speech.[33] So language makes reality meaningful to us – but it stumbles when it tries to express what lies beyond its reach.

It was said that the Veda had been sounding from all eternity, but that the rishis were the first human beings who were able to hear it.[34] With the help of soma and, perhaps, an early form of yoga, they had sensed the mysterious force that pulled the cosmos together. They left no account of the process, but they had probably cultivated this insight deliberately. The word 'mysticism' derives from the Greek verb *muo* ('to close'). Later contemplatives explained that they would 'close' or 'turn off' the analytical and propositional activity that we now know to be characteristic of the brain's left hemisphere. The Flemish mystic Johannes Ruysbroek (1293–1381) described this practice in Christian terminology:

The revelation of the Father, in fact, *raises the soul above reason*, to an image-less nakedness. The soul there is simple, pure and spotless, empty of all things and it is in this state of *absolute emptiness* that the Father shows his divine brightness. *To this brightness neither reason nor sense nor remark nor distinction may serve; all that must remain below.*[35]

Once the mind is 'emptied' in this way, the holistic vision of the right hemisphere has free play. Ruysbroek sees this activity as orchestrated by what he calls 'the Father'; in India, mystics regarded it as a human initiative. Breath control, which, as we shall see, is crucial to yoga, has also been found to elicit 'internally focused states'.[36] The hymns of the Rig Veda seem to reflect a right-brain vision of the numinous interconnection of the disparate parts of the cosmos. From this very early date, the truths imparted by scripture differed from the factual knowledge we derive from our normal, left-brain appraisal of the world, which is only a representation of a far more complex reality.

The hymns of the Rig Veda say that they 'heard' Vac, a sacred sound that bore no relation to human speech, because they also 'saw' it with *dhi* ('inner vision', 'insight'). They spoke of an 'inner eye' that somehow 'visualised' a 'knowledge' (*veda*) that lay beyond the competence of ordinary language and bore little relation to our regular methods of absorbing and processing information.[37] What did the rishis 'see'? It seems that they had lightning glimpses of *rta*, embodied in the luminous forms of the *devas* riding in chariots and sitting on golden thrones in the heavens. They tried, haltingly, to express these 'visions', which came to them in a series of static, unconnected pictures, in faltering human language: 'Then verily we saw with our power of vision [*dhi*], in your seats, something golden, with our mind, through our own eyes, through the eyes proper to Soma.'[38] It was '*something golden*' that did not quite relate to any mundane object. There was no attempt to describe the *devas*' activities in a clear, linear narrative. Instead, the Word erupted into a rishi's mind in a rapid succession of 'stills' with no logical or temporal coherence. What he saw transcended time and could refer equally to past, present or future – or all at once.[39] So the hymns of the Rig Veda proceed in flashes of insight, often couched in riddles, paradoxes and conundrums with no clear message.[40] The people of India still believe that true knowledge cannot be accessed by reason alone, because the divine transcends intellect, dogma and experience.

This, however, was not a private revelation but was given to the rishi for the sake of his community. In India, it is said that a visionary must always 'return to the marketplace'. He or she must revert to normality and transmit these mystical insights in a form that ordinary people can understand. The *rishi* or 'seer', therefore, had to become a *kavi* ('poet'). He somehow had to achieve a 'verbal formula' (*brahman*) that expressed the ineffable in mundane language. Sometimes he would ask one of the *devas* to help him.[41] The word *brahman* derives from a root which means 'to swell' or 'to grow'. The poets seem to have felt something very powerful surging up from within. They described themselves fashioning their hymns as a tailor created a 'fair and well-made robe ... as a deft craftsman makes a chariot',[42] fitting disparate pieces of already-existing things together to make something new.[43]

A rishi was only able to convey this indescribable vision because he somehow embodied it:[44] he was called *vipra*, because he 'trembled' or 'vibrated' with the rhythms of *rta*.[45] His transcendent vision was not simply an encounter with another form of existence; he had himself in some way become divinised. The whole point of gaining transcendent vision was to achieve this personal transformation. The right hemisphere reveals the profound interconnection of all things, so there is no gulf dividing the sacred from the profane, divinity from humanity. This is the world of meta-phor, which unites apparently diverse things, so that we see each differently; to say that a human being is a god means that our understanding of both humanity and divinity is altered. In India, truth is still primarily experienced in a man or woman who somehow incarnates divine wisdom.[46]

When the Aryans recited the rishis' hymns during their sacrificial rituals they returned them, in the spirit of rta, to the devas who had helped to create them. Those who truly hear scripture must always give something back. From their visions of the devas at work in the heavens the rishis concluded that they had all taken a solemn vow (vrata) to uphold cosmic order. Every morning Mitra and Varuna raised the sun up into the heavens,[47] while Varuna held the sky above the earth, making it possible for rain to fall and fructify the soil.[48] While the devas performed a cosmic liturgy to keep the world in being, the Aryans' offerings of food and soma, which Agni conveyed to the heavenly world, would support and strengthen them in their task.[49] The mythos and its accompanying ritual helped the Aryans to cultivate an attitude of reverence and gratitude that refused to take the planet for granted. Instead of exploiting the natural world for their own advantage, they had a dharma, a 'moral responsibility' to help sustain the cosmos. By personalising the unseen forces of nature and associating specific devas with the wind, sun, sea and stars, they were expressing their sense of affinity with the cosmic mystery.[50]

From the very beginning, therefore, Indian ritual was inseparable from the experience of scripture. Our knowledge of Vedic ritual at this early stage is limited, but we have some information about the festival held at the turning of the New Year, when, it was thought, the cosmos was in danger of reverting to primal chaos.[51] To strengthen rta in its battle against the forces of darkness, the Aryans competed ferociously with one another in ritualised chariot races, target-shooting, tugs-of-war, dicing and mock battles.[52] One of these contests was a poetry competition, in which the rishis composed extempore, relying on the inspiration of their patronal devas, vying with each other so aggressively that one poet compared the struggle with Indra's battle with Vritra.[53] The death of the old year raised the spectre of human mortality, which filled Aryans with a deep anxiety so the poets' task was to produce a brahman, a 'verbal formula' expressing an insight that could allay this terror of extinction.[54]

In one hymn, a young, inexperienced poet, standing on the platform beside his opponents, admits that he is afraid. He has the required insight: he knew that at the critical moment of the year's turning, Agni would 'push back the darkness with his light like a king'.[55] But did he have the skill to create a *brahman* that would assuage the fears of his audience? He was also worried about upstaging his elders, but as he reached the third stanza of his hymn, he suddenly realised it would not be he but Agni who would compose and utter the *brahman*, because in the moment of revelation, he and Agni were one:

> *He* knows how to stretch the thread and weave the cloth;
> *he* will speak fine words correctly.
> Who understands this [wisdom] is the protector of immortality
> though he moves below, he still sees higher than any other.[56]

Agni was not a distant deity in whom this young man had to believe: Agni *was* the experience of transcendence that flooded his heart and mind with the light of a vision that lay beyond the reach of normal speech. 'What shall I say?' he cried. 'What shall I think?'[57]

Vedic society was deeply agonistic. This young poet – so nervous of humiliating his elders – knew that the poetry contest often resulted in a catastrophic loss of face: to appear *amati* ('dull-minded') at this crucial moment could result in deprivation of priestly status.[58] But another hymn insists that instead of being divisive, poetry should bind the community together. This had been the greatest achievement of the first seven rishis:

> When they set in motion the first beginning of speech, giving names, their
> most pure and perfectly guarded secret was revealed through love.
> When the wise-ones fashioned speech with their thought, sifting it as grain
> is sifted through a sieve, then friends recognised their friendship. A good
> sign was placed on their speech.[59]

The crafting of a poem is compared to the ceremonial filtering of the soma plant that enabled the sacred liquor to gush forth. It was extremely difficult to strain the divine Word through the poet's limited mind and if motivated solely by self-interest, he would fail because inspiration was born of love. Sacred Speech (Vac) 'reveals itself to someone as a loving wife, beautifully dressed, reveals her body to her husband'.[60] So revelation should bring people together. The rishi castigates a poet who 'has grown awkward and heavy in this friendship', because true enlightenment is incompatible with animosity:[61] 'A man that abandons a friend who has learned with him no longer has a share in Speech.'[62]

During the tenth century BCE, the Aryans refined their idea of the supreme reality, which they now called the Brahman. As we have seen, this word had originally referred to a poetic formula but was now applied to the energy that pervaded the universe: the Brahman enabled all things to grow, expand and thrive, because it was life itself.[63] Like *rta*, the Brahman was not a *deva* but a force that was higher, deeper and more fundamental than the gods.[64] It could never be defined or described because it was all-encompassing: human beings could not get outside it and see it whole. But it could be experienced intuitively in the drama of ritual. The sacrificial rite often concluded now with a ritualised competition known as the *brahmodya*, in which the poet-priests challenged one another to find a 'verbal formula' (*brahman*) to define the ineffable Brahman. The challenger would ask a difficult question and his opponent would respond with an equally obscure query. The match continued until one of the contestants asked a question that reduced the entire company to silence. He was the victor, but not because of his brilliance, learning and acumen. Rather, he had tipped the participants into an apprehension of the ineffable. The ensuing quiet was, perhaps, not unlike the beat of silence in the concert hall after the last notes of the symphony have died away. It was full, pregnant and numinous because the Brahman was present. The priests' clever thoughts and learned aphorisms faded, their busy minds were stilled, and for a few moments, they felt at one with the mysterious force that held the whole of reality together. Transcending all human categories, the Brahman could be experienced only in the stunning realisation of the impotence of speech.[65]

One of the late hymns of the Rig Veda is a *brahmodya*. It begins by suggesting that in the beginning there was nothing – neither existence nor non-existence. How then, the rishi asks in a series of baffling questions, did an ordered, viable cosmos emerge from this abysmal void?

Who really knows? Who will here proclaim it? Whence was it produced? Whence is this creation? The gods came afterwards, with the creation of the universe. Who then knows whence it has arisen? – perhaps it formed itself, or perhaps it did not – the one who looks down on it, in the highest heaven, only he knows – or perhaps he does not know.[66]

Finally, the rishi falls silent and admits that he has come up against the ineffable. Not even the *devas* could answer these questions. The competitive and voluble Aryans had learned an important truth about scripture. Not even a revealed text has all the answers; all religious language – even the inspired words of scripture – must eventually segue into the silence that is an expression of awe, wonder and unknowing.

*

By the ninth century BCE, the Aryans had moved further east and established two small kingdoms between the rivers Ganges and Yamuna: one founded by a confederation of the Kuru and Panchala clans, the other by the Yadava. The Aryans now ruled regular agrarian states. Hitherto, Aryan society had not been rigidly stratified but agriculture required social specialisation. It had to incorporate the *dasas*, the indigenous peoples who had farming expertise, so the old mythology that demonised the *dasas* had become obsolete. Only elite warriors were now sent on annual raids, while the rest stayed at home. Some of these erstwhile warriors worked in the fields alongside the *dasas*; others became potters, tanners, metal-smiths and weavers. There were now four classes in Aryan society. Topping the hierarchy were the Brahmins, the priests who presided over the rituals; next came the warriors (Rajanya – later called Kshatriya: 'the empowered ones'); then the ordinary clansmen (Vaishya); and, finally, the *dasas* who had become Shudra ('the servants').

The priests now had more leisure to refine their concept of divinity and they developed a ritual science that focused on the rites rather than the *devas*. They recorded their insights in the Brahmanas, a new set of texts that were finally codified in about 600 BCE and made it clear that scripture was ancillary to ritual.[67] Their purpose was simply to instruct the priests in the technicalities of the *yajna*, the sacrifice.[68] The Veda now comprised four sets of texts. The first was the Rig Veda; the others were the Sama Veda, a collection of songs (*samen*) with instructions for their recitation during the sacrifice; the Yajur Veda, a compilation of short prose formulae used in the *yajna*; and the Atharva Veda, an anthology of hymns and magical formulae. Each of the four priestly schools was responsible for the memor- isation and transmission of one of these Vedas and each supplied an officiant for the rite.[69] The *hotr* priest, who specialised in the Rig Veda, performed the main recitation, assisted by the *udgatr*, who 'chanted aloud' songs from the Sama Veda, while the *advaryu* priest, who performed the sacrificial actions, focused on the Yajur Veda. The fourth priest, the *brahmin*, remained silent throughout the rite, but his presence was essential. He had to watch the action, ensuring that the rites were performed correctly and if there was a mistake, he healed the fractured rite in his mind.[70] His silence was said to be 'half of the sacrifice'.[71] Despite the Brahmanas' emphasis on the spoken word, silence, which pointed to the ineffable, still lay at the heart of every ritualised utterance.[72]

The new rites were powered by a yearning for personal transformation. The old boisterous ritualised contests had been replaced by a symbolic heavenly journey in which the 'sacrificer' or 'patron' – a Kshatriya or a Vaishya – who financed the ritual was led through the ceremony, by the four officiating priests, and achieved temporary divine status.[73] First, he was bathed, anointed with fresh butter and ushered into the Hut of the Consecrated beside the sacrificial fire. There, warmed by *tapas*, a creative heat that filled his body with sacred power, he was symbolically reborn into the world of the gods.[74] The new ritual was based on *bandhus*, 'connec-tions' between heavenly and earthly phenomena. Every single action, utensil and hymn in the rite was linked to a cosmic reality. It was an attempt to incarnate the rishis' holistic vision of the universe. When performed with full consciousness of these 'connections', the liturgy bridged the gulf between heaven and earth by yoking gods with humans, humans with animals, the visible with the invisible, and the transcendent with the mundane.[75]

The two hemispheres of the frontal brain work in tandem. The Brahmanas' ritual science, which explained, systematised and analysed the right hemi-sphere's intuitive grasp of the inter-relatedness of all things, was a left-brain project. But the drama and sensory experience of the ritual, all enhanced by a draught of soma, returned this analytical account of the *bandhus* to the right brain, so that the patron experienced these 'connections' physically and emotionally. He thus had intimations of the transcendent Brahman that informed the disparate elements of the universe and pulled them into a sacred unity. As he went through the rite, the patron had to make himself aware that every single implement – such as a fire stick – was linked to the utensils used in the primordial sacrifice that had brought the cosmos into being. He had to imagine that he was inseparable from the ghee that he fed into the sacrificial fire, so that he was really offering *himself* to the gods and was ascending in the smoke to the heavenly world. He had to identify with the animal victim so closely that its death became his own and – at least for the duration of the rite – he was no longer plagued by fear of mortality:[76] 'Becoming himself the sacrifice, the sacrificer frees himself from death.'[77]

The patron also reminded himself that he was walking in the footsteps of the *devas*, who in primordial time had themselves achieved divine status and immortality by means of these rituals. 'It was done then by the gods. So, now it is done by men.'[78] The gods, however, could perform the rites perfectly, a feat that was well-nigh impossible for mere mortals. The ritual procedure was so complex and so many things could go wrong that some ritualists doubted that any human being had ever achieved this heavenly journey – and even if he did, he could not remain in the world of the gods while inhabiting his body. The rite could only take the sacrificer there long enough to reserve a place for himself in heaven after death.[79] And to secure post-mortem immortality, the sacrificer had to go through the rite again and again. A succession of correctly performed ritual 'actions' (*karma*) performed over a lifetime, it was believed, would result in permanent residence in the world of the gods.[80]

Some of the poets had been refining their conception of the *devas* and they expressed these insights in new hymns that were added to the Rig Veda in the tenth century BCE and became the charter myths of the new ritual science. The first took the form of a *brahmodya*, posing a succession of unanswerable questions that segued into a silent apprehension of the mystery that lay at the heart of existence. 'Who [*Ka*] is the god whom we should worship with this oblation?' asked the rishi, a question that is repeated like a refrain throughout the hymn. None of the *devas* seemed to measure up. Who was the true lord of men and cattle? Who owned the snow-capped mountains and the ocean? Could any one of the *devas* support the heavens? Finally, the poet saw a *deva* emerging from the primal chaos who personified the ultimate Brahman. His name was Prajapati, 'the All', because he was identical with the universe, the force that sustained it and the seed of consciousness in the human mind. Yet personifying this ultimate reality did not detract from its ineffability; because human minds cannot comprehend 'the All', there was very little that anybody could say about Prajapati.[81] Indeed, it was said that his real name was the question asked at the beginning of the hymn: '*Ka?*': 'Who?'

At the beginning of the twentieth century it was thought that, after clearing up a few outstanding problems in the Newtonian system, our understanding of the cosmos would soon be complete. Then Albert Einstein (1879–1955) developed quantum physics, which contradicted nearly every major postulate of Newtonian science and unveiled an incomprehensible universe. This did not disturb Einstein, however. Like the rishis, he was content to marvel – indeed, he insisted, anyone 'to whom this emotion is a stranger ... is as good as dead':

> To know that what is impenetrable to us really exists, manifesting itself to us as the highest wisdom and the most radiant beauty, which our dull faculties can comprehend only in their most primitive forms – this knowledge, this feeling is at the centre of all true religiousness.[82]

The rishis' *brahmodya* was neither delusional nor a willed obscurantism, but was rather a realistic assessment of our ability to understand the cosmos. Indeed, modern physics has indicated that some problems will remain insoluble. 'The structure of nature may eventually be such that our processes of thought do not correspond to it sufficiently to permit us to think about it at all,' wrote the American physicist Percy Bridgman (1882–1961). 'The world fades out and eludes us ... We are confronted with something truly ineffable.'[83]

The second hymn added to the Rig Veda drew on an ancient Aryan myth that claimed that the voluntary self-sacrifice of the First Man – an act of divine kenosis – had brought the world into being. The rishi described this primordial 'Person' (Purusha) walking of his own free will into the sacrificial area, lying down on the freshly mown grass and allowing the gods to kill him. His body was broken up and its dismembered parts became the cosmos and everything in it, including the *devas* and the classes of Aryan society:

> His mouth became the Brahmin; his arms were made into the Warrior [Kshatriya], his thighs the People [Vaishya], and from his feet the Servants [Shudra] were born.
> The moon was born from his mind; from his eye, the sun was born. Indra and Agni came from his mouth, and from his vital breath the Wind was born. From his navel the middle realm of space arose; from his head the sky evolved. From his two feet came the earth, and the quarters of the sky from his ear.[84]

Even the Four Vedas emerged from Purusha's corpse: 'From that sacrifice, in which everything was offered, the verses and chants and the metres were born from it, and from it the formulas were born.'[85] This hymn celebrated the interdependence and the inherent sacrality of all things, since everything and every person was derived from a single body that was both human and divine. It is an early instance of a common scriptural theme, which sees the human being as the supreme reality in whom the entire universe comes together. Early Christians would see the glorified Jesus, who also died in a kenotic manner, in this way.[86] It is also uncannily like the modern perception of the human being as a microcosm in which the macrocosm is present as a hologram.

By the ninth century BCE, Purusha and Prajapati had merged in the Vedic imagination but their story had become darker. The Brahmanas describe Prajapati, 'the All', bringing forth the three worlds – earth, middle-space and heaven – from himself by means of ritualised *tapas*;[87] he then 're-entered' everything he had made so that he became its breath, body and its innermost self or *atman*.[88] All this confirms the vision of the original hymns. But in other passages, Prajapati is no longer serene and confident: he is lonely and vulnerable. He creates because he is yearning for company and his creation is a mess. His creatures are weak and sickly: some cannot breathe, others are tormented by demons;[89] they fight and eat one another; and some run away from Prajapati, who is so enfeebled by his creative emission that he has to be revived by the very gods that he had created.[90] 'Put me back together again,' he pleads, so Agni built him up, piece by piece, rather as the Brahmins ritually constructed the Fire Altar: 'When [the priest] builds up the five layers, it is also with these five body parts that he builds up Prajapati.'[91]

There is never a single version of a myth. Scriptures often juxtapose different accounts of a single mythical event, each of which contains important insights. These new stories emphasise Prajapati's vulnerability and the fragility of the cosmos but other Brahmanas make a different point and give human beings a cosmic mission. They claim that Prajapati created the three worlds by uttering three sacred sounds – *bhu*, *bhuvah* and *svah* – that had no semantic meaning but which represented the mystical essence of the Vedas.[92] They present Prajapati as the first rishi to 'see' the Vedic hymns, meters and rituals[93] and then perform them – intoning the Vedic hymns like the *hotr* priest, chanting the songs like the *udgatr* and uttering the sacred formulae like the *advaryu*[94] – so that when the priests chanted these mantras, they sustained Prajapati's broken world and kept it in being.[95]

By the ninth century BCE, the 'insightful word' (*manisa*) that had assuaged the anxiety of the Aryans at the New Year Festival, had acquired a creative power that – like the three sounds uttered by Prajapati – was entirely unconnected with its meaning. It simply had to be spoken aloud by a rishi and pronounced correctly. The source of this power was *rta*, the sacred force that stabilised the universe.[96] It is difficult to define mantra. For the Dutch scholar Jan Gonda it is a general name for sequences of words that 'are believed to have magical, religious or spiritual efficacy [and] are recited, muttered, or sung in Vedic ritual'.[97] Mantra bears no relation to prayer, which uses human language to bring the transcendent within our conceptual grasp, and has nothing in common with scriptural narrative that personalises the divine. Mantra is impersonal, practical and – to modern minds – hopelessly irrational.[98] The Indologist Fritz Staal has claimed that mantras are essentially meaningless, like Prajapati's *bhu*, *bhuvah* and *svah*. Like trance, ecstasy or a baby's babbling, they are simply reversions to a prelinguistic state.[99]

In the modern West, words have a one-to-one connection with objective realities, but in India, language is experienced as an event. Its purpose is not to name something but rather to do something – that is, to transform us.[100] Unless we try to understand and accept this, our notion of scripture will remain incomplete.[101] The German scholar Jan Assmann cites the Syrian philosopher Iamblichus (*c*.250–338 CE), who explained that the magical words used by Egyptian priests only seem nonsensical to us because we have forgotten their meaning. But the gods still understand them, so when the priest speaks their language, he is raised to the divine level. Sacred speech, therefore, has a transformative power irrespective of its meaning and when we speak or hear it, we are ourselves transformed.[102]

In India, the recitation of a mantra is used to achieve the transition from the wordy, analytic left hemisphere of the brain to a deeper and more intuitive form of consciousness. The meditator will sit in a comfortable position, his back straight, eyes closed, and repeats the mantra given to him by his teacher. The meaning of the words is not important because the mantra is symbolic and points to something other than itself. It is rather the physical vibrations of the recitation that over time stills the rational activity of the brain by the sheer monotony of the exercise. If the practitioner becomes too interested in the meaning of his mantra, he may want to stay in the discursive world of the left brain, but if monotony predominates, the switch to a more intuitive mode of perception in the right hemisphere can elicit a deeper insight.[103]

Gonda points out that in India there is in principle no difference between the experience of the first great rishis, who 'heard' and 'saw' sacred Speech, and that of the contemporary listener and reciter, since verbal formulae, rhythmically pronounced, are themselves 'bearers of power' that do not

give us information about the *devas* but are 'the essence of the gods'.[104]
They correspond to what Christians call a sacrament, which incarnates the
sacred physically and materially.[105] It might be helpful to see a mantra as a
sonoral temple.[106] A sacred place, sealed off from other locations, is a zone
of contact with the divine, which surrounds and envelops us in holiness.
Powerful sound can similarly engulf us, reverberating within us viscerally.
In the all-encompassing sound of an orchestral concert we experience
intimations of transcendence that move us physically and emotionally, lifting
us momentarily beyond ourselves.

But contemplation and the attainment of transcendent insight must
always lead to dedicated activity. In ancient India, this meant the performance of ritual. In the mythical story Prajapati, the Brahman – everything
that is – had to be put together again by the gods.[107] Our world, therefore,
had to be healed daily in the Vedic sacrificial ritual that re-enacted his story:

> The same Prajapati who became broken is this very fire we now build [on
> the altar]. That very fire-pan over there which lies empty before being
> retracted is just like Prajapati as he lay collapsed ... He [the priest] warms
> [the empty pot] on the fire, just as the gods once warmed [Prajapati].[108]

The sacrificial arena replicated his body: '[The altar] should measure the
distance of the outstretched arms ... for that is the size of a man, and it
should be the size of a man.'[109] Two offertory vessels represent the hands,
two milk pots the ears, two pieces of gold the eyes. Other ritual implements stood in for the flanks, intestines, buttocks, thighs and penis.[110]
Morning and evening, the priest kindled sticks to supply Prajapati with
food: 'These same acts should be performed for a whole year ... unless he
wants to see our father Prajapati torn apart.'[111] The Aryans deliberately
cultivated a sense of the fragility and sacrality of the cosmos. It was not
something that men and women could treat with impunity but had to be
revered and rescued daily.[112]

But when enacted ritually, the myth of Prajapati reinforced in the minds
of participants an appreciation of the interconnection – indeed, the profound
identity – of the divine, human and natural worlds:

> Whatever fire there is in this world is his inward breath; the atmosphere is
> his body; whatever winds there may be are his body's vital breath. The
> sky is his head, the sun and moon are his eyes ... Now that same firm

foundation which the gods put together is here, even to today, and will be so hereafter." [3]

The altar was shaped like a bird that could fly to the celestial realms, linking the disparate parts of the universe together, just as the human chants of the liturgy rose to the heavenly realm. But the Brahmanas made large claims when they said that if a person performed enough ritual 'actions' (*karma*), he would win a place in the world of the gods after his death, and over the years, these doubts became more acute. To address these fears, ritualists would begin to explore their interior world and produce a new set of scriptures.

3

CHINA: THE PRIMACY OF RITUAL

By the end of the third millennium BCE, a civilisation had developed in the lower valley of the Yangtze River. It left no archaeological trace, but tradition claims that it was ruled by the Xia dynasty (c. 2207–1600 BCE). The first historical Chinese regime was founded by the Shang, a nomadic hunting people from northern Iran, who seized control of the Great Plain between the Huai Valley and modern Shantung in about 1600 BCE.[1] The Shang established a typical agrarian economy, subsidised by plunder and hunting. Their kingdom consisted of a series of small towns, each governed by a member of the royal family and each designed to replicate the cosmos, its four walls carefully oriented to the compass directions. As in India, though differently expressed, we find a concern to align human life with the cosmic order. The king was revered as the son of the High God, Di Shang Di ('God Most High'), while the princes, who governed the cities in his name, represented Di's heavenly vassals – the 'gods' of wind, clouds, sun, moon and stars in the sky, and the 'spirits' of the rivers and mountains on earth. The king alone was permitted to approach Di, who had no other contact with human beings and administered earthly affairs through the 'gods', the 'spirits' and the deceased Shang kings. To court the goodwill of their ancestors and keep them onside, the Shang held huge 'hosting' (bin) ceremonies, sacrificing vast numbers of beasts and cooking the meat in magnificently crafted bronze vessels.[2] Then 'gods', 'spirits', the Shang ancestors and their living descendants shared a feast.[3]

Like most premodern aristocrats, the Shang regarded their peasants, known as the min ('the little people'), as an inferior species. The peasants never set foot in the cities but lived quite separately from the nobility in subterranean dwelling-pits in the countryside. They had their own cults and rituals of which we know little. The min farmed the land and the Shang seized their surplus to fund their cultural activities. Even though peasants were routinely exploited in any agrarian economy, the Shang's ill-treatment of the 'little people' would become proverbial in Chinese scripture.

Unlike the Aryans, the Chinese were not averse to writing, which played a crucial role in their political and religious life, and it is in China, perhaps, that we find the earliest 'scriptures' in the modern sense of written sacred texts. The Shang relied on Di to provide the harvests that were essential to the economy, but, perversely, Di often sent droughts, floods and other disasters, and the ancestors were equally unreliable. Indeed, the Shang believed that the spirits of the newly dead were potentially dangerous, so special rites were devised to transform a troublesome ghost into a helpful ally. To assess the likelihood of Di's support before embarking on a project, therefore, the Shang resorted to a divinatory practice that had long been used in north Asia. The king, or his diviner, would address a charge to a god or spirit on a specially prepared turtle shell or cattle bone while applying a hot poker. 'Today it will not rain,' he might say; or 'Today there will not be the coming of bad news from the border regions.'[4] Sometimes the charge was directed to an ancestor who seemed to be the cause of the problem: 'There is a sick tooth; it is not Father Yi [the twentieth Shang king] who is harming it.'[5] The king would then study the cracks which had developed in the shell and contained the cryptic divine response; his job was to interpret them and announce whether the oracle was auspicious or not. Afterwards, the royal engravers carved the king's charge into the shell; sometimes they also recorded the god's prognosis; and – very occasionally – they documented the outcome.

About 150,000 of these oracle bones have been unearthed at Yin (modern Anyang), the Shang capital. Irrational as it may seem, this was a serious attempt to create a science of precedents to see if an underlying pattern emerged that could help the king predict Di's behaviour. The legitimacy of the dynasty depended in large part on the king's ability to define and control reality, so this collection represented an archive, compiled by colleges of soothsayers and scribes to make their prognostications more accurate and exert some control over the future.[6] The fact that very few records of the king's failed predictions have survived, while his successful forecasts were inscribed in especially ornate script, suggests that the archive was also designed to demonstrate his efficacy as an intermediary with the divine world. Some of the shells, however, do show a commitment to accurate record-keeping – as, for example, the prediction that the queen would bear a son when in fact she gave birth to a girl and the god got the date wrong.[7]

These oracle inscriptions are the earliest examples in China of the use of linked graphs in a written text. Indeed, the script itself was modelled on the cracks that appeared in the turtle shells. Insofar as they expressed the divine Word in writing, these oracle bones have a claim to being the world's first written 'scriptures'. Certainly, their use in divination gave the graphs a numinous aura and their link with royal power would place writing at the heart of Chinese civilisation.[8] But this was very different from the rishis' reception of sacred knowledge. These human/divine communications seem crudely pragmatic, blatantly goal-related and unashamedly self-interested. They reveal the bureaucratic mentality of logos and the brain's left frontal hemisphere – they are contractual, rational, routinised, mathematical and compartmentalised.[9] Later, as we shall see, the Chinese would develop a holistic spirituality that depicted the divine, the natural world and humanity as a mutually dependent sacred triad, a vision that would be essential to their scriptural canon.[10] But the Shang's relationship with the divine world was characterised by hostility rather than intimacy and love. True, Di was sometimes cooperative and sent propitious rain, but one oracle also complained: 'It is Di who is harming our harvests.'[11] Di even helped the Shang's enemies. 'The Fang are harming and attacking us,' another oracle lamented; 'it is Di who orders them to make disasters for us.'[12] Certainly, it is difficult to regard Di as a force for moral good. He was perplexing, inscrutable and inspired neither faith nor confidence. Shang society was a strange mixture of refinement and barbarity. When a Shang king died, hundreds of his servants and retainers were buried with him. Their exquisite bronze vessels reveal a tender appreciation of the animal world, yet they slaughtered beasts with such reckless abandon during their hunting expeditions that they decimated the region's rich wildlife.

The Chinese would later remember the Shang's last years as a disastrous decline. In about 1050 BCE, while the last Shang king was fighting barbarians in the Huai region, the Zhou, a warlike and less sophisticated clan who ruled a principality in the western Wei Valley, invaded the Shang domain. Tragically, the Zhou monarch, King Wen, was killed during the campaign and was succeeded by his son Wu, who defeated the Shang and executed the last Shang king at Muye to the north of the Yellow River – a battle hailed in Zhou tradition as the triumph of good over evil. After his victory, King Wu divided the spoils: he would remain in the old Zhou capital in the west; his son Cheng would govern Yin; and the other Shang cities were entrusted to Wugeng, son of the late Shang king. When King Wu died shortly after the campaign, he was succeeded by Cheng, who was still a minor. Wugeng attempted a revolt, but this was crushed by King Wen's brother, Dan, usually known as the duke of Zhou. The Shang now lost control of the Great Plain but retained a foothold in the city of Song.[13]

After the victory, the duke of Zhou, acting as regent for the young king, devised a quasi-feudal system. Princes and allies of the Zhou were each given one of the Shang cities as a personal fief and the Zhou built a new capital named Chengzhou to maintain a presence in their new eastern territories. The duke himself ruled the city of Lu in Shantung, to the north-east of the Zhou domain. In the ancient world, continuity was essential for a successful transfer of power so at first the new regime probably differed little from the old. Like the Shang, the Zhou enjoyed hunting, archery, chariot-driving and lavish parties; Zhou cities were organised on the Shang model; and the Zhou worshipped the Shang ancestors and continued to revere Di, claiming that he was identical with their own High God, whom they called Heaven (Tian).

The Zhou also adopted a form of divination that had probably developed during the Shang's last years. In this new procedure, bone oracles were replaced by the casting and manipulation of sticks made from yarrow stems. Even or odd numbers of these stalks made it possible to construct sixty-four figures composed of six continuous or broken lines; these hexagrams would later symbolise all the possible forces of the cosmos and were thought to have dynamic power.[14] This was the origin of one of the six Chinese 'Classics', a collection of ancient texts whose authority was as unassailable as any scripture. Each of the Zhou cities had its own version of yarrow divination, but the system developed in the Zhou capital was the only one to survive; for centuries, it was known as the *Zhouyi* ('Changes of Zhou') because mastery of the hexagrams was thought to give adepts a measure of control over the dynamic of change. Over time, Zhou ritualists composed short, cryptic elucidations of each hexagram, which they attributed to the duke of Zhou. It is now well-nigh impossible to decipher the original meaning of these 'line-statements' but, as we shall see, they would later inspire ten complex commentaries that presented the cosmic order as a totality of opposing and complementary forces. These essays were added as 'wings' to the original statements and this massively extended book became the *Yijing*, the 'Classic of Changes'.

The word 'classic' needs some explanation. When Jesuit missionaries from Europe arrived in China during the seventeenth century CE, they were introduced to the Chinese word *jing*, which attributed transcendent status and value to a book. The Europeans were happy to translate *jing* as 'scripture' if the works were Buddhist or Daoist, but because the texts that formed the Confucian canon did not conform to their own notion of 'religion', they regarded them as secular 'classics', like the Homeric epics. It is still common in the West to regard Confucianism as a secular philosophy. But for some 3,000 years the Chinese have treated their Classics as scripture, have experienced transcendence in the *jing*, and have found that they make the sacred accessible to them and help them to nurture it in their own lives.[15]

We do not know how the *Zhouyi* was used in the early Zhou period, but it has been suggested that it originally consisted of the oracles that had persuaded them to undertake their momentous campaign against the Shang. These were carefully preserved and could have been recited during the ritualised re-enactment of the conquest. It was said that the system of the hexagrams had been revealed to King Wen while he had been, briefly, a prisoner of the Shang king. Later, when Wen sought advice about the feasibility of war against the Shang, the line-statements of the early Hexagrams urged caution – 'Do Not Act', 'Rest in Steadfastness' – and advised Wen to build alliances and gain allies first. But in Hexagram Five, we hear that 'All is Auspicious', and in Hexagram Six that 'The Army sets out in orderly fashion.' The phrase 'cross the [Yellow] river' occurs seven times in the *Yijing*. The Yellow River was both a physical and mental barrier and its crossing represented the point of no return. The sense of rising expectation climaxes in Hexagram Thirty ('Judgement'), the concluding hexagram of the first section of the *Yijing*: 'The king goes to war. There is a celebration. Heads are cut off, troops are captured. No harm.'[16]

After their victory, it is said that the Zhou established an official educational system (*guan xue*) to provide their state with a skilled bureaucracy and an ideology based on their achievements. The duke of Zhou is traditionally given the credit for this and he may indeed have given the Shang ritual system a clearer political and moral orientation.[17] But in fact the new curriculum took time to evolve. At some point, court scribes and archivists (*shi*) began to collect speeches and announcements expressing the ideals and principles of government which were attributed to the founders of the Zhou dynasty. These discourses, originally inscribed on sacrificial vessels and in 'books' consisting of bamboo and wooden strips tied together, were eventually anthologised in the *Shujing* ('Classic of Documents'), also known as *Shangshu* ('Most Venerable Book'). These speeches were almost certainly not delivered by the founders, however, but were composed long afterwards;

later still, during the fourth and third centuries BCE, other texts in a different dialect were added. These have been denounced as 'forgeries', but as we have seen, ancient scriptures were regularly updated so that they could speak to the concerns of later times.

The Chinese would look back on the early years of the Zhou as a golden age, but in truth we know little about the first century of Zhou rule except that more 'barbarian' territories were conquered and more land put under cultivation. It is hard to imagine that the Zhou were markedly different from their predecessors and unlikely that they could overcome the inherent injustice of the agrarian state. But one of their innovations made an indelible impression on Chinese culture and figures importantly in *Documents*. The Mandate of Heaven is an early example of a scripture insisting on a practical, political programme of action. It is most fully expressed in 'The Shao Announcement', a speech said to have been delivered by the duke of Zhou, when he was acting as young King Cheng's regent during the consecration of the new capital.

The duke explained that the Shang kings had ruled for hundreds of years with the blessing of Heaven (Tian), but that by the end of their reign they had become tyrannical and corrupt. The common people had suffered so greatly that in their anguish they cried out to Heaven and Heaven 'too grieved for the people of all the lands', revoked the Shang's mandate to rule and decided to bestow it on the Zhou because they were deeply committed to justice. King Cheng had now become the 'Son of Heaven'. It was a heavy responsibility for the young man. The mandate required him to be 'reverently careful' and it was especially important that he was 'in harmony with the *min*' – the 'little people' – because Heaven would take away its mandate from an oppressive ruler and give it to a more deserving dynasty, so Cheng could not afford to be complacent:

Dwelling in this new city, let the king have reverent care for his virtue. If it is virtue that the king uses, he may pray to Heaven for an enduring mandate. As he functions as king, let him not, because the common people stray and do what is wrong, then presume to govern them by harsh capital punishments. In this way, he will achieve much. In being king, let him take his position in the primacy of virtue. The little people will then pattern themselves on him throughout the world. The king will therefore be illustrious.[18]

The Zhou had introduced an ethical ideal into Chinese religion, which had hitherto been unconcerned with morality. Unlike the visions of the

Aryan rishis, this important insight was not a divine revelation from on high, but resulted from the Zhou's study of Chinese history. Meditating on the fall of the Shang and their own extraordinary victory, they concluded that Heaven was not impressed by the slaughter of pigs and oxen, but demanded compassion and justice instead. The Mandate of Heaven would become an important ideal in Chinese scripture. It was potentially subversive, because, in theory, the people could demand that any ruler who did not measure up to this ideal could be deposed. The Mandate also implied that if a king were wise, humane and truly concerned for the welfare of his subjects, news of his virtue (*de*) would spread and people would flock to his kingdom from all over the world.

There was never any question of Chinese scripture separating religion from politics, because suffering, injustice, cruelty and the welfare of society were matters of sacred import. The quest for wisdom, enlightenment and transformation would nearly always be inseparable from a concern with the inherent political problems of society. Chinese scripture insisted that a ruler's policies must conform to the 'Way [Dao] of Heaven' – that is, to the fundamental rhythms of life. Once he had achieved this harmony with the ultimate and all-pervasive reality of Heaven, there was nothing that he could not do, because he would be aligned with the Way things ought to be. Indeed, his mere presence could rectify hearts and minds. This virtue had near-magical efficacy, since it enabled a king to subdue his enemies, attract loyal followers and impose his authority effortlessly. This may sound hopelessly naïve to us today, but in the not too distant past, we have seen the power of perceived moral charisma in Mahatma Gandhi, Martin Luther King and Nelson Mandela.

This ideal took time to develop. In the early texts of *Documents*, the main concern was still to establish a ritual procedure that would itself safeguard the correct balance between Heaven and Earth:

> Heaven has decreed the five duties of obligation and hierarchy for us, with their concomitant responsibilities. Heaven has mandated the five levels of the universe and those give rise to the five rites, which we have to conduct accordingly. If these are properly observed, then all life is united in harmony.[19]

Here Heaven is simply a force of cosmic order, not unlike *rta*, except that it seems unconcerned about human morality. But with the idea of the Mandate, Heaven acquired humanlike characteristics and its Way would always include justice and compassion, especially for the *min*. But Heaven never became a wholly personalised 'god' and always retained its status as an omnipresent cosmic potency – so much so that some translators prefer to translate Tian as 'Nature'.[20] Given the dynamics of the agrarian system, it was probably impossible to implement the Mandate fully but it caught the imagination of the Chinese. By emphasising the Mandate, therefore, *Documents* compelled the Chinese to look at the gulf that existed between the ideal human order and the grim reality, helping them to cultivate a critical attitude towards their civilisation.[21] This was scripture that nurtured a divine discontent and demanded a practical response.

Documents is not a sacred text like the Rig Veda, in which the divine directly discloses itself; rather, it is what some scholars have termed a 'cultural text' that enshrines traditions which bind people and create a communal identity. The anthropologist Claude Lévi-Strauss distinguished between 'cold' societies that deliberately block out the past, and 'hot' societies that have internalised their history and made it a driving force for development.[22] Our natural tendency is probably to forget the past but scripture tells us what we must remember: it evokes the past to give meaning to the present and, in the process, obliterates some things and gives prominence to others.[23] These early Chinese scriptures, therefore, did not attempt modern historical realism. Doubtless, during the Zhou conquest, which was celebrated as a sacred event, there were shameful and horrifying episodes that were deliberately 'forgotten'. The myth of the Zhou conquest, therefore, challenged each generation to consider the implications of the Mandate. But the speeches of *Documents* would not have become central to the identity and imagination of ancient China if they had simply been inscribed on bamboo strips and sacrificial vessels. A sacred text is always embedded in ritual. In an age when few people were literate, scripture became a compelling force only if recited and performed.[24]

The events of the conquest were internalised – first by the Zhou nobility and later by a larger segment of the population – by means of ritualised gestures, music and dancing. The conquest was acted out annually in the Temple of the Ancestors, accompanied by songs from another early Chinese scripture, the *Shijing* ('Classic of Odes') during the ritual 'hosting' (*bin*) of the ancestors. After the feast, sixty-four dancers, arranged in eight rows and each dressed in a tunic embroidered with dragons, danced with the king, who took the role of his ancestor King Wu. First, they mimed the departure of the army from the old Zhou capital, while a choir of blind musicians[25] sang an ode recalling the Zhou kings' reception of the mandate.

> Heaven had a firm charge
> Two monarchs received it.
> Nor did King Cheng stay idle ...
> Ah! The Bright Splendour
> Hardened his will.[26]

Later scenes enacted the defeat of the Shang, with the dancers leaping and jabbing the earth with their spears, and the victorious march back to Zhou territory. The establishment of Zhou rule was celebrated, with the choir praising King Wen's achievements and urging the audience to emulate them: 'May his descendants hold them fast!'[27] The rite concluded with the great Dance of Peace while the choir sang an ode entitled 'Martial', which reminded the audience of their own political responsibilities:[28]

> Oh, great were you King Wu!
> None so doughty in glorious deeds.
> A strong toiler was King Wen;
> Well he opened the Way for those that followed him.
> Firmly founded were his works.[29]

Centuries after the conquest, this ode could still challenge an audience, as a text written in the fourth century BCE explains:

> As for 'Martial' it consists of quelling the rapacious, putting away the weapons, protecting the great, stabilising the work, bringing peace to the people, bringing harmony to the masses, and making abundant the resources, thereby causing the descendants not to forget its stanzas.[30]

For centuries, the rite urged participants not to forget the inconvenient truth that justice and peace, however difficult to realise, were required of them by Heaven, the ultimate and all-pervasive force of life.

In the tenth century BCE, poetry was not read in solitude but was, rather, a collective enterprise that expressed the values of the community and was performed in public ritual. The Chinese character *shi* ('ode') began as a combination of the graphs for hand and foot, symbolising the dancer's gestures. Later, as the words became more important, the graphs for mouth (*kuo*) and speech (*yan*) were added.[31] The earliest odes, which were probably composed during the first century of Zhou rule, frequently use the personal pronoun 'we', suggesting that they were sung in unison by participants in a 'concelebration'.

Crucial to the experience of the *Odes*, as of nearly all scripture, was the fact that these poems were not merely recited but sung. Where language is a recent evolutionary development, music is far more fundamental for human beings; it is thought that protohumans may have communicated by singing before they could speak.[32] A product of the right hemisphere of the brain and deeply rooted in the body, music brings about physical responses in different people at the same time, so it can draw groups together at a level deeper than the purely rational. As the psychologist Anthony Storr explains, 'it has the effect of intensifying and underlining the emotion which a particular event calls forth, by simultaneously coordinating the emotions of a group of people'.[33] It would certainly have bonded the Zhou nobility during the *bin*. Music creates a state of heightened awareness that is enthusiastically sought and almost universally experienced as life-enhancing. In music as in poetry, rhythm evokes a sense of immediacy, of 'getting ready', which is absent in prose. As the literary critic I. A. Richards explains, it creates a 'texture of expectations, satisfactions, disappointments, surprisals'.[34] All this would have added to the sense of urgency and commitment that the *Odes* were trying to convey.

The *Odes* were not the only scripture to be performed in this way. The 'Gu ming', two chapters of *Documents*, provide a detailed account of the inauguration of King Kung (who succeeded Cheng in about 1005 BCE) and may describe the Zhou coronation rite.[35] When told that he must succeed his father, Kung bows twice, saying: 'I am nothing, nobody, just a child. How can I rule the four corners of the land and assure reverence to Heaven's glory?'[36] The choir responds with an ode:

> Pity me, your child,
> Inheritor of a House unfinished
> O august elders,
> All my days I will be pious ...
> O august kings
> The succession shall not stop.[37]

The princes then remind Kung that he must now respect the mandate, at which point, the choir would burst into another ode:

> Respect it! Respect it!
> By Heaven all is seen;
> Its charge is not easy to hold.[38]

And when the king replied that he would indeed strive to 'manifest the brightness' of his illustrious ancestors, the choir sang the ode's concluding words: 'I learn from those that show bright splendour, O radiance, O light, Help these my strivings.'[39]

Neurophysicists tell us that bodily movement is one of the most important means of discovering ourselves and learning about the world.[40] If a ritual brings the carefully remembered past into the present, the physical actions of the participants inscribe the past in the body, which becomes, in a sense, entextualised. A skilfully devised rite can also yield a transcendent experience, in which the participant goes beyond the self in an *ekstasis* and experiences a profound transformation. The *bin* ritual that 'hosted' the ancestors created an earthly replica of the Heavenly Court. At the beginning of the rite, the younger members of the royal family, each impersonating an ancestor, were led into the courtyard by a priest, where they were greeted with reverence, and, to the accompaniment of beautiful music, were escorted to their seats to watch the dancing. This was a holy communion with their departed forebears. By taking on the personae of their divinised ancestors, the young royals were taught to cultivate their own *shen*, the sacred core within themselves. By playing a role, we become other than ourselves; by taking on a different persona, we momentarily leave the self behind. By conforming physically to the tradition, we learn to embody it at a level deeper than the rational.[41]

The *Odes* emphasised the significance of the smallest gesture: 'Every custom and rite is observed, every smile, every word is in place.'[42]

> Very hard have we striven
> That the rites may be without mistake ...
> The spirits enjoyed their drink and food
> They assign to you a hundred blessings.
> According to their hopes, to their rules
> All was orderly and swift.

> All was straight and sure.
> Forever they will bestow on you good store.[43]

In conforming to the ideal world of the rite, participants laid aside the confusions, inconsistencies and perplexities of the mundane and felt caught up in something larger, momentous and more perfect. The rites were a theophany, a vision of sacred harmony achieved on earth. The *Classic of Rites*, a document of the third or second centuries BCE, explained that while the Shang had put the spirits in the first place and the rites second, the Zhou had reversed this order.[44] The Shang had tried to manipulate the spirits, but the Zhou discovered that the transformative effect of the ritual was more important, because it induced a form of kenosis that enabled participants to become aware of their own sacred potential. But this ritual response was 'very hard': the internalisation of a scriptural imperative demanded sustained effort, precision and discipline.

By the middle of the tenth century BCE, there seems to have been a ritual reform. Hitherto, the royal rites had been confined to the ruling class – to the royal household and the princes who ruled the cities of the Great Plain. But after about 950 BCE, instead of a 'concelebration', the rites were performed by specialists before a large audience. The *Odes* composed in this period changed too: instead of praying directly to the ancestors in the first-person plural, ritual specialists now described to the spectators what was going on, explaining what it all meant.[45]

> There are the blind drummers
> Pan pipes and flutes are ready, and begin.
> Sweetly blend the tones
> Solemn the melody of their bird music.
> The ancestors are listening;
> As our guests, they have come
> To gaze upon their victories.[46]

There had been no need for such explanations before. In another ode, the *shi* announces the arrival of the king:

> He comes in solemn state,
> He arrives in all gravity
> By rulers as lords attended
> The Son of Heaven, mysterious.[47]

And when the royal family approach the king, representing their ancestors, the *shi* made the audience aware of the importance of the presence of their departed forebears:

> May they grant us long life,
> Vouchsafe for us manifold securities;
> May they help us, the glorious elders.[48]

By this time, the Zhou dynasty had begun its long and slow decline. Some of the princes and their retainers were becoming estranged from the king and no longer understood the royal rites, and it is possible that a more socially varied audience was invited to enhance the popularity of the monarchy. Eventually all agrarian-based empires outrun their economic resources, which cannot expand beyond a certain point, but the Zhou had a special problem. At first, the princes had remained loyal to the dynasty, but by the tenth century BCE, some had started to assert their independence. The eastern colonies were now governed by cousins of the king twice or thrice removed who were becoming restive. Unable to rely on his personal charisma, the king's power was mediated by a faceless bureaucracy and by the end of the ninth century BCE, new odes lamented:

> The great Mandate is about at an end,
> Nothing to look ahead to or back upon.
> The host of dukes and past rulers
> Does not help us.
> As for mother and father ancestors,
> How can they treat us so?[49]

The memory of the Zhou's golden years did not die, however, and would long set a standard against which contemporary affairs would be judged. The *shi* consulted *Odes* and *Documents* to discover what had gone wrong, adding more speeches and stories that expressed the old ideals in a new form and reinterpreted the *Odes* so that they could address the troubled present and keep the ideal of the Mandate alive: if it had been realised once, it could be revived again.

*

In 771 BCE, the Qong Rang barbarians, from Shensi, attacked the western Zhou capital and killed King Yon. The Zhou kings managed to regroup in their eastern capital under King Ping, the heir apparent, but this was the beginning of the end. The king retained a symbolic aura, but the lords of the cities, who had long been restive, now had de facto power and steadily enlarged their territories. About a dozen small but powerful principalities developed in the Great Plain, including Song, Wei, Lu and Zai, alongside many virtually autonomous cities. The Zhou would remain nominal rulers until the late third century BCE, but the defeat in 771 marked the start of a long period of fragmentation. China seemed chronically broken, but with hindsight we can see that, without a fundamental break in continuity, it was undergoing the complex and painful process of evolving from an archaic monarchy to a unified centralised state.[50]

Thus began the period known as Spring and Autumn (Chunqiu). This was also the name given to the Temple Annals of the principality of Lu, which would later become one of the Chinese Classics. Since the ninth century BCE, ritual specialists (*shi*) in the cities and principalities had recorded important events in writing and ceremonially recited them, day by day, to the ancestors in their temple. Like the bone oracles, these annals were another attempt to build an archive that could guide policy in diplomacy and war and the interpretation of natural disasters. And like the bone oracles, the entries were dry and laconic – seemingly unpromising material for scripture. The *Spring and Autumn Annals* was the only one of these records to survive. It charts events from 722 to 481 BCE and took its name from the seasons listed in the headings of each section. Together with the late-fourth-century-BCE *Zuo Commentary*, which would transform these archives into a powerful scripture, the *Spring and Autumn Annals* are our only historical source for this period.[51]

Now that the king was little more than a symbol of unity, the widely scattered cities and principalities of the Great Plain created a communal identity that united them by means of a code of ritual practices (*li*) governing every aspect of life, public and private. The *li* functioned rather like international law, controlling the conduct of wars, vendettas and treaties and supervising the interchange of goods and services. At a time when Chinese society appeared to be fragmenting, ritual seemed the only way of holding it together. By the eighth century BCE, the Chinese no longer relied on gods and ancestors to avert disaster. Instead, there was a widespread conviction that morally correct actions were in themselves the key to survival and success. Heaven or Nature (Tian) was thought to operate automatically, almost like a natural law, so virtuous conduct that was properly aligned with Heaven should result routinely in good fortune.[52] During the early Zhou period, the nobility had developed a set of customs to promote social harmony that had probably evolved more by trial and error than by conscious design. There were some things that an aristocrat (*junzi*) did and other things that he did not do. Now, during the Spring and Autumn period, schools of ritual specialists turned this mass of customal law into a coherent system.[53]

These specialists belonged to the *shi*, minor officials from the lower ranks of the aristocracy. Originally, they had managed the estates of the nobility, supervised the sacrifices and ritual dances, and functioned as soothsayers and diviners. During the eighth century BCE, they became more specialised, and the *shi* who focused on ceremonial ritual, known as the *ru* ('ritualists' or 'literati'), began to codify the principles of aristocratic life. The *li*, which can also be translated as 'principles of appropriate behaviour', were now obligatory and, the *ru* insisted, failure to observe them could be disastrous for interstate relations. Every nobleman needed a competent master of ceremonies who understood both the intricate details of the *li* and the general spirit underlying the entire system.[54] The training of a ritual specialist began under a master at an early age. Details of the traditional rites were transmitted orally from one generation to the next, together with commentaries that explained their transcendent significance. The *ru* also kept alive the memory of bloody struggles between the great feudal lords, because these battles showed what happened when people abandoned the rules of 'appropriate behaviour'. Over the years, the school of Lu became famous for its ritualists. A small, militarily weak state in Shantung, it had hitherto played only a minor political role in the Great Plain but by the eighth century BCE, because of its connection with the duke of Zhou, its literati had become respected custodians of the august past. They compiled an anthology of ritual practices that became another of the Chinese Classics, alongside *Documents* and *Odes*. The *Liji*, the 'Classic of Rites', epitomised the indissoluble link in China between scripture and ritual.

The Shang and early Zhou had lived extravagantly, flaunting their wealth and power. But the newly codified rites insisted on moderation and restraint, because the old lavish lifestyle was no longer 'appropriate'. The eighth century BCE had seen an environmental crisis. The Zhou had made great progress in clearing the land for cultivation, but intense deforestation had destroyed the natural habitat of many species; centuries of profligate hunting had decimated the wildlife of the region; and there was less land for the breeding of sheep and cattle. Slaughtering hundreds of animals for the sacrificial banquets was no longer acceptable since the shock of this new scarcity had made the Chinese wary of such ostentation. The ritualists now strictly controlled the number of sacrificial victims and limited hunting to a carefully defined season. The economy depended more on agriculture than raiding. Wars became more ceremonial and less violent than before. With fewer military and hunting expeditions, the *junzi* spent more time at court, increasingly preoccupied with protocol and etiquette.[55] To a modern sensibility, these rituals seem arbitrary, pointless and even absurd. But the environmental crisis had led the Chinese to recognise the folly of exploiting the natural world and they felt compelled to repair the damage. Moderation and self-control became the order of the day.

But this would not have been achieved merely by verbal instruction. A *junzi* had to incorporate the rules of 'appropriate behaviour' physically, at a level deeper than the purely rational, because, as we have seen, we learn a great deal through bodily movement. Every detail of court life was now strictly regulated; it had become a stylised performance that transformed the mess of everyday life into an art form.[56] Each *junzi* had to know exactly where to stand at a royal gathering, what to say and how to say it, because the smallest infringement of costume, deportment or tone of voice was potentially disastrous. The court now centred on the local prince, who represented the Zhou king. A mystical power or virtue emanated from him but had to be protected from contamination. Consequently, he led an isolated life, his vassals forming a protective barrier between him and the rest of the world. No one could address him directly – indeed, no one should even speak in his presence. If he required advice, it must be offered tortuously 'in a roundabout manner'.[57] There were strict rules governing the way a vassal looked at the prince: 'To look fixedly over the head is arrogant; to look below the girdle is to show vexation; to look sideways is to display evil sentiment'; eyes must be fixed at a spot 'higher than the point of the chin'.[58]

Life at court had become an elaborate ritual. In the prince's presence, an official must 'stand with body bent, the ends of his sash hanging to the ground, his feet seeming to tread upon the hem of his garment. The chin must be stretched out like gargoyles on a roof.'[59] Before entering his presence, vassals must purify themselves, abstain from sex, and wash their hands five times daily.[60] For his part, the prince was forbidden to fool around or joke. He could listen only to strictly regulated music, must eat only carefully prescribed meals, sit on a mat that had been correctly arranged, and walk with a stride that did not exceed six inches.[61] His vassals, on the other hand, activated by the potency of his moral charisma, should walk swiftly, 'with their elbows spread out like the wings of a bird', while their prince, weighed down by the gravity of his position, remained motionless and speechless.[62]

It was probably the ritualists of Lu who added 'The Canons of Yao and Shun' to Documents.[63] These two kings, founders of the Xia dynasty, were said to have ruled the Great Plain in the twenty-third century BCE and, unlike the other Chinese heroes of the ancient past, they fought no battles and killed no monsters, but had reigned by their 'virtue' or 'charisma' alone. The canons open with a description of Yao:

> He was reverent, intelligent, accomplished, sincere, and mild. He was sincerely respectful and capable of modesty. His light covered the four extremities of the empire and extended to heaven above and the earth below.[64]

Henceforth, the Chinese sage deliberately placed himself in relationship first with the mundane political world and then with Heaven-and-Earth. Yet again, politics and reverence for the cosmos was essential to the pursuit of human perfection. In a pattern that will become familiar to us, it was said that Yao's gentle 'virtue' radiated outward in concentric circles, as he extended his affection first to his family, next to his clan, and finally to foreign states, making humankind a united, loving family. Yao commissioned officials to study the movements of the celestial bodies and the four seasons so that the lives of the people would be aligned with these cosmic rhythms. As a result: 'The whole world lived in balance and harmony. This meant that everyone lived in a state of enlightenment and even the surrounding states and tribes lived peacefully.'[65] Instead of creating a self-interested and exploitative government, Yao had established the Great Peace (Dai Ping).

Yao's transcendence of self-interest was especially clear when he refused to allow his own son, who was deceitful and quarrelsome, to succeed him, passing the succession instead to Shun, a man of humble origin, who was well known for his forbearance and self-control. Even though his father had mistreated and even tried to kill him, Shun had refused to retaliate so that, as Yao's ministers reported, 'He has managed to create such harmony within the home that all of them have become better people as a result.'[66] As king, Shun 'was passionate about ensuring harmony and balance'. He punctiliously observed the rituals that honoured the natural order and carefully supervised his officials, punishing those who abused their power but consistently moderating severity with compassion.[67]

The ritualists of Lu were convinced that the *li* could transform the Chinese nobility into humane men like Yao and Shun. The ideal *junzi* was 'grave, majestic, imposing, distinguished ... his face ... sweet and calm'.[68] His moderation, self-control and generosity would hold violence, hubris and chauvinism in check, because 'Rites obviate disorders, as dykes obviate floods.'[69] But the *li* must be performed with 'sincerity' and observed so precisely that they became integral to the *junzi*'s personality; he must surrender himself to these rites as wholeheartedly as the participants in the great ritual dramas relinquished their individuality when they impersonated their ancestors. His body thus became a walking, breathing icon of the harmony and order that he observed in the cosmos.[70]

In the modern world, we tend to think that moral transformation begins in our minds and hearts and is merely reflected in our physical demeanour. But neurophysicists argue that bodily movements create our ideas and feelings: 'Gestures do not merely reflect thought, but help constitute thought,' one psychologist explains; 'without them the world would be altered and incomplete.'[71] Others insist that body and mind are inseparable and that many of our fundamental concepts are derived from bodily experience. An hour after birth, a baby can already imitate adult gestures and clearly enjoys the response she elicits, so there must be an intimate connection between the bodily acts of others and our own internal states. We do not outgrow this, but build upon it in later life.[72]

During the Spring and Autumn period, when the decline of the Zhou threatened the ideological basis of society, the physical disciplines of the *li* strove to recreate the world. The attempt to behave in a courteous and self-less manner kept the ideal of social order alive, and, at the same time, it made the Chinese aware of how far they fell short of that ideal. The gestures of the *li* were designed to develop an attitude of yielding (*rang*). Instead of competing aggressively for status and flaunting their achievements, the prince's counsellors were expected to defer to one another. Family life was regulated in the same spirit. The eldest son must serve and revere his father as a future ancestor; indeed, his meticulous performance of the *li* of filial piety would create within his parent the numinous, sacred quality (*shen*) that would enable him to become a divine ancestor. He, therefore, waited on his parents, preparing their food, mending their clothes, and addressing them always in a low, humble voice. If his father was irritable, he should refrain from anger, like Shun, and try instead to empathise with him, happy when he was content, sad when he was upset, and fasting when he was sick.[73]

This may be repugnant to our modern sensibility, but the *li* also qualified the father's authority, requiring him to behave fairly, kindly and courteously to his children. Indeed, a son was never expected to submit to a father's wrongdoing. The system was so designed that each family member received a measure of reverence and respect. The chief duty of a younger son was not to serve his father but to support his older brother. The eldest son would become a father himself and receive homage from his children at the same time as he was serving his father; when his father died, he represented him during the *bin* ritual because he had helped to create the *shen* that had made him an ancestor. Underlying the family rituals was perhaps the psychological truth that if people are treated with absolute respect they acquire a sense of their intrinsic value.[74]

We do not know how punctiliously the Chinese observed the *li*, but by the seventh century BCE, Zhou extravagance seems to have been replaced by a new ethos of moderation and self-restraint.[75] The *li* also halted the total disintegration of the Zhou empire. In their distant eastern capital, the Zhou kings could no longer unite the Great Plain politically, but because the principalities now re-enacted the great liturgical ceremonies of the imperial court, the kings were represented ritually. At the same time, their speeches were preserved and transmitted in *Documents*, their hymns in *Odes* and their rituals in *Rites*. These Classics, together with martial arts and the study of Zhou music, created a curriculum that formed an aristocratic elite with a distinctively Chinese identity.

This did not mean, of course, that Chinese aristocrats had all become like Yao and Shun. 'Yielding' does not come easily to human beings, and it seems that mastery of the *li* sometimes became a mode of self-promotion – a competition to see who could yield the most. The *li* of battle demanded an external attitude of submission to the enemy, but the rites were often performed in a spirit of pride and bravado, the sport being to bully their opponents with acts of kindness. Before a battle, warriors boasted loudly of their enemy's prowess, hurled pots of wine over the city wall as gifts to their adversaries, doffing their helmets ostentatiously if they caught sight of their prince.[76] The same happened at the great archery contest, at the end of which both archers wept: the winner out of pity for his defeated rival and the vanquished out of sorrow for the victor – who was the real loser since a true *junzi* shot to miss.

But while the small principalities in the centre of the Great Plain were cultivating the *li*, three kingdoms on the periphery had been infiltrating the neighbouring barbarian lands and were acquiring large, rich territories there: Jin, in the mountainous north; Qi, a maritime state in the north-west; and Chu, a huge southern state in the middle Yangtze. Their new indigenous subjects had no time for the rites, and their rulers too were gradually relinquishing the rules of 'appropriate behaviour'. By the seventh century BCE, while barbarian tribes in the north were invading Chinese territory more aggressively than ever before, Chu, intent on its own expansion, had become a major threat to some of the vulnerable principalities. Surrounded by these powerful states led by rulers who had no intention of yielding, the principalities of the Great Plain clung to their customs tenaciously, and because they could not hope to defend themselves militarily, they relied increasingly on diplomacy in their struggle to survive.

The *Odes* played a significant role in this diplomatic strategy. Our only source for the period is the *Zuo Commentary*, which was composed in the fourth century BCE, but scholars believe that its reports are substantially reliable.[77] Some of the *ru* in the princely courts had specialised in the *Odes*, learning them by heart, transmitting them and composing new poems.[78] Because the *Odes* were an important element in the curriculum that initiated young men into the nobility, an adroit quotation from an ode in public assemblies and court debates proved that the speaker was a true *junzi*, and not only helped him to engage with his audience emotionally but also gave him the opportunity to compete with other aristocrats for pre-eminence and prestige.[79] The *Odes* thus acquired a secular role, becoming a tool for self-promotion rather than 'yielding'.

The new fashion of presenting odes (*fu shi*) depended upon a strategy known as 'breaking apart the stanza to extract a meaning' (*duan zhang qu yi*), which demolished the original meaning of the poem and gave it an entirely new significance.[80] This did not worry the Chinese, who, like most premodern peoples, valued a text that could be transformed to address a new problem. They took it for granted that the original meaning would change over time and their use of *fu shi* paved the way for later innovative commentaries on the *Odes*. The emotional power of the *Odes* proved to be extremely effective in diplomacy.[81] When the energetic diplomat Mu Shu was trying to persuade Jin to protect Lu from the menacing incursions of Qi, his dry, factual description of Lu's strategic vulnerability fell on deaf ears. But when he later recited, to the same envoys, one ode that criticised an official for cruelly abandoning a distressed population, and another that compared the desolation of warfare to the plaintive cry of wild geese, the poignancy of these verses worked their magic and he secured the military help that Lu required.[82] At the same time, while failure to recognise a quotation from one of the odes could be politically damaging, in other circumstances, responding to an ode incorrectly was hailed as a sign of virtue.[83] The issues were so complex that even the authors of the *Zuo Commentary* struggled to understand their rationale. Yet in none of these accounts are the *Odes* used to teach reverence or yielding.

However, the *Zhouyi* ('Changes of Zhou'), the ancient text based on yarrow-stalk divination which we discussed earlier, did occasionally inspire ethical interpretation. Unlike *Documents* and *Odes*, there are no uplifting speeches, tales of heroic deeds, or evocative poems in the cryptic 'line-statements' of *Changes*, but by the late Spring and Autumn period, people were just beginning to invest divination with a moral dimension. In the *Zuo Commentary*, there are two dozen references to *Changes* interpretation, dating from the seventh to the early fifth century BCE. By this time, divination it seems was no longer the preserve of trained specialists but was also practised by politically minded aristocrats. In several stories in the *Zuo Commentary*, a *junzi* whose predictions are based on moral considerations as well as stalk-casting is shown to be the more accurate diviner. In one case, a woman under house arrest contradicts the royal astrologers who had predicted her imminent release. The line-statement reads: 'Eminent, penetrating, successful, beneficent, pure. No blame', but the lady retorted, 'I am a woman and have participated in a rebellion ... Having chosen evil, how can I be "*without blame*"?'[84] When Duke Hui of Jin was imprisoned for neglecting his duties, he complained that if he had followed the predictions of his astrologers, he would have escaped this plight. But his companion disagreed: 'The *Odes* says, "The calamities of men are not sent down by Heaven. Whether they come together in civil speech or turn from another in hatred, the responsibility is with men."'[85] It seems that morality was becoming more central to Chinese religion and would soon add a new dimension to the aristocratic cult of the *li*.

*

By the sixth century BCE, all three of the regions we have considered were undergoing major social, political and economic transformation. In China, the rulers of the three large, peripheral states were casting off the restraints of ritual and 'yielding', their ultimate objective to displace the increasingly impotent Zhou kings. The Ganges Plain in India was on the cusp of an economic revolution, which would render many of the ancient Aryan ideals irrelevant. And in 597 BCE, the people of Israel had lost their land after a rebellion against King Nebuchadnezzar II, and the aristocracy and their retainers were deported to Babylonia. Ten years later, after another ill-considered rebellion, the Babylonians destroyed the city of Jerusalem and burned its temple to the ground. As the Israelites struggled to adapt to their drastically altered circumstances, they turned to scripture.

PART TWO

Mythos

4

NEW STORY; NEW SELF

The priest Ezekiel was in the first batch of Israelite deportees to arrive in Babylonia in 597 BCE; five years later, he had a terrifying vision that smashed to pieces the Israelites' relatively comfortable image of their God. Hitherto Yahweh had always been Israel's friend, but he was now unrecognisable, terrifying and impossible to define. The Sacred had become fearsomely other. Ezekiel gazed into a murky obscurity – deep cloud, fierce winds, flashes of lightning – in which everything was disturbingly unfamiliar, but he could just make out what seemed to be a war chariot. On the chariot was something that might have been a throne and seated upon it was a being that shone like bronze yet strangely resembled a man:

> And from what seemed his loins downwards I saw what looked like fire, and
> a light all round like a bow in the clouds on rainy days; that is how the surrounding
> light appeared. It was something that looked like the glory of Yahweh.[1]

A hand appeared, clasping a scroll on which were written 'lamentations, wailings, moanings', and a voice commanded Ezekiel to eat it. He was told to ingest its message of sorrow and devastation and then regurgitate it by reciting it to his fellow exiles.

When Ezekiel swallowed the scroll, it tasted as sweet as honey yet when he left the divine presence, he recalled, 'my heart ... overflowed with bitterness and anger and the hand of Yahweh lay heavy upon me'.[2] The German theologian Rudolf Otto has described the sacred as *mysterium terribile et fascinans*, fearful yet enthralling: it can appear 'an object of horror and dread, but at the same time it is no less something that allures with a potent charm':

> The creature who trembles before it, utterly cowed and cast down, has
> always at the same time the impulse to turn to it, nay even to make it

somehow his own. The 'mystery' is for him not merely something to be wondered at but something that entrances him.[3]

This mystical vision had not been elicited by carefully crafted mental disciplines; rather, it had broken upon Ezekiel unsolicited, its brutal dislocation of normal categories reflecting the devastating shock of exile. Yahweh had appeared as wholly alien: stunningly separate from Ezekiel. Yet before he could prophesy, Ezekiel had to internalise this devastating revelation, transforming it into a force within himself and discovering its sweetness.

The Israelite exiles were not too badly treated in Babylon. Their king retained his royal title and lived in the imperial court[4] and most of the deportees were settled in attractive suburbs near the Chebar canal. Ezekiel himself lived in a district that the exiles named Tel Aviv ('Springtime Hill'). But exile is a spiritual and physical trauma. Once the fixed point of 'home' has gone, a fundamental lack of orientation makes everything appear alien and oddly irrelevant. Cut off from the roots of their culture and identity, exiles can feel that they are disintegrating and have become insubstantial.[5] Trauma has been defined as an 'explosion of the psyche so catastrophic that there is no "I" that can experience it ... The psyche's templates cannot comprehend it.'[6] It is 'the confrontation with an event that in its unexpectedness or horror, cannot be placed within schemes of prior knowledge'. It is 'speechless terror . . . history that has no place'.[7] Significantly, the Israelites, who had always recorded their history hitherto, never described their life in Babylon.

Yet, as the American scholar David Carr himself discovered after a harrowing accident, the shock of such suffering can 'teach forms of wisdom that transcend their original contexts', precisely because it strips away illusions and pushes one into a different mode of consciousness.[8] A century after the Israelites went into exile, we shall see that the Greek tragedian Aeschylus would make the same point: 'We must suffer, suffer into truth ... and we resist, but ripeness comes as well.'[9] The Israelite exiles expressed this 'ripeness' in their scriptures. Even though it did not record the events of the exile, nearly every book in the Hebrew Bible bears the impact of this destructive experience.[10] Ezekiel's personal disturbance is clear in the aberrant actions which, at Yahweh's command, he performed to bring the nature of their predicament home to the deportees. He lay for 390 days on one side facing Jerusalem, without once turning over;[11] he shaved his head and burnt his hair as a sign of what would soon happen to Jerusalem; and when his wife died, he refused to mourn her, because, he explained to his fellow exiles, soon their children would all be put to the sword and when that happened they would find that the shock rendered them numb.[12]

We have seen that ritual can provide symbolic healing, but without their temple, the exiles could seek comfort only in their oral traditions. But the texts of the traditional curriculum, such as the Song of the Sea and the Royal Psalms, were triumphant celebrations, and the calm confidence of Solomon's wisdom could not speak to their extremity. The prophets' predictions of doom, however, were all too relevant and helped the exiles to look steadfastly at past mistakes and ponder the reasons for this catastrophe in the hope of finding a better stratagem for the future.[13] In the writings of the Deuteronomists, the exiles learned that they had been closer to Yahweh as landless refugees than at any time in their hitherto triumphant history. Above all, Moses had urged them to *remember*. All the deportees could do now was 'remember Zion': memory would become their main resource.[14]

Some modern scholars have imagined exiled editors sifting through written manuscripts of the documents known to us as 'J' and 'E' which they had brought with them to Babylonia, but it would have been impossible for the deportees to have lugged heavy, cumbersome scrolls on their forced march from Judah to Babylonia – a journey of some 500 miles. But somehow, they put the multifarious stories, hymns, laws and genealogies that they had memorised together in a way that gave them new significance. We do not know whether there was a single author or a team of editors. All we have is the final product: the Hebrew Bible. It is made up of three large literary units: a long narrative section, which traces Israel's history from the creation to the exile and includes some priestly legislation; the collected oracles of the prophets; and a miscellaneous section of psalms and other Wisdom writings. The jewel in the crown, on which the whole depends, is the narrative history, which has the book of Deuteronomy as its 'spine', with the Tetrateuch (Genesis, Exodus, Leviticus and Numbers) on one side, and the historical books of Joshua through Kings on the other.[15] We have seen that these tales had been circulating among the people with different emphases for centuries. Northern and southern traditions had begun to merge after the fall of the kingdom of Israel in 722 BCE, but during the exile the editors reassembled them in a way that reflected their own tragic circumstances but which was also, against all odds, heroically creative.

This project was a prime example of the forward-thrusting dynamic of scripture, which has no qualms about abandoning the 'original' vision but ransacks the past to find meaning in the present. The editors were trying to discover why things had gone so tragically wrong, but they were chiefly concerned about the future. Would the community of exiles (*golah*) survive as a people or would they simply vanish like the deportees in 722 BCE? How could Judah keep its national culture alive in an alien, hostile land? And, if the exiles allowed themselves to hope, how could they prepare for their return? By about 550 BCE, the texts they had preserved and rearranged had become the repository of their deepest fears and aspirations.[16]

The newly edited history, now dominated by the theme of exile and return, clearly reflected both the trauma and the yearnings of the *golah*, giving the biblical narrative – for perhaps the first time – a strong, internal coherence.[17] Adam and Eve were expelled from the Garden of Eden. The Tower of Babel – a Babylonian ziggurat, now a horribly familiar sight – was destroyed and its people dispersed. Yahweh commanded Abraham to migrate from his home in civilised Babylonia, and live as a foreigner in Canaan. Famine forced each one of the patriarchs – Abraham, Isaac and Jacob – to leave the Promised Land and seek grain in Egypt. Jacob's favourite son Joseph was sold into slavery in Egypt by his jealous brothers; a few years later famine forced the whole family to settle in Egypt, where they were forcibly detained. Their descendants had languished in slavery there for 500 years before Moses liberated them. After forty years in the wilderness, they finally returned to their land, bringing the bones of Jacob and Joseph back home. But the history ended in tragedy, recording how the northern kingdom of Israel had been destroyed by the Assyrians in 722 BCE and the deported Israelites had disappeared forever into the Assyrian empire, while in 597 BCE the aristocracy of the southern kingdom of Judah were deported to Babylonia.

In putting together this new history, the editors focused on the heroes of the distant past who had never known Jerusalem. Perhaps the memories of the city were too painful and it was easier to concentrate on the patri- archs and on Moses, who never made it to the Promised Land.[18] Yet at the beginning of the exile, Ezekiel had warned the *golah* not to dwell too much on Abraham's story. It seems that those Israelites who had not been deported in 597 BCE claimed that they could now rule the nation, saying: 'Abraham was alone when he was given possession of the Land. Now we are many and we hold the country as our domain.'[19] But the exile gave the editors a very different view of Abraham's story, and they had no qualms about giving these old tales a new twist.[20]

Whatever the original story of Abraham may have been, the editors now focused on the fact that when God commanded him to leave his home in Mesopotamia, he went willingly into a self-imposed exile – and that was why Yahweh favoured him.[21] The *golah* was painfully aware that Abraham's descendants were now universally regarded as a 'laughing stock'.[22] But the editors insisted on Yahweh's promise, which they repeated incessantly, that eventually Abraham would be universally revered: 'All the tribes of the earth shall bless themselves by you.'[23] As soon as Abraham arrived in Canaan, the editors made Yahweh promise to give the entire Land to his descendants – and that its borders would stretch to Babylonia itself![24] Like themselves, Abraham had been an exile, but wherever he went God had protected and enriched him, even though Abraham frequently expressed grave doubts about how these fine promises could possibly be fulfilled – just as the exiles did.[25]

The story of Abraham's willingness to sacrifice his son Isaac spoke directly to the extremity of the exiles' despair. As time passed and more and more of them died in Babylonia, it must have been increasingly difficult for the *golah* to have any faith in Yahweh's promises. So when God told Abraham to kill his son – 'your only son, Isaac, whom you love'[26] – the cruelty of this command would have resonated deeply with the deportees. God seemed to be leading Abraham to the brink of meaninglessness. If Isaac had indeed died, God's promise could not have been fulfilled and Abraham's entire life of devotion and obedience to Yahweh would have been utterly pointless. Yet Abraham, who usually not only questioned Yahweh but even argued with him, obeyed Yahweh's cruel command without demur, until, at the very last moment, Yahweh intervened and repeated the terms of his promise more emphatically than ever before:

I will shower blessings upon you, I will make your descendants as many as the stars of heaven and the grains of sand on the seashore. Your descendants shall gain possession of the gates of their enemies. All the nations of the earth shall bless themselves by your descendants, as a reward for your obedience.[27]

This troubling story reflects the doubts of a traumatised people, whose faith was deeply shaken. But it also told them never to lose hope, since an unexpected reprieve could come even at the eleventh hour. Abraham's story now bound the entire history together. Originally a southern hero, Abraham seems to have had only a minor role in the northern traditions.

But the new history made it clear that Yahweh's care for Isaac, Jacob and the generation of the Exodus all sprang from the original promise to Abraham.[28]

This is a scripture that gives no clear answer to the question of who or what is God. Indeed, the whole of the book of Genesis could be read as a systematic deconstruction of the conventional, reassuring depiction of the Creator in Chapter One – a deity presented as omnipotent, ubiquitous and wholly benign; who blesses every single one of his creatures and finds them all, even his old enemy Leviathan, 'good'; and who is effortlessly in command of the world. But by the end of Chapter Three, Yahweh has completely lost control of his creation and the fair-minded, impartial God is guilty of monstrous favouritism. We are made to feel the pain of those whom he quite arbitrarily and cruelly rejects – Cain, Esau, Hagar and Ishmael. The kindly Creator God becomes a cruel destroyer during the Flood, when, in a fit of pique, he eliminates almost the entire human species. Finally, the God who was ever-present in the early chapters vanishes and – like the exiles – Joseph and his brothers must rely on their own dreams and insights.

Nearly all Yahweh's encounters with his people in the Pentateuch are disturbing and ambiguous. Why did Yahweh so summarily reject Cain's sacrifice? And why did Yahweh meet Moses on the road one night and try to kill him?[29] And who exactly was the enigmatic stranger who, without any provocation, fought all night with Jacob beside the Jabbok River at the place that he would rename Peniel ('Face of God')? The next day Jacob was due to be reunited with his twin brother Esau whom he had gravely wronged, and, uneasy at the prospect, he had already sent Esau a huge gift of livestock:

> For [Jacob] said to himself;
> I will wipe [the anger from] his face
> with the gift that goes ahead of my face;
> afterward, when I see his face,
> perhaps he will lift up my face.[30]

These urgent repetitions enable the reader to link the face of Esau with Jacob's numinous encounter at Peniel. Perhaps, as he slept that night, bracing himself for this momentous meeting, Jacob recalled, in some deep reach of his memory, that he had wrestled with Esau while they were still in their mother's womb.[31] That night he wrestled again, this time with the stranger, who wounded him, refused to reveal his name, but blessed and empowered him. 'So, Jacob called the place Peniel, saying, "For I have seen God face to face, and yet my life is preserved."'[32] The text is subtly hinting that the 'face' of God and the 'faces' of Jacob and Esau are somehow one and the same, the divine and human inseparable. By reconciling with his brother, Jacob would glimpse the sacred dimension that informed the whole of reality. When the brothers finally meet the following day, Jacob tells Esau: 'Truly, to see your face is like seeing the face of God.'

In the Hebrew Bible, Yahweh is often as elusive, baffling and incomprehensible as he was in Ezekiel's vision. When Yahweh appeared in the Burning Bush and Moses asked for his name and credentials, he received only an aggressively cryptic reply: 'I Am who I Am!' (*Ehyeh asher ehyeh*), a Hebrew idiom to express deliberate vagueness.[33] In the ancient world, knowing a person's name gave you a certain power over him, but Yahweh had replied, in effect: 'Never mind who I am!' or even: 'Mind your own business!' Furthermore, we learn that in Moses, Yahweh has chosen a man with a speech impediment: 'No man of words am I,' Moses pleads, 'not from yesterday, not from the day-before, not (even) since you have spoken to your servant, for heavy of mouth and heavy of tongue am I!'[34] A prophet is someone who speaks on behalf of his God, but Yahweh had chosen a stammerer as his spokesperson, because the divine lies beyond the reach of language. *Theologia* ('speech about God') is, therefore, always potentially idolatrous. Significantly, it is Moses' brother Aaron who can speak well, who will be Moses' 'prophet', speaking *for him* to the people.[35] And it is the fluent, voluble Aaron who commits the archetypal act of idolatry by encouraging the people to worship the golden calf.[36]

The stories of Moses were already well developed by the sixth century BCE, but during the exile, the editors seem to have introduced new elements. Hitherto, the oral traditions had focused on the crossing of the Sea of Reeds, the Sinai revelation and the years in the wilderness. But the exiled Judahites seem to have added new details about the Israelites' enslavement in Egypt, which closely mirrored their own experience in Babylon. In this final version, 'Egypt' really *does* mean Egypt, not the Egyptian-controlled city states of southern Canaan. Like the exiles, the Israelite slaves suffer in a foreign land under a cruel imperial power, and, like the Judahites who had been recruited into Nebuchadnezzar's labour bands, they are forced into Pharaoh's corvée. The Egyptians' policy of killing all male Israelite infants spoke strongly to the exiles' fear of their nation's extinction, and Moses, saved from death by an Egyptian princess, embodied the destiny of the entire people. Especially relevant is the fact that the enslaved Israelites must wait a very long time for their liberation. Moses is forced to go back and forth frequently to plead with Pharaoh, who breaks his promise time after time. All this would have resonated with the exiles, as their sojourn in Babylonia continued, year after year.[37]

The Ten Plagues sent by Yahweh on the Egyptians do not seem to have figured in the original story, and the final plague, when the Angel of Death passes over the homes of the Israelites but slaughters all the firstborn Egyptian children, perhaps reflects a form of 'survivor's guilt': why should the exiled Judahites dream of liberation when the Israelites deported in 722 BCE had not survived as a people? Originally, the spring festival of Pesah had celebrated the barley harvest[38] but the trauma of exile gave Passover a darker significance. Moses told the Israelites that they must never forget that last night in captivity, when Yahweh's angel had 'spared our houses' but had killed the hapless Egyptian children.[39] When it became clear to the Judahite exiles that they had a chance to go home, they may well have asked why Yahweh had favoured them. It was certainly not because of their superior virtue. Where Hosea had depicted the wilderness years as a time of loving intimacy with their god, the exilic editors presented their ancestors as 'stiff-necked and stubborn', ungrateful, constantly complaining and hankering after the fleshpots of Egypt.[40]

The history calls Israel 'holy' (*qaddosh*) but this does not imply virtue. *Qaddosh* means 'separate', 'other': just as Yahweh was 'holy', that is, radically separate from all contingent beings, the exiled Israelites must share that otherness, living apart from their Babylonian neighbours so that they could survive as a nation. This 'holiness' is reflected in the priestly legislation of Leviticus and Numbers. The exiles learned to observe the purity rituals formerly observed only by priests who served the Presence (Shekhinah) in the temple. Indeed, without these rites, the insights of the new history might have remained purely notional. Ritual transforms a historical memory into mythos, something that happens *all the time*, by liberating it from the past and bringing it into the present. While the temple still stood, it had given the Judahites access to the sacred. Now, by observing these priestly rites *as if* they were still serving the Shekhinah in this foreign land, the exiles could realise within themselves the intimacy that Adam and Eve had enjoyed in Eden, when Yahweh had walked in their midst. In the priestly traditions of Leviticus and Numbers, known as 'P', Yahweh is not confined to his temple: he is a god on the move, his 'glory' comes and goes, and his 'place' is with the community. For P, the portable Tabernacle he commanded

Moses to build assured the exiles that he would accompany his people wherever they were:[41] 'I will build my Tabernacle in your midst and I myself will walk about among you.'[42] In the priestly tradition, this accompanying Presence is just as important as the *torah*.[43] Nevertheless, the detailed bodily practices and prohibitions of the *torah* created within the exiles such a strong sense of the divine presence that, when the time came, many of them would feel no need to return to Jerusalem.[44]

Priestly holiness also had a strongly ethical dimension. The purpose of scripture is not simply to comfort or save the individual: it always demands ethical and empathic action. For P, the holiness of God is not confined to a distant, personalised deity but is immanent in the whole of creation. This required an absolute and practically expressed reverence for the 'holiness' of every single creature. P asked the exiles to recall the radical egalitarianism that had inspired early Israel – before it had achieved statehood – to devise such practices as the Jubilee Year, when all slaves were to be liberated and all debts cancelled, and insisted that nothing could be enslaved or owned – not even the land.[45] The Israelites' 'holy' lives must not encourage tribal exclusivity; the exiles must never forget the experience of living as an ostracised minority in a foreign land:

> If a stranger should live with you in your land, do not molest him. You must treat him like one of your own people and love him as yourselves. For you were strangers in Egypt.[46]

This command was very different from the 'love' (*hesed*) demanded by the Assyrian kings or Hosea's cultic loyalty.

In 530 BCE, Cyrus II, king of Persia, conquered the Babylonian empire and issued an edict that permitted the deported peoples to return to their homeland and rebuild their national shrines. A prophet known as 'Second Isaiah'[47] hailed Cyrus as a *messhiah*, a man specially 'anointed' by Yahweh to end Israel's long exile.[48] He drew his fellow exiles' attention to the 'Servant', a figure apparently known to the *golah*, who seemed to embody the pain of the exiled community:

> Without beauty, without majesty (we saw him),
> no looks to attract our eyes;
> a thing despised and rejected by men,
> a man of sorrows and familiar with suffering,
> a man to make people screen their faces.[49]

Yet, Yahweh exclaims, 'My servant will prosper!' Some people had reviled him, because they assumed that he was being punished for a sin of his own; now they understood that he had suffered on their behalf: 'On him lies the punishment that brings us peace and through his wounds we are healed.'[50]

Second Isaiah believed that the exiles' triumphant return would usher in a new age, when 'the glory of Yahweh would be revealed and all mankind shall see it'.[51] But, after the splendour and sophistication of Babylonia, many of the returnees found Judah bleak and alien. Harvests were bad and when the meagre foundations of Yahweh's new temple were finally laid, many were so disappointed that they burst into tears during the opening ceremony. The 'people of the land' (*am ha-aretz*) – those Israelites who had not been deported and whose religious outlook was now very different from that of the *golah* – bitterly resented the newcomers. Jerusalem was still in a ruinous state, dangerously underpopulated and harried by aggressive neighbours. When this news reached the Judahites who had chosen to remain in what was now the Persian empire, they were extremely disturbed and requested King Xerxes to commission Nehemiah, one of their community leaders, to bring stability to the province of Yehud. Nehemiah, therefore, travelled from Babylonia to Yehud as the envoy of the Persian government. When he arrived in Jerusalem in about 445 BCE, he was appalled by the lack of morale and security and masterminded an impressive building project to strengthen the city walls. But a spiritual revival was also essential.

In the very first years of the fourth century BCE, the Persian king dispatched Ezra, priest and scribe, to Jerusalem with a mandate to enforce the *torah* of Moses as the law of the land.[52] The Persians could have been reviewing the legal systems of their subjects to ensure that they were compatible with imperial security, and Ezra may have worked out a satisfactory modus vivendi between Mosaic law and Persian jurisprudence. Like Nehemiah before him, he was horrified by the lack of morale in Judah, and to the dismay of the Jerusalemites, tore his garments and sat in the street in an attitude of deep mourning until it was time for the evening sacrifice. He then summoned the entire population to a meeting on New Year's Day. Everybody had to attend – men, women, children and the elderly – on pain of confiscation of property or expulsion from the community.

When the congregation had assembled, Ezra stood on a specially constructed wooden dais, so that he towered over the people, and read the new law aloud. We have no idea what this text was, but in the biblical account we find an old verb given an entirely new meaning: Ezra had 'set his heart to investigate [*li-drosh*]' the *torah* of Yahweh, to practise it and teach its laws and customs to Israel.[53] *Li-drosh* was originally a term used in divination: priests had 'consulted' Yahweh by casting lots.[54] But now Ezra was 'investigating' the *torah*, that is, going in search of something that was not self-evident. From *li-drosh*, we get the noun *midrash* ('exegesis'), a discipline that, as we shall see, would always retain a sense of expectant enquiry – its purpose was to find something new. We are told twice that 'the hand of Yahweh' rested on Ezra, a phrase that indicates divine inspiration.[55] So when he stood on the dais to read the *torah*, Ezra was not reciting a traditional, familiar teaching. Rather, he was 'investigating' the scriptures with the people to find an entirely different message that would speak directly to their present predicament. Furthermore, Ezra was not simply an exegete; his midrash – his commentary on scripture – was itself divinely inspired.

Ezra not only 'read from the Law of God'; he also interpreted it in a running commentary, 'translating and giving the sense so that the people understood what was read'.[56] At the same time, the Levite priests, the teachers of Israel, circulated amongst the crowd and 'explained the *torah* to the people, while the people remained standing'.[57] The task of the exegete was not to hark back to what had been written in the past, but to find fresh teachings in these ancient writings. The people had clearly never heard this *torah* before and they were dismayed: 'they were all in tears as they listened', shocked, perhaps, by the challenge of the new. 'Do not be sad,' Ezra consoled them: this was the festival of Sukkoth and they must feast, drink sweet wine and give generously to those who had nothing.[58]

The next day, the clan heads, priests and Levites gathered before Ezra for more *midrash*. This time they learned that Yahweh had instructed Moses that during the seventh month Israelites should live in leafy shelters (*sukkoth*) in memory of their ancestors' years in the wilderness. This was a complete innovation: 'Israel had never done such a thing from the days of Joshua, son of Nun, to the present.'[59] In the past, Sukkoth seems to have been celebrated quite differently in the temple. But the people were delighted. They rushed out and 'brought back branches and made themselves shelters, each man on his own roof, in their courtyards, in the precincts of the Temple of God ... and there was great merrymaking'.[60] Yet again, ritual transformed a vague historical memory into a myth, liberating it from the past and making it a vibrant and, in this case, a joyous reality in the present. This new rite helped the *golah* to identify with their ancestors who had made their own painful transition to an unknown and frightening future. It also provided a ritualised context for Ezra's *midrash* on the *torah*, which he delivered from morning to night for the next seven days. Indeed, the story suggests that without an accompanying ritual that brought the community together, scripture could be alarming and even alienating.

During the post-exilic period, several of the old cultural texts were rewritten so that they could address the contemporary situation.[61] Jeremiah's letters were altered to reflect Jerusalem's destruction and the ensuing exile. The two books of Chronicles, composed by priestly authors, glossed passages of Genesis, Samuel and Kings, giving them new meaning. In the Septuagint, the Greek translation of the Hebrew Bible, these books were called *paralipomena* ('the things omitted'); the authors were reading between the lines of the old texts and adding new reflections that made them both more complex and more credible. Ezra would be remembered as a creator of scripture as well as an exegete. It was said that when the Babylonians had burned the temple to the ground in 586 BCE, all Israel's sacred texts had been destroyed. But, writing under divine inspiration, Ezra had restored them, spending forty days dictating ninety-four of these books to the scribes. But he withheld seventy important texts that could be imparted at some future time only to the wisest Israelites.[62] These texts were never disclosed. This was a myth that expressed an important truth: in scripture, there was always something left unsaid.

*

We left the Chinese on the brink of major change. The rulers of the states on the periphery of the Great Plain – Qi, Chu and Jin – were intent on enlarging their territories, since, in an agrarian economy, the only way a state could become more wealthy and powerful was by acquiring more arable land. Besides extending their rule into 'barbarian' territory, these ambitious rulers were also bent on conquering the small principalities in the centre of the Great Plain. They felt no loyalty to the declining Zhou monarchs – some of them were even beginning to style themselves 'king' – and had no desire to model themselves on Yao and Shun, the 'Sage Kings' who had brought peace to the world in primordial time by aligning their rule with the Way of Heaven. They no longer revered kings Wen and Wu or the duke of Zhou and had no time for the *li*, the rites that promoted an ethos of 'yielding' (*rang*), kenosis and self-restraint that had held the Zhou empire together.

In the small states of the Great Plain, therefore, people lived in constant fear of annihilation. In the old days, warfare had been ceremonially ritualised, but military violence was now so extreme that during a prolonged siege the people of Song had been forced to eat their own children. In some of the principalities, the aristocracy was developing an appetite for luxury that fatally undermined the economy. As a result, some of the lower nobility were reduced to the rank of commoners and an alarming number of the aristocracy's retainers were so impoverished that they had to leave the privileged enclave of the city and live with the 'little people', in the countryside.

For conservative literati, of course, this was not simply a political and economic crisis, because this rampant egotism violated the Way of Heaven or Nature that governed the cosmos. One of the *ru* was so appalled that he decided to retire from public life. Kong Qiu (551–479 BCE) was one of the impoverished retainers. His parents had belonged to the ducal house of Song, but were forced to emigrate to Lu, where Kong was brought up in genteel poverty. He had hoped to attain high office, but was probably too honest to succeed at court and he achieved only menial posts in various principalities. When he retired from politics, at the age of sixty-eight, he devoted the rest of his life to teaching, founding one of the first of the philosophical schools to emerge during this critical time. These schools held aloof from the disordered princely states and developed alternative models of society and personal conduct. Here the Master became the 'ruler' of his disciples, transmitting his teachings orally, while his disciples committed them to writing in the hope of reaching a wider audience and future generations.[63]

Kong Qiu's disciples called him Kong fuzi ('our Master Kong'), so in the West we call him Confucius. His pupils were not boys – some held government posts – and it was they who began to compile the anthology of short aphorisms attributed to Confucius that became the *Lun yu* (or *Analects*), one of China's most important scriptures. It was once thought to have been assembled shortly after his death but it seems that the text was several centuries in the making, undergoing many transformations before reaching its final form. Confucian tradition, therefore, did not cling slavishly to the Master's *ipsissima verba*, but developed his ideas so that they could address current challenges. The *Analects* was not what we would call a 'book'. Chinese texts were still inscribed on strips of silk or bamboo that functioned rather like a loose-leaf folder, so it was easy to add new material. The text of the *Analects* passed through many hands over several generations, as various Confucian schools preserved and developed different maxims to support their own ethos. In the extant Classic, we can see these groups competing with one another. Some passages show the Master singling out certain disciples as being especially perceptive.[64] Others present several students asking Confucius the same question – on the meaning of filial piety, for example – and getting quite different answers.[65] There was, therefore, no overall Confucian orthodoxy; instead we find varied perspectives coexisting democratically side by side.

Indeed, the Master was not the author. The real author, the silent recorder of Confucius' conversations, remains unknown and invisible: Confucius was 'written up', like a character in a novel, known to us only by the words that his disciples, who clearly had ideas of their own, attributed to him. It would be well over a century before a master wrote down his own thoughts; until that time, people wrote about him and he became the soil in which his followers planted their own theories. Because Confucius does not have a consistent voice, we shall see that he himself became the ultimate object of enquiry, as readers struggled to find solid 'Confucian' principles underlying these seemingly irreconcilable differences.[66] Little regarded in his own time, Confucius became a mysterious, numinous figure, both he and his ideas firmly eluding clear definitions or official doctrines in a way that challenges our modern notion of a religious tradition.

The *Analects* opens with Confucius asking his disciples:

> To learn and then have occasion to practice what you learn – is this not satisfying? To have friends arrive from afar – is this not a joy? To be patient even when others do not understand, is this not the mark of a gentleman?[67]

This was a community of friends: learning (*xue*) was a communal rather than a solitary activity and it was certainly not an abstract pursuit of truth. The goal was 'to practise' what has been learned, so the acquisition of Confucian knowledge was inseparable from a profound personal transformation. Confucius' favourite disciple was the mystically inclined Yan Hui, a man of humble origins. Confucius once said that Yan Hui was the only member of his school who truly loved 'learning' – not because he had mastered a set of doctrines but because his behaviour towards others had changed. He took note of his failures, amended his conduct accordingly and made steady progress: 'He did not vent his anger on an innocent person, nor did he make the same mistake twice.'[68] Confucius once told his ebullient disciple Zigong that learning meant acting in such a way that you never had to regret anything you had done.[69] As Zengzi, another disciple, explained, the learning process was accompanied by a constant rigorous appraisal not of your interior state of soul but of your dealings with others:[70]

> Every day I examine myself on three counts: in what I have undertaken on another's behalf, have I failed to do my best? In my dealings with my friends, have I failed to be trustworthy in what I say? Have I passed on to others anything that I have not tried out myself?[71]

Confucius' disciples studied the Classics – *Documents*, *Odes*, *Rites* and *Music*[72] – but this textual study was inseparable from the constant practice of kindness and consideration. And as kindness and consideration had to be enacted towards others, this process could not be solitary. 'In order to establish oneself, one should try to establish others,' Confucius explained. 'In order to enlarge oneself, one should try to enlarge others.'[73] This creative partnership was essential because the goal was transcendence of ego. It was an *ekstasis*, a 'stepping outside' the self – but in the form of courtesy and compassion instead of a dramatically ecstatic vision like Ezekiel's. Unless a *junzi* responded wholeheartedly to the needs of his fellows, he would remain self-centred in a closed and shuttered world.[74]

Scriptural study was, therefore, all about *ren*, a word that Confucius refused to define because its true meaning could not be contained within the familiar categories of his time.[75] The only way you could understand it was to practise it perfectly, like Yao and Shun. The Zhou had used *ren* ('noble') to distinguish the *junzi* from the commoners, but Confucius gave the concept a moral meaning: he believed that *ren* was the 'power of the Way' (*Daode*) that had enabled the Sage Kings to rule without force, because they had acted in accordance with the laws of Heaven or Nature. How can we acquire *ren*? asked Yan Hui. '*Keji fuli*,' Confucius replied: 'Curb your ego and surrender to *li*.'[76]

Yielding to others does not come naturally; nor does an attitude of reverence and constant consideration for the needs of our fellow human beings. Confucius understood that simply meditating on the importance of kenosis, reverence and consideration would not be sufficient to curb that egotistic drive and, like today's neurophysicists, he knew that we learn a great deal from bodily gestures and discipline. The stylised gestures of the *li* would enable the *junzi* to cultivate the habit of 'yielding' to others. Instead of aggressive posturing and self-promotion, the *li*'s physical discipline of external respect would enable him to develop an interior attitude of reverence for others. The rites lifted ordinary biological actions onto a different plane. By ensuring that we did not treat others perfunctorily, they endowed mundane affairs with a ceremonial dignity that made people aware of the holiness of life. A reformed ritualism, which cut out obsession with status and pre-eminence, would restore dignity and grace to human intercourse. The rites also conferred sanctity on others. Confucius understood the psychological truth that lay behind the ancient belief that the rites of filial piety created the divine *shen* that enabled a mortal man to become an ancestor.

The *li* also taught people to deal with one another as equals, partners in the same ceremony in which even the person who plays a minor role contributes to the beauty of the whole. Hence ritual was not simply a means of self-cultivation, but had political relevance. When one of his disciples asked Confucius how *ren* applied to political life, he replied:

> When abroad behave as though you were receiving an important guest. When employing the services of the common people behave as though you were officiating at an important sacrifice. Do not impose on others what you yourself do not desire. In this way, you will be free from ill will whether in the state or in a noble family.[77]

For Confucians, personal cultivation always involved the rectification of society. The *li*, Confucius believed, would make China humane again. 'If a ruler could curb his ego and submit to the *li* for a single day,' he insisted, 'everyone under heaven would respond to his goodness.'[78]

Confucius may have been the first to enunciate the Golden Rule in a pithy, memorable formula: 'Do not impose on others what you yourself do not desire.' When Zigong asked him: 'Is there one word that can serve as a guide to one's entire life?', Confucius replied that the word was 'reciprocity' (*shu*):[79] 'The Way of the Master consists in doing one's best for others,' Zengzi explained, 'and in using oneself as a measure to gauge the needs of others.'[80] Instead of placing yourself in a special, privileged category, look within, discover what distresses you, and then refrain from inflicting that pain on anybody else. To be truly transformative, this altruism must become habitual, performed not simply when convenient but 'all day and every day'.[81] It sounded easy, but laying the clamorous ego to rest was a lifelong struggle, Yan Hui admitted:

> The more I look up at it, the higher it seems; the more I delve into it, the harder it becomes. Catching a glimpse of it before me, I then find it suddenly

at my back. The master is skilled at gradually leading me on, step by step. He broadens me with culture and restrains me with the rites, so that even if I wanted to give up, I could not. Having exhausted all my strength, it seems as if there is still something left, looming up ahead of me. Though I desire to follow it, there seems to be no way through![82]

Yan Hui was describing a transcendent experience: *ren* was not something that you 'got' but something that you gave 'all day and every day'. *Ren* was itself the transcendence you sought, because living an empathic life took you beyond yourself in a kenosis that laid the self to one side. Empathy and compassion, as we have seen, are derived from the right hemisphere of the brain, which sees the profound interconnection of all things. As he tried to realise this ideal, 'all day and every day', Yan Hui had momentary glimpses of a sacred reality that was both immanent and transcendent, rising from within, but which was also an exacting presence, 'looming up ahead of me'. There could be no 'born again' Confucians. The Master himself explained that it was some fifty years before the *li* and the virtues of *shu* and *ren* became second nature to him.[83]

At the age of fifteen, Confucius had begun his education with the study of the *Odes*, *Documents*, *Rites* and *Music*. Confucius always insisted that he was not an original thinker but relied wholly on the teachings of the past: 'I transmit rather than innovate; I trust in and love the ancient ways.'[84] His study of *Documents* as a young man, supplemented by the practice of the *Rites*, had convinced him that Yao and Shun had created the perfect ethico-political order. And if Yao's Great Peace had been achieved once, it could be achieved again. History, therefore, was not an antiquarian exercise, but a call to dedicated political action in the troubled present. When Confucius, sickened by the egotistic violence that engulfed the principalities of the Great Plain, had retired from public life, he was convinced that the reformation of China could be effected only by an educated elite who would make these ancient texts directly applicable to public life. In the past, Chinese aristocrats had often quoted the *Odes* to promote their own interests, but in the *Analects*, we see Confucius and his disciples imbuing the *Odes* with an ethical teaching not found in the original: they believed the scriptures had to speak to the moral issues of their own time.[85] Confucius had founded his school to establish a cadre of disciplined scholars, who could educate princes in the Way of Yao and Shun so that they could implement the Mandate of Heaven.[86] But they could not achieve this unless they had first transformed themselves in a long, disciplined process of self-cultivation.

There was no easy answer to the current predicament of China. Indeed, the *Analects* left the Chinese with a healthy suspicion of definitions, absolute truths and immutable rules.[87] Confucius rarely answers a question directly. When asked about *ren*, he gives two different answers – one to Yan Hui, the other to Xhongyong – and then caps these with a third definition to Sima Niu.[88] When asked to distinguish the *junzi* from the 'small person' (*xiao ren*), Confucius gives a different definition every time.[89] When asked what makes a good son, he offers no general principles, but provides disparate, unconnected examples of filiality.[90] Such an avoidance of generalisation and definition would become a hallmark of Chinese scripture. Western readers have found this exasperating, but the overall message of the *Analects* is that clever talk and learned definitions are irrelevant. The world needs people who have fully cultivated their humanity rather than facile orators.

Confucius famously said: 'I am thinking of giving up speech.' When Zigong objected, 'If you did not speak, what would there be for us, your disciples, to transmit?', Confucius simply replied that Heaven did not speak – yet look how effective Nature was: 'What does Heaven ever say? Yet there are the four seasons going round and there are the hundred things coming into being. What does Heaven ever say?'[91] Yao, he believed, had ruled, as Heaven does, without words, and transformed his people simply by the force of example, his virtue reaching out efficaciously to the entire world.[92] *Ren* was not simply a matter of behaving empathically to your own people. This was clear in Yao's concentric circles of compassion. The family is the school of empathy, which we learn to practise habitually by caring for parents and siblings according to the *li*. But it cannot stop there. Chinese scripture insists that we abandon our tribal instincts and think globally. Caring for his family enlarges the heart of the *junzi*, so that he feels empathy with more and more people – with his immediate community, then with the state in which he lives, and finally with the entire world.[93]

*

The Aryans had originally designed their rituals to support the gods in their task of maintaining cosmic order (*rta*). In the ninth century BCE, the ritual specialists had developed the concept of the Brahman, the ultimate and ineffable reality that pulled the disparate forces of the universe together. Yet increasingly, their rites aimed not only to prevent the disintegration of the cosmos, but also to give participants posthumous life. It was thought that a lifetime of impeccably performed ritual actions (*karma*) would result in rebirth after death in the world of the gods. Yet people were becoming doubtful about the efficacy of these ritualised *karma* and during the sixth century BCE, a new set of scriptures addressed these problems.

These scriptures were known collectively as the *Vedanta*, the 'end of the Vedas', for two reasons. First, they marked the closure of the revelation (*shruti*: 'that which is heard'), which had been received by the rishis and was recorded and amplified in the Vedas. After the *Vedanta*, the revelatory process could only be remembered (*smrti*). But this 'end' was a long time coming. There are nearly 250 Upanishads, as these new scriptures were called. The twelve 'classical' Upanishads were composed between the sixth and the first centuries BCE but new Upanishads continued and continue to appear. Hence, it seems, a scriptural canon does not always achieve full closure. Second, if we define 'end' as 'goal', then the Upanishads certainly represented the 'end' of Vedic *shruti*, because they tell us what the visions of the early rishis and the ritual speculations of the Brahmanas had been about. 'These, clearly, are the very essences of essences,' explains an early Upanishad, 'for the essences are the Vedas and these are their essence.'[94] Because the 'end' of the Vedas is ineffable, it could neither be expressed nor ended definitively.

The Upanishads have sometimes been viewed in the West as a quasi-Protestant rejection of early Vedic ritualism. It is true that they are often dismissive of earlier ceremonial practices, but in fact the Upanishads are a continuation and deepening of the earlier ritual science. The first two Upanishads probably appeared during the sixth century BCE, a period of intense social and economic change in the Ganges region. The *Chandogya Upanishad* originated in the Kuru-Panchala region, while the *Brhadaranyaka Upanishad* was composed in the kingdom of Videha, a frontier state on the most easterly point of Aryan expansion. Here their authors met people with very different traditions: Aryan settlers from earlier waves of migration; Iranian tribes known as the Malla, Vajji and Sakya; as well as the indigenous peoples of India. This was also a time of rapid urbanisation: the *Brhadaranyaka* and the *Chandogya* scarcely mention agriculture but frequently allude to urban crafts. Improved transport made it possible for people to travel long distances to consult the new sages. The old class divisions were beginning to erode: many of the debates recorded in these early Upanishads take place in the court of a raja, which suggests a degree of Kshatriya input.[95]

These first two Upanishads are anthologies of earlier writings put together by editors and presented as the formal instructions of famous teachers: Yajnavalkya in the case of the *Brhadaranyaka*, and Uddalaka Aruni in the *Chandogya*. Both are Brahmin householders but other teachers, such as King Ajatashastra, are members of the Kshatriya warrior class, which has prompted some scholars to suggest that these Upanishads were pioneered by Kshatriyas. It is more likely, however, that urbanisation simply led to greater social interaction. These teachings are still deeply embedded in the priestly assumptions of the Brahmanas.[96] The word *upanishad* is often translated as 'esoteric teaching', its etymology *upa-ni-shad* ('to sit near to') suggesting that this advanced knowledge was imparted by mystically inclined sages to a few gifted pupils who sat at their feet. But this view is now regarded as untenable, since the earliest use of the term *upanishad* was 'equivalence', 'resemblance' or 'correspondence'.[97] This suggests that these new scriptures were developing the science of 'connections' (*bandhus*) developed by the ritual specialists, which had cultivated a sense of the profound unity of reality by linking earthly and heavenly realities together.

This is clear in the *Brhadaranyaka*, the Upanishad of the *advaryu* priests who performed the sacrificial actions, so it begins with a meditation on the famous Horse Sacrifice, a fertility rite that celebrated a raja's authority. In a series of priestly *bandhus*, the horse is equated with the entire cosmos: its limbs are the seasons, its flesh the clouds, its forequarters the rising sun; and its neighing is Vac ('Speech'), the supreme deity itself.[98] The *Chandogya*, however, is the Upanishad of the *udgatr* priests, so it starts by contemplating the sacred mantra *AUM*, with which the *udgatr* began each of his chants. *AUM* represents the quintessence of reality – of the earth, the waters, the plants and the human being whose deepest essence is Vac.[99] Vedic priests had long been instructed to meditate on the meaning of their rituals and the task of the *brahman* priest had been to perform the entire liturgy in his mind. Now the Upanishadic sages extended this priestly contemplation of the cosmos to include the exploration of the inner self, using older Vedic texts to support their discoveries.[100]

The Upanishadic project is, therefore, an extended meditation on Vedic scripture: these sages were trying to experience for themselves the visions enjoyed by the early rishis, who had tried to describe a reality that lay beyond the reach of language. For these new sages, therefore, the inspired words of the Rig Veda were 'seeds' from which new ideas and experiences could germinate.[101] The first rishis had claimed to have seen and heard these truths, so they had described the Brahman in sensual imagery, calling it the 'germ of the world'[102] or the 'Lord of creation'.[103] The Upanishadic sages, however, believed that revelation involved the mind rather than the senses, so they referred to it more abstractly, as the *atman*, the indescribable essence of reality that pervades all things.[104] Our knowledge of the *atman*, therefore, has nothing in common with the empirical knowledge that we derive from sense perception and it transcends all mundane categories. The *atman* is both immanent and transcendent and yet it is neither – nor is it a combination of the two. It was only possible to grasp this subtle insight after a lifetime of intensive training under a skilled teacher, which systematically pushed the student's perception beyond everyday conceptual thought, until eventually he or she acquired a different mode of consciousness, more dependent upon the right hemisphere, which glimpses the transcendent unity of reality.[105]

These new rishis were developing a different notion of selfhood, claiming that – because all things are One – the *atman*, the sacred core of everybody and everything, was inseparable from the immortal Brahman that sustained the entire cosmos. They recalled the myth in the Brahmanas in which Prajapati ('the All') had united the fragile world he had created by projecting his own *atman*, his 'self' or 'inner essence', into all his creatures, thus making the entire cosmos essentially divine. If we could penetrate to the depth of our being, therefore, we would enter the 'place' where Brahman, the ultimate reality, and *atman*, the individual essence of the human being, merged and became one. This required the sage to go beyond the body, beyond conceptual thought and beyond emotion to discover the sacred 'I' that was one with the Brahman in the very core of his or her being. The first rishis had embodied the sacred Word that they had 'heard' and 'seen', but now the Upanishadic sages would go further, claiming '*Ayam atma Brahman*': 'This self is Brahman.'[106]

But how could you access the core of the self, which, Yajnavalkya explained, was inaccessible to normal consciousness?

> You can't see the Seer who does the seeing. You can't hear the Hearer who does the hearing; you can't think with the Thinker who does the thinking; and you can't perceive the Perceiver, who does the perceiving. The Self within the All [Brahman] is this *atman* of yours.[107]

The mystic had to engage in a long period of training, as we would say, systematically denying the categorisation and analytical definitions of mundane thought. 'About this *atman*, one can only say "not ... not" [*neti ...*

neti],' Yajnavalkya insisted. 'He is ungraspable, for he cannot be grasped. He is undecaying, for he is not subject to decay ... He is not bound; yet he neither trembles in fear nor suffers injury.'[108] Eventually, he or she would glimpse the profound oneness of all things, and realise that the human self and the divine were therefore inseparable. This was inaccessible to ordinary logic, so instead of reasoned arguments, the Upanishads give us accounts of experiences and visions, aphorisms and riddles that are deliberately hard to penetrate. They often present a debate ending with one of the participants at a loss for words – seguing into the silence of *brahmodya*.

The essential message of the Upanishads, therefore, is that the human self is itself divine, wholly inseparable from the ultimate reality.[109] Monotheists sometimes dismiss this claim as 'mere pantheism', but their own mystics have also experienced this identity. The German mystic Meister Eckhart (*c*.1260–1327) said: 'There is something in the soul so closely akin to God that it is already one with Him and need never be united to Him.' If this state could be fully realised, he insisted, a Christian 'would be both uncreated and unlike any other creature'.[110] Yajnavalkya also believed that the Upanishadic disciplines could wholly divinise the human practitioner. He could *become* the sacred reality that he sought.

The old Vedic rituals had tried to construct a 'self' that would survive in the heavenly world by oft-repeated ritual actions (*karma*), and which was the result, therefore, of a stock of perfectly executed sacrifices. But Yajnavalkya believed that the 'self' was a product of *all* our actions – not just ritual *karma*; this included our mental activities, our impulses and desires, and our feelings of attraction or hatred. A person whose desires were still fixated on this world when she died would be reborn on earth after a brief stay in heaven. But a person who systematically sought only his immortal 'self', his *atman*, was already one with the Brahman – 'Brahman he is, and to Brahman he goes' – and would never again return to this world of pain, sorrow and mortality.[111] This is the first time we hear of the doctrine of *karma* in which the term refers to mental and physical activities instead of ritual performances. It would become crucial to Indian spirituality. All desire for the mundane must be expunged from the psyche, and this could be achieved only by completely altering one's day-to-day existence and by lifelong instruction from a guru.

In India, the study of scripture would always require the presence of a teacher who could introduce his disciples to a wholly different way of life that would enable them to cultivate a refined level of consciousness that bore no relation to ordinary sense perception. A guru could not teach his disciple what the *atman* was; he could only show him how to attain this 'knowledge' for himself in a form of midwifery that brought a new self to birth within him.[112] To achieve this, the student had to leave home and live in his teacher's house, collect fuel for his sacred fire and tend it, live chastely and commit no act of violence. Moreover, this knowledge was not achieved simply by thinking but rather by doing physical things: chanting mantras, performing menial tasks, and taking part in ascetical exercises under the guru's direction. Because the guru 'knew' his *atman*, he was a living embodiment of the Brahman, and by imitating his way of life – his chastity, his *ahimsa* ('non-violence') and his benign reverence for all creatures (all of whom also incarnated the Brahman) – the disciple would eventually realise that the Brahman was, in fact, inseparable from his own deepest self.[113]

The teaching of the Upanishads, therefore, only makes sense in the context of this intensive transmission. From now on, sacred texts in India would often take the form of sutras – short, pithy aphorisms designed to be used by a guru in one-on-one oral instruction but which are incomprehensible to an outsider.[114] Teaching often took the form of a Q&A designed to remove systematically all rational and logical obstructions from the student's mind until he achieved a moment of illumination. But this was not for everybody. A student had to have a tranquil disposition and be prepared for a long, arduous apprenticeship and the daily performance of dull, servile tasks. The fact that so many young men – and, during the early Upanishadic period, even a few women – were willing to undergo this gruelling regime bears witness to the deeply rooted desire for transformation – indeed, the yearning for divinisation – that lies at the heart of the religious quest.

Together guru and student were cultivating a psychological state that is natural to humanity but extremely difficult to achieve. The appearance of the Upanishads in India coincided with the development of the bodily and psychological disciplines of yoga, which would enable practitioners to take the 'I' out of their thinking and thus realise the Brahman. The *atman* is often translated as 'soul', but the *atman* was conceived in a physical way and the body played a crucial role in this transformative process. The Upanishads saw the human body as the 'city of Brahman',[115] so arduous disciplines of breathing and sitting were just as important as meditative exercises. Gurus used different methods to initiate their students. Yajnavalkya told his pupils to reflect upon their dreams, which would make them alert to the unconscious mind. In a dreaming state, we often feel freer and have intimations of a higher self, but we also have nightmares when we become aware of the pain and fear that we suppress in our waking lives. But in deep sleep, Yajnavalkya explained, we achieve a unified consciousness that is a foretaste of the adept's final liberation, when he would become 'calm, composed, cool, patient and collected' because he was one with the Brahman, and 'free from evil, free from stain and free from doubts'.[116]

In the *Chandogya Upanishad*, Uddalaka had a different approach. When he initiated his son, he made him fast for fifteen days until Shvetaketu was so weak that he could no longer recite the Vedic texts by heart as he once had been able to do. In this way, Shvetaketu learned that the *atman* was a physical and spiritual unity, and that his mind consisted 'of food, of breath, of water, speech and teeth'.[117] Uddalaka then showed him that the identity of any object was inseparable from the material of which it was composed, such as clay, copper or iron. The same was true of everything that exists, since the Brahman was the true self of every single creature. 'The finest essence here – *That* constitutes the self of this whole world,' Uddalaka explained again and again. '*That* is the truth; *That* is the *atman*; and you are *That*, Shvetaketu.'[118] These sentences run like a refrain throughout the Upanishad, underlining the fact that Shvetaketu, like everything and every-body else, was Brahman, 'the All'. The Brahman was the subtle essence of the banyan seed, from which a giant tree grows – even though it is barely visible to the eye – just as it was the *atman* of every single human being.

The Upanishadic disciplines were making adepts aware that because all creatures shared the same sacred core, they were all profoundly intercon-nected. That was why the practice of non-violence was essential. But most people, Uddalaka explained to Shvetaketu, were blind to this reality. They thought they were unique and clung to the particularities that made them so precious and interesting. Yet these characteristics, Uddalaka explained, were no more durable or significant than rivers that flowed into the sea. Once they had merged, they became 'just the ocean' and no longer cried: 'I am this river!' or 'I am that river!' Whatever we are – tigers, wolves, people or gnats – we all merge into *that*, because *that* is all we can ever be. We have to let go of our self in kenosis, because clinging tenaciously to this fictitious self is a delusion that can result only in pain and confusion which we can avoid only by acquiring the deep, liberating 'knowledge' that the Brahman is our *atman*, the truest thing about us.[119]

The most common method of acquiring this 'knowledge', however, was by reciting the words of scripture as a mantra. The Upanishads rarely attempt to interpret these sacred words, because the liberating insight was not achieved by verbal analysis. Rather, the monotony of the exercise stilled such analytical activity, and the physical practice of chanting as well as the breath control it required introduced a student to a different mode of consciousness.[120] Four great mantras summed up Upanishadic teaching: 'Whoever knows thus "I am Brahman" [aham Brahmasmi] becomes this All';[121] 'Tat tvam Asi [You are That]'; 'Ayam atma Brahman: "This self is Brahman"';[122] and 'Prajnanam Brahman': "Wisdom is Brahman!"'[123] As the student became viscerally aware of the sound resonating through his body, the mantric statement became incarnate within him, and was present in his breath, speech, hearing, sight and mind. Becoming aware of all these 'connections' (bandhus), he himself experienced the Brahman making him divine, immortal and free from fear. The sacred was no longer a distant reality because the absolute had become immanent:

> It is large, heavenly of inconceivable form;
>   Yet it appears more minute than the minute;
> It is farther than the farthest,
>   Yet it is here at hand;
> It is right here within those who see,
>   Hidden within the cave of their heart.[124]

The rishi no longer looked outside himself for the divine but turned within, 'for in reality, each of these gods is his own creation, for he himself is all these gods'.[125]

5

EMPATHY

In 453 BCE, three Chinese families in the state of Jin rebelled against their prince and created three new breakaway states in Jin territory: Han, Wei and Zhao. This marked the start of a long and terrifying era known in China as the Warring States period. The powerful states on the periphery of the Great Plain — Chu in the south, Qin in the west, Qi in the north and the new 'Three Jin' — fought one another in a desperate struggle to achieve hegemony. In the process, one state after another was eliminated. But this was also a creative period, because the horror of these wars, conducted now with deadly efficiency and backed by abundant resources, intensified the quest for religious vision. Important new texts were produced, some of which would become major scriptures.

As we have seen, the rulers of the big peripheral 'warring states' had no time for moderation, ritual and restraint. Duke Wen (446–395 BCE), ruler of the new state of Wei, was a patron of learning and supported a school of literati to advise him on matters of protocol: Zixia, Confucius' disciple, was one of his protégés. But the other 'warring' rulers found Confucianism ludicrously idealistic and sought the advice of the new military theoreticians (*xie*), who roamed the countryside and were prepared to serve anybody for the right salary. Thousands of peasants were drafted into the infantry, which now bore the brunt of the fighting. In the old days of ritualised warfare, killing women, children or the elderly was considered ungentlemanly, but now massive civilian casualties became routine.

Yet during the early fourth century BCE, one of the peripatetic *xie* began preaching a radical message of non-violence. He was called Mozi, 'Master Mo' (*c*.480–390 BCE).' We know very little about him. He seems to have been the leader of a disciplined brotherhood of 180 men, who intervened in military campaigns to defend the more vulnerable cities. Indeed, Mozi devoted nine chapters of his book to defensive strategy and the construction of siege equipment to protect city walls. Like the *Analects*, the *Mozi* was a composite work that developed over time; its sections on logic and military science were probably composed much later.[2] It would not become one of the Chinese Classics, but during the Warring States period, Mohism and Confucianism were the most prominent of the philosophical schools that held aloof from the state as they watched their world seemingly heading for catastrophe. The *Mozi* also shows that the ideals of empathy and compassion were not confined to the Confucian literati but were also preached, albeit with different emphases, by their strongest critics, the *xie*.

In the core chapters of his book, Mozi mounted a sustained attack on the Confucians, the 'literati' or *ru*; he had no time for the duke of Zhou, and was irritated beyond measure by the elaborate rituals of the nobility, especially their expensive funerals and the three-year mourning period. Aristocrats might be able to afford such things, but it would ruin a working man and if everybody indulged in them, these absurd customs would devastate the economy and weaken the state.[3] Mozi, however, did approve of the Sage Kings, who, he was convinced, had not participated in this nonsense. His favourite was Shun's protégé Yu, a practical man who had worked night and day to develop a technology to prevent flooding. Mozi also cited an ancient text about Yao to support his contempt for elaborate funeral rites. When Yao died, his corpse had been wrapped in three meagre pieces of cloth and placed in a simple coffin, with no wailing during the burial.[4] He quoted the Zhou scriptures to validate the point, noting that in one of the *Odes*, Heaven had commended King Wen for his simple lifestyle:

> Though renowned, you do not make a display
> Though leader of your land, you do not change.[5]

Mozi, however, preferred to call Heaven 'God'. The aristocracy had carefully cultivated an impersonal conception of the divine, but Mozi probably reflected the ideas of the *min*, the 'little people', who worshipped Heaven as a personal deity. What is more, he insisted, the Zhou scriptures agreed with him. Did not the *Ode* say: 'King Wen ascends and descends on the left and right of God'?[6]

Mozi is unique among the Warring States scholars in his enthusiasm for the written word: he insisted very strongly that the *Odes* had been committed to writing:[7]

Such deeds were recorded on bamboo and silk, engraved on metal and stone, inscribed on bowls and basins, and handed down to posterity in the generations after. Why was this done? It was done so that men would know how these rulers loved and benefited others and obeyed the will of Heaven and won Heaven's reward.[8]

Because the Sage Kings had inscribed these texts and preserved them for posterity, Mozi and his generation could correct the false claims of the *ru*. He was particularly incensed by the Confucians' preoccupation with family and filial piety – this clannish spirit, he believed, was to blame for many social problems. Instead, Mozi preached *jian ai*, which is often translated as 'universal love' but this is probably too emotive for the pragmatic Mozi.[9] A better rendering would be 'concern for everybody'. 'Others must be regarded as like the self,' Mozi insisted; goodwill and empathy could not be confined to friends and family but must be 'all-embracing and exclude nobody'.[10] The Chinese would only stop slaughtering one another if they carefully cultivated *jian ai*: 'If men were to regard the states of others as they regard their own, then who would raise up his state to attack the state of another? It would be like attacking his own.' So, Mozi concluded, 'partiality should be replaced by universality'.[11]

This was another attempt to overcome the tribalism inherent in human nature and develop a more universal outlook. To support this teaching, Mozi quoted a now-lost section of *Documents*: 'King Wen was like the sun and moon, shedding his bright light in the four quarters and over the western land.' In this way, Mozi commented, his benevolence 'shone upon the whole world without partiality'.[12] He also cited *Odes*: 'Broad, broad is the way of the King, neither partial nor partisan.'[13] The *Odes* and *Documents* known to Mozi were different from our extant versions, because many texts were lost during the turbulence of the Warring States era. But at the time the Chinese were clearly using these writings, which by this time were over five hundred years old, as scripture, referring to them to endorse and illuminate current concerns and investing them with their highest hopes and ideals.

Despite the tragic violence of these times, China was undergoing an astonishing political and economic transformation. During the fourth century BCE, the Chinese learned to cast iron and with their strong iron tools cleared an immense amount of forest land; as a result, the harvests improved, and there was rapid population growth. A new class of merchants, working closely with the rulers, built foundries, developed mines and established large trading empires. Cities were no longer primarily cultic domains but crowded centres of trade and industry.[14] Many were delighted with these changes, but others found them disturbing. Increasingly, politics reflected the shrewd pragmatism of the developing commercial ethos. The *Rites* had insisted that a king must rely on the 'virtue' (*de*) of his office, like Yao, and 'do nothing' (*wu wei*). But the new rulers pursued their policies energetically, and the king of Wei replaced the hereditary aristocracy with a salaried civil service. Unsatisfactory ministers could now be summarily executed or sent into exile.

These changes inevitably caused social disruption. Village economies were damaged when peasants were drafted into the army and when the rulers purloined land where peasants had traditionally fished, hunted or gathered wood. Many of them were put to work in the new factories and mines. Now that they were being replaced by salaried officials, some aristocratic families became redundant, lost influence and declined. As the world changed, some sought new answers while others simply retired from urban life. In the Mediterranean around the same time, the Athenians were developing democracy as an antidote to authoritarian rule, but in China the anti-authoritarian impulse was expressed in a wholesale rejection of the political. Convinced that the only solution was to abolish government altogether, some philosophers simply walked out of the cities and headed for the forest.[15] These hermits represented the first phase of philosophical Daoism.

Their hero was Shen Nong, one of the mythical Sage Kings who had preceded Yao and Shun at the beginning of time, and had invented agriculture.[16] Daoists claimed that instead of centralising his empire, Shen Nong had allowed each fiefdom to remain autonomous and, instead of terrorising and exploiting his people, he ruled by 'doing nothing' (*wu-wei*). Daoists believed that putting your life in danger defied Heaven, which had allotted humans a fixed lifespan, so now that political life had become so perilous, it was clearly wrong to seek office. In the later sections of the *Analects*, probably composed in the mid-fourth century BCE, we see Confucius arguing with hermits, called 'men who shun the world' (*yin-zhe*), who mocked him for the 'frustrated purpose' of his attempts to save society.[17] These anchorites developed a philosophy to justify their retreat and the earliest of them was Yangzi ('Master Yang'). His dates are uncertain and he left no texts, but fragments of his teachings have survived in later works. The great Confucian philosopher Mencius (361–288 BCE) summed up Yangzi's philosophy as 'Every man for himself'[18] and dismissed it as pure egotism, claiming that Yangzi had said that 'Even if he could benefit the Empire by pulling out one hair he would not do it.'[19] This is almost certainly a distortion of Yangzi's words. What he probably meant was that he would not give up a single hair in exchange for all the pleasures of empire. Others claimed that Yangzi 'valued self' or that he 'despised things and valued life'. For him life was so precious that all the wealth in the world could not compare with it; so, to preserve it was a sacred duty.[20] Later Daoists would echo such sentiments.[21] It is easy to dismiss Yangists as self-indulgent hippies, but they clearly disturbed their contemporaries. Moreover, even their critics noted that, as the big Warring States were developing strong political ideologies, their determination to force their people to conform to an unnatural norm seemed equally unrealistic. The early Yangists may therefore have been struggling towards a deeper understanding of the limits of despotism and totalitarian rule.[22]

Yangism was much discussed in the Jixia Academy, founded by the rulers of Qi. The Confucians were deeply troubled by the new movement. If Yangzi was right, the Sage Kings, who had suffered hardship for the sake of the people, had been foolish. How could the world improve if humans were fundamentally selfish? Was the Confucian ideal of self-cultivation unnatural and perverse? Two scholars of the academy came to radically different conclusions. One was Shen Dao (c.350–275 BCE), founder of a school known as 'Legalism', who saw the new institutions in the Warring States as a manifestation of the Way of Heaven that must not be impeded by mere humans: the ruler must practise *wu wei* and refrain from any personal intervention in government that might block the mechanical working of the system. Legalist ideas had already been implemented in Qin by Lord Shang (d. 338 BCE), who had no time for the Sage Kings or compassionate government. His sole aim was the enrichment of the state and the strengthening of its military capacity.[23] The morality of the ruler was entirely irrelevant – indeed, a virtuous sage, Shang believed, would be a disastrous king. Legalism made Qin the most powerful state in China and it would later become an important ideology in the Chinese empire.

But Mencius, who was also at the academy, was convinced that Confucianism was the only way forward and his book became one of the most important Chinese Classics.[24] Like Confucius, he failed to influence any of the rulers of his day, but he had an almost messianic conviction of the importance of his mission. He reckoned that a true king arose every 500 years, yet it was now 700 years since the Zhou had founded their dynasty: 'The appearance of a true king has never been longer overdue than it is today,' he lamented, 'and the people have never suffered more under tyrannical government than today.' Yet Mencius was convinced that if a ruler finally established a benevolent government, 'the people would rejoice as if they had been released from hanging by the heels' and would rally en masse to his state. He backed up this claim with a quote from Confucius: 'The influence of virtue spreads faster than an order transmitted through posting stations.'[25]

Like Confucius, Mencius was not the author of his own book, which is also an anthology compiled by his disciples that purports to record his discussions with pupils, kings and opponents. Unlike the pithy statements of the *Analects*, however, the *Mencius* develops its arguments in detail. Like Mozi, Mencius quotes *Documents* and *Odes* to give scriptural authority to his ideas, but he also included Confucius among these authorities. Confucianism was neither a powerful, popular nor even a united movement – there were about eight 'Confucian' schools, each with sharply divergent views[26] – but Mencius was hugely optimistic about its potential. The world had changed since Confucius' day, so Mencius did not cling slavishly to the Master's ideas but adapted them quite radically to the present. Where Confucius had a broad, mystical understanding of *ren*, Mencius narrowed its meaning to 'benevolence'; where Confucius had hoped to revive the Sage Kings' idealism, Mencius simply wanted political and economic reform.

In this time of technological progress, instead of praising their ritual proficiency, as Confucius had done, Mencius revered Yao and Shun as practical men of action. Still, he pointed out that, unlike the ruthless kings of his own day, they had been motivated by compassion, feeling the people's suffering as if it were their own. When the Great Plain had been devastated by a disastrous flood, Yao 'was filled with anxiety' and this discomfort had inspired not *wu wei* but technological innovation.[27] He cut channels so that the water could flow into the sea and the land became habitable. Yu, Shun's chief minister, had spent eight years dredging the rivers, deepening their beds and building new dykes, and in all that time, even though he was newly married, he never once slept in his own house.[28] For Mencius, the first sign of incipient sagehood in Yao, Shun and Yu had been their empathic concern for the people. Each one had 'a heart sensitive to the pain of others ... and this manifested itself in compassionate government'. They had ruled by *ren*, which Mencius defined as 'the extension of one's scope of activity to include others'.[29] The man of *ren* did not simply act for himself, but made himself benevolently aware of the needs and rights of his fellows.

Compassion, Mencius believed, was a natural impulse, deeply rooted in human nature. Everyone, without exception, had four fundamental 'impulses' (*tuan*) which were as essential to our humanity as our arms and legs and, if properly cultivated, would develop naturally into the four cardinal virtues: benevolence (*ren*), justice, courtesy and the ability to distinguish right from wrong. If a man saw a child teetering on the edge of a well, about to fall in, he would instinctively lunge forward to save her. There would be something radically amiss with someone who could watch her fall to her death without a flicker of disquiet. Similarly, a person who had no sense of shame or who lacked any rudimentary sense of right and wrong would be a defective human being. You could stamp on these 'impulses' – just as you could cripple or deform yourself – but, if properly nurtured, they acquired a dynamic power of their own, 'like fire starting up or a spring coming through'. A *junzi* who had fully developed this empathic instinct could save the world.[30]

There was nothing supernatural about Mencius' Confucianism, no infusion of divine grace. The *junzi* simply revealed a potential that was inherent in everyone. As Mencius put it, the *junzi* had acquired this moral charisma by aligning himself with Heaven-and-Earth, the fundamental rhythms that governed the universe, and so, naturally, he exerted a profound influence on everyone he encountered: 'A *junzi* transforms where he passes, and works wonders where he abides. He is in the same stream as Heaven above and Earth below. Can he be said to bring but small benefit?'[31] Confucius had believed that sagehood had been achieved only by the great kings of the distant past. But Mencius insisted that it was possible for everybody here and now: anyone could be like Yao and Shun. 'If you wear the clothes of Yao, speak the words of Yao, and behave like Yao,' Mencius argued, 'then you *are* a Yao.'[32] The Dao, the Way of Heaven, was not an external rule imposed from without, but something that you discovered within yourself by daily, hourly compassionate action and practice of the Golden Rule, which made the *junzi* aware of his profound connection with all things.

> All the ten thousand things are there in me. There is no greater joy for me to find, on examination, that I am true to myself. Try your best to treat others as you would wish to be treated yourself, and you will find that this the shortest way to humanity [*ren*].[33]

All too often, however, a person loses touch with this inherent sagehood and 'allows his heart to go astray'. The only way to recover the lost heart is by 'learning' (*xie*), which was not a matter of studying complex doctrines but a disciplined enhancement of our humanity.[34]

Transformation and sagehood, therefore, were within the reach of every-body. They could also be acquired by the tacit knowledge acquired by ritual: the term 'self-cultivation' (*xie shen*) literally means 'cultivation of the body'.[35] By observing the *li*, we learn how to stand, move and eat, how to refine our commonplace selves and inspire others to do the same. Mencius recalled that Shun had grown up in the countryside with pigs and deer, but when he experienced the graceful speech and ritualised action of Yao's court, the effect on him was overwhelming: 'It was like water causing a breach in the dykes of the Yangtze or the Yellow River. Nothing could withstand it.'[36] A meticulous observance of the rites enabled the *junzi* to so embody compas-sion that he was completely transformed, with *ren* being manifest 'in his face, giving it a sleek appearance. It also shows in his back and extends to his limbs, rendering their message intelligible without words.'[37] True insight, Mencius believed, was achieved by silent example rather than words. In his list of the five modes of education, verbal teaching comes second to last:

> A *junzi* teaches five ways. The first is by transforming influence, like that of timely rain. The second is by helping his student to realise his virtue to the full. The third is by helping him to develop his talent. The fourth by answering his questions. And the fifth is by setting an example that others not in contact with him can emulate.[38]

Mencius deplored the pedantic and aggressive style of contemporary reli-gious debate: Mohists and Yangists were continually trying to force their teachings on others. But he admitted ruefully that, in these troubled times, he sometimes had to resort to this type of disputation himself to 'rectify the hearts of men ... and banish excessive views'.[39]

He then made a surprising claim. Confucius, he said, had also felt compelled to correct the errors of the day, so he had composed the *Spring and Autumn Annals*, which 'struck terror into the hearts of rebellious subjects and undutiful sons' and brought a measure of peace to Chinese society.[40] Scholars believe that the *Annals* may have originated in an ancient practice, dating, perhaps, to the ninth century BCE: throughout the year, it seems, brief accounts of current events were announced daily to the Zhou kings and their ancestors in the ancestral temple. Why would Mencius attribute them to Confucius? Originally, he explained, the Zhou kings had supervised the writing of history, but officials had been dispatched to the villages to collect the songs of the *min*, which were then circulated to the rest of the population, ensuring that the voices of the 'little people' were heard. But later kings had discontinued this custom and failed to live up to the Mandate

of Heaven, so Confucius had felt obliged to write the *Annals* to denounce
the tyranny and corruption of his day:[41]

> There were instances of regicides and parricides. Confucius was apprehensive
> and composed the *Spring and Autumn Annals*. Strictly speaking, this was the
> Emperor's prerogative. That is why Confucius said, 'Those who understand
> me will do so through the *Spring and Autumn Annals*; those who condemn me
> will do so because of the *Spring and Autumn Annals*.'[42]

The sage had a duty to challenge the problems of his time. The ancient
Sage Kings had taken practical action after the flood; the duke of Zhou had
restored stability after the conquest by subduing the barbarians; and
Confucius had rectified hearts and minds by composing a scripture. Even
though Confucius had explicitly stated that he had never composed an
original work but simply transmitted the wisdom of the ancients, his author-
ship of the *Annals* was now taken for granted, making this arcane text an
important Chinese scripture.

*

By the late fifth century BCE, the old Aryan chiefdoms in the Eastern
Ganges region had been absorbed into the large and constantly expanding
kingdoms that had developed beside the River Ganges: Koshala to the north
with Kashi and Magadha to the south. Further east, several 'republics' had
developed – Malla, Koliya, Videha, Vajji, Shakya and Licchavi – ruled by an
assembly (*sangha*) of aristocrats. Increased urbanisation saw the emergence
of a merchant class, formed of Vaishyas and Shudras, which no longer fitted
neatly into the old class system. City life encouraged innovation and experi-
mentation in practical as well as religious matters. But urban life was also
blighted by overcrowding, disease and death. Many were disturbed by the
growing violence and ruthlessness of this new world, where kings could
force their will on the people and the economy was fuelled by greed.
Increasingly, they felt that life was *dukkha* – 'unsatisfactory', 'flawed', 'awry'.

The rapidity of these developments had made city-dwellers acutely aware
of the pace of change. In the countryside, where life was ruled by the
seasons, everybody did the same things year in and year out. But in
the towns, where life was being dramatically transformed, people could
see for themselves that their 'actions' (*karma*) could have long-term consequences. A new religious idea had taken firm hold in India. The traditional

sacrificial rite had claimed that if a person completed enough perfectly executed sacrifices, he would win a permanent place in the world of the gods. But people were fast losing faith in the efficacy of these elaborate and time-consuming rituals, which seemed out of step with urban life. By the fifth century BCE, it was generally accepted that everybody, without exception, would have to return to this world of sickness, pain and death again and again; they would not only have to undergo a traumatic death once, but must endure sickness, old age and death repeatedly with no hope of final release. After death, men, women and animals would be reborn into a new state on earth that would be determined by the quality of their actions in their most recent life. Bad *karma* would cause you to be reborn as a slave, an animal or even a plant; good *karma* meant that you could be a king or even a god next time. But even a god would one day exhaust the good *karma* that had divinised him. He would then die and be reborn in a less advantageous position here on earth. All beings, therefore, were caught up in an endless cycle of *samsara* ('keeping going'), which propelled them from one life to another.[43]

People were hungry for new solutions and increasingly the 'renouncers' became the men of the hour. As early as the seventh century BCE, some of the sacrificers, who had made the ritualised journey to heaven as prescribed by the Brahmanas, had been reluctant to return to profane life after the ritual. Instead, they decided to remain in the world of the Brahman and abandoned profane life, leaving their families, retiring to the forests, living rough, owning no property and begging for their food. Some lived in communities, tending the traditional sacred fire; others were hostile to the official cult.[44] On the day he left home, a renouncer would throw one last offering into the fire and extinguish it; he would then set out to find a guru to initiate him into the life of a 'silent sage' (*muni*), seeking an 'enlightenment' (*yathabhuta*) that was an 'awakening' to his true and more authentic self.[45] By the fifth century BCE, the 'renouncers' became the main agents of religious change in India.[46]

Many ascetical schools developed, each clustered round a teacher who promised liberation (*moksha*) from *samsara*. We know little about these schools but it seems that all renouncers took four vows, promising not to kill and to abstain from lying, stealing and sex. They seem to have taught that life was indeed *dukkha* but that certain forms of asceticism or meditation could free you from the desire that compelled you to act and thus bound you to *samsara*. There were no complex scriptures to memorise, because the 'teaching' (*dharma*) was based on a guru's personal experience.

If his teaching worked for you, you achieved *moksha*; if not, you simply looked for another teacher.

But two of these schools eventually produced important scriptures. Interestingly, their founders both came from the tribal 'republics' that were less dominated by the old Vedic ideas. The first was Vardhamana Jnanatraputra (497–425 BCE), whose disciples renamed him Mahavira ('Great Man'), the title given to an intrepid warrior.[47] We know little about his life, since our earliest sources date only from the second and first centuries BCE. It seems that he was the son of a Kshatriya chieftain, was destined for a military career, but at the age of thirty became a renouncer and for over twelve years struggled alone, without a guru, to attain *moksha* by means of fasting, sleep-deprivation and exposing his naked body to the torrid heat of summer and the cold of winter. But it was not this draconian regime that brought him enlightenment; instead, he achieved *moksha* by developing a new way of looking at the world, which overturned the martial ethos of his early life.

His insight can be summed up in a single word: *ahimsa* – 'harmlessness', 'non-violence'.[48] Every human being, animal, plant or insect, without exception – even a drop of water or a rock – had a *jiva* trapped within it, a living entity that was luminous and intelligent, and had been brought to its current state by the accumulated *karma* of its former lives. Every single entity, therefore, must be treated with kindness, consideration and respect because, like human beings, they all had the potential to be reborn into a better state. For men and women, *moksha* was possible only if they did not harm their fellow creatures:

> All breathing, existing, living, sentient beings should not be slain, nor treated with violence, nor abused, nor tormented, nor driven away. This is the pure, unchangeable, eternal law, which the clever ones, which understood the world, have proclaimed.[49]

Mahavira achieved the transformation he sought when he identified empathically with the plight of every single entity on the planet. He had allowed the pain, torment and terror experienced by his fellow creatures to penetrate his very being, and it was through this disciplined compassion that he became a *jina*, a spiritual 'conqueror'.

Mahavira had laboriously dismantled the shield that we instinctively construct to protect ourselves from the discomfort of witnessing the suffering of others.[50] By focusing so intensively on the plight of every single creature he encountered in a kenosis that put his self to one side, Mahavira had achieved what the Jain scriptures call 'omniscience' (*kevala*), enabling him to see all levels of reality simultaneously in every dimension of time and space. It was a state of mind that was ineffable and indefinable, from which 'words return in vain, about which no statements can be made, and which the mind cannot fathom'.[51] It consisted simply of absolute friendliness and reverence for everything and everybody.

It is often said that Jainism is atheistic. Certainly, it has no concept of a modern Western-style God who oversees the cosmos; for Mahavira, a *deva* was simply a being who had achieved divinity by honouring the sacred essence of every single creature. Furthermore, Mahavira was convinced that anybody who followed his regimen would automatically sacralise his humanity, and become a 'Great Man'. Later, Jains would develop a complex cosmology that viewed *karma* as a form of fine matter, like dust, that weighed the soul down. They would see Mahavira as just one in a long line of 'Ford-makers' (Tirthankara) who had crossed the river of *dukkha* and preached *ahimsa*. But the earliest Jain texts show no sign of these doctrines, though they do refer to 'clever ones' who had preached *ahimsa* in the past. It seems that for Mahavira, the path to enlightenment was simply *ahimsa tout court*.

Jains were convinced that human beings were defined not by their Vedic class, but by their deeds.[52] They had no interest in the Vedas and did not regard them as divinely inspired. They condemned the ritualism of the Brahmanas as the 'science of violence' – their texts and mantras did not neutralise the cruelty of sacrificing hapless cattle.[53] They developed rituals of their own, which were far more important to them than scripture because they enabled them to acquire the disturbing awareness that everything around them – even seemingly inert objects – had a *jiva* capable of suffering. Jains, therefore, always walked with consummate caution lest they carelessly trampled on an insect; they laid down objects with extreme care, and never moved around in the darkness lest they inadvertently crushed a fellow creature. Like all renouncers, Jains took the four vows that abjured killing, lying, theft and sex, but added elements that nurtured a habit of empathy. Not only must a Jain refrain from lying, he or she (Jains admitted women into their *sangha*) must never speak unkindly or impatiently. It was not enough to forgo stealing: a Jain was forbidden to own anything at all because every single being had a *jiva* that was sovereign and free.[54]

Instead of spending hours practising yoga, like other renouncers, Jains developed their own form of meditation, standing motionless, in the posture of the Ford-makers, their arms hanging by their sides, systematically suppressing every hostile thought and impulse and, at the same time, making a conscious effort to fill their minds with love and kindness for all creatures.[55] Experienced Jains sought to achieve a state that they called *samakiya* ('equanimity'), in which they *knew*, at every level of their being, that all objects, animals and people enjoyed equal status, and realised their responsibility for any creature, however lowly or unpleasant.

Jain ritual was so demanding that there was little time for scripture. Jains did not experience the divine in their sacred texts, but cultivated an awareness of the sacredness of all things instead. Over the centuries, they would develop an ambivalent attitude to scripture. They agreed that it might help the unenlightened by making them aware of the importance of *ahimsa*, but once you were committed to the Jain path, the scriptures no longer played a significant role. Most Jains had little desire to read them. Indeed, for the uninitiated, scripture could be dangerous.[56] To this day some Jain sects do not allow the laity to read their scriptures and even Jain nuns are given access only to anthologies of carefully selected quotations. There is a concern that people might imagine that they have mastered the message simply by grasping it intellectually.[57]

The Jain term that comes closest to 'scripture' is *agama*, the 'coming' of a body of doctrine by transmission through a line of authoritative teachers, the 'enlightened' persons who had discovered the truth of *ahimsa*. *Agama* is summed up in the oft-quoted statement: 'The Worthy One enunciates the meaning, then the disciples form the sacred text [*sutta*], and then the sacred text proceeds for the good of the doctrine.'[58] The meaning of a text is therefore separate from its words. Moreover, *sutta* means 'indication' – something that merely suggests or points to the meaning that is fully imparted only by a qualified teacher.[59] We see this three-tiered process at work in Mahavira's story. After his enlightenment, he is said to have preached at the shrine of a tree spirit to the king and queen of Champa and a huge crowd of ascetics, gods, laypeople and animals. Later Mahavira's disciples, who had heard the sermon, transmitted the message orally, so that it became a *sutta*. But this was only an 'indication' of Mahavira's words. He had enunciated an eternal, fixed truth, which, like the universe itself, had no beginning and had already been preached by 'enlightened ones' in previous eras. So, the *sutta* does not record Mahavira's actual words but was merely a commentary on his message.

This perhaps explains the strong Jain belief that their scriptures are incomplete and that important truths have been mislaid – a theme we will also encounter in other traditions. Each of the twenty-four Ford-makers, it was said, had preached the doctrine of *ahimsa* to his own circle of disciples, and each time they had recorded his teachings in fourteen scriptures. But – tragically – after the death of every single Ford-maker, the disciples who were responsible for the transmission of his teachings died during a famine, so crucial instructions were lost.[60] After the passing of each Ford-maker, therefore, Jains were always left with an incomplete scriptural canon. The remaining scriptures were not committed to writing until the eleventh century CE. Some Jains believe that the few scriptures that had survived preserved the less essential doctrines and were intended for women and children, since only men could comprehend the more advanced teachings.[61] Jains tried to rectify the weak transmission of their scriptures in a series of councils (*vacana*). The first was held in the mid-third century BCE at Pataliputra and the second and third were convened during the fourth and fifth centuries CE. A more accurate translation of *vacana* is 'recitation'. There were no learned debates at these assemblies; instead participants listened to monks chanting the scriptures they had memorised.

The Jains' frank admission of the ongoing disintegration of their scriptural corpus means that they have no concept of a fixed canon. Virtually any text of reasonable antiquity can command a degree of authority and while it is almost impossible to date them, very few claim to go back to the time of Mahavira. Western scholars have often dismissed these late texts as inauthentic and have assumed that the *Kalpa Sutra* is a crucial Jain scripture because it has been preserved in so many richly illustrated manuscripts. It is indeed important to Jains, but not because it records Mahavira's words; nor is it revered for its message, since very few Jains can understand the archaic Prakrit dialect. Its status depends entirely on its role in the festival of Pargushan ('Abiding'), the most important day in the year for lay Jains. It celebrates the coming of the monsoon, the time when ascetics stop wandering and settle down among the laity, who celebrate their arrival. The *Kalpa Sutra* is recited as an act of solidarity to bind the community together. In Gujarat today, during the first seven days of the festival that are thinly attended, the extracts from the Sutra are recited in the vernacular translation. But on the eighth day, when the crowds come out, the monks recite the entire Sutra in the original Prakrit at such breakneck speed that nobody – even a Prakrit expert – could possibly understand it, while during the reading, illustrated manuscripts of the Sutra are paraded through the streets as objects of worship.[62] This scripture is significant for Jains not because of its teachings but because of its role in ritual.

The second renouncer school that would become a major religious trad-ition was founded by Siddatta Gotama, a younger contemporary of Mahavira,

who became known as the Buddha, or the 'Enlightened One'. He probably
died, according to modern scholarly reckoning, in about 400 BCE. Mahavira
and Gotama had much in common. Both were Kshatriyas (Gotama came
from an aristocratic family in the republic of Sakka); both accepted the
doctrines of *karma* and rebirth; and both achieved an enlightenment without
a teacher by their own unaided efforts. They both denied the divine origin
of the Vedas and both claimed to teach an ancient truth, realised by 'clever
ones' in the past: there had been multiple Buddhas before Gotama, and
both he and Mahavira insisted that anybody could reach this sublime state
if they followed the correct regimen. Both, therefore, founded communities
of disciples, which they called *gana* ('troop') or *sangha* ('assembly');
these were Kshatriya terms for the warrior-brotherhoods of young men in
traditional Aryan life, but both eschewed violence and emphasised the
importance of compassion for all creatures.

The Buddhist scriptures give us no continuous narrative of the Buddha's
life nor do they tell us much about his forty-five-year teaching mission. Yet
the early Buddhists thought deeply about selected incidents of his career
which are recounted in detail in the Pali scriptures – his renunciation of
family life, his long struggle for nirvana, his enlightenment experience itself,
his teaching career and his death – because these episodes told them what
they must do to attain enlightenment. This call to dedicated action transformed the history of the Buddha's life into a myth that did not attempt
an accurate biography of Gotama but rather revealed a timeless truth.
Nirvana was not an impossible goal; it was built into our human nature
and could be achieved by anybody who followed the Buddha's example.
Like any myth, its meaning would remain opaque unless it was put into
practice, hour by hour, day by day.

While Jains had little interest in complex meditative techniques, the
Buddha achieved nirvana through a specialised form of yoga. The scriptures
tell us that after leaving home, he was trained by some of the most profi-
cient yogins of the day. By this time, yoga had become a carefully crafted
science, which enabled a yogin to push himself into a transcendent state
by doing the opposite of what came naturally.[63] In practising *asana*, the
yogin refused to move: our bodies are in constant motion – even in sleep
we are never truly still – so when the yogin sat motionless in the correct
posture for hours on end, he seemed more like a plant or a statue than a
human being. When practising *pranayama*, he thwarted the most instinctive
of our bodily functions by radically controlling his breathing, and found
that this physical discipline induced sensations of grandeur, expansiveness

and calm nobility. He was then ready for *ekagrata*, concentration 'on a single point'. Our minds are in constant flux, with ideas and emotions flickering endlessly through our consciousness, so the yogin learned to focus on a single object with the intellect alone, his senses quiescent, rigorously excluding any emotion or association until he entered a tranced state (*jhana*), where he would find that he was impervious to desire, pleasure or pain. In later stages, he would experience a sense of infinity and a perception of absence that was, paradoxically, a plenitude. Very gifted yogins would enter a series of 'meditative states' (*ayatanas*) that were so intense that they felt they had entered the realm of the gods, because they bore no relation to anything in profane life; they experienced a pure consciousness that was aware only of itself.

Gotama, a gifted student, achieved these higher states very quickly, but because he knew that he had manufactured them himself, he could not believe that they were truly transcendent. When he emerged from his trance, he found that he was still subject to ordinary passions and had achieved only a brief respite from the *dukkha* of ordinary life. Nirvana, he decided, could not be temporary. He therefore abandoned traditional yoga, subjecting himself instead to a gruelling ascetical programme that nearly killed him. Finally, he admitted that the established methods had failed him and that in future he would rely only on his own instincts. As soon as he had made this decision, a new solution declared itself to him.

He recalled an incident from his childhood, when his father had taken him to watch the first ritualised ploughing of the fields. Left alone, under the shade of a rose-apple tree, the young Gotama had noticed that the ploughing had torn up the young grass and that the insects and the eggs they had laid there had all been destroyed. He felt a piercing sorrow, as though his own relatives had been killed. Yet in this surge of empathy, he experienced a yogic *ekstasis*.[64] Henceforth, he decided, when meditating he would simply cultivate 'helpful' (*kusala*) emotions, such as compassion, and rigorously exclude such 'unhelpful' (*akusala*) states as envy, hatred or greed – he would be working with his natural humanity instead of subverting it. Based on that childhood memory, Gotama developed a yogic practice known as 'the immeasurables': at each stage of his descent into the depths of his mind, he would deliberately evoke the emotion of love, and direct it to the furthest corners of the world, not omitting a single plant, animal, friend or foe from this radius of empathy until he finally achieved a state of total equanimity. This exercise in kenosis brought him an insight that forever changed him and liberated him from the deadly cycle of *samsara*.

This insight is traditionally known as the Four Noble Truths. The first three – that life is *dukkha*, that greed and desire are the cause of *dukkha*, and that enlightenment would liberate us from this state – were held by nearly all renouncers. The real advance was the fourth truth. The Buddha claimed that he had found a way out of the cycle by a method that he called the Noble Eightfold Path, which he rationalised into a threefold plan of action: morality (*sila*) cultivated *kusala* states in speech, action and lifestyle; meditation (*samadhi*) was practised according to Gotama's revised yogic disciplines; and wisdom (*prana*) consisted of a correct understanding of the Path and a determination to achieve it by integrating it directly into the aspirant's way of life.

Buddhism is a remarkable instance of the right and left hemispheres of the brain working creatively together. The Buddha's 'immeasurables' and his final transcendent insight seem to have come from the right-hemispheric vision of the profound interconnection of all things, but the Buddhist prescription is 'scientific' in its clarity, analysis and precision. Countless Buddhists have 'realised' the Four Truths by making them a reality in their own lives. Still subject to sickness, sorrow and death, they have nevertheless achieved an inner serenity that enables them to live serenely with their pain. Nirvana, the Buddha always insisted, was an entirely natural state and could be reached by anybody who cultivated the path as energetically as he did.

But nirvana was not the end of the story. The Pali scriptures tell us that after he had achieved enlightenment, the Buddha was tempted to relish his new-found peace in solitude. But the god Brahma issued a call to action, begging him to 'look down at humanity which is drowning in pain and to travel far and wide throughout the world' to teach others how to deal with their suffering.[65] It was, after all, his yogic cultivation of loving-kindness that had brought Gotama to nirvana, and this required him to 'return to the marketplace' to help others. For the next forty years of his life, he tramped tirelessly through the cities and towns of the Ganges region, bringing his teaching to gods, animals, men and women alike, and made the same demand of his disciples. 'Go now,' he told his monks who had achieved enlightenment:

And travel for the welfare and happiness of the people, out of compassion for the world, for the benefit, welfare and happiness of gods and men … Teach the *dharma*, monks, and meditate on the holy life. There are beings with only a little desire left within them who are languishing for lack of hearing the Teaching [*dharma*]; they will understand it.[66]

While the Buddha was alive, there was no need for scripture, because he was himself a living, walking icon of his teaching: 'He who sees me sees the *dharma*,' he told his monks, 'and he who sees the *dharma* sees me.'[67] After his death, it seems that the monks met fortnightly to chant the *Buddhavacana* ('the Word of the Buddha') together as a formal act of remembrance.[68] Tradition has it that a year after the Buddha's death, they held a council at Rajagriha to codify the first collection of Buddhist scripture, which, like the councils of the Jains, was primarily a recitation in which some 500 monks chanted and thus codified the official *dharma*. It is said that Ananda, who had been the Buddha's constant companion, recited all the utterances of the Buddha that he could remember, giving each a historical setting. Each *sutta* begins: 'Thus I [Ananda] have heard at one time: The Lord dwelt in . . .' The aim was to establish the situation which had prompted a teaching rather than to preserve the Buddha's actual words. In this way, the kernel of the message was transmitted, but the monks could vary and modify it, using the original historical context to adapt it to different cultural contexts in the future.[69]

Yet from the first, there was uneasiness about the very notion of a Buddhist scripture.[70] Some of the monks pointed out that they already had what was necessary to reach nirvana. They quoted the Buddha's dying words to Ananda:

You may be thinking, Ananda, the word of the Teacher is now a thing of the past; now we have no more Teacher. But that is not how you should see it. Let the *dharma* and the discipline that I have taught you be your teacher when I am gone.[71]

Nevertheless, some fifty years after the First Council, monks in the eastern regions of northern India had developed methods of memorising the Buddha's sermons and the detailed rules of the Order. They adopted a formal, repetitive style, still evident in the written texts, to aid memorisation and divided the texts into distinct but overlapping collections. Certain monks were given the task of learning one of these anthologies by heart and transmitting it to the next generation. Thus developed the Pali Canon, so called because it was composed in the north Indian dialect that may have been spoken by the Buddha. It is also called the Tripitaka ('Three Baskets') because when these scriptures were eventually written down in the first century BCE, different categories of texts were kept in three separate receptacles: the Basket of Discourses (Sutta Pitaka) consists of five collections of *nikaya*s ('sermons'); the Basket of Disciplines (Vinaya Pitaka) contains the rules of the monastic order; and the Parivara is a miscellaneous body of classified rules. Even after they were committed to writing, however, these texts continued to be recited aloud and were memorised so that the scriptures became embedded in the monks' minds.

The Pali Canon may have been called 'the Word of the Buddha', but it also included discourses by some of his more advanced disciples. Indeed, one of the *suttas* claims that *any* teaching that leads to enlightenment is the 'word of the Buddha', no matter who uttered it.[72] Some 300 years after the Buddha's death, an entirely new section, the Abidharma ('Further Utterances'), was added to the third 'basket', which analysed the original teachings philosophically, drawing out fresh implications. With the word Buddha simply meaning 'enlightened', *Buddhavacana* could usefully be translated as 'enlightened teachings', since the authors of these texts claimed to have achieved the same enlightenment as Gotama.[73]

The Buddha had always believed that his task was simply to make the *dharma* accessible to as many people as possible. In the Pali scriptures, therefore, we often find him adapting his teachings to the needs of his audience, using terminology and ideas that they could understand and relate to. Even though he had no time for Vedic ritual, in his famous 'Fire Sermon', addressed to a congregation of Brahmins, he drew upon the image of the three ritual fires that a Brahmin householder was obliged to keep alight and tend daily. 'Everything is burning,' he began. Senses, desires and passions were all ablaze. What caused this conflagration? The three 'fires' of greed, hatred and delusion.[74] If people continued to feed these flames, they would never reach the coolness of nirvana, for the word literally means 'extinguishing; blowing out'. He also punned on the word *upadana* ('clinging'), whose root meaning was 'fuel'. It was our grasping desire for the things of this world that kept us afire and impeded our enlightenment. In a similar reinterpretation of Vedic tradition, the Buddha changed the meaning of *karma* from 'ritual action' to 'intention', so that it pointed to an interior state of mind rather than an external rite.[75]

In his second sermon, delivered to five of his former renouncer companions, he introduced his doctrine of *anatta* (in Sanskrit, *anatman*), or 'no self'. This was a direct challenge to the Upanishadic quest for the 'self', the imperishable *atman*/Brahman.[76] Nobody, the Buddha argued, has a permanent, unchanging self. He pointed out that our emotions were in constant flux, altering from one moment to the next, and compared the human mind to a monkey ranging through the forest, grabbing at one branch after another.[77] There could, therefore, be no permanent *atman*; moreover, if there was, there would be no possibility of transformation. By ceasing to identify with his selfhood, by sitting loose to it, the Buddha explained, a monk would find that he was ripe for enlightenment. And indeed, the Pali scriptures tell us that when they heard this teaching, all five monks were filled with joy and immediately attained nirvana.[78] When the Buddha's disciples began to live as though the ego did not exist they found that they were happier and, paradoxically, experienced an enhancement of being.

The Buddha seems always to have addressed people where they were, not where he thought they ought to be. One day, he came across a group of Brahmins who were intent on achieving a vision of Brahma, whom they revered as the highest *deva*.[79] Instead of chiding them for their devotion to the *devas*, the Buddha introduced these Brahmins to his yogic practice of the 'immeasurables'. This disciplined empathy, he explained, was the essence of that ecstatic 'release of the mind' (*cetto-vimutti*) that constitutes true enlightenment, so instead of arguing about Brahma, they should try this method that would so enlarge their minds that they became every bit as 'extensive, magnified, and boundless' as the *deva* they were seeking.[80]

This technique of the Buddha, known as *upaya* ('skill in means'), itself epitomised the 'release of the mind' that constituted enlightenment. A discourse that set out to prove that our opponents were wrong was 'unhelpful' (*akusala*) because it fed the ego and, instead of transforming us, imprisoned us in a petty and limited version of ourselves. *Upaya*, however, was a courteous and compassionate method that respected the dignity of the other, attacked none of his cherished beliefs, but used them instead as a starting point from which he could progress.[81] Buddhist scriptures, therefore, do not enunciate clear doctrines, nor do they stridently insist on a belief system. A person's theological opinions were a matter of complete indifference to the Buddha; indeed, to accept a dogma on somebody else's authority was *akusala* because a religious idea could become a mental idol, something to cling to, whereas the point of the Buddha's teaching was to help people to let go. He always insisted that his disciples test everything he taught them against their own experience and, if a teaching or practice did nothing for them, to put it gently to one side. He had no interest in developing theories about the creation of the world or the existence of the *devas*: these were fascinating topics but such a discussion would not bring a monk any closer to nirvana.

The Buddha's teachings were directed only to his monks, however, because the Four Noble Truths could not be achieved without an intensive yogic discipline that was impossible in the noise and bustle of an Indian household. Many of his lay followers were merchants, whose commercial activities were fuelled by desire and competitiveness, so they could not hope to extinguish the fires of greed. The best these laypeople could expect was rebirth in more promising circumstances and a *dharma* was designed to help them achieve this. They must live morally, undertaking a milder version of the Five Vows taken by the renouncers by avoiding stealing or cheating, lying, sexual promiscuity and intoxicants. But such a two-tier system was not an ideal solution and Buddhists would later seek an alternative.

Many monks prepared to attain nirvana by practising mindfulness (*sati*). This has acquired a new vogue today since people find that regular sessions help them to feel more centred and self-aware and deal with stress and anxiety. But Buddhist monks were required to scrutinise their behaviour at every moment of the day, noting the ebb and flow of their emotions and sensations, to make themselves aware of the ephemeral nature of the self.[82] Buddhist spirituality was rooted in bodily practices that formed new rituals. A monk must move always with the grace and harmony that expressed the tranquillity of nirvana.[83] In rather the same way as the Chinese *li*, the practice of *kaya* ('mindfulness of the body') transformed mundane activities into a ceremony of spiritual beauty. Unlike some other renouncers, with their matted hair and filthy bodies, the Buddhist monk had to keep his body and robe scrupulously clean, and walk slowly and thoughtfully, constantly aware of his physical movements:[84]

> A monk exercises clear comprehension when moving and returning, when looking ahead and looking to the side, when drawing in and extending the limbs; when wearing his robes and carrying his outer robe and bowl; when eating and drinking, chewing his food and tasting it; when defecating and urinating; when walking and standing, sitting, falling asleep, waking up, speaking and keeping silent.[85]

In this way, a monk's body instructed his mind in the *dharma*'s wisdom. By becoming so acutely aware of his physical life, he developed a calm detachment towards both it and the prospect of its eventual demise. Buddhist scriptures alone could not bring people the release they sought. They could only direct people to the rigorous ritualised disciplines that brought out the full potential of the human being.

*

At this point, Greece should enter the story. The Greeks were not a people of scripture, even though the Homeric epics – the *Iliad* and the *Odyssey* – functioned as 'cultural texts' to initiate elite youths into the Hellenic ethos. But they were an Aryan people and, like their cousins in India, had always seen the divine as merged indissolubly with humanity. The ancient rishis had been revered as incarnations of *rta*; the young poet knew that Agni was present in the inspiration that invaded his mind during the poetry contest; and the Upanishadic sages had insisted that the Brahman was identical with the *atman* of every single creature. The Greeks too experienced the divine in any outstanding human achievement. When a warrior was carried away by the *ekstasis* of battle, he knew that he was possessed by Ares; when his world was transfigured by the overwhelming power of erotic love, he called this 'Aphrodite'. The divine craftsman Hephaestus was revealed in the work of an artist and Athena was present in every cultural attainment.[86] But this was not simply an Aryan insight. In Israel too, Yahweh was mysteriously present in the stranger who wrestled with Jacob, and the prophets had experienced the divine as an overpowering imperative that compelled them, sometimes against their will, to speak out. In China, the sacred force of *ren* that welled up within Yan Hui was identical with humanity and every man or woman embodied the divine principle of *shen*. But in the fifth century BCE, the Greeks developed the very first secular psychology.

This startling innovation was rooted in the democratic political system, established in Athens by Solon (638–559 BCE), who, during a period of economic distress, had reformed the Greek city state's constitution on a more egalitarian basis. By the late sixth century BCE, Athenian citizens were represented by the Council of 500, whose members were elected annually from the middle classes. This body could challenge any abuse of power on the part of the aristocratic Council of Elders, who met on the rocky hillock of the Acropolis. Nearby, on the southern slope, a theatre, seating some 14,000 people, had been hollowed out of the hillside beside the temple of Dionysus. This was the birthplace of Greek tragic drama. Originally citizens had gathered there on the festival of Dionysus to hear a choral recitation of his sufferings, while a narrator explained their esoteric meaning. By the early fifth century BCE, this had been replaced by a drama contest in which three poets each presented a trilogy of plays. This annual event was both a communal meditation and a civic duty, since all male citizens were obliged to attend.

The Greeks had always believed that the sharing of grief created a valuable bond between people; the tragic experience therefore bound the citizen body together.[87] At the City Dionysia, Athenians realised that they were not alone in their sorrow and wept loudly and unashamedly. By witnessing the anguish of the hero, depicted on stage, they learned to appreciate the pain of others. As Aeschylus (c.525–456 BCE), one of the earliest tragedians, explained in his 'Prayer to Zeus', suffering enabled mortals to acquire a divine perspective:

> We must suffer, suffer into truth.
> We cannot sleep, and drop by drop at the heart
> The pain of pain remembered comes again,
> And we resist, but ripeness comes as well.
> From the gods enthroned on the awesome rowing bench
> There comes a violent love.[88]

Aeschylus' play *The Persians*, the earliest of the tragedies to come down to us, was presented at the City Dionysia of 472 BCE. It commemorated the recent war between Athens and Persia, when the Persian army had rampaged through the city, smashing its buildings and desecrating its holy places until, finally, the Athenian navy had defeated the Persians in the landmark Battle of Salamis (480 BCE). In the play, there was no chauvinistic righteousness, no gloating. Instead, the audience was urged to weep for the Persians, who were presented as a noble people in mourning, and Greece and Persia were described as 'sisters of one race ... flawless in beauty and grace'.[89]

But this seems to have been the last play to have depicted a current event. Instead, poets dramatised the ancient myths of the great Homeric heroes – Agamemnon, Orestes, Achilles, Oedipus, Theseus and Ajax – in a way that utterly transformed them. The cult of the hero was a unique feature of Greek religion. These ancient kings and warriors were revered as demigods, their tombs occupying a place of honour in most of the city states. Enraged by his death, the hero had to endure a shadowy existence in the underworld; a disturbing aura emanated from his grave and rites were devised to appease him. But the memory of his exceptional qualities lived on and he remained an inspiration to the community.[90] By the fifth century BCE, however, the hero, who had embodied the aristocratic values of the old order, had become something of an embarrassment in the demo-cratic *polis* ('city state'; plural *poleis*). In the tragedies, he now became a disquieting, problematic figure, but he still retained a place in the hearts and minds of the people, who found this new perspective painful and disturbing.[91]

Each tragedy took the form of a debate between the hero, his family and colleagues, who were played by professional actors, and a Chorus, a collective, anonymous group representing the Athenian citizenry. And while the Chorus spoke in the lyrical style of the poetry that had celebrated the heroic ethos, the hero's lines were more prosaic. He sounded like a regular citizen and thus seemed closer to the audience than the Chorus that was supposed to represent them. This made both audience and actors acutely aware of the complexity of their relationship with a past whose values still had resonance and had contributed to the birth of the *polis*.[92]

The tragedies left the audience in a state of *aporia*, a dizzying and disorienting doubt about fundamental issues that was not unlike the profound uncertainty that, as we shall see in the next chapter, would shortly assail the Aryans of India. In Greece, tragic drama had developed in response to the new legal system of the *polis*, which was based on the concept of personal responsibility and distinguished an 'intentional' crime from one that was 'excusable'. Athenian men – women, of course, did not figure in Athenian law – were therefore required to regard themselves as masters of their own actions, no longer prey to the influence of the gods.[93] Today we take human autonomy for granted, so it is difficult for us to understand how disturbing this concept was in the ancient world where people believed they had only minimal control of their destiny. Most Athenians were still convinced that without the efficacy that was the exclusive prerogative of the gods, all human action was chronically impotent.

Indeed, so engrained was this attitude that the Greeks had no word for 'will', 'choice' or 'responsibility'.[94] The Greek *hekon*, although often translated as 'will', included any action not imposed by outside pressure but it could result from impulse as well as conscious deliberation. *Hekon* and *akon* ('that which is not willed') were legal terms designed to regulate the practice of honour-killing. They distinguished a murder that was wholly reprehensible from one that was defensible. Traditional ideas were still so dominant, however, that the *polis* had to make provision for *hamartia*, a mental sickness inflicted by a religious power that took possession of the individual, and could extend to his entire family or city. A human being, therefore, was not a free, autonomous agent; he could not simply 'will' his crime, because it also existed outside and beyond him.[95] As the scholar André Rivier has argued, these supernatural powers were not external to the tragic hero but operated at the heart of his decision. He could not 'choose' or 'make up his mind', because his decision was always determined by the gods and was conditioned by a reverential fear of the sacred. His task was simply to recognise that the imperative that compelled him was divine. But, Rivier insists, there was nothing mechanical about this. A hero like Orestes, who was driven to murder by the Furies, was not passive; rather, his dependence on these divine forces and his relationship with them gave greater depth to his action and increased his moral energy and commitment.[96]

In asking the citizen to regard himself, however minimally, as a free agent, therefore, the *polis* was attempting a radical break with tradition. It would be at least a hundred years – the century in which tragedy flourished – before the Greeks were able fully to accept and internalise it. They experienced their consciousness as so deeply interfused with the divine that without it they would not exist. Our modern secular consciousness, therefore, was hard-won. It was not a natural development but carefully cultivated. The old mythical consciousness later reasserted itself in Europe and, as we shall see, in the early modern period, Descartes' heroic assertion of mental autonomy would involve considerable psychological strain. It seems to have been more natural and instinctive to see the divine as an all-pervasive force that 'flows through all things', including the human psyche, and eludes the analytical categorisation of logos.

The Greeks expressed their unease with this secularised psychology in the genre of tragedy, which depicted the hero operating simultaneously on two levels, human and divine.[97] The playwrights were clearly preoccupied by the new legal system. Bloodshed was a favourite theme and the plays often included a trial or judgement. Whatever the *polis* said about his personal responsibility, the hero's mind and intentions were still suffused with divine forces that were indistinguishable from his mental activities. Our word 'drama' is derived from the Doric *dram* ('to act'): in Attic Greek, this would become *prattein*. The hero was required to decide on a course of action, only to discover that it had an intrinsic dynamic that, through no fault of his own, recoiled upon him hideously. The genre of tragedy, the French scholar John-Pierre Vernant explains, flourished in a 'border zone', an era that began with Solon and ended with Euripides (d. *c*.407 BCE). The new ideas had been implemented in the law courts but the old still retained their hold on the Greek psyche. In the hero's mind, the divine and human activities were sufficiently distinct to clash but also inseparable. As he wrestles with these conflicting forces, the tragic hero feels estranged from himself. He is presented as a *thauma* or *deinon*, a 'baffling monster', who is both agent and acted upon, guilty and innocent, lucid and yet blinded by a frenzy inflicted by the gods. By the fourth century BCE, when the secularised psychology had become more established, Plato and Aristotle could no longer understand the purpose of tragedy.[98]

The hero's dilemma is clear in Sophocles' masterpiece *Oedipus Turannos* (often translated as 'Oedipus the King'), which was presented at the City Dionysia in 429 BCE. During the Homeric period, Oedipus had not been regarded as a tragic character. A *turannos* was not a 'tyrant' in our modern sense, but a ruler who did not gain the throne by natural heredity. The original story, a magical tale of a foundling who made good, was exactly the kind of legend that was often attached to a *turannos*. At his birth, it had been predicted that Oedipus would kill his father, so, not surprisingly, perhaps, his father Laius, king of Thebes, had the baby's ankles pinned together and commanded one of his herdsmen to take him up Mount Cithaeron and leave him to die there. But the herdsman, out of pity, handed the child to a shepherd who took him to Corinth. There Oedipus was adopted by the childless king and queen and grew up believing that this royal couple were his true parents. But later he consulted the Delphic oracle, who predicted that he would not only slay his father but also marry his mother. Determined to avoid these terrible crimes, Oedipus vowed never to return to Corinth but on the road to Thebes a chariot aggressively forced him off the road. In the ensuing fight Oedipus killed the charioteer, who just happened to be his birth father Laius. Unaware that he was guilty of parricide, Oedipus arrived in Thebes, where the monstrous Sphinx was ravaging the city, devouring anyone who failed to interpret her riddle. Oedipus solved the riddle and the grateful city rewarded him with the hand of the newly widowed Queen Jocasta. He thus became king of Thebes. In the play, Oedipus claims that he was the favoured son of Tuchē ('Luck' or 'Chance'), 'the great goddess, giver of all good things', who had marked him out for his high destiny.[99] In the original story, he was not disgraced when the truth of his situation came to light; nor did he blind himself in despair. Homer describes him ruling Thebes until his death.[100]

Aeschylus and Sophocles (c.496–405 BCE), however, transformed Oedipus into a tragic figure. Sophocles takes up the story some years after his accession to the throne, when Thebes is in the grip of a devastating plague. Oedipus sends Creon, his brother-in-law, to consult the oracle, who proclaims that the pestilence will continue until the murderer of the late King Laius is unmasked. Oedipus at once initiates a forensic inquiry. The investigation begins by asking 'Who killed Laius?', but, as he interrogates the herdsman and the shepherd who had played such a crucial role in his story, it ends with the question: 'Who is Oedipus?' At the beginning of the inquiry, Oedipus confidently declares: '*Ego phano!*' – 'I'll bring it all to light!'[101] The audience, of course, knew the story and would have spotted the tragic irony: Oedipus would indeed bring the truth to light but in an entirely unexpected way. And at the end of the play he would never see daylight again.

Oedipus, solver of riddles, finds that he is the greatest riddle of all and that he is the opposite of what he thought he was. He intrepidly leads a juridical investigation only to discover that he himself is its object.[102] He sees himself as the doctor who will heal Thebes by his scientifically conducted inquiry, but he proves to be the disease (*hamartia*) that has brought death to the city.[103] At the beginning of the play he is hailed as the 'first of men'. Serenely convinced of his righteousness, he scornfully dismisses the hints of the blind seer Tiresias, who knows the terrible truth. He must learn that all along, albeit through no fault of his own, he was in fact the 'worst of men'.[104] The king revered as almost godlike by his subjects becomes the scapegoat, the *pharmakos* who must be cast out to remove the contagion. His very name indicates the ambiguity of his existence. 'Oedipus' derives from *oida* ('I know'), a phrase that he confidently repeats during the early stages of the inquiry,[105] and *pous* ('swollen foot'), the mark of the unwanted child. Oedipus must experience a kenosis that punctures his lofty sense of self. His childhood was not a romantic fairy tale; he was and will remain a defiled and polluted outcast.[106] He is described as a hunter, intrepidly tracking down the truth during the investigation,[107] but when he finally discovers that his marriage with Jocasta is incestuous he wanders off the stage, howling like a wild animal[108] before blinding himself and fleeing to the mountains.[109] The erstwhile hero has become a paradigm of ambiguous, tragic humanity.

For Sophocles, the unspeakable and unthinkable reality lies just beneath the surface of Oedipus' consciousness, so that he often speaks the truth without realising it. Knowing his story, the audience would have appreciated the fearful irony. At the beginning of the inquiry, Oedipus serenely proclaims that he is exactly the right person to uncover the truth: 'I am the land's avenger by all right, and Apollo's champion too', not realising how very true that was. He immediately adds that the murderer of King Laius might be tempted to raise his 'violent hand' against him – and, of course, Oedipus, the slayer of Laius, does indeed lift his hand violently against himself when he tears out his eyes.[110] At one point, he threatens Creon, whom he suspects of plotting against him: 'If you think you can abuse a kinsman, and then escape the penalty, you are insane.'[111] He is about to learn that he himself will pay the penalty for not only abusing but killing his own father. Unlike Oedipus, the audience can appreciate the *double entendre*. The gods' thoughts are so deeply entwined with Oedipus' own psychic processes that, without knowing it, he is uttering words that they, who alone know the entire truth, would utter. So, as Vernant explains, in Oedipus' speech we see that 'two different types of discourse, a human and a divine one, are interwoven'.[112] When the truth finally comes to light, Oedipus realises that he has never been the master of his actions: all along he has merely been the plaything of the gods. His actions, which he sincerely believed to have authored himself, have in fact been inspired by an inimical divine force. He has never been in command of his life. 'What man alive more miserable than I? More hated by the gods!' he exclaims. 'But why, why? Wouldn't a man of judgement say – and wouldn't he be right? – that some savage power [*daimon*] has brought this down upon my head?'[113]

As the truth emerges, the audience achieves a tragic world view, becoming aware of the terrifying ambiguity of the human condition. This is no criticism of the gods; the gods are often benign, but they are also savage and cruel because life itself is terrible and humans helpless before their power. But in the *polis*, the citizens of Athens were being taught that they must take responsibility for their actions. So, when the Messenger arrives on stage to describe Jocasta's suicide and Oedipus' self-blinding in horrible detail, he assumes that Oedipus acted on his own volition and was in command of his conduct. These deeds were indeed

> terrible things, and none done blindly now,
> all done with a will. The pains
> we inflict upon ourselves hurt most of all.[114]

But the Chorus cannot accept this. When Oedipus is led out, blind and bleeding, they revert to the traditional position:

> What madness [*mania*] swept over you? What god,
> what dark power leapt beyond bounds ...
> has crowned your destiny that was the work of an evil *daimon*?[115]

Oedipus too now realises that all the actions that he sincerely believed he had initiated had in fact been masterminded by a divine force, with whom he had merely cooperated; he addresses this *daimon*: 'My destiny, my dark power, what a leap you have made!'[116] When the Chorus asks him, 'What superhuman power drove you on?', Oedipus replies:

> Apollo, friends, Apollo –
> He ordained my agonies – these are my pains on pains!
> But the hand that stuck my eyes was mine,
> mine alone, no one else.[117]

The origin of Oedipus' actions had always lain elsewhere. They had always been directed by a divine order that alone give human projects meaning and direction. Humanity and divinity were inseparable.

Oedipus tore out his eyes because he had been guilty of hubris, a pride that had made him blind to the truth, which had lain just under the surface throughout the investigation. He is as physically blind as he had been figuratively and like the blind Tiresias, he can now 'see' clearly. But like a true tragic hero, he has the freedom to 'suffer into truth' and learns that, with suffering, 'ripeness comes as well' – though this too was a divine gift:

> From the gods enthroned on the awesome rowing bench
> there comes a violent love.

A new element has entered the play. When he is led onto the stage, ruined and blinded, the Messenger warns the Chorus: 'You are about to see a sight, a horror even his mortal enemy would pity.'[118] 'I pity you,' the Chorus cries, distraught, 'but cannot bear to look.' Oedipus now addresses them with a tenderness and appreciation that we have not heard from him before:

> Dear friends, still here?
> Standing by me, still with a care for me,
> the blind man? Such compassion,
>   loyal to the last.[119]

His self-mutilation has taken Oedipus to the limits of the knowledge that had been his hallmark, and his blindness has given him an entirely new emotional vulnerability.[120] His speech is larded with wordless exclamations ('*Ion … ion! Aiai … aiah!*') and the Chorus responds in kind, tenderly addressing him as 'friend' and 'dear one'.[121] When Oedipus reaches out to his distraught daughters, Antigone and Ismene, he momentarily forgets himself in sympathy for their plight. Moreover, in tragedy, the compassion expressed on stage is a direction to the audience, instructing them to sympathise with a man guilty of crimes that would normally fill them with disgust. When the audience wept for Oedipus, they would experience the catharsis, the purifying transformation effected by tragedy in the *ekstasis* of empathy.

Oedipus had accepted his undeserved punishment with courage, serenity and compassion. The apparent sagacity that had brought him such prestige had been ruthlessly dismantled. But there was a strange reversal. Cut off from other human beings by his pollution (*hamartia*), he had, in the logic of Greek religion, become taboo, a figure separate, apart and, therefore, holy. In *Oedipus at Colonus*, a play that Sophocles wrote at the very end of his life, Oedipus would be exalted – almost deified – in death and his grave would become a source of blessing to the *polis* of Athens, which had given him asylum.

By this time, the era of tragedy was nearing its end. The *polis* relinquished the tragic world view, which was replaced by the philosophical logos pioneered by Socrates (*c.*469–399 BCE), Plato (*c.*427–347 BCE) and Aristotle (*c.*384–322 BCE). Plato would even make Socrates expel the tragic poets from his ideal Republic. But old habits die hard. Firstly, Plato presents Socrates' dialogues as a philosophical version of the ancient Aryan *brahmodya* ritual. When people came to Socrates, they believed that they knew exactly what they were talking about, but after half an hour of Socrates' relentless questioning they discovered that they did not know the first thing about such basic concepts as justice, goodness or beauty. A Socratic dialogue often ends with the participants experiencing a vertiginous doubt (*aporia*) and at that moment, Socrates insisted, they had become philosophers, because they longed for greater insight but realised humbly that they did not have it. Indeed, many of his pupils found that this initial vertigo led to *ekstasis*, because they had 'stepped outside' their former selves.

Socrates was eventually accused of impiety and of corrupting Athenian youth. Yet after the Athenian judges had pronounced the sentence of execution at his trial, Socrates, the founder of Western rationalism, made it clear that he did not regard his mind as an autonomous entity. He told his judges that he had always relied on a *daimon*, a term that Plato's modern translators have rendered as 'prophetic power' or a 'spiritual manifestation'. Throughout his life, Socrates had listened intently to this *daimon*, who had 'frequently opposed me when I was about to do something wrong'. But he drew comfort from the fact that during his trial, his *daimon* 'has not opposed me, either when I left home at dawn, or when I came into court, or at any time that I was about to say something during my speech'. He interpreted the silence of his *daimon* as a divine but tacit endorsement of his stance, which also suggested to him that death was not an evil, but could even be 'a great advantage'. That, he concluded, was 'why my *daimon* did not oppose me on any point'.[122] Throughout his life, therefore, Socrates, champion of logos, had experienced a divine presence in his mind, sometimes in tune with his own ideas and sometimes not, but always fused with his most profound and momentous deliberations.

6

UNKNOWING

After the Buddha's death, the idea of an imperial state took root in India. King Bimbisara of Magadha, the Buddha's friend, was murdered by his son Ajatashattu, who promptly annexed the kingdoms of Koshala and Kashi. Parricide would now become a regular feature of monarchical succession: the five kings who succeeded Ajatashattu all killed their fathers. Finally, a low-caste Shudra, Mahapadma Nanda, founded the first non-Kshatriya dynasty and extended the borders of his realm still further. When Chandragupta Maurya, also a Shudra, usurped the Nandas in 321 BCE, the kingdom of Magadha became the Mauryan empire. No premodern empire could maintain its rule without ceaseless military activity, since the subject peoples were always liable to revolt. In addition, the forcible acquisition of more arable land was essential to the economy and prisoners of war provided essential manpower.[1] The rise of the Shudra emperors made it clear that the old Vedic system of four distinct classes, each with its clearly defined role, status and *dharma*, was dead. Indeed, the world seemed to have succumbed to *adharma* and had become terrifying and lawless.

Yet the ideal of *ahimsa* ('non-violence') lived on, in strange counterpoint with an ethos of extermination. The Nanda rulers had vowed to slaughter the entire Kshatriya class to prevent them from regaining power.[2] Mahapadma Nanda, who became known as *sarva kshatrantaka* ('annihilator of the Kshatriyas'), predicted that in future 'the kings of the earth will all be Shudra'.[3] But, paradoxically, the last Nanda emperor was killed by Kautalya, a Brahmin whose caste was vowed to *ahimsa*. Perhaps stranger still, the first three Mauryan kings, all of whom had slain their fathers to acquire the throne, had patronised Jains and Buddhists, who abjured all violence. Ashoka Maurya, who came to the throne in 268 BCE after murdering two of his brothers, had a reputation for cruelty and lived a dissolute life. But in 260 BCE, while accompanying his army to put down a rebellion in Orissa, he was so horrified by the violence he witnessed that he inscribed massive edicts preaching 'abstention from killing living beings' on cliff faces and cylindrical pillars throughout his empire. But he could not disband his army, of course.⁴ The last Mauryan king was also killed by a Brahmin, Pashyamistra, who founded the Sunga dynasty. Then followed centuries of warfare, invasion and chronic disorder until, finally, the Gupta dynasty (320–540 CE) created a more decentralised system of government and ushered in India's classical age.

This is the turbulent background of India's great epic, the *Mahabharata*, which reflects a world in which the assassination of kings is taken for granted, extermination an accepted monarchical practice, and the institution of *dharma* – the duties incumbent on each class of society – a dead letter. Significantly, this massive epic – eight times the length of the *Iliad* and *Odyssey* combined – is one of the most popular of India's sacred texts. Set in the Ganges region in the Late Vedic period, probably, according to some modern estimates, from the tenth to the ninth centuries BCE,⁵ it depicts the struggle for succession between two sets of cousins in the ruling Bharata family: the Kauravas (the hundred sons of the blind ruler Dhrtarashtra) versus the epic's heroes, the five sons of the impotent King Pandu, who were conceived by five *devas*. Dharma, patron of cosmic order, fathered Yudhishthira; Vayu, god of physical force, conceived Bhima; Arjuna was the son of Indra; and the twins, Sahadeva and Nakula, were the offspring of the Ashvins, the divine guardians of fertility. In the world of the epic, divine and human intermingle so thoroughly that it is impossible to regard them as distinct categories. Rather, divinity gives humanity a third dimension, symbolising that numinous aspect of our lives that constantly eludes our grasp.

The succession issue is not clear-cut, since both Pandu and Dhrtarashtra have ruled in turn, but events segue into open warfare. Eighteen books of the epic are devoted to this catastrophic conflict which results in the extermination of almost the entire Kshatriya class and heralds the beginning of the Kali Yuga, the deeply flawed dark age that continues to this day. This is a scripture that gives no easy answers, no neat doctrines, no final certainty. It offers no hopeful panacea, but brings both its heroes and its audience to the brink of despair. It is impossible to summarise its 'message': as the Indologist Wendy Doniger explains, 'It is a contested text, a brilliantly orchestrated hybrid narrative with no single party line on any subject ... The contradictions at its heart are not the mistakes of a sloppy editor, but enduring dilemmas that no author could ever resolve.'⁶

This is not what many expect of scripture today, but the epic has enthralled the people of India for centuries and this should make us perhaps question our modern Western view of scripture. It was always performed rather than read privately. During the 1990s, it was even produced in serial form on national television in India and attracted huge audiences. Ancient Indian philosophers called drama 'visual poetry' because abstruse ideas are transmitted by carefully articulated gestures, especially of the hands and eyes, in a presentation that is simultaneously ceremonial and spontaneous.[7] The intensity of the experience gives both actors and spectators intimations of a higher level of reality that may resolve some of the epic's many contradictions but eludes rational analysis.

Reading this epic from start to finish is probably an impossible task (one attempted only by Western scholars). It took centuries to evolve, each generation contributing its own insights, so that it is more encyclopaedia than regular narrative. Its composition is much debated. Most scholars believe it to be an oral work, transmitted between 400 BCE and 400 CE, which probably began as a Kshatriya saga exploring the mythology and *dharma* of the warrior class. But the epic we have now bears little resemblance to the original, since over the centuries a mass of didactic tales and priestly myths were added.[8] Some of this new material included tales of gods who had, at best, only a tangential relationship with the Vedas: Vishnu, for example, makes only a fleeting appearance in the Rig Veda, while Rudra-Shiva appears in just one of the later Upanishads. But the tales of Vishnu and Shiva had probably been transmitted outside Brahmin circles for centuries and eventually they would both become major deities in India. But in the epic, Shiva is overshadowed by Vishnu, since it transpires that Krishna, the Pandavas' cousin, who plays a major role in the action, is an avatar or incarnation of Vishnu.[9]

It seems, therefore, that the original Kshatriya saga was taken over and completed by Brahmins over a very long period. But a theory of the scholar Alf Hiltebeitel has recently attracted much attention. He suggests that instead of being transmitted orally, the epic was composed in writing between the mid-second century BCE and the early Common Era 'in committee', as it were, by Brahmins who enjoyed royal patronage. To conform to Vedic orthodoxy, however, they wanted it to *appear* to be an oral text, and they even called it the 'Fifth Veda'. So while the epic was always performed orally, Hiltebeitel argues that it was in fact composed by priestly scholars who were proud of their grasp of grammar and their ability to produce a written text.[10]

Throughout, the epic emphasises the importance of oral recitation and its reception by an audience. At the very beginning, we are presented with two different accounts of the epic's transmission, which 'frame' the entire story and influence the way it is received by the listeners. In the first account, the bard Ugrashravas arrives in the Namisa Forest, where the Brahmin Shaunaka and his companions are performing a twelve-year Vedic ritual. It was customary for priests to tell stories in the intervals between rites, so the Brahmins gather around him, eagerly hoping for a tale. Ugrashravas explains that he has just attended a highly irregular 'snake sacrifice' held by the Pandavas' only surviving descendant, King Janemajaya. There Ugrashravas had heard another bard, Vaishampayana, reciting an epic tale that *he* had heard from its original composer, the great rishi Vyasa, the Pandavas' grandfather. Ugrashravas asks the priests if they would like to hear this story and they eagerly accept. The purpose of this 'Outer Frame' is to establish Ugrashravas' credentials. He will narrate the epic story of the Kauravas and Pandavas to us as well as to Shaunaka and his Brahmins, but – importantly – Shaunaka will constantly interrupt him, asking questions or requesting clarification.[11] In this way, the 'present' (Shaunaka's ritual in the Namisa Forest) becomes entwined with the events of the tragic past and this reminds us that past and present are inextricably entwined. Actions are never over and done with because what happened in the past inevitably impacts the future.[12]

But a little later, we learn something significant: it transpires that Shaunaka is no ordinary Brahmin. He is rather a *bhugu* (plural *bhgavas*), a priest regarded as deeply flawed because he did not conform to the Brahmin *dharma*. *Bhgavas* married Kshatriya women, dabbled in black magic, and instead of observing *ahimsa*, they specialised in the martial arts. Furthermore, it transpires that nearly all the Brahmins in the *Mahabharata* are *bhgavas* so the Pandavas were instructed in morality and warfare by flawed priests who – like the Brahmins who killed the Nandan and Mauryan kings – did not observe the rules of their class. The Pandavas' mission is to restore *dharma* in a world that is spinning out of control; yet the situation is so bad that the only Brahmins who can guide and educate them are debased and adharmic.[13]

So much for the 'Outer Frame' that encircles the epic. The 'Inner Frame' is the strange 'snake sacrifice' where Ugrashravas first heard the story of the *Mahabharata*, narrated by the bard Vaishampayana to King Janemajaya, the Pandavas' sole descendant. We will hear Vaishampayana's account of the epic war as well as Ugrashravas'. But we discover that while Janemajaya is listening to the tragic story of his ancestors, he is carrying out a gruesome vendetta. Because the king of snakes had killed his father, Janemajaya had vowed to slaughter all the snakes in the world. So while Vaishampayana is reciting his version of the epic – to us as well as to Janemajaya – snakes are being pushed into the sacrificial fire in a systematic attempt to exterminate the entire species. The epic violence of the past, therefore, comes to us framed by a modern atrocity, which horrifies even the Brahmins who are participating in it. We are not allowed to forget this, because, like Shaunaka, Janemajaya frequently interrupts Vaisampayana with questions and comments.[14] This raises an important issue. The war between the Pandavas and Kauravas was supposed to put the world to rights. Yet the last surviving Pandava is performing a cruel, adharmic sacrifice. Was the epic battle, which resulted in such massive casualties, worth it? Do people learn from the past? Are human beings capable of progress or are they addicted to cruelty, vengeance and massacre? Again, the epic has no answer.

In the epic, we are constantly coming up against such imponderable issues. One of its translators, J. A. B. van Buitenen, remarks: 'The epic is a series of precisely stated problems imprecisely and inconclusively resolved, with every resolution raising a new problem until the very end.'[15] It is said that when Vyasa composed the epic, he dictated it to Ganesha, the one-tusked elephant god, but told him not to write down anything that he did not understand. To rest from the rigours of dictation, Vyasa deliberately wove 'knots' – enigmatic, riddling passages – into the story that were so complex that even the omniscient Ganesha had to pause and deliberate for a moment.[16] The riddles of the epic are, therefore, intentional and the questions raised are by no means trivial. Do human beings have any control over their destiny or are they mere puppets, driven by forces beyond their ken? Does correct action really lead to happiness, and, if not, why follow one's *dharma*? Why, despite the good intentions of nearly all concerned, did events turn out so tragically? Instead of inspiring faith, the epic plunges us into radical doubt.[17] The horror of the *Mahabharata* is so great that to this day, copies of the epic are never stored in the house and it is recited only outside on the porch – and here never from start to finish, since the inexorable progression of tragic events is not only overwhelming but is considered inauspicious.[18]

During the disturbing and violent period in which the *Mahabharata* was created, Indian scriptures had one objective: to deal practically with the problem of human suffering. The Buddha had drawn attention to the ubiquity of *dukkha* in the First Noble Truth and had given the word *dharma* an ethical dimension. Jains and Buddhists had both insisted that it was compassion, interior equanimity and *ahimsa* that liberated you from the *dukkha* inherent in existence. In response, the Brahmins had also ethicised the concept of *dharma*, which became the focus of much debate. Some of this new '*dharma* literature' still argued that observing the moral and ritual duties of your class would liberate you from suffering in this life and guarantee your place in heaven.[19] It was the growing tension between these two ideals, some scholars believe, that inspired the composition of the *Mahabharata*.[20] The epic makes it clear that the Brahminic concept of *dharma* was no longer viable. Most of its characters are either victims of suffering or discover that their pursuit of *dharma* is responsible for the misery of others. Furthermore, as we shall see, the epic also suggests that the idea of a heavenly rebirth may well be an illusion. Perhaps, as the Buddha had explained, any religiosity that focuses on salvation and the survival of the self in celestial conditions is 'unskilful', since it embeds you in the ego that, according to the renouncers, you must transcend if you wish to achieve peace and enlightenment.

Nearly every one of the epic's heroes, who are committed to the old *dharma* ideal, either dies a violent death or survives the war overwhelmed with grief. The *Mahabharata* forces us to witness human suffering on an epic scale but without heroics. Five whole books are devoted to the savagery of an eighteen-day battle, in which death is squalid and degrading.

> Some were pierced by spears and some by battle-axes, and some were crushed by elephants and others were trampled by horses. Some were cut by car-wheels and some by sharp arrows, and they cried out everywhere for their relatives ... And many entrails were scattered and their thighs were broken ... And others, with arms torn off and their sides split open were seen wailing. Thirsty, they desired to live, and others, overwhelmed with thirst, with little strength, fell on the battlefield on the bare ground and begged for water.[21]

When the battle is over, Ashwattaman, a *bhugu* Brahmin, vows to avenge the tragic death of his noble father, Drona, in which the Pandava heroes, despite their good intentions, were deeply implicated. Ashwattaman enters the Pandava camp while everybody is asleep, and slaughters men, women and children. His first victim is the man who had decapitated his father: Ashwattaman 'trampled him in his rage, crushing his vital organs with appalling blows from his feet, like a lion mauling a rutting elephant'.[22] His victims are murdered in their beds, begging for mercy, and grovelling in the dirt. After the massacre, Ashwattaman fires off a *brahmasiris*, a weapon of mass destruction that, had it not been intercepted by the prayers of two compassionate rishis, would have destroyed the whole world.

Not surprisingly, the Pandava heroes are stupefied with sorrow and fear as they see their valiant efforts to observe their *dharma* and save the world recoil horribly upon themselves, their kinsfolk and their hapless victims. But their wise counsellors do not allow them to succumb to despair. 'Grief destroys beauty, grief destroys wisdom, grief brings on disease,' Vidura tells his brother Dhrtarashtra, the blind king. This, perhaps, is the epic's central message: suffering is a fact of life and must be accepted with courage and equanimity. This is a scripture that weans us from our craving for easy, self-serving answers. It asks us to stand back from our distress, because if we despair, we simply suffer more ourselves and, perhaps, increase the pain of others. Vidura continues:

> Nothing is gained by sorrowing; the body just suffers and one's enemies exult: do not give into grief.
>> Again and again, man dies and is born,
>> Again and again man rises and falls.
>> Again and again man asks and is asked,
>> Again and again man mourns and is mourned.
> Happiness and misery, good fortune and bad, profit and loss, death and life touch everyone in turn – therefore a wise man neither rejoices or grieves.[23]

If you abandon yourself to your grief, you are likely to make appalling decisions, as Ashwattaman did. The epic requires us to move beyond our own sorrow and acknowledge the pain of others – even that of our enemies.[24]

Yudhishthira epitomises the tension between the old spirituality and the new. He is the son of the god Dharma so he knows that because he is destined to be king, he is required to fight to regain the throne. But none of his enemies, however ignoble, he insists, deserves to die, and to gain the kingdom Yudhishthira will have to kill his kinsmen, friends and gurus.[25] He seems incapacitated – almost paralysed – by the insoluble conflict between the traditional Kshatriya *dharma* and the new ideal of non-violence. Nowhere is his moral paralysis more evident than during the game of dice that is the pivotal, and, perhaps, the most perplexing, event of the entire epic.[26]

The Pandavas and Kauravas were raised together; but, led by Duryodhana – Yudhishthira's rival for the throne – the Kauravas come to resent their cousins and plot to kill them. Eventually, their father, King Dhrtarashtra, reluctantly gives the Pandavas the eastern half of his kingdom, so they establish their capital at Indraprastha and build a magnificent assembly hall there. But this reawakens Duryodhana's jealousy and he plots with his uncle, Sakuni, to rob the Pandavas of their kingdom. They challenge Yudhishthira to a game of dice, and even though he has serious doubts, Yudhishthira accepts because he believes that it is somehow fated and knows that his *dharma* requires a king to accept any challenge. Yet he seems stupefied by his dilemma and, with hideous consequences, appears to sleepwalk through the entire event.

The game takes place in Dhrtarashtra's assembly hall in Hastinapura. The dice are rigged, and during the game, Yudhishthira pledges – and loses – his kingdom, his wealth, his brothers and, above all, his integrity. It is as though he has become an automaton, abandoning basic moral imperatives to fulfil the demands of his *dharma* and propelled forward by events, lost to common decency. Finally, he pledges – and loses – Draupadi, the common wife of all five Pandava brothers. There follows a shocking scene. Draupadi, who was not present at the game since women may not enter the hall, is dragged before the assembled kings and princes by Duryodhana's brother, her hair undone and her sari stained with menstrual blood, only to be raped by Duryodhana while the entire nobility, including the Pandavas, watch – and do nothing.

All the characters are implicated in this crime. Duryodhana is consumed with jealousy, but there are mitigating circumstances because the Pandavas (though not Yudhishthira) treated him cruelly when he visited Indraprastha. King Dhrtarashtra at first opposed the dice game, but – at the precise moment when he foresaw that it would have disastrous consequences – he gave in. His silence during the rape indicates tacit consent. But most disturbing of all is the conduct of Yudhishthira, the *dharma* king. When the dicing began, he was cautious, but he quickly became disoriented and unhinged, gambling recklessly and, in a way that was highly uncharacteristic of this usually sensitive man, boasting of his wealth. One by one, he pledged – and lost – each of his beloved brothers but when he finally pledged his wife, with a paean of praise for her beauty, the elders in the hall cried 'Woe! Woe!' and the wise counsellor Vidura almost fainted with horror. Yet nobody stepped forward to prevent the coming outrage.

When the usher was dispatched to bring Draupadi into the hall, she sent him back with an enigmatic message for Yudhishthira: 'Whom did you lose first, yourself or me?' It is a pertinent question, since in his fidelity to the royal *dharma*, Yudhishthira has indeed lost his best and true self – but he 'did not stir, as though he had lost consciousness and made no reply'.[27]

Throughout the rape he seemed barely conscious – 'silent and motionless' – and did not respond to Draupadi's magnificent speech in which she asked the assembled company that had silently witnessed her violation: 'What is left of the *dharma* of kings?'[28] None of the elders – all of them well versed in the new *dharma* sutras – could reply. Her question reverberates throughout the entire epic. If none of the ritualists, wise counsellors, gurus and Vedic specialists present could speak in Draupadi's defence, then *dharma*, which was supposed to provide protection, happiness and security, was indeed impotent.

The appalling silence was ended by the inauspicious howling of jackals outside and this seemed to awaken Dhrtarashtra, who granted Draupadi her freedom and released her husbands. But he then recalled them for one last throw. Once more, Yudhishthira felt obliged to play; and this time too he lost and the Pandavas were forced into exile for twelve years. When they returned, the war broke out. But what had happened to Yudhishthira? And where was their kinsman Krishna, avatar of the god Vishnu? Could he have prevented the disaster – or were the *devas*' powers also limited? Perhaps the *devas* even condoned the crime? Again, these questions remain unanswered.

Krishna remains an ambiguous figure throughout the epic. We are told that whenever *dharma* is in decline, Vishnu descends to earth to restore it. And yet during the war, instead of restoring *dharma*, Krishna encouraged the Pandavas to behave immorally – to lie to their kinsmen and gurus. This resulted in the deaths of two Kaurava generals who had inflicted severe casualties on the Pandava side. Bhishma and Drona, who had tutored the Pandavas in the martial arts when they were boys, were both *bhugu* Brahmins with magical powers, so they could not be defeated by normal methods. But neither was so lost to decency that he would dream of lying or breaking an oath and they would both have found it incredible that Yudhishthira, the *dharma* king, would lie to them. Yet Krishna argued that the war could not be won by ordinary means so he persuaded Yudhishthira to trick Bhishma into revealing the only way it was possible to kill him and to tell Drona that Drona's son had been killed in action. In his shock and grief, Drona had laid down his arms and made himself vulnerable to attack. 'A lie would be better than the truth,' Krishna argued, 'and he that speaks a lie in order to live is not contaminated by it.'[29] But the consequences were appalling: Drona's son – Ashwattaman – would avenge his death. And despite Krishna's reassurance, Yudhishthira was tarnished. His chariot had always floated the width of four fingers from the ground, but as soon as he lied to Drona, it came sharply down to earth, while Drona, who died a saintly death, was taken directly up to heaven. The contrast between Yudhishthira's fall from grace and Drona's ecstatic ascension was devastating and Arjuna bitterly berated his brother: his vile lie would taint them all.[30]

The Pandavas escaped Ashwattaman's massacre, because – again acting ambiguously – Krishna advised them to sleep outside the camp that night. At the close of the war, 1,660,020,000 Kshatriyas had died, leaving a mere handful standing on each side.[31] And despite Krishna's reassurances, Yudhishthira was indelibly tarnished. After the war, he reigned for fifteen years, but the light had gone out of his life. For centuries, the epic has compelled its audience to face up steadily to the moral ambiguity of warfare and the tragedy of imperial rule, refusing to mitigate its horror with pious platitudes.

Unanswerable questions and riddles continue right up to the end.[32] Thirty years after the war, the Pandavas hear of Krishna's death and Vyasa, the author of the epic, tells them that their work in the world is over. The five brothers, Draupadi and Yudhishthira's pet dog set off on their final journey, circumambulating the world in a suicidal ritual that continued until participants dropped dead of exhaustion. When they reached Mount Meru, Draupadi died, followed successively by Sahadeva, Nakula and Arjuna. 'Why?' Bhima asked Yudhishthira in anguish after each death. But each time, as if indifferent, Yudhishthira coldly pointed out a moral flaw of the deceased. His failure to mourn was alienating. When Bhima too fell, Yudhishthira marched on alone with his dog.

Suddenly Indra appeared and invited Yudhishthira to climb into his chariot, telling him that kings have the privilege of entering heaven in bodily form; his kinsfolk, having shed their bodies, await him there. But Yudhishthira refused to leave his faithful dog behind. At this, the dog threw off his disguise and revealed that he is the god Dharma, Yudhishthira's father, and cried:

> You are of noble birth, king of kings ... Now you have given up a chariot
> to heaven because a mere dog is devoted to you. For this, lord of men, no
> one in heaven is equal to you. Therefore, best heir of Bharata, the imperish-
> able realms are yours, even in your own body, and you have attained the
> highest celestial state.[33]

It is a delightful turn of events, but our unease remains. Indra had already promised Yudhishthira the privilege of entering heaven in the body because he was a king; now Dharma tells him that he has this honour because of his kindness to animals. But this is a world of tests and tricks. When Yudhishthira arrived in heaven, he saw not his family but his enemy Duryodhana enthroned 'in royal glory'.[34] Wanting no part of such a heaven, Yudhishthira demanded to be taken to his kinsfolk, was led down a grim and ominous path, and to his horror, heard the voices of the damned, begging him to stay to alleviate their pain. Yudhishthira agreed – only to find that the sufferers were his brothers and Draupadi. Beside himself with rage, Yudhishthira reviled the gods, vowing to stay in hell and comfort his beloved family.

Immediately the gods arrived, the horrors of hell vanished, and a sweet, cool breeze began to blow. 'Come, tiger-like hero, it is finished,' Indra announced. 'You have attained perfection, king, and the imperishable realms are yours.'[35] But our doubts remain. Is this yet another trick? The epic leaves us bewildered and unmoored. Perhaps it is inviting us to shed our desire for clear-cut answers and religious certainty, as well as self-centred fantasies of afterlife. By focusing on the fact that human life is *dukkha* we learn that the only solution is to respond to this inexorable truth without rage or excessive sorrow but with compassion for others and courageous acceptance.

*

During the Warring States period in China, the Yangists, who had challenged the Confucian ideal of public service and retired from political life, had asked how they could preserve their lives in an era of ever-increasing violence. In this first phase of Daoism, the answer was to escape. By fleeing to the mountains and forests, Yangzi thought, it was possible to avoid the evil and destruction of the human world. But sickness, disaster and death also occur in the world of nature. Thus later Daoists went deeper. We could perhaps survive, they thought, if we understood the laws that govern the universe and regulated our behaviour accordingly. This second phase of Daoism is expressed in the *Daodejing* ('The Classic of the Way and its Potency'), which became a major Daoist scripture. Composed probably in the mid-third century BCE, it seems to be a collection of sayings used by teachers committed to self-cultivation through meditation and the reform of current political practice.[36] It is the first Chinese text we have considered that explicitly defines itself as *jing*, as a 'Classic' – a work of unique spiritual importance. Originally *jing* was a term used in weaving – it was the warp that defined and supported the structure of a fabric – but in the late Warring

States period, *jing* was applied metaphorically to a text or a body of writings that expressed a universal truth and could, therefore, strengthen and order society.[37]

In the first poem of the *Daodejing*, Laozi, the presumed author, forces his readers to recognise the limits of their understanding by distinguishing being (*yu*) from non-being (*wu*):

> The way [Dao] that can be spoken of
> Is not the constant way;
> The name that can be named
> Is not the constant name.
> The nameless was the beginning of heaven and earth;
> The named was the mother of the myriad creatures.[38]

Laozi is not speaking of a Creator God or the origin of species: he is making an ontological rather than a temporal or factual statement. Because there are beings, there must be that by which all things came to be but about which we know nothing:

> Silent and void
> It stands alone and does not change,
> Goes round and does not weary.
> It is capable of being the mother of the world.
> I know not its name
> So I style it 'the way'.[39]

The Dao is ineffable, and if we want to talk about it we can only give it a name that is not really a name at all.[40] Perhaps, Laozi suggests, we should simply call it 'the Dark' to remind ourselves of its impenetrable obscurity.[41] Ordinary rational thought is useless when it confronts transcendent reality. The *Daodejing* deliberately subverts the analytical logic of the left hemisphere of the brain, forcing us to consider antitheses that not only reverse conventional assumptions but which have nothing to do with logic or reasoning. We find that inaction is superior to action, ignorance to knowledge, female to male, and emptiness to fullness.[42] By holding these contradictions in his mind, the sage learns to think beyond normal categories and can thus have intimations of the Unknowable. Laozi did not trace the steps that led to these insights: these cryptic remarks are only points for meditation; his readers had to make this journey themselves.

But Laozi did explain how the sage should live. There is a Chinese saying that 'when a thing reaches an extreme, it reverts from it',[43] or, as Laozi expresses it: 'Turning back is how the way moves.'[44] When anything reaches extremity, it retracts: 'A gusty wind cannot last all morning, and a sudden downpour cannot last all day.'[45] This is a fundamental law of life. When people eat too much, they get sick; a student who imagines he has learned everything, cannot advance; and arrogance is a sign that one's progress has reached a limit and that it is time to retract. As Laozi put it:

> To be overbearing when one has wealth and position
> Is to bring calamity upon oneself.
> To retire when the task is accomplished
> Is the way of heaven.[46]

So, a wise person will avoid disaster by living humbly and being content with little, avoiding 'excess, extravagance, and arrogance'.[47] He will therefore prosper, because he is submitting to the fundamental law of life: he 'puts his person last and it comes first':[48]

> He does not show himself, and so he is conspicuous;
> He does not consider himself right, and so is illustrious;
> He does not brag, and so has merit;
> He does not boast, and so endures.[49]

For Laozi, *wu-wei* did not mean 'doing nothing'; it meant restricting activity to what was necessary and avoiding extremity. But, in an important passage, he suggested that there was a deeper solution. It was selfhood or ego that caused our pain: 'The reason there is great affliction, is that I have a self. If I have no self, what affliction would I have?'[50]

The third and final phase of Daoism would explore this insight in the book attributed to Zhuangzi (c.369–286 BCE), one of the most brilliant and ebullient philosophers of the period.[51] He is usually considered the author of its first seven chapters, but this Classic is an anthology of various Daoist writings, which was compiled at the beginning of the early Han empire (206 BCE–24 CE). Like the Yangists, Zhuangzi had retired to the forest to escape the dangers of the political world, but soon discovered that the countryside was no haven of tranquillity. In the forest, creatures preyed ceaselessly on one another, seemingly unaware that they themselves would be killed and eaten in their turn.[52] These creatures did not agonise about their condition like human beings but just went with the flow. So, Zhuangzi concluded, humans must also align themselves with Heaven and the inevitable rhythms of the Dao without repining. He gave up worrying about death. When his wife died, he refused to mourn: she was at peace in the bosom of the endlessly evolving Dao. To weep and rage would be at odds with the viewpoint of Heaven, the Way things really were.[53]

Most people, Zhuangzi noted, were in love with their opinions. They distinguish 'this' from 'that'; what 'is' from what 'is not'; 'death' from 'life'. But the sage will have nothing to do with this relentless left-brain analysis, with its pointless distinctions and quarrelsome discussions:

> The sage does not go down this way, but sheds the light of heaven upon such issues. 'This' is also 'that' and 'that' is also 'this'. The 'that' is on the one hand also 'this', and 'this' is, on the other hand, 'that' ... When 'this' and 'that' do not stand against one another, this is called the pivot [i.e. the essence] of the Dao. The pivot provides the centre of the circle, which is without end, for it can react equally to that which is and to that which is not.[54]

The sage stands in the centre of that circle, aware of everything that is going on within it, but uninvolved – not out of laziness or cynicism, but because he has achieved the point of view of what we would call the brain's right hemisphere. Once we lay this analytical mentality aside, we glimpse the Whole, the unity of all things in the undifferentiable One.

Zhuangzi told a story about Yan Hui, Confucius' beloved disciple, who announced one day to his Master that: 'I sit quietly and forget.'

> I let the body fade away and the intellect fade. I throw out form, abandon understanding – and then move freely, blending away into the Great Change [of the Dao]. That is what I mean by 'sit quietly and forget'.[55]

'Forgetting' is not absent-mindedness; it is rather an achievement – a deliberate curtailment for a while of our rational and logical faculties, which enables us to 'blend' with the transcendence of the world that surrounds us. We should learn from the sounds of Nature, Zhuangzi believed. Each one is unique; it is what it is, without being influenced by any of the others. But words (*yen*) always represent ideas and opinions that conflict with others. We thus boost the ego that is the cause of so much misery to ourselves and other people. Everyone has his own one-sided point of view. People argue ceaselessly about 'this' and 'that', making some ideas absolute, condemning others, and forming cast-iron opinions that they claim are indubitably 'right':

> They struggle with their minds day after day ... sometimes straying wildly, sometimes probing deeply, sometimes calculating ... Then, making judgements about 'right' and 'wrong', their minds shoot off like a crossbow pellet. They cling to opinions as if they had taken a holy oath.[56]

How sad and pointless it is to jostle with each other this way, forming rival parties – Mohists versus Confucians! Because the Dao eludes such definition, the only consistent position is unknowing, since nobody can be certain about what or who is 'right'. When we deliberately 'forget' these distinctions, becoming aware of the unity of all things in the Dao, we lose that obsessive need to flaunt our opinions. Zhuangzi seems to have deliberately 'closed down' the analytic activity in the left hemisphere of his brain and achieved the more panoptic vision of the right, which is capable of holding different views of reality at the same time. He did not walk around in a hazy, impractical trance, however: there were times when he had to evaluate situations and make distinctions like everybody else.[57] But his carefully nurtured holistic vision enabled him to feel attuned to the Way, at one with the 'root' from which all things grow and the axis around which they revolved.

The quest for certainty often makes people dogmatic and intolerant of the beliefs of others and this, Zhuangzi says, precludes our transformation. What we should do is relinquish our obsession with the self and cultivate empathy instead. 'The perfect man has no self,' Zhuangzi explained.[58] Because he has lost any sense of himself as separate and special, he 'regards other people as I': 'People cry so he cries – he considers everything as his own being.' Without the distorting lens of egotism, he had achieved the unselfconscious benevolence that is the essence of enlightenment.[59]

Daoism had come full circle. The Yangists had gone to great lengths to preserve the self but then Laozi realised that this was the cause of our sorrow. Finally, Zhuangzi had discovered that seeing things from the perspective of the Dao meant abandoning clamorous self-assertion. He did not achieve this insight by intensive yogic introspection. The *Zhuangzi* tells many stories of humble peasants and artisans who are thoroughly embodied, so intent on their physical work – be it trapping cicadas with a sticky pole, carving a roast ox or crafting a wheel – that they effortlessly achieve *ekstasis*, a self-forgetfulness that enabled them to be in complete communion with the Way things work without their having to think about it. They could not explain how they performed these tasks so perfectly. It was simply a 'knack' acquired by keeping the mind empty of dogmatism and letting the deeper rhythms of life take over.

The last great Confucian thinker of the Warring States period was Xunzi (340–245 BCE), who created a powerful synthesis of the intellectual and spiritual thought of his time. The *Xunzi* never became a canonical scripture but for the first time it lists the *jing* that would become the Chinese Classics, which, Xunzi believed, were essential to the cultivation of humanity (*ren*):[60] 'Learning [*xie*] begins with the recitation of the Classics [*jing*] and ends with the reading of the ritual texts; it begins by learning to be a man of breeding and ends with learning to be a sage.'[61] As always, Confucian learning was inseparable from self-cultivation. Xunzi also supported the growing conviction that sagehood was not an achievement of such men as Yao, Shun and Yu in the distant past, as Confucius had believed, but was possible for anybody: by the daily, even hourly, practice of benevolence (*ren*) and righteousness (*yi*), Xunzi insisted, 'The man in the street can become a Yu.'[62]

Ritual was also an essential component of sagehood and it was not confined to the rites of filial piety and the mourning ceremonies for the dead. It was essential to give one's full attention to the physical minutiae of life: 'the placing of the goblet filled with water in the highest place, the laying out of raw fish on the offering table, the presentation of the unflavoured soup – all these acts have the same significance.' Such actions build within us an attitude of respect for each element of the meal, creating a habit of reverence not only for our fellow humans but also for everything in the natural world.[63]

The five *jing*, Xunzi taught, represent the highest part of the Way and its power':

> The reverence and order of the *Rites*, the fitness and harmony of *Music*, the breadth of the *Odes* and *Documents*, the subtlety of the *Spring and Autumn Annals* – these encompass all that is between heaven and earth.[64]

But it was futile to study scriptures without ritual. 'To lay aside the *Rites* and try to attain your objective with the *Odes* and *Documents* alone is like trying to measure the depth of a river with your finger, to pound millet with a spear-point, or to eat a pot of stew with an awl. You will get nowhere.'[65] Study of the Classics had to reach the depths of our bodily as

well as our intellectual being. 'The learning of the petty man enters his ear
and comes out of his mouth,' Xunzi complained; he hears the scripture and
immediately starts discoursing upon it. But the Classic has affected only
'the four inches between ear and mouth', and failed to penetrate the rest
of the body.[66] Such a person was simply using his learning to impress others
and advance his career. The learning of a *junzi*, however, 'enters his ear,
clings to his mind, spreads through his four limbs, and manifests itself in
his actions'.[67] It involves the whole human being, not simply the cerebral
part of his mind. Scripture had to engage all our mental and physical
capacities, otherwise there would be no transformation.

The appalling violence of the late Warring States period led Xunzi to
conclude that human nature was fundamentally evil. In 260 BCE, the army
of Qin conquered the state of Zhao, Xunzi's birthplace, and massacred
400,000 prisoners of war by burying them alive. Yet Xunzi did not give up
on humanity: the catastrophe only made the cultivation of our full humanity
more urgent than ever. He pointed out that Yao, Shun and Yu realised that
they could end the intolerable misery they witnessed only by making a
massive intellectual effort. They had created the rites of reverence, courtesy
and 'yielding' to bring order and harmony to social relations.[68] Daoists
believed that Confucian ritual imposed a set of alien and unnatural rules,
but in fact the rites humanised the emotions, bringing form and beauty out
of unpromising material: they 'trim what is too long, and stretch out what
is too short, eliminate surplus and repair deficiency, extend the force of
love and reverence, and step by step, bring to fulfilment the beauties
of proper conduct'.[69]

Rituals presuppose the presence of others: self-cultivation cannot be
achieved alone. Xunzi would have agreed with the people of India – without
a teacher, scripture was impenetrable:

> *Ritual* and *Music* present us with problems but no explanations; the *Odes* and
> *Documents* deal with ancient matters and are not always pertinent; the *Spring*
> *and Autumn Annals* is terse and cannot be quickly understood ... Therefore,
> I say that in learning nothing is more profitable than to associate with those
> who are learned, and of the roads to learning, none is quicker than to love
> such men.[70]

A warm, emotional rapport with your teacher was indispensable: 'If you
are first unable to love such men and secondly are incapable of ritual, then
you will only be learning a mass of jumbled facts, blindly following the

Odes and *Documents* and nothing more.'[71] Like Zhuangzi, Xunzi deplored what he called 'obsession', an egotistic insistence on one doctrinal position rather than another, which must be countered by the 'yielding' of ritual and the love of your teacher.

Xunzi was a Confucian through and through, but he was also profoundly influenced by Daoism. Like Zhuangzi and Laozi, he was convinced that the Way could be comprehended by 'closing' the critical activity of his mind, so that it became 'empty, unified and still'. Such a mind would be 'empty' in remaining ever open to new impressions instead of clinging to the familiar and by cultivating a profound responsiveness to the Other – to everything that is not ourselves; it would be 'unified' in its refusal to force the complexity of reality into a tidy, self-serving system, forming certainties based on abstraction; and 'still' in refusing to indulge in egotistic 'dreams and noisy fantasies'. 'These', Xunzi concluded, 'are the qualities of a great and pure enlightenment.'[72] By carefully dismantling small-minded, self-centred thinking, any human being could achieve the panoptic vision of a sage:

> He who has such enlightenment may sit in his room and view the entire area within the four seas, may dwell in the present and yet discourse on distant ages. He has a penetrating insight into all beings and understands their true nature, studies the ages of order and disorder and comprehends the principle behind them. He surveys all heaven and earth, governs all being, and masters the great principle and all that is in the universe.[73]

A person who had achieved this enlightenment was not a 'god'; he had simply fulfilled the potential of his humanity: 'Broad and vast – who knows his virtue? Shadowy and ever-changing – who knows his form? His bright-ness matches the sun and moon, his greatness fills the eight directions. Such is the Great Man.'[74]

Xunzi did not mention the *Zhouyi* ('Changes of Zhou'), the ancient divinatory text that was about to be transformed into the *Yijing*, the sixth Chinese Classic. During the third and second centuries BCE, a set of commentaries known as the 'Ten Wings' or 'Appendices' had given the enigmatic line-statements of the *Zhouyi* new significance, transforming it from a divinatory text into a proto-scientific, rational account of a well-ordered, dynamic and benign universe that was the source of goodness.[75] The 'Wings' were designed to reassure and encourage; they presented the cosmos as engaged in a ceaseless process of change and transformation that was impersonal, tranquil and simple – the *yi* of the title also means 'easy'. The 'Great Ultimate' (Taiji), the indescribable and unknowable source of being, engenders two forces, yin and yang, which are, respectively, passive and female, active and male. The first of the patterns that evolved from yin and yang were the Eight Trigrams, three-line diagrams of broken and unbroken lines: in the 'Wings', they no longer represented good or bad fortune but had become cosmic, heavenly forces. The Trigrams then multiplied to become the Sixty-Four Hexagrams, which represented all possible forms of change, situations, possibilities and institutions on earth.

Instead of being controlled by perverse and irrational spirits, whose intentions could be discerned only by arcane and unreliable divination, the Chinese had now developed a system that, as the First Wing explains, could be predicted objectively:

> The system of *Change* [i.e. the *Yijing*] is tantamount to heaven and earth, and therefore can always handle and adjust the way of heaven and earth. Looking up, we observe the pattern of the heavens; looking down, we examine the order of the earth. Thus we know the causes of what is hidden and what is manifest. If we investigate the cycle of things, we shall understand the concepts of life and death.[76]

The 'spirits' of old had been transformed into orderly natural forces, and there is now 'no disagreement' between them. The science of the *Yijing*, therefore, 'embraces all things and in its way, helps all under heaven, and therefore there is no mistake.' It understands and rejoices in Tian ('Heaven' or 'Nature'), so it 'understands destiny. Therefore, there is no worry. As [things] are contented in their stations and earnest in practicing kindness, there can be love.'[77]

This may seem simplistic but the philosophy is clear: human beings are firmly embedded in the cosmos. You cannot say 'Nature' or 'Heaven' without also saying 'Human': they form an inseparable triad, so every earthly event must be interpreted in this holistic context. In the 'Great Appendix' (Dazhuan), the most important of the Wings, we find the sage described as a person who understands things from their beginnings to their endings:

> There is a similarity between him and heaven and earth, and hence there is no contrariety to them ... He comprehends as in a mould or enclosure the transformation of heaven and earth without any error; by an ever-varying

adaptation he completes all things without exception ... It is thus that his
operation is spirit-like, unconditioned by place, while the changes he produces
are not restricted to any form.[78]

The Wings position humanity firmly in the natural order and the sage, the
fully developed person, has aligned himself so perfectly with Heaven-and-
Earth that he has himself become divine – just as described by Xunzi.

The Great Appendix goes on to describe Fu Xi, the first Sage King,
becoming aware of the interaction within the sacred triad.

> He looked up to examine the images [*guan xiang*] in Heaven, and down to
> examine the models [*fa*] on Earth. He examined the markings *wen* ['patterns']
> of the birds and the beasts and their suitability to the terrain. Near at hand,
> he took it from himself, and at a distance from objects. Thereupon he created
> the eight trigrams to communicate with the powers of spirit intelligence,
> and to categorize the natures of the myriad objects.[79]

Fu Xi's royal 'virtue' (*de*) enabled him to read and interpret the cosmos
like a text. When he looked up at the stars, he saw the archetypal 'images'
of the cosmos and created his own 'patterns' in the Trigrams. But he could
also see that these cosmic 'images' corresponded to earthly 'patterns' (*wen*)
in the markings of birds and animals that enabled them to blend with their
natural habitat. This perception of the sympathy that existed between Heaven
and Earth inspired Fu Xi to create technologies that helped human beings
to live productively in the world. 'He invented the knotted cords [to make
records] and made nets and squares for hunting and fishing. He probably
took [the idea for] this from the hexagram *li* [Hexagram 30: "Fire", of the
Yijing].'[80]

Fu Xi had created a human sign-system that paralleled the universe, so
that each revealed the truth of the other. This encouraged the sages who
came after him to create increasingly sophisticated technologies. By contemplating *Yi* (Hexagram 42: 'Increase'), Shen Nong invented the science of
agriculture that made the earth productive. Yao and Shun brought the Great
Peace to the world by meditating on the first two Hexagrams, 'Heaven'
(Tian) and 'Earth' (Kun), and realising that their harmonious interaction
must be replicated in human affairs. Other Hexagrams motivated them to
build boats and tame oxen; and Hexagram 38, *Gui* ('Opposition'), gave them
the idea of bows and arrows that would keep violent intruders at bay. Their
last invention was writing (derived from Hexagram 43: *Guai*, 'Resolution'),

which they used to create government documents and contracts so that 'officials were controlled and the people supervised'.[81] *Changes*, therefore, explored the interrelationship of monarchy, scholarship, technology and civilisation. The Sage Kings knew that human flourishing depended on the imitation of these cosmic patterns which enabled them to live in harmony with the whole.

The *Spring and Autumn Annals*, which now claimed Confucius as its author, also became linked with divination. During the Warring States period, three important commentaries on the *Annals* were transmitted orally: the *Gongyang*, the *Guliang* and the *Zuozhuan*.[82] Divination, the interpretation of dreams, and exegesis are related in many cultures, because they all require an interpreter to find a hidden meaning in obscure imagery.[83] In the *Annals*, eclipses, fires and floods had often portended political disaster and the *Gongyang* and *Guliang* both saw these ancient omens as a warning for the rulers of their own day.[84] Originally, the *Zuo Commentary*, which we encountered earlier, was probably an independent chronicle of the Spring and Autumn period that was later adapted to fit the *Annals* when exegesis became prestigious.[85] It claimed that the *Annals'* laconic entries represented teachings of Confucius that he had transmitted secretly to avoid the reprisals of tyrannical rulers. So, at a time when kingship was in decline, scripture had performed the task of a monarch: *Odes* by helping to shape policy and *Rites* by bringing order to the states.[86]

The *Annals*, of course, had simply recorded births, marriages, deaths, diplomatic meetings and military campaigns, but this dry historical record had always had a numinous aura because of its ritual function. Now attributed to Confucius, it became a link with Heaven and, like all scripture, it was radically reinterpreted to throw light on the present. The *Gongyang* was convinced that the *Annals* had transformative power 'for restoring order in chaotic times and effecting a return to what is correct'.[87] Confucius had reported portentous natural disasters to admonish the rulers of his day and now Warring States exegetes studied these same omens to critique current abuses, adding insights of their own.[88] The *Gongyang* believed that because China had been without an effective king during the Spring and Autumn period, monarchy had survived only in the judgements of the *Annals*.[89] By the end of the Warring States period, the idea that a sacred text could be the sole repository of political authority had taken firm root in China.[90]

*

For almost 200 years, Greece had consisted politically of a loosely related confederation of self-governing, independent city states, but it entered a new phase in 334 BCE, when Alexander, king of Macedon (356–323 BCE), crossed over to Asia Minor, liberated the Greek *polis* of Ephesus from Persian control and defeated the massive army of Darius III, king of Persia, the following year. When he died, some ten years later, the empire of Alexander the Great extended as far as India and Afghanistan. In the confusion following his death, his leading generals, known as the *diadochoi* ('successors'), fought one another for control of the empire and in 301 BCE the province of Judah fell to Ptolemy I Soter, who had established a power base in Egypt. The Ptolemies did not interfere much in local affairs, but in the wake of the army, Greek colonists arrived in the region and established democratic city states in Gaza, Schechem, Marissa and Amman. Greek soldiers, merchants and businessmen settled in the region, and the local people learned to speak Greek; some even became 'Hellenes' themselves, entering the lower ranks of the imperial armies and local government.

Even though the *polis* was alien to deep-rooted Near Eastern traditions – Greek society was ruled by a secular intelligentsia rather than a divinely appointed king or a priestly elite – Hellenism gained ground in the region. Egyptians, Persians and Judahites could become 'Greek' by studying in the local *gymnasia*, where they memorised extracts from the *Iliad*. Far more crucial to the creation of a Greek citizen, however, were the physical exercises that enabled elite young men to embody the heroic ideals of the Homeric tradition, teaching them to master their bodies in a way that would reflect their mastery of others.[91] Some of the local people learned to feel at home with Greek culture, blending it creatively with their own traditions. The famous philosopher Philo of Alexandria (*c.*20 BCE–50 CE), for example, applied the Greek discipline of *allegoria* to the stories and laws of *torah*. But others aggressively asserted and redefined their own literary heritage. In Judah, textual study had traditionally been confined to a scribal elite, but now, in a bid to resist Hellenisation, study groups for male Israelites developed outside the temple. But the reading of scripture remained an aristocratic, priestly art: laymen were simply instructed in the general principles of their Hebrew traditions.[92]

Yet in the writings of Ben Sira, a priest and scribe in Jerusalem from the late third to the early second centuries BCE, we see a merging of Greek and Hebrew traditions that was different from Philo's.[93] His students were destined to become scribal retainers, ministering to the priestly aristocracy who governed the temple state under the auspices of the Ptolemies. This instruction was still conducted orally, but Ben Sira committed his lessons to writing in the hope of reaching future generations.[94] He tells his pupils to 'listen' and 'hear' his words, his aim being to engrave the texts on their hearts. Wisdom was acquired only by one who 'practises' the teachings of *torah* and allowed them to change him.[95] Ben Sirah may have been the first Judahite to link the traditional 'wisdom' of Israel with the Greek idea of a primordial Wisdom embodied in the laws of the cosmos – a synthesis that gave Israel's scripture a suprahistorical dimension.

For Ben Sira, *torah*, the traditional 'teaching' of Israel, was identical with the eternal wisdom of God.[96] He personified this divine Wisdom in a female figure who sings her own praises in the Divine Council in a hymn that was clearly meant to be performed and, possibly, sung. She describes herself coming forth from the mouth of Elohim as the divine Word that had brought the whole of creation into existence. She then wandered through the world in search of a home until God commanded her to settle with the people of Israel. That is how she came to be established on Mount Zion, ministering before God in the temple, an inexhaustible source of insight and confidence.

> They who drink me will thirst for more.
> Whoever listens to me will never have to blush
> Whoever acts as I dictate will never sin.[97]

This hymn clearly draws on another hymn, which was probably added to the ancient Wisdom texts of Israel during the early Hellenistic period (*c.*330–250 BCE).[98] Here too, Wisdom claims that Yahweh 'created me when his purpose first unfolded, before the oldest of his works', and that she had been at his side at every stage of the creative process, 'a master craftsman, delighting him day after day, ever at play in his presence'.[99]

This is a very different scriptural world from the dark, perplexing universe of the *Mahabharata*. Nor are we guided through a Daoist maze of carefully cultivated ambiguities that plunge us into a cloud of unknowing. Ben Sira was no Zhuangzi or Laozi; he was a civil servant training a new generation of obedient scribes who, like himself, were in love with the temple and its rituals. Ben Sira does not seem to have been working with a definitive biblical text: there was as yet no official biblical canon. But his grandson, who would preserve and edit his book, lived in a far more perplexing time, when Jerusalem's rulers tried to force a scriptural canon on their reluctant subjects.

7

CANON

In 221 BCE, the Qin dynasty defeated the last of its rivals, ending the long nightmare of the Warring States period by uniting the entire country in the first Chinese empire. The so-called First Emperor was not particularly versed in the Six Classics; nor was he a ritualist or a sage. He had adopted Lord Shang's pragmatic 'Legalism' and believed that the welfare of the state depended on agriculture and warfare rather than *ren*. He achieved sole rule by eliminating the aristocracy, forcing the 120,000 princely families to reside in the capital and confiscating their weapons. The empire was divided into thirty-six commanderies ruled by officials who answered to central government. The Zhou rites were abolished and replaced by ceremonies that focused on the emperor.[1] When the court historian objected to this innovation, Prime Minister Li Si (a former student of Xunzi) advised the emperor that any school that opposed the Legalist programme must be abolished and its texts confiscated.[2] The historian Sima Qian, who held office between 140 and 110 BCE, would later claim that there was a massive book-burning and that 460 teachers were executed, but some modern historians believe that the emperor simply forbade private individuals and schools to own the prohibited books. The Classics were entrusted to the regime's official philosophers, and could be studied only under strict supervision. This concentration of intellectual authority in an imperial library and a body of scholars was the first step towards the formation of an official canon to serve the state.[3]

But in attempting to establish a ruthlessly autocratic government, the First Emperor had miscalculated. When he died in 210 BCE, the people rose in rebellion, and after three anarchic years, Liu Bang, one of the imperial magistrates, founded the Han dynasty. He wanted to preserve the centralised state and knew that the empire needed Legalist realism, but he was also aware that a more inspirational ideology was necessary. His solution was a combination of Daoist and Legalist principles.[4] There would be 'empty', open-minded governance and strict penal law, but no draconian punishments.

In his account of the philosophical schools of China, the historian Liu Xin (c.46 BCE–23 CE) argued that each had its strengths and weaknesses. He regarded the literati (*ru*) as the 'loftiest', since they were rooted in China's most distinguished traditions: they cultivated the Classics, promoted *ren* and *yi*, transmitted the traditions of Yao and Shun, regarded kings Wen and Wu as authorities and Confucius as their founder. But they did not have the whole truth: 'There are gaps in [their] knowledge, which can be filled by the other schools.' Daoists were the most spiritual: they knew how to 'maintain oneself by clarity and emptiness, uphold oneself by humility and yielding', but they underestimated the importance of ritual and the rules of morality. Legalists understood that government depended on laws and deterrents, but were mistaken in jettisoning *ren* and *yi*. Liu Xin approved of the Mohists' condemnation of extravagance and their promotion of 'universal love' (*jian ai*) but not of their failure to appreciate 'the distinction between kin and stranger'.[5]

In the West, religious traditions are distinct and usually opposed to one another, but in China, synthesis was the norm. Like Xunzi, one could be a Confucian by day and a Daoist by night. Legalists shared many Daoist ideas, arguing that the truly enlightened ruler 'waits in stillness and emptiness', and practised *wu wei* by letting 'the tasks of themselves be fixed'. He was simply the Prime Mover, remaining immobile but setting his ministers and subjects in motion.[6] This clearly resembled the idealised Confucian prince who silently emitted his 'virtue' but neither acted nor spoke. Chinese scriptures differed in emphasis, but shared a conviction that it was essential for humans to align themselves with the Way of 'Heaven' or 'Nature'; they saw no distinction between the spiritual and the physical, the sacred and the profane.[7] But – an important distinction – this did not mean that their scriptures were 'secular', as Western scholars once assumed, but rather that the secular was sacred.[8]

The Daoism promoted by Liu Bang as the state religion differed greatly from the spirituality of Zhuangzi and Laozi. It focused on the ancient Sage King known as the Yellow Emperor (Huang Lo), and seems to have been an amalgam of various cults, advocating minimalist government, low taxes and simplified legal codes. At court, the preferred texts were *Daodejing* and the *Zhuangzi* but there was also a vogue for 'Neo-Daoist' rituals claiming to contact spirits and enhance longevity. In his youth, however, Liu Bang had studied Confucian ritual and, at the beginning of his reign, he commissioned the *ru* to devise a court ceremonial. When it was performed for the first time, he exclaimed: 'Now I realise the nobility of being a Son of Heaven!'[9] The literati slowly gained ground at court, and there was a growing desire for more solid moral guidance.[10]

The psychological effects of the First Emperor's prohibition of the Classics were profound, however.[11] The trauma of this imperial 'assault' had made many of the *ru* nervous about the integrity of the *jing*; many were convinced that the *jing* had survived only in a defective condition, and since it was virtually impossible to establish a definitive text before the advent of printing, it was not easy to allay these fears. Inevitably, perhaps, some portions of the *jing* were lost over time. We have seen that Mozi and Mencius both quoted 'scriptures' and maxims of Confucius that are no longer extant. This widespread anxiety about the status of the Classics both created and was fed by the myth of the 'book-burning' but it also motivated the establishment of an official canon. Some of the literati tried to reconstruct the *Yuejing*, the 'Classic of Music', which had indeed been lost, or recover lost fragments of the *jing*. Others attempted to amalgamate the five surviving *jing* – Documents, Odes, Rites, Changes and Spring and Autumn Annals – into a single text or tried to prove that they were not an arbitrary collection of disparate writings but had a common thread. Most of the *ru*, however, tended to focus on one of the Classics, which they reinterpreted so that it addressed the new reality of the Chinese empire.

One of these scholars was Dong Zhongshu (179–104 BCE), who specialised in the *Annals* as interpreted by the *Gongyang* commentary. He was convinced that, supplemented by some of the new cosmological ideas, this Classic could become the blueprint for a new Han ideology.[12] In a work entitled *Chunqiu fanlu* ('The Luxuriant Gems of Spring and Autumn'), Dong and his disciples argued that the Confucian scriptures were essential to the process that enabled human beings to embody Heaven. Confucius had left a blueprint for the perfect polity in the enigmatic judgements of the *Annals* but had deliberately veiled these ideas in esoteric language. Only a skilled exegete, therefore, could unlock the dynamic power of this sagely text. In the *Analects*, Confucius had reminded us that even though Heaven did not speak, we could discern the Way of Heaven by observing the rhythms of Nature. But discovering the hidden meaning of the *Annals* required a massive intellectual effort:

> Now if eyes do not look, they will not see. If the mind does not deliberate,
> it will not understand. Even if the world's greatest delicacy is before you,

if you do not taste it, you will not know its excellence. Even if the greatest
principles of the sages are set before you, if you do not deliberate you will
not know their righteous principles.[13]

Scholars could not be content with a superficial reading of *Annals*, but must
infer (*tui*) new meanings in the text.

The emperor's 'virtue' (*de*) had always been essential to the well-being
of the state; now Dong insisted that the Han emperor must rule as the
direct instrument of Heaven. Because he was the link that drew the triad
of Heaven, Earth and Humanity together, the emperor's task was to use
his unique intellectual gifts to align his subjects with Heaven's Way.[14] If he
failed to provide them with security and happiness, Heaven would withdraw
its Mandate, but would issue warnings in the form of natural disasters –
floods, plagues and earthquakes – before doing so. The *Annals* showed how
the monarch's partnership with Heaven had worked during the Spring and
Autumn period, so it could now help the emperor to decipher current
signs of Heaven's will. It was, therefore, essential that a cadre of scholars
able to interpret the otherwise impenetrable *Annals* had the power to ensure
that imperial policy was based on their exegesis.

When Dong wrote the *Luxuriant Gems*, Huang-Lo ideology was still dominant at court, so there was no hope of this coming to pass until the young
Emperor Wu (r. 141–87 BCE), who was favourably disposed to the Confucians,
succeeded to the throne. Wu appointed specialists in the Five Classics to
imperial office and Dong came to court. He suggested to the emperor that
there were too many competing ideologies and recommended that the
Confucian scriptures become official state teaching. Confucius, he explained,
had intended the *Annals* to perform the task of a king at a time when the
monarchy was in abeyance. The emperor should establish an academy of
scholars whose study of the *Annals* would reveal what Confucius would have
done in his place. Dong is often credited with making Confucianism the
official ideology of the Chinese empire, but in fact he fell from favour and
never achieved high office. Wu did establish an academy, as Dong requested,
but it did not become an important institution until 124 BCE, when the
Confucian scholar Gongsan Hong suggested that the study of ritual and history
would produce more insightful state officials, requesting that fifty of his own
students be recruited to the academy, where they would be tested on the
Classics and, if they performed satisfactorily, appointed to public office.[15]

The triumph of Confucianism was a long time coming. Wu was never
wholly committed to the Confucian ideal – he also promoted the Daoist

rites – and was motivated chiefly by political considerations. He delegated very little and the scholars he patronised became a new elite at court.[16] But he did not make the mistakes of the First Emperor: there was no sectarian intolerance and Wu continued to see merit in all the schools. Initially, the *ru* could make little headway against the prestige of the army but by the end of the first century BCE, there would be over a thousand young men studying the Classics in the academy and by 140 CE, the numbers had risen to 30,000.[17] Gradually, familiarity with the Confucian scriptures became the hallmark of the most influential officials.[18]

But Confucianism changed during this transitional period – some would claim that it had lost its way. The officials' interpretation of the Classics was, perhaps inevitably, rationalistic and pragmatic and, in the process, Confucius himself was transformed. Sima Qian, Grand Historian of the imperial court, was the first to articulate the new Confucian mythos.[19] He claimed that by Confucius' time, the *Rites* were no longer practised and only fragments of *Odes* and *Documents* had survived. But Confucius had heroically restored these lost scriptures by researching the ancient lore of the Xia, Shang and early Zhou dynasties; he had also reassembled the texts of *Rites* and *Music* and added the stories of Yao and Shun to *Documents*. Textual scholarship, of course, was the prerogative of the ruler, but since the monarchy was in decline, Confucius had had no option but to perform this royal duty. 'From this time,' Sima Qian concluded, 'the [rules of] *Ritual* and *Music* could be presented, and he thereby completed the Kingly Way and perfected the Six Arts.'[20]

Sima Qian also insisted that Confucius had been a sage as well as an editor, but he had to contend with the fact that the great sages – Fu Xi, the Yellow Emperor, Yao and Shun – had all been either kings or the founders of dynasties; Confucius, of course, had been neither. Yet in his extraordinary biography of the Master, Sima Qian explained that only a sage had the ability to combine civil (*wen*) with martial (*wu*) power – ordinary mortals simply excelled in one or the other. He went on to claim that Confucius (who, in fact, had never held high office) had not just been a brilliant minister but, in accordance with the warrior ethos, had ruthlessly carried out executions. Clearly, he had been the sage of his time. Even though he had not been a king, Sima Qian insisted that Confucius had predicted that his judgements in the *Annals* would one day be implemented by a Han emperor: 'As for the meaning of the [*Annals'*] condemnations, later there will be a king who will take it and open it. The righteousness of the *Annals* will be put into practice and the world's religious ministers and rulers will fear it.'[21]

By the first century BCE, the Chinese had a canon, which consisted of the Five Classics that would be used to train civil servants until the 1911 Revolution. But it was a mixed blessing. The canon included neither the *Analects* nor the *Mencius*, which had emphasised the importance of spirituality and self-cultivation. Instead, the canonical texts focused on the political and the external. *Documents* recorded the words and deeds of noble statesmen but said nothing about the interior development that had led them to these views. *Rites* prescribed the rules of ritual without, in the main, elaborating on their spiritual effects. *Changes* presented a body of supposedly objective knowledge that enabled a *junzi* to conduct himself morally in the world. And *Annals*, a historical text, had a purely pragmatic role. Many of the *Odes*, it is true, did reflect the affective, interior life, but in the early Han period, the *Odes* were generally used to provide rulers and officials with ethical or political advice.[22]

The texts selected were made to focus on the mundane. Where Mencius had experienced Heaven as a spiritual reality within himself, for Dong, Heaven was chiefly evident in the patterns of history and the natural world. In seeking to establish the official faith of an agrarian empire, Confucians had provided the Chinese state with a moral and political message, but for over a millennium, those Chinese who wanted to explore the inner life and achieve the profound transformation that had been so crucial to Confucius would turn to the Daoist spirituality of Zhuangzi and Laozi. Others were drawn to Mahayana Buddhism.

*

Buddhists approached their canon very differently. The First Council, held shortly after the Buddha's death, had affirmed the Pali Canon but not to everybody's satisfaction. 'The Doctrine and the Discipline have been well chanted by the Elders,' said one of the monks. 'Nevertheless, I maintain that I retain the doctrine in my memory, just as *I* heard it ... from the lips of the Blessed One.'[23] Buddhism would never have a single, authoritative 'doctrine'. The Buddha had always altered his teachings to meet the needs and circumstances of different people and Buddhism was now spreading to other regions – to Sri Lanka, along the trade routes, and to Han China – where, following the Buddha's example, the monks adapted the tradition they had inherited to these new environments.[24]

At the Second Council (*c.*330 BCE), the Theravadins, the 'elders' of the Sangha, accused some of the monks of relaxing the monastic rules.

The monk Mahadeva had put forward five objections to the claims of the *arahant* ('the worthy') who had attained nirvana. These points were debated a few decades later at a Third Council convened by the emperor Ashoka at Pataliputra. Theravadins maintained that every Buddhist could achieve an enlightenment that was identical to Gotama's, but the 'majority' (*maha-sanghitas*) believed that the Buddha's enlightenment was unique and that the *arahant* had achieved only a penultimate state. He was still subject to desire, Mahadeva had claimed, still had erotic dreams, was not omniscient in mundane matters, still had doubts, and could still profit from instruction.[25] When the vote went against them, the Theravadins withdrew from the majority, but for many years there was no formal breach and Theravadins and those monks who inclined to what they called the Mahayana, the 'Greater Vehicle', because they found it a more adequate expression of the Buddha's teaching, continued to live together in the same monasteries.[26]

Ashoka had urged Buddhist monks to cultivate a close relationship with their lay patrons, and it is possible that this made some more sensitive to the plight of the laity, who had no hope of achieving enlightenment. Warriors and merchants could not spend hours in meditation nor could they realistically detach themselves from the desires that tied all beings to the endless cycle of death and rebirth. The Pali texts include a poignant story about Anathapindika, a generous patron of the early Sangha. When he was dying, the great *arahant* Sariputta had visited him and had preached a short sermon on detachment, which reduced Anathapindika to tears. Why had he never heard this teaching before? Because it was for monks only, Sariputta explained. That is not right, Anathapindika protested; many householders were ripe for nirvana and could attain it, if they were taught how.[27] He died that night and was reborn in heaven with only seven more lives ahead of him. This seemed a blessing to the editors of the Pali Canon, but to others – monks as well as laypeople – it must have seemed a poor reward for his devotion and generosity. This sentiment may have contributed to the development of the Mahayana.[28]

This was a very gradual process lasting centuries. As we have seen, two factors were at issue: compassion for the laity and a diminution of the *arahant*'s status, which in turn was accompanied by an enhancement of that of the Buddha. Gotama's attainments were now deemed exceptional.[29] This did not mean that he had become a god – because in India an enlightened man is superior to the *devas* – but he was no longer regarded as an ordinary mortal. In the Pali scriptures, the Buddha is presented as a regular human being, but as the Mahayana developed, he acquired superhuman attributes. It was said that he was conceived without intercourse, had been born from his mother's side at the level of her heart, had lived in a constant meditative state and had only seemed to wash, eat or sleep.

Stories also circulated about his previous lives as a bodhisattva, which were collected in the *Jatarka* ('Birth Tales') and included in the Pali Canon. A bodhisattva is a person who has vowed to attain nirvana, an achievement that could take many lifespans. The Buddha, it was said, had previously lived as an animal, a layman and even a woman, and his chief attribute had always been compassion, often voluntarily enduring pain to help other suffering beings. Consequently, the Mahayana argued that Buddhists should not retire from the world as the Theravadins did. Had not the Buddha commanded his monks to go forth to a suffering world? In the Pali Canon, the Buddha was called the Tathagata, because he had 'gone' and had transcended the pain of life. But the Mahayana insisted that he had not 'gone' at all: his death was just another simulacrum and he was still present, helping all sentient beings deal with the inescapable sorrow of existence. Both the Theravadins and the Mahayana preserved essential aspects of the Buddha's life and vision. He had indeed lived for years as a solitary ascetic and had renounced society while seeking enlightenment. But he had also spent forty years tirelessly teaching others how to liberate themselves from their pain. The Mahayana developed new traditions about the innumerable Buddhas who had attained nirvana before Gotama and circulated tales of bodhisattvas who remained in the world after attaining enlightenment to help suffering creatures.

Over time, the Mahayana became the dominant and most popular form of Buddhism. Its success was, perhaps, due to the essential dynamic of scripture, which insists that its teachings be practically implemented. For the Mahayana, to thwart this mandate and retreat, like an *arahant*, into one's own inner peace was a deviation. The Pali Canon continued to grow, notably in the Abidharma, which explored the philosophical implications of the Buddha's life. But the Mahayana's appeal was due in no small measure to its massive scriptural corpus which, if printed in English, would fill 150 volumes.[30] Nobody, however, was expected to read all these scriptures and most Mahayanists focus on only one. These texts are not perused silently but are chanted out loud, and, as always in India, a teacher is essential, since they make no sense unless accompanied by meditative and ethical practices that require careful supervision. The texts are also a focus of worship because each represents the 'body' of the

Buddha. In both Pali and Sanskrit – as in English – the word 'body' (*kaya*) can refer to a group or collection of elements, so the '*dharma*-body' of the Buddha is composed of those qualities and teachings which represent the Truth that he embodied.

How could the multifarious Mahayana scriptures, which frequently disagree, express the essential truth of the tradition? The Mahayana has never regarded itself as a 'school' with a clear doctrinal objective. It was, rather, an undirected spiritual movement that developed incrementally over centuries and took many forms. It had no ambition to seek the 'essential' truth of Buddhism, since it regards essentialism as a fallacy that impedes our understanding of reality.[31] Essentialism is crucial to the sciences, but when we are confronted with the messiness of human experience, it can lead to an unrealistic and unsustainable quest for certainty. Mahayana scripture, on the other hand, revels in difference and regards variety and the dissolution of categories as a virtue. Mahayanists have no desire either to close or pare down their canon, because its irrepressible proliferation leaves the door open for fresh experiences.[32]

Instead of consigning the historical Buddha to the past, the Mahayana scriptures released him into the present, where he and the bodhisattvas play havoc with received ideas that give us an illusion of stability. Making the Buddha an effective force that could console, clarify or protect here and now may have been a response to the turmoil following the collapse of the Mauryan empire – the terrifying world of the *Mahabharata* – in which enlightenment could seem difficult, if not impossible, without the Buddha's presence.[33] But this was never a vague, self-indulgent yearning. Both Theravadins and Mahayanists cultivated a sense of the Buddha's presence in a disciplined meditative practice known as *Buddhanasmrti* ('recollection of the Buddha').[34] In one of the oldest texts of the Pali Canon, the monk Pingiya, now too old to travel with the Buddha, had discovered a way of being in his presence continually: 'With constant and careful vigilance, it is possible for me to see him with my mind as clearly as with my eyes, in night as well as day.'[35] In the fifth century CE, the great Theravadin exegete Buddhaghosa would instruct the meditator to go to a solitary place and call the Buddha to mind, dwelling systematically and in detail on his physical features with such concentration that he eventually becomes one with him. In this way, 'he conquers fear and dread ... He comes to feel as if he were living in the Master's presence, and his [own] body ... becomes as worthy of veneration as a shrine room.'[36]

An early Mahayana scripture explains that this practice hastens enlight-enment and that by living in seclusion and focusing solely on the Buddha's person, Buddhists could acquire a more extensive vision:

> They should keep their bodies erect, and, facing the direction of the Buddha, meditate upon him continuously. If they maintain mindfulness of the Buddha without interruption from moment to moment, then they will be able to see *all the Buddhas of the past, present and future, right in each moment.* [37]

This practice was essential to the production of the Mahayana scriptures and enabled them to claim that they were indeed presenting *Buddhavacana* ('enlightened teachings'). Because the Buddha and the other innumerable Buddhas and bodhisattvas were still in the world, they could communicate with Mahayanists in dreams and visions. [38] The Mahayana scriptures do not narrate historical or empirical facts. Instead they describe the visionary ex-periences of meditators who have practised *Buddhanasmrti* and seen an entirely different version of the cosmos. The Mahayana envisages millions of worlds besides our own, some of which have become 'Buddha-fields', regions where a Buddha has exerted his enlightened influence. The scriptures often describe Gotama Buddha as seen in such visions, preaching to or conversing with thousands of fellow Buddhas or bodhisattvas who are active in other universes.

This was possible because of the Mahayana concept of 'emptiness', which is discussed in the vast anthology of early scriptures known as the *Prajnaparamita* ('Perfection of Wisdom'). Containing some 150,000 verses, it was compiled between 100 BCE and 100 CE but new writings continued to be added for another two centuries. [39] 'Wisdom' (*prajna*) was a state of consciousness, achieved by meditative disciplines that applied the Buddha's teaching of *anatta* ('no-self') to all other realities. Their meditative experiences had convinced Mahayanists that what they called the *dharmas*, the categories that are essen-tial to our ordinary experience of the world, had no solid foundation: the world was essentially 'empty', lacking in substance. This 'emptiness' was neither bleak nor nihilistic, however, but opened the practitioner to new forms of perception. As the American scholar Stephen Beyer explains:

> The metaphysics of the *Prajnaparamita* is in fact the metaphysics of the vision and the dream: a universe of glittering and quicksilver change is precisely one that can only be described as empty. The vision and the dream become the tools to dismantle the hard categories we impose upon reality, to reveal the eternal, flowing possibility in which the bodhisattva lives. [40]

Subhuti, a contemporary of the Buddha who was famous for his loving-kindness, is the principal speaker in the earliest portions of the *Perfection*. He explains that the Abidharma section of the Pali Canon had got stuck in conceptual thought and that 'emptiness', the realisation that everything we see and imagine is illusory, could be achieved only by disciplined intuition. Subhuti had learned this directly from the Buddha but it was accessible to anyone who assiduously practised *Buddhanasmrti*. They 'will hear this perception, take it up, study it, spread, recite and write it, and ... will honour, revere, adore and worship it'.[41]

'Emptiness' was not an abstruse, metaphysical idea but a carefully cultivated state of mind. Practitioners would experience 'nothing' – an existential vertigo with nothing to hold on to and nothing to aim for.

> In form, in feeling, will, perception, and awareness
> Nowhere in them they find a place to rest on.
> Without a home they wander, *dharmas* never hold them
> Nor do they grasp at them.[42]

That, Subhuti explained, is why many are 'frightened and terrified' and made 'anxious' by this teaching.[43] It was the ultimate renunciation, because practitioners had to 'let go' of everything, even their attachment to nirvana as something that 'I' will achieve and enjoy. Just as the 'self' was illusory, they had to realise that nirvana was also 'like an illusion, like a dream'.[44]

An early chapter of the *Perfection* explains that the *arahants* have never really 'let go'. Far from being 'empty', they are full of themselves: 'They make up their minds that "one single self shall we tame ... one single self shall lead to nirvana."' It did not seem to occur to them that after enlightenment, they had a duty to guide other suffering beings to nirvana. The bodhisattva, however, becomes enlightened precisely because of his concern for others, although he must derive no self-satisfaction from this:

> He surveys countless beings with his heavenly eye, and what he sees fills him
> with great agitation ... And he attends to them with the thought that: 'I
> shall become a saviour to all those beings, I shall release them from all their
> sufferings!' But he does not make either this or anything else into a sign to
> which he becomes partial.[45]

He must quash any hint of self-congratulation by reminding himself that neither he nor anybody else has any substantial reality at all. So, while it is true that innumerable people have been led to nirvana by a bodhisattva, it is also true that 'no being at all has been led to nirvana'.[46] It is this ultimate detachment that makes a true bodhisattva.

Obviously, the bodhisattva cannot go around insisting that suffering beings must adopt *his* doctrines and practices, nor must he imagine that they are universally applicable. Like the Buddha, he employs *upaya-kaushalhya*, usually translated as 'skilful means', a 'clever' or 'expedient' form of pedagogy (*upaya*) designed to enable a particular audience to achieve nirvana. For the Mahayana, the Buddha's teaching was essentially provisional so it could vary or be altered, because what is appropriate in one situation may not be so in another. The bodhisattva, therefore, adapts his teaching to the needs of those whom he addresses, abandoning any doctrinal preference of his own. An attachment to cherished beliefs is another symptom of the egotism that blocks enlightenment. Bodhisattvas are prepared to go to any lengths to liberate suffering beings from their pain. In the *Perfection* and other Mahayana sutras we read of bodhisattvas tearing out their eyes or chopping off limbs to heal the suffering of others. These tales cannot be read literally, of course, because these eyes and limbs are also 'empty', but their very extremity can shock the listener into an appreciation of what Buddhist renunciation involves.

The doctrine of 'skilful means' was first developed in the *Lotus Sutra* (*Saddharmapudarika*), which is probably the most important of all the Mahayana scriptures, revered not only in India, where it was originally composed, but also in China, Korea and Japan.[47] It is a dramatic sutra, which opens with Gotama Buddha sitting in a deep meditative trance, surrounded by 12,000 *arahants*, 6,000 nuns, 8,000 bodhisattvas, 60,000 gods, and hundreds of thousands of heavenly beings – a cosmic vision clearly arising from *Buddhanasmrti*. The whole universe is trembling, flowers rain down and perfume pervades the atmosphere. Then the Buddha begins to explain his practice of *upaya*: his teachings must be adapted to the needs of each of his audiences to enable everybody to achieve enlightenment. There were not one but three 'vehicles' or dispensations – for monks, the laity and the bodhisattva – each enabling people to follow the path to nirvana at their own pace.

The bodhisattva acts solely out of compassion. He will go anywhere and do anything to help sentient beings find release from their pain. This ideal is beautifully described in Chapter 25 of the *Lotus Sutra*, which is devoted to bodhisattva Avalokishvara (known as Guanyin in China and Kannon in Japan). He incarnates the Buddha's compassion and comes to the aid of anyone who calls on him. He has saved people from fire, storms, rivers, demons and prison (even when they are guilty). He appears in different forms – as a Buddha, a hero or a god – adapting the Buddha's teachings to the unique circumstances of each suffering individual. He even became a bird so that birds could hear the *dharma*. Some Buddhists would claim that Avalokishvara took the form of Jesus; Tibetans claim that he is now incarnate in the present Dalai Lama.

In the *Lotus Sutra*, the Buddha explains *upaya-kaushalhya* to the huge assembly in simple parables that bring it to life. His doctrine, he says, is like rain that descends on all plants equally but is absorbed differently by each according to its nature and capacity.[48] He is like a guide leading human beings to a utopian land; when his followers tire and want to give up, the guide becomes a magician who creates an enchanted city where they can rest before they reach their destination. The magical city stands for arahant-ship, which is not an end in itself but only a temporary way station.[49]

Then suddenly, to the astonishment of the assembly, another Buddha appears in the sky who introduces himself as Buddha Prabhutaratna, explaining that he admires the *Lotus Sutra* so much that he has vowed to be present whenever it is preached. It turns out that the *Lotus* is not a new scripture but has been part of the teaching of every single Buddha in every age. According to the teachings of some Buddhists, Prabhutaratna died aeons ago but here he is – patently, vibrantly alive; like Gotama Buddha, he is still present in the world.[50] And Prabhutaratna's arrival demonstrates the extraordinary power of the *Lotus Sutra*: we are told that if a person hears a single word of this scripture and rejoices in it, even for a moment, he or she will gain enlightenment. This sutra should not merely be recited but must be worshipped as if it were the Buddha himself with 'sundry offerings of flowers, perfume necklaces, powdered incense, paste, burnt incense, silk canopies and bananas, garments or music'.[51] It makes the Buddha an effective force of salvation in this world of *dukkha*. But the *Lotus* must be preached in the correct spirit: with a serene, honest, brave and joyful heart; with uprightness and great compassion.[52] One of the reasons for the popularity of the *Lotus* is that it suggests that the smallest act of devotion can have a disproportionately positive result. If somebody merely raises their hand and says, 'Adoration to the Buddha', they are on the road to enlightenment.[53]

The *Lotus* does not discuss 'emptiness', but its magical quality reflects the glittering, visionary world that is unveiled once we have let go of rigid categorisation. Emptiness is, however, a major theme of the *Vimilakirti Sutra*, one of the most beloved of the Mahayana scriptures.[54] At the beginning, we learn that Vimilakirti, a wealthy householder of Vaishali, is much respected for his philosophical learning, though some think he talks too much. But he is ailing and complains that the Buddha's disciples no longer visit him, so a huge throng of Buddhists, led by bodhisattva Manjushri, famous for his great compassion, leave the Buddha's house and pour into Vimilakirti's home for a discussion of emptiness. The whole sutra demonstrates the freedom we experience once we realise that nothing has substantial existence. Vimilakirti argues that once you abandon dualistic habits of mind that separate matter and spirit, human and divine, one universe from another, you enter an existence in which anything is possible. You realise that nirvana is so close to the heart of everything and everyone around us that we fail to notice it.

In the 'empty' world of this sutra, we watch the Buddha transforming 500 jewelled parasols into a dome that reflects the entire universe, and are amazed to see thousands of the Buddha's followers fitting miraculously into Vimilakirti's modest house. Vimilakirti summons the Goddess of Wisdom, who blesses the audience with flowers and teases the great *arahant* Sariputta, whose misogynism is well known, by arguing that maleness and femaleness have no intrinsic reality. Vimilakirti orders lunch from another universe, which is delivered by bodhisattvas from the Buddha-land of the great Buddha Sugardhakuta. Finally, Vimilakirti miniaturises the entire assembly, picks it up in his hand, and places it gently back into the Buddha's presence. It then transpires that Vimilakirti is no ordinary householder but an incarnation of Akhshobhya Buddha and has his own marvellous Buddha-land, known as Abhirati ('Intense Delight').

The light-hearted charm of this sutra challenges some of our preconceptions of scripture: there are no stern commandments, no terrifying revelations or condemnations, no grim prophecies. But hard questions are asked. If our world is the Buddha-land of Gotama Buddha, why is it still so full of suffering? Does it mean that our Buddha was ineffective and inferior to Buddha Sugardhakuta who had created a Perfume Universe? Vimilakirti points out that Gotama Buddha had only forty years to save our world and that our perception of it comes from our own unenlightened mentality. But he also insists that our dark world is more conducive to the achievement of enlightenment than the 'perfumed' and 'delight-full' Buddha-lands, because the suffering we witness inspires our compassion. It fills us with discomfort and acts as a goad, impelling us to make the bodhisattva vow instead of retreating into the solitary nirvana of arahantship.

One question on the truth of non-duality, the Ultimate Truth, is so profound that it reduces even the voluble Vimilakirti to a 'thunderous silence' – not unlike the silence at the end of the *brahmodya*. The Mahayana produced many voluminous scriptures but its shortest sutra consists of only three sentences. It begins, as usual, with the Buddha sitting before an assembly of 1,250 monks and billions of bodhisattvas, but he announces that this discourse will consist of a single sound – 'a' – and the audience responds with joy.[55] As the first letter in the Sanskrit alphabet, 'a' is inherent in each consonant and – being both infinite and indeterminate – is a symbol of emptiness.[56] Others went even further. The great Indian philosopher Nagarjuna (d. *c*.250 CE) echoes Vimilakirti's silence by arguing that the Buddha was silent throughout his entire life: 'The Buddha did not teach any doctrine anywhere to anyone.'[57] Others have compared the Word of the Buddha to the sound of a wind chime, which, without being activated by anyone, produces its sound when stirred by the wind. So, too, the words of scripture, which like all phenomena are empty of substance, become a reality only when it touches the minds and hearts of sentient beings, according to the different needs of each.[58]

*

When Ben Sira's grandson translated his book into Greek in about 130 BCE, he was aware that the intellectual and social climate of Judah had become tragically narrow. He wanted to reveal the generous breadth of his grandfather's vision to the wider world of Israel. Ben Sira, he explained emphatically, had devoted himself 'more and more to reading the Law and the Prophets *and the other writings succeeding to the prophets*'.[59] But a series of tumultuous political events in Judah and the surrounding regions had resulted in the creation of a less inclusive canon. Ben Sira had believed that his insights were on a par with the visions of the ancient prophets, but now the religious authorities claimed that the era of prophecy had ended with Ezra.[60] Many Judahites, however, refused to accept this.

By the end of the third century BCE, more Judahites were acquiring a Greek education. Instead of belonging to a chosen people, they hoped to become citizens of the world and found the traditional *torah* archaic and inhibiting. In Jerusalem, the Tobiads, one of the aristocratic clans of the ruling class, wanted their city to discard its Hebrew traditions. By this time, the Ptolemies had lost their Syrian territories to the Seleucid kingdom, founded in Mesopotamia by another of Alexander's 'successors'. The

Seleucids controlled the population through a network of *poleis* scattered through their kingdom, all equipped with *gymnasia* to enculturate the local people and create a Hellenised ruling class. When Antiochus IV succeeded to the Seleucid throne in 175 BCE, he inherited an impoverished kingdom and his policies would be dictated as much by finance as ideology. The Tobiads were eager to make Jerusalem a *polis*, since this would bring them considerable tax benefits. Their leader Joshua, who had adopted the Greek name Jason, gained the office of high priest by offering Antiochus a huge sum of money from the temple treasury; in return, Jerusalem received *polis* status. A few years later, Jason's rival Menelaus, who was not of Aaronide descent, secured the high priesthood for himself by offering Antiochus double tribute, and civil war broke out. Eventually Antiochus drove back Jason's army and, in gratitude, Menelaus escorted Antiochus into the Devir, the 'Holy of Holies' in the temple, where the king seized the equivalent of six years of tribute from the treasury.[61]

The religion practised by the people of Judah was not yet 'Judaism' as we know it today, a faith in which the divine is experienced primarily through the study of sacred texts. The scriptures were important but, as we have seen, they were chiefly the preserve of the scribes and members of the ruling class. The majority faith was still a predominantly temple religion, centred on the divine presence (Shekhinah) enshrined in the Holy of Holies. The Psalms show that when they entered the sacred precincts, Israelite worshippers felt that they had stepped into another dimension, which they believed existed contemporaneously with the mundane world. The Jerusalem temple was holy (*qaddosh*) – that is, it was 'other' and 'set apart' from profane space. The plan of the building represented a three-tiered approach to the sacred, beginning in the courtyard, proceeding through the cult-hall and culminating in the Holy of Holies, which was accessible only to priests. While the Tobiads and their colleagues were beginning to cultivate a more secular vision, most Judahites were profoundly disturbed by Antiochus' violation of their holy place, which was the centre of their world. But worse was to come.

Neither the Ptolemies nor the Seleucids had interfered with the religious observance of their subjects. But in 170 BCE, for reasons that are hard to fathom, Antiochus installed a new Hellenistic cult in the temple and banned the traditional Judahite dietary laws, circumcision and Sabbath observance. The Hasmonean priestly family, led by Judas Maccabeus, led a rebellion and by 165 BCE had managed not only to wrest Judah and Jerusalem from Seleucid control but also to establish a small empire by conquering neighbouring Idumea, Samaria and Galilee.[62] But despite its pious beginnings, the Hasmonean empire (165–63 BCE) was no more just or humane than any other agrarian state. And while the Maccabees had initially been hostile to Hellenism, their own government had distinctly Hellenistic characteristics. To incorporate the conquered Nabateans, Galileans and Idumeans into their empire, they transformed Judahism, hitherto a strictly ethnic category, into a more inclusive identity open to others to reflect what the Greeks called a *politeia*.[63]

Scripture, however, was very important to the Hasmoneans, who needed to affirm their religious legitimacy.[64] Following the example of Alexander the Great, who had created a *kanon* of Hellenistic texts, they insisted that they alone had the power to endorse some Judahite books as authoritative and exclude others, and they firmly declared that the era of prophecy was over. The temple was still the focal point of Judahite religion, but the Hasmoneans had installed their own high priest, which violated Judahite law because he was not descended from Aaron. A group of scribes and priests, therefore, seceded from the Jerusalem temple, now regarded as irreparably compromised, and with their leader, the Teacher of Righteousness, withdrew to Qumran by the shores of the Dead Sea, to create a spiritual temple and a renewed Mosaic covenant.

Other scribes refused to accept the Hasmonean ban on the production of new scriptures and defiantly produced new texts, all preoccupied by the problem of the temple and its priesthood. Scribes usually had distinct areas of expertise. Where Ben Sira's speciality had been Wisdom, these scribes focused on prophecy, insisting that whatever the Hasmoneans decreed, the era of prophecy was *not* over – indeed, in these troubled times, it was more necessary than ever. But instead of speaking in their own voice, like Amos and Hosea, these visionary scribes attributed their prophecies to figures of the primordial past, such as Enoch, Shem or Baruch, who made only a fleeting appearance in the biblical narratives. These texts were not 'forgeries', however: like Ben Sira, the scribes were convinced that their own writings were equal to those of the prophets of old. Relying on their own visions, they interpreted the old stories inventively, reimagining the biblical narratives and making them speak to the present. They regarded this inventive exegesis as an *apocalupsis* – an 'unveiling' or 'revelation'.[65] First and foremost, they were addressing the big issue of the day: how could they access the divine presence, now that the temple had been so tragically polluted? The popularity and longevity of their copious writings showed that many Judahites shared their concern.

These 'prophetic' scribes tried to fill the gaps in the biblical narrative. They were, for example, intrigued by the story of Enoch, the father of Methuselah, who was born six generations after Adam:

> Enoch walked with God. After the birth of Methuselah, he lived for three
> hundred years and became the father of sons and daughters. In all, Enoch
> lived three hundred and sixty-five years. Enoch walked with God. Then he
> vanished because God took him.[66]

What did 'walking with God' mean? How did Enoch 'vanish'? And where did he go when God 'took him'? Had he been taken up to heaven? The scribes believed they knew the answer. From the second century BCE until well into the Common Era, they portrayed Enoch and other biblical heroes as ascending to God's temple in the heavens and being radically transformed by the experience.

These texts present Enoch variously as a priest, scribe, prophet and even an angel.[67] In one, he ascends to the Heavenly Temple, where he saw a 'lofty throne' and heard a voice saying: 'Do not fear, Enoch, righteous man, scribe of righteousness, come near to me and hear my voice.'[68] What Enoch 'saw' was not Yahweh himself, of course, but the 'great glory' (*kavod*), a reflection of the divine essence that had appeared so long ago to Ezekiel in a form 'like a son of man'.[69] In the book of Daniel, composed during the Maccabean wars, the prophet had a vision of 'one of great age' seated on the heavenly throne[70] and saw 'one like a son of man' coming to liberate Judahites from imperial tyranny.[71] Philo of Alexandria had described Moses as 'god and king of the whole nation' who 'entered, we are told, into the darkness where God was'.[72] A cluster of ideas was now forming in which a human being ascended to heaven, entered the Presence, was transformed – even divinised – and became a redemptive figure.

Because of the Hasmoneans' attempt to create a scriptural canon, from the early second century BCE, we find, for the first time, standardised manuscripts that are almost identical with the Hebrew Bible we have today. The Hasmonean canon, however, also included the blatantly propagandist books of the Maccabees, which carefully portrayed their heroic resistance to the Seleucids as a war for scripture – for the 'book of the Law'.[73] We hear that Judas Maccabeus quoted from 'the Torah and the Prophets' when exhorting the troops.[74] But – a significant change – the term *torah* now refers specifically to the Pentateuch, and 'the Prophets' span only from Moses to Ezra; all later works written in Greek, such as Ben Sira's book, are excluded.[75] Henceforth, the Hebrew Bible would be referred to as the 'Law and the Prophets'.

The Qumran sectarians refused to accept the Hasmonean Bible.[76] Their library shows that they acknowledged the 'Law and the Prophets' but it also included scriptures of their own composition. The *Temple Scroll* claims to have been dictated by the Angel of the Presence. Although the story is set in Sinai, the temple it describes will be built by God at some future date and bears no relation to the Tabernacle constructed in the wilderness nor to any other Israelite shrine. Like the *War Scroll*, which describes the final battle between the Sons of Light and the Sons of Darkness, it is a vengeful text that looks forward to the destruction of Yahweh's enemies. Yet it is important to note that there is no indication that Qumran was planning a holy war: God, not the community, would take the initiative in the End Time.[77]

While they affirmed Mosaic law, the sectarians focused on their own legal texts, the *Community Rule* and the *Damascus Rule*, insisting that their 'New Covenant' was more authentic than the Hasmoneans' canon. Instead of confining revelation to the distant past, they claimed that their own Teacher of Righteousness was the last of the prophets. They developed a form of exegesis that they called *pesher* ('interpretation') to show that the ancient prophets had foretold the coming of their Teacher, the Final Battle and the New Temple. Qumranites celebrated their New Covenant with Yahweh in a ritualised meal:

> Wherever there are ten men of the Council of the Community, there shall not lack a Priest among them. And they shall all sit before him according to their rank and shall be asked their counsel in all things in that order. And when the table has been prepared for eating and new wine for drinking, the Priest shall be the first to stretch out his hand to bless the first fruits of the bread and new wine.[78]

Every night a quorum of priestly leaders, set apart from the rest of the community, engaged in a long recitation of scripture, during which they experienced new revelations based on a creative exegesis of the sacred texts.[79] The *torah* of God was not confined to the pre-Hellenistic past, as the Hasmoneans claimed, but was an ongoing revelation derived from an innovative interpretation of scripture.

In 63 BCE, the Hasmonean regime fell to the Roman armies and hatred of the Greeks segued into anti-Roman feeling. The Romans inaugurated a harsh regime, with heavy taxation that impoverished the lower classes, especially in Galilee. The slightest infringement was punished with crucifixion. Like the Persians and the Greeks, the Romans ruled through the priestly aristocracy in Jerusalem, but they also installed a puppet king in Herod (r. 40–4 BCE), an Idumean prince and a recent convert to Judahism. Herod embarked on an extensive building programme which included a magnificent new temple that attracted pilgrims from all over the diaspora in the Near and Middle East, and devoted considerable resources to the support of Judahite communities outside Palestine.[80] New scriptures appeared, written in Greek, including such texts as *Tobit* and the *Wisdom of Solomon*.

Our main source for this period is the Jewish historian Flavius Josephus (*c.*37–100 CE), who was at home in both Greek and Hebrew literature. He came from a priestly family, but also belonged to the new sect of the Pharisees. We know very little about the movement at this early date. Josephus simply says that the Pharisees were expert in 'the traditions of the elders':[81] it seems that they were scribes who, in the usual manner of their class, studied these traditions inventively.[82] Josephus suggests that by this time, many – if not all – Judeans, Galileans and Idumeans had accepted 'the Law and the Prophets', a contained scriptural corpus of pre-Hellenistic scriptures:

> We do not possess myriads of inconsistent books, conflicting with one another; but our books, those which are justly believed, are only twenty-two, and contain the record of all time. Of these, five are the books of Moses ... From the death of Artaxerxes, who followed Xerxes as king of Persia, the prophets after Moses wrote the events of their own times in thirteen books. The remaining four books contain hymns to God and precepts for the conduct of human life.[83]

But some still insisted that the era of prophecy was not over. Josephus records the escalation of non-violent movements against Roman rule, led by self-styled 'prophets', who were inspired by a resentment of its heavy taxation as much as by religious fervour.

During the 50s CE, for example, one Theudas led a New Exodus of 400 people into the Judean desert, convinced that if the people took the initiative, God would send deliverance. Another unnamed prophet marched a crowd of 30,000 unarmed people through the Judean desert to the Mount of Olives, determined to storm Jerusalem and overwhelm the Roman

garrison, not with weapons but by the power of God.[84] But these movements had little political leverage and were ruthlessly suppressed. Josephus
does not mention Jesus of Nazareth, hailed as a prophet and healer, who
was sentenced to death by crucifixion in about 30 CE by the Roman governor
Pontius Pilate after leading a provocative procession into Jerusalem at
Passover, welcomed by an excited crowd as their king. Within days, his
disciples had visions of him, utterly transformed, standing, like Enoch,
beside God's throne in the Heavenly Temple; this convinced them that God
had 'anointed' him as the *messhiah*, and that he would shortly return to
establish God's kingdom on earth.

In 66 CE, a widespread revolt against Roman rule erupted in the province of Judea after the Roman governor had commandeered money from
the temple treasury. The war culminated in the siege of Jerusalem.
Eventually, Titus, son of the newly elected Roman emperor Vespasian, forced
the insurgents to surrender and on 28 August 70 CE, the Roman army
burned the city to the ground. Yet again the people of Judah had lost their
temple, and this time it would not be rebuilt. This could have been the end
of the religion of Israel but instead, a group of Pharisees engaged in a
textual revolution that replaced the temple with a new scripture.

8

MIDRASH

In the ancient Middle East, a temple was so crucial to a people's identity that national life was inconceivable without it.[1] But during their exile in Babylonia, the compilation of a coherent scripture had given the exiled Judahites hope and purpose. The destruction of the Second Temple in 70 CE led to another surge of textual creativity and inspired two new movements. The scriptures produced by Jesus of Nazareth's followers announced that his death had inaugurated a new 'testament' or covenant between God and humanity. But most Judeans felt no need to abandon the Sinai revelation and found new ways of expressing it first in the Mishnah and then in the Talmuds, which gave birth to rabbinic Judaism.

The Pharisees had not supported the war against Rome. Their remarkable leader, Yohanan ben Zakkai, a member of the Great Sanhedrin (a political assembly of the leading men of the city), managed to escape from besieged Jerusalem. Tradition has it that he went to see Vespasian, who was commanding the siege, prophesied that he would soon become emperor, and that, when this prediction proved correct, Vespasian allowed him to establish a centre of learning at Yavne to the east of Jerusalem. After the fall of Jerusalem, Pharisees assembled there and the academy would also welcome scribes and priests, who had lost much of their prestige now that the temple had gone. The learned among them were called *rabbi*, 'my master'. In the early years, the academy was led by Rabbi Yohanan and his two gifted pupils, Rabbi Eliezer and Rabbi Joshua, who would be succeeded by Rabbi Akiva and Rabbi Ishmael. At first, the rabbis still hoped that the temple would be rebuilt for a second time: perhaps God would appoint another *messhiah* like Cyrus? In the meantime, they would preserve the memory of its practices and rituals so that the cult could be immediately resumed. At the same time, they embarked on a massive project to revise the Torah to serve their people in their tragically altered world.[2]

We have seen that when Ezra read Yahweh's Torah to the people after the Babylonian exile, his explanation of the text merged with his performance of the scripture. The text of the Torah (known as *miqra*: 'that which is recited') had thus fused seamlessly in the minds of the audience with the reciter's running commentary, which seemed equally inspired. Now, in the new rabbinic ideology, a sage no longer derived authority from his priestly status or scribal skills but from the wisdom he had inherited from a chain of masters.[3] Scripture was identified with the *written* Torah that had once been stored in the temple. But its interpretation (*midrash*) became the *oral* tradition that a rabbinic student received from his mentor, learned by heart, and passed on to his own pupils. Interpretation was something that you 'recited' (*shna*) carefully and accurately from one generation to the next; it was, therefore, a *mishnah* ('repeated tradition') derived not from an inscribed scroll but from an inspired human being.

At Yavne, therefore, the rabbis who cultivated this *mishnah* were called *tannaim* ('reciters'). The written text of scripture was there for all to see, but it was the 'repeated traditions' that brought its words to life. But 'repetition' did not imply that a rabbi was obliged to reproduce his master's insights verbatim. Once he had thoroughly absorbed them, he could improvise and shape them anew, so that they spoke to the political and intellectual challenges of his own time. A rabbi would impart these new insights to his own pupils, who would later transform them again in their turn. The *mishnah*, therefore, was a living and constantly developing body of knowledge.[4]

The rabbis were not interested in abstruse theology. Their issues were intensely practical. Their task was to develop a legal system that would enable Jews to be faithful to the Mosaic tradition in a tragically altered world, so they could not afford the luxury of relying nostalgically on the past. A ruling about tithing obligations in Transjordan, for example, was defined during a clamorous debate that had no warrant at all in scripture. Yet Rabbi Eliezer greeted it with delight: "'The mystery of the Lord is with those who fear Him and His Covenant shall inform them!"[5] Go and tell the sages! Do not distrust your decision!'[6] The Mishnah was deliberately moving away from the canonical Hebrew Bible. Instead of quoting scripture, the rabbis preferred to cite Hillel and Shammai, who had been active in Jerusalem during the early first century CE. The Mishnah never claimed that its entire body of rulings derived from Moses. That idea would emerge only later.[7]

Exegesis was not a solitary study but a noisy, communal affair. Students learned the 'repeated traditions' of their teachers by reciting them aloud and arguing about them vehemently. A Palestinian rabbi would later describe the scene: 'Words fly back and forth when the sages come into a house of study and discuss Torah, one stating his view, still another stating another view, and another stating a different view', their ideas flying back and forth 'like a shuttlecock'.[8] Even though a legal decision would be carried by a majority vote, minority views were carefully preserved because revelation was conceived as open-ended.[9] An opinion might not be valid right now but could well be needed in a future debate. It was even said that God himself had to study these 'repeated traditions' to make sure that he grasped their implications for the future.[10] As a later rabbi would explain, there could be no last word:

> If the Torah were handed down cut and dried, we would not have a leg to stand on. What is the scriptural basis for that statement? [It is]: 'And the Lord spoke to Moses' ... Moses said to Him, 'Lord of the World, teach me the Law.' He said to him, 'Follow the majority [to declare the Law]. If the majority finds the accused innocent, find him innocent; if guilty, guilty.' So, the Torah may be decided in forty-nine ways siding with a decision of uncleanness and in forty-nine ways favouring a decision of cleanness.[11]

God had given the Torah to Moses with multiple meanings; it was up to the interpreter, the *tanna*, to apply it according to the needs of the time.

But the text alone could not provide the wisdom required to interpret the Torah correctly. As in India and China, a student learned its true significance by living with his teacher, serving him, observing his behaviour and seeing the Torah in action in the minutiae of daily life. One unfortunate student, who had misunderstood one text and ignored another, misinterpreted a scriptural ruling on ritual purity and thus failed to observe one of the commandments (*mitzvoth*). His mistake was to rely on the texts. If he had watched his rabbi performing the *mitzvah* in question, he would have grasped its underlying significance intuitively. Scripture was often difficult to understand, but your teacher embodied it in every moment of his life. By watching how he ate, spoke, moved or prayed, you saw the Torah incarnate.

The Mishnah is not an attractive scripture. It lacks the emotive language of the Bible and consists of dry legal rulings instead of intriguing stories. But the idea of narrative, in which one event led inexorably to another, was too painful for the rabbis because they knew only too well how the story ended. The Mishnah, it has been said, is a cocktail of raw pain and false hope – a means of keeping despair and terror at bay.[12] Facing a shattered world, the rabbis could only pick up the pieces. They wanted nothing to do with the tales of the Heavenly Temple that scribes were still composing, but clung to the mundane reality, arguing, for example, about the function of a room in the temple complex[13] or how the night-watch had patrolled the premises.[14]

A crucial figure was Rabbi Akiva, who perfected a system of *midrash* that often gave the 'Law and the Prophets' a meaning that differed dramatically from the intentions of the biblical authors. In one story, which circulated long after his death, it was said that the fame of his genius reached heaven and that Moses decided to attend his class, only to find, to his intense embarrassment, that he could not understand a word of Akiva's explanation of the Torah that had been given to *him* on Mount Sinai. 'My sons have surpassed me,' he said proudly as he made his way back to heaven.[15] Rabbi Ishmael believed that Akiva sometimes went too far. It was, surely, better to be as faithful as possible to the original text?[16] But Rabbi Akiva's method won the day, because it kept scripture open: God's word was infinite and could not be confined to a single interpretation.

But Akiva was a tragic figure, whose fate demonstrated the fragility of the rabbis' hopes. In 130, the Roman emperor Publius Aelius Hadrianus visited Palestine during an imperial progress. It was his custom to leave a permanent memento of his visit in the form of a building and when he arrived in Jerusalem, which was still in ruins, he decided that his gift would be a brand-new city named Aelia Capitolina after himself and the gods of the Roman Capitol – a prospect that naturally filled Jews with horror. The following year, Hadrian issued a set of edicts banning circumcision, Torah-teaching and rabbinic ordination. Even the most moderate rabbis realised that another war with Rome was now inevitable. The revolt was led by Simon Bar Koseba, a hard-headed soldier who managed to hold the Romans at bay for three years. Rabbi Akiva hailed him as the Messiah and renamed him Bar Kochba, 'Son of a Star'. The Roman legions systematically wiped out one Jewish stronghold after another. Jews were henceforth barred from Judea and Rabbi Akiva died a martyr, flayed alive by the Romans for supporting the revolt.

The rabbis had to move to Usha in Lower Galilee. Even though the new emperor, Antoninus Pius (r. 158–61), relaxed Hadrian's legislation, they realised now that the temple would never be rebuilt and turned their work into a new scripture, which they called the Mishnah. It seems likely that there was a written version of their discussions at Yavne, which was combined with their later, more sober deliberations.[17] Oral discussion and transmission remained the norm, but after the destruction of the Bar Kochba revolt the rabbis felt that it was essential to have a permanent record of their traditions. They regarded the original Hebrew scriptures – the Tanakh – as belonging to a phase of history that had gone forever, but could be used selectively to legitimise their own vision. The completed text of the Mishnah was a formidable collection of the rabbis' legislation for this new world, arranged in six *sedarim* ('orders'): Zeraim ('Seeds'), Moed ('Festivals'), Nashim ('Women'), Niziqin ('Damages'), Qodeshim ('Holy Things') and Tohorsh ('Purity Rules'). These were then subdivided into sixty-three tractates. The Mishnah held proudly aloof from the Bible and rarely quoted or appealed to it. It never claimed to derive its authority from Moses, never discussed its origins or authority, but loftily assumed that its competence was beyond question. Because the rabbis were living incarnations of Torah, their rulings needed no biblical support.[18] After the Bar Kochba disaster, they had no time for apocalyptic fervour or messianic dreams of redemption. The temple may have gone for good, but Jews made themselves aware of the divine presence by ritualising their daily lives, as the exiles had done in Babylonia. The Mishnah helped them to live as if the temple were still standing. Indeed, the Six Orders were constructed as a textual temple.[19] The first and sixth dealt respectively with the holiness of the land and the people. The two innermost orders – Nashim and Niziqin – legislated for the private, domestic lives of Jews and their business relationships. But the second and fifth ('Festivals' and 'Holy Things') were the load-bearing pillars on which the entire textual edifice depended.

But to live as if the Shekhinah were still enshrined in the Holy of Holies, when all that remained were a few charred ruins, demanded a degree of heroism. Thousands of new rulings worked out the implications of the temple's virtual presence for everyday life. How should Jews deal with Gentiles? Could women take over the priestly task of ensuring that every Jewish home was a holy place? How could these homely rituals possibly compare with the splendid ceremonies of old?[20] The rabbis used the ancient liturgical calendar to give these domestic rites a lustrous aura. The Mishnah carefully described the Passover celebrations in the temple, while making it clear that these could now be adapted to every humble home. Henceforth every Jewish village replicated Jerusalem and every home the temple. At the same time, the rabbis seem to have put together the final text of the Bible, which reflected the new sober mood. Before the loss of Jerusalem, some of the apocalyptic tales of the Heavenly Temple had been regarded as scriptural. These were now rigorously excluded from the canon. Only the book of Daniel, a historical character, was retained. These decisions may have been influenced by the emerging scriptures of the Jesus movement that were more attuned to apocalypse and retained books that the rabbis rejected.

The rabbis had achieved the extraordinary feat of transforming temple ritual into a spirituality of the mind. They would not have been able to persuade people to observe these rites had they not been effective. Communal study would now introduce Jews to the divine presence: 'If two sit together and interchange words of Torah, the Shekhinah abides among them.'[21] We do not find this emotive spirituality in the dry pages of the Mishnah, but in *Pirke Avot* ('Sayings of the Fathers'), an anthology compiled after the completion of the Mishnah in about 220. A much-loved text, it traces the pedigree of the great rabbis back to Hillel and Shammai and describes the transformative experience of Torah study. Rabbi Meir, one of Rabbi Akiva's most distinguished pupils, described the transformation and near-divinisation wrought by Torah study:

> Whoever studies the Torah for its own sake merits many things, not only for this but [one can even say] that the entire world is found deserving for his sake. He is called the Beloved Companion who loves the Divine Presence and loves all creatures [and] who makes the Divine Presence glad and makes glad all creatures. And it robes him in humility and fear ... And people shall benefit from his counsel, discernment, understanding and fortitude ... And the mysteries of the Torah are revealed to him and he becomes an overflowing and ceaseless torrent ... and it makes him great and lifts him above the entire creation.[22]

Ben Azzai, another pupil of Rabbi Akiva, also had mystical leanings. While expounding a text one day, he was seen caught up in a nimbus of flame. He had been creating a *horoz*, he explained, a 'chain' that linked together passages of scripture that had no connection in the original text, but which, once 'enchained', revealed an integral, dynamic unity.

> I was only linking the words with one another and then with the words of the Prophets, and the Prophets with the Writings, and the words rejoiced, as when they were delivered at Sinai, and they were sweet as at their original utterance.[23]

The practice of *horoz*, when activated by a human voice, revitalised the Torah and gave it new fire and relevance, translating a historical narra-

tive into a mythos that made it an eternal truth. In the *horoz*, scriptural
verses were woven together to create either a narrative or an argument
that made sense of the tragic present by rooting new insights into the
sacred past.

To this end, the rabbis felt free to change the wording of scripture,
telling their pupils: 'Do not read *this*, but *that*.'[24] In *Sifre*, a collection of
exegetical texts from the third century, for example, we find Rabbi Meir
completely reversing the meaning of a harsh ruling in Deuteronomy which
decreed that a criminal who had been hanged must be buried before night-
fall, because he was 'cursed by God [*qilelat Elohim*] and his corpse would
pollute the Land'.[25] But, Rabbi Meir protested, 'Do not read *qilelat Elohim*'
but substitute '*qallat Elohim*' ('the pain of God'). The grim law was made
to evoke a God who suffered with his creatures. 'When a person is in grave
trouble, what does the Shekhinah say?' asked Rabbi Meir. 'It says, as it were
[*kiryatol*], "My head is in pain, my arm is in pain."'[26]

Compassion was central to rabbinic spirituality. *Pirke Avot* presents Simon
the Just, a revered high priest of the third century BCE, explaining that the
world order depended 'Upon the Torah, upon the Temple Service and upon
the doing of acts of kindness'.[27] This theme was developed in a story in
Avot de Rabbi Nathan, a later text, which describes Rabbi Yohanan walking
in Jerusalem with Rabbi Joshua, who cried aloud in distress as they passed
the temple ruins. How could Israel atone for its sins without the sacrificial
rituals? To reassure him that acts of loving kindness would be just as effective, Rabbi Yohanan created a *horoz*: first, completely reversing the sense of
the original, he quoted God's words to Hosea, 'I desire love [*hesed*] and not
sacrifice'; he linked this with Simon the Just's maxim, and ended with a
verse from Psalms, slightly altered for the occasion: 'The world is built
by love.'[28]

It is in *Sifre* that we first encounter the doctrine of the two Torahs – one
oral, the other written – that would inform later rabbinic exegesis.

> Just as the same rain falls upon trees and gives to each distinctive flavour
> – vines in accord with their nature, olives in accord with their nature – so
> too the words of the Torah are all one – yet they contain [the distinct char-
> acteristics of] scripture: Mishnah, *halakhot* and *aggadot*.[29]

There is no distinction here between the Mishnah (the 'repeated traditions'
of the rabbis), their legal rulings (*halakhot*, sing. *halakha*) and the stories
that illuminate their teaching (*aggadot*). All have the status and authority of

scripture. Another rabbi explained: 'Two Torahs were given to Israel; one by mouth, the other by script.'[30] By the third century, the rabbis were beginning to regard their oral traditions as a continuation of the same revelatory process that had produced the original Torah. Even when engaged in heated debate about the Torah, a committed student knew that, in some sense, both he and his opponent were continuing a conversation that had begun on Sinai: 'The words of those and of the other sages, all of them were given by Moses the Shepherd from what he received from the Unique One of the Universe.'[31]

*

Meanwhile the followers of Jesus of Nazareth were taking the Jewish tradition in a different direction. Originally this was a party of the 'little people': while the rabbis belonged to the elite, Jesus and his first followers came from the peasantry. Despite extensive research into the historical Jesus, we know little about him. He seems to have founded a popular movement of itinerant preachers and healers who ministered to the economically marginalised people of Galilee during the late 20s CE. In an agrarian state, the aristocracy lived separately from the masses, whose religion, therefore, tended to be rather different. But even though they could neither read nor study the scriptures like rabbinical students, Jesus and his disciples would have been familiar with psalms sung at Passover and on pilgrimage to Jerusalem. They certainly knew the story of the Exodus and some of the prophetic teachings, but the prophets they honoured most were men of the people: Moses, who had delivered their ancestors from slavery; and Elijah, who had preached in northern Palestine and was revered as a local hero in Galilee, and was expected to return one day to restore true piety in Israel.[32]

Jesus was born into a society traumatised by state violence. He was brought up in Nazareth, a hamlet near Sepphoris which had been destroyed by Roman troops during an uprising in Galilee after King Herod's death. Galilee was now governed by Herod's son, Antipas, who imposed heavy taxes to fund his own extensive building projects. Failure to pay was punished by confiscation of land, so many peasants were forced into banditry while others – Jesus' father, Joseph the carpenter, possibly among them – turned to menial labour. The crowds who thronged around Jesus for healing were hungry, distressed and sick, many afflicted with neurological and psychological disorders attributed to demons. In Jesus' parables, we see a society split between the very rich and the very poor. People are desperate for loans, heavily indebted, and forced to hire themselves out as day-labourers.[33]

It seems that Jesus called for a renewal of the original covenant with Yahweh, champion of the 'little people'. The Kingdom of God he proclaimed was based on justice and equity, and his followers should behave as if it had already arrived.[34] In God's Kingdom, the poor would be first and the rich and powerful last. But, Jesus taught, those who feared indebtedness must themselves release those indebted to them and they must love even their enemies. Instead of responding with violent reprisals to wrongdoing, like the Romans, they must turn the other cheek, give to everyone who asked for help, and refrain from asking a robber to return what he had stolen. Jesus' followers should live compassionately, and observe the Golden Rule, treating others as they would wish to be treated themselves.[35] Jesus is said to have told his followers to give all their possessions to the poor. Practically expressed compassion was essential to his message. He predicted that the people admitted to the Kingdom of God would not be those who had the correct beliefs but those who had given food to the hungry, drink to the thirsty, who made the stranger welcome, clothed the naked, cared for the sick and visited those in prison.[36]

This was an inherently political message. Jesus was not preaching armed resistance, but his teaching of the Kingdom of God was an implicit critique of imperial power. When asked whether it was permissible to pay taxes to Caesar, he answered equivocally: 'Give back to Caesar what belongs to Caesar and to God what belongs to God.'[37] This statement was in fact more provocative – and politically dangerous – than it sounds to us today. Here Jesus was not advocating a neat separation of church and state. Nearly all the uprisings in Palestine against Rome during the first century CE had been sparked by Roman taxation, which was deemed illegitimate since the Holy Land and its produce belonged to God. There was, therefore, Jesus implied, precious little to 'give back' to Caesar.[38] The event that may have led to his death, however, was his provocative entrance into Jerusalem, when he was hailed by the crowds as king of Israel. He then staged a demonstration in the temple, turning over the money-changers' tables and declaring that God's house was a 'den of thieves'.[39] The temple had been an instrument of imperial control since the Persian period and the tribute extorted from the population was stored there.[40] Within days, Jesus was sentenced to crucifixion by Pontius Pilate, the Roman governor of Judea.

Crucifixion was the Romans' instrument of state terror, a powerful deterrent, usually inflicted on slaves, violent criminals and insurgents. The public display of the victim, his broken body hanging at a crossroads or in an amphitheatre and left as food for birds of prey or wild beasts, demonstrated the pitiless might of Rome. In 4 BCE, after uprisings following Herod's death, 2,000 rebels had been crucified outside the walls of Jerusalem.[41] In the New Testament, the gospels claim that Jesus was tried at a special meeting of the Sanhedrin and that Pilate valiantly tried to save his life. But it is most unlikely that a mere Galilean peasant would be treated with such consideration, especially by a governor who was later recalled to Rome for reckless cruelty. Jesus' disciples, who fled after his arrest, probably never knew the details of his death. In the Roman empire, crucifixions were everyday occurrences and Jesus was probably dispatched without trial, with few, if any, eyewitnesses, and with a casual brutality that is hard for us to imagine.[42]

The gospels are not historical documents: they do not attempt to give us the facts of Jesus' life. They too are *midrash*, weaving scriptural verses together to create a story that injected meaning and hope into the perplexing present. The earliest extant New Testament texts, however, are the letters that Paul, a former Pharisee, wrote to the early Christian communities he founded in the eastern Mediterranean during the 50s, some twenty years after Jesus' death. These show that from a very early date Jesus' followers used the Hebrew scriptures to interpret the events of his life. Paul tells his disciples in Corinth:

> I taught you what I had been taught myself, namely that Christ died for our sins, *in accordance with the scriptures*; that he was buried; and that he was raised to life on the third day, *in accordance with the scriptures*.[43]

There was no explicit prophecy of these events in the Hebrew Bible, but like the Qumran sectarians, the early Christians read the ancient scriptural texts as predictions of current events.

It seems that after the crucifixion, Jesus' followers experienced visions in which they saw him standing, like Enoch, beside God's Throne. These visions inspired an *ekstasis* which they felt to be an outpouring of the Spirit of God. From a very early date, Christians turned to a cluster of texts that seemed to predict Jesus' extraordinary exaltation. Two came from psalms originally performed during the coronation of a new king: 'The Lord said to my lord, "Sit at my right hand until I make your enemies your footstool.'"[44] The other proclaimed the new king's adoption by Yahweh: 'You are my son; today I have become your father.'[45] His disciples remembered that Jesus had often described himself as the 'son of man', which recalled Psalm 8, in which the wonders of creation inspired the psalmist to ask why God should have raised a 'son of man' – a mere human being – to the eminence that, as they had seen with their own eyes, Jesus now enjoyed:

> ... you have made him little less than a god,
> you crowned him with glory and splendour,
> made him lord over the work of your hands,
> set all things under his feet.[46]

This also reminded them of Daniel's vision of a figure 'like a son of man' who had been endowed with 'sovereignty, glory and kingship, and men of all peoples, languages and nations became his servants'.[47] With truly remarkable speed, the titles 'lord', 'son of man' and 'son of God' were attributed to Jesus, who was now recognised as the *messhiah* (in Greek, *christos*, 'the anointed one').[48]

Like rabbinic *midrash*, this exegesis was not conducted in a spirit of cool academic enquiry. The first Christians believed that they were living in the last days before Jesus returned to inaugurate the Kingdom of God, and that the *ekstasis* they experienced had been foretold by the prophet Joel:

> I [Yahweh] will pour out my spirit on all mankind.
> Your sons and daughters shall prophesy,
> your old men dream dreams,
> and your young men see visions.
> Even on your slaves, men and women,
> I will pour out my spirit in these days.[49]

In the past, prophets had usually belonged to the aristocracy, but now the Spirit was inspiring humble peasants, fishermen and artisans.

A very early text, which scholars call 'Q' (from the German *Quelle*, 'source'), has survived only in the gospels attributed to Matthew and Luke. This was simply a collection of Jesus' teachings and did not tell the story of his life. Significantly, it never mentions his death and resurrection. But scholars have long assumed that an account of Jesus' crucifixion also circulated at an early date and was used by the four evangelists. Recently, however, the American scholar Arthur Dewey has argued that there is no hard evidence for this: the horror of Jesus' execution may have been so traumatic that the early Christians rarely spoke of it and it seems that there was no established story that described it in any detail. But, as Paul's letters reveal, in Syria Christians did commemorate his death in a ritualised meal. During his last meal with his disciples, it was said, Jesus had broken a loaf of bread, saying: 'This is my body, which is for you: do this as a memorial of me.' The wine was 'the new covenant in my blood'. 'Every time you eat this bread and drink this cup,' Paul explained to his Corinthian converts, 'you are proclaiming his death.'[50] To make a solemn libation in honour of a man executed by the state as a common criminal was extraordinary.

The Cross had huge implications for Paul. Originally opposed to the Jesus movement, he was converted by a vision in which he too saw Jesus' degraded, broken body raised by God to the highest place in heaven. For Paul, this was an *apocalupsis*, a 'revelation'. Old rules no longer applied. Ethnic, social, cultural and gender divisions had been obliterated: 'There is no such thing as Jew or Greek, slave or freeman, male or female, for you are all one person in Christ Jesus.'[51] But Paul never described the crucifixion in detail. Dewey points out that until the early fifth century, there were only two pictorial representations of the Cross – one a mocking graffito, the other a magical charm.[52] The first Christians did not dwell on Jesus' death, therefore; their focus was his resurrection and exaltation.

We find the first detailed account of Jesus' death in Mark's gospel, composed in about 70 CE but originally performed orally to audiences in Galilee and Syria, the narrator improvising in response to the audience's reactions.[53] This gospel presents Jesus as a popular prophet of the 'little people': like Elijah, he spent forty days in the wilderness, struggling with Satan; his walking on the waters of the Sea of Galilee recalled the Exodus from Egypt; and his miraculous feeding of the crowds was reminiscent of the manna that fed the Israelites in the wilderness. Like Moses, he issued new commandments from a mountaintop and his twelve disciples repre-sented the tribes of Israel. Writing shortly after the horrific destruction of the temple, Mark was trying to counter the inflammatory messianism that had fuelled the tragic Jewish war. He presents Jesus as a suffering, defeated Messiah, his mission a journey to the Cross, the narrative punctuated with predictions of his death.[54]

Crucifixion had been a hideous feature of the siege of Jerusalem. Josephus records that as the starving people fled the city, they were seized by the Romans and, like Jesus, they 'were first whipped, and then tormented with all sorts of tortures ... and were then crucified, before the wall of the city'. The entire city was soon encircled by crosses, their victims deliberately pinioned in grotesque positions.

> So the soldiers, out of the wrath and hatred they bore the Jews, nailed those they caught, one after one way, and another after another, to the crosses, by way of jest; when their number was so great, that room was lacking for the crosses and crosses lacking for the bodies.[55]

News of this atrocity would have resonated throughout the region. For Mark, Jesus' death was a mythos – just one more instance of the suffering of the innocent that happens all the time – and his account of Jesus' crucifixion is a *horoz* of scriptural texts.[56] His chief source was Psalm 22, the lament of a virtuous man who has become the 'scorn of mankind, jest of the people':

> All who see me, jeer at me,
> They toss their heads and sneer,
> 'He relied on Yahweh, let Yahweh save him!
> If Yahweh is his friend, let him rescue him!'[57]

Mark attributes this abuse to 'the chief priests and scribes' standing at the foot of Jesus' Cross;[58] as in the psalm, he has the Roman soldiers casting lots for Jesus' clothing;[59] and he is the only evangelist who put on Jesus' lips the psalmist's terrible cry of dereliction: 'My God, my God, why have you deserted me?'[60] Mark also draws on other psalms: Jesus was betrayed by his friends,[61] experienced sorrow and anguish,[62] and, in his extremity, was given sour wine to drink.[63]

Mark linked Jesus' death inextricably with the tragedy of Jerusalem. Shortly before his arrest, Jesus had predicted the destruction of the city and as he died 'the veil of the Temple was torn in two from top to bottom'.[64] Mark makes it clear that in a world dominated by Rome, Jesus' followers must expect to suffer. Election to divine sonship no longer meant kingship but ignominy and suffering:[65]

> Be on your guard: they will hand you over to Sanhedrins; you will be beaten in synagogues; and you will stand before governors and kings for my sake, to bear witness before them, since the Good News must first be proclaimed to all the nations … You will be hated by all men on account of my name, but the man who stands firm to the end will be saved.[66]

God's Kingdom *will* come: Mark has Jesus predict that Jerusalem's destruction is the beginning of the End, and his followers will see the Son of Man, coming on the clouds of heaven 'to gather his chosen from the four winds, from the ends of the world to the ends of heaven'.[67]

The gospels of Matthew and Luke, based on Mark and Q, are also *midrashim*. Matthew presents Jesus as the Messiah for Gentiles as well as Jews, so in his account of Jesus' birth the Persian Magi are the first to honour him. He never misses a chance to quote a scriptural precedent for events in Jesus' life. He applies the Greek translation of Isaiah's prediction of the birth of Hezekiah to Jesus' miraculous birth: 'The virgin will conceive and give birth to a son and they will call him Immanuel (God-with-us).'[68] When the Magi ask Herod where they will find the Messiah, Matthew quotes Micah's prophecy that 'a leader who will shepherd my people Israel' will come from Bethlehem.[69] Indeed, Matthew's entire gospel is designed to show that the whole scriptural corpus of Israel points to Jesus, God's ultimate revelation. In the Sermon on the Mount, Jesus becomes the new Moses, who promulgates a New Law in a commentary on the Old that indicates its inadequacy: 'You have heard what was said to our ancestors ... but I say to you ...'[70] The ancient law of retaliation – 'eye for eye and tooth for tooth' – becomes 'turn the other cheek';[71] 'love your neighbour' is transmuted to 'love your enemies'.[72] This could have been a riposte to the rabbis at Yavne, whose influence was just beginning to be felt. The Jesus movement, Matthew argues, trumps Yavne: 'For I tell you, if your virtue goes no deeper than that of the scribes and Pharisees, you will never get into the Kingdom of Heaven.'[73]

Luke's *midrash* is less relentless than Matthew's but he also shows the scriptures pointing to Jesus as the ultimate revelation to Israel. Mary's triumphant song while pregnant with Jesus looks forward to the coming Kingdom: it is a long *horoz*, predicting the imminent triumph of the 'little people', which enchains disparate biblical fragments and gives them an entirely new significance.[74] By this time – Matthew was writing in the 80s, Luke, perhaps, in the early second century – Christians claimed that after Jesus rose from the dead, he had appeared to his disciples before ascending to heaven. One of these apparitions, described by Luke, gives us a glimpse of the experience of early Christian *midrash*.

A few days after Jesus' death, Luke says, two of his disciples were walking sadly from Jerusalem to Emmaus and were joined by a stranger, who asked them why they were so distressed. When they told him the tragic story of their Messiah's disgraceful death, he chided them for failing 'to believe the full message of the prophets', which had 'ordained that the Christ should suffer and so enter into his glory'. Then, 'starting with Moses and going through all the prophets', the stranger showed that all these scriptures had predicted a suffering Messiah.[75] When they arrived at their destination, the disciples begged their new friend to lodge with them and when he blessed the bread, broke it, and handed it to them, 'their eyes were opened', and they realised that their companion was none other than the risen Christ. At once he vanished from their sight. 'Did not our hearts burn within us,' they said to one another, 'as he talked to us on the road and explicated the scriptures to us?'[76]

In *Pirke Avot*, the rabbis claimed that when two or three people studied Torah together, the Shekhinah was in their midst. Jesus' two followers had a similar experience, but for them the Presence once enshrined in the lost temple was now embodied in the person of Jesus. Exegesis was an emotional experience that made their hearts 'burn'. They would experience this Presence in the ritualised meal that reproduced his death, in the insights that came to them as disparate scriptural texts blended numinously together, and in their dealings with the stranger. This would be especially significant in Luke's mixed community of Jews and Gentiles, who in overcoming their prejudices and preconceptions were 'opening their eyes' to larger horizons.

The three synoptic gospels – Mark, Matthew and Luke – all describe an incident in which three of the disciples – Peter, James and John – saw Jesus ablaze with divine light: 'There in their presence, he was transfigured: his face shone like the sun and his clothes became white as light.'[77] Moses and Elijah appeared beside him and a heavenly voice proclaimed: 'This is my Son, the Beloved; he enjoys my favour. Listen to him.'[78] This could be a description of the disciples' Easter visions or a vision experienced by members of the Jesus movement during their midrashic sessions.[79] It is clearly reminiscent of Ezekiel's vision of 'a being that looked like a man', surrounded by light and 'something that looked like the glory [*kavod*] of Yahweh'. The early Christians seem to have glimpsed something of the divine 'glory', a luminous reflection of the divine, in the man Jesus. John's gospel (written *c.* 100 CE) reflects a different tradition, possibly from Asia Minor, but its prologue, which depicts Jesus as the pre-existent Word (Logos) of God, may originally have been a separate document in general use among the churches:[80]

In the beginning was the Word: the Word was with God and the Word was
God. He was with God in the beginning. Through him all things came to
be, not one thing had its being but through him.[81]

The Word *was* God but not identical with God since it was also *with*
God. The Word, an agent of creation, like Wisdom, had now become incarnate: 'The Word was made flesh; he pitched his tent among us, and we saw
his glory, the glory that is his as the only Son of the Father, full of grace
and truth.'[82]

Paul's letters show that right from the beginning, in their communal
worship the members of the Jesus movement experienced eternal and heavenly realities as already present.[83] People spoke in strange tongues, had visions,
prophesied, delivered divine instructions, performed miracles of healing and
preached extemporaneously under the inspiration of the Spirit.[84] In his letter
to the Philippians, written some twenty-five years after Jesus' death, Paul
quoted a very early hymn, probably used in Christian ritual, which suggests
that John's Christology, as expressed in the Prologue, was not a 'late development'. It is clear in the gospels that in their *pesher* exegesis, early Christians
identified Jesus with the mysterious Servant eulogised by Second Isaiah: 'a
man of sorrows and familiar with suffering' who would be 'lifted up; exalted,
rise to great heights'.[85] The hymn quoted by Paul states that Jesus had been
with God from the beginning but, in a supreme act of kenosis, had voluntarily
descended to earth and assumed the status of a servant:

> His state was divine,
> yet he did not cling
> to his equality with God
> but emptied himself [*heauton ekenosen*]
> to assume the condition of a slave ...
> And was humbler, yet, even to accepting death, death on a cross.[86]

But, the hymn continued, God 'raised him high' so that 'every tongue
should acclaim Jesus Christ as Lord, to the glory of God the Father'.[87] Paul
was not giving the Philippians a theological lesson, however, but was telling
them to practise kenosis themselves: 'There must be no competition among
you, no conceit, but everybody is to be self-effacing. Always consider the
other person to be better than yourself, so that nobody thinks of his own
interests first, but everybody thinks of other people's interests instead. In
your minds, you must be the same as Christ Jesus.'[88]

Paul had taken his gospel to the Gentile world, convinced that the Messiah would return to establish the Kingdom of God on earth in his own lifetime. His utopian vision of gender, racial and social equality must be seen in this light; the world as he knew it was passing away. In the meantime, he and his disciples should live as if the new order had already arrived. But he was not a rabble-rouser; he told his converts to live quietly and attend to their business. Nothing must be done that might lead the authorities to a massive repression of the Messiah's followers, since this would impede the coming of the Kingdom. It is, perhaps, in this light, that we should read his instructions to the Romans:

> You must all obey the governing authorities. Since all government comes from God, the civil authorities were appointed by God, and so anyone who resists authority is rebelling against God's decision, and such an act is bound to be punished ... The state is here to serve God for your benefit.[89]

Paul was no friend of the Roman empire that had killed Jesus, but until Christ's return, Roman rule was God's will. This, however, was only a temporary arrangement. The status quo would be abrogated when Christ dragged the mighty from their thrones.[90] It is also significant that Paul immediately insisted that political as well as ethical activity must be submitted to the rule of charity: 'Love cannot avenge a neighbour; therefore, love is the fulfilment of the law.'[91] Jesus had taught his followers to love even their enemies; political hatred, with its concomitant, righteous superiority, had no place in the Messiah's community.

But eventually it became all too clear that Jesus' followers faced a long period of coexistence with Graeco-Roman society, so new scriptures tried to adapt Paul's radical teachings to this sober reality. Paul wrote only seven of the letters attributed to him in the New Testament.[92] In the early second century, writing in Paul's name, the authors of the epistles to the Colossians and Ephesians urged Christians to conform to mainstream social norms. Where Paul's egalitarian gospel had insisted that there was neither male nor female, slave nor freeman, these new 'Pauline' directives conformed closely to the household codes promoted by Graeco-Roman philosophers: Christian wives must obey their husbands and slaves their masters.[93] Convinced that Paul was the only author who had truly understood Jesus' teaching, Marcion (d. 169), a well-educated shipbuilder from Sinope on the Black Sea, put together a 'New Testament' to replace the Hebrew Bible, which, he argued, preached a violent, vengeful God: it consisted of a single

gospel, based on Luke, and the Pauline letters. Other Christians, opposed
to Marcion, composed the so-called 'Pastoral Epistles' – also written in
Paul's name – to Titus and Timothy. They clearly disapproved of the women
who preached and officiated in Marcion's communities: 'Their role is to
learn, listening quietly and with due submission.'[94]

Marcion had made some Gentile Christians uneasy about their relationship with Judaism.[95] The synoptic gospels present Jesus engaged in a fierce
polemic against the 'scribes and Pharisees'.[96] Jewish leaders are reported
to have plotted against Jesus, and in Matthew's gospel, when Pilate is
reluctant to take responsibility for Jesus' execution, the Jewish crowd 'to
a man' shout back: 'His blood be on us and on our children!'[97] Later, these
words would regularly inspire European Christians to attack Jewish
communities on Good Friday. But in their original context, this was not
'anti-Semitic' because most 'Christians' were still Jews. The polemic,
therefore, reflects an internal Jewish debate in the immediate post-temple
period between the rabbis and the Jesus movement.[98] Jesus' sharp rhetoric
in the synoptic gospels resembles some of the intense halakhic debates in
the Mishnah.[99] 'Jesus himself was a Jew speaking to other Jews,' the
American scholar Amy-Jill Levine points out. 'His teachings comport with
the tradition of Israel's prophets. Judaism has always had a self-critical
component.'[100]

But John's gospel, as distinct from its Prologue, may reflect a conflict
within the Jesus movement. In the synoptic gospels, Jesus keeps his
messiahship a secret, but John has Jesus declare on every possible occasion that he works with the Father, agrees with him, and acts as his agent
so closely that the two are one.[101] In one scene, Jesus seems to be goading
his Jewish interlocutors into rejecting him – telling them that they are
not true children of Abraham and that their father is the Devil.[102] Some
members of John's community may have been alarmed by its new, more
extreme claims about Jesus that seemed incompatible with Jewish monotheism.[103] Both the gospel and the three epistles attributed to John suggest
that this community felt beleaguered. In the gospel, there is a dualism
that suggests a cosmic battle, pitting light against darkness, world against
spirit, and life against death. Threatened by 'the world', these Johannine
Christians felt their most important duty was to cling together and love
one another.[104] There seems to have been a painful schism in which some
members found the community's teachings 'intolerable' and were regarded
by the faithful as 'antichrists', filled with murderous hatred of the
Messiah.[105]

In the book of Revelation, 'Johannine' dualism has morphed into a cosmic battle between good and evil forces. Satan and his cohorts attack Michael and his angelic army in heaven, while the wicked assail the good on earth. The author, John of Patmos, assures his readers that God will intervene at the critical moment and vanquish the group's enemies. He had received a special revelation (*apocalupsis*) that would 'unveil' the true state of affairs, so that the faithful would know how to conduct themselves in the Last Days. Satan will give his authority to a Beast who will rise from the depths of the sea, demanding universal obeisance. But while the angels poured seven plagues upon the earth, Jesus, the Lamb, would come to the rescue. The Word of God would ride into battle like a Roman general, fight the Beast, and fling him into a pit of fire. For 1,000 years, Jesus would rule the earth with his saints, but finally God would release Satan. There would be more destruction and more battles until peace was restored and the New Jerusalem descended from heaven to earth.

Undermining the non-violent ethic of the synoptic gospels, this disturbing text draws heavily on the imagery of the Roman arena, where gladiators were forced to fight to the death before a large audience.[106] A dramatic enactment of Roman power, the gladiatorial games displayed the merciless force that upheld the Roman empire. John of Patmos was not alone in using the games as an image of eschatological violence. A fifth-century Palestinian rabbi would also envision the Judgement as a dramatic eschatological reversal of the games:

> R. Aha said ... When the Day arrives about which it is written 'the sinners are afraid in Zion' [Isaiah 33:14], you will be among the viewers and not among the viewed; you will be among the spectators rather than the gladiators.[107]

Righteous Jews would not be hapless gladiators but would become the elite, watching the agony of their former imperial masters from their privileged seats. In Revelation too, there is an unpleasant *Schadenfreude*. Those who have worshipped the Beast 'will be tortured in the presence of the holy angels and the Lamb, and the smoke of their torture will go up for ever and ever'.[108] The Lamb, a cruel and conquering hero, is a horrifying antithesis of the vulnerable 'lamb of God that takes away the sins of the world'.[109] Like Titus after his destruction of Jerusalem, he enjoys a Roman triumph, riding at the head of the celestial cavalry, his cloak soaked with the blood of the victims.[110]

John is offering his fellow Christians a vision of an alternative future at a time when Roman power seemed invincible. But Rabbi Aha was writing at a time when Palestine was ruled by Christian Roman emperors who were similarly merciless to the subject peoples. The book of Revelation overturns the kenotic vision of the New Testament and many church leaders were reluctant to include it in the canon; to this day Greek and Russian Orthodox Christians will not have it read during the liturgy. But we shall see that it has become the scripture of choice for many Protestant Christians today, especially in the United States.

There is much talk these days of the violence inherent in scripture. We are an aggressive species and, despite their message of empathy and compassion, all scriptures, without exception, have a belligerent strain that can easily be exploited. But we cannot lay the blame for so-called 'religious violence' entirely on scripture, as Rabbi Jonathan Sacks points out:

> Every scriptural canon has within it texts which, read literally, can be taken to endorse narrow particularism, suspicion of strangers, and intolerance toward those who believe differently than we do. Each also has within it sources that emphasise kinship with the stranger, empathy with the outsider, the courage that leads people to extend a hand across boundaries of hatred and hostility. The choice is ours. Will the generous texts of our tradition serve as interpretive keys to the rest, or will the abrasive passages determine our ideas of what we are and what we are called to do?[11]

Tragically, Christians have often made the wrong choice. The disastrous history of Christian antagonism to Jews should make them wary of castigating other faith traditions for the supposed intolerance of their scriptures.

*

At about the same time as the Christian canon was evolving, another – quite different – revelation on a battlefield announced the birth of a new religious passion in India. In the *Bhagavad Gita*, a late work incorporated into the *Mahabharata*, we have the first indication of *bhakti* ('devotion'), a spirituality that spread irresistibly throughout the subcontinent in a peaceable revolution that overturned the abstruse ritual science of the Brahmins, replacing it with a faith centred on loving devotion to a *deva*. Like the *Mahabharata* itself, *bhakti* may also have been a response to the violent and turbulent period that followed the collapse of the Mauryan empire. Like the epic, it offers no easy answers about the legitimacy of either warfare or *ahimsa*. We will see that in the early twentieth century, people would look to the *Gita* for guidance on these matters and draw very different conclusions.

The context of the *Gita* is the Great Battle of the *Mahabharata*. The opposing armies are forming their battle lines, when Arjuna, normally an intrepid warrior, has one of those '*Mahabharata* moments' in which a character is suddenly paralysed with sorrow and dread. Turning to his cousin Krishna, his charioteer, he declares that he cannot fight. They are trying to save the world, yet in the enemy ranks he sees his friends, gurus and kinsmen – 'fathers, grandfathers, teachers, uncles, brothers, sons, grandsons and friends'.[112] How can they heal an adharmic world if they violate the 'timeless laws of family duty'?[113] Overcome with grief, Arjuna slumps into his chariot and throws down his weapons. Krishna tries to hearten him, citing all the traditional arguments for a just war, but Arjuna is unimpressed, so Krishna introduces a novel idea. In such circumstances, he tells Arjuna, a warrior must simply dissociate himself from the effects of his actions and perform his duty kenotically, without personal animus. Like a yogin, he must take the 'I' out of his thoughts and deeds, so that he acts impersonally – indeed, *he* will not be acting at all since even in the frenzy of battle, he will remain fearless, stripped of desire and personal animus.

Arjuna listens politely, but is too disturbed to achieve such detached equanimity, so Krishna proposes an even more revolutionary option. Arjuna should enter this meditative state by focusing on Krishna himself. He is not what he seems. Yes, he has a 'lower nature' like everybody else, so that he looks like a perfectly ordinary man, but in fact he is nothing less than 'the life force that sustains the universe'.[114] He, Krishna – Arjuna's friend and kinsman – is the avatar of Vishnu, the ground of being: 'All that exists is woven on me, like a web of pearls on a thread.'[115] He is also Indra, Shiva and the sacred mountain Meru; he is the eternal syllable *AUM*, the essence of all things, sacred and profane, 'the great ritual chant, the meters of sacred song . . . the dice-game of gamblers, the lucidity of lucid men'.[116] The entire universe 'and whatever else you wish to see; all stands here in my body'.[117] The all-pervasive reality that sustains the universe had been revealed in a human being.

Arjuna bows before his cousin, his hair bristling with terror: 'I see the gods in your body, O God, and hordes of varied creatures!'[118] He sees that all things – human and divine – are present in the body of Krishna. Everything that exists rushes inexorably towards him, as rivers are drawn towards the

sea and moths fly haplessly into a flame. And, to his horror, Arjuna sees the
Pandava and Kaurava warriors too, all hurtling into Vishnu's blazing mouth.
From a limited human perspective, the Great Battle had not yet begun, but
Arjuna realises that in the timeless realm of the sacred, Krishna had already
annihilated both armies. Not only did Arjuna have a duty to fight; he had
already fulfilled that obligation.

This was the culmination of a long process in India, which had begun
when the early rishis had embodied the sacred sound of the Vedas. Krishna
now tells Arjuna that he, Vishnu, had descended into an earthly body and had
been born, lived and died time and time again to save humanity from itself.

> Whenever sacred duty [*dharma*] decays
> and chaos prevails,
> then, I create
> myself, Arjuna.
> To protect men of virtue
> and destroy men who do evil,
> to set the standard of sacred duty
> I appear in age after age.[119]

That is why, at this moment of chaos and *adharma*, he had come to earth
again to fight the battle that would usher in the Kali Yuga, the fourth and
final 'age' of our current world-cycle, a period of escalating disease, disorder
and distress.

Krishna could rescue those who loved him from the ill effects of their
karma — but only if they achieved an attitude of complete equanimity:

> Acting only for me, intent on me,
> Free from attachment,
> Hostile to no creature, Arjuna,
> A man of devotion can come to me.[120]

Hitherto, *moksha* had been only for elite priests and a few heroic ascetics
but now selfless devotion to Krishna was possible even for the 'little people':
'women, Vaishyas, Shudras, even men born in the womb of evil'.[121] Whatever
his caste or however great his karmic burden, anybody inspired by the love
of Krishna could learn to transcend greed, selfishness and partiality in the
ordinary duties of daily life. Indeed, the entire material universe was a
battlefield in which mortals struggle for peace and enlightenment with the

weapons of humility, non-violence, honesty and self-restraint.[122] Knowledge (*veda*) was no longer an esoteric pursuit but could be acquired in the practice of simple virtues – reverence for one's teacher, 'constant equanimity in fulfilment and frustration' – and by retreating occasionally to a solitary place to meditate on the mystery of Krishna.[123] The *Bhagavad Gita* did not negate the insights of the earlier scriptures; it made Vedic spirituality possible for everybody.

9

EMBODIMENT

Gods, it seems, could take human form – but could human beings become divine? The Christian doctrine of the incarnation of God in the man Jesus was inspired and impelled by a longing for this very transformation. By the third century CE, men and women from the elite classes of the Mediterranean world were attracted to Christianity, and the study of scripture became a sophisticated art form. Most of these early theologians were Platonists, who took it for granted that men and women could transcend the limitations of the physical world by their own natural powers. The Alexandrian philosopher Origen (c.185–254) believed that we had all fallen from a state of original perfection. Destined to be angelic spirits standing before God rapt in contemplation, we had chosen to neglect – or, in the case of demons, to reject – the divine by making ourselves the centre of our world. Only Jesus had remained steadfastly united to God. But, Origen insisted, it was possible to regain this angelic status by the study of scripture.[1] His exegetical method would dominate both Eastern and Western Christianity for over a millennium.

Origen's message was clear: 'I beseech you, therefore, be transformed. Resolve to know that in you there is a capacity to be transformed.'[2] It was pointless to read scripture unless you were determined to achieve an enhanced humanity. Origen was well versed in Alexandrian *allegoria*, and after moving to Palestine, where he set up his own academy, he also studied *midrash* with the rabbis of Caesarea. For Origen, every single word of scripture had in some sense been spoken by Christ, the Word of God, and summoned the reader to follow him. The interpreter's task was to make that divine voice audible. Origen did not neglect the literal sense of scripture. He produced an edition of the Hebrew Bible that placed the original text alongside five different Greek translations; and he was fascinated by the geography, flora and fauna of Palestine. But he insisted that the reading of scripture was essentially a spiritual process and that, if we were indeed

to transcend our recalcitrant selves, it required 'the utmost purity and
sobriety and ... nights of watching' and was impossible without prayer
and virtue.[3] The meaning of the Bible could not be discovered by the intellect alone; it also required intensive moral cultivation. But if the exegete
persevered, pondering the scriptures 'with all the attention and reverence
they deserve, it is certain that, in the very act of reading and diligently
studying them, his mind and feelings will be touched by a divine breath
and he will recognise that the words he is reading are not the utterances
of a man but the language of God'.[4]

In the Prologue to his *Commentary on the Song of Songs*, Origen suggested
that three of the 'wisdom' books attributed to Solomon – Proverbs,
Ecclesiastes and the Song of Songs itself – represented the three stages of
the journey to the angelic state. Scripture had a body, a psyche and a spirit,
which corresponded to the three 'senses' of the biblical text. Proverbs
represented the body of scripture and expressed the *literal* sense of the
text; it was essential to master this thoroughly before attempting anything
further. Ecclesiastes worked at the level of the psyche, the natural powers
of mind and heart; its author taught us to see the vanity of earthly things
and showed us how futile it was to place all our hopes in the material
world. By teaching us how to behave, it represented the *moral* sense of
scripture. Only a Christian who had been through this preliminary initiation
could advance to the *spiritual* or *allegorical* sense.

In his treatise on the Song of Songs, Origen explained that the opening
verse – 'Let him kiss me with the kisses of his mouth' – *literally* spoke of
a bride longing for her groom; but when interpreted *morally*, the bride
became the model for all Christians, who must teach themselves to yearn
ceaselessly for this return to their original state. *Allegorically*, the bride
symbolised the people of Israel, who had received the 'Law and the Prophets'
as a dowry, but were still waiting for the Word that fulfilled them. Applied
to the individual, these words expressed the hope that his 'pure and virginal
soul may be enlightened by the illumination and visitation of the Word
himself'.[5] As a Platonist, Origen was convinced that the practice of *theoria*
('contemplation') enabled human beings to ascend to the divine world by
their own natural powers, so Christians should meditate on this verse until
they had made themselves 'capable of receiving the principles of truth'.[6] If
Origen's commentaries seem inconclusive, it is because his teachings could
only place his pupils in the correct spiritual posture; he could not do this
intensive meditation for them. Furthermore, as in traditional Greek *philosophia*, exegesis also required a disciplined lifestyle. Origen's pupils could

grasp the true meaning of scripture only by selflessly living out its implications in daily life.[7]

Origen lived at a time when Christians were still a despised minority suffering sporadic persecution. By the fourth century, however, the church had become a significant organisation, had ejected some of its wilder elements, and like the Roman empire itself, was multiracial, international and administered by clergy who had become efficient bureaucrats.[8] In 306, Valerius Aurelius Constantinus (274–337) became one of the two rulers of the empire's western provinces. Determined to achieve sole rule, he campaigned against his co-emperor Maxentius and in 312, on the eve of their final battle, Constantine saw a flaming cross in the sky embellished with the words 'By this, conquer!' He attributed his victory to this miraculous omen and legalised Christianity later that year. In 323 he went on to defeat Licinius, emperor of the eastern provinces, became sole ruler of the empire, and moved his capital from Rome to the new city of Constantinople in Byzantium on the Bosporus. Christians regarded this development as providential. They were no longer marginal citizens in the empire and could now make a distinctive contribution to public life. Many believed that Constantine would establish the Kingdom of God on earth.

Constantine had hoped that Christianity would be a unifying force in the empire but found that in the eastern Mediterranean the church was torn apart by a bitter quarrel about the person and nature of Jesus. Hitherto there had been no single 'rule of faith', and while Jesus had long been revered as the Word of God, there was no official view of what this really meant. We cannot trace these intricate discussions in detail here. What is important for us is that it proved to be difficult – indeed, impossible – to find a solution in scripture. Arius (c.250–336), the charismatic presbyter of Alexandria who sparked the crisis in 320, was a learned exegete. Very few of his works have survived, so we must rely on the writings of his opponents, who almost certainly distorted them. Today Arius is usually regarded as a heretic but at the start of the controversy, there was no official Christian orthodoxy and nobody knew who was right.

Because they believed that the Hebrew scriptures had predicted Jesus' coming, Christians followed Origen in regarding many of the psalms and prophecies as – in some effable sense – spoken by Christ, who was described in the prologue to John's gospel as the Word of God.[9] The Arian conflict began with a disagreement over a verse in the book of Proverbs where 'Wisdom' declares that 'Yahweh created me when his purpose first unfolded, before the oldest of his works.'[10] It seemed clear to Arius that Christ, the

Word and 'Wisdom' of God, was explaining here that he had been created by God. Arius, therefore, told his bishop, Alexander, that the Son of God had many divine qualities: like the Father, he was unchangeable (*atraptos*) and inalienable (*analloiotos*), but he was clearly not unbegotten (*agennetos*).[11] He wrote to Eusebius (*c*.260–340), bishop of Caesarea, that logically the Father must have existed before his Son so Jesus must have been created out of nothing; otherwise he would be a second God.[12] A verse from Psalm 45, now thought by Christians to have been addressed to Christos, 'the anointed one', supported this position:

> This is why God, your God, has anointed you
> With the oil of gladness, above all your rivals.[13]

God had, as it were, 'promoted' the Word, the firstborn of all creatures, to exceptionally high status. Arius ended his letter by quoting the hymn cited by Paul in his letter to the Philippians: God's elevation of Jesus meant that 'every tongue should acclaim him as Lord to the glory of God the Father'.[14]

As far as scripture went, this was perfectly acceptable. Jesus had always called God his Father, implying that he was indeed *gennetos* ('begotten'); he had said clearly that the Father was greater than he. Unexceptionable too was Arius' concern to safeguard the transcendence of God, who was 'unique' – 'the only unbegotten, the only eternal, the only one without beginning, the only true, the only one who has immortality; the only wise, the only good'.[15] Origen would have had no problem with this and Eusebius, like most bishops, held similar views. Some of Arius' more extreme supporters may have claimed that Jesus was a mere human being, whose exemplary virtue had been rewarded by promotion to near-divine status; this too had scriptural backing, especially in Paul's letters. But it was too radical for Arius, who was simply trying to develop a consistent, rational and scripture-based theology.[16] He set his ideas to music and soon sailors, barbers and travellers were singing popular songs proclaiming that the Father was God by nature and had given life to the Son, the divine Word and Wisdom, who was neither co-eternal nor uncreated. But Arius had been schooled in Origen's *philosophia*, which was rapidly being replaced by a 'new philosophy' developing in the Syrian and Egyptian deserts.

In 270, Antony (*c*.250–356), a young Egyptian peasant, had been troubled by Jesus' words to the rich young man: 'If you wish to be perfect, go and sell what you own, and give money to the poor, and you will have treasure in heaven.'[17] He immediately relinquished his property and embarked on a quest for freedom and holiness in the Egyptian desert, replicating the lifestyle of the very first Christians as described in the Acts of the Apostles: 'The whole group of believers was united, heart and soul; no one claimed for his own use anything that he had, as everything they owned was held in common.'[18] Monasticism was a direct challenge to the worldliness and splendour of Constantine's imperial Christianity.[19] Arius was opposed by Athanasius (c.296–373), the assistant of Bishop Alexander, who was deeply inspired by the monastic ideal and would write Antony's biography.

At the Council of Nicaea summoned by Constantine in 325, Athanasius carried the day when it was declared that Jesus, the Logos, was not 'created' from nothingness, like everything else, but had been begotten 'in an ineffable, indescribable manner' from the *ousia* or 'essence' of God. Thus he was 'from God' but different from all other creatures. This had no scriptural backing. Indeed, the word that described the status of Christ in the Nicene Creed did not appear in the Bible: Jesus, the creed asserted, was *homoousios*, 'of the same nature' as the Father. Many of the bishops were uneasy about this decision but succumbed to imperial pressure. Only Arius and two of his colleagues refused to toe the line; the rest returned to their dioceses but continued to teach as they had always done – for the most part, midway between Arius and Athanasius. It took another fifty years of acrimony, negotiation, compromise and even violence before the Nicene Creed, with alterations, was finally accepted as the official doctrine of the church. To this day many Eastern Christians find it unacceptable.[20]

The Nicene doctrine was rooted not in scripture but in ritual. Athanasius was determined to safeguard the liturgical practice of the church, which regularly directed its prayers to Jesus and revered him, albeit imprecisely, as divine. If, he argued, the Arians truly believed that the Christ was a mere creature, were they not guilty of idolatry when they worshipped him?[21] Whatever scripture said, the man Jesus was an image (*eikon*) of the divine and had given Christians a glimpse of what the utterly transcendent and otherwise unknowable God was like. More importantly, Christians were convinced that in their liturgy they had experienced a hitherto unexplored dimension of their humanity which – in some sense – enabled them to participate in the divine life. In the fourth century, they called this experience *theosis* ('deification'): like the incarnate Logos, they too had become sons of God, as Paul had clearly stated.

But did this mean that the wholly spiritual God had taken human flesh? By the fourth century, many Christians were turning away from Origen's Platonism and no longer believed that humans could aspire to the divine by their own efforts. Instead of seeing a Chain of Being emanating eternally from the divine to the material world, many now felt that the cosmos was separated from God by a vast, unbridgeable chasm.[22] The universe was experienced as so fragile, moribund and contingent that it could have nothing in common with the God that was Being itself. And yet, their new Eucharistic ritual had given Christians intimations of *theosis* and they could not – surely? – have experienced this had not the God that had called all things into being from an abysmal nothingness somehow bridged that immense gulf when 'the Word was made flesh and lived among us'. Athanasius argued that Christians could neither have experienced 'deification' nor even imagined the unknowable God, had not God entered the realm of his fragile creatures. 'The Word became human that we might become divine,' he insisted. 'He revealed himself through a body that we might receive an idea of the invisible Father.'[23]

We have seen that both mystical intuition and the study of scripture have always been rooted in physical practices: human beings have repeatedly felt that they embodied the divine. Their contemplative practices relied on the input of the right hemisphere of the brain, which, unlike the left, is at home with the body and the physical. Platonism, with its sharp division of matter and spirit, had severed that link, and the exegesis of Origen, the Platonist, had represented an ascent from the body of the text to its spirit. Yet their new status under Constantine had given Christians a stake in the mundane world. They could now build imposing basilicas and develop a dramatic liturgy in which the splendour of the imperial court blended with biblical descriptions of Solomon's temple. The simple Eucharistic meal of the early Christians had become a feast for the senses, with spectacular processions, massed choirs and clouds of perfumed incense.[24] Christian spirituality had been reunited with the body. During the fourth century, there was an explosion of such tangible devotions as the veneration of relics. Pilgrims flocked from all over the Christian world to pray in the new churches in Jerusalem and Palestine and to walk physically in Jesus' footsteps.

Most importantly, the monks of the desert claimed to have returned to their original angelic state not by Origen's Platonic ascent but by an intensely corporal asceticism that transformed their very flesh. In his biography,

Athanasius described Antony's extraordinary appearance when, after twenty years of solitude, he finally emerged from his cell:

> And they, when they saw him, wondered at the sight, for he had the same habit of body as before and was neither fat, like a man without exercise, nor lean from fasting and striving with demons, but he was just the same as they had known him before his retirement. And again, his soul was free from blemish, for it was neither contracted, as if by grief, nor relaxed by pleasure ... But he was altogether even, as being guided by reason [*logos*] and abiding in a natural state.[25]

The British historian Peter Brown has argued that theologians of the fourth and fifth centuries would not have pursued the huge intellectual problems raised by the incarnation of the Word 'with such ferocious intellectual energy had the joining of human and divine in a single person ... not been sensed by them as a haunting emblem of the enigmatic joining of body and soul within themselves'.[26]

Ephraim (*c*.306–73), the most important Syrian theologian of the period, insisted that the Christian received the knowledge of God not through scripture alone but through the liturgy in which the divine was apprehended through the senses rather than the intellect. In the Eucharist, Christ's body

> was newly mingled with our bodies
> and His pure blood was poured into our veins,
> and His voice into our ears, and His brightness into our eyes.
> All of this has now been mixed with all of us by his compassion.[27]

In the incarnation, God had poured himself into a body and in the bread and wine of the Eucharist he enters the body of the Christian, so that nothing separated the believer's body from his:

> Ears even heard Him, eyes saw Him,
> hands even touched Him, the mouth ate him.
> Limbs and senses gave thanks to
> The One Who came and revived all that is corporeal.[28]

The sanctification of the corporeal in the new Christian ritual made Christ's incarnation central to the Christian experience. It is true that in the western provinces of the Roman empire, Christians had inherited the ancient

Mediterranean conviction that the body was a source of moral danger. This is clear in the writings of such Latin theologians as Tertullian, Augustine and Jerome. Their denunciation of the physical has attracted much scholarly attention but the liturgical developments in Eastern Christendom that endowed bodily experience with positive spiritual value have often been overlooked.[29]

Arius may have been attempting to rein in this new enthusiasm, hoping that scriptural clarification would persuade the more mature Platonic Christians to hold aloof from this populist piety and insist on a more rigorous interpretation of the biblical texts. But Athanasius and his colleagues agreed that the new theological formulae – such as *homoousios* – represented a deeper understanding of the Christian tradition. The theology of the church was rooted in ritual as well as in scripture and must, therefore, reflect the Christian experience of *theosis*. But the doctrine of Christ's incarnation presented huge intellectual difficulties, which were thrashed out in the intense debates of the fourth and fifth centuries.

Christians in the western provinces lacked the linguistic and philosophical experience to participate in these discussions. At the Council of Chalcedon (451), Pope Leo – who for Eastern Christians was simply the bishop of Rome – tried to resolve the problem in a common-sense definition: Christ had two natures, one human, the other divine, which were united in one person and one substance. This satisfied Latin-speaking Christians, but in the east the council's endorsement of Leo's *Tome* was little more than an agreement to disagree. It failed to do justice to the experience of Eastern Christians for whom the point of the debates was the divine potential of humanity rather than abstruse technicalities about the nature of God.

As the Orthodox theologian Vladimir Lossky explains, in Eastern Christianity dogma is inseparable from spirituality: the official teaching of the church would have no hold on the people if it did not in some way reflect their interior experience:

> We must live the dogma expressing a revealed truth, which appears to us an unfathomable mystery, in such a fashion that instead of assimilating the mystery to our mode of understanding, we should, on the contrary, look for a profound change, an inner transformation of spirit, enabling us to experience it mystically.[30]

Greek Christians argued about the doctrine of Christ's incarnation so fiercely because they had experienced their own *theosis* – an enhancement of their humanity that was as crucial to their theology as the achievement of nirvana had always been to Buddhists.

The Greek position was definitively expressed by Maximus the Confessor (580–662), who claimed that Jesus was the first human being to be wholly 'deified' – entirely possessed and permeated by the divine – and that we could all be like him, even in this life. For Maximus, human deification is based on the fusion of the divine and human nature in Jesus – in rather the same way as body and soul are united in the human being:

> The whole human being [*anthropos*] should become God, deified by the grace of God-become-man, becoming a whole human being, soul and body, by nature, and becoming wholly divine, soul and body, by grace.[31]

For Maximus, the man Jesus gave us our only glimpse of what the indescribable God was like but he had also revealed what human beings could become. Yet this would have made no sense without the profound experience of the liturgy and the physical disciplines of the committed ascetic. It could not be simply deduced from the sacred texts. Maximus made it clear that scripture could not issue clear teachings and lucid information about the transcendence that we call 'God'. It was only because we did not know what God was that we could say that human beings could, in some way, share the divine nature. Even when we contemplated Jesus the man, 'God' remained opaque and elusive. Any clear conception of divinity could, therefore, only be idolatrous. The purpose of scripture was to make us appreciate the ineffability of God. It was no good looking for proof texts, as Arius had done; these matters could not be settled by doctrinal or scriptural formulations, because human language was not adequate to express the divine.[32]

Here Maximus was in full agreement with Gregory (c.335–94), bishop of Nyssa in Cappadocia, who had insisted that scripture, the Word of God, paradoxically asserted the unknowability of the divine:

> Following the instructions of Holy Scripture, we have been taught that [the nature of God] is beyond names and human speech. We say that every [divine] name, be it invested by human custom or handed onto us by the tradition of the scriptures, represents our conceptions of the divine nature, but does not convey the meaning of that nature in itself.[33]

Gregory's older brother Basil (c.329–79), bishop of Caesarea in Cappadocia, distinguished *dogma*, which he defined as everything about God that could *not* be said, from *kerygma*, the public teaching of the church based on the scriptures. *Dogma* represented the deeper meaning of biblical truth, which could be apprehended only through the experience of contemplation and the liturgy. In the West, however, the word 'dogma' would come to mean 'a body of opinion, formulated and emphatically stated', and a 'dogmatic' person 'one who confidently asserts his or her opinions in an authoritative and arrogant manner'.[34]

Basil and Gregory both emphasised the importance of the 'tradition' that accompanies scripture. Tradition – the truths that are handed down orally from one generation to another – reflected the Christian community's ever-developing understanding of the scriptural message. Basil believed that alongside the clear message of the gospels, there had always existed a private and esoteric teaching 'which our holy fathers have preserved in a silence that prevents anxiety and curiosity ... so as to safeguard by this silence the sacred character of the mystery'.[35] In the Greek-speaking world, a 'mystery' was not a hazy irrational conundrum: the word *musterion* was closely related to *myesis* ('initiation'), an experience achieved by ritual.[36] For centuries, Greeks had found that the rituals of Eleusis, a carefully constructed psychodrama, gave *mustai* ('initiates') a direct and overwhelming experience of the sacred that, in many cases, transformed their perception of life and death. In Greek Christianity, a 'mystery' was a truth that brought people up against the limits of language but which could be intuited by the ritualised drama of the liturgy.

The 'mystery' of the Trinity was a prime example. The gospels speak of Father, Son and Spirit, but they certainly do not endorse the elaborate Trinitarian doctrine formulated by Basil, Gregory and their friend Gregory (c.329–90), bishop of Nazianzus. These three Cappadocians distinguished between the *ousia* of a thing, its inner nature, and its *hypostases*, its external qualities. In God, there was, as it were, a single, divine self-consciousness that remained unknowable, unspeakable and unnameable. But Christians had experienced this ineffability in *hypostases* – outward manifestations of the inscrutable Godhead – that had translated it into something more accessible to human beings. God had one *ousia*, but three *hypostases* – Father, Son and Spirit. We could never know God's *ousia*; indeed, we should not even speak of it. But we could recognise God's activities (*energeiai*) in the world. 'Father' represents the source of being – like the Brahman – in which all creatures participate; we glimpse something of the unknowable divine essence in the 'son' Jesus, and in the immanent divine presence within each one of us that scripture calls the Holy Spirit. The biblical terms 'Father',

'Son' and 'Spirit', Gregory of Nyssa explained, are simply 'terms that we use', to describe the way the utterly unknowable Godhead has made itself known to us.[37]

But nobody was asked simply to 'believe' this. Like any *musterion* it became a reality only in a ritual that inducted Christians into a different way of thinking about the divine. After their baptism, the new *mustai* were introduced to a mental rite to be performed during the Eucharistic liturgy, which kept their minds in continuous motion, swinging back and forth between the unknowable One and the symbolically glimpsed Three until they had an intuitive grasp of the *musterion*. As Gregory of Nazianzus explained, this was not a purely cerebral exercise but elicited intense emotion:

> No sooner do I conceive of the One than I am illumined by the Splendour of the Three; no sooner do I distinguish the Three than I am carried back into the One. When I think of any of the Three I think of it as the whole, and my eyes are filled with tears, and the greater part of what I am thinking escapes me. I cannot grasp the greatness of that One so as to attribute a greater greatness to the rest. When I see the Three together, I see but one Torch, and cannot divine or measure the undivided light.[38]

Without this meditation, the Trinity made no sense. That is probably why for many Western Christians, who have not experienced this rite, the Trinity remains baffling and unscriptural.

The conflict between Arius and Athanasius had shown that scripture alone could not resolve such theological disputes. As the British theologian Rowan Williams explains, the scriptures 'need to be made more difficult, before we can actually grasp their simplicities and this admission that scripture and tradition do not necessarily make sense – is one of the most fundamental tasks of theology'.[39] But perhaps the rank and file wanted their scriptures to 'make sense'. Did not the new enthusiasm for pilgrimage to the Holy Land indicate an interest in the simple facts of Christian history? One of the first of these pilgrims to arrive in Jerusalem in about 333 came from Bordeaux. During his visit to the ruined Temple Mount, he stated, in a laconic, matter-of-fact manner, that he was shown the stone which the psalmist had described as 'rejected by the builders',[40] as well as the site of the murder of the prophet Zechariah (complete with blood-stains on the pavement) and the palm tree whose branches were strewn before Jesus during his triumphal procession into Jerusalem.[41] A modern pilgrim, whose thinking is dominated by logos, would find these claims outrageous but these early visitors seem entirely unperturbed, because they were thinking mythically. The distant past became present for these pilgrims, who did not assess the holy places critically but with *affectio*, a word that recurs in their memoirs. At these sites their memories of scripture were experienced *diligentius* ('more feelingly') so that it felt like a homecoming.[42]

Even Jerome (c. 342–420), an exegete who focused on the literal sense of the Bible, did not approach these sites like a modern historian. Here the past became present: 'Whenever we enter the Holy Sepulchre, we see the Lord lying in his winding sheet and, dwelling a little longer, again we see the angel at his feet, the cloth wrapped at the head.'[43] The biblical events formed a timeless backcloth to the present and could be brought to the foreground of consciousness in an act of willed devotion. Egeria, a devout Spanish pilgrim, arrived in Constantinople in 381, just as the bishops were assembling for the council that would make Athanasius' doctrine the official teaching of the church. On her long trip around the Near East, she and her companions always read the appropriate biblical passage 'on the very spot' (*in ipso loco*). This reading was a sacramental re-enactment that made the past a present reality. Egeria describes huge crowds of pilgrims marching in procession in the streets of Jerusalem, singing hymns and psalms in a ritualised 'walkabout' through the Bible that was a liturgical *horoz* linking disparate events instead of biblical verses in an entirely unhistorical manner: the place where Elijah was taken up to heaven was next to the site of Jesus' baptism; the altar on which Abraham bound Isaac was beside the site of the crucifixion.[44]

*

Jerome was one of the refugees who left Europe during the barbarian invasions of the fourth century, founding a monastery in Bethlehem, where he translated the Hebrew Bible into Latin.[45] His Vulgate ('Vernacular') would remain the standard biblical text in western Europe until the sixteenth century. Jerome had begun by translating the Septuagint, the Greek translation of the 'Old Testament' used by Eastern Christians, but when he discovered that the local rabbis considered it inaccurate, he started working from what he called *Hebraica veritas* ('the truth in Hebrew'). Initially attracted to allegorical exegesis, his close textual work brought him back to the literal or plain sense of scripture.

His friend Augustine (354–430), bishop of Hippo in North Africa, was a Platonist naturally inclined to *allegoria*, but he explored the historical context of the biblical texts more thoroughly than Jerome. This made it clear to him that morality was historically conditioned, an insight that led him to the 'principle of charity' which, he insisted, was crucial to biblical exegesis. Christians should not haughtily condemn the polygamy of the Jewish patriarchs, for example, because it was a common practice among primitive peoples. It was also inappropriate to allegorise the story of King David's adultery, because we all – even the best of us – commit sin.[46] Righteous condemnation was a sign of self-satisfaction and a major impediment to our understanding of scripture. Instead, Augustus insisted, 'we must meditate on what we read until an interpretation can be found that tends to establish the reign of charity'.[47] Like Buddhists, Jains and Confucians, Augustine insisted that scripture was pointless if it did not lead to compassionate thinking and behaviour.

Western Christians practised a version of Jewish *pesher*, reading the 'Old Testament' as a prediction of the 'New'.[48] Irenaeus (*c.*130–200), bishop of Lyons, had called this the 'rule of faith':

> If anyone reads the Scriptures ... with attention, he will find in them an account of Christ and a foreshadowing of a new calling. For Christ is the treasure that was hidden in the field; that is, in this world ('for the field is the world'[49]). And Christ was the treasure hidden in the scriptures that is pointed out to us by analogies and parables.[50]

Augustine agreed, to a point: 'Our whole purpose when we read the Psalms, the Prophets and the Law is to see Jesus there.'[51] But for Augustine, the 'rule of faith' was not a dogma. Rather, our interpretation of scripture must be guided by the 'principle of charity', even if it contradicts the plain sense:

> Whoever thinks that he understands the divine scriptures or any part of them so that it does not build the double love of God and of our neighbour does not understand it at all. Whoever finds a lesson there useful to the building of charity, even though he has not said what the author may be shown to have intended in that place, has not been deceived.[52]

The principle of charity taught us to put ourselves constantly in the place of others and thus build up a habit of *com passio*, the ability to 'feel with' the other: 'Scripture teaches nothing but charity, nor condemns anything except cupidity, and in this way, shapes the minds of men.'[53]

Augustine had been trained in classical rhetoric and at first had found the Bible's lack of stylistic refinement embarrassing. But he came to realise that scripture was accessible only to those who shared the humility of Christ, the Word of God, who had stooped to our level.[54] In scripture, the timeless Word had been revealed in words written by fallible, mortal men. Scripture, therefore, could never yield absolute truth and its meaning will only become clear at the end of time.[55] After Adam's fall, God could teach us about spiritual matters only through objects and historical events.[56] So the language of scripture is conditioned by the inadequacy of human nature. Both are limited, so quarrelling about the interpretation of the Bible was foolish and destructive since the purpose of scripture was to create a bond between Christians.[57] Augustine had no time for people who believed that they alone understood the meaning of scripture.[58] Their pride and egotism had isolated them from the community; rather, the diversity of possible interpretations should unite Christians whose views may otherwise differ together in love.[59]

No theologian, apart from Paul, has been more influential in the Western world than Augustine. Even though he focused on the literal and historical sense of scripture, Augustine was no diehard literalist: his 'principle of accommodation' would dominate biblical interpretation in the West well into the early modern period. He explained that God had adapted his revelation to the cultural norms of the people who first received it.[60] One of the psalms, for example, reflects the ancient view, long outmoded by Augustine's time, that there was a body of water above the earth that caused rainfall.[61] It would, Augustine insisted, be ridiculous to interpret this verse literally. God had simply accommodated his revelation to the science of the day so that the people of Israel could understand it. If the literal meaning of scripture clashed with reliable scientific information, Augustine ruled, the interpreter must respect the integrity of science or he would bring scripture into disrepute.[62] A great deal of trouble could have been avoided if later Christians had taken this advice seriously.

In the last years of Augustine's life, the Vandals besieged his home town of Hippo. As he watched the western provinces of the Roman empire falling helplessly before the invading tribes, plunging western Europe into a Dark Age that would last some 700 years, his vision darkened. This is the context of his fateful doctrine of original sin. Adam's fall had condemned all his descendants to eternal damnation and, despite our redemption by Christ, had permanently damaged our human nature. For a Western Christian like Augustine, there was no prospect of deification and no delight in either the body or the senses. Adam's sin, he taught, was transmitted through the sexual act, when men and women take irrational pleasure in each other instead of God – just as Rome, the source of order and civilisation, had been brought low by lawless barbarians. Each of us, therefore, was conceived and born 'in sin':

> God created man aright, for God is the author of all natures, though he is certainly not responsible for their defects. But man was willingly perverted and justly condemned, and so begot perverted and condemned offspring. For we all *were* that one man who fell into sin, through the woman who was made from him before the first sin.[63]

Our 'seminal nature', therefore, had been utterly corrupted; we were now 'bound with death's fetters' and could not be born in any other state.[64] Only those saved by Christ could be liberated from the second death of eternal perdition.

The Greek-speaking theologians in Byzantium found Augustine's exegesis tragically mistaken. Every human being was free to turn towards the good, Maximus insisted.[65] He also pointed out that Jerome's translation of the proof text in Romans, cited by Augustine to back up his claim, was inaccurate. Paul explained that Adam's sin had indeed brought death into the world, but he went on to say that the reason that we all died was that *everyone* – not just Adam – was guilty of sin during their lives. Jerome, Maximus pointed out, had translated '*eph ho pantes hermarton*' ('everyone has sinned'[66]) as '*in quo omnes peccaverunt*' ('in whom [i.e. Adam] all have sinned'). The Greeks, therefore, would interpret the practice of infant baptism quite differently from the Latins. In the West, it was performed to expunge the sin of Adam, but for Theodoret of Cyrus, Augustine's contemporary, a newborn was without sin and baptism simply a promise of her future deification.[67]

Some of the rabbis believed that building the Tower of Babel had been humanity's first sin. Some argued that the 'original sin' had occurred when 'the sons of God, looking at the daughters of men, saw they were pleasing ... and had children by them'. It was immediately after this that God decided to destroy humanity in the Flood.[68] But other rabbis not only accepted human weakness as a fact of life but believed that it had positive potential. They claimed that on the last day of creation, God had said that his work was '*very* good'[69] precisely because God had created the 'evil inclination' (*yetzer ha ra*) that day. 'But *is* the evil inclination "very good"?' the rabbis asked. Yes, they decided, because, paradoxically, it contributed to human creativity, progress and endeavour. 'For if it were not for the evil inclination, a man would not build a house or take a wife or beget a child, or engage in business, as it says: "All labour or skilful work comes of a man's rivalry with his neighbour."'[70]

Western Christianity is unique in its catastrophic view of Adam's sin. Both Augustine and Origen were Platonists, who regarded the body as inferior to the soul – a dualism that is entirely alien to the Bible. They both concluded that an original failing had separated humanity from the divine and saw the body as a symptom of that primal lapse. Origen was convinced that transformation was within our natural powers, but Augustine had come to regard human nature as so hopelessly corrupted that, even after Christ's redemptive death, it remained chronically impaired. Tragically, Augustine bequeathed to Western Christianity an indelible guilt that the Buddha would have called 'unskilful' (*akusala*), because guilt embedded us in the ego that we should try to transcend.

*

During the fifth and sixth centuries, the rabbis in Babylonia and Palestine completed the two Talmuds. Jews were continuing to move steadily away from the Hebrew Bible: the Mishnah had rarely quoted it, while the Tosefta ('Supplement') was a commentary on the Mishnah, not the Bible. The Talmuds were less dismissive of the Tanakh, but their focus too was the Mishnah, making it clear that the rabbis' oral traditions could not be subordinated to the Written Torah. The Palestinian rabbis completed the Yerushalmi, the Jerusalem Talmud, in about 400 CE. It is less comprehensive than the Bavli, the Babylonian Talmud, and this probably reflects the insecurity of the Jewish communities of the Roman empire after Constantine's conversion. Palestinian Jews had to watch Jerusalem being transformed into a Christian holy city while Constantine launched an aggressive missionary offensive in Jewish Galilee. His successors introduced legislation prohibiting marriage between Jews and Christians and making it illegal for Jews to own slaves, which damaged their economy. Finally, in 353, Constantius II outlawed conversion to Judaism, describing Jews as 'savage', 'abominable' and 'blasphemous'.[71]

The Yerushalmi is a commentary (*gemara*) on the Mishnah. By this time, the idea that God had revealed an Oral as well as the Written Torah to Moses on Sinai had taken root in Palestine, reflecting the Jewish conviction that the Torah must be revivified by living voices in each generation. A ruling from Rabbi Yohanan's circle made it clear that the rabbis' 'repeated traditions' were superior to the Written Torah: 'Matters derived from what is taught by mouth are more precious than those derived from scripture.'[72] The ongoing revelation of the Oral Torah cemented Jews' relationship with God and, unlike the Bible, which had been appropriated by Gentile Christians, it was accessible only to the rabbinic elite.[73] Rabbi Jehoshua ben Levi went further. Commenting on Moses' words in Deuteronomy that 'Yahweh gave me the two stone tablets inscribed with the finger of God and on them was written all the words which the Lord spoke to you on Sinai',[74] he argued that this not only applied to every single rabbinic ruling – past, present and future – but that even a young rabbinic student discussing Torah with his teacher was repeating the divine words spoken to Moses: 'Even what a trained disciple will in future expound before his master – all were already spoken to Moses on Mount Sinai.'[75]

Revelation was not confined to the distant past, therefore: it was an ongoing – and essentially physical – process that occurred every time a Jew applied his mind to the Torah. It was said that after a rabbi had died and his pupils recited his traditions to their own students, the deceased's 'lips move[d] simultaneously in the grave' and he felt sensuous pleasure, 'like someone drinking honeyed wine'.[76] When a rabbi passed on his master's teachings to his pupils, the Yerushalmi urged him to picture his master standing beside him in a practice not dissimilar to *Buddhanasmrti*.[77] By imagining his teacher, who had embodied the Torah in word and deed, at his side while he recited his traditions, a rabbi would give him posthumous life. Rabbinic learning was never simply a study of ancient texts; it was rather a living dialogue with the sages of the past.[78]

The Bavli was completed in about 600 CE. The Jews of Babylonia maintained close ties with the Palestinians, so the two Talmuds resemble one another, but the Parthians, an Iranian dynasty, allowed the Jewish community a measure of self-government and this made the Bavli more confident and self-assured. It would become the key text of rabbinic Judaism. Like the Yerushalmi, the Bavli used the Hebrew Bible to support the Oral Torah, using only those portions of the Tanakh that it found useful and ignoring the rest. None of the authorities of the past were sacrosanct. The Bavli's editors felt free to reverse the legislation of the Mishnah, play one rabbi off against another, and point out gaps in their arguments. They even changed the Written Torah in favour of their own rulings, saying what the Tanakh should have said.

The rabbis regarded themselves as the prophets of their time: 'Since the day the Temple was destroyed, prophecy has been taken from the prophets and given to the sages.'[79] In the Bavli, Abraham, Moses, the prophets, the Pharisees and the rabbis are not presented as belonging to a particular historical period, but are brought together on the same page, so that they seem to be debating – and often vehemently disagreeing – with one another across the centuries. There could be no definitive answers. In one seminal story, we find Rabbi Eliezer engaged in an intractable argument with his colleagues about a fine point of Jewish ritual. When they refused to accept his opinion, he asked God to back him up by performing some spectacular miracles. Before long, a carob tree moved 400 cubits of its own accord, water in a conduit flowed uphill, and the walls of the House of Studies shook so dramatically that they seemed about to collapse. But the other rabbis were not impressed. Finally, in desperation, Rabbi Eliezer asked for a voice from heaven (bat qol) to endorse his view, and a divine voice obligingly declared: 'What is your quarrel with R. Eliezer? The legal decision [halakha] is always according to his view.' But Rabbi Joshua demurred with a quotation from Deuteronomy, referring to the Torah: 'It is not in heaven.' The Torah no longer belonged to God: once promulgated on Sinai, it was the inalienable possession of every single Jew, 'so we pay no attention to a bat qol'.[80] No one could have the last word on the divine and no theology was definitive.

The Bavli has been described as the first interactive text.[81] When eventually it was committed to writing and, later, became a printed book, it was set so that the portion of the Mishnah under discussion was placed centre-page and was surrounded by the comments of sages from the distant and more recent past. Each page also left a space for the student to add his own commentary. When studying the Bible through the Bavli, he learned that truth was constantly changing and that while tradition was numinous, it should not constrict his powers of judgement. If a student failed to add his own gemara, the line of tradition would be broken. Even when embroiled in a heated debate with his colleagues, a student was aware that he was participating in a conversation that stretched back to Moses and would continue as God's revelation developed over time.

*

Meanwhile, merchants and peripatetic monks had brought Mahayana Buddhism to China. Indian and Chinese culture had long mingled in Central Asia, where the Iranian Kushana empire, centred in Bactria, stretched from the Ganges Valley to the Silk Route. But in China itself, Buddhism was dismissed as a religion of barbarians. The Confucians, especially, found the monks' renunciation of family ties repugnant and their idea of rebirth called the ancestor cult into question. Nevertheless, during the Period of Disunity (221–581) that followed the collapse of the Han dynasty, Buddhism began to attract people who were interested in advanced meditative techniques. Daoism, of course, had not disappeared once the Confucian canon had been established. Its mystical ideas still appealed to members of the aristocracy, who found a distinct similarity between Buddhism and the Daoism of Zhuangzi. The Mahayana concept of 'emptiness' seemed wholly compatible with the Daoist ideal that the mind should be 'empty, unified and still'. It was also said that Laozi had visited India at the end of his life, where he had instructed the Buddha – or even become the Buddha himself.[82]

In Chinese Buddhism, therefore, we find a creative synthesis between Indian and Chinese mystical traditions. During the Period of Disunity many found that Buddhist meditative techniques provided relief from the political uncertainty and, during the third and fourth centuries, an increasing number of such Buddhist texts as the *Perfection of Wisdom* were translated into Chinese. Inevitably, perhaps, Buddhist ideas were explained in terms of Daoist philo-sophical categories in a process known as *goyi*, or 'interpretation by analogy'. The monastic ideal became more appealing to some, and from the fourth century, Chinese Buddhists formed what was essentially a monastic society, separate from the mainstream.

But during the fifth century, a massive translation effort brought the Buddhist scriptures to a wider audience. It seems that over half of Buddhist monks became translators, exegetes, specialists in *vinaya* ('monastic rule'), sutra-reciters, sutra-masters and chanters. They tended to focus on a single text, which became the benchmark by which they evaluated other scriptures: the basic theme of that key text would be identified, and other texts, with similar themes, could be organised around it.[83] Some of the translators came from abroad, including the great Central Asian Buddhist Kumarajiva, who lived and taught in modern Sian from 401 until his death in 413 and whose Chinese disciples became extremely influential. Kumarajiva had introduced them to more traditional Buddhist teachings, but, true to the Mahayana emphasis on 'skilful means' (*upaya-kaushalhya*), he continued to use such Daoist terminology as *yu* ('being', 'existence'), *wu* ('non-being'), *yu-wei* ('purposeful action') and *wu-wei* ('restricted action'). This method differed from the old *goyi* analogy, where the similarities had been only verbal, because Kumarajiva's pupils understood the deeper connection of these ideas. The result was not a distortion or misrepresentation of Buddhism but rather a synthesis of Indian Buddhism with Chinese Daoism that led eventually to a uniquely Chinese form of Buddhism.[84]

Two of Kumarajiva's disciples developed ideas that would become central to Chinese Buddhism. One was Sengzhao (384–414), who had studied the writings of Laozi and Zhuangzi for years before becoming Kumarajiva's pupil. He wrote two essays, 'There Is No Real Uncertainty' and 'On the Immutability of Things', in which crucial Buddhist doctrines blended with Daoist teachings. All things are in constant flux, he taught, changing from moment to moment; the knowledge of a sage is not like secular knowledge, in which the object of thought is external to the knower; and to have knowledge of *wu* is to be at one with it and it was this knowledge that constituted the state of nirvana – but because such knowledge transcends language, nothing could be said about it.

Sengzhao died at the age of thirty, but his fellow student Daosheng (d.434) became a monk of great brilliance; it was said that when he taught, even the stones nodded in agreement. His teachings were so revolutionary that he was banished from his monastery, though he was later reinstated when new scriptural translations of Indian Buddhist texts affirmed his ideas. His teachings, like those of Sengzhao, laid the foundations of the Chan Buddhism (known as Zen in Japan) that would develop during the ninth century. One of his key doctrines was that the achievement of enlighten-ment did not occur gradually, over time, but happened instantaneously – like leaping over a chasm. This was because nirvana is not an objective 'thing' that could be divided into parts. You could not gain a little bit of nirvana today and more tomorrow: it either came all at once or not at all. Daosheng also insisted that every sentient being possesses a Buddha nature, but that most people do not realise this. The Buddha-world is right here, he taught, in our present existence. Even the *icchantika*, the opponent of Buddhism, could attain Buddhahood, because he or she has a Buddha nature. An essay attributed to Sengzhao explained this theory:

> Suppose there is a man who, in a treasure house of golden utensils, sees the golden utensils, but pays no attention to their shapes and features. Or even if he does pay attention to their shapes and features, he still realises they are all gold. He is not confused by their varying appearances, and therefore is able to rid himself of their [superficial] distinctions. He always sees that their underlying substance is gold, and does not suffer any illusion. This is an illustration of what a sage is.[85]

The Buddha-nature, therefore, is not only *in* the phenomenal world – there is no other reality.

There is a Chinese Buddhist tradition that the Buddha developed an esoteric teaching that was never written down but was transmitted secretly to a disciple, who imparted it to one of his own pupils, until finally it reached Bodhidharma, the 28th Chan patriarch, who brought it to China in about 520 CE. There is no documentary evidence to support this, however, and no scholar today takes it very seriously, because the ground for Chan Buddhism had already been prepared by Sengzhao and Daosheng. Scripture played little part in the instruction of the Chan masters. Because nirvana cannot be discussed, it cannot be expressed in texts nor could it be achieved by conscious effort (*yu-wei*) or by rituals and prayers. When the student was ready, his master could shock or even beat him into the psychological awareness of his Buddha nature that was enlightenment. He then continues with his life as before, but everything has a different significance for him.

The ideas of Sengzhao and Daosheng would also influence Confucianism. The *Analects* had made it clear that *ren* or human-heartedness was fundamental to our humanity; it was indefinable, transcendent, but near at hand – in rather the same way as nirvana. Daosheng taught that anybody could become a Buddha, just as Mencius and Xunzi had insisted that even the man in the street could become a Yao or Shun. Chinese Buddhism is an arresting demonstration of the profound similarity of the religious and spiritual experience of human beings. Each culture will express it according to its own genius and in its own scriptures. In the case of Chan/Zen, no scriptures are necessary, however, because the capacity for transcendence is already implanted in the human mind. This sacred reality is not locked away in a spiritual world, in paradise or heaven, but is inherent in our humanity and all we need to do is cultivate it. The sacred, the divine, Buddhahood or nirvana are states that we all embody. Scripture is only one of the ways in which we realise this reality that is inseparable from our deepest selves. As a new Arabic scripture would have it, it is closer to us than our jugular vein.[86]

10

RECITATION AND *INTENTIO*

The scriptural revolution in the Middle East, which had begun in the first century CE with the Mishnah and the New Testament, culminated in Arabia during the month of Ramadan in 610, when a merchant of Mecca, a commercial city in the Hijaz, had a terrifying vision in a mountain cave and found the first words of a new Arabic scripture pouring, as if unbidden, from his lips. Later, he would call that momentous night Layla al-Qadr, 'Night of Destiny', because it had made him a messenger of Allah, the high god of Arabia whom the Arabs now identified with the God of the Jews and Christians. Muhammad was devastated by the experience and ran in terror down the rocky hillside of Mount Hira to his wife Khadija, who told him firmly that he had received a divine revelation.

In the fifth century, Sozemon, a Palestinian Christian historian, reported that some of the Arabs had rediscovered the ancient monotheism of Abraham, which was known as the *hanifiyyah*, the 'pure religion'. There were communities of Jews and Christians in Arabia, who were known as the *ahl al-kitab* ('the people of scripture'), and it was widely accepted in the region that the Arabs were descended from Ishmael, Abraham's elder son. God had commanded Abraham to abandon him and his mother Hagar in the desert but had promised that Ishmael would also be the father of a great people.[1] Later, according to Arab folklore, Abraham had visited Ishmael in the wilderness and together they had rebuilt the Kabah, the cube-shaped shrine in the middle of Mecca, which had originally been built by Adam. From all over the peninsula, pagan and Christian Arabs alike congregated to perform ancient rites around the Kabah during the month of the hajj pilgrimage.

There was a form of Arabian paganism that was probably stronger in Mecca than elsewhere. But the Bedouin tribes had little time for religion. In their view, everything was controlled by time or fate; all things passed away, and even the most heroic warrior would die. But the Meccans worshipped several gods. Allah, like most high gods, was a rather abstract deity and had no specific cult: it was said that he had created the world, was the giver of rain, and quickened the embryo in the womb. People might pray to him in an emergency but tended to forget him after the crisis.[2] The Meccans also worshipped three goddesses, the daughters of Allah – Allat, Al-Uzza and Manat – represented by large standing stones in the nearby oasis cities of Taif, Nakhlah and Qudayd.

During the early sixth century, the Quraysh, Muhammad's tribe, had made Mecca a centre of trade. They had been able to abandon nomadic life by servicing the foreign caravans that traversed the desert, bringing goods from India to the settled lands of the Middle East. Over time, the Quraysh began to send their own caravans into Syria and Yemen, and this meant that they had to extract themselves from the chronic cycle of inter-tribal warfare and make Mecca a haven of peace where people could trade without fearing a vendetta. With consummate skill and diplomacy, they had established the Haram ('Sanctuary'), a zone with a twenty-mile radius centred on the Kabah, where all violence was forbidden.[3] They also made special agreements with Bedouin tribes, who promised that they would not attack the caravans during the 'forbidden months' when markets were held in various parts of the peninsula, culminating in five consecutive fairs or *suqs* in and around Mecca. The last fair of the year was held in nearby Ukaz, immediately before the month of the hajj, so the trading cycle concluded with the merchants performing the ancient rites at the Kabah and visiting their own deities, whose effigies were installed in the Haram.

This was not a cynical exploitation of religion. The Quraysh believed that trade had saved them from the hardships of nomadic life, making them rich beyond their wildest dreams. Trade, therefore, had its own sacrality and, some believed, offered a hope of immortality. It was an unusual view of faith, perhaps, but the Arabs enjoyed a unique independence. Neither Persia nor Byzantium, the great powers of the region, had any interest in the barren deserts of Arabia, so the Quraysh could develop their fledgling market economy freely, without imperial control. They could also cultivate their own religious ideology and interpret the theological ideas of their more sophisticated neighbours as they saw fit. They had retained the proud self-sufficiency (*istighna*) that was the hallmark of Arab life and firmly resisted any attempted domination. Trade had also taught them to appreciate the values and ideals of others: an object was tradeable only because other people, for a variety of reasons, coveted it, so the exchange of goods was also an exchange of ideas and world views.

There was an openness in Arabia that we do not find in either the Hebrew Bible or the New Testament.[4]

Because of this more pluralistic outlook, the idea of an exclusive religion was alien to the Quraysh. Arabia was surrounded by Christians – in Syria, Mesopotamia, Abyssinia and Yemen – most of whom had rejected the orthodoxy of the Council of Chalcedon and had their own views of Jesus. Jews had migrated to Arabia after the destruction of Jerusalem and had acculturated with Arab tribal life. They practised their own form of Judaism and over the years had also developed independent traditions. Arab tribesmen were all familiar with such Jewish lore as the story of Abraham and Ishmael but they did not regard any of these traditions – Judaism, Christianity, paganism or the *hanifiyyah* – as discrete or self-sufficient. They were, rather, seen as strands of thought and practice that were open-ended, flexible and still in flux. They had little experience of hard-and-fast scriptural tenets and relied more on oral pronouncements. The first word of the scripture dictated by God to Muhammad on Mount Hira had been '*Iqrah!*', 'Recite!' Many of the succeeding revelations also commanded Muhammad to proclaim the divine message orally: 'Say!'[5] He would listen to the inspired words, memorise them and then recite them to his followers. Eventually these revelations were collected in the scripture that we call the Quran, the 'Recitation'.

This revelation was, therefore, the culmination of two processes in Arabia, which fused in the Quran: one was the scriptural revolution of the Middle East, which had enlivened the scriptural genre in the region; the other was Arabs' habit of regarding the religious ideas of their neighbours as tendencies that were still in the process of development rather than hard-line doctrines. The astonishing – indeed, unprecedented – speed with which Islam took off, within and outside Arabia, suggests that it spoke to widespread but undeveloped desires and a dissatisfaction with the hard-line state orthodoxy that had by this time developed in Byzantium. The Quran proudly and repeatedly announces itself as a 'scripture'[6] – something that we do not find in either the Hebrew Bible or the New Testament. Above all, it was an *Arabic* scripture. Arabic was a literary language, shared by all the tribes: it was the lingua franca of the peninsula.[7] Poetry was the supreme art form in Arabia. Inspired by the *jinn*, the fiery sprites who haunted the steppes, the poet was 'one who knows', because he had access to what others could not see.[8] Tribal poetry focused on honour, courage, love, sex, wine-drinking and idyllic descriptions of nature. It was also used to strike terror in the hearts of enemies. Like other pre-literate peoples, the Arabs could memorise large quantities of verse and its recitation was felt to have numinous power.

Muhammad always insisted that he was not a poet. He believed that poetry smacked too much of the old tribal *jahiliyyah* ('irascibility' or 'aggression') – a chronic obsession with honour and prestige and, above all, a tendency to violence and retaliation.[9] In both style and content, the Quran would differ from conventional Arabic poetry, but Muhammad was reciting to people who had developed 'one of the most finely tuned and scrutinising tastes in the history of prophetic speech'.[10] They would know how to listen to the inspired words, how to appreciate the multiple layers of meaning in almost every phrase, and how to memorise it, taking it into their hearts.

For some years before the first revelation, Muhammad and Khadija had made an annual retreat on Mount Hira, just outside Mecca. There he had given alms to the poor and performed rituals, which may have included prostrations before Allah.[11] Muhammad seems to have been gravely preoccupied about the state of the world. Tribal warfare had escalated in the peninsula, and, further afield, the great empires of Persia and Byzantium seemed bent on destroying one another in a series of devastating wars. Within Mecca, too, there was spiritual malaise and dissatisfaction. Some Qurayshi clans were becoming rich, but others felt increasingly marginalised. The communal spirit that had been essential to the tribe's survival in the desert had been undermined by the market economy, which depended on ruthless competition, greed and individual enterprise. Ignoring the plight of poorer tribesmen, some were building fortunes; they even exploited orphans and widows, absorbing their inheritance into their own estates. It seemed that the Quraysh had jettisoned the best and retained only the worst of the tribal ethos – the *jahili* recklessness, arrogance and egotism that were morally destructive and could lead only to ruin.

The Quranic solution to the problems of Mecca began to unfold in the very first revelation:

> Recite in the name of your lord who created –
> From an embryo created the human ...
> The human being is a tyrant
> He thinks his possessions makes him secure
> To your lord is the return of everything[12]

This verse developed the Quraysh's somewhat notional belief that Allah had created each one of them but declared their proud self-sufficiency to be delusory because humans were entirely dependent upon God. Allah insisted that he was not a distant, absent 'high god'. His creatures must 'come near' so that he could guide them, and abandon their proud istighna: 'Touch your head to the ground!' God commanded at the end of the surah (chapter).[13] Thus was born the religion of Islam, which demands the 'surrender' (islam) of the ego. A muslim was a man or woman who had made that existential surrender.

But this 'surrender' must be expressed in practically expressed compassion. The Prophet began nearly every recitation of the Quran with the invocation: 'In the name of God, the Compassionate [al-Rahman], the Merciful [al-Rahim]'; these divine attributes had to be incarnated in Muslim society. The Quran gave the Prophet a political mandate, demanding that human beings behave to one another with justice and equity and distribute their wealth fairly. This, the divine voice insisted, had been the central message of all the great scriptures of the past. The experience of building such a society (ummah) and living in it would give Muslims intimations of the divine, because they would be in harmony with the way things ought to be. Thus, the political well-being of the ummah was a matter of sacred importance, and politics was what Christians would call a sacrament that enabled the divine to function effectively in the world.

The Quran frequently refers to the Semitic notion of the Umm al-Kitab, the 'Source of Scripture', an archetypal Book that had been with God from all eternity.[14] The Quran regards this root of scripture (asl al-kitab) as the text from which all human scriptures are derived. Consequently, the Quran regards all scriptures as inspired by God and transmitted through a line of prophets to different groups of people. The Psalms were revealed to David, the Torah to Moses, the Gospel to Jesus, and now, finally, the Quran to Muhammad. Later, Muslims would acknowledge the validity of the Zoroastrian Avesta and the Indian Vedas. Where Jews and Christians tended to be more exclusive in their idea of revelation, the Quran insisted that Muslims must honour the revelations received by every single one of God's messengers:

Say: 'We believe in God and in what has been sent down to us and to Abraham, Ishmael, Isaac, Jacob, and the Tribes. We believe in what has been given to Moses, Jesus and the Prophets from their Lord. We do not make a distinction between any of them. It is to Him that we devote ourselves. If anyone seeks a religion other than complete devotion [islam] to God it will not be accepted from him.'[15]

The last sentence is often quoted to 'prove' that the Quran insists that Islam is the one true faith. But Islam was not yet the official name for Muhammad's religion. Here the word simply refers to the total 'surrender' of the self to God; so, when read in context, this verse clearly rejects the idea of an exclusive faith. In the Quran, each of the revealed religions is said to have its own *din*, its own practices and insights. Religious pluralism, therefore, was God's will: 'We have assigned a law [*din*] and a path to each one of you. If God had so willed, He would have made you one community [*ummah*].'[16] God was not the exclusive property of any one tradition, but was rather the source of all human knowledge. 'God is the light of the heavens and the earth,' proclaimed one of the most mystical verses in the Quran. The divine light could not be confined to a single lamp but was enshrined in every vessel of illumination.[17]

For twenty-three years until his death, Muhammad continued to receive revelations. Revelation was a painful experience. He used to sweat, even on a cold day, and faint with the effort of translating the divine utterance into human speech. Some revelations referred allusively to stories that were familiar to the Arabs from their contacts with Jews and Christians. These tales of Abraham, Joseph, Moses, Jesus and Mary resemble but also differ from the biblical versions. They are not 'borrowings' that distort the 'original'; rather, they reflect the Arabian habit of regarding such stories and doctrines as 'work in progress' that could morph fluidly into different modes to meet particular needs. For the Arabs, Judaism and Christianity were not exclusive traditions but reflected spiritual tendencies that seemed entirely compatible with Arabian notions.

The earliest revelations focused on the Judgement at the end of time, an idea that clearly derived from Jewish and Christian traditions. But it also differed from them, because it was designed specifically to challenge the glum pessimism of Arab paganism and its vision of life as inescapably moribund. The Quran insisted that at the Judgement, the human being encountered 'the Lord of the daybreak' and stepped into life.[18] But the 'Day of Reckoning' (Yawm ad-Din) was not presented simply as a future event, because the Arabic *din* can also mean a 'moment of truth' that compels you to make life-changing decisions here and now.[19] At the Final Judgement, there would be a dramatic ontological reversal: everything that had seemed solid and permanent would become ephemeral, while behaviour that seemed unimportant at the time would prove to be momentous: 'Whoever does a mote's weight good will see it; whoever does a mote's weight wrong will see it.'[20] A seemingly insignificant selfish action or an unconsidered act of generosity would be the measure of a human life: 'To free a slave, to feed the destitute on a day of hunger, a kinsman, orphan, or a stranger, out of luck, in need.'[21] The Quran insistently asks: 'Where are you going with your life?'[22] The probing, intimate questioning and the constant use of the present tense obliged the Prophet's audience to see their lives differently. But human beings are forgetful and tend to push inconvenient truths to the back of their minds. 'Remind them,' God urged Muhammad. 'All you can do is be a reminder.'[23]

The Quran made it clear that it was not teaching anything new. It was simply a reminder (*dhikr*) of what everybody knew already. The old tribal ideal had emphasised the importance of caring for every single one of its members, but the market economy was making people forget this. Like the Hebrew prophets, Jesus and Paul, the Quran insists on social equity. People would not be judged for their private beliefs or sexual misdemeanours, but on their fidelity to the 'works of justice'. The bedrock message of the Quran is that it is wrong to build a private fortune and good to share your wealth, creating a society in which the poor and vulnerable are treated with respect. The Quran has harsh words for the *kafir*, a word often mistranslated as 'unbeliever' but which derives from the root *KFR* ('ingratitude') and implies a churlish refusal of something offered with kindness and generosity.[24] The Quran does not berate *kafirun* for their unbelief but for their arrogance, haughtiness, self-importance, insolence and unkindness:[25]

> Do you see him who calls the Reckoning a lie?
> He is the one who casts the orphan away
> who fails to urge the feeding of one in need ...
> who make of themselves a big show
> but hold back the small kindness.[26]

The Muslim, however, practised the traditional Arab virtue of *hilm* and was forbearing, patient and merciful.[27] Unlike the *kafirun*, Muslims must control their anger, care for the poor, and feed the destitute, even when hungry themselves.[28]

After a while, the Quran began to include stories of the prophets, especially Abraham, who was neither a Jew nor a Christian since he had lived before the Torah and the Gospel.[29] Muhammad experienced hostility and rejection from some of the *ahl al-kitab* in Arabia. Because he had no conception of an exclusive religion, he assumed that the idea of a 'chosen people' or the conviction that *only* Jews or Christians would enter Paradise were the views of misguided individuals.[30] He was also bewildered to learn that some Christians believed that God was a Trinity and that Jesus was the son of Allah and, again, believed that they had simply misinterpreted their scriptures.[31]

In Mecca, Muhammad encountered not only opposition but persecution and the position of the Muslim community became insupportable, so in 622 he accepted the invitation of Arabs in the agricultural oasis of Yathrib, some 250 miles to the north.[32] The oasis had been torn apart by chronic tribal warfare and Muhammad was brought in as an impartial arbitrator. Soon after the Muslims' arrival, the Prophet renamed it *al-Madinah al-Munawarah*, the 'Illuminated City' or, more briefly, Medina. There he could implement his moral and social reforms in a way that had been impossible in Mecca. During the last ten years of his life, therefore, the Quran changed: its surahs became longer and more concerned with legislation. But the *ummah* was extremely vulnerable and these were frightening years. Muslims would experience nothing like this until the modern colonial period, when, once again, the *ummah* felt surrounded by powerful enemies. In Medina, Muhammad faced virulent opposition from some of the pagan and Jewish tribes, who resented the newcomers. There were attempts on the Prophet's life, while in Mecca his own tribe, the Quraysh, vowed vengeance.

The Muslim emigrants had to find a new source of income or they would become a burdensome drain on the Medinese. They were bankers and merchants, with no agricultural expertise, and, in any case, all the available arable land in the oasis was taken. The obvious solution was the *ghazu*, the acquisition raid, which was the time-honoured way of making ends meet in a time of scarcity in the peninsula. Fighters would carry off food and animals, taking care not to kill a tribesman as that would result in a vendetta. Nobody would have found this reprehensible – the *ghazu* was regarded almost as a national sport. The only difference was that the Muslims were attacking their own tribe. Muhammad, therefore, dispatched raiding parties to the trading caravans of the Quraysh, at first with little success as they were inexperienced warriors. They achieved their first major victory in March 624 at the Well of Badr, but it was a terrifying experience since the Quraysh had dispatched their powerful cavalry to defend their caravan and the Muslims were seriously outnumbered by well-trained troops. The Quraysh, who were determined to eradicate the *ummah*, inflicted severe defeats on the Muslims during the next three years. At one point, in March 627, before the tide turned in Muhammad's favour, a huge Meccan army and their Bedouin allies – some 10,000 men – besieged Medina for an entire month.

The Quran records the Muslims' terror: 'They massed against you from above and below; your eyes rolled [with fear], your hearts rose into your throats and you thought [ill] thoughts of God. There the believers were sorely tested and deeply shaken.'[33]

But Muhammad managed to build a strong confederation of friendly Bedouin tribes by means of diplomacy and negotiation, and in 628, he led 1,000 Muslim pilgrims from Medina to Mecca to make the hajj pilgrimage. Since all violence was forbidden in the Haram, especially during the pilgrimage, the Muslims were going virtually unarmed into enemy territory. The Quraysh dispatched their cavalry to attack the pilgrims, but their Bedouin allies led them into Mecca by a back way. At the Well of Hudaybiyyah, they rested and awaited developments. Knowing that they would lose all credibility in Arabia if they massacred bona fide pilgrims in their sacred territory, the Quraysh eventually sent an envoy to negotiate and, to the dismay of the Muslim pilgrims, Muhammad gave away most of the advantages gained during the war. But support for the *ummah* in Arabia had become an irreversible trend. Two years later Mecca voluntarily opened its gates to the Muslim army and many of Muhammad's Qurayshi opponents embraced Islam. When he died in 632, he had united the whole of war-torn Arabia in the Pax Islamica.

Islam had prevailed, however, neither through conquest nor Muhammad's personal charisma, but through the power of the Quran. This is difficult for non-Muslims to understand, because to an outsider the Quran can seem an unattractive and bewildering scripture. Europeans and North Americans, who bring to the Quran a biblically based understanding of scripture, are often baffled. There is no coherent narrative: anecdotes about the prophets are scattered throughout the text, with no sense of progression. Themes are not developed logically; there is no systematic treatment of doctrines; and its constant repetitions seem wearisome. Its surahs have been arranged seemingly arbitrarily, starting with the longest and finishing with the shortest. There is little sense of time: the prophets, whose lifetimes span a millennium or more, are all treated as contemporaries.

But the Quran is an orally transmitted scripture and designed to be performed, not read silently or sequentially. Well versed in the art of oral recitation, Muhammad's audience would have been able to pick up verbal signals that are lost in written codification (and in translation). They would find that themes, words, phrases and sound patterns recurred again and again – like variations in a piece of music, that subtly amplify the original melody and add layer upon layer of complexity. The Quran is designed to be repetitive. Its ideas, imagery and stories are bound together by internal echoes, which reinforce its central teachings with instructive emphasis. Verbal repetitions link disparate passages in the listener's mind and integrate the different strands of the text, as one verse delicately qualifies or supplements others.

The Quran was not imparting facts that could be conveyed instantaneously. Like Muhammad himself, listeners had to absorb its teachings slowly, their understanding growing more profound and refined over time. The rich, allusive language and rhythms of the Arabic helped them to slow down their habitual mental processes and enter a different mode of consciousness. In the early Meccan surahs, the Quran spoke intimately to the individual, often preferring to pose teachings in the form of a question – 'Have you not heard?', 'Do you consider?', 'Have you not seen?' Each listener was thus invited to interrogate themself. Any response to these queries was usually grammatically ambiguous or indefinite, leaving the audience with an image on which to meditate but no decisive answer. The Quran was not attempting to impart metaphysical certainty but inviting its audience to develop a different kind of awareness. As the American scholar Marshall G. S. Hodgson explains:

> The Qur'ân was never designed to be read for information or even for inspiration, but to be recited as an act of commitment in worship; nor did it become a mere sacred source of authority ... What one did with the Qur'ân was not to peruse it but to worship by means of it; not to passively receive it, but in reciting to reaffirm it for oneself; the event of revelation was renewed every time one of the faithful in the act of worship relived [i.e. re-spoke] the Qur'ânic affirmations ... it continued to be an event, an act, rather than a statement of facts or norms.[34]

The Quran united two scriptural forms. One, as we have seen, was the Semitic tradition of the Heavenly Book. The other was the eastern tradition of sacred sound. Quranic language had the power of an Indian mantra. When Muhammad received a revelation, he was instructed to listen intently until its meaning became apparent.[35] Muhammad would recite each new revelation to his Companions until they too knew it by heart – the traditional mode of transmitting Arabic poetry. They had to allow the sound to percolate through their consciousness and the beauty of the words to fill them with awe. The object, as Hodgson explains, was not intellectual conviction but, rather, commitment and worship.[36]

The Quran records its effect on Muhammad's first audiences. Some were puzzled, even shocked, by it because it was so unlike traditional Arabic poetry. Others were emotionally transported: they 'fell to their knees and wept'; the recitation caused 'the skins of those in awe of their Lord to quiver ... their hearts soften at the mention of God', their eyes 'overflowing with tears because they recognise the Truth [in it]'.[37] Umar ibn al-Khattab, who would become the second caliph, was originally hostile to the Prophet's message, but one evening when he saw Muhammad reciting the Quran quietly to himself beside the Kabah, he crept under the damask cloth that covered the shrine and edged his way around until he was standing directly in front of him: 'There was nothing between us but the cover of the Kabah,' he recalled. 'When I heard the Quran my heart was softened and I wept, and Islam entered into me.'[38] The recitation was a form of music, which, it has been said, is intrinsically sad. The Greek philosopher Gorgias (c.485–380 BCE) maintained that those who listen to poetry – which, of course, was always sung in ancient Greece – experience 'awe and tearful pity and mournful desire'.[39] The philosopher Suzanne Langer said that music had the power to evoke 'emotions and moods we have not felt, passions we did not know before'.[40] Sorrow and the empathy that feeds our sense of justice are deeply connected,[41] so the very sound of the Quran endorsed at a level deeper than the merely rational its ethical imperative.

For centuries, Muslims have experienced the Quran as what Christians call a sacrament, a perpetual breaking-through of the transcendent into the mundane.[42] While Christians see the Word of God embodied in the man Jesus, for Muslims the Word is present in the sound of the Quranic text as recited in communal worship. When they learn it by heart, they take it into themselves in a holy communion. Muslims have worked hard to spread literacy, and the calligraphic copying of the text is a sacred art form, but a Muslim's most important duty is to learn the Quranic message by heart.[43] For many, this is a lifelong task. It cannot be memorised from a written text but by listening to its recitation, every one of which is a re-enactment of the revelation, a symbolic participation in the mystery of God's concern for humanity.[44]

In the modern West, we rely on empirical thought and discursive reasoning, which proceeds logically from premises to conclusions. This has been essential to our scientific and technological achievements. But, as we have seen, human beings also acquire meaning from physical movement, so Muslims also learn from bodily rituals.[45] The 'Five Pillars', the essential practices of Islam, are corporal as well as mental disciplines. The obligatory prayers that interrupt all mundane activities at five precisely prescribed times each day include ritualised physical movements. At the sound of the muezzin calling them to prayer (*salat*), Muslims must first determine the direction (*qibla*) of Mecca and position themselves accordingly, a physical 'reminder' (*dhikr*) of their true orientation. They then recite Quranic verses, while bowing forward, sitting on the backs of their legs, and touching the ground with their foreheads – all of which impress on the mind and heart what is required in the 'surrender' to God. The Ramadan fast, which reverses the usual sequences of space and time, is another 'reminder' of the ultimate. During the day, austerity is the rule: food, drink and sex are prohibited, while the night is for communal celebration. The ritual circumambulations of the hajj pilgrimage around the Kabah, another physical *dhikr*, enacts the spiritual centring of life around the transcendent.

After the Prophet's death in 632, his confederacy broke up and his 'successor' (*khalifa*), Abu Bakr, fought the defecting tribes to prevent Arabia from regressing into chronic warfare. Within two years, he had restored the Pax Islamica, and after his death, Umar ibn al-Khattab (r.634–44) was convinced that peace could be preserved only by an outwardly directed offensive. These military campaigns were not religiously inspired – there is nothing in the Quran to suggest that Muslims are committed to world conquest. Umar's motives were purely economic. In times of scarcity, the *ghazu*, the acquisition raid, had been the traditional way of redistributing limited resources in Arabia, but because Muslims were forbidden to fight one another, it was no longer possible. The solution, Umar decided, was to raid the rich settled lands, which, as the Arabs were aware, were in disarray after the debilitating Persian–Byzantine wars. As expected, they met little opposition. The armies of both powers had been decimated and the subject peoples disaffected. Within a remarkably short period, the Arabs had forced the Byzantine army to retreat from Syria and Palestine (636) and crushed the depleted Persian army in a single battle (637). In 641, they conquered Egypt, and though it took some fifteen years to pacify the whole of Iran, they were eventually victorious. Only Byzantium, now a rump state shorn of its southern provinces, held out. Thus, twenty-five years after Muhammad's death, the Muslims found themselves masters of a huge empire, encompassing Mesopotamia, Syria, Palestine and Egypt.

The Arabs had no experience of state-building and simply adapted Persian and Byzantine systems of land tenure, taxation and government. As in Persia, the 'people of the book' – Jews, Christians and Zoroastrians – became *dhimmis* ('protected subjects'), managing their own affairs and paying a poll tax in return for military protection. Islam was the religion of the conquerors, in the same way as Zoroastrianism, which had developed from the revelations of the Aryan prophet Zarathustra, who was active in the Caucasus in about 1200 BCE, had been the exclusive faith of the Persian ruling class.[46] Indeed, for the first hundred years, conversion to Islam was discouraged for religious as well as economic reasons. But empire was a religious challenge. How could the systemic inequity of the agrarian empire be squared with Quranic justice? Umar did not permit his officers to establish estates in the rich land of the Iraq. Instead, Muslim soldiers lived in strategically placed garrison towns: Kufah in Iraq, Basra and Damascus in Syria, Qum in Iran, and Fustat in Egypt. But by the reign of the third caliph, Uthman (r.644–56), troops had become mutinous and discontented. Uthman was also concerned about the integrity of the Quran.

There is some evidence to suggest that in the last year of his life, Muhammad had begun to anthologise his revelations in a written text, with the help of his scribe Zayd ibn Thabit, but did not live to see the project completed.[47] The preservation of the Quran became problematic almost immediately after his death, when many of the leading Quran-reciters, who knew the scripture by heart, were killed during the 'successor wars'. Abu Bakr, Zayd and the remaining reciters collected the surviving scripted fragments to create a written text. They were confident that they had memorised the entire Quran because they had chanted it with the Prophet during his last year. After Abu Bakr's death, this text passed to Umar, who, in turn, bequeathed it to his daughter Hafsa, one of Muhammad's wives.

But this was not the only copy in circulation. In Iraq, Muslims preferred the version of Abdallah ibn Masud, a greatly respected companion of the Prophet, while Muslims in Syria claimed that their own text was superior. Uthman therefore commissioned a council of prominent scribes and reciters, including Zayd ibn Thabit, to compile an authorised text. Queries about phrasing or content were resolved by those who had learned the disputed passage from the Prophet himself. When the task was complete, Uthman kept one copy in Medina and dispatched others to Kufa, Damascus, Basra and Mecca, each accompanied by an official reciter, and ordered that all other copies be burned. Tradition has it that this was done everywhere except Mesopotamia, which remained loyal to Ibn Masud's text.

But Uthman's would become the standard version. The revelations are divided into 114 surahs, arranged according to length rather than content. Within the surahs, verses (ayat) preserve the traditional rhyming prose, rhythm and musical quality of the Quran. Apart from Surah 9, each surah begins with the *bismillah* ('In the Name of God, the Compassionate, the Merciful'), the formula used by the Prophet. Yet Uthman's text is acknowledged to be defective. There are variants that are due not to scribal error but to the inadequacy of the Arabic script at this early date. For its first 400 years, the Quran was written in Kufic script, which differed from later cursive Arabic. Because, like Hebrew, Arabic is a consonantal script, vowels had to be inserted by the reciter. Also, some of the consonants at this stage looked so alike that diacritical marks were later inserted to distinguish them. Muslims accept these different readings as de facto, so 'canonical' variants, each regarded as valid, were listed side by side.[48] None of them makes a substantive difference to the meaning – it was even said that the Prophet had recited the same passage differently on certain occasions. Oral transmission was still the preferred mode, and Muslim interpreters regarded the variants as a blessing since they all came from Muhammad.[49]

It was probably inevitable that, as Muslims made their astonishingly swift transition from penury to imperial rule, there would be leadership problems.[50] In 656, Uthman was killed during a mutiny and a war for the succession broke out between Ali, the Prophet's cousin and son-in-law, and Muawiyyah, the son of one of Muhammad's most obdurate enemies. Finally, arbitration went against Ali, who was deposed by Muawiyyah and murdered in 661. The trauma of this civil war has permanently marked Islamic life. Most Muslims agreed that the unity of the *ummah* must take priority. Even if this meant accommodating a degree of injustice, they would follow the Sunnah, the 'customary practice' of the Prophet; henceforth they would be known as the Sunni. But others, who called themselves the Shiah i-Ali ('the Partisans of Ali'), henceforth known as Shiis, claimed that his blood descendants were the true leaders of the *ummah* and regarded Ali's death as symptomatic of the chronic injustice of political life. This conviction was later confirmed in 681 when Ali's son Husain, together with his family and companions, were slaughtered at Karbala near Kufa by the troops of Caliph Yazid, Muawiyyah's son and successor.

Muawiyyah had moved his capital from Medina to Damascus and founded a hereditary dynasty, and the Umayyad empire gradually became a typical agrarian state with a privileged aristocracy, an unequal distribution of wealth, and a standing army dedicated to territorial expansion. But the more thoughtful Muslims continued to engage in intense discussions about the morality of imperial rule and it was from these debates that key institutions and pious practices of Islam, as we know it today, began to emerge. These principled deliberations about the role the political leadership of the *ummah* played in Islam were as decisive as the great Christological debates in Byzantium. For Muslims, politics was not a distraction from the religious life but was the arena in which they experienced God and which enabled the divine to function effectively in the world. Thus, an ascetical movement developed in reaction to the luxury of aristocratic life; like the Prophet, ascetics wore the coarse woollen garments (*tasawwuf*) of the poor so they were known as Sufis. The Shiis too developed a piety of protest, insisting that only a descendant of the Prophet could be the true imam ('leader') of the *ummah*: some therefore withdrew from political activity, while others militarily opposed the cruelty and injustice of imperial life.

Islamic jurisprudence (*fiqh*) was another response to the dilemma of imperial rule. The early jurists wanted to create legal norms that would make the Quranic teachings that were God's revealed will a realistic possibility in human affairs. The problem was that the Quran had made no hard-and-fast rulings; it contained very little legislation and what laws there were had been designed for a small and much simpler society. It was also far too lenient for a viable empire – or, indeed, for any state. The Quran, for example, prescribed capital punishment for murder or treason – but if the miscreant atoned, judges must remember that Allah was forgiving and merciful.[51] Theft should be punished in the traditional Arabian way by amputation of the hand – 'but if anyone repents after his wrongdoing and makes amends, God will accept his repentance'.[52] During the war with Mecca, the Quran had issued rulings for conduct during a battle – though these too were always followed by a verse urging forbearance: 'but if they incline towards peace, you must also incline towards it and put your trust in God ... If they intend to deceive you, God is enough for you.'[53]

In the early days, Muslims in the garrison towns could ask Muhammad's Companions what he would have said or done in a problematic situation, but when the first generation had died, jurists began to collect news or reports (hadith), which recorded the Prophet's words on a given occasion and his habitual mode of behaviour (Sunnah).[54] The hadith became crucial to Islamic *fiqh*.[55] Some of these 'reports' were used to support the new forms of Islamic piety that had developed in opposition to Umayyad imperialism; others provided historical evidence to support state policy. These reports multiplied during the eighth and ninth centuries, until a bewildering number of hadith circulated throughout the empire, covering everyday matters, metaphysics, cosmology and theology as well as politics.

These were finally collected and anthologised. The most famous editors were Muhammad ibn Ismail al-Bukhari (d. 870) and Muslim ibn al-Hajjaj (d. 875), who developed criteria to judge the credibility of each hadith based on its chain (*isnad*) of transmitters, which began with the Prophet or one of his Companions and ended with a present-day authority. Experts carefully examined each link in the chain to assess the reliability of these transmitters. In this way, a hadith was declared sound (*sahih*), acceptable (*hasan*) or weak (*daif*).

Because many, indeed most, of the hadith reflect theological or legal debates that occurred after the Prophet's death, some Western scholars have dismissed them as fabrications or even forgeries. Yet we do not speak of the gospels in this way, even though they too were produced decades after Jesus' lifetime and reflect later conditions.[56] Both the gospels and the hadith were attempts to ground the present in the sacred events of the past that had inspired the movement. The gospels, like the hadith, are a commentary on the original revelation, which for Christians is the incarnate Word and for Muslims the Word recorded in the Quran.[57] The hadith were vigorously promoted by a populist contingent known as the Ahl al-Hadith ('Hadith People') who insisted that Muslim law be rooted in these eyewitness reports instead of the 'independent reasoning' (*ijtihad*) developed by the jurists. Their piety appalled the more rationally inclined Muslims, since it threatened their strict sense of the divine unity, but these practices also resembled the way Christians had come to think about Jesus. The Hadith People believed that the Quran was an earthly embodiment of the Word of God that had existed with him from all eternity. They could hear the voice of God whenever they listened to a Quranic recitation; and when they recited the Quran, God's speech was on their tongue and in their mouths. They held the Word in their hands when they carried a copy of the sacred text.

Today, terrorist atrocities committed in the name of Islam have led many people in the West to assume that the Quran is an inherently violent scripture and addicted to jihad, which, they believe, means 'holy war'. In fact, jihad means 'struggle', 'striving' or 'endeavour'. The word and its derivatives occur only forty-one times in the Quran and in only ten of these instances does jihad refer unequivocally to warfare.[58] The 'surrender' of Islam required a constant struggle against innate selfishness. Sometimes, as in the war with Mecca, this involved 'fighting' (*qital*), but giving to the poor in times of personal hardship was also a jihad. In the Quran, the word jihad is always preceded with the definite article (*al-*) and followed by the phrase *fi sabil*

Allah, and should be translated not as 'fighting' but as '*striving* in the path of God'. The word *harb* ('fighting') appears only four times in the Quran and is never used with the phrase 'in the path of God'; only once does it refer to a righteous war waged by the Prophet.[59]

Significantly, the phrase *al-jihad fi sabil Allah* is usually linked with *sabr* ('patience', 'forbearance', 'steadfastness'). In Mecca, Muslims were often abused, physically and verbally, by their opponents. Instead of retaliating violently, the Quran exhorts them to make an effort – to 'struggle' – to respond to such ill-treatment with quiet, long-suffering patience:[60] 'You who believe, be steadfast [*asbiru*], more steadfast than others [*sabaru*], be ready [*rabitu*] and revere God so that you may prosper.'[61] The earliest major commentators on the Quran – Mujahid ibn Jabr of Mecca (d.722), Muqatil ibn Sulayman (d.767) and Abd al-Razzaq al-Sunani (d.827) – all explain that *sabr* referred to the self-control that Muslims were required to show when abused. Later *rabitu* would acquire military connotations, but in the Quran, it always refers to the Muslims' steadfastness in continuing to make the required prayers even when physically assaulted for doing so.[62] Again, those Muslims who had been compelled to leave their homes during the Prophet's migratory *hijrah* from Mecca to Medina are told to 'strive' (*jihadu*) and remain 'patient' (*sabaru*). In the Quran, therefore, jihad is chiefly associated not with warfare but with non-violent resistance.

From an early date, Muslim commentators were sensitive to context and developed the exegetical strategy of linking each verse of the Quran to an event in Muhammad's life so that the historical setting of a revelation could establish a general principle. Most of the early exegetes – Muqatil, Mujahid and the *Tanwir al-Miqbas*, attributed to Muhammad ibn Abbas – emphasise the defensive character of Muslim warfare, as is clear in this early verse: 'Those who have been attacked are permitted to take up arms because they have been wronged – God has the power to help them – those who have been unjustly driven from their homes only for saying "Our Lord is God."'[63] Significantly, this verse goes on to equate Jewish and Christian worship with Muslim prayer, pointing out that had such violence not been vigorously opposed, 'many monasteries, churches, synagogues and mosques, wherein God's name is much invoked, would have been destroyed'.[64]

The early exegetes placed one apparently aggressive verse firmly in its historical context, explaining that it was revealed during the Treaty of Hudaybiyyah, when Muslims were preparing to enter enemy territory, virtually unarmed.[65] It begins with an emphatic command: 'Do not commit aggression [*wa la ta tadu*].'[66] If it became necessary, Muslims could fight in the Meccan Haram, where all violence was usually prohibited, but only if they were attacked there first:

> Kill them wherever you encounter them, and drive them out from where they drove you, for persecution is more serious than killing. Do not fight them in the Sacred Mosque unless they fight you there. If they do fight you, kill them – this is what such disbelievers deserve – but if they stop, then God is most forgiving and merciful. Fight them until there is no more persecution and worship is devoted to God.[67]

Far from seeing this verse as justifying aggressive warfare, the early exegetes insisted that it was obsolete because it applied only to the extraordinary circumstances at Hudaybiyyah. Similarly, the *Tanwir al-Miqbas* interprets the verse 'Fighting is ordained for you, though it is hard for you'[68] as restricted to the time of Muhammad. These early interpreters also contextualised the oft-quoted 'Sword Verse', claiming that it applied only to the war with Mecca and had no current relevance: 'When the four "forbidden months" are over, wherever you encounter the idolaters [*mushrikin*], kill them, seize them, besiege them, wait for them at every lookout post.'[69] For the first 400 years of Islamic history, this verse, quoted so frequently today by critics of Islam, was seldom discussed. Those exegetes who did address it did so perfunctorily, explaining that the *mushrikin* referred to the Quraysh and that the verse was now irrelevant because there were no longer any Arab 'idolaters'.[70] It is worth noting that even the ferocious 'Sword Verse' ends with a call to reconciliation: 'But if they repent, maintain the prayer, and pay the prescribed alms, let them go on their way, for God is most merciful and forgiving.'[71]

But this peaceable attitude was not conducive to empire-building. In the eighth century, after the Umayyad armies had failed to defeat Byzantium, hawkish scholars connected with the imperial government began to find loopholes in the Quranic prohibition of aggression. The Medinan exegete Zayd ibn Aslam (d.753), an advisor to Caliph Yazid, argued that verses that seemed to urge forbearance rather than violent retaliation in fact simply urged patience during a military jihad. Thus, in Quran 22:39–40, cited above, he glossed *rabitu*: '*Be firm* in the path of God with your enemies and the enemies of your religion', arguing that the verbal noun *ribat* was an early reference to the deployment of cavalry to secure the frontier, but failing to mention the fact that in the Prophet's time there was no 'frontier'.[72]

Many of the hadith that militarised the Quranic notion of jihad originated in imperial circles. Some of these claimed that fighting was the Sixth Pillar of Islam, since it was God's way of spreading the faith, while others argued that fighting was far more precious in God's sight than praying all night beside the Kabah or fasting during Ramadan.[73] They predicted that in paradise the martyr will wear silk clothes, drink wine and bask in the sexual delights he had forsaken when he joined the Umayyad army by being married to seventy-two of the women of paradise; these hadith were traditionally judged to be 'weak' but they have acquired special notoriety since 11 September 2001.[74] In Mecca and Medina, however, where the frontier was a distant reality, almsgiving and compassion for the poor remained the most important form of jihad.

This aggressive exegesis became more pronounced under the Abbasids, who defeated the Umayyads in 750 and moved the Muslim capital to Baghdad. Even though the Abbasids realised that the empire could expand no further, it was still essential to defend the border. The celebrated Abbasid jurist Muhammad Idris al-Shafii (d.820) formulated what would become the classical doctrine of jihad: humanity was divided into the Dar al-Islam ('the Abode of Islam') and the Dar al-Harb ('the Abode of War') and there could be no final peace between the two, though a temporary truce was permissible. The goal of jihad was not to convert the subject peoples, since the *ummah* was only one of many divinely guided communities; its purpose was to extend the values of the Quran to the rest of humanity, liberating all peoples from the tyranny of states run on worldly principles.[75] There is nothing to this effect in the Quran. This division of the world into two potentially hostile camps – the rulers and the ruled – is a typical imperialist ideology. The great exegete Abu Jafar al-Tabari (d.923), who was closely associated with the Abbasid elite, dutifully noted the irenic interpretations of the early exegetes, but leaned towards the more aggressive view of jihad, which was becoming an irreversible trend in some circles.[76] It would become even more prominent in later centuries, when Muslims were surrounded by hostile enemies.

*

Meanwhile in India, a new scriptural genre was developing which was inspired by *bhakti*, the loving 'devotion' to a deity.[77] Like the *Mahabharata*, these scriptures were known as a 'Fifth Veda'; it was claimed that they were not 'new' at all but were *puranas* ('ancient tales'). These stories may indeed have circulated orally among the lower classes for centuries. It is also possible that they developed from the *phalashruti* ('fruits of hearing'), narratives recited during the great festivals, which describe the benefits of chanting or hearing a certain mantra.[78] It was important for a priest to be familiar with the history of a mantra he was about to recite and make the public aware of its efficacy in the past. The Puranas were, however, extensions of the mantra tradition, because unlike the classical mantra, where the sound alone was transformative, the meaning of a Purana was also important. In one of the most popular Puranas, for example, Vishnu recites a mantra claiming that he is the supreme reality:

> I alone was in the beginning; there was nothing else at all,
>> Manifest or non-manifest.
> What exists now as the universe is I Myself; what will
>> Remain in the end is simply Myself.[79]

But the Devi, the Mother Goddess, makes the same claim in her Purana: 'All this universe is just I Myself, there is nothing else eternal.'[80] Both emphasise the sacred oneness of all things but they are also making sectarian claims that are important to their devotees, so in the Puranic mantra we have a synthesis of sound and meaning.

The Puranas claimed to be older than the Vedas. It was said that the first scripture uttered by Brahma, the *deva* who personified the *brahman*, was not the Veda but the primordial Purana, which had been so long that Vyasa, the rishi who edited the scriptures, had to divide it into the eighteen 'Great Puranas' to make it accessible to human beings. Western scholars have sometimes dismissed the Puranas as mere compilations, but in India the arrangement and rearrangement of material is the highest form of creation. A single narrative, such as the story of Prajapati, can, as we have seen, be told in innumerable ways, and recast again and again.[81] So while the material of a Purana may be ancient, there is no unique 'master' version. Hence the maxim '*Purapi navam bharati puranam*': 'What, though formed long ago, becomes new? – a Purana!'[82]

Officially, there are only eighteen Great Puranas but in fact there are many, many more and there is no agreement about which texts comprise the canon of eighteen. Puranas are extremely difficult to date, because ancient material often coexists with more recent additions. Some of the stories could be even older than the Rig Veda, but in their extant form, they were all edited between 400 and 1000 CE.[83] Concern with dating, however, is a modern Western preoccupation; from an Indian perspective, it is irrelevant. The American scholar C. Mackenzie Brown has suggested that instead of seeing the eighteen Puranas as a closed canon, it is probably more accurate to see the Puranic genre as a stream with many channels that part, diverge and come together again later in different ways. It is an ongoing attempt to update tradition by reinterpreting ancient truths in a way that speaks to the present. As Brown explains: 'In the Hindu tradition, history is seen as a playground ... Like a carousel, history goes round and round. The actual details of any one cycle are less significant than the principle that governs the cycles as a whole.' What we find in the Puranas, therefore, is 'creative history' which 'discloses the nature of the human condition vis-à-vis the divine reality'.[84]

Each Purana is said to have five topics (*lakshanas*): the Primary Creation (cosmogony); the Secondary Creation (the cycle of destruction and renovation of worlds); the genealogies of gods and patriarchs; the reigns of the Manus (the fourteen primordial kings); and later history. These topics are indeed discussed in some of the early Puranas but do not appear significantly in others. What the *lakshanas* provide is not subject matter, but the world view that governs the story. These prehistoric events presuppose and lead up to the 'present' of the 'ancient tale' but the Puranas are always ready to transform their own premises and never insist on an absolute, objective account of the past.[85]

The Puranas are also very conscious that they are written texts, which, in India, almost amounts to the breaking of a taboo.[86] Strangely enough, this was a bid for greater spiritual equity because a written text can be transmitted to a larger audience. It was said that Brahma had ordered Vyasa to dictate the text of the *Mahabharata* to Ganesha because he wanted the epic to become a book that would be accessible to more people. The Brahmins had transmitted the Vedas – orally – only to other priests, but the Puranas were open to everybody, even Shudras and women, who were debarred from the Vedas. It was also said that a devotee acquires merit by worshipping the scripture in her own home, because the book which contains the 'ancient tale' is itself sacred.[87] It was particularly meritorious to copy the text of a Purana and give the manuscript away as an act of charity, especially if the recipient was a Brahmin priest. This was a defiant bouleversement. The lower classes were appropriating the aristocracy's monopoly of the recitation and transmission of scripture, since now a mere Shudra can give a Brahmin a copy of a Purana.[88]

Where the mantra had embodied the invisible, transcendent Brahman in the form of sound, the holy book was revered as a visible manifestation of the *deva* it celebrated. When Krishna, the avatar of Vishnu, was about to leave the world, his companion Uddhava asked him how his devotees could endure the loss of his presence. Krishna's answer was to present Uddhava with a copy of the *Bhagavata Purana* into which he had infused his own energy: 'Therefore, this is the verbal image of Shri Hari here on earth, which rids a person of sin.'[89] An iconic image of Krishna or Vishnu was ritually instilled with divinity, making the Supreme God present to his devotees. In the same way, the book that celebrates Vishnu's love for his *bhakta* ('devotee') is imbued with his presence: the devotee must look through the physical reality to find the divinity within.

Like the *Mahabharata*, the Puranas proceed in question-and-answer form, between a narrator and his audience, as part of a living oral tradition. This is *smrti*, transmission through an act of remembering that authenticates the present. In the *Bhagavata Purana*, Shuka, the narrator, is telling Krishna's story to King Parikshit, the child Krishna had rescued from Ashwattaman's Night Massacre so that the Pandava line could continue. Parikshit was fated to die of a snake bite and he is listening to Shuka's story beside the Ganges at the very end of his life. So, the story is relayed to an audience suspended – as are we all – between life and death. These are the last words Parikshit will hear and they reconcile him to his fate.[90] He tells Shuka, 'The more I hear you, the more I drink the nectar of Krishna's stories that flows from your mouth; my body grows livelier; my grief is gone; I feel neither hunger nor thirst; my heart is pleased.' Shuka replies that the story purifies the man who enjoys it, like the water that flows from Vishnu's foot. This is no longer an edifying instruction; nor does it, like the epic, fill us with fear and foreboding. It is, rather, a holy communion.[91]

In the *Bhagavad Gita*, Krishna had described *bhakti* as an austere yogic discipline. But in the *Bhagavata Purana*, *bhakti* has absorbed the wilder, emotional spirituality of southern India and aristocratic yogic concentration has been replaced by an ecstatic and intimate love that breaks down the barriers of class. The *Bhagavata Purana* presents itself as the culmination of the Vedas. It self-consciously uses Vedic language, expressing the emotional spirituality of the south Indian Tamils in archaic Sanskrit, saying, in effect: 'Not only do I conform to Vedic orthodoxy, I even sound like the Veda.'[92] Indeed, it claims to be the crowning achievement of Vyasa.[93] It explains that after Vyasa had divided the Veda into four texts, composed the *Mahabharata*, and compiled the eighteen Puranas, he felt strangely unfulfilled. Suddenly the divine rishi Narada appeared and explained that Vyasa was dissatisfied because he had not yet sung the praises of Krishna. Vyasa, therefore, returned to his hermitage, meditated, and finally had a vision of the Purusha, the archetypal, divine 'Person'. He then composed the *Bhagavata Purana*, his heart overflowing with joy as he celebrated Vishnu-Krishna, Lord of creation.[94]

Purusha, the primordial 'Person' of the Rig Veda, was now thought to be incarnate in Lord Krishna, who was *purushottama* ('Vishnu *person*-ified'). Purusha's body had contained all the worlds: all gods, demons, sages and kings; all rituals; all truth and, significantly, all the Vedic mantras, meters and chants.[95] So Vishnu/Krishna was not only the fulfilment of the Veda, he *was* the Veda in human form: 'Asceticism is my heart; mantra is my body; knowledge assumes the shape of my activity; sacrifices are my limbs; the *dharma* born from sacrifices is my essence [*atman*]; the gods are my various breaths.'[96] The abstruse lore of the Brahmins had now blended with the yearnings of the ordinary people, who had been excluded from the Vedic rites. The goal is no longer a disciplined, mystical absorption in the inscrutable Brahman, but ecstatic union with Krishna.

By far the most popular part of the *Bhagavad Purana* is the tenth book, which, drawing on the *Harivamsha*, a third-century supplement to the *Mahabharata*, tells the story of Krishna's childhood. This Krishna bears no resemblance to the daunting, aristocratic Krishna of the epic. The divine child is born with the four arms and weapons of Vishnu, the Supreme God,[97] and his parents immediately recognise him as the Brahman incarnate.[98] Baby Krishna kicks over a heavy cart during his birth ceremony and uproots trees to liberate the spirits trapped inside.[99] Boy Krishna is an inveterate butter-thief; he displaces a mountain with his fingertip; and when his mother looks inside his mouth she sees the entire universe there.[100] When he and his brother Rama walk down the street of Mathura, the townsfolk immediately recognise them as the greatest of the gods.[101] Krishna, the cowherd, has a devastating effect on women: as soon as the women of Mathura see him, they become utterly confused and abandon their domestic duties.[102] He steals the clothes of the *gopis*, the herder-women, while they are bathing,[103] assumes different forms so that he can have sex with every single one of them – though, we are assured, he is acting out of compassion rather than lust – and at the sound of his flute, the *gopis* leave their milking unfinished, let milk boil over and even abandon the babies they are suckling.[104]

When Indra threatens to punish the village for neglecting his cult with a devastating rainstorm, Krishna fights on its behalf. But this is nothing like Indra's battles with Vritra. Krishna just picks up Mount Gorendhara and holds it aloft like a giant umbrella to shelter the community. His most famous battle is with Kaliya, a many-headed monster who was poisoning the stream in which he lived and killing the cattle. Krishna jumps into the water, baiting Kaliya until he finally emerges from his lair. Instead of fighting, Krishna dances around him until Kaliya's heads droop with exhaustion. He admits defeat, and Krishna banishes him to a distant island.

Play (*lila*) is Krishna's mode of being. A far cry from the law-giving God of the monotheistic religions, Krishna expresses the unconditioned nature of the divine, which is not bound by human conventions.[105] He exemplifies the imaginative, rich and creative activity of the sacred that is spontaneous and free. This theophany reveals a divinity that does not demand pomp and sycophantic praise, does not govern the world from a majestic throne, and neither needs nor desires elaborate rituals. Instead, the divine transcends human conventions and class divisions and invites us to question them. Krishna's flute is a summons that mocks our self-important sense of duty and invites men and women alike to a realm of beauty and carnival that even the gods cannot resist. The *gopis* express that yearning for transcendence that is built into our nature and our desire for an *ekstasis* that is impossible in the humdrum world of the habitual. In short, the *Bhagavad Purana* challenges the stereotypical image of Indian spirituality as meditative, yogic and still. Its abiding popularity suggests that it expresses a central insight. All too often scripture is used to confirm our preconceptions, whereas in fact its real function may be to subvert them.

*

In China, the Song dynasty (960–1279) had developed the most sophisticated economy in the world at this time but the northern territories, which included the Great Plain, were repeatedly invaded by their barbarian neighbours and the Song government lost sixteen prefectures south of the Great Wall, while the Tanqat tribe established their own state in the north-west. Reform of the institutions and techniques of government seemed essential. Wang Anshi (1021–86) was convinced that the problem was merely military and fiscal, while Sima Guang (1019–86) looked back to the *Spring and Autumn Annals* to find the underlying 'principle' (*li*) of government that would reveal what strategies had succeeded in the past and could, therefore, guide current policy.

But a group of Confucians in the north, who were initially involved in these political reforms, believed that a deeper solution was essential. Change must be based on the sacred principle or ultimate reality that pervaded the cosmos, influenced everything that happened and was also present in each human being. Only if people were aligned to this fundamental principle would their affairs accord with the Way of Heaven. For some time now, Buddhists had dominated the philosophical scene and Chinese Buddhists insisted that one must achieve enlightenment before undertaking political action. But the Confucian Han Yu (768–824) had challenged this, citing a chapter in the *Classic of Rites* known as the *Great Learning (Daxue)* which prepared a *junzi* step by step for his social and political responsibility. More recently, the great statesman Fan Zhongyan (989–1052) had pointed out that according to Mencius, Yao, Shun and Yu acquired sagehood precisely because of their compassionate concern for the people and the practical steps they took to assuage their suffering. Instead of making your own peace of mind the priority, like the Buddhists, he argued, the Confucian path to self-fulfilment lay in an active struggle for the welfare of the general population.

By the tenth century, more Confucians were beginning to study the *Great Learning*, which spoke precisely to this predicament by insisting that political engagement was essential to the process of self-cultivation. It begins with a pithy sentence combining the two: 'The Way of the *Great Learning* lies in illuminating virtue, treating the people with affection, and resting in perfect goodness [*ren*].'[106] You acquire a clear, luminous character not by retiring from the world but by loving the people and making *ren* ('human-heartedness') the foundation of your life.[107] Like a tree, rooted in the mysterious earth, the man of *ren* aspires to Heaven but, at the same time, he reaches out compassionately to the people.[108] Five terse paragraphs set out this programme. It was essential to establish clear priorities: 'Knowing what to put first and what to put last, one comes near to the Way.'[109] The 'elders' – Yao, Shun, Yu and the duke of Zhou – had begun by ensuring that all was well in their own families, but to achieve that, they had to reform their own minds and hearts. This involved *gewu* ('the investigation of things'), the extension of their knowledge of the Way of Heaven, which, of course, since Heaven permeated all things, included an understanding of earthly affairs. The *Great Learning*, therefore, prescribed an eightfold programme that began with individual self-cultivation but ended with the establishment of world peace:

It is only when things are investigated that knowledge is extended; when knowledge is extended, that thoughts become sincere; when thoughts become sincere that the mind is rectified; when the mind is rectified that the person is cultivated; when the person is cultivated that order is brought to the family; when order is brought to the family that the state is well governed; when the state is well governed, that peace is brought to the world.[110]

This was not simply a project for the ruling class. Everybody – 'from the Son of Heaven to the ordinary people' – had a responsibility to cultivate *ren*, which was the 'root' and 'foundation' of the world: 'It can never happen that the root is disordered and the branches are ordered.' Unless the ruler and his people cultivated their humanity assiduously together, the entire political edifice would remain corrupt and anarchic.

Han Yu had also recommended another chapter of the *Rites*, known as the *Doctrine of the Mean* (*Zhongyong*), a more psychological, metaphysical and mystical text, which Confucius was said to have transmitted to his grandson Zisi, who passed it on to Mencius.[111] *Zhong* ('moderation') is a state of equilibrium, it taught, in which such emotions as pleasure, anger, sorrow and joy are held in perfect balance:

> When these feelings are aroused and each and all attain due measure and degree, it is called harmony [*he*]. When equilibrium and harmony are realised in the highest degree, Heaven and Earth will attain their proper order and all things will flourish.[112]

The rule established by the Sage Kings and the early Zhou followed the pattern of Nature or Heaven – the Way of Heaven-and-Earth – in which 'all things are produced and developed without injuring one another. The courses of the seasons, the sun and moon, are pursued without conflict.'[113] This must be reproduced in political life, because the Way of Heaven-and-Earth is also the Way of human beings. It is essential to our very nature – it 'cannot be separated from us for a moment' – so we can and must develop the stability and harmony we see in Nature in our own lives and refrain from damaging one another.[114] Unlike Buddhist nirvana, this requires no extraordinary effort; indeed, the word *yong* in the chapter title means 'ordinary'. Following the Way is simply a matter of doing normal things – such as eating, drinking and conversing – correctly, making ourselves aware of the importance of these mundane activities at every moment of the day.

Self-cultivation, therefore, consists of the sanctification of daily life. Rulers, subjects and even the *min* ('little people') must observe the rites of family, public and private life, being 'reverent to strangers from far countries', trustworthy to friends and obedient to parents. The Way of

Heaven-and-Earth requires us to be scrupulously honest with ourselves, behaving decently, kindly and respectfully to all.[115] The Way is manifest in the cosmic order, so we must study it extensively, enquire into it accurately and practise it so earnestly that it becomes second nature to us.[116] It will not make us extraordinary; instead, the objective is *cheng*, 'authenticity' or 'sincerity'. We simply perfect our nature, becoming our most complete selves:

> Sincerity is the Way of Heaven. To think how to be sincere is the way of man. He who is sincere is one who hits upon what is right without effort and apprehends without thinking. He is naturally and easily in harmony with the Way. Such a man is a sage. He who tries to be sincere is one who chooses the good and holds on to it.[117]

Sagehood was not an exceptional state: Mencius and Xunzi had both insisted that it was possible for everybody, even the *min*.

Whereas Daoists and Buddhists sought enlightenment by withdrawing from society, the *Mean*, like Confucius, insisted that we need each other to achieve full humanity. You cannot perfect yourself without, at the same time, working for the perfection of all other beings: 'Sincerity is not only the completion of one's own self, it is that by which all things are completed. The completion of the self means humanity [*ren*].'[118] *Cheng* is, therefore, an active force that enables us to cooperate with Heaven-and-Earth, by perfecting each other and transforming the world:

> Only those who are absolutely sincere can fully develop their nature. If they can fully develop their nature, then they can fully develop the nature of others, they can then fully develop the nature of things, they can then assist in the transforming and nourishing of Heaven and Earth. They can thus form a trinity with Heaven and Earth.[119]

Yong also means that which is universal: so, while the word *zhong* in the title refers to ordinary human nature, *yong* directs us to humanity's partnership with the sacred forces of Heaven-and-Earth and the essential unity of humanity and divinity.

These two scriptures were crucial to the eleventh-century Confucian reformers in northern China. Zhou Dunyi (1017–73), however, was first inspired by the *Changes*, which he believed was 'the source of the Five Classics ... the deep and dark abode of Heaven, Earth and Spiritual beings'.[120] He argued that the hexagrams had enabled Confucius to 'form a trinity with Heaven-and-Earth and become equal to the Four Seasons'.[121] Zhou was so deeply aware of his intimate relationship with all things that, it was said, he refused to cut the grass that grew under his window. Zhang Zai (1020–77) expressed his vision of the fundamental unity and equity of things in the 'Western Inscription' ('Ximing'), so called because it was inscribed on the western wall of his study:

> Heaven is my father and Earth is my mother, and even such a small creature as I finds an intimate place in their midst.
>
> Therefore, that which extends through the universe I regard as my body and that which directs the universe I consider as my nature.
>
> All people are my brothers and sisters, and all things are my companions.
>
> The great ruler [the emperor] is the eldest son of my parents [Heaven and Earth], and the great ministers are his stewards. Respect the aged – this is the way to treat them as elders should be treated. Show affection toward the orphaned and weak – this is the way to treat them as the young should be treated ... Even those who are tired and infirm, crippled and sick, those who have no brothers or sisters, wives or husbands, are all my brothers who are in distress and have no one to turn to.

This vision of the unity of all things was, therefore, an imperative to compassionate action. The 'Western Inscription' ends: 'In life, I follow and serve [Heaven and Earth]. In death, I will be at peace.'[122]

Zhang Zai was the uncle and teacher of the Cheng brothers. 'When they were fourteen or fifteen,' he recalled later, 'the two Chengs were already free [from wrong ideas] and wanted to learn to be sages.'[123] They were convinced that the 'Western Inscription' recorded a lost teaching of Confucius and that sagehood was not confined to the ancient past but could be achieved by anybody in the present. Cheng Yi (1033–1108) wrote of his elder brother Cheng Hao (1032–85) that after studying with Zhang Zai, he gave up his preparation for the Civil Service examinations and for ten years drifted between Daoism and Buddhism before returning to the Classics.[124] After long and deep study, Cheng Hao concluded that the vision of the 'oneness of all things' was essential to the achievement and practice of *ren*, which made him one with Nature: 'The man of *ren* takes Heaven and Earth as being one with himself; to him there is nothing that is not himself. Having recognised them as himself, what can he not do for them?'[125]

We have seen that the state curriculum, consisting of the five Confucian Classics, had marginalised the spirituality of Confucius and Mencius and, by encouraging an 'exam mentality', it had meant that the Classics were approached in a pragmatic spirit. Cheng Yi presented his brother's discovery as the heroic recovery of this lost tradition. After Mencius, he argued, the learning of the great sages had been lost, so Cheng Hao 'took it as his own responsibility to restore the cultural tradition':

> Since the Way has not been illuminated, perverse and strange doctrines have arisen in rivalry, have thrown mud at the eyes and ears of the people, and have submerged the world in dirt. Even people of great ability and bright intelligence have been tarnished by what they see and hear ... All this forms clusters of overgrowth and weeds in the correct path and an obstruction to the gate of the sage. We must clear them away before people can enter the Way.[126]

After 1,400 years, therefore, the Way had been rediscovered and must now be defended strenuously in this decadent and dangerous period of history. Regardless of what the Han teachers had taught, sagehood was possible for everybody: 'In the way of learning, the first thing is to know where to go and then act vigorously in order that they may arrive at sagehood.'[127]

The Chengs called their philosophy *Daoxue* ('Dao learning') and it had immediate appeal for those literati who longed for a more spiritual interpretation of their tradition. The response was extraordinary: 'Those engaged in learning shouldered satchels and hiked up their garments [in hurrying] to personally receive their instructions, spreading it to the four directions. Some in secret, some openly – none can exhaust the record!'[128] There was exuberance, excitement and hope. Cheng Yi claimed that his doctrine of 'principle' (*li*), which was very different from that of the political reformers, was the lost teaching of the sages. It had been expressed in a concise sixteen-character statement attributed to Yao and Shun in *Documents*: 'The human mind is precarious; the Dao mind is stable. Be discriminating, be undivided, that you may sincerely hold fast to the *Mean*!'[129]

The neo-Confucians believed that we all have two minds: our human mind and the mind of Heaven with which we were all endowed at birth. Our heavenly mind embodies the *li*, the heavenly principle, and the Way we ought to be. As the *Mean* explained:

> What Heaven imparts to man is called human nature. To follow our nature is called the Way. Cultivating the Way is called education. The Way cannot be separated from us for a moment.[130]

It is tempting to equate these two minds with the left and right hemispheres of the brain. The Chengs urged their pupils to control what we would call the busy left hemisphere and achieve the vision of the unity and interconnectedness of the Dao mind, resident in the right hemisphere, which inspired the 'Western Inscription'. Our human mind is 'precarious': our selfish desires, prejudices and instability constantly separate us from our Dao mind, so we must control it, uniting it to our heavenly Dao mind by means of *jing* ('attentiveness' or 'reverence'). 'I've been troubled by unsettled thoughts,' Su Jiming, a member of the Cheng circle, confessed. 'At times, before I think through one matter, other matters occur to me, entangled like hemp fibres. What's to be done?' 'This must be avoided; it is the source of disintegration. You must practice,' Cheng Yi replied. 'When practicing, you become capable of concentrating, things will be all right. Whether in thought or action, you must always seek unity.'[131]

A *jing* mind is unified and whole, and to be *jing*, one must be always in the moment. Whatever you are doing – serving a parent, washing, doing calligraphy, eating or enjoying the scenery – *jing* requires us to control our errant human mind and focus on this task to the exclusion of all else. Certain physical practices can help us to acquire this attentiveness. Cheng Yi advised his students 'to be orderly and solemn', 'control your countenance', 'regulate your dress and dignify your gaze'.[132] In the Chinese tradition, where there is no body/mind divide, our physical demeanour helps us to develop spiritual states. 'To be dignified and grave is not the way of inner mental attentiveness,' Cheng Yi explained, 'but to practise *jing* you must begin here.'[133] The body, therefore, can guide and sustain the mind until it is finally emptied of selfishness and can reflect the Dao in the same way as still water mirrors the sky.

The Chengs developed Zhang Zai's vision of the unity and equity of all things. As Cheng Hao insisted in his book *On Understanding Ren*: 'A person of *ren* is undifferentiatedly the same body [*tongti*] together with all things.'[134] Empathy, we have seen, is a product of the right hemisphere of the brain, which is profoundly attuned to the Other and sees all reality as deeply interconnected. Because we form 'one body' with all other beings, we should feel their suffering as our own, just as we respond immediately to pain or an itch in our own bodies: 'Not to feel disinterested sympathy with others is to lose the consciousness that they are one substance with myself.'[135] Once aware of your unity with Heaven-and-Earth and all things, Chang Hao insisted, you have 'no mind [of your own]'.[136] This was different from Buddhist *anatta* ('no mind'), which denies the stable existence of the human mind. Chang Hao taught his students to empty their minds of selfishness so that they could be filled with the mind of Heaven-and-Earth. This was achieved by constant moral effort and by *jing*, which also implies 'reverence', a profound sense of religious awe. We cultivate it by *gewu*, the 'investigation of things', a deep study of the 'principle' of Heaven that exists in all its manifestations, since Heaven speaks to us through its creatures.[137] As Cheng Yi explained, *gewu* required you to look beneath the surface:

> In each thing, there is a manifestation of principle — it is necessary to probe principle to the utmost. There are many ways of probing principle — the study of books, and the explanation of moral principles in them; the discussion of prominent figures, past and present, and distinguishing what is right and wrong in their actions; handling practical affairs and managing them appropriately. All are ways of probing principle.[138]

For Cheng Yi, it also meant a deep study of the natural world: 'every blade of grass and every tree possesses principle and should be examined'.[139]

The 'study of books' was a crucial activity in the Cheng circle.[140] The Classics were essential to this quest, but the Chengs believed that the way they were read in the state syllabus completely distorted them. Instead of soullessly memorising these texts to pass examinations, students must 'savour' them, probe their original meaning, and see how they speak to us here and now. When Cheng Hao taught the *Odes*, he didn't analyse them intellectually, one of his students explained, he just 'savours them in a carefree way, intoning them high and low, and thus brings it about that people get something from it'.[141] The Chengs compared the 'taste' and 'flavour' of the text to a sensuous experience in the mouth. Their performance of the scriptures reunited the written text with the living voice, especially when they were studying the *Analects* because it recreated and continued the discussions that Confucius had begun with his disciples. Cheng Yi explained:

> Just take the sage's words and savour them for a while, then naturally there will be something gained. You ought to look deeply in the *Analects*, taking the disciples' questions as your own questions and the sage's answers as what your ears have heard today, then naturally you will get something out of it. If Confucius or Mencius were alive today, they would not go beyond this in reaching people.[142]

Learning must be a communal rather than a solitary experience, because students were learning how to be people of *ren*, who did not set themselves apart but were one with each other.

Above all, the study of scripture must be transformative. 'If after studying the *Analects*, one is still just the same old person as before,' said Cheng Yi, 'that's to have never studied it.'[143] It was essential that 'the study of books' be integrated with the 'investigation of things' in the natural world in a steady, cumulative process. 'One must investigate an item today and another tomorrow,' he explained. 'When one has accumulated much knowledge, he will naturally achieve a thorough understanding, like a sudden release.'[144] After a long period of intensive study, there would come a moment of insight when everything suddenly fell into place. Unlike Buddhist enlightenment, which went beyond thought and feeling, the neo-Confucians found it impossible to separate moral, intellectual and emotional insight. Even for a rationalist like Cheng Yi, the study of scripture had physical resonance:

> In reading the *Analects* and *Mencius*, do so thoroughly and get the real taste of them. Apply the words of the sage to yourself earnestly. Do not treat them as so many words ... There are people who have read the *Analects* without having anything happen to them. There are others who are happy after having understood a sentence or two. There are still others who, having read the book, unconsciously dance with their hands and feet.

To further this process, the Chengs introduced the habit of 'quiet-sitting' (*jingzuo*), adapted from Chan and Daoist meditation as a more relaxed form of yoga. It did not require sitting in the lotus position; the goal was simply to empty the restless human mind as part of the daily, hourly practice of *jing*.[145] One of his students said that when Cheng Hao sat still in this way, 'he was like an earthen statue, but when he associated with people he was completely a sphere of peaceful disposition'.[146] The Chengs taught chiefly by example. It was said of Cheng Hao that 'He would not do to others what he did not wish others to do to him':[147]

> His self-cultivation was so complete that he was thoroughly imbued with the spirit of peacefulness, which was revealed in his voice and countenance. However, as one looked at him, he was so lofty and deep that none could treat him with disrespect.[148]

Cheng Hao so thoroughly embodied the scriptures that he had become their living, walking reality.

*

After the fall of the western provinces of the Roman empire, Europe was constantly attacked by Norsemen, Magyars and pirates, and its monasteries became often the only islands of stability. In the early fifth century, John Cassian (*c.*360–435) had founded monastic communities in southern France, introducing Western Christians to Origen's method of exegesis and the spirituality of the Desert Monks, based on the memorisation and constant repetition of biblical texts. The Egyptian monks had called this *mneme theou* ('the memory of God'), but, as the medieval scholar Mary Carruthers has explained, *memoria* was not simply the recollection of past events but implied creativity and invention.[149] Once scripture had been learned by heart, it became the base on which you crafted new ideas of your own. This violates our modern scholarly preoccupation with objectivity and respect for the integrity of an ancient text. In the premodern world, it was not only permissible but essential to make ancient writings say something new; as we have seen, the goal was not fidelity to the past but edification for the future.

In a passage that became crucial to Western hermeneutics, Paul had compared himself to an architect:

> I laid the foundations, on which someone else is doing the building. Everyone doing the building must work carefully. For the foundation, nobody can lay any other than the one which has already been laid, that is Jesus Christ. On this foundation, you can build in gold, silver and jewels, or in wood, grass or straw.[150]

Paul had laid the foundations, but others would complete the building, using materials of their choice. 'Didn't you realise', he asked the Corinthians, 'that *you* were God's temple and that the Spirit of God was living among you?'[151] We have seen that in all traditions, the aim of scriptural study was personal transformation. Paul was reminding his converts that they were not constructing an edifice of orthodox doctrines and practices: they *were* the building. Each one of them was developing the Spirit of Christ within themself, and in this quintessentially personal project there could be no set rules incumbent upon everybody. A Christian must improvise, each responding to their unique circumstances. The foundation laid by Paul was only the beginning; it must not be confused with the final structure.

Pope Gregory the Great (c.540–604) referred to Paul's metaphor in his explanation of Origen's three 'senses' of scripture – literal, moral (or typological) and allegorical.

> First, we put in place the foundations of literal meaning [*historia*]; then through typological interpretation, we build up the fabric of our mind in the walled city of faith; and, at the end, through the grace of our moral understanding, as though with added colour, we clothe the building.[152]

The literal sense of scripture was simply the foundation. Its efficacy lay in the creative use we make of it in the 'fabrication' and 'colour' we add during the process of our personal edification. Gregory regarded the historical books of the Bible as the 'foundation' of scripture, but he had little interest in their factual content. The purpose of scripture was not to instruct us in the history of Israel or the life of the early church but to effect a radical change within ourselves: 'We ought to transform what we read within our very selves, so that when our mind is stirred by what it hears, our life may concur by practising what has been heard.'[153] Unless and until our interpretation of scripture resulted in a major life change, it was incomplete. Scripture was a mirror, in which we see both our ugliness and beauty: 'There we know how much we have gained, there how far we lie from our goal.'[154] Its purpose was not to teach us about God's work in the past but to spur our own quest for holiness in the present. Peter Chrysologus, the fifth-century bishop of Ravenna, experienced scripture as a dynamic force that, once injected into our consciousness, set our minds and hearts ablaze: 'If we would only sow this grain of mustard-seed in our memories in such a way that it will grow into a great tree of knowledge ... Thus, it will burn for us with all the fire of its seed, and break into flame in our heart.'[155] Scripture must be so deeply internalised that it became part of oneself that changed our entire outlook.

In the West, the monastery was no longer a desert outpost, but a school for the education of youth. Benedict of Nursia (c.480–547) had composed his monastic rule when civil society in Italy seemed on the point of collapse. His aim was to create communities of obedience, stability and *religio* (which should be translated as 'reverence' or 'bonding'). His Rule provided *disciplina*, a set of physical rituals carefully designed to restructure emotion and generate an interior attitude of humility.[156] Later, Benedictine *disciplina* would appeal to Charlemagne (r.772–84), the Frankish king who restored order in northern Italy, Gaul and central Europe and became the first 'Holy Roman Emperor'. He and his successors knew that they owed their achievements to highly disciplined troops and they promoted Benedictine monasticism throughout their domains to reform Europe in an educational curriculum based on scripture. Monasteries that signed up for the Carolingian reform were all presented with lavish lectern Bibles, although they bore no resemblance to the Bible as we know it.[157] They consisted of biblical excerpts arranged for use in the monastic liturgy and the performance of the Divine Office – *Opus Dei*, the 'Work of God' – which was central to the Carolingian educational reform.[158]

In the Divine Office, which punctuated the monastic day, Benedictines chanted the entire book of Psalms, interspersed with scriptural readings, every week. Of special importance was the Night Office, in which the whole biblical canon was supposed to be recited each year, but, as the English reformer Aelfric confessed, 'because we are lazy and slothful servants' the Bible also had to be read during meals to meet this requirement.[159] This performance of scripture was not, as has sometimes been claimed, a mechanical exercise. In his Rule, Benedict had explained:

> We believe that the divine presence is everywhere, and that in every place the eyes of the Lord are watching the good and the wicked. But beyond the least doubt, we should believe this to be especially true when we celebrate the Divine Office. Let us consider then how we ought to behave in the presence of God and his angels, and let us stand to sing the psalms in such a way that our minds are in harmony with our voices.[160]

The Office, Benedict insisted, was a monk's chief occupation.[161] Monks soon came to know the entire psalter by heart and the rhythms of the Gregorian chant gave the psalms and anthems an emotional timbre that enhanced their semantic meaning.[162] As in the chanting of an Indian mantra, the monotony and regular rhythm of the chant restricted the rational consciousness of the left hemisphere of the brain, enabling a more intuitive mode of consciousness. But unlike India, where the meaning of the mantra was unimportant, Western monasticism never rejected the semantic meaning of the psalms; the aim was to go beyond the rational to a deeper, primordial understanding of the scriptural words.[163]

The monks also dramatised the biblical stories. During Lent, they walked in procession, covered in ashes, contemplating Jesus' forty days in the desert; and on Palm Sunday, they re-enacted Jesus' fateful entry into Jerusalem. During the vigil on Easter Saturday night, the laity were invited into the monastic church to participate in a ritual that made the meaning of the resurrection clear to them by dramatic alternations of light and darkness, silence and exuberant music. The *Regularis Concordia* (the 'Monastic Agreement') composed in England in 973 emphasised its importance for the laity in 'setting forth clearly both the terror of the darkness, which, at our Lord's Passion struck the tripartite world with unwonted fear, and the consolation of that apostolic preaching which revealed to the whole world Christ obedient to his Father even unto death'.[164] On Easter Sunday morning, monks enacted for the laity the women's discovery of the empty tomb and their meeting with the angel who told them that Jesus had risen. Monks made the Bible a living reality for the laity in rituals and gestures that were probably their chief link with scripture.[165] Of special importance was their re-enactment of Jesus' washing of his disciples' feet the night before his death. In some monasteries, the entire community took it in turns to wash the feet of the poor throughout the year and the Rule also instructed them to wash the feet of their guests, as if they were Christ himself.[166]

A monk spent two to three hours each day in *lectio divina* ('divine study').[167] He would imagine himself standing beside Moses on Sinai or at the foot of Jesus' Cross.[168] Instead of simply running his eyes over the page, he would mouth the words, murmuring them subvocally, a practice recommended by classical rhetoricians as an aid to memorisation. Monks compared *lectio divina* to a cow's rumination – a metaphor possibly suggested by the 'chewing' movement of the mouth.[169] Memory was the stomach and scripture the sweet-smelling cud that, ingested, became a part of himself and, when required, could be recalled from the stomach to the palate and spoken aloud.[170] The text, therefore, became integral to the monk. A good monk, wrote a twelfth-century abbot, will 'devour and digest the holy books ... because their memory does not let go of the rules of life'.[171] The whisper of *lectio* became the voice of meditation – rather as the bridegroom in the Song of Songs summoned his spouse in a low voice (*sono depresso*) or the divine voice spoke to Elijah in the whispering breath of a gentle wind.[172]

Meditation also had a vigour and urgency that was suspenseful, purposeful and focused, giving the peaceful rumination a forward, practical momentum.[173] This required *intentio* ('concentration'), in which the monk fastened on every word of scripture. Augustine recalled that his mentor, Bishop Ambrose of Milan, read silently while his 'recollecting mind cracked

open [*rimabatur*] the sense', breaking each word to pieces until he had
exhausted its potential before storing it away in his memory.[174] Because, as
Augustine had insisted, scripture taught nothing but charity, during his
meditation a monk deliberately turned his *intentio* away from ego towards
his fellow human beings.[175] *Intentio*, therefore, expressed the dynamism of
the scriptural art, which is not complete unless it drives the practitioner
to work energetically for a more altruistic and compassionate world.

But the monasteries also fostered biblical scholarship. At this date, each
book of the Bible was presented in individual manuscripts, prefaced by a
commentary by one of the Fathers of the church, whose interpretations
often differed. During the twelfth century, therefore, some French monks
tried to devise a standard set of commentaries. Anselm of Laon (d. 1117)
interpreted the Psalms, Paul's letters and John's gospel; his brother Ralph
(d. 1133) glossed Matthew; while his pupil, Gilbert of Auxerre (d. 1144),
tackled Jeremiah's Lamentations and the twelve minor prophets. All followed
the same method: brief explanations were inserted between the lines
of the biblical text with a more extended commentary in the margins. The
formula became so popular in the monastic schools that it was known as
Glossa Ordinaria ('the Ordinary Gloss').

At the Abbey of St Victor in Paris, exegesis became more adventurous
and forward-looking. Hugh of St Victor (d. 1141), who added a fourth 'sense'
of scripture to Origen's three, defined meditation as 'the ability of a keen
and curious mind to explore the obscurities and perplexities that we find
in scripture'.[176] One began with an intensive study of the *littera*, the literal
sense, which included the study of grammar and rhetoric, but at this point,
a student should also apply the spiritual sense, *allegoria*, because events in
the Old Testament foreshadowed those in the New. He would thus learn
that the present contained the seeds of things to come. Next came the
moral or tropological sense, when he would discover what this scripture
meant for him personally. Finally, in meditation, he developed the *intentio*
that impelled him to the compassionate action in the present that would
create a better future.[177]

Meanwhile, the Jewish communities of northern France were developing
an entirely different form of exegesis. Rabbi Shlomo Yitzhak (d. 1105),
known as Rashi, had abandoned *midrash* and focused entirely on the literal
sense of scripture, dwelling on individual words which, when scrutinised,
raised fresh questions.[178] *Bereshit* (the first word of Genesis), could mean
'In the beginning *of*', so the sentence could read: 'In the beginning of God's
creation of Heaven and Earth, the Earth was a formless void [*tohu vabohu*].'

Did this mean that the raw materials of the world were already in existence? An alternative reading of *bereshit* was 'Because of the beginning', and
in the Bible, Israel and the Torah were also called *bereshit*. Could we, therefore, infer that God had created the world specifically to give Israel the
Torah? Rashi's successors were more radical. Joseph Karo (d.1130) argued
that an interpreter who departed from the plain text was like a drowning
man clutching at a straw, and Joseph Bekhar Shor made a point of finding
a natural explanation for biblical signs and wonders. Lot's wife was simply
enveloped by lava issuing from the volcanic explosion that destroyed Sodom
and Gomorrah; Joseph had dreamed of future greatness because he was an
ambitious young man, and anybody with a modicum of intelligence could
have interpreted Pharaoh's dreams.

This strictly literal approach intrigued Andrew of St Victor (1110–75),
Hugh's most gifted pupil, who became the first Christian scholar to attempt
a wholly literal interpretation of the Bible.[179] Andrew had nothing against
allegory but it simply did not interest him, so, like Rashi, he focused on
semantics and the geographical or historical factors that illuminated the
plain sense. He agreed with Rashi that Isaiah had predicted that a 'young
woman', not a virgin, would bear Immanu-El; did not even mention Jesus
in his commentary on the Song of Songs; and saw the Servant as a symbolic
representation of the entire people of Israel rather than a precursor of
Christ. Instead of regarding Ezekiel's vision of one 'like the son of man' as
a prophecy of the incarnation, Andrew simply wondered what the Judabite
exiles had made of this peculiar vision.

Something was happening to Western spirituality. *Lectio divina* was still
essential to the spiritual life of Anselm of Bec (1033–1109), yet he also
developed the famous ontological proof, which had nothing to do with
scripture, but relied on the new metaphysics that were becoming fashion-
able in Europe. Anselm defined God as 'that thing than which nothing more
perfect can be thought' ('*aliquid quo nihil maius cogitari possit*').[180] Not only
had this no basis in scripture, but it called God a 'thing', a being whose
existence was capable of left-hemispheric proof. Anselm wrote no commentary on scripture and in his theological writings he simply used the Bible
to support his own ideas – an early instance, perhaps, of 'proof-texting'.[181]
Most notably, in *Why Did God Become Man?* Anselm used biblical texts to
support a wholly logical rationale for the incarnation and crucifixion: Adam's
sin required atonement; because God was just, a human being must atone;
but because the original sin was so grave, only God could make reparation.
If he wanted to save the world, therefore, God had to become man. The

logic was impeccable but it was bad theology, because Anselm was making 'God' think and reason like a human being.

Augustine's doctrine of original sin did not yet loom large in Western spirituality, but Anselm's prayers showed what might happen if it did:

> Alas, I am indeed wretched, one of those wretched sons of Eve, separated from God! What have I begun, and what accomplished? ... I sought after goodness, and lo, here is turmoil; I was going towards God, and I was my own impediment. I sought for peace within myself, and in the depths of my heart I found trouble and sorrow.[182]

The emphasis on the first-person pronoun is striking; his conviction of inherited guilt seems to have embedded Anselm in the ego he should be trying to transcend. Instead of his *intentio* impelling him kenotically to compassion for others, it was driving Anselm back into himself in a way that would become all too common in Western Christianity.

INEFFABILITY

The rationalism of Rashi, Andrew and Ambrose signalled a change in the spirituality of Europe, which was beginning its lengthy transition from an agrarian to a capitalist economy fuelled by critical and empirical thinking. Already, traditional social structures were being undermined. As cities became centres of prosperity, power and creativity, bankers and financiers of humble birth became rich at the expense of the aristocracy, while some townsfolk were reduced to abject poverty.[1] Rich and poor lived in such proximity that the disparity was becoming intolerable. The conditions of peasants had also gravely deteriorated. A few had migrated to the towns and become rich but landless villagers roamed the countryside desperately seeking employment.[2]

Although nearly all the scriptures we have discussed insist on social justice and concern for the 'little people', there had always been a limit to the extent that this could be implemented in an agrarian economy. The new capitalism would not improve matters. Love of money, in common use by the late eleventh century, was regarded as the 'root of all evil', and in popular iconography, the deadly sin of avarice inspired visceral loathing.[3] In this climate, the wealth of the aristocratic clergy, which violated the egalitarian ethic of the gospels, had become particularly offensive and was vehemently denounced by dissident groups condemned by the church as heretical. The followers of Valdes, a rich businessman of Lyons who had given all his wealth to the poor, held everything in common like the early Christians and, like Jesus' apostles, travelled from one town to another in pairs, barefoot and begging for their food. The Cathari, the 'Pure Ones', founded alternative churches dedicated to poverty, chastity and non-violence in the major cities of northern and central Italy, Languedoc and Provence.

In a bid to control the poverty movement, Pope Innocent III approved the Order of Friars Minor founded by Francis of Assisi (c. 1 1 8 1 – 1 2 2 6), the son of a well-to-do merchant who had renounced his patrimony after a serious illness. He and his followers dedicated themselves to the service of the poor in the cities, and their early Rule consisted almost entirely of biblical quotations. As his biographer Thomas of Celano explained, Francis's spirituality was based on *lectio divina*:

> Whenever he read the Sacred Books, and something was once tossed into his mind, he indelibly wrote it on his heart. He had a memory for [whole] books because having heard something once he took it in not idly, but with continued devout attentions, his emotion-memory [*affectus*] chewed on it. This, he said, was the fruitful method for teaching and reading, not to have wandered about through a thousand learned discussions.[4]

As we have seen, monastic meditation on scripture concluded with a focused *intentio* towards charity. While Benedictines had invited laypeople into the monastery, a haven of *stabilitas* and *caritas* in a violent, unstable world, Francis's meditations on the Gospel drove him to the turbulent cities. In the same spirit, Dominic Guzman (1170–1221) and his Order of Preachers took the Gospel to the people of southern France and Spain.

From the start, the Dominicans knew that they needed sound biblical knowledge to counter the Cathars' arguments, but the Franciscans also came to realise that, if they did not want to be regarded as the 'counterfeit apostles' and 'false prophets' denounced in the New Testament,[5] they needed a different kind of discourse. Many of the church's teachings were not grounded in scripture: how could the friars explain this discrepancy? How could they harmonise the teachings of the Fathers, which were so often contradictory? *Lectio divina* was no help here; instead, the friars decided that they needed what the French philosopher Peter Abelard (1079–1142) had called *theologia*, a 'discourse about God' that required a more analytical approach to religious truth and was supported by logically compelling arguments.[6] The Friars became a major force in the new 'universities', so called because they were seeking a universal conception of truth that integrated many different fields of knowledge. The Friars began to apply their new skills to the Bible, composing *postillae*, line-by-line commentaries that covered topics not included in the *Glossa Ordinaria*, and, drawing on the work of Rashi and Andrew of St Victor, they tried to establish a more accurate edition of Jerome's Vulgate. They also attempted to integrate the traditional monastic curriculum with the new scientific disciplines that scholars had brought back from Muslim Spain.[7]

Since the tenth century, European scholars had been travelling to Cordova to study with the mullahs and here they encountered the medicine, mathematics and science of ancient Greece that had been lost to Europe during the Dark Ages. Muslims had translated Greek texts into Arabic during the eighth and ninth centuries and their study of Aristotle had inspired some Muslims to develop a new Islamic tradition that they called *falsafah*. Roughly translated as 'philosophy', it was really an entire way of life. The *faylasufs* wanted to live in accordance with the rational laws that, they believed, governed the cosmos, integrating their scientific knowledge with Quranic teaching. There were conflicts, of course: Aristotelian science contradicted the Quranic doctrine of creation *ex nihilo*, but the *faylasufs* did not despise the traditional view. Both scripture and science, they believed, were valid paths to God, because they served the needs of different people. But *falsafah* was more developed because it purged the idea of God of anthropomorphism. The distinguished *faylasuf* Abu Ali ibn Sina (*c*.980–1037), known in the West as Avicenna, came to a very different conclusion from his contemporary Anselm of Bec, arguing that the Divine Unity meant that Allah was perfectly simple, and had, therefore, no attributes distinct from his essence, so analytic reason had absolutely nothing to say about him.

European Christians, who encountered Aristotle through the commentaries of devout, mystically inclined *faylasufs* like Avicenna, found it exhilarating. They translated Aristotle's works from Arabic into Latin, and by the early thirteenth century these were being studied in the universities of Paris, Bologna, Oxford and Cambridge, and gave Western Christians exactly what they were looking for. For the first time, they encountered an intellectual vision that embraced theology, cosmology, logic, ethics, physics, metaphysics and politics in a single system.[8] They now included moral and natural philosophy and metaphysics in the university curriculum. Oxford and Cambridge also introduced medicine, law and theology, training physicians to tend the sick, lawyers to administer justice, and pastors to teach the faith. Everything must be brought under the sacred canopy of the divine – and Aristotle showed that it was possible to integrate this new knowledge and demonstrate its truth rationally.

Some scholars, however, were wary of Aristotelian science, which maintained that the universe had always existed and had simply been set in motion by the Prime Mover, which Aristotle equated with 'God'. But during the mid-thirteenth century, Bonaventure of Fidanza (1221–74), a Franciscan, and the Dominican scholar Thomas Aquinas (1225–74) effectively baptised Aristotle. Thomas understood the challenge of Aristotelianism, and in his treatise *On the Science of Holy Scripture* he argued that theology could become a rational, Aristotelian science – but with a difference. For Aristotle, scientific knowledge started with general first principles from which all other truths could be logically deduced. But the biblical revelation, based on stories and events, focused on particulars instead of universals. The exegete could either regard biblical events as signifying universal truths or conclude that theology was a form of wisdom but not a science. Thomas chose the first option, adding the new rational science of *theologia* to the traditional four 'senses' of scripture. The meaning of the inspired words provided the *literal* sense of scripture, and the realities to which they pointed yielded the *spiritual* sense, which must always be grounded in the literal.

Aristotle had defined God as the 'First Mover'; for Thomas, God was the 'First Author' of the Bible. The human authors, who had translated the divine Word into earthly speech, were God's instruments and God had, as it were, set them in motion too – though they were responsible only for the style and literary form of a text. The exegete could learn a great deal from the literal sense of scripture, which now included a rational study of biblical vocabulary and rhetoric. But unlike human authors who could communicate only with words, God could also orchestrate historical events. The *literal* sense of the Old Testament could be found in the words used by the biblical authors, but its *spiritual* meaning came to light only in such events as the Exodus or the institution of the Paschal Lamb, which prefigured the redemptive work of Christ.

But the exciting techniques of Aristotelian logic could take us only so far. Whenever a theologian made a statement about God, Thomas insisted, he must remember that his words were inherently and inescapably inadequate because what we called 'God' was transcendent – that is, it lay beyond our conceptual grasp. *Theologia*, literally 'speech about God', should therefore finally reduce both the speaker and his audience to silent awe. If the new science of *theologia* did not make it clear that the reality we call 'God' lay beyond the grasp of the human mind, its statements were idolatrous. At the very beginning of the *Summa Theologiae*, his magnum opus, Thomas listed, somewhat perfunctorily, five 'proofs' (or, as he preferred to call them, five 'ways') for the existence of a Prime Mover, an Efficient Cause, a Necessary Being, the Highest Excellence and the Intelligent Overseer, as demonstrated by Aristotle and the *faylasufs*. But no sooner had Thomas apparently settled the matter than he undermined the entire project, by pointing out that we did not know what we had proved. We had simply come up against an insoluble mystery:

> There is no proving that men and skies and rocks did not always exist, so it is well to remember this so that one does not try to prove what cannot be proved and give non-believers grounds for mockery and for thinking the reasons we give are our reasons for believing.[9]

Even scripture could tell us nothing about God – indeed, its task was to make us realise that God was unknowable. 'Man's utmost knowledge is to know that we do not know Him,' Thomas explained, 'for then alone do we know God truly when we believe that it is far above all that man can possibly think of God.'[10]

Even Jesus, God's supreme revelation, eluded us. Had not Paul insisted that the Christ was 'far above ... any name that can be named'? During his ascension to heaven, scripture said that Jesus was hidden in a cloud. When he left the world, therefore, the Word was concealed from us again in a realm beyond the reach of our intellect and would remain perpetually unknowable and unnameable.[11] Thomas's entire *oeuvre* can be read as an attempt to counter the tendency that we found in Anselm to domesticate transcendence. His long and, to a modern mind, tortuous analyses should be read as an intellectual ritual that leads his readers through a labyrinth of thought that culminates in a final *musterion* or *ekstasis*.[12] For Thomas, faith clearly did not mean uncritical belief. Meditation was a state of intense, aroused attention, which Thomas defined as *solicitudo* ('worry'). Like a dog worrying a bone, it arouses *curiositas*, which is not 'idle curiosity' but is better translated as 'carefulness' or 'attentive mindfulness', a state of intellectual arousal in which the emotions were also deeply involved.[13]

Thomas greatly revered and often quoted the writings of an anonymous sixth-century Greek theologian who had adopted the pseudonym Denys the Areopagite, St Paul's first Athenian convert.[14] Denys's work had been translated into Latin and influenced nearly every major Western theologian before the Reformation. The fact that so few people have even heard of him today may be a symptom of our current difficulties with religion. Denys made Christians sensitive to the limitations of language. He pointed out that in the Bible God was given fifty-two names.[15] He was called a rock and a warrior and compared with the sky and the sea. Because what we call 'God' was ubiquitous and continually poured itself into its creations, any one of these can tell us something about God. A rock, for example, spoke of God's stability and permanence – but it was clearly wrong to say that God *was* a rock. The more sophisticated names we give to God, such as Unity, Goodness, Trinity and the like, were more problematic and could even be dangerous, because they gave us the misleading impression that we know what God is like. But God is not 'good' in any way that we can understand and is unlike any kind of triad in our experience. Even though God has revealed these 'names' to us in the scriptures, we must remind ourselves that we have no idea what they mean.

The mythical language of scripture, Denys explained, supplies God 'with horses and chariots and provides him with delicately prepared banquets' as if he were a human being, so we can easily get into the habit of thinking of God as a being like ourselves, writ large, with appetites and opinions like our own. The Bible also tells us of 'God's fits of anger, His griefs, His various oaths, His moments of repentance, His curses, His wraths, and manifold and crooked reasons are given for His failure to fulfil promises'.[16] All this is so clearly inadequate that it should shock us into an appreciation of the inherent incompetence of more sophisticated theological speech.[17] When listening to the scriptures, we must attend critically to what is being said, realise that we are babbling incoherently, and fall into an embarrassed but reverent silence.

The next step is to repudiate these names, and in so doing, make an ascent from earthly modes of perception to the divine. Denying the physical names is easy, because God is clearly not a rock, a gentle breeze or a warrior. Nor is he anything like a human creator or artisan. But we must also deny God's more abstract names, because God is not Mind, Greatness, Power, Light, Life, Truth or even Goodness as we know it.[18] We certainly cannot say that God 'exists' because our experience of existence is based on limited and moribund beings rather than Being itself:

> God is known by knowledge and by unknowing; of Him there *is* understanding, reason, knowledge, touch, perception, opinion, imagination, name and many other things, but He is *not* understood, *nothing* can be said of him, he cannot be named. He is *not* one of the things that are; He is all things in everything and *nothing* in anything.[19]

This was not simply an arid conundrum orchestrated by the left hemisphere of the brain. Denys taught his Greek congregation to engage in this discipline during the Eucharist, when they were touched sensually and emotionally by the evocative music, drama and ritualised solemnity that transposed it into the intuitive world of the right brain. In such a context, Denys's practice could induce an *ekstasis* like that of the *brahmodya*.

In the medieval West, Denys's apophatic or 'silent' theology existed as a corrective counterpoint to Aristotelian *theologia*. Bonaventure, an Italian Franciscan who lectured in Paris at the same time as Thomas, also insisted that Christ, God's supreme revelation, did not make the divine any clearer. 'Take care', he warned, 'that you do not believe that you can understand the incomprehensible.'[20] The Word spoken by God in Christ and in scripture segued inexorably into unknowing, by leading us to the unknowable Father.[21] Revelation yielded no clarity but plunged us into obscurity. Instead of presenting Jesus' death as a logical necessity, like Anselm, Bonaventure argued that the crucifixion of the Word reflected the brokenness of all language about God. We too 'must die and enter into this darkness. Let us silence all our care and our imagining. Let us "pass out of this world to be with the Father"[22] ... For he who loves this death can see God, for it is absolutely true that man shall not see God and live.'[23] The language of scripture, Bonaventure insisted, always pointed beyond itself. Certainly, the natural sciences, logic and ethics could contribute to our understanding of the divine, but only if we recognised the limitations of *theologia* in an interior discipline that overturned our normal ways of thinking and seeing.

This was valuable – indeed essential – advice. Provided that the ineffability of God was safeguarded, Thomas and Bonaventure saw no incompatibility between scientific rationality and scripture. They had developed a scholastic theology modelled on scientific discourse, which insisted that *theologia* had logical coherence, was keenly analytic, and proceeded by relentless question-and-answer. But a generation after Thomas and Bonaventure, some Europeans were beginning to cultivate an exclusively left-hemispheric vision not only of the world but also of God. By this time, university students studied logic, mathematics and Aristotelian science before they began their theological studies, and when they arrived in the divinity school they were so well versed in scientific methodology that they tried to solve theological problems mathematically.[24] In England, the Franciscan theologian John Duns Scotus (1265–1308) was convinced, like Plato, that reason could prove anything and that it was possible to arrive at an adequate understanding of God by our natural reasoning powers. Thomas had claimed that while what we call 'God' must 'exist', we have no idea what the word 'exists' can mean in that context – and the same applied to any of the divine attributes.[25] But Scotus insisted that 'existence' had the same meaning, whether it applied to God, men, mountains, animals or trees. Thomas had regarded such thinking as potentially idolatrous, since if we assumed that God was a mere being, it was all too easy to project our own ideas onto him and create an idol in our own likeness. William of Ockham (c.1285–1349), another English Franciscan, also insisted that our doctrinal statements were literally true and should be subjected to stringent rational enquiry.

The medieval scholastics, however, failed to realise that scientifically acquired knowledge of the natural world is essentially different from knowledge derived from texts. It can proceed only through empirical observation, which tests its findings experimentally, and is de facto subject to constant revision.[26] As the scientific method developed in Europe, this would lead to tension in the future. Eventually, the great scientists of the seventeenth and eighteenth centuries would scornfully reject Aristotelian science, but, ironically, it was their academic grounding in Aristotelianism that enabled them to do this.[27]

*

Islamic mysticism focused entirely on the Quran. Jafar al-Sadiq (d.765), the great-great-great-grandson of the Prophet Muhammad, was revered by the Shiis as the true leader of the *ummah*, but he developed a form of mystical exegesis that was also crucial to Sufi mysticism. These meditational techniques enabled his disciples to intuit a hidden (*batin*) wisdom in every single Quranic verse – a spirituality that was not designed to replace but rather to supplement the literal exegesis of a scholar like Tabari. Jafar called the process *tawil* ('carrying back'), because the interpreter made himself able to hear the Quran as it was recited in the heavenly realm. Henri Corbin, the historian of Iranian Shiism, has compared it to musical polyphony: interpreters could hear the human Arabic words at the same time as they intuited the Quran's divine essence. By listening (*sama*) in this way, the exegete stilled his critical faculties and became aware of the numinous silence surrounding the words of scripture, acutely conscious now of the gulf that existed between our idea of God and the ineffable reality.[28]

Shiism was fuelled by an acute anxiety about Quranic transmission. Because the Quranic text was, as we have seen, problematic, Shiis believed that interpretation required a prophetic insight.[29] They claimed that Muhammad had imparted an esoteric knowledge (*ilm*) of the Quran to his cousin and son-in-law Ali; and that each of Ali's descendants had imparted this to his own son and successor. The leader of the *ummah* must have this special understanding of scripture to enable him to update the Quran, to make it speak to different times and circumstances.[30] Shiis argued that the Quran itself endorsed the necessity of the imamate in the verses addressed to the Prophet's family, the *ahl al-beit*, and in references to an imam who would guide the *ummah*.[31] In the mystical verse describing God as the light of the world, 'fuelled from the blessed olive tree', the olive was said to refer to the imams.[32] While ordinary Muslims could comprehend the clear and obvious meaning of the Quran, only the imams who had this special knowledge could discern the hidden meaning of each Quranic verse.[33]

After Jafar's death, there was a rift in the Shiah. Most Shiis revered a succession of twelve imams descended from Ali. As Abbasid power declined, the caliphs could not permit the imams to remain at large so the Tenth and Eleventh Imams were imprisoned and probably poisoned but the Twelfth Imam simply disappeared. It was said that he had been miraculously concealed by God – had gone into 'occultation' – and would return, shortly before the Final Judgement, to establish a rule of justice. Other Shiis, however, believed that Ali's line had ended with Ismail, Jafar's eldest son who had died before his father and, unlike the 'Twelvers', the 'Ismailis' did not accept the legitimacy of Jafar's second son.

Abu Yaqub al-Sijistani (d. 971), an important Ismaili thinker, was disturbed by the anthropomorphic language applied to God in the Quran, so he devised a dialectical exercise that, when put into practice, elicited a sense of the transcendent by making the reciter aware of the stumbling inadequacy of logos when it was applied to the divine. It began by talking about God in negative terms – God is non-being rather than being, not-ignorant rather than wise. But this left us with an arid abstraction, so we must deny the negation, saying that God was 'not-not ignorant' or 'not-not Nothing'.

Sufi *tawil* was less historically focused, but it too was rooted in the Quran. Sufis wanted to experience something of what the Prophet had felt when he had received the Quranic revelations so they looked for a hidden (*batin*) meaning in the Quranic verses that might throw light on Muhammad's interior state. Emphasising God's mercy and love rather than God's stern judgement, they devised practices that enabled everybody – not just a mystical elite – to experience an awareness of the transcendent. The most popular of these devotions was *dhikr*, the communal 'remembrance' of the divine presence achieved by chanting Allah's name like a mantra. The monotony and repetitive rhythm of the exercise together with the powerful physical reverberations of the chant, stilled rational habits of mind, making participants open to the more embodied mode of thought in the brain's right hemisphere. Posture and breathing were carefully monitored and participants were instructed to focus on a given part of the body as they exhaled and inhaled. *Sama* ('listening'), another important Sufi practice, used music and devotional song to cultivate this awareness.

The archetypal mythos of Islamic mysticism was the story of Muhammad's 'Night Journey' from Mecca to Jerusalem and his spiritual ascent to God's throne. This episode is referred to only allusively in the Quran,[34] but commentators greatly expanded it, so that it became an allegory of the return that we all must make to the Source whence we came. This required the 'annihilation' (*fana*) of the ego and its consequent 'revival' (*baqa*) when the mystic realised that he was inseparable from the divine. The early Sufi Abu Yazid al-Bistami (d. 874) described how he had to peel away one egotistic preoccupation after another until he seemed to merge with the divine presence that said to him: 'I am thine through thee; there is no God but Thou.'[35]

Sufis were criticised for ignoring the plain sense of the Quran but they responded by citing a Quranic verse in which God describes the complexity of scripture:

> Some of its verses are definite in meaning – these are the cornerstone of the Scripture – and others are ambiguous. The perverse at heart eagerly pursue the ambiguities in their attempt to make trouble and to pin down a specific meaning of their own: only God knows the true meaning. Those firmly grounded in knowledge say, 'We believe in it: it is all from our Lord' – only those with real perception will take heed.[36]

Because the Quran was God's speech, it was infinite and could not be confined to a single interpretation, so these 'ambiguous verses' could be grasped only by those 'firmly grounded in knowledge' who had 'real perception'.[37] When they recited the Quran, Sufis imagined themselves ascending from earth to heaven, as the Prophet had done when he transmitted the Quran in Mecca and Medina, when Gabriel, the angel of revelation, had recited it to him, and, finally, when he had heard it directly from God. As one Sufi explained:

> I used to read the Quran but found no sweetness in it until I recited it as if I were hearing the Messenger of God reciting it to his companions. Then I rose to a station above it and I recited it as if I was hearing Gabriel presenting

it to the Messenger of God. Then God brought me to another way station and now I hear it from the Speaker. Here I found from it a blessing and delight that I could not resist.[38]

The experience could be as devastating as it had been for the Prophet: like Muhammad, Jafar used to lose consciousness but, he explained, 'I kept repeating the verse in my heart until I heard it from the Speaker and my body was unable to stand firm.'[39]

Some Muslims objected to Sufi exegesis. Tabari argued that many of the 'ambiguous verses' were explained quite satisfactorily elsewhere in the Quran and that delving into obscurity could only cause discord.[40] The Persian scholar Fakhr al-Din ar-Razi (d. 1210) thought that exegetes should simply accept the most obvious reading of a difficult verse.[41] But Abu Hamid al-Ghazzali (d. 1111), the greatest theologian of his day, gave Sufism its imprimatur. By this time, Sufism had become a popular movement throughout the empire, attracting Muslims from every social class. The Sufi masters seem to have tapped an authentic and essential dynamic in the Quran. Ordinary folk now gathered for *dhikr* and revered their *pirs*, praying and holding *dhikr*s at their tombs. Each town now had a *khanqah* ('convent') where local people gathered for instruction. Sufi Orders (*tariqas*) were created, with branches all over the Muslim world. Al-Ghazzali realised that the Sufis' contemplative rituals helped people to develop an interior spir-ituality: 'those firmly grounded in knowledge', he said, were Muslims who engaged in the Sufi disciplines, which, if diligently observed, yielded a knowledge that transcended the conceptual. Sufism had become an unstop-pable force. Even its critics, such as the arch literalist Ahmed ibn Taymiyyah (d. 1328), were initiated into Sufi Orders. Until the nineteenth century, Sufi practices remained the chief lens through which Muslims experienced the Quran.

The Persian poet Jalal al-Din Rumi (c. 1207–73), founder of the Sufi Order popularly known as the 'Whirling Dervishes', made some of the more abstruse Sufi ideas accessible to ordinary Muslims. Known to his disciples as Mawlana ('Our Master'), his great poem, the *Masnawi*, suggested that, knowingly or not, everybody was searching for the absent God, obscurely aware that he or she was separated from the source of being.[42] The *Masnawi* challenged Muslims to look through the appearances of every-thing around them to discover the transcendence within. Did not the Quran urge them to regard all the elements of the natural world as 'signs' pointing to the divine? Rumi cited the Quran more frequently than any other Sufi poet and invariably clarified its meaning,[43] so much so that the *Masnawi* was said to be 'the Quran in Persian poetry'.[44] This was not a blasphemous statement. Commenting on a hadith in which the Prophet says, 'The Quran has an outer and an inner dimension and its inner dimension has seven layers', Rumi explained:

> There is an outer form to the Qur'an
>> Its inner is more powerful though, good man,
> And inside that there's even a third layer –
>> All intellects would lose themselves in there.
> The fourth layer inside none have seen at all
>> But God, Who's peerless and incomparable.[45]

Because its deepest meaning is known only to the illimitable God, the Quran constantly yields fresh meaning. Revelation was not confined to the distant past, therefore, but occurred whenever a Sufi opened themself to the sacred text.

This idea was central to the thought of the Spanish mystic and philosopher Muid ad-Din Ibn al-Arabi (d. 1240), who was convinced that everybody, not just a mystical or theological expert, should seek out the hidden meaning of scripture. 'The Quran is perpetually new for those who recite it,' he insisted; indeed, anyone who reads a Quranic verse in the same way twice had not understood it correctly.[46] Truly attentive Muslims will find fresh meaning in a Quranic verse every time they recite it, because they are hearing exactly what God intends for them at that precise moment.[47] Muslims must remember that God's Spirit was present in every recitation, so the Quran is not just a text but 'a divine attribute – and the attribute is inseparable from that which it qualifies. [When it] descends upon the heart, then He Whose Word the Quran Is descends with it.'[48] This applied not only to the Quran but to all the scriptures that had preceded it – the Torah, the Psalms, the Gospel and the Vedas.[49]

No interpretation of the Quran, therefore, could be exclusive. Anyone who recites a verse 'acquires a new judgement; with each reading he is the reciter who, in his own existence, follows God'.[50] Nobody should feel bound to accept anybody else's interpretation.[51] The Quran encourages everybody to seek out the deepest meanings of its verses (*ayat*), which, like the 'signs' (*ayat*) of nature, are 'signs for those who reflect'.[52] Some people, Ibn al-Arabi explained, break open the shell of a nut to find the richness of the kernel, while others are content with the shell – and that is God's will for them.[53] There must be no elitism or exclusivity, because the Quran is infinite – 'an ocean without a shore'.[54] But mysticism required careful thought – there could be no hazy sentimentality. Reason (*aql*) must always complement intuitive insight and the Quranic words must be understood correctly as they were in the Prophet's time.[55] A Muslim must aspire to *become* the Quran as the Prophet did: his wife Aisha said of him that 'His nature was the Quran.'[56]

As the *bismillah* emphasised at the beginning of each recitation, the Quran recorded the speech of a God of mercy. Unlike the jurists, who emphasised God's justice, Ibn al-Arabi repeatedly quoted the Sacred Hadith in which God says: 'My mercy takes precedence over my wrath.' Did not the Quran itself insist that God sent Muhammad as 'a mercy' to the world?[57] Ibn al-Arabi emphasised the divine mercy so forcefully that he even insisted that the sufferings of hell could not be permanent.[58] This insistence on the divine compassion lay behind his conviction that all faith traditions were equally valid:

> My heart is capable of every form:
> A cloister for the monk, a fane for idols,
> A pasture for gazelles, the votary's Kabah,
> The Tables of the Torah, the Koran.
> God is the faith I hold: wherever turn
> His camels, still the one true faith is mine.[59]

Sufism, which was becoming the dominant form of Islam, would develop an outstanding appreciation of other faiths.

But other Muslims could not share this generous view of other religious traditions. In July 1099, the Crusaders from Europe had descended upon Jerusalem, where Jews, Christians and Muslims had lived in reasonable harmony for over 400 years, and slaughtered some 30,000 people in three days. In Europe, the historian Robert the Monk made the extraordinary claim that the importance of this conquest was exceeded only by the creation of the world and the crucifixion.[60] Before the Crusade, most Europeans had known next to nothing about Islam; afterwards, Muslims were excoriated in the West as a 'vile and abominable race', 'despicable', 'degenerate and enslaved by demons'.[61] Yet despite the appalling massacre of 1099, there was no concerted Muslim offensive against the 'Franks' for over fifty years. The Crusaders who settled in the Levant established small kingdoms and principalities, and the local emirs, who went on fighting one another as usual for territory, had no qualms about making alliances with Frankish princes. Far from being programmed for holy war by their scripture, Muslims seemed to have had little appetite for a military jihad. Not until the arrival of the massive armies of the Second Crusade in 1148 did some of the emirs become uneasy. Even so, it took Nur ad-Din (d.1174) and Salah ad-Din (d.1193) a good forty years to create a popular enthusiasm for a religiously inspired war against the Franks. Jihad, which had been all but dead, was resurrected not by the inherent violence of the Quran but by a sustained assault from the West.[62]

At the same time as the Muslims of the Levant were fighting off the Crusaders, the Mongol armies were conquering vast swathes of Muslim territory in Mesopotamia, the Iranian mountains, the Syr-Oxus Basin and the Volga region, where they established four large states. Any ruler who failed to submit immediately saw his cities laid waste and his subjects massacred. Both Ibn Taymiyyah and Rumi were refugees who had fled their homes to escape the Mongol advance, which was finally checked by the Muslim Mamluk army at the Battle of Ain Jalut in Galilee in 1250.

It was during this fearful time that Muslim scholars began to interpret the Quranic verses on warfare more aggressively. Earlier exegetes, as we have seen, had insisted on the defensive nature of military combat. But, writing in Spain during the Christian Reconquista, which was bent on expelling Muslims from Iberia, Muhammad al-Qurtubi (d. 1278) argued that Quran 22:39–40, which pointed out that 'many monasteries, churches, synagogues and mosques' would have been destroyed had there not been a show of force, had abrogated all the verses ordering Muslims to make peace with their enemies. Fakhr ad-Din ar-Razi, however, argued that monasteries, churches and synagogues could not be considered places 'where God's name is much invoked', because God was worshipped correctly only in mosques. Again, the early exegetes had concluded that the charge in Quran 2:190–93 – 'Do not overstep the limits [la ta tadu]' – had put a brake on initiating hostilities and responding disproportionately to aggression. They had also ruled that these verses applied only to the unique circumstances of the extraordinary expedition when, it will be recalled, Muhammad had led a thousand virtually unarmed Muslims into enemy territory and had, against all odds, signed a decisive peace treaty with the Quraysh at the Well of Hudaybiyyah. The Muslims who had accompanied the Prophet on this high-risk mission were concerned about how they should respond if the Quraysh attacked them in the Meccan Haram, where fighting was forbidden. In these unique circumstances, the Quran gave them permission to fight back: 'Kill them wherever you encounter them', even in the sacred precincts, but *only* if the enemy opened hostilities. Now, however, al-Qurtubi took the verses out of their historical context and claimed that the Quran had issued an absolute command: Muslims must fight all 'unbelievers' whether they attacked first or not.[63]

Previous commentators had given little attention to Quran 2:216 ('Fighting has been ordained for you [*alaykum*], though it is hard for you'). Indeed, until well into the eighth century, most exegetes had concluded that after the death of the Prophet and his Companions, fighting was no longer a prescribed duty. But now ar-Razi argued that the word *alaykum* ('upon you') made fighting a general obligation, which, like the Ramadan fast, was incumbent on all Muslims – a view that gained currency during his lifetime, which witnessed the Third and Fourth Crusades. Al-Qurtubi agreed, pointing out that the Christians had managed to seize Andalusian territory only because Spanish Muslims had been reluctant to fight. Earlier exegetes had decided that Quran 9:5 ('Wherever you encounter the idol-aters, kill them, seize them, besiege them, wait for them at every lookout post') had applied only to those Quraysh who had broken the Hudaybiyyah pact. But again ar-Razi took the verse out of context, insisting that it was a general injunction, incumbent on Muslims in the present. He did not, however, claim that it abrogated the Quranic commands to coexist peace-fully and courteously with non-Muslims.[64]

*

There had always been a mystical element in rabbinic Judaism. Rabbi Akiva had sought out the Torah's hidden spiritual significance and when Rabbi Yohanan had discussed Ezekiel's vision of the heavenly chariot with his disciples, fire had fallen from heaven and an angel had spoken to them from the flames.[65] When Jews studied Torah, it was said that they were repeating the Sinai theophany in which God had revealed his glory (*kavod*) and Presence (Shekhinah) to the people of Israel.[66] This type of speculation intensified after the Muslim conquest of Palestine, perhaps influenced by the story of Muhammad's ascent to the throne of God. Rabbis began to meditate on the cosmic role of the Torah.[67] The *Pesikta Rabbati*, produced in Palestine during the seventh century, claimed that because the Torah was identical with Wisdom, God's 'master craftsman' in creation, when God had said 'Let *us* make man in *our* own image' he was addressing his helpmeet, the Torah. And if the Torah's words were identical with the divine speech that had brought the world into being, then when Jews studied it they were aligned with the sacred rhythms of the cosmos.[68] The eighth-century *Pirke de Rabbi Eliezer* endowed even the script and letters of the Torah with cosmic power.[69] Torah study was acquiring theurgic significance: not only did it keep the world in existence, it even strengthened God himself. In the Talmud, we hear that Rabbi Ishmael had warned Rabbi Meir that he was doing heaven's work when he committed the Torah to writing, and that if he omitted or added a single letter he would destroy the entire world. All letters – be they crooked or curved, large or small – were the forms of God himself, so a single error disqualified a scroll because it was no longer in God's image.[70]

Jews living in the Islamic empire had created their own version of *falsafah*, though they also found it difficult to reconcile Aristotle's Prime Mover with the God of the Bible. How, demanded Saadia ben Joseph (882–942), leader of the Babylonian Jewish community and the first Talmudist to undertake a philosophical interpretation of Judaism, could a wholly spiritual God have created a material world? At a certain point, reason stalled; it could only present the teachings of scripture logically and systematically.[71] The Spanish-born Moses ben Maimon (1185–1204), known as Maimonides, was also aware of the conflict between Aristotle and the Bible.[72] But he concluded that because the divine essence was ineffable, it could be adequately expressed only in the rational abstractions of *falsafah* and the arcane symbolism of mysticism, both of which required intellectual sophistication and meditative expertise. It was therefore impossible to share these insights with the ordinary people; they must remain esoteric, hidden within the apparently simple language of the Bible. The prophets themselves had been compelled to use allegorical or figurative language, because the mystery that was 'God' bore no resemblance to any mundane being.

It was, therefore, Maimonides argued, better to use negative terminology when we spoke of God. Our experience of 'existence' was so limited that instead of saying 'God exists', we should say that God does not *not* exist. It was also impossible to say that God was 'wise', 'perfect' or 'powerful' and preferable to say that God was 'not ignorant', 'not imperfect' or 'not impotent'. Otherwise, we would project our limited notions of power, perfection and wisdom onto God. But this method could be applied only to God's attributes and never to God's essence – God's innermost self – which lay beyond the reach of speech.[73] Like the Ismailis, Maimonides found that this method yielded intermittent sparks of insight. It was so designed 'that the truths be glimpsed and then again be concealed', he explained;

'the subject matter will appear, flash and then be hidden again'.[74] The clumsiness of these statements, which brought practitioners up against the limits of language, tipped one into an apprehension of transcendence. Maimonides spoke of his own 'trembling excitement' when confronted with the ineffability of the divine.[75]

Maimonides' exclusion of the masses offends our egalitarian ethos, but it was standard in agrarian society, where the educational gulf between the peasants and the aristocracy was well-nigh insuperable. Maimonides in fact developed a 'creed' for the unlettered – a list of beliefs essential for salvation, which affirmed the existence, unity, spirituality and eternity of God; prohibited idolatry and validated prophecy; claimed that God knew how people behaved and would judge them accordingly; and looked forward to the coming of the Messiah and the resurrection of the dead.[76] The Muslim *faylasuf* Abu al-Walid ibn Ahmad ibn Rushd (1126–97), known in the West as Averroës, produced a similar creed, but neither made much impact. Today we expect 'religion' to define its beliefs in this way, but this was not the case in the premodern period when religious truth was chiefly experienced and expressed in ritualised action.

Maimonides himself certainly did not experience Judaism as a static set of required dogmas but saw it as cumulative and dynamic. Each generation added new laws and norms and controversy and debate were essential to this process. In their intense discussions, the early rabbis had not been desperately trying to retrieve essential but forgotten teachings, as some Jews claimed; rather they were grappling with the problems of the post-temple world when old norms no longer applied.[77] Nor did Maimonides subscribe to the more recent divinisation of the Hebrew language; Hebrew was simply a human creation and, therefore, equivocal, concealing as much as it revealed. Instead Maimonides relied on the rational language of *falsafah*, which could probe the underlying significance of biblical ambiguities and bring to light their hidden meaning. But he was also convinced that the intuitions of prophecy and mysticism, which relied on the imagination, yielded a more exalted vision of God.

In the late thirteenth century, a small group of Jews in Spain and Provence pioneered a new mystical discipline, which they called Kabbalah ('inherited tradition'), because, like rabbinic learning, it was transmitted from teacher to pupil. Moses de Leon, Isaac de Latif and Joseph Gikatilla had little experience of the Talmud but had been excited by *falsafah* until they decided that it bore no relation to their own experience. Instead, they looked back to Rabbi Akiva, the hero of a mysterious story in the Talmud, which described four sages entering an 'orchard' (*pardes*), which clearly symbolised a dangerous spiritual experiment. Only Rabbi Akiva had emerged unscathed, so the Kabbalists concluded that their spirituality, based firmly on the Bible, was the only safe form of mysticism.[78] They called it PaRDeS, an acronym for the four 'senses' of scripture: *peshat*, the literal sense; *remez*, allegory; *darash*, the moral sense; and *sod*, their own mystical interpretation of Torah. It sounds like Christian exegesis but in fact each 'sense' represented a prior phase of Jewish hermeneutics. *Peshat* referred to Rashi's literal interpretation; *remez* to the *faylasufs'* more abstruse exegesis; and *darash* to later commentarial texts, such as *Pesikta Rabbati*. While politely acknowledging earlier attempts to interpret scripture, therefore, the Kabbalists presented *sod*, their own mystical exegesis based firmly on the Bible, as the only safe way of encountering the divine.

Unlike the Christian system, in which interpreters used each 'sense' in turn, the Kabbalists never produced literal, moral or allegorical commentaries, but focused solely on the mystical. Yet they created a powerful synthesis.[79] They revived the mystical element in rabbinic tradition, which some rabbis and *faylasufs* tended to downplay, and drew on *faylasuf* cosmology, which had depicted the material world emerging from the indefinable God in ten emanations that concluded in the production of our material world. In Kabbalah, however, revelation no longer bridged an ontological abyss; rather, these emanations occurred continuously in everyone. Creation too was not an occurrence in the distant past, but a timeless process, in which we all participate. It was a profound attempt to express the unity of reality that is glimpsed only darkly when our analytical faculties are stilled and we enter the vision of the right hemisphere of the brain.

Scripture was crucial to Kabbalah. Whenever he studied scripture, the Kabbalist descended into the text and into himself – a descent that was also an ascent to the source of being. God and scripture were inseparable, because scripture embodied the divine in human language, and the biblical stories were the 'garments' of Torah. Most people could not see beyond these narratives, but the Kabbalist, like a new husband, stripped away the garments of his bride until he and his beloved were one.[80] While the rabbis had sought God's will in scripture, the Kabbalists sought the divine presence there, discovering an esoteric interpretation in every single verse of the Bible. Like the *faylasufs*, they knew that words could not define God, but God could be experienced – if not known – in the symbols of scripture. Because there was an intrinsic connection between a word and what it

symbolised, the Tetragrammaton – the four letters of the ineffable Name –
was the essence of God.[81] The Torah was in fact a living texture of all the
names woven from God's unknowable Name, so God had, as it were,
compressed itself into the scripture and *was* the scripture.[82]

Kabbalists called God's innermost essence En Sof ('Without End'). En
Sof was utterly unknowable and was not even mentioned in either the Bible
or the Talmud. During the creation, it had erupted from its impenetrable
concealment like a massive tree, whose branches manifested its attributes.
There were ten such emanations, which the Kabbalists called *sefiroth*
('numerations', sing. *sefirah*), each revealing an aspect of En Sof, which lay
beyond the reach of speech, each one more comprehensible than the last
as they approached the material world. But they were not 'segments' of
the divine, because each encapsulated the entire mystery of divinity under
a different heading.

This mythos was designed to throw light on the indescribable process
whereby the unknowable God made itself known to us. The emanations
were not a ladder, linking our world with the divine. Rather, they informed
our world and enclosed it, and because they were also present in the human
psyche, they represented the process whereby the impersonal En Sof became
the personalised God of the Bible. The Kabbalists took the problematic
doctrine of creation 'out of nothing' very seriously, but turned it on its
head. This 'nothing' was within En Sof and everything followed from it.
The first *sefirah*, Keter, the dark flame that began the creative-revelatory
process, was called 'Nothing' because it did not correspond to any reality
that we could conceive. It was the divine itself, a hidden and inexpressible
reality, whose 'face' is turned inward and away from us – a transcendence
that always eludes our understanding.[83] Next Hokhmah ('Wisdom'),
the second *sefirah*, representing the utmost limit of our understanding,
broke through the impenetrable darkness, followed by Bimah, the divine
'Intelligence'. Then the seven lower *sefiroth* followed in succession: Rekhamin
('Compassion'), Din ('Stern Judgement'), Hesed ('Mercy'), Netsakh
('Patience'), Hod ('Majesty') and finally Malkuth ('Kingdom'), also called
Shekhinah.

When Adam was created, he was supposed to contemplate the entire
mystery of the Godhead on the first Sabbath, but instead he took the easier
option, meditating only on the Shekhinah, the most accessible *sefirah*. Not
only did this result in Adam's fall; it also ripped the Shekhinah away from
the other *sefiroth* so that it was exiled from the divine world. But by devoting
themselves to the task that Adam should have performed, Kabbalists learned

to contemplate the divine mystery concealed in the Bible, which became a coded account of the interaction of the *sefiroth*. For example, Abraham's binding of Isaac showed how Judgement (Din) and Mercy (Hesed) always act together, each tempering the other. Joseph, who rose to power by resisting sexual temptation, showed us that in the divine psyche, restraint (Din) was always balanced by Grace and Compassion (Rekhamin), while the Song of Songs symbolised the yearning for harmony and unity that throbs through all levels of existence.[84] The Kabbalists thus explored the different levels of scripture in the same way and at the same time as they contemplated the 'layers' of divinity.

The *Zohar* ('Book of Splendour'), ascribed to Moses of Leon, took the form of a novel set in the second century CE. It depicts Simeon ben Yohai, one of the early rabbis, wandering around Palestine and meeting up with his companions to discuss the Torah. These conversations show that as the Kabbalist descends layer by layer into the text, he discovers that he is ascending to the source of being. The process is described in an allegory in which a beautiful maiden, secluded in a palace, had a secret lover who was perpetually walking up and down in the street outside, hoping to catch a glimpse of her. So, she would open the door – just for a second – and then withdraw. First, she gave him a sign and spoke with him 'from behind the veil which she hangs before her words, so that they suit the manner of understanding in order that he may progress gradually'.[85] The Kabbalist too must progress gradually from one level to another, the veils becoming progressively less opaque, until, at last, the beloved 'stands disclosed, face to face, with him, and holds converse with him concerning all of her secret mysteries'.[86] Like an ardent bridegroom, he had to strip away the garments of Torah – the biblical stories, laws and genealogies:

> People without understanding see only the narratives, the garment; those somewhat more penetrating see also the body. But the truly wise, those who serve the most high King and stand on Mount Sinai, pierce all the way through to the soul, the true Torah, which is the root principle of all.[87]

At first, the Torah seems flawed and incomplete; only diligent exegesis could reveal its indwelling divinity.

The mythos of Kabbalah became a reality by means of ritual, which took the form of vigils, fasts and constant self-examination. Most importantly, Kabbalists had to live together in fellowship, repressing selfishness and egotism, because anger shattered the divine harmony that each was trying to build within himself. It was impossible to experience the unity of the *sefiroth* in a divided, fragmented state.[88] The love of friendship is so crucial to the *ekstasis* of Kabbalah that one of the signs of a successful interpretation of scripture in the *Zohar* is the cry of joy of an exegete's colleagues when they hear the divine truth and when, finally, the exegetes embrace and kiss one another before continuing their mystical journey. Kabbalah began as a tiny esoteric pursuit, but it would become a mass movement in Judaism, its mythos appealing even to Jews who had no mystical talent. In rather the same way as the Sufis had tapped into an essential dynamic of Islam, the Kabbalists had clearly touched a vital nerve in the Jewish psyche.

*

The Chengs had also stirred something deep in the Confucian soul, when they had insisted that anybody could discover the heavenly mind within them and become a sage. But their movement remained marginal until Zhu Xi (1130–1200) grounded their quest for 'principle' firmly in scripture. His version of neo-Confucianism would dominate the Chinese intellectual world until the 1911 revolution. Born in modern Anshi, Zhu was educated at home by his father, who introduced him to the writings of the Chengs. After his father's death, Zhu passed the Civil Service exams at the precocious age of nineteen and studied Buddhism and Daoism before taking up an official post. He was especially drawn to Chan Buddhism, but experienced a conversion that convinced him that he was at heart a Confucian.

Like the Chengs, Zhu believed that Confucians had lost sight of essential teachings. In his commentary on the *Doctrine of the Mean*, he explained that Zisi, Confucius' grandson, had written it 'because he was worried lest the transmission of the "learning of the Way" [*Daoxue*] be lost'. Zhu reminded his readers that Confucius had not been a powerful minister, as Sima Qian had claimed, but was a virtual outcast in his own day, and this made his recovery of the true significance of the Way even more heroic than that of Yao and Shun. Yet only two of his disciples – Yan Hui and Zeng Can – had fully understood his message and after Mencius, it was forgotten. Fortunately, the *Mean* had survived and had given the Cheng brothers something to work with. They had courageously 'picked up the threads' of its message, but, alas, their own explanations were now in eclipse. Zhu admitted that he himself had struggled to 'piece together' the true message of the *Mean* from the fragmentary material available to him. 'Repossessing the Way'

(*Daotong*), therefore, had required the dedicated effort of inspired individuals who had almost literally 'linked' or 'stitched' it together again.[89]

After his conversion, Zhu studied under Li Tong (1088–1158), a disciple of Cheng Yi, who introduced him to the practice of quiet-sitting which, he said, would enable him to encounter the 'principle of Heaven' (*Tianli*) in the ground of his being.[90] But Zhu had reservations about quiet-sitting, because it too closely resembled Chan meditation; he recommended it to his students but only as part of their cultivation of *jing* ('reverent attention'). Li Tong also advised Zhu to study the Classics and their rational discourse about morality.[91] Zhu wholly endorsed Cheng Hao's doctrine of 'forming one body with all things' but feared that if the moral implications of this truth were insufficiently emphasised, it could degenerate into a hazy, self-indulgent nature mysticism:

> To talk about *ren* in general terms of the self and things as 'one body' may lead one to be vague, confused, neglectful and make no effort to be vigilant . . .
> On the other hand, to talk about love exclusively in terms of consciousness will lead people to be nervous, impatient and devoid of any quality of depth.[92]

Zhang Zai had made it clear that the 'unity of all things' must be realised in moral action – in filiality to parents, respectful service of an elder brother, and in a loyal and serious performance of duty. Confucius had said: 'Curb your ego and surrender to the ritual [*li*]' which governed all our dealings with others. 'This means', Zhu explained, 'that if we can overcome selfishness and return to the "principle of Heaven", then the substance of this mind [i.e. *ren*] will be present everywhere.'[93]

Zhu would always insist that the neo-Confucian quest for the 'principle of Heaven' in the human mind was inseparable from morality and dedicated action in society. He refused to equate *ren* with Buddhist 'compassion' (*ci*) because Buddhism did not have a practical programme, which implied that 'principle' and 'practice' were separate. What distinguished Confucianism from Chan was what Zhu called *liqi fenshu* – 'the unity of principle and the diversity of its particularisation'. The discovery of the Dao of Heaven-and-Earth in your 'human' mind was inseparable from your own unique circumstances that came with duties and responsibilities that were yours alone. Li Tong had taught Zhu that the achievement of enlightenment was not a precondition for serving the world, as Chinese Buddhists maintained. You did not postpone your engagement with the mess of human affairs until after you had gained nirvana. True self-realisation and spiritual freedom were attained in the practical performance of our service to others.[94]

Zhu pointed out that learning was inseparable from affection for the people and involvement in the political activity of ordering the state and bringing peace to the world. Self-cultivation – the 'extension of knowledge' and the 'investigation of things' – led inexorably to social action in the world of affairs. The Chengs had explained that learning was a cumulative process that brought about 'a sudden release' when everything fell into place. At a certain point, Zhu taught, one experiences a 'breakthrough to integral comprehension' (*huoran guantong*) – what we might call the wisdom of the right hemisphere of the brain – when one abruptly perceives the undifferentiated 'wholeness' described by Zhang Zai and the Chengs. There was no longer any dichotomy between oneself and others, between inner and outer, and you understood your unique place in the 'whole substance and great functioning' of Heaven-and-Earth and the very particular obligations that this brought. Because of *liqi fenshu*, this experience would be different for everybody: 'At a certain stage in the pursuit of learning … one's understanding finally brings about a sense of being at home with oneself and the world … where nothing in the world seems alien to one.'[95] It comes with a sense of awe at the wondrous functioning of creation in the most ordinary things – an experience which, as the Chengs explained, compounded the physical and the emotional, the moral and the rational. But Cheng Yi had arrived at his 'release' by studying the world 'out there', searching for principle in every blade of grass. Zhu would insist that his disciples achieve this transformative insight by immersing themselves in the Confucian scriptures.

Zhu understood that the process of learning must be carefully orchestrated: students must begin with simpler texts and progress to more complex works only when they had advanced sufficiently. For some time now, Confucians had been focusing on the *Great Learning*, the *Mean*, *Analects* and the *Mencius*, texts that addressed their desire for self-transformation more directly than the Five Classics. In 1190, Zhu published these four scriptures in a single volume called *Four Masters* (*Sizi*), together with a commentary that bound them together, instructing his students to master these texts first.

The *Four Masters* must be read in a certain order, Zhu explained:[96]

I want people first of all to read the *Great Learning* to set a pattern; next to read the *Analects* to establish a foundation; next to read the *Mencius* to observe its development, and next to read the *Mean* to seek the subtle points of the ancients.[97]

The first two books emphasised the importance of self-cultivation and the effect of moral leadership on society at large. In the *Mencius*, students considered ren and morality in greater depth, and finally, in the *Mean*, they reflected on the interior life of the sage, achieved only by immense effort.

Alongside the *Four Masters*, beginners studied a few basic texts. One was Zhu Xi's *Reflections on Things at Hand*, a concise anthology of quotations that helped students who were not yet ready for metaphysics to understand the process of self-cultivation. What was revolutionary about *Reflections*, however, was that there was no mention of Yao, Shun, Yu or even the duke of Zhou. Instead, the focus was on the 'moderns' – on Zhou Dunyi, Zhang Zai and the Chengs – who proved that sagehood was attainable here and now. In addition, the *Lower Education* (*Xiaoyixue*) introduced students to the social and moral prerequisites for advanced philosophical study, while in *The Outline and Digest of the 'General Mirror'* (*Tongjian Gang mu*) Zhu summarised Sima Qian's massive history, making its lessons clearer by omitting its more abstruse details. His pupils were all members of the ruling class and destined for public office. This carefully designed curriculum balanced moral with intellectual training, preparing pupils for a lifelong devotion to learning that, Zhu believed, was essential to the service of others and the health of the state.[98] After they had mastered these preliminary texts, they could embark on the Five Classics.

Zhu was disturbed by the state of learning in China. Too many of the literati simply wanted to gain a reputation for brilliance and ingenuity and some of these belletrists had never even read the Classics. The Civil Service examinations encouraged an 'exam mentality' that was morally enervating, and Zhu also believed that Chan teachers, who did not encourage serious study, gave students the impression that learning and enlightenment were easy.[99] Moreover, he was worried about the insidious effects of printing. Even though the Chinese had invented the printing press in the eighth century, this technology had only recently become widespread.[100] Certainly, it was an advantage to have texts that were cheap and readily available but there were now too many books; students no longer had to memorise them and assumed that they had mastered a text after a single reading. As a government official, Zhu took a keen interest in education, founded nine academies and taught in others, his aim being to encourage more disinterested learning. The rapid spread of similar academies during the twelfth century indicated that he had addressed a need felt by many of the literati.[101]

Zhu was a great believer in the transformative power of scripture. 'If people today simply did ten days of reading, lowering their heads and ignoring all unrelated matters, I guarantee that they'd become transformed people.'[102] But it was not sufficient simply to become familiar with the content of a text. Students must embody it so thoroughly that 'the words seem to come from our own mouths. We should then continue to reflect upon it so that its ideas seem to come from our own minds. Only then can there be real understanding.'[103] If a passage seemed obscure, the student must wrestle with it, not leaving it until he had fully grasped its meaning, reading slowly with full concentration.[104] When he was their age, he told his students, he used to recite the *Great Learning* and the *Mean* ten times every morning; they too should recite each of the four books so repetitively that it became part of themselves.[105]

Like the Chengs, Zhu instructed his students to 'savour' the texts. Repeated recitation, performed slowly, meditatively and deliberately, enabled the reader to internalise the words of the sages. Like Benedictine monks, Zhu drew on the imagery of rumination. The reader should 'chew' the words, over and over, relishing their flavour; the more slowly he read, the longer the flavour would last.[106] Just as 'we are what we eat', Zhu hoped that the words of the sages would in this way transform us into our true sagely selves. Like the Chengs, he compared reading the sages' texts to 'speaking with them face to face',[107] so a student should approach their books with reverence. Making their words his own, he would not only become one with the scripture but with the mind of the sage who had authored it.

Students must not read their personal beliefs into scripture. 'Nowadays people usually have an idea in their own minds first, then take what other men have said to explain their idea. What doesn't conform to their idea they forcibly make it to conform.'[108] A student must divest himself of his own ideas 'and read for the meaning of the ancients'.[109] If students found that they were struggling with a text, it could be that the traditionally accepted view (which they had unthinkingly absorbed) was blocking their understanding. They should read the commentaries critically, because they all contained mistakes.

Doubt, Zhu insisted, was the starting point for the achievement of enlightenment. All received ideas should be scrubbed from the mind, so 'that it becomes like a clear mirror that reflects the divine principle within'.[110] Half the day should be spent in reading and the other half in quiet-sitting, since this cleansed the mind of the self-interest that impeded impartial study and helped students to cultivate *jing*. Like the Chengs, Zhu believed that physical posture could control the chronically restless

mind – the head upright, feet and hands respectful, one's bearing solemn.[111]
Study was a dialectical process in which, after many readings, two distinct
things – the text and the reader – fused in the moment of enlightenment.[112]
In China, transcendence was not the discovery of an 'other' realm, but was
rather the realisation of the authentic self that awakened the sage inherent
within all of us and enabled us to discover our fundamental connection
with all beings in the universe.[113]

*

At the very end of the fifteenth century, a young man had a divine revelation in a village near Lahore, which was then part of the Muslim Mughal
empire. Nanak had been born in 1469, three years after the publication of
the Gutenberg Bible in Europe. His father had hoped that he would become
an accountant or a herdsman, but he was a solitary young man who spent
hours each day in meditation and tended to give away whatever money he
earned. One day, while bathing in the river, he vanished and his family
feared that he had drowned but three days later he stepped out of the water.
His first words were: 'There is no Hindu, there is no Muslim, so whose
path shall I follow? I shall follow God's path.'[114] He later described his
experience:

> I was a minstrel out of work; he had assigned me the task of singing the
> Divine Word day and night. He summoned me to the court and bestowed
> on me a role of honour for singing his praises. On me, he bestowed the
> Divine Nectar in a cup, the nectar of his true and holy Name.[115]

For years after this revelation Nanak travelled extensively, reaching Assam
in the east and Mecca in the west, composing and reciting his inspired
poetry, and conversing with Hindus and Muslims at pilgrimage sites in
Baghdad and Benares, before returning home. On his return to the Punjab
in 1519, Guru Nanak, as his *shikshya* ('disciples') called him, established a
community at Kartarpur.

Early Sikh doctrines and practice combined many of the themes we have
found in other scriptures. They insist on the absolute ineffability of the
supreme reality, which Nanak called Akal Purakh ('Beyond Time').
The Creator cared for all men and women, regardless of their caste or faith
tradition. Human life was filled with sorrow and the goal of the religious
quest was *mukti* ('release') from the cycle of suffering and rebirth (*samsara*).

Nanak communicated his message in hymns of great beauty, which he ascribed to the 'holy word' (*shabad*), insisting that he himself had no part in their creation.[116] The Sikhs passed their time in communal singing, chanting the divine name as a mantra – a practice not dissimilar to Muslim *dhikr* – and serving the poor. When Nanak died in 1539, he appointed a successor, founding a lineage that would last for 170 years. Significantly, however, he left no official scripture. Indeed, he repudiated the very idea of a canonical text, be it the Vedas or the Quran. Instead of hearing the divine message delivered externally, a Sikh should hear the divine word with his inner ear.

The emphasis on ineffability in these scriptures brings us back to the rishis we encountered at the beginning of our story, who had pioneered the art of scripture. Ever since, people had continued to chant or to listen to their sacred texts to have intimations of the ultimate reality that lay beyond the reach of speech, realising that to achieve this they had to culti-vate forms of thought and feeling that differed from the way we normally process information. As Nanak explained, they had to listen with their 'inner ear'. They were not consulting scripture to have their own ideas confirmed, but were pressing forward to achieve new insights, making the sacred texts say something different, and pushing their traditions forward into uncharted waters. The experience of transcendence was also dependent on the prac-tice of compassion and, in China especially, a sense of the interdependence of humanity, the natural world and the cosmos. Nanak was even ready to abandon conventional scripture, but in western Europe, which at the time was experiencing major social, economic and political change, people were coming to rely on the sacred text exclusively, without the rites and practices that had traditionally supported it.

PART THREE

Logos

12

SOLA SCRIPTURA

By the early sixteenth century, Europeans realised that their societies were undergoing major change. They had discovered new continents; they were penetrating the mysteries of the cosmos with unparalleled accuracy; and, with the aid of new techniques, could express their insights more brilliantly in painting and sculpture than ever before. Humanity, the biblical scholar Gianozzo Manetti was convinced, was evolving to a sublime state:

> Everything that surrounds us is our work, the work of man: houses, castles, cities, magnificent buildings over all the earth. They resemble the work of angels rather than man; nevertheless, they are the work of man ... And when we see these marvels, we realise that we are able to make better things, more beautiful things.[1]

But others were fearful. Between 1347 and 1350 the Black Death had killed a third of the population of Europe; in 1453, the Ottoman Turks had conquered the Byzantine empire and were now encroaching on European territory; and the scandal of the Great Schism (1378–1417), when as many as three pontiffs vied unscrupulously for the papacy, had alienated many from the church. Italy, the home of the Renaissance, was harassed by invasion and internecine warfare. Human beings 'endure continually the most cruel conflicts with temptation', wrote the Italian poet Francesco Petrarch (1304–74); they 'lie always open to many grievous perils, and are never secure before they die'.[2]

When they studied the classics of ancient Greece and Rome, the humanists were astonished to discover how different Europe had been in the past. This made them realise that radical change was possible, even in religion. They were men of letters, preoccupied above all with literary style, and they rejected the writings of Thomas Aquinas not on doctrinal grounds but because of their inelegance. Knowledge, they believed, was acquired not by the intellect alone but also by the heart and the senses. Scripture too must be appreciated emotionally and aesthetically as well as theologically, because, as Petrarch wrote to his brother: 'One might say that theology is actually poetry, poetry concerning God.'[3]

To revivify their faith, the Renaissance humanists looked back to the wellsprings (ad fontes) of Christianity and that meant reading the Bible in the original languages.[4] Lorenzo Valla (c. 1406–57) produced an anthology of the New Testament 'proof texts' currently in use in the universities to support church doctrine. When he set Jerome's Latin translation of these texts alongside the original Greek, it was clear that they did not always verify what was claimed for them. Valla's Collatio circulated initially in manuscript form, but Desiderius Erasmus (1466–1536), a Dutch humanist, produced a printed version that reached a far wider audience. Erasmus also published the Greek text of the New Testament, which he translated into stylish Ciceronian Latin. Thanks to the printing press, anyone who knew Greek and Latin could now read the gospels in the original. Scholars could also review a translation more quickly than ever before and suggest improvements, and Erasmus profited from this, publishing several more editions of his New Testament. The humanists were especially attracted to Paul, whose letters acquired new vitality in the original koine Greek. Hitherto, although they had always recognised Paul's importance, Christians had often found him baffling because his ideas and intricate arguments were difficult to transmit orally. But, once liberated from Jerome's cumbersome translation, his writings came to life. Erasmus was convinced that an appreciation of the emotional impact of scripture could reform the church and that laymen like himself were key to this reformation.[5]

The commercial economy, which had been developing in northern Europe since the fourteenth century, was also affecting the way people thought and experienced the world. Inventions and innovations, none of which seemed particularly decisive at the time, were occurring simultaneously in different fields, and their cumulative effect would be conclusive. All these discoveries were characterised by a pragmatic, logos-driven mentality that was undermining the traditional mythical ethos. People had started to make precise instruments – the compass, the telescope, the magnifying lens – that produced more accurate maps and charts, improved navigational techniques and revealed hitherto unseen worlds. The Dutch microscopist Antony van Leeuwenhoek's observation of bacteria, spermatozoa and other microorganisms raised new questions about the processes of generation and decay, life and death. By 1600, inventions were occurring on such a scale that progress had become irreversible. Capitalism would eventually enable the West to replicate its resources indefinitely and free it from the limitations of the agrarian economy. When this process finally resulted in the industrial revolution of the nineteenth century, social, political, economic and intellectual change had become part of an interlocking process, each element dependent on the others.[6]

But fundamental yet imperceptible change can be disorienting. People cannot see the direction their society is taking but experience its slow transformation in incoherent and disturbing ways.[7] Some felt that the pieties and rituals that had sustained Western Christians for more than a millennium were out of kilter with this new world and, perhaps because the fifteenth century was probably more devout than any previous century in Europe, there was a new sensitivity to clerical venality and a growing concern that the Roman Church had little to do with the church founded by Christ. Some feared that the End of Days was nigh and were convinced that only a thoroughgoing reformation could save Christendom from divine vengeance.[8]

Martin Luther (1483–1546), professor of scripture and philosophy at the University of Wittenberg, epitomised this dis-ease. As a young friar, he had observed the rules of his order faithfully, but found that these practices, formed in a very different world, could not assuage his near-pathological terror of death.[9] He found relief in exegesis. While preparing a series of lectures on the Psalms, he interpreted the literal sense of a verse in Psalm 71 – 'In your righteousness [*justitia*], deliver me'[10] – as a prayer of Christ to his Father. But then he turned to the moral sense, transforming this verse into the prayer of a believer to Christ, and, to his immense excitement, realised that it implied that Christ could bestow his *own* righteousness upon the sinner.[11] Not long afterwards, while interpreting the Epistle to the Romans in his study in the monastery tower, he was puzzled by a quotation that Paul had chosen from the prophet Habakkuk:

> For I am not ashamed of the Good News: it is the power of God saving all who have faith – Jews first, but Greeks as well – since this is what reveals the justice of God to us: it shows how faith leads to faith, or, as scripture says, *The righteous man finds life through faith.*[12]

Luther had always assumed that God's righteousness (*justitia*) was the divine justice that condemned a sinner to hell. How could that be 'good news'? And how was 'righteousness' linked to 'faith'? He then recalled Psalm 71 and everything fell into place. Paul, he believed, was saying that God would bestow his *own* righteousness on the sinner who had faith in Christ. 'I felt as though I had been born again,' Luther wrote later, 'and as though I had entered through open gates into paradise itself.'[13]

Luther's signature doctrine of justification by faith alone meant that if a sinner had faith, he could say: 'Christ has done enough for me. He is just. He is my defence. He has died for me. He has made his righteousness my righteousness.'[14] By faith (*fides*), Luther did not mean 'belief' in a set of doctrines. He was using the word in its original sense of commitment and trust. 'Faith does not require information, knowledge and certainty,' he explained, 'but a free surrender and a joyful bet on [God's] unfelt, untried, and unknown goodness.'[15] His interpretation of Paul's words differed from their original meaning, but Luther was engaging in the traditional art of scriptural exegesis, giving them a new significance that spoke directly to his situation. But there was an important difference. The art of scripture also required kenosis, an 'emptying' of self, accompanied by compassionate outreach to others. This interpretation of Romans, however, was all about Luther − *his* faith, *his* salvation, *his* fear of death − and compassion, as we shall see, was not one of Luther's virtues.

The Protestant Reformation began on 31 October 1517, when Luther nailed his ninety-five theses to the door of the castle church of Wittenberg. They fiercely challenged the penitential and sacramental practices of the Roman Church that had no biblical sanction. Two years later, in a public debate in Leipzig with Johann Eck, professor of theology at Ingolstadt, Luther formulated the new doctrine of *sola scriptura* ('scripture alone'). The Roman Church claimed that only popes and councils of bishops were competent to interpret the Bible. Indeed, asked Eck, how was it possible to understand scripture without the guidance of the popes, councils and universities who had been entrusted with the complex art of scriptural interpretation? 'A simple layman armed with scripture is to be believed above a pope or a council without it,' was Luther's reply.[16] This stirring rallying cry appealed immediately to democratically minded townsfolk who were sick of clerics extorting money from gullible people. The towns of central and southern Germany had become important commercial centres and were therefore in a position of strength to declare and achieve de facto independence from Rome.[17] The more intellectual clergy spread Luther's ideas in their own books, which, thanks to the new technology of printing, circulated with unprecedented speed, creating one of the world's first mass movements.

Sola scriptura was the revolutionary cry that launched the Protestant Reformation. Hitherto, as we have seen, scripture had never been experienced by itself. It was traditionally performed and enacted in rituals that were sometimes more important than the texts themselves. But scripture was now very much in vogue. The Gutenberg Bible had made it more accessible than ever before and the humanists had sparked their own scriptural renaissance, as a result of which the Protestant reformers were all well versed in Hebrew and Greek.[18] Indeed, in Switzerland the Reformation had begun in humanist study groups. Swiss reformers were less interested in dogma than Luther and simply wanted a moral reformation. But like Luther, Huldrych Zwingli (1484–1531) of Geneva was convinced that this could be effected only by a direct encounter with the Bible. 'The Word of God, as soon as it shines upon an individual's understanding, illuminates it in such a way that he understands it,' he wrote in 1522.[19] The Bible needed no interpretation: 'It is certain and may not fail. It is clear and will not leave us to err in darkness. It teaches itself on its own.'[20]

Balthazar Hubmaier (*c.*1480–1528), a colleague of Zwingli, agreed:

> In all divisive matters and controversies, only scripture, canonised and made holy by God himself, should and must be the judge, no one else ... For sacred scripture alone is the true light and lantern through which all human argument, darkness and objections are recognised.[21]

But we have seen that in fact scripture did *not* 'teach itself'; instead, it often segued deliberately into silence and unknowing. It did not settle dogmatic disputes: Greek theologians were unable to prove the divinity of Christ by scripture alone, and Muslim legists had to exercise 'independent reasoning' (*ijtihad*) when they developed Islamic jurisprudence. The rabbis had found no clear answers to the post-temple world in the Bible and had created the Mishnah instead; and, finding their scriptures fallible, Jains had relied on their compassionate rituals.

Not surprisingly, therefore, the reformers soon discovered that despite their biblical expertise, they could not agree about what scripture taught. Luther and Zwingli, for example, argued vehemently about the Eucharist. What had Jesus meant when he said: 'This is my body'?[22] Luther, who still believed in the real presence of Christ in the Eucharistic elements, interpreted this literally – 'This loaf *is* my body' – but Zwingli insisted that the 'natural' sense was: 'This loaf *signifies* my body' or 'This loaf is *like* my body, broken for you.'[23] Between 1525 and 1529, reformers published twenty-eight treatises opposing Luther's view. This was not a trivial matter, because it meant that the reformers could not worship together, so from the very start, the Protestant Reformation split into warring camps.

The Reformation, it has been said, signalled a resurgence of the left hemisphere of the brain, which, as we have seen, had begun in Europe during the thirteenth century.[24] The Eucharistic quarrels represented a flight from the metaphorical to a literalistic mode of thought. The reformers were grappling with the implausible doctrine of transubstantiation, an unhappy attempt by medieval theologians to make sense of the Eucharist in Aristotelian terms, which was never accepted by Greek Christians. It claimed that when the priest spoke the words of consecration, the 'substance' (the underlying reality) of the bread and wine *literally* became the body and blood of Christ, while leaving their 'accidents' (their outward appearance) intact.

Transubstantiation represented an 'unskilful' flight from metaphor, the natural mode of expression of the brain's right hemisphere which sees the interconnectedness of things. Metaphor links the whole of one thing with the whole of another so that we see both differently.[25] When we call a man a wolf, the wolf becomes more human and a man more animal, and when we say that a human being is divine, we gain a new understanding of both humanity and divinity. This metaphoric insight occurs before the information is processed in the left hemisphere.[26] Traditional Catholic ritual was deliberately metaphorical, implicit and indecipherable, enabling participants tacitly to glimpse the unity of reality. The Reformation, however, heralded the triumph of the written Word and a preference for clarity and definition. Christ's words would now mean that the bread could *only* be a loaf – a mode of thought that resulted in an emphasis on the word rather than the image, on the literal rather than the metaphorical, and an insistence on the explicit meaning of scripture. Instead of 'cracking open' the words of scripture to glimpse something Beyond, like Ambrose of Milan, the reformers abandoned the traditional four 'senses', focusing instead on the literal, historical reading. Allegory was permitted only if it did not jeopardise the plain meaning of the text – a decision that would subject the Western Christian mind to a tension that would soon become intolerable.

The new literalism was also evident in the reformers' vehement disagreement about infant baptism, which the Anabaptists, the more radical reformers, claimed was 'unscriptural'. True, there was no explicit mention of this practice in the New Testament, but it had been accepted, for different reasons, by both Eastern and Western Christians who had felt free to improvise and innovate. But the reformers debated this issue with an anger and self-righteousness that embedded them in the ego that the art of scripture obliged them to transcend. Konrad Grebel denounced the baptism of children as 'a senseless, blasphemous abomination, against all scripture', while Felix Mantz declared that it was 'against God, an insult to Christ, and a trampling underfoot of his own true eternal word'. For Hans Hut it was an immoral 'defrauding of simple people, a cunning trick on all Christendom, and an arch-rogue's cover for all the godless', while Michael Sattler, a former Benedictine monk, condemned it as 'the pope's greatest and first abomination'.[27]

The reformers seem to have forgotten Valla's warning about the fallibility of proof texts: the warring parties all cited scriptural maxims to incriminate their opponents, who, of course, hurled back other texts to endorse their own position. One wonders what Zhuangzi, Xunzi, the Buddha or the rabbis would have made of these disputes. They had all, in different ways, argued that this kind of aggressive, egotistic sparring was 'unskilful', that it was dangerous to be in love with your own opinions, and that strident certainty was drastically misplaced and could become an 'obsession'. Zhu Xi had specifically warned his pupils *not* to read their own ideas into the texts, as the reformers were doing. The art of scripture was designed to effect radical change in those who studied it, not to give divine sanction to their own inescapably limited views. The reformers all revered Augustine, but seem to have forgotten his insistence that scripture taught nothing but charity. 'Beware of Zwingli and avoid his books as the hellish poison of Satan,' Luther warned his colleagues, 'for the man is completely perverted and has completely lost Christ.'[28]

Luther claimed that the Bible had only one meaning. 'In the whole of scripture, there is nothing else but Christ, either in plain words or involved words.'[29] But he soon became aware that some books of the Bible were more Christological than others. His solution was to create a 'canon within the canon', privileging books that supported his own theology. Here he clashed with the Wittenberg theologian Andreas Karlstadt, who objected strongly to Luther's marginalisation of the Epistle of James which challenged his doctrine of justification by faith alone. 'Take the case, my brothers, of someone who has never done a single good act but claims that he has faith. Will that faith save him?' James had asked. Could faith save a man who did nothing to help those who lacked the necessities of life? 'If good works do not go with it', James had concluded, faith is 'quite dead'.[30] We have seen

that scripture was always a call to action and that the monotheistic traditions had always stressed the importance of social justice. The Mahayana
had opposed the *arahants* because they had felt no obligation to help others
find relief from their suffering, and the neo-Confucians had insisted that a
practical compassionate outreach to the ends of the earth was essential to
enlightenment.

Ever since the duke of Zhou had introduced the idea of the Mandate of
Heaven, scripture had had a political dynamic, since the injustice, inequity
and oppression of the state were matters of sacred import. During the
Reformation, this issue came to a head during the Peasants' Revolt.[31]
The peasants of southern and central Germany had resisted the centralising
policies of their princes, which deprived them of traditional rights. Some
had won concessions by hard-headed bargaining, but between March and
May 1525, lawless bands of peasants looted and burned church properties.
Luther had no sympathy with the peasants' cause, maintaining that suffering
was their lot: they must obey the Gospel, turn the other cheek and accept
the loss of their lives and property.[32] But the peasants could also quote
scripture and had the temerity to retort that Christ had made all men free.
For Luther, this defiance proved that they were in thrall to Satan so he
counselled the princes:

> Let everyone who can, smite, slay and stab, secretly or openly, remembering
> that nothing can be more poisoned, hurtful or devilish than a rebel. It is just
> as when one must kill a mad dog: if you do not strike him, he will strike
> you and the whole land with you.[33]

Indeed, he argued, killing the rebels was an act of mercy, because it would
liberate them from satanic bondage. Some 100,000 peasants may have lost
their lives before the uprising was quashed. Luther was the first Christian
to advocate the separation of religion from politics. He believed that
Christians, justified by a personal act of faith in God's redemptive power,
belonged to the Kingdom of God and must hold aloof from the political
affairs of the sinful world. But these true Christians were few and far
between; most so-called Christians still belonged to the Kingdom of the
World, a realm of selfishness and violence, ruled by the Devil, and must
be forcibly restrained by the state.[34]

Scriptural interpretation, of course, had always been, perhaps inescapably,
the preserve of the literate and leisured elite. After the Peasants' Revolt,
Luther withdrew his bold claim that 'a simple layman' could interpret the

Bible for himself. Anabaptists would continue to insist that all Christians had the right to read scripture, but during the 1530s, the 'Magisterial Reformation' which followed Luther and Zwingli decreed that only those Christians who were fluent in Hebrew, Greek and Latin could read the Bible. The rest must acquire biblical teachings through such 'filters' as Luther's *Lesser Catechism* (1529).[35] Later, the French reformer John Calvin (1509–64) agreed that most Christians were incapable of reading scripture, and his *Institutes of the Christian Religion* (1559) became the standard Protestant guide to the Bible.[36]

Calvin was no diehard literalist, however. He continued to respect Augustine's 'principle of accommodation', arguing that the divine Word was conditioned by the historical circumstances in which it was uttered. The creation story was a prime example of the divine *balbative* ('baby talk') that adapted immensely complex processes to the mentality of simple, uneducated people.[37] The discoveries of modern astronomers, Calvin argued, should not be condemned 'simply because some frantic persons are wont boldly to reject whatever is unknown to them'. Moses, for example, had described the sun and moon as the largest of the heavenly bodies, but now scientists believed Saturn to be larger than the moon:

> Herein lies the difference; Moses wrote in a popular style things which, without instruction, all ordinary persons, endued with common sense, are able to understand; but astronomers investigate with great labour whatever the sagacity of the human mind can comprehend.

Revelation, Calvin believed, was a gradual, evolutionary process. At each stage, God had adapted his truth to the limited capacity of human beings, so his teaching had changed and developed over time, becoming progressively more spiritual.[38] But where Luther had regarded the 'Old' Testament simply as a prelude to Christ, Calvin respected the integrity of the revelation to Israel and made the Hebrew scriptures more important in themselves to Western Christians than ever before.

At the Council of Trent (1545–63), the Roman Church affirmed its traditional conception of scripture against the reformers. The bishops refuted *sola scriptura*, insisting that the chain of tradition was an essential supplement to the Bible; claimed that the Protestant canon was insufficient; affirmed the authority of the Vulgate and the church's prerogative to interpret it; and ruled that no one could publish a commentary on scripture unless it was vetted by his superior, a decision that crippled Catholic biblical scholarship for centuries. Like the Protestants, the Catholic Church also issued a series of 'filters' and catechisms which attempted to 'freeze' the scriptural message in a single historical moment, putting a brake on the innovative interpretation that had hitherto enabled exegetes to make scripture responsive to changing circumstances.[39] Printing would also change people's attitude to scripture.[40] As the printed book gradually replaced oral methods of communication, religious knowledge became depersonalised and, perhaps, less flexible than when truth had developed in dynamic relation between master and pupil. The printed page was itself a model of precision and exactitude, a symptom of the mental outlook of the new logos-driven, commercial ethos.[41]

In Spain, there was a Catholic reformation of a different kind. Teresa of Ávila (1515–82) radically transformed monastic life for women in her reformed Carmelite order, ensuring that women were properly educated in scripture and the psychology of mysticism so that they did not succumb to the hysteria that was rife in medieval convents. John of the Cross (1542–91), her friend and mentor, described the transition that the mystic must make from everyday consciousness to the mystical:

> In this state of contemplation which the soul enters when it forsakes medi-
> tation for the state of the proficient, it is God who is now working in the
> soul; he binds its interior faculties and allows it not to cling to the *under-*
> *standing, nor to have delight in the will, nor to reason with memory*.[42]

This was clearly a disciplined withdrawal from the dominance of the left hemisphere; the contemplative 'binds' or controls its focus on the rational, the conceptual and its willed enhancement of the self. Teresa described a similar process:

> When all the faculties of the soul are in union ... they can do nothing
> whatever, because the understanding is, as it were, surprised. The will loves
> more than the understanding knows; but the understanding does not know
> what the will loves, nor what it is doing ... As to the memory, the soul, I
> think, has none then, nor any power of thinking, nor are the senses awake,
> but rather as lost.[43]

Like the Upanishads, these Carmelite reformers were teaching adepts to transcend normal modes of perception to discover their identity with Brahman – 'the All'.

But this did not entail a total retreat from the world; Teresa did not share Luther's disdain for good works: 'This ... is the aim of prayer; this is the purpose of the Spiritual Marriage of which are born good works and good works alone ... We should desire and engage in prayer not for our enjoyment but for the sake of acquiring this strength which fits us for service.'[44] Another Spanish reformer, Ignatius of Loyola (1495–1556), founder of the Society of Jesus, created his *Spiritual Exercises* with the sole purpose of inspiring his Jesuits to action; it was by missionary work in the far-flung reaches of the known world – even, as we shall see later in this chapter, in China – that they would gain enlightenment. Ignatius had experienced a visionary moment, in which 'he was left with his under-standing so enlightened that he seemed to be another man with another mind'.[45] But, as a former soldier, he was also a man of the left hemisphere. His *Spiritual Exercises* guided each Jesuit through a controlled thirty-day interior journey, precisely signposted; his theology and spirituality were preoccupied with system, analysis and definition – a cast of mind that made Jesuits leading figures in the development of early modern science.

The quarrels of the Reformation had resulted in a deep hostility between Catholics and Protestants, which was magnified by the so-called 'Wars of Religion'. After the Reformation, north-eastern Germany and Scandinavia were, roughly speaking, Lutheran; England, Scotland, the northern Netherlands, the Rhineland and southern France were chiefly Calvinist, while the rest of the continent remained Catholic. This inevitably exacer-bated international relations, but many of the German princes were also alarmed by the ambitions of the Hapsburgs, who now ruled the German territories, Spain and the southern Netherlands. The emperor Charles V (r.1519–56), a Catholic, was bent on achieving trans-European hegemony on the Ottoman model, while the German princes were equally determined to build strong, sovereign states on the model of France and England. The Catholic kings of France tried to thwart the Hapsburgs' ambitions and for over thirty years engaged in military campaigns against the Catholic emperor, who eventually had to admit defeat and sign the Peace of Augsburg in 1555. Henceforth in Europe the religious allegiance of the local ruler would determine the faith of his subjects – a principle enshrined in the maxim *Cuius regio, eius religio* ('He who controls the region, controls its religion').[46]

In the minds of the participants, however, these wars were certainly experienced as a life-and-death struggle between Protestants and Catholics, but if the conflict had been inspired solely by religion, we would not expect to find Protestants and Catholics fighting on the same side. Yet, in fact, they often did so, and, therefore, killed their co-religionists. The same was true of the French Wars of Religion (1562–98), which segued into the Thirty Years War (1618–48) that killed about thirty-five per cent of the population of central Europe.[47] But the trauma of these conflicts convinced many Europeans that the theological differences between Catholics and Protestants were insoluble and that they must find common ground in a truth that had nothing to do with religion.

Many, therefore, welcomed the solution of the French philosopher René Descartes (1596–1650), which was crafted on the battlefield of the Thirty Years War. Even though he remained a devout Catholic until his death, Descartes agreed that religion was part of the problem rather than the solution and was haunted by the challenge issued by the French sceptic Michel de Montaigne (1553–92) at the end of his essay 'The Apology of Raymond Sebond': unless we could find a truth that yielded absolute certainty, we could not be sure about anything at all. In 1619, while Descartes was serving as a gentleman-soldier, heavy snowfall forced him off the road at Ulm on the Danube, where he lodged in a small room heated by a stove. There, he had three luminous dreams, which inspired him to create a science that brought together all the disciplines – theology, arithmetic, astronomy, music, geometry, optics and physics – under the mantle of mathematics.

Instead of *sola scriptura*, Descartes proffered *sola ratio* ('reason alone'). His solution discounted all revelation and traditional theology, and offered his contemporaries an idea that, he was convinced, was self-evident, clear and distinct but which began with radical doubt. We could not rely upon the evidence of our senses – indeed, we could not even be sure that the objects in our immediate vicinity truly existed: we could be dreaming when we thought we saw, heard or touched them. So Descartes systematically emptied his mind of everything that he thought he knew; but while he was thinking and doubting in this way, he became aware of the reality of his *own* existence.[48] His disciplined, sceptical ascesis had enabled the ego to rise ineluctably from the depths of his mind:

> Remarking that this truth, *cogito, ergo sum* ['I think, therefore I am'] was so certain and so assured that all the most extravagant suppositions brought forward by the sceptics were incapable of shaking it, I came to the conclusion that I could rescue it without scruple as the first principle of the philosophy for which I was seeking.[49]

The thinking self was solitary, autonomous and a world unto itself, unaffected by outside influence and separate from all other existing things.

Descartes' *cogito* marked the beginning of the European Enlightenment, but unlike the scriptural transformation effected by kenosis, the enlightenment achieved by 'reason alone' was a triumphant self-assertion.

From this nub of certainty – *cogito, ergo sum* – Descartes went on to prove the existence of God and the reality of the external world. The only animate thing in the entire universe was the thinking self, so the material universe, which was lifeless, godless and inert, could tell us nothing about God. There was no need for scripture, revelation or theology, because 'God' was a clear and distinct idea in the human mind, and because God was Truth itself, Descartes explained in a somewhat circular argument, he would not allow us to be in error about such an important matter as his existence. Where Avicenna, Maimonides, Denys and Thomas Aquinas had all insisted that God was not a being, Descartes had no qualms about calling God the 'first and sovereign being', thus shrinking the ineffable and omnipresent Reality of sages, rabbis and mystics to fit the confines of the human mind.[50]

When he dedicated his *Meditations on First Philosophy* to the scholars of the Sacred Faculty of Theology in Paris, Descartes calmly informed these eminent theologians that scientists like himself were more qualified than they to discuss the divine. They were only too happy to agree. Descartes had offered his contemporaries a real hope of extracting themselves from the apparent impasse of incompatible dogmas. *Sola scriptura* had inspired a mass of irreconcilable opinions simply because the reformers had fallen in love with their own ideas but found that their proof texts proved nothing. But Descartes could argue: 'It is at least as certain that God who is a Being so perfect, is, or exists, as any demonstration of geometry can possibly be.'[51] Descartes believed that it was the task of science to dispel the awe and reverence for the natural world that scripture had sought to inspire. Indeed, his philosophy would make us lords and masters of nature. Cosmic phenomena were simply the product of physical necessity, he insisted, and soon, thanks to scientific *ratio*, 'we will no longer have occasion to wonder at anything that can be seen of them ... we will easily believe that it is similarly possible to find the causes of everything that is most admirable above the earth'.[52]

Schizophrenia has been defined as an excess of rationality; it is not a regression to a more primitive, unselfconscious mode of thought, but 'an excessively detached, hyper-rational, reflexively self-aware, disembodied and alienated condition' that occurs when a person makes a deliberate effort to distance himself from his surroundings, and suspend 'all normal assumptions and subject them to a detached scrutiny'.[53] Descartes' symptoms, if not indicative of mental illness, suggest that his reliance on *sola ratio* might have put excessive strain on his psychological balance. He described himself looking through his window at men passing in the street and wondering why he took it for granted that they were human beings rather than automata: 'I do not really see them, but infer that what I see is men ... yet what do I see from the window but hats and coats, which may carry automatic machines? Yet I judge these to be men.'[54] He found it incomprehensible that 'this mysterious pinching of the stomach which I call hunger causes me to desire to eat'.[55] Indeed, he struggled to convince himself that he had a body at all. He could make a 'probable conjecture' that his body existed, but it was 'only a probability' and he had no 'clear and distinct idea' of his corporeal nature.[56]

Descartes had heroically pioneered the Age of Reason, which would bring about spectacular advances in science, philosophy and technology, but it would also transform the way Western people experienced their scriptures. Hitherto, scripture had been an art form that had relied on the bodily gestures of ritual, on communal chanting and on music, the most physical of the arts; it had also demanded an empathic concern for humanity rather than Cartesian withdrawal and detachment.

*

In the West, therefore, theology and scripture would increasingly be translated into a rational idiom that was alien to them. Logos cannot assuage our sorrow or evoke our sense of the transcendent, so it cannot convince us that, despite all the rational evidence to the contrary, our lives have meaning and value. True, the music of Johann Sebastian Bach (1685–1750) and George Frederick Handel (1685–1759) would help to return the biblical text to the right hemisphere of the brain, and the magnificent prose of the King James Bible, besides providing readers with a text that was (relatively) free of polemic, would separate sacred language from mundane speech. But increasingly, Catholics and Protestants alike would read the biblical mythoi as if they were logoi. Not surprisingly, perhaps, some poets, artists and dramatists retained a more traditional approach to scripture. While theologians tended to focus increasingly on the original meaning of the biblical text, they continued to interpret its narratives freely so that they could address current issues and effect within the reader the personal transformation that is essential to religion.

John Milton (1608–74), a poet hailed as second only to Homer and Virgil in his own lifetime, radically reinterpreted the biblical story of the Fall of Adam and Eve in his epic poem *Paradise Lost*, which was published in 1667. A humanist as well as a child of the Reformation, Milton embodied the two great movements of the day, yet he was also a transitional figure. A devout Protestant and committed to *sola scriptura*, by the end of his life he had become disgusted with sectarian dogmatism and espoused the passion for political and intellectual liberty that would become central to the eighteenth-century Enlightenment. Yet he utterly rejected Descartes' *sola ratio* – after all, he pointed out, Paul had made it clear that Christianity was essentially irrational.[57] 'When discussing sacred matters, let us disregard reason,' he urged in his treatise *On Christian Doctrine*, 'and follow exclusively what the Bible teaches.'[58] But he refused to accept both Luther's reliance on faith alone to the detriment of 'good works' and his insistence that true Christians should not involve themselves in political matters. We were certainly justified by faith, Milton argued, 'but by a living faith not a dead one'; faith, he believed, 'has its own works', and the greatest of these was politics. Milton was deeply involved in the political turmoil of his day. After the English Civil War (1642–49), which resulted in the execution of King Charles I and the creation of a short-lived Puritan republic, he served in Oliver Cromwell's government and published essays on political theory.

After the restoration of the monarchy in 1660, Milton was forced to retire from political life so he devoted himself entirely to poetry. It was during these years that he composed *Paradise Lost*. In 1652, he had lost his sight and, from dawn to dusk each day, he dictated the poem to his secretary or his long-suffering daughters. For Milton, this was not simply a literary endeavour; it was rather a 'good work' inspired by faith and its purpose was essentially political. Poets, he claimed in his famous pamphlet *Areopagitica*, were better teachers than scholars because instead of merely imparting facts, poetry worked by indirection; it appealed to what we would call the subconscious mind, enabling readers to imbibe its lessons at a level deeper than the purely rational.[59] Milton believed that the religious and moral education of its citizens was far more important to the health of the state than constitutional arrangements. The task of government was 'to make the people fittest to chuse, and the chosen fittest to govern ... to mend our corrupt and faulty education to teach the people faith, not without virtue'.[60] Blind, disgraced and politically impotent, creating this epic poem was the only way he could do God's work.

Milton had read the Bible in the original languages and he expected his readers to be scripturally literate, praying that he would 'fit audience find, though few'.[61] Yet he took great liberties with the biblical text, introducing entirely new elements into the story of the Fall, because he felt himself to be as inspired by his celestial muse as the biblical authors. *Paradise Lost* is a work of *midrash*: like the rabbis, Milton filled the gaps in the biblical tale to make it address conditions in England after the turmoil of the Civil War and the Restoration.

Like the great classical epics, *Paradise Lost* begins *in medias res*, after Satan and his rebel angels had been defeated in the great war in heaven and find themselves in hell. Rousing his defeated troops, Satan plots to seduce the newly created human race and extend his power into its brave new world. Travelling through the terrifying realm of primal Chaos, he arrives in Eden, where he spies on Adam and Eve in their unfallen state. Halfway through the epic, the plot swings back to the very beginning of the story, when Satan declares war on God, making a republican bid for liberty against God the Father who had just promoted his Son to the highest place in heaven. We then witness the tragic Fall of Adam and Eve but the epic ends with the archangel Michael giving Adam a history lesson that reveals not only the consequences of the Fall but the promise of regeneration.

The subject of the poem, Milton declares at the outset, is Augustine's doctrine of original sin:

> Of Mans First Disobedience, and the Fruit
> Of that Forbidd'n Tree, whose mortal taste
> Brought Death into the World, and all our woe,
> With loss of Eden.[62]

As we have seen, the Eastern Church had firmly rejected Augustine's interpretation of Genesis and, even though his doctrine had been amplified by Anselm, it did not impinge much on Western spirituality until the early modern period, when it became central to the faith of both Catholics and Protestants. Emphasising the ineradicable guilt of human beings, it was a dark and pessimistic doctrine; even after baptism, Augustine had maintained, our humanity remained severely impaired. Where the Eastern Church has never doubted the possibility of the *theosis* ('deification') of every Christian in his or her own lifetime, such transformation was felt to be well-nigh impossible in the West.

By Milton's time, the situation had become even more fraught, since the doctrine of predestination, although it had not been important to Calvin himself, had become a distinguishing mark of Calvinism. Theodore Beza (1519–1605), who took the leadership of his church after Calvin's death, had maintained that humans could contribute nothing towards their own salvation and that because God's decrees were changeless, he had decided from all eternity to save some and predestined the rest to everlasting damnation. Conversion became a tortured drama in which the 'sinner' often experienced a psychological abreaction, a dangerous swing from extreme desolation to hysterical rapture. Convinced that they were damned, some fell into a suicidal depression that was seen as the work of Satan, who seemed as powerful and implacable as God.[63]

Milton would have none of this. This merciless Calvinist God violated the ideals of his humanist education. 'Whence does it happen that Adam's fall irremediably involved so many, many peoples,' he demanded indignantly, 'together with their infant offspring, in eternal death?'[64] His most effective riposte, however, was his depiction of Satan, who makes only a few fleeting appearances in scripture. In the Bible, he is not named as the tempter of Adam and Eve, who, as we have seen, was simply a talking snake. In the Hebrew scriptures, the origin of evil is usually attributed to the rebellion of a hitherto subordinate god or hero, such as Leviathan, the king of Babylon or the prince of Tyre.[65] Satan is presented as the enemy of Jesus in the gospels, but really does not come into his own until the book of Revelation. Despite the Protestant emphasis on *sola scriptura*, however, the minor scriptural figure of Satan dominated the Christian imagination during the early modern period and he is easily the most powerful figure in *Paradise Lost*.

From the very beginning critics were unable to agree about Milton's Satan, some regarding him as the epitome of evil, others maintaining that he was its epic hero. In fact, the secret of Satan's fascination is that he remains an 'insolubly ambivalent' enigma, his character constantly shifting from defiant evil to moving pathos.[66] Like most human beings, his character eludes us. When addressing his fellow devils in hell, he is passionate and grand in his fury, but when he first sees Eve, in her beauty and innocence, he becomes 'stupidly good', momentarily abstracted from the evil that, he declares, now defines his nature, before he 'recollects' himself and reassumes his satanic pose.[67] The narrator tells us that his rage and courage masks an ever-deepening despair.[68] Milton gives Satan soliloquies worthy of Hamlet or Macbeth that reveal his inner torment and remorse so eloquently that we find ourselves not only sympathising with him but admiring the courage involved in his constantly stifled pain:

> Which way I flie is Hell, my self am Hell;
> And in the lowest deep a lower deep
> Still threatning to devour me op'ns wide
> To which the Hell I suffer seems a Heav'n.[69]

Satan is the most developed character in the poem – the one we come to know most intimately – precisely because he is the most human. Like any human being, he remains complex, opaque and contradictory. Milton attempts to puncture the monstrous nightmare that was driving terrified Puritans to suicide by making Satan human.

Milton's treatment of Satan reminds us of the rabbis' description of the 'evil inclination' that is inextricably combined with human progress and productivity. Satan embodies many of the achievements of early modernity. When he embarks on his dangerous journey through Chaos, he becomes an intrepid early modern explorer, courageously seeking a New World; in his plan to invade Eden, he becomes a European coloniser; and, of course, he shares Milton's passion for republican liberty when he inveighs against the monarchical elevation of the Son. Looking back on his moment of rebellion, he declares that he 'sdeind [i.e. disdained] subjection': 'Will ye submit your necks, and chuse to bend / The supple knee?' he asks his fellow angels:

> Who can in reason then or right assume
> Monarchie over such as live by right
> His equals, if in power and splendor less,
> In freedom equal?[70]

Like the rabbis, Milton implied that evil was not an alien, omnipotent force; it was rather intricately combined with the creativity and inventiveness that were essential to human nature and its achievements. As he explained in *Areopagitica*:

Good and evil we know in the field of this world grow up together almost inseparably, and the knowledge of the good is so involved and interwoven with the knowledge of evil, and in so many cunning resemblances hardly to be discerned ... It was out of the rind of one apple tasted, that the knowledge of good and evil, as two twins cleaving together, leaped forth into the world, and perhaps this is the doom that Adam fell into of knowing good and evil, that is to say, of knowing good by evil.[71]

By projecting evil onto the monstrous figure of Satan, early modern Christians were disowning the evil that was not only inherent but an essential part of their humanity. Milton's Satan invited them, in effect, to own the evil that is a peculiarly human characteristic and adopt the more balanced and realistic rabbinic perspective.

Satan overhears Adam explaining to Eve that they must obey God's command that they not eat the fruit of the tree of knowledge, because it is the one and only 'easie prohibition' that God had imposed on them. Not surprisingly, Satan, ardent republican as he is, concludes that this is yet another sign of God's arbitrary injustice. But for Adam, it is a 'sign of our obedience'[72] – a symbolic reminder of the fact that, like their fellow creatures, they are not autonomous, 'self-begotten, self-raised',[73] but owe their existence and status to God, so their authority over the natural world cannot be a mandate for domination and exploitation.[74] When Eve succumbs to Satan's arguments and plucks the apple, Milton explains that she has set in motion the tragic history of the human abuse and corruption of Nature:

> Earth felt the wound, and Nature from her seat
> Sighing thru' all her Words gave signs of woe,
> That all was lost.[75]

But, Milton argues, all was *not* lost. As they leave the Garden, the archangel Michael promises Adam and Eve that 'thou ... shalt possess / A paradise within thee, happier farr',[76] a transformation they will achieve by practically reordering their relationship with one another and their fellow creatures.

In the last two books of Milton's epic, Michael reveals to Adam the future history of humanity. He begins by showing him six biblical scenes, starting with Cain's murder of his brother Abel and ending with Noah's flood. At first, Adam is horrified to see the suffering that his lapse has inflicted on his hapless descendants, but gradually, under Michael's tutelage, he realises that in every case what seemed a catastrophe leads ultimately to rebirth, transformation and regeneration. Interestingly, in this final section of the epic, Milton does not emphasise the fact that the suffering and death of the Son (which was discussed in heaven earlier) is crucial to this redemptive process.[77] Adam's enlightenment comes from his compassionate response to the distress of his fellow human beings[78] and it is this that gives him hope.[79] Feeling that he has finally achieved enlightenment, he cries:

> Henceforth I learne, that to obey is best,
> And love with feare the onely God, to walk
> As in his presence, ever to observe
> His providence, and on him sole depend.[80]

But Michael immediately corrects him. A purely internal, spiritualised transformation is not enough. Adam must express this insight in 'good works'; disciplined and persevering effort must, the archangel repeats emphatically, be *added* to faith:[81]

> onely add
> Deeds to thy knowledge answerable, add Faith,
> Add Vertue, Patience, Temperance, add Love.[82]

The 'paradise within' that Adam and Eve will experience cannot simply be a private, interior serenity. Humankind must make a practical effort – political and social – to reshape on earth in whatever form it can the paradisal life for which human beings were created.

Milton had magnificently rebutted the damaging depiction of Satan that had become current in Calvinist circles. He succumbed, however, to the inadequate notion of God that was beginning to take hold in Western Christianity and would, increasingly, make God religiously and intellectually problematic. Milton had grave doubts about the Trinity, for example, which, as we have seen, has no sound scriptural basis, but so deeply entrenched was Trinitarian terminology in the Christian psyche that he could not avoid it. The result was deeply unsatisfactory, intellectually and theologically. Western Christians had never grasped the mystical basis of the Greek conception of the Trinity, in which 'Father', 'Son' and 'Spirit' were simply 'terms that we use' to express the way in which the utterly transcendent and unknowable God makes itself known to us – partial and incomplete glimpses of the Divine Nature (*ousia*) that lies far beyond all imagery and conceptualisation. It is never clear in Milton's epic whether the Son is a second divine being or a mere creature like the angels. As in other early modern depictions of the Trinity, Father and Son are seated side by side in the heavens – presumably on celestial chairs – two entirely separate person-alities who must engage in lengthy conversations of deep tedium to learn each other's intentions, even though the Son is the acknowledged Word and Wisdom of the Father.

The Father's language is strangely unscriptural. While the Son makes oddly proleptic references to scriptural events that have not yet occurred but which prefigure the salvation that he will at some time in the future bring to the world, the Father's speeches are mechanical, casuistical, repetitive, frigid and dull. The Fall has not yet occurred, but already he shows little warmth towards the human species that he has created:

> So will fall
> Hee and his faithless Progenie: whose fault?
> Whose but his own? ingrate, he had of mee
> All he could have; I made him just and right,
> Sufficient to have stood, though free to fall.[83]

He soundly quashes any suggestion that, as an omnipotent Creator, he could prevent this future catastrophe:

> if I foreknew,
> Foreknowledge had no influence on their fault,
> Which had no less prov'd certain unforeknown.
> So without least impulse or shadow of Fate,
> Or aught by mee immutablie foreseen,
> They trespass, Authors to themselves in all
> Both what they judge and what they choose.[84]

This cannot but remind the reader of the absurd theological debates that now preoccupy some of the devils in Milton's hell – on 'Providence, Preknowledge, Will, and Fate, / Fixt Fate, free Will, Foreknowledge absolute' – which the narrator dismisses as 'Vain wisdom all, and false Philosophie'.[85]

Milton's God is the doctrinal deity created by the catechisms and 'filters' that were designed in the aftermath of the Reformation to impose strict orthodoxy. The Father comes across as callous, self-righteous and entirely lacking in the compassion that his religion was supposed to inspire. Once we make what we call 'God' think and reason as we do, 'he' is no longer Being itself but merely *a* being like ourselves writ large, an idol that we have constructed in our own image. It is disconcerting to hear Father and Son and, indeed, Michael discoursing at length on tragic events in the history of Israel that are determined in advance; it inevitably occurs to the reader that there must be an easier and more merciful way to save the world. Forcing God to speak and think like one of us shows the inadequacy of an anthropomorphic conception of the divine that would become increasingly widespread in the Western world. In *Paradise Lost*, we have, in embryo, the irate 'Old Man in the Sky' that would eventually make religion impossible for many Europeans. There is no sign here of the ineffable God of Denys, Thomas Aquinas or Bonaventure or the inscrutable En Sof of the Kabbalists. But in other parts of the world, a more traditional theology and the art of reading sacred texts were still alive and well.

*

On 2 January 1492, the Christian armies of the Reconquista had conquered the city state of Granada, the last Muslim stronghold in Europe, and on 31 March the Catholic monarchs Ferdinand and Isabella signed the Edict of Expulsion, which gave Spanish Jews the option of baptism or deportation. Many were so attached to al-Andalus that they converted to Christianity and remained in Spain, but about 80,000 Jews crossed the border into Portugal, while 50,000 fled to the Ottoman empire.[86] Ferdinand and Isabella were creating a modern centralised state that could not tolerate such autonomous institutions as the medieval guild and the Jewish community, so the unification of Spain was completed by an act of ethnic cleansing. In 1499, the Muslims of Spain were given the same choice as the Jews, and for several centuries, western Europe became Muslim-free. For some, modernity, therefore, would be empowering, liberating and enlightening, but others would experience it as coercive, invasive and destructive.

Jewish communities throughout the world mourned the extinction of Spanish Jewry, which seemed to put the Torah itself in jeopardy. Maimonides had feared that the Jews' dispersion over so many lands would result in the fragmentation of the Torah, so he had composed the *Mishneh Torah* ('Second Law'), a summary of the entire Oral Law. Now Joseph Karo (1488–1575), a leading scholar of Sefad in northern Palestine, produced a similar precis, the *Shulkhan Arukh* ('Prepared Table'), which consisted of thirty short sections that could be read daily, ensuring that throughout the scattered Jewish communities there would be only One Torah. Thanks to the printing press, there were now too many books and too many opinions:

> As the days passed and we were poured from one vessel into another ... and troubles came upon us, until, because of our sins, the prophecy was

fulfilled and the wisdom of the sages shall be lost, and the Torah and the
students are powerless, for the Torah is now not like two laws [the Oral and
the Written Torahs] but rather like many laws, because of the many books
explaining its rules and ordinances.[87]

In Poland, Rabbi Moshe Isserles, known as Rasa, produced a similar code
for his Ashkenazi students, because he also deplored this proliferation of
Torah interpretations, all claiming to be divinely inspired: 'Time passes and
their words do not perish ... and afterwards these books themselves
and the one who reads them claims they are all given in Sinai.'[88]

Like the new 'filters' and catechisms that were being produced in Christian
Europe, these rabbinic codes were trying to stem the flow of innovation.
But, significantly, in the Jewish world, there were immediate objections to
these summaries. Scholars insisted that it was wrong to present the Talmud
as a streamlined legal system. Rabbis Jacob Polak and Shalom Shachne,
founders of Talmudic learning in Poland, refused to create such a 'filter'
for their students, because it would inhibit their ability to innovate and
respond creatively to a new situation. 'I do not want the world to depend
on me,' Rabbi Jacob protested:

> When there is disagreement between rabbinic authorities, a rabbi should
> decide or entertain his own opinion, since, 'The judge should only follow
> that which he sees with his own eyes.' Everyone, therefore, should rule
> according to the needs of the hour as his heart desires.[89]

Unlike the reformers and the Tridentine Fathers, the rabbis did not
expect – indeed, they abhorred – uniformity of opinion and were not at
all disturbed by the possibility of disagreement or innovation, because the
Talmud not only allowed for but actively encouraged diverse points of view.
As Solomon ben Jehiel (1510–74), known as Maharshal, explained, scripture
was the Word of God, so that even if the heavens and the oceans were ink,
they would not suffice to expound a single passage of scripture, record all
the doubts arising from it, and the many new ideas that it inspired. It was
unrealistic to expect explanations of all the puzzling passages of the Torah,
because it was deliberately composed in a terse, enigmatic style that had
created the necessity for intense oral discussion and disagreement.[90]

The rabbis had a deep, instinctive appreciation of the forward-thrusting
dynamic of scripture, which European Christians seemed intent on forgetting. Jews had always believed that the Torah came to life in the oral

discussions that inspired new interpretations. Rabbi Chaim Bezalel criticised Rasa's code as an act of censorship that would condemn all previous texts to oblivion. The genius of Halakha (the system of Jewish law and jurisprudence), he insisted, was that it was open-ended and could not be tied down because both Torah and Halakha were God's words and therefore infinite. Without a closed code, a rabbi did not have to try to be consistent but could respond wisely and creatively to the needs of the moment. 'He might not rule today as he did yesterday,' Bezalel explained. 'This does not imply change or deficiency. On the contrary, this is the very path of Torah.'[91] As we have seen, most of the discussions recorded in the Bavli (the Babylonian Talmud) avoid definitive answers to questions raised. Instead they deliberately preserve the wealth of difference and variety in the approach to any problem, to give later generations, who would be living in a very different world, the opportunity to respond to their circumstances creatively.

There were, however, disagreements about the scriptural curriculum. In France, the rise of Talmudic learning had led to a decline in the study of the Bible. 'No Jew should study anything but Talmud,' ruled the sixteenth-century rabbi Aharon Land – not 'even the twenty-four books' that made up the Bible.[92] A more nuanced view from Poland helps to explain this preference. The obscurity of the ancient biblical texts did not help a Jew to cultivate piety and reverence, so it was better to stick to the Talmud: 'Bible study does not cause anyone to be pious, because we cannot understand [it] ... Even a little Talmud is enough to bring fear of God than much learning of other subjects.'[93] Clearly, there was no desire to return *ad fontes*: Maharshal pointed out the progressive evolution of scripture. The Mishnah had recorded the Oral Torah and this had resulted in the creation of the Talmud, a still greater text, which in turn had inspired the Tosefta, which clarified the Talmudic debates. It is regrettable, however, that the prestige of the Bavli minimised the study of the Bible, the foundational written text.

There were arguments too about whether the Bavli could be studied alongside *falsafah* and Kabbalah. Maimonides, as we have seen, had believed that *falsafah* was a safeguard and corrective to the anthropomorphic presentation of God in the Bible. He had also argued that the study of the Talmud was inferior to the mystical study of metaphysics, regarding it as a way station to higher disciplines. For Kabbalists, the goal was *devekut*, union with God through meditational techniques, which could be hindered by the intensely analytical focus of Talmudic study. But Joseph Karo, a great Talmudist and mystic, maintained that there was no conflict between mystical intuition and traditional meditation, 'for the study of Torah strengthens the communion'; indeed, to interrupt Torah study was to fall away from the mystical state.[94]

The Sephardi Jews who migrated to the Ottoman empire after their expulsion from Spain had a different experience from their Ashkenazi brethren. Some settled in Safed in Palestine, where they met Isaac Luria (1534–72), a frail, northern European Jew who had developed a form of Kabbalah that spoke directly to their predicament. Their deportation had inflicted a psychic wound that made the world appear alien, with everything in the wrong place.[95] While Western Christians were developing a wholly literal and historical understanding of scripture, Luria was still able to interpret the Bible mythically, bringing out its underlying significance in a creation myth that bore no resemblance to the orderly cosmogony of Genesis. While the scriptural value of kenosis was disappearing in Christian Europe, Luria depicted the creation as an act of self-emptying. Because God was omnipresent, there had been no place for the world, so En Sof, the unknowable Godhead, had contracted into itself, as it were, in a voluntary withdrawal (*zimzum*), to create such a space, making itself less so that its creatures might flourish and be.

Luria's creation story proceeded in a series of cosmic accidents, explosions and false starts. Sparks of divine light had fallen into the vacuum created by *zimzum*, everything ended up in the wrong place, and the Shekhinah wandered through the world, yearning to be reunited with the Godhead.[96] Luria's story may differ from the biblical myth, but it seemed a more accurate depiction of the arbitrary world that Jews now inhabited than the Genesis account. Yet it was also true to the underlying spirit of the biblical history, which had presented the people of Israel suffering one painful migration and deportation after another. This myth gave meaning to the experience of the traumatised exiles, suggesting that their tragedy was in tune with the basic rhythms of existence since even God was exiled from itself. Instead of being discarded outcasts, Jews were central actors in a process that could heal their broken world, because their precise observance of Torah could end this universal displacement and effect the 'restoration' (*tikkun*) of the Shekhinah to the Godhead, the Jews to their Land, and the rest of the world to its rightful state.[97] By 1650, Lurianic Kabbalah had become a mass movement in the Jewish world from Poland to Iran – the only Jewish interpretation of scripture in the early modern period that commanded such wholehearted acceptance.[98]

In the Protestant world, ritual was gradually being discarded or downgraded. But Luria's myth would have remained a senseless fiction without the rites he devised to make it a healing reality. Kabbalists made night vigils, weeping and rubbing their faces in the dust as a way of owning their sorrow. They lay awake all night, calling out to God in their abandonment, and took long walks around Galilee, enacting their essential homelessness. But they had to work through their pain in a disciplined manner. Vigils always ended at dawn with a meditation on the end of humanity's exile from the divine in which they practised exercises of concentration (*kawwanoth*) that elicited a sense of wonder and delight. Compassion was a crucial Lurianic virtue and there were severe penances for injuring others. Jews who had suffered so much themselves must not add to the sum of the world's sorrow.[99]

*

It is often said in the West that Islam has never had a proper 'reformation', but movements of *islah* ('reform') and *tajdid* ('renewal') had always punctuated Islamic history. They had often occurred during a period of cultural change or in the wake of such political disasters as the Mongol invasions, when old answers no longer sufficed and reformers used *ijtihad* ('independent reasoning') to address the new status quo.[100] Ibn Taymiyyah, for example, had tried to reform shariah law to meet the needs of Muslims living under Mongol rule. Like the Protestant reformers, he returned *ad fontes*, to the Quran and the Sunnah, challenging the medieval jurisprudence that was now considered sacred. But, unlike the Christians, Muslim reformers usually focused on practice rather than dogma.

Another such moment occurred after the discovery of gunpowder when the new military technology gave rulers more power over their subjects and enabled them to build larger, more centralised states. During the late fifteenth and early sixteenth centuries, three powerful new Islamic empires were created: the Safavid empire in Iran, the Moghul empire in India, and the Ottoman empire in Anatolia, Syria, North Africa and Arabia, which all differed from the old Muslim empires in one important respect. The Abbasid administration had never implemented shariah law, nor had it evolved its own Islamic ideology, but the rulers of these new empires all had a distinct Islamic orientation. In Safavid Iran, Shiism became the state religion; *falsafah* and Sufism were dominant in Moghul polity; and the Ottoman empire was the first state to attempt to rule by shariah law. Of special interest to us are seventeenth- and eighteenth-century 'reformations' in Iran and Arabia.

The spectacular military successes of Shah Ismail, who conquered Iran in the early sixteenth century, had shocked the Muslim world. Hitherto, most Shiis had been Arabs and most Iranians were Sunnis, though there were Shii centres in Rayy, Kashan, Khurasan and the old garrison town of Qum. Since the time of Jafar al-Sadiq, Shiis had made a principled withdrawal from politics, so, Muslims asked one another, how could there be 'state Shiism'? But Shah Ismail set about creating an establishment Shiism that had little in common with traditional Twelver orthodoxy. Hitherto, Shiis and Sufis had been close but now Sufi Orders (*tariqas*) were suppressed in Iran, and Sunni *ulema* (scholars specialising in theology and sacred law) either executed or deported. Ismail probably knew very little about regular Shiism. The Safavids subscribed to the 'extremist' (*ghuluww*) theology prevalent in the *ghazi* states on the fringes of Mongol territory, which acknowledged the Mongols as overlords but ran their own emirates. They all had a strong Sufi orientation, developing Sufi Orders that combined extravagant forms of Sufism with the revolutionary ethos of the very early Shiah. They revered Ali as an incarnation of the divine and claimed that, like the Hidden Imam, the deceased imams of their *tariqa* were in 'occultation'. Like other *ghuluww* leaders, Ismail may have believed that he *was* the Hidden Imam, who had returned to found a Shii empire and establish a reign of justice.

But now that they ruled a large agrarian empire, the Safavids soon realised that their 'extremist' ideology was no longer viable. Shah Abbas I (1588–1629) expelled all *ghuluww* officials and imported Arab Shiis from Lebanon to instruct his people in Twelver orthodoxy. Under Abbas, Isfahan, his capital, enjoyed a cultural renaissance that, like the European Renaissance, looked *ad fontes* for inspiration, which for Abbas meant pre-Islamic Persian culture. But the Arab *ulema* found themselves in an anomalous position. Because Shiis regarded all government as inherently unjust, they had traditionally held aloof from society and had no mosques or madrasas of their own but had simply met in one another's homes in private study groups. Now they found themselves in charge of the state educational and legal system which was generously funded by the shahs, who built them magnificent madrasas. They compromised by refusing official government posts and insisting on ranking as subjects, at the same time making it clear that it was they – not the shahs – who were the true representatives of the Hidden Imam.

But their new wealth compromised the egalitarian spirit of the Shiah. Some, like Muhammad Baqir Majlisi (d. 1700), who set in motion a Shii reformation, became authoritarian and even bigoted. Over the years, the

Shiah had developed a mystical spirituality, influenced by both Sufism and *falsafah*, which Majlisi regarded as a corrupt innovation. He insisted on a return to fundamentals, relentlessly persecuted the remaining Sufis and was passionately hostile to the Sunni Ottomans. He also tried to suppress the teaching of *falsafah* and mystical theology in Isfahan, pressuring the *ulema* to focus on jurisprudence (*fiqh*) instead. Many of the *ulema*, therefore, would develop a legalistic, literalist and rationalist ethos.[101] Unlike the Protestant reformers, however, whose focus was scripture, Majlisi concentrated on ritual. He outlawed Sufi *dhikr* and the cult of Sufi saints, and introduced into Iran, which was still predominantly Sunni, the Shii mourning rites for Imam Husain – carefully taming this potentially subversive ritual to make it serve the imperial cause.

During the month of Muharram, Shiis had long staged ritual processions commemorating the martyrdom of Husain, the Prophet's grandson, who had been murdered by the troops of Caliph Yazid at Karbala. Weeping, moaning and slapping their foreheads, mourners expressed the passion for justice that lies at the heart of Shii spirituality, and their frustration with imperial inequity. By the sixteenth century, these rituals had become more elaborate. Tearful women and children representing Husain's bereaved family rode on camels. The coffins of the imam and his martyred companions were followed by the local governor and notables, while large crowds of men sobbed, wailed and slashed themselves with knives.[102] The *Rawdat ash-Shuhada*, an emotional account of the Karbala tragedy, was recited to similar lamentation. Majlisi, however, had as little sympathy for poor Iranians as Luther had for rebellious peasants. Instead of inspiring the masses to follow Husain in the struggle against tyranny, Majlisi taught them to revere him as a patron who could secure their admission to paradise. These doctored rites now endorsed the status quo, tacitly encouraging the people to curry favour with the powerful and focus on their personal salvation instead of the political welfare of the *ummah*.[103]

During the seventeenth century, a rift developed within Iranian Shiism.[104] Most Iranian Shiis followed the Akbaris, who tried to oppose the growing power of *ulema* like Majlisi by returning *ad fontes* – to the Quran as interpreted by the imams. In the process, however, the Akbaris lost touch with the mythical character of traditional Shiism, and tended to reduce scripture to a set of explicit directives.[105] The Akbaris were particularly alarmed by a new idea, which assumed that most Muslims were incapable of interpreting the fundamentals (*usul*) of Islam for themselves. The Usulis, who represented this somewhat pessimistic view, opposed the Akbaris, fearing that they were so in thrall to the past that they were unable to meet the challenges arising from the decline of Safavid power. In the absence of the Hidden Imam, the Usulis argued, no jurist could have the last word and no precedent could be binding, so ordinary Muslims must follow the rulings of a living authority – a *mujtahid* who was deemed capable of exercising *ijtihad*.

But at about the same time as Descartes was creating his creed of *sola ratio*, Mir Dimad (d.1631) and Mulla Sadra (d.1640) founded a new school of mystical philosophy in Isfahan that opposed the shrinking horizons of the Usulis.[106] In Europe, Catholics and Protestants were insisting that the faithful submit to their doctrines, but for Mir Dimad and Mulla Sadra true knowledge could never be achieved by intellectual conformity. Instead, they developed a synthesis of mysticism and the rationalism of *falsafah* – in modern terms, a creative partnership of the two frontal hemispheres of the brain. Mulla Sadra criticised the *ulema* for belittling mystical intuition and berated the Sufis for rejecting rational thought, while Mir Dimad was a natural scientist as well as a mystic. A true *faylasuf* should be as rational as Aristotle but then go beyond him in an ecstatic apprehension of transcendent truth.

Both emphasised the role of the imagination and the unconscious, which they described as a state that existed between the realm of sense perception and rational abstraction. Sufis had called it the *alam al-mithal*, the world of pure images, which surfaces in our dreams but can also be experienced by mystical techniques. These experiences should not be dismissed as illusions, because, even though they cannot be analysed logically, they are part of our human nature and profoundly affect our behaviour and personality. Truth is not confined to ideas that can be logically or practically demonstrated: it has an interior dimension that transcends our normal waking consciousness.

The hard-line *ulema* drove Mulla Sadra from Isfahan, and for ten years he lived in isolation in a small village near Qum. Like Luther in his tower and Descartes in his lodgings, he worked out his philosophy in solitude, realising that, despite his commitment to mystical philosophy, his approach to religion was still too abstract and cerebral. When he began to practise the disciplined mental exercises that enabled him to descend deeply into the *alam al-mithal*, his mind, he said, caught fire and he found that he could apprehend mysteries that had hitherto seemed incomprehensible. Mulla Sadra believed that, by making an immense effort, human beings could be utterly transformed, acquiring a measure of divinity by embodying the attributes of God as the prophets and the imams had done.[107]

But this did not imply a rejection of the secular world. Having attained this transformation, the mystic could not remain in *ekstasis* but must return to political life, working practically to create a more just society in what Buddhists would call a 'return to the marketplace'. In *The Four Journeys of the Soul*, Mulla Sadra described the progress of such a charismatic leader. First, he must abandon the empirical thinking of what we call the left hemisphere of the brain and enter the holistic, imaginative realm of the *alam al-mithal*. There he should contemplate each of the divine attributes revealed in the Quran in turn, until he discovered their essential unity – an insight that would transform him. In his third journey, the mystical *faylasuf* returned to humankind, and discovered that he now saw the world quite differently. His final task was to preach God's word, finding new ways to implement the Quran and reorder society in accordance with God's will.[108] For Mulla Sadra, justice and equity could not be achieved without a mystical and religious underpinning. This new vision of Shii leadership regarded the rational effort that was essential for the transform-ation of society as inseparable from the mythical and mystical context that gave it meaning. His quest, which began as a profound exploration of his mind, ended with a principled return to the political world to realise Quranic principles.

A later, eighteenth-century Islamic reformation in Arabia, which has greatly impacted modern Islam, attempted, like the Protestant Reformation, to return *ad fontes*. At that time, the Ottoman empire was beginning to unravel on its fringes, and the ensuing disruption inspired several reform movements, all characterised by a return to the Quran and the Hadith. Convinced that the current unrest was due to the deterioration of orthodox practice and the importation of such foreign rites as honouring the tombs of Sufi saints, their goal was the social and moral reconstruction of society. Even though the Quran was central to this project, the reformers were not calling for a doggedly literalist interpretation. While Western Christians were introducing 'filters' for the unlearned, these reformers urged all Muslims to study scripture directly instead of relying on commentaries and handbooks, using their powers of *ijtihad* to discover what a Quranic ruling or a hadith had meant in its original context.[109]

One of the most important of these reformers in Arabia was Muhammad ibn Abd al-Wahhab (1702–91). He was opposed by the more conservative *ulema*, who feared that once Muslims began studying the Quran indepen-dently, their authority would be diminished. They also accused him of promoting violence, but Ibn Abd al-Wahhab always denied this. His 'struggle' (*jihad*) began with education and fighting could only be a last resort. Because he needed a protector, he formed an alliance with Muhammad ibn Saud of Najd in 1744: he was to be responsible for religious practice while Ibn Saud managed political and military affairs. Ultimately this arrangement failed, because Ibn Abd al-Wahhab would not endorse all Ibn Saud's military campaigns, insisting that true jihad was not a means of acquiring wealth and power. He himself conducted an epistolary jihad, inviting local leaders, scholars and rulers to join his movement and Wahhabi ideas spread through the peninsula.[110]

Ibn Abd al-Wahhab required all Muslims – men and women alike – to study scripture for themselves; but he urged them not to waste time on the obscure, 'ambiguous' verses, but to concentrate on Quranic teachings that were clear and direct. At the same time, they were to study the Five Pillars. The Shahada, the First Pillar, is a declaration: 'There is no god but Allah.' This was not merely a matter of 'belief'; rather, it insisted that a Muslim's first and only priority was Allah rather than such false 'gods' as wealth, power and status. Once students had truly grasped this and ordered their lives accordingly, they could proceed to *salat*, the five canonical prayers. Then they could practise *zakat* ('almsgiving') and by this time, a student had become a true Muslim and must turn his or her attention outwardly to the creation of a just and compassionate society.[111]

In advocating the study of scripture, Ibn Abd al-Wahhab always emphasised the importance of discussion, argument and careful attention to the meaning of Quranic words. Ibn Taymiyyah had been the first Muslim to rule that anybody who did not accept his views was a *kafir*, an unbeliever, and some of Ibn Abd al-Wahhab's disciples inclined to this maverick view, but he himself always insisted that God alone knew what was in a person's heart so nobody could say whether a person was or was not a Muslim. Nor did he agree with those of his followers who were cultivating a more militant understanding of Islam. Like the early exegetes, he interpreted the jihad verses in their historical context in a way that placed limitations on warfare.[112] But the more aggressive Wahhabis sided with Ibn Saud, who was bent on carving out a large kingdom for himself in Arabia. It was due to their influence that Ibn Taymiyyah's writings were admitted to the Wahhabi canon in the early nineteenth century, a decision that would lead Wahhabis to a more intransigent interpretation of the Quran.

*

While Western Christians were becoming aggressively sectarian, India had been moving in the opposite direction. Akbar (1542–1605), the third Moghul emperor, founded a House of Worship, where scholars from all religious traditions met to discuss spiritual matters, and a Sufi Order dedicated to 'divine monotheism' (*tawhid-e-ilahi*), based on the conviction that the One God reveals itself in any rightly guided religion. In November 1598, Akbar, with an entourage of scribes, artists, painters and musicians, visited Arjan, the Fifth Sikh Guru, in Goindval in the Punjab. During his visit, the imperial manuscripts would have been displayed as a demonstration of Moghul power, and this may have inspired Guru Arjan to edit the hymns and writings of his four predecessors, together with over 2,000 hymns of his own, thus creating the first official Sikh scripture. The First Guru, Nanak, had, of course, repudiated the very idea of a scriptural canon, but Amar Das, the Third Guru, had paved the way by commissioning a two-volume hymnal consisting of the poems of all three Gurus and some medieval poets. It seems that some of Guru Arjan's enemies were circulating spurious works in Nanak's name to entice Sikhs away from the legitimate succession, so Arjan was preparing an authorised version bearing his own imprimatur.[113] Starting immediately after Akbar's visit, this massive editorial effort resulted in the *Adi Granth*, the 'First Volume' of Sikh scriptures, which was enshrined in the Golden Temple at Amritsar.

In this new scripture, we find many of the values that we have seen differently expressed in other traditions, but which the modern West was beginning to relinquish. Descartes had devised his philosophical insight by engaging in an intense dialogue with himself, relying entirely upon his own mind. In a sense, Nanak had done the same. He received no revelation from an external deity; rather, his transcendent experience was the result of a profound reconfiguration of his consciousness by means of an internal conversation in which one part of his mind addressed another.[114] Nearly every section of the *Adi Granth* begins: 'O Nanak!' but the speaker is not a personalised 'God' or an external force. In a process that is not unlike the neo-Confucians' doctrine of 'two minds', we hear Nanak's unconscious mind addressing his unredeemed mind, beseeching, cajoling and wooing it like a lover.

The triumphant conclusion of Descartes' solitary struggle had been a strong affirmation of ego: *cogito, ergo sum*. But Nanak's unredeemed mind had become estranged from its better half precisely because it was perpetually engaged in the preservation and promotion of the ego, calculating, blazing out in anger, manipulating others to secure its advantage, and indulging in negative emotions – haunted always by the knowledge of its eventual extinction:

> The mind is an elephant raging in rut
> Through the jungle, seduced by the charms of this world.
> It roams here and there under pressure of death,
> Through the guru, it's able to find its way home.[115]

The true 'home' of the unredeemed mind is the unconscious mind, which has come to terms with death, mortality and impermanence. It understands what the *Adi Granth* calls the 'command' (*hakam*): the fact that extinction is a fundamental law of life. We can only transcend the ego and experience the transcendence that the Sikh scriptures call the 'One', 'the Name' or 'the Word', when we wholeheartedly accept the fact that everything that exists, including ourselves, will pass away:

> No idea of Him can be conceived through thousands of thoughts
> Ultimate silence evades the most deep meditation
> To heap up the wealth of the world does not lessen man's hunger
> And multiple cleverness will not assist us hereafter.
> Nanak says: 'How to be cleared? How to break down the wall of the ego?
> Follow the command [*hakam*], as ordained from the beginning.'[116]

While Descartes believed that he had found an incontrovertible proof for God's existence, the Sikh scriptures make it clear that the ultimate reality is beyond human reckoning. It cannot be attained by 'thousands of thoughts', intensive 'meditation' or 'multiple cleverness' but only by transcending the ego.

This cannot be achieved by straining our mental processes, as Descartes did. Nanak's approach is gentler, though, like Descartes, he looks no further than his own mind for salvation: 'Though ego's an illness that's chronic, it also contains its own cure.'[117] This is because, at the deepest core of our being, in the unconscious mind, we know and accept the 'command', the law of life and death. To get beyond the clamorous ego, the Ten Gurus devised a practice called *nam simerum* ('remembrance of the Name'). *Simerum* derives from the Indo-European root *SMR* ('to remember') but is also cognate with *MR* ('to die'), so in this discipline, we remind ourselves constantly of our own mortality and that of everything and everybody

around us – a process not unlike Buddhist mindfulness that enables practitioners to realise the ephemeral nature of the self.

Descartes' quest was deliberately – almost aggressively – solitary, but
scripture has always emphasised the importance of community. The hymns
and reflective writings of the *Adi Granth* also make it clear that the
acknowledgement of the essential impermanence of existence must lead
to sympathy, respect and fellow feeling for all living things, who are
profoundly interconnected by sharing this common fate. The Gurus called
this intimate link between self and other '*nam*'. Descartes' rigorous
ascesis had made him a solitary 'thinking thing', unable even to believe
in the humanity of passers-by and alienated from his own body. His
embrace of *sola ratio* had made awe and wonder distasteful. But for the
Ten Gurus:

> The Word adorns the tongue
> Which chants 'How wonderful!' ...
> Folk come to honour those
> Made lovely by this chant.
> Grace grants 'How wonderful'
> With honour at the gate.[118]

Sikh scriptures called this state *sargan* and it derives from a vision of the
divinity inherent in all things. We do not experience the Absolute by separating ourselves from the world, but by discovering it within and then
projecting this sacrality into our daily experience.

Sikhs neither renounce the world nor separate religion from secular
and political life, because if mystical experience fails to actualise itself in
contingent events in the mundane world it remains sterile. Descartes'
cultivated self-ownership could easily lead to a sense of our entitlement
to the ownership of other things – an attitude that would be crucial to
capitalist society. But the practice of *nam simerum* helped Sikhs to develop
a consciousness of finitude that lets go of things. Because this countered
the economic drive of society, it was a political concept. Sikh scripture
develops a vision of a society based on divine justice without oppression
of any kind.

But politics would soon become extremely perilous in the Punjab. Akbar's
visit was the climax of good relations between Muslims and Sikhs. After
his death, the Moghul empire began its slow decline. Akbar's son Jahangir
(r. 1605–27) had to put down one rebellion after another and resented the

increasing power of Guru Arjan, whom Sikhs often addressed as 'Emperor'. Arjan's enemies fanned this hostility and he was charged with sedition, tortured, and executed in 1606. Four years later, Jahangir imprisoned his successor, Guru Hargobind (d.1644), who felt obliged to arm the Sikh Panth ('community') to defend itself.

Much of the seventeenth century was marked by political and military conflict, which culminated in the execution of the Ninth Guru, Tegh Bahadan, in 1675. His son and successor, Gobind Singh, added the writings of his father to the *Adi Granth* and shortly before his death, after years of fighting the Moghuls, he terminated the traditional line of personal Gurus and declared that their scripture would become the Sikhs' eternal Guru. It was renamed the *Guru Granth Sahib* ('The Guru of the Sikhs'), because it embodied the spirit of the Ten Gurus. The Sikhs had extended the meaning of the word guru: it referred not only to an inspiring teacher but to the spirit that had inspired all the Gurus, which Sikhs can experience in their writings. Worship of a book, therefore, is not 'idolatry', as one Sikh scholar explains: 'There were not ten different Gurus. Guru is one and the same spirit, and that is the spirit of Nanak. It is manifested in ten historical persons. Finally, it resides in the word of God in the *Guru Granth Sahib*.'[119]

The *Guru Granth Sahib* is housed in its own building, the Gurdwara, in the Golden Temple, placed on a cushion, wrapped in a special cloth and covered by a canopy. It is treated in rather the same way as the images of Shiva and Vishnu, which also enshrine a divine presence. Sikhs bow before it and remove their shoes before entering the Gurdwara, preparing themselves for an encounter with the sacred.[120] In the Hindu tradition, the divine is chiefly experienced in a human being – in a rishi or a guru – who humanises the divine Word and adapts it to the special needs of his disciples. While Nanak and his successors ruled the Panth, they probably transmitted the Word in this way. Now a written text had taken their place. Just as Hindus ask their guru for personal advice, Sikhs consult their scripture in a ceremony known as *vak lao* ('taking God's Word'), a daily devotion that also occurs at weddings, initiations or the naming of a child. The presiding priest opens the sacred book at random and begins to recite from the first verse on the top left-hand page. When spoken aloud, the verse is received as a message conveying the divine will for this unique event.

On one famous occasion, a group of Untouchables asked to join the Panth, but the more conservative Sikhs objected. They agreed to consult the Guru. The book was opened at random in the usual way, and the priest read aloud the following:

> Upon the worthless He bestows his grace, brother, if they will save the true Guru. Exalted is the service of the true Guru, brother, to hold in remembrance the divine name. God himself offers grace and mystic union. We are worthless sinners, brother, yet the True Guru has drawn us to that blissful union.[121]

The divine message was clear. To the modern Western mind, this would merely be a fortunate coincidence, but Sikhs regard this randomness as a way of removing egotism and personal bias, making room, as it were, for the divine will. A Sikh takes a *vak lao* every morning, regarding it as a personal message which he or she contemplates throughout the day. In the evening, it is understood as the Guru's comment on the day's happenings.[122]

This is clearly very different from the modern Western emphasis on the intelligibility of scripture. It belongs with the Indian spirituality of mantra, *bhakti* and sacred sound. The Sikh scriptures have transformative power only if they are recited in precisely the same way as they were first uttered by the Gurus. Like Hindus, Sikhs are more concerned with hearing and reciting the Word than understanding it semantically; but unlike Hindus, they only recently developed an interpretive tradition – probably the result of Western influence. It is a reminder that the modern Western understanding of scripture, which was beginning to emerge during the Reformation, is far from universal and should not, perhaps, be universalised.[123]

*

While spiritual horizons were shrinking in western Europe, in late sixteenth- and early seventeenth-century China, there was an openness to new ideas and a diminution of sectarian hostility. Where the Chengs and Zhu Xi had often been dismissive of Daoism and Buddhism in their effort to renew the Confucian spirit, late-Ming Confucians usually affirmed the 'Three Teachings', insisting that they were complementary and that no one tradition was the sole bearer of truth. In the West – as well as in modern China – neo-Confucianism has often been regarded as inherently unscientific, but that view has recently been challenged. The American sinologist Wm. Theodore de Bary has argued that a certain aptitude for scientific thinking had been present in Confucianism from the start. The drive to

transcendence that was essential to Cheng–Zhu learning was easily transmuted into a willingness to go beyond preconceived ideas. The practice of
'emptying' the mind and the conviction that a *junzi* had 'no mind of his
own' could encourage an intellectual attitude of impartiality and objectivity.
Similarly, the scriptural emphasis on 'the extension of knowledge' and the
'investigation of things', alongside Zhu's belief in the creative importance
of doubt, encouraged a scientific exploration of the natural world as well
as a critical stance towards scripture that, in some cases, led to a rebellion
against the very tradition that had nurtured these attitudes.[124]

This critical attitude was already evident in Zhu's commentary on the
Doctrine of the Mean, which urged the Confucian to 'study ... intensively,
inquire ... accurately, think ... carefully, sift clearly and practice earnestly'.[125]
Zhu had expanded on this:

> After one has studied extensively, he can have the principles of all things
> before him. He can, therefore, examine them and compare them to get the
> right questions to ask. Then, as he asks accurately, his teachers and friends
> will wholeheartedly engage in give-and-take with him, thus stimulating
> him and he will begin to think. As he thinks carefully, his thoughts will be
> refined and free from impurities. Then he achieves something for himself.
> He can now sift what he has achieved. He can, therefore, be free from doubts
> and can put his thoughts into action.[126]

Like Descartes, the neo-Confucian scholar had become doubt-free, but this
was not a Cartesian solitary quest since he seeks input from 'teachers and
friends' in a process of 'give-and-take', which is not purely cerebral but
engaged in 'wholeheartedly'. This is no dutiful submission to a received
doctrine. The scholar achieves 'something for himself'.

While in Europe, Catholics and Protestants were increasingly at odds,
the Chinese were becoming more pluralistic. Ni Yuanlu, a late-Ming
statesman who at the end of the dynasty was ready to die for his ruler and
was passionately intent on reasserting traditional Confucianism during this
turbulent period, was also a devout Buddhist. Jiao Hong (*c*.1540–1620),
an outstanding example of the new spirit, was also a sincere believer in
the 'Three Teachings'.[127] He regarded Buddhism as a commentary on
Confucianism, disapproved of Zhu's hostility to it, and was strongly influenced by Daoism. There was no *sola scriptura* for Jiao: the Way, he insisted,
is a dynamic, existential process that lay beyond the reach of words, doctrines
and texts. The scriptures are like a fish trap or a rabbit snare, which you

can forget once the fish or animal has been caught. In pursuing the Way, you should be like a horse, perpetually galloping forward, led by texts and teachings but always going beyond them.[128] Verbal teachings are only 'traces' (*ji*) and 'images' (*xiang*) which can suggest what the Way is like but can never fully express it.[129]

In stark contrast to the West during the seventeenth century, Jiao believed that a scholar should not be attached to any one set of teachings; still less should he argue about them. Jiao believed that the ancient sages had understood this. They never quarrelled about orthodoxy because they knew that any teaching was inescapably inadequate: they simply learned from one another.[130] Confucians, he pointed out, often claimed that Confucius had campaigned against Buddhists and Daoists, but there *was* no Buddhism in China in his time and Confucius had never criticised Laozi.[131] It was Mencius' hostility to Mozi and Yangzi that had introduced this intolerance into the tradition, even though both these philosophers had derived their teachings from ancient sages: Mozi from Yu, and Yangzi from the Yellow Emperor.

The emphasis on the ineffability of the ultimate clearly reflects Daoist and Buddhist influence. This syncretism was also common among the more radical members of the 'School of Mind' founded by Wang Yangming (1472–1579), who were known as 'Wild Chanists' even though they retained some Confucian values. For all his doubts about the ultimate value of their teachings, Jiao regarded sacred texts as indispensable, because 'the fish and the rabbit have yet to be caught, the trap and the snare cannot be done away with'.[132] He emphasised the ineffability of the Way to demonstrate the validity of all teachings, each of which reflected the Truth in its own manner. This concern led him to challenge the neo-Confucian curriculum, urging students to study the Five Classics without relying on the standard commentaries. This was, of course, a return *ad fontes* – but with a difference. Where the Protestants had retreated from their original determination to let all Christians read the scriptures for themselves and insisted on the use of catechisms as explanatory substitutes, Jiao pointed out that commentary had become habitual only under the Han and had made Confucian scholarship more superficial: 'As the commentaries explain more, the student of the Classics thinks less.'[133] Jiao did not want to prevent scholars from commenting on the Classics – he himself discussed them at great length, keeping his remarks separate from the original texts – but he did object to the way many of the officially recognised exegetes claimed to speak for the sages while expounding ideas of their own. The older commentaries,

Jiao pointed out, 'explained the words and the language without trying to unravel the meaning of the Classics, which the reader should perceive for himself through deep reflection'.[134]

In his attempts to return to this original type of exegesis, Jiao became one of the first pioneers of the scientific textual criticism that would become so important in Europe during the nineteenth century. The *Odes*, he argued, 'should be discovered in terms of its sound, and the rest of the Classics be understood by way of the language'.[135] A prolific author and bibliophile, Jiao collected ancient editions and compiled a monumental work on Chinese bibliography. He explained the Classics by attempting a scholarly reconstruction of their original historical setting and made an important discovery about the pronunciation of ancient Chinese by analysing the rhymes of the *Odes*.

Fang Yizhi (1611–71) expressed the emerging scientific orientation of the late Ming period differently.[136] He had received the usual education in the Classics and was widely read in philosophy, though he preferred poetry. He had doubts about a career in public life, especially after his father was imprisoned in Beijing – Fang's lachrymose plea for clemency persuaded the emperor to transmute the sentence from execution to banishment – but became tutor to the emperor's third son. When the Manchu Qing troops converged on the capital in 1644, however, Fang had himself tonsured as a Buddhist monk – a stratagem adopted by many of the Chinese to demonstrate their determination not to serve the new Qing dynasty. But, it is said, although he lived as a monk for the last twenty years of his life, he never forgot that he was a Confucian and in his writings continued to minimise the difference between the two traditions.

Fang was also influenced by the Jesuit missionaries from the 'Far West' who presented themselves as the peers of the Chinese literati and catered to their growing interest in European mathematics, astronomy and natural philosophy. Fang was already conversant with Western science: his father had prepared an imperially sponsored collection of European astronomical studies. But, like a true Confucian, Fang approached the new science from the standpoint of the *Great Learning*. Zhu Xi had rearranged the third paragraph of this scripture to make it clear that *gewu*, 'the investigation of things', was the root of both moral and political action:

The men of old who wished to make bright virtue plain throughout the world first put their countries in order, for which they first had to regulate their families, and for that to improve themselves as individuals, and for that to correct their hearts, and for that to give integrity to their intentions, and for that to extend their knowledge. *The extension of knowledge lies in the investigation of things.*[137]

But Fang disagreed with Zhu's understanding of 'things' (*wu*), which Zhu had confined to the discovery of the heavenly 'principle' in the human mind through scripture. This had become the standard neo-Confucian interpretation, but Fang thought it too narrow, since it neglected the study of natural phenomena.[138] He also disagreed with Wang Yangming, who had insisted that *gewu* must be explored only in the mind and that exploration of the natural world was irrelevant to self-cultivation. Fang argued that 'things' must include everything in the world, physical as well as spiritual:

'Things' are that which fill the space between Heaven and Earth. Here is where human beings attain life. Life being contained in our bodies and our bodies being centred in the real world, all that we experience of events [*shih*]. Events [or activities] are a class of 'things'.[139]

The mind is also a 'thing'; nature is a 'thing'; so too are 'Heaven-and-Earth together'.[140] Fang pointed out that the ancient sage kings had made technological discoveries as well as exploring their inner world: they had 'made implements [*qi*] and developed useful methods so that the lives of human beings would be eased'.[141] He found it 'laughable' that people should consider these inventions as 'impractical and without benefit'.[142] Fang was not discounting Zhu's quest for 'principle' in scripture but simply maintained that it should be anchored within this broader context.

Where Descartes had retreated into his mind to achieve certainty, Fang had a wider, more inclusive perspective and, like Zhu Xi, he envisaged it as a communal rather than a solitary effort. It was essential to see one's 'self' in the context of all 'things' in Heaven-and-Earth:

If I had worldly riches, I would set up a rude [i.e. simple] place of study and provide stipends to the most talented minds of the empire. We would utilise the strong points and ramifications of causes in such fields as classical exegesis, principles of nature, principles of things, literature, economics, philology, technical skills, music, calendrical knowledge, and medicine. We would arrange the important points and make details known about specific phenomena.[143]

Fang was open to learning from the West. He seems to have accepted without demur the notion that the earth was spherical and part of a heliocentric universe, and absorbed the ideas of both Copernicus and Tycho Brahe. The Chinese who held on to the ancient theory that 'the earth floats on water and the heavens enclose the water' were, he said, 'in error in not examining the matter'.[144]

But he had reservations about Western philosophy. The West is 'detailed in material investigation', he concluded, but deficient in 'comprehending seminal forces'.[145] By 'seminal forces', Fang referred to what is 'unknowable', 'the recondite', and the 'uniting reality underlying layers of mysteries'[146] – in short, what Jiao and others called the unknowable Dao. Fang would have been horrified by Descartes' claim that his proof of God's existence was as obvious as a geometrical demonstration. Descartes had, of course, eliminated 'wonder' from the world because he – and an increasing number of Western philosophers – was losing a sense of the ineffable and was confining the ultimate within a human system of thought.

Fang was happy to consider such Western ideas as the orbital heavens, the existence of the Primum Mobile, the relative positions of the celestial bodies, the phases of Venus, and the distance and dimensions of heavenly bodies other than the sun. But he could not follow the Jesuits in their belief in a tenth 'quiescent' heaven, the home of an absurdly inadequate 'God' whom the Jesuits called 'Lord of Creation'. The scientifically minded Jesuits had succumbed to the circumscribed, left-hemispheric 'God' of Scotus and Ockham, which Aquinas would have regarded as an idol. Instead of the Dao – which was unnameable and unknowable, dynamic, endlessly evolving, inherent in all that exists, and the reality that 'rolls through all things' – the Jesuits' 'Lord of Creation' was boxed into a single sector of the universe he had supposedly created – a deity not unlike Milton's God. In the West, the ineffable God of the Cappadocians, Denys, Thomas and Bonaventure was becoming a mere being, one among others. The Jesuits, Fang concluded, had not realised the limitations of language when speaking of the ultimate: 'Frequently, their meanings are encumbered by their words.'[147]

13

SOLA RATIO

The first freethinkers and atheists in Europe were not Enlightenment *philo-sophes* but Spanish Jews who were forced to convert to Christianity during the Spanish Inquisition and were derisively known as Marranos ('pigs'), a term of abuse that they adopted as a badge of pride. Most had accepted Christianity only under duress, were now forbidden to leave Spain and were closely watched by the Inquisition for signs of reversion. Lighting candles on Friday evening or refusing to eat shellfish could mean imprisonment, torture or even death. Not surprisingly, many of these *conversos* ('converts') would never wholeheartedly accept Christianity and were thrust into a spiritual limbo. After the Edict of Expulsion in 1492, 80,000 Jews were granted asylum in Portugal by King João II, but when Manuel I succeeded to the Portuguese throne three years later, Ferdinand and Isabella, his parents-in-law, ordered him to have the Jews in his kingdom forcibly baptised. Manuel, however, granted them immunity from the Inquisition for fifty years, which gave the *conversos* time to form an underground move-ment in which a dedicated minority continued to practise Judaism secretly and tried to win other Jews back to the faith.

But inevitably over the years, their understanding of Judaism became attenuated. They had received a Catholic education and their minds were filled with Christian symbols and doctrines, so many of these closet Jews ended up with a hybrid faith that was neither Jewish nor Christian.[1] Without access to Jewish worship, Marranos could perform very few of the rituals and practices that made the Torah a lived reality. Some had studied logic, physics, medicine and mathematics in Portuguese universities and brought a rational, empirical mindset to religion. Their God was the Aristotelian Prime Mover, who never intervened in earthly affairs and issued no commandments, since the laws of nature were accessible to everybody.[2]

Francisco Sanchez (1550–1623), a *converso* who was still drawn to Judaism, became rector of the College of Guyenne in south-western France. He was the first modern thinker to reject the scholastic notion of *auctoritas* ('authority'), which insisted on submission to the ideas of 'authors' – such as Aristotle in physics or Galen in medicine.[3] His Marrano experience had made him allergic to censorship in any form. 'Don't ask me for many authorities or reverence for "authors",' he wrote in 1581, 'since this is of a servile and unlearned spirit, rather than of one who is free and wants to know the truth. I shall follow only the reason of nature.' Here, perhaps for the first time, we hear the voice of *sola ratio*, rendered hostile to religion by cruelty and oppression: 'The object of authority is to believe, of reason is to demonstrate. One is for faith, the other is for science.'[4]

We hear this voice again in Baruch Spinoza (1632–77), the first scholar to study the Bible scientifically and who managed, unusually in Europe at this time, to live successfully beyond the reach of established religion. When *conversos* were permitted to leave Iberia at the end of the sixteenth century, his parents had settled in Amsterdam, which many Jews regarded as the New Jerusalem. The Dutch Republic had solved the problem of the European confessional state in which the religious allegiance of the ruler – Catholic, Lutheran or Calvinist – became the official faith of the nation. This system had failed to reduce denominational tension. Moreover, the Dutch noted that Christian rulers, mindful of the gospels' condemnation of Mammon, tended to be lukewarm in their support of trade. For purely pragmatic reasons, therefore, the Dutch Republic separated church and state: it supported the Reformed Protestant Church but did not oust the Catholic clergy because this would antagonise the Catholic states with whom they hoped to trade. As a result, the Dutch not only prospered materially but became world leaders. They extended this religious freedom to Jews, many of whom were attracted to Amsterdam for its social and economic opportunities. Some of these Marranos, however, were eager to return to the full practice of Judaism. This was not easy, since they had to be entirely re-educated in the faith and it is a tribute to the Dutch rabbis that most, despite initial tension, were able to make the transition.

But a significant number were not and their experience is instructive. To some sophisticated Portuguese Marranos, the 613 commandments of the Pentateuch seemed not only arbitrary but absurd, and the arcane dietary laws and purification rites barbaric. They had perforce become accustomed to thinking things out for themselves and found it difficult to accept the rabbis' explanations. As we know, the process of intensive Torah study gave Jews intimations of the sacred, and the practice of the *mitzvoth* brought a divine imperative into the minutiae of daily life. But to the critical Marranos, these rites, which had no biblical sanction, seemed bizarre. Their dilemma reminds us that the mythos of religion is unsustainable without the insights that come from ethical practice, the bodily disciplines of ritual and the intellectual ascesis of study, contemplation and prayer.

Spinoza's parents had managed the transition and at first their son seemed well adjusted and devout. He had never experienced persecution, had attended the excellent Keter Torah school, and studied mathematics, astronomy and physics. But at the age of twenty-two, he began to voice doubts. There were contradictions in the biblical texts, he argued, which could not therefore be of divine origin. Indeed, revelation itself was a chimera, since 'God' was simply the totality of Nature itself. Eventually, on 27 July 1656, Spinoza was excommunicated from the synagogue and was glad to go. He had powerful patrons, and enjoyed the friendship of leading scientists, philosophers and politicians. But at this date, there was no secular alternative in Europe. You could adopt another faith, but unless you were an exceptional human being – like Spinoza – it was almost impossible to live without belonging to a religious community. There were tragic cases of Marranos who were unable to survive outside the synagogue: we hear of one who lived miserably alone, shunned by Jews and Christians alike, and eventually shot himself in the head; and of a defiant Marrano who failed to integrate with the Jewish community and may have taken the desperate step of attempting reconciliation with the Catholic Church he had shunned all his life.[5] Certainly Jews and Christians alike found Spinoza's irreligion profoundly disconcerting.[6]

Spinoza was not the first Marrano to interpret the Bible by reason alone. Isaac La Peyrene (1596–1676) had applied Sanchez's scientific methodology to the study of the Bible, pointing out that the text was corrupt, contained inaccuracies and could not have been written by Moses.[7] But Spinoza went further. Like Sanchez, he had no time for authority:

> The supreme authority in explaining religion, and in passing judgement thereon, is lodged with the individual because it concerns individual rights. As the authority of Scriptural interpretation belongs to every man, the rule for such an interpretation should be nothing but the actual light of reason which is common to all – not any supernatural nor any external authority.[8]

Spinoza believed that the meaning of scripture could be ascertained 'solely by means of the signification of the words or by a reason acknowledging no foundation but scripture'.[9] There must be no inventive *midrash* and no imposition of post-biblical doctrines onto the biblical text. Scripture must be interpreted by the rational rules that had been so fruitfully applied to the investigation of the natural world:

> The method of interpreting Scripture does not differ from the method of interpreting nature. For as the interpretation of nature consists in drawing up a history [i.e. a systematic account of the data] of nature and therefrom inferring definitions of natural phenomena, so Scriptural interpretation naturally proceeds in drawing up a true history of Scripture.[10]

The real subject of scripture was not the events related in the biblical stories but its theological and moral teachings. These should be judged by natural reason, which tells us that a supreme being exists, who must be obeyed and worshipped by the practice of justice and love of one's neighbour. Scripture is not the supreme authority, therefore; it is subservient to *sola ratio*. As we have seen, theology has traditionally required intuition and imagination together with ritual and other disciplines that encourage empathy, but as the Age of Reason progressed, the concept of religion – and, therefore, the understanding of scripture – was becoming attenuated.

Frustrated by the theological debates of the Reformation, many Christians turned to the new discoveries of science, which they hoped could confirm their beliefs in an objective, empirical God and put it beyond question. In a magnificent synthesis, Sir Isaac Newton (1642–1727) brought together Cartesian physics, the laws of planetary motion discovered by the German astronomer Johannes Kepler (1571–1630), and Galileo's laws of terrestrial movement. Gravity was the force that integrated this cosmic activity, preventing the planets from flying into space and pulling them towards the sun, and drawing the moon and the oceans towards the earth. But – Newton argued – this intricate system 'could only proceed from the counsel and domination of an intelligent and powerful Being'.[11] This was a very different deity from Luria's self-emptying En Sof or the kenotic Word of the New Testament. It was an overwhelming force that mastered and controlled the universe, whose chief quality was Dominion: 'It is the domination of a spiritual being that constitutes a god,' Newton claimed.[12] The Creator must also have intelligence, perfection, eternity, infinity, omniscience and omnipotence.

As the Chinese philosopher Fang Yizhan had feared, the God of the 'Far West' had been reduced to a scientific explanation and given a limited, definable function in the cosmos, controlling matter as the will regulates the body. God's existence was now a rational consequence of the world's design and God was immanently present in the laws 'he' had devised: gravity was simply the activity of God himself. So who needed scripture? Not Newton, for whom science was the only means of arriving at a proper understanding of the divine: 'For there is no way to come to ye knowledge of a deity but by ye forms of Nature.'[13] Scientific rationalism, he believed, was the original religion of humankind, but it had been corrupted by 'monstrous Legends, false miracles, veneration of reliques, charmes, ye doctrine of Ghosts or Daemons and their intercession, invocation & worship of other superstitions'.[14] Newton composed a treatise entitled *The Philosophical Origins of Gentile Theology*, arguing that this 'fundamental religion' had been founded by a man whom the Jews called Noah but who had been given a different name by other peoples. Noah and his sons had worshipped in temples that replicated the cosmos: 'The whole heavens they recconed to be ye true & real temple of God & therefore ... they framed it so as in the fittest manner to represent the whole systeme then wch. nothing can be more rational.'[15]

Jews, Newton argued, had originally followed this faith that had inspired them to study the universe rationally, but they had lapsed time and again into superstition and had repeatedly to be recalled to the religion of reason by the prophets. Jesus had been one of these prophets but his Religion of Nature had been corrupted by Athanasius, who had devised the doctrines of the Incarnation and the Trinity to win over the heathens. In the book of Revelation, God had predicted that the rise of Trinitarianism – 'this strange religion of ye west', 'the cult of three equal gods' – would incur divine wrath.[16] There was no need for ritual or meditation in Newton's 'fundamental religion', which required only 'belief', a word that Newton persistently used in its modern sense of an intellectual assent to a somewhat dubious proposition. Hitherto, 'belief' had meant loyalty and commitment to the practices of the faith that made its theology intuitively comprehensible.[17] For Newton, belief was simply an intellectual acceptance of doctrine. 'When I wrote my treatise about our Systeme,' he wrote to the classicist Richard Bentley, 'I had an eye upon which such Principles as might work with considering men for the beliefe in a Deity and nothing can rejoyce me more than to find it usefull for that purpose.'[18] Belief required no leap of faith, because it was obvious that the solar system depended upon a 'voluntary Agent' to balance its various forces, who was 'very well skilled in Mechanicks and Geometry'.[19]

Newton had clearly created a god in his own image and likeness. But, wearied by the quarrels of the Reformation, Christian leaders were eager to exchange *sola scriptura* – which had led only to fruitless conflict – for *sola ratio*. During the early eighteenth century, a new theism based entirely on reason and Newtonian science emerged. Like Newton, the deists claimed to have uncovered the primordial faith that lay hidden beneath the biblical tale. Matthew Tindal (1655–1733) and John Toland (1670–1722) in the British Isles, the French philosopher Voltaire (1694–1778), and Benjamin Franklin (1706–90) and Thomas Jefferson (1743–1826) in the American colonies all sought to bring religion under the mantle of reason – their goal being to enable every single person to think logically, discriminate judiciously and grasp the truths revealed by science.[20]

Like Spinoza, John Locke (1632–1704) denied the necessity for revelation or allegory, so he argued that the biblical accounts of the Creation and the Fall should be understood as factual and expressing our need of redemption. Because logical statements could not mean several things at the same time, there must be no figurative exegesis, which instead should conform to the rules of rational language, so that everybody could discover the truth for himself:

> For our simple ideas ... which are the foundation and sole matter of all our notions and knowledge, we must depend wholly on our reason, I mean our natural faculties, and can by no means receive them, or any of them, from traditional revelation.[21]

Locke also gave a rational sanction to Luther's separation of religion and politics. The Wars of Religion, he believed, had been caused by a fatal inability to entertain other points of view, whereas religion was a 'private search' so could not be policed by the government. To mingle religion and politics was a dangerous and existential error:

> The church itself is a thing absolutely separate and distinct from the commonwealth. The boundaries on both sides are fixed and immoveable. He jumbles heaven and earth together, the things most remote and opposite, who mixes these two societies, which are in their original end, business, and in everything perfectly and infinitely different from one another.[22]

This, however, would have been anything but self-evident to most of his contemporaries, since religion had always been a call to social and political action. But modern 'religion', as defined by Luther and Locke, would try to subvert this scriptural dynamic by turning the seeker in upon themself.

Liberal philosophers like Locke took it for granted that rational methods of exegesis could uncover the original meaning of the biblical texts, a common-sense view that would prevail throughout the eighteenth century. The principles of interpretation were clear, explained Johann Salomo Semler (1725–91), professor of theology at the University of Halle:

> Hermeneutical skill depends upon one's knowing the Bible's use of language properly and precisely, as well as distinguishing and representing to oneself the historical circumstances of a biblical discourse; and on one's being able to speak today of these matters in such a way as the changed times and circumstances of our fellow men demand.[23]

Those who could not accept the historicity of the biblical narratives still insisted that the truths of Christianity were spiritually important. 'The religion is not true because the Evangelists and Apostles taught it', the German man of letters Gotthold Lessing (1729–81) argued, 'but they taught it because it is true.'[24]

But Locke's friend Anthony Collins (1676–1729) signalled a change in attitude. In *A Discourse on the Grounds and Reason of the Christian Tradition* (1724), he dismissed the traditional idea that the prophets of Israel had predicted the life and death of Jesus. They were ordinary human beings, so they could not foretell the future, and Isaiah's prediction that a virgin would conceive simply referred to a young woman living in the time of King Ahab – not the Virgin Mary. A rational statement could not mean several things at the same time, so the true meaning of the Bible depended on the intentions of its human authors.[25] This, however, threatened the unity of the biblical canon, since from the very beginning, Christians had seamlessly joined the 'Old' Testament with the 'New'. In a groundbreaking essay in 1775, Semler went even further, arguing that the Bible was not identical with the Word of God and that the canon was simply a human creation. If each book was assessed in the light of its own historical context rather than from our modern perspective, it would become clear that some of the biblical writings had little religious value for us today – so human beings should decide for themselves what was in the Bible.[26]

The rational ethos of the Enlightenment was making scriptural exegesis a lost art. So too was the troubling debate about the historical reliability of the biblical stories, which was especially acute in England and Germany. The notion of history was changing. For the first time, academic historians could use modern scientific methods to uncover an accurate picture of the past, backing up their findings with empirical evidence. Because the new history was 'true', claimed the Scottish philosopher David Hume (1711–76), it 'improves the understanding and ... strengthens virtue'.[27] The classical Greek and Roman historians, who had sought practical lessons for the present from their research into the past, were widely read.[28] But where did this leave the biblical accounts, which included outlandish tales of miracles and other dubious phenomena? In the past, as we have seen, people did not expect historical accuracy because these tales were mythoi, important because of their meaning. But if they were not factual, people were now beginning to suspect that they must be 'false'. Discussion focused on those narratives that most directly impacted Christian theology, such as the Genesis account of the Creation and the Fall of Adam and Eve and the miracle stories in the gospels.

Some, such as Siegmund Jakob Baumgarten (1706–57), took a more robust line, insisting that recent scientific discoveries did not conflict in any way with the biblical account and that even the words of scripture and the literary form of each book were directly inspired by God. Baumgarten was professor of theology at the University of Halle, which had been founded by a Protestant movement known as Pietism shortly after the Thirty Years War. Pietists were reacting against the rigid, confessional orthodoxy that had marred the Reformation, focusing instead on good works and a holy life. Halle scholars produced the *Biblia Pentapla* to encourage a trans-denominational reading of scripture, with five different translations printed side by side, so that Lutherans, Calvinists and Catholics could read their preferred version, but could consult another if the wording was unclear. This liberal approach had encouraged Semler to adopt a more secular view of scripture, but devout Pietists, who attached great importance to individual Bible study, were convinced that every single word contained a germ of absolute truth and, if read devoutly, yielded a numinous experience. Paradoxically, this paved the way in Germany for a deep interest in the Bible as a written document, which persisted long after the critical study of scripture became a chiefly secular pursuit.[29]

There was nothing like Pietism in England; instead, there was a growing scepticism about the biblical text. In 1745, William Whiston (1667–1752) published a version of the New Testament that omitted all references to the Trinity or the Incarnation. The Irish deist John Toland tried to replace the New Testament with an ancient manuscript, which claimed to be the long-lost gospel of St Barnabas and denied Christ's divinity. Others argued that the text of the New Testament was so corrupt that it was impossible to determine what the Bible really taught. But Newton's friend Richard Bentley (1662–1742) applied the new critical techniques for analysing Graeco-Roman literature to the Bible, arguing that it was possible to reconstruct the original manuscripts by collating and analysing the variants.[30]

Most English scholars, however, were more concerned about the factual than the textual reliability of the gospels. Either the stories of Jesus' miracles and his resurrection proved that he was divine or they should be dismissed as unhistorical fantasies. Yet, strangely, none of them thought of comparing the Gospel stories to the narratives of a new literary genre currently developing in England and France that was attracting much popular attention. These fictions purported to relate actual happenings, but they were clearly not historical. Yet they explored profound truths about the human condition and were discussed seriously with increasingly sophisticated critical acumen. Could not the biblical tales make sense in rather the same way as the novels of Samuel Richardson (1689–1761), Henry Fielding (1707–54) and, later, Jane Austen (1775–1817)?[31] There was of course a difference. The biblical stories had narrated humanity's experience of transcendence in the tragedies and vicissitudes of history. The novel, however, depicted the impact on ordinary individuals of the immense social, historical and political changes occurring in England and France, which defined and enhanced these fictional characters but also constricted them. The huge popularity of the novel showed that it gave readers a much-needed insight into their painful, exhilarating and often baffling transition to modernity.

The novelists carefully linked their fictions with the new vogue for historical writing, celebrated by Hume as morally edifying. Richardson's masterpiece, *Clarissa* (1747–49), was subtitled *The History of a Young Lady*, and takes the form of a collection of letters that appear to have been critically anthologised to display different perspectives on the situation. Fielding's *chef-d'oeuvre* was entitled *The History of Tom Jones*. Both authors were concerned with morality and meaning. In his dedication of *Tom Jones* to the politician George Lyttelton, Fielding declared that, despite his hero's outrageous sexual escapades, 'to recommend goodness and innocence hath been my sincere endeavour in this history'. As in the biblical narratives, the reader is encouraged to empathise with these fictional people, experience their joys and sorrows and meditate upon the baffling complexities of the human predicament. But the new emphasis on *sola ratio* did not permit scholars to treat the biblical stories as imaginary. The only person to approach the biblical stories as a genre that was similar to the new fiction was the German poet Johann Gottfried Herder (1744–1803), who insisted that the only way to understand the Bible was to identify emotionally with its characters.

> Become shepherds with a shepherd, with the people of the sod a man of the land, with the ancients of the Orient an Easterner, if you wish to relish these writings in the atmosphere of their origin; and be on your guard especially against abstractions of dull, new academic prisons.[32]

Yet Herder was also committed to the historical truth of the Bible and never fully reconciled these two very different approaches.

He clearly detested the 'dull, new academic prisons' in which German scholars of the so-called 'Higher Criticism' applied scientific techniques for the analysis of ancient manuscripts to the Bible. They concluded that Moses was certainly not the author of the entire Pentateuch, which was rather the work of several different authors, each with a distinctive style and message. They noted that there were duplicate narratives, obviously by different hands, such as the two creation accounts in Genesis. Jean Astruc (1684–1766), a Paris physician, and Johann Gottfried Eichhorn (1752–1827), professor of oriental languages at Jena University, argued that Genesis contained two documents: one which called God 'Yahweh' (J); while the other preferred the title 'Elohim' (E). But other scholars, including Johann Severin Vater (1771–1826) and Wilhelm de Wette (1780–1849), maintained that the Pentateuch consisted of numerous fragments, which had been anthologised by a redactor. By the nineteenth century, it was generally agreed that it combined four originally independent sources. De Wette believed that Deuteronomy (D) was the latest book of the Pentateuch, while the Halle professor Hermann Hupfeld (1796–1866) argued that the 'Elohist' source consisted of two separate documents: the oldest was E1 (a priestly work), which was followed, in chronological order, by E2, J and D.

But Karl Heinrich Graf (1815–69) was convinced that the priestly document (E1) was in fact the latest of the four sources and Julius Wellhausen (1844–1918) seized upon this theory because it solved a problem that had long troubled him. Why did the prophets never refer to the Mosaic law? And why was the Deuteronomist, who was clearly familiar with the Yahwist and Elohist, ignorant of the priestly document? All this could be explained if the priestly source (E1) was a late composition. Wellhausen also showed that the four-document theory was too simplistic. There had been additions to all four sources before they had been combined into a single narrative. His work was regarded by his contemporaries as the culmination of the critical method, but Wellhausen himself realised that research had only just begun; in fact, it continues to the present day.

Historical criticism has greatly enhanced our understanding of the Bible and the way it was put together over time. But this critical preoccupation with the text could lead to a diminution of the transcendent experience of scripture – a loss that would become part of the modern experience. Yet the scholars' findings had moral as well as academic value: they showed that when the editors put the biblical texts together, everybody's insights were included and respected, even when they held contradictory views, such as southern alongside northern traditions in Israel. History would have been very different if Protestant and Catholic reformers, who had split the Reformation into warring camps, had been similarly inclusive.

Because their theologians were unable to agree on basic matters of faith, Europeans had turned in relief to Descartes' *sola ratio* in their quest for common ground.[33] In America, the philosophers and statesmen who led the 1776 revolution against British rule – George Washington, John and Samuel Adams, Thomas Jefferson, James Madison and Benjamin Franklin – were deists, rationalists and men of the Enlightenment, inspired by the ideas of Locke and Scottish Common Sense philosophy. The Declaration of Independence, drafted by Jefferson with Franklin and John Adams, was based on Locke's ideal of human rights, which he had defined as life, liberty and property (the last was later changed to 'the pursuit of happiness'). These natural human rights were declared to be 'self-evident'. But were they? As it turned out, the *philosophes* held widely different views of human nature, so *sola ratio*, like *sola scriptura*, did not necessarily bring unanimity; nor could it produce a clear, distinct and incontrovertible *raison d'être* for human rights.

Locke was convinced that liberty and equality were fundamental human rights. In their natural state, he argued, men had lived 'in a state of perfect freedom to order their actions and dispose of their possessions as they think fit, within the bounds of the law of nature'. Their societies were egalitarian, 'there being nothing more evident than that creatures of the same species and rank ... should also be the equal one amongst another, without subordination or subjection'.[34] But that was not the view of Thomas Hobbes (1588–1679), who believed that in the state of nature, human beings may indeed have been born equal in ability, but this simply led them 'to destroy and subdue one another'. Left to himself, without strong governmental control, 'the life of man [is] solitary, poore, nasty, brutish, and short'.[35] Jean-Jacques Rousseau (1712–78) came to the opposite conclusion: human nature was good and it was our political institutions that had made us bad.[36]

Similarly, the American Founders did not agree about such basic issues as democracy. John Adams, the second president of the United States, was wary of any policy that might lead to the impoverishment of the aristocracy, while the followers of Jefferson insisted that freedom and autonomy must be enjoyed by Americans of all classes.[37]

This disagreement about supposedly 'self-evident' truths would not have surprised the German philosopher Immanuel Kant (1724–1804), whose *Critique of Pure Reason* (1781) undercut the Enlightenment project by claiming that all our ideas were essentially and inescapably subjective. Like today's neuroscientists, he understood that the order we think we discern in nature probably bears little relation to the reality. We could devise a viable rational vision to satisfy our minds, but there was no such thing as an objective truth that was the same for everybody. Kant had issued the classic definition: 'Enlightenment is man's exodus from his self-incurred tutelage. Tutelage is man's inability to make use of his own understanding, without direction from another.'[38] The Enlightenment has been described by a modern scholar as a 'great leap to human autonomy and self-management', which began 'with the human resolve to take history under human administration and control'. It was, of course, a child of the brain's left hemisphere: its 'weapon' was 'reason ... the flawless human facility to know, to predict, to calculate, and so to raise the "is" to the "ought"'.[39]

Jefferson, especially, was resolved to liberate human politics from the thrall of God's so-called representatives and place history under human control. But most Americans were devoutly religious Protestants of various hues – Presbyterians, Anglicans, Puritans and Congregationalists – all still adhering to *sola scriptura* and looking askance at Jefferson's deist approach to the Bible. Like most eighteenth-century thinkers, he still believed that it had spiritual value, but in 1787 he urged his nephew Peter Carr to subject each of its books to 'the tribunal of reason':

> those facts in the Bible which contradict the laws of nature must be examined with more care and under a variety of faces. Here you must recur to the pretensions of the writer to inspiration from God. Examine upon what evidence his pretensions are founded, and whether the evidence is so strong, as that its falsehood would be more improbable than a change in the laws of nature, in the case he related.[40]

One could not, for example, credit the story of Joshua making the sun stand still. Jefferson also urged Carr to consider the 'pretensions' of such

Christian doctrines as Jesus' divinity, virgin birth and bodily ascension to heaven and not to worry if he concluded that God did not exist: 'Your own reason is the only oracle given you by heaven, and you are answerable, not for the rightness, but for the uprightness of the decision.'[41] Jefferson's strong commitment to *sola ratio* had made him incapable of appreciating the role of mythos in religion – in his version of the New Testament, he cut out all the miracles, the virgin birth and the resurrection, focusing solely on Jesus' teachings.[42]

So bitter had been the disputes arising from *sola scriptura* that Jefferson realised that the federal constitution could never gain the support of all the states if it made any single Protestant denomination the official faith of the Union. Like Locke, he was convinced that the segregation of religion from government was 'above all things necessary for the creation of a peaceful society'.[43] In 1786, Jefferson disestablished the Anglican Church in Virginia, declaring that coercion in matters of faith was sinful and tyrannical. Truth would prevail only if people could form their own opinions, so there must be a 'wall of separation' between religion and politics.[44] The lapidary clause of the First Amendment to the US Constitution in the Bill of Rights decreed that 'Congress shall make no law respecting the establishment of religion, or prohibiting the free exercise thereof.' This would liberate religion from the inherent injustice and violence of the state, but it could also encourage a retreat from the world's pain into a privatised spirituality centred on oneself. The Founding Fathers claimed that they had derived their understanding of human dignity and equality from reason alone; but they had also clearly imbibed these ideals, at least in part, from the Jewish and Christian scriptures which they still, however minimally, respected. It is certainly true that Christian rulers had rarely lived up to the ideal of justice and equity proclaimed in their scriptures. But secularist philosophers and governments would also fail their sacred texts. In *A Letter Concerning Toleration*, an Enlightenment classic, Locke had been adamant that the liberal state could tolerate neither Catholicism nor Islam.[45] He also insisted that a master had 'Absolute, Arbitrary, Despotical Power' over a slave, which included 'the power to kill him at any time', and that the native 'kings' of America had neither legal jurisdiction nor right of ownership of their land.[46] The American Declaration of Independence had insisted that all men were created equal, but there would be no equality for Native Americans, African slaves, or the poorer Americans living on the frontiers, whom the Founders taxed as harshly as the British had done.[47]

The modernisation process in the West was often punctuated with outbreaks of extreme irrationality and, as I have discussed at length elsewhere, secularist disdain has frequently distorted religion.[48] Most Americans could not share the rational ethos of the Founders and tried to accommodate their new secular ideals religiously. In the past, ritual – now either rejected or greatly reduced by some Protestants – had helped people to deal with the turbulence of their inner world. The rites of Lurianic Kabbalah, for example, had guided the Sephardic exiles through their trauma, enabling them to absorb it, act it out, and learn to live with it kindly and creatively. But without the support of such disciplined ritual, some American Protestants would experience radical change in a wrenching process that the Buddha might have considered *akusala* – 'unhelpful' or 'unwholesome'.

The learned Calvinist minister Jonathan Edwards (1703–58) believed that the religious revival known as the First Great Awakening that had swept through Connecticut, Massachusetts and Long Island in 1734 had introduced the less educated Americans to the Enlightenment ideal of the pursuit of happiness,[49] leaving them with the memory of a blissful state that they called 'liberty'.[50] But this *ekstasis* had nothing in common with the disciplined yoga that had brought the Buddha to 'enlightenment' or Guru Nanak's dialogue with his unconscious mind; instead it was a dangerous surrender to emotion. During Edwards' sermons, the congregation screamed and yelled, writhed in the aisles, and crowded round his pulpit begging him to stop. Some 300 people, their emotions alternating between soaring highs and devastating lows, were 'born again'. Convinced that they were damned, some committed suicide out of despair while others, Edwards reported, went mad with 'strange enthusiastic delusions'.[51] There could be no liberating kenosis, because this dangerous surrender to the unconscious was all about the individual – *my* repentance, *my* salvation, *my* damnation.

The Second Great Awakening in the 1790s, however, was a rebellion orchestrated by poorer Americans on the frontiers against the rational ethos of the aristocratic Founders. Its prophets had no time for *sola ratio*: they had found the ideals of freedom and equity clearly expressed in the Bible and, naturally, they emphasised the radical teachings of the New Testament far more vigorously than aristocratic exegetes. Their highly emotional piety certainly resembled that of the First Great Awakening, but they rejected intellectuals like Edwards, who believed that only scholars had the right to interpret the Bible, pointing out that Jesus and his disciples did not have college degrees. At first glance, these new prophets seemed to belong to a bygone age, because they relied on everything that the *philosophes* deplored: dreams, visions, signs, wonders and miracles. But they also presented the modern ideals of democracy, equality, free speech and independence in a biblical idiom. There were torchlight processions and mass rallies in which the new Gospel Songs transported the crowds into ecstasy, so that they wept and rocked violently backward and forward, shouting for joy, in the emotional extremity that would become a hallmark of American Christianity.[52]

During the 1840s, Charles Finney (1792–1875) brought this frontier spirituality to the middle classes, and by the mid-nineteenth century, 'Evangelical Christianity', based on a literal reading of scripture, had become the dominant religion of the United States.[53] Evangelicals did not find Jefferson's separation of religion and politics a self-evident truth, but at least in the northern states, they made the ideal of inalienable human rights a biblical mandate, campaigning against slavery and liquor and for educational and penal reform and equal rights for women, creating a hybrid that some scholars have called 'Enlightenment Protestantism'.[54]

All too often, though, modern exegesis forgot Augustine's insistence on the 'principle of charity'. This was clear in a biblical doctrine that took root in America during the late nineteenth century and became known as *pre*millennialism, because it claimed that Christ would return to earth *before* he established his 1,000-year reign, as prophesied in Revelation. Premillennialism was the creation of John Nelson Darby (1800–82), an Englishman who had found few takers at home but toured America six times to great acclaim between 1859 and 1877. Humanity, he claimed, was becoming so depraved that God would soon destroy the world, but faithful Christians would emerge triumphant and enjoy Christ's final victory in the Kingdom.[55]

Premillennialism is a prime example of a literalistic, supposedly 'rational' interpretation of scripture, which, like the Great Awakening, bordered on insanity. For Darby, the prophets, St Paul and the author of Revelation were not speaking metaphorically but were making precise predictions that could be deciphered analytically. Darby divided the entire history of the Bible into seven 'dispensations' or epochs, each of which ended in such catastrophes as the Fall, the Flood or the crucifixion. Humankind was presently living in the sixth, penultimate dispensation, Darby explained, which would end in unprecedented horror. Antichrist, the false redeemer whose coming Paul had foretold,[56] would shortly inaugurate a seven-year period of Tribulation, massacring untold numbers of people until, as predicted in Revelation, Jesus descended to earth, defeated Antichrist and fought Satan on the plain of Armageddon outside Jerusalem. He would then inaugurate the Seventh Dispensation, ruling the world in peace and justice for 1,000 years until the Last Judgement brought history to a close.

Evangelical Christians were predisposed to Darby's mission, because they were morbidly yearning for the extinction of modern society. William Miller (1782–1849), a farmer in upstate New York, was convinced that the biblical prophecies could be deciphered with scientific, mathematical precision, and in 1831 he issued a pamphlet, announcing that Christ's Second Coming would occur in 1843. Miller too believed that all Christians had the right to interpret the Bible and he encouraged his readers to challenge his calculations. Few did, however, and some 50,000 Americans became dedicated 'Millerites'. They were distraught when Christ failed to show up in 1843, but other sects, such as the Seventh Day Adventists, adjusted the eschatological timetable – wisely avoiding precise predictions – and enabled generations of Americans to look forward to the imminent End.[57]

Darby's premillennialism, however, had the added attraction of enabling the elect to avoid the End Time ordeals. Seizing upon a chance remark of St Paul, who, in a lyrical description of Jesus' Second Coming, had told his Thessalonian converts that they would be 'taken up in the clouds ... to meet Christ in the air',[58] Darby concluded that shortly before Tribulation, there would be a 'Rapture' in which true Christians would be snatched up to heaven. Presenting their exegesis as rational and scientific, premillennialists have developed a detailed scenario of the Rapture: aeroplanes, cars and trains will crash as born-again pilots and drivers are whisked into the air while their hapless passengers die in agony; markets will plummet and governments will fall. Those 'left behind' will realise – too late – that the true Christians, whose beliefs they had scorned, had been right all along. Premillennialism is cruel and divisive: the elect complacently imagine themselves gazing down upon the sufferings of those who had ridiculed them and now get their just deserts.

There is also a drastic loss of transcendence. Previous exegetes had insisted that when we speak about God we do not know what we are talking about. But Darby showed no such reticence: his God is a sadistic, vengeful human being, writ large, whose actions could be predicted to the last detail. He embodied the resentment of the 'little people' of America, who felt ignored and despised by the supposedly egalitarian establishment. Yet, strangely, premillennialism was in tune with more sophisticated nineteenth-century scientific and political thought. Darby's contemporaries Georg Wilhelm Hegel (1770–1831), Karl Marx (1818–83) and Charles Darwin (1809–82) had all argued that development is the result of conflict. Like Darby, they had divided history into different eras and Marx had looked forward to a utopian finale. Discovering successive epochs of the earth's development in the strata of fossilised fauna and flora in rocks and cliffs, some geologists had concluded that each had ended in catastrophe. Premillennialism was also modern in its literalism and democracy. There were no hidden or symbolic meanings in the Bible, accessible only to an elite who had the leisure and education to ferret it out. Scripture meant exactly what it said. A millennium meant ten centuries; 485 years meant precisely that. When the prophets spoke of 'Israel', they were not referring to the Christian Church, but to the Jews. And if Revelation foretold a battle between Jesus and Satan outside Jerusalem, that was exactly what would happen.[59] A premillennial reading of the Bible would become even easier for ordinary Christians after the publication of the *Scofield Reference Bible* (1909), which explained this dispensational history in copious notes attached to the biblical text and became an instant bestseller.

Scripture, an art form originally designed to be interpreted imaginatively, had now to be as rational as science if it was to be taken seriously. But science itself was changing. Because Darwin's theories were largely hypothetical, some Christians dismissed them as 'unscientific'. They looked back to the philosopher Francis Bacon (1561–1626), for whom the task of science had been simply to categorise known phenomena and organise its findings into theories based on facts that were obvious to everybody.[60] The nineteenth-century Baptist preacher Arthur Pierson, for example, wanted the Bible to be interpreted in 'a truly impartial and scientific spirit':

> I like a Biblical Theology that ... does not begin with an hypothesis and then wraps the facts and the philosophy to fit the crook of its dogma, but a Baconian system, which first gathers the teachings of the word of God, and then seeks to deduce some general law upon which the facts can be arranged.[61]

But biblical truths had never pretended to be amenable to scientific demonstration, so a 'scientific' approach to scripture could only produce a caricature of rational discourse that would bring religion into disrepute.[62]

In 1873, Charles Hodge, professor of theology at the New Light Seminary in Princeton, New Jersey, was the first theologian to attack Darwin's theory of evolution. At this point, very few Christians appreciated the full implications of Darwin's hypothesis. For the liberal American theologian Henry Ward Beecher (1813–87), God was present in the natural processes, so evolution could be regarded as evidence of God's loving concern for his creation. Later, however, when it was clear that innumerable species had been destroyed in the process of natural selection, evolution would seem less benign. But for the Baconian Hodge, Darwinism was simply bad science. Scientists, he said, had become so immersed in the study of nature that they believed only in natural causes and did not appreciate that religious truth was also factual. He feared for the future, when scientists no longer saw God as the ultimate explanation: religion, he said, 'has to fight for its life against a large class of scientific men'.[63] But this would not have been so had Christians not allowed themselves to become dependent upon a scientific method that was alien to traditional exegesis.

Far more worrying to Evangelicals at this date was the Higher Criticism of the Bible, however. In 1860, the year after the publication of *On the Origin of Species*, seven Anglican clergymen published *Essays and Reviews*, a series of articles that made German scholarship available to the public. It created a sensation, selling 22,000 copies in two years – more than *Origin* in the first twenty years of its publication – and inspired 400 books and articles in response.[64] The most important essay in the book was by Benjamin Jowett, master of Balliol College, Oxford, who argued that the Bible must be subjected to the same rigorous scrutiny as any other ancient text. Evangelical Protestants in Britain as well as America found these ideas disturbing. In 1888, the English novelist Mrs Humphry Ward published *Robert Elsmere*, the story of a clergyman whose faith was destroyed by the Higher Criticism. At one point, his wife complains: 'If the Gospels are not true in fact, as history, I cannot see how they are true at all, or of any value.'[65] The novel became a bestseller in England, suggesting that many people shared her fears.

In the United States, the Princeton theologians headed the fight against the Higher Criticism.[66] In 1873, Hodge published the first volume of his two-volume work *Systematic Theology*. Overturning centuries of scriptural interpretation, Hodge argued that the task of the theologian was not to look for a meaning *beyond* the words, but simply to arrange the clear teachings of the Bible into a Baconian system of general truths. Every single word of the Bible was divinely inspired and infallibly true, so must not be distorted by allegorical or symbolic exegesis. Until the Reformation, Western Christians had experienced biblical interpretation as an ascent to the divine; the plain sense of the words was only the first rung in a ladder leading to the ineffable. Neither Jews nor Christians had ever experienced biblical teachings as clear because they pointed to the inexpressible. Now, however, the Bible had to be marshalled into a rational system.

In 1811, Charles's son, Archibald Hodge, and a younger colleague, Benjamin Warfield, published a defence of the literal truth of the Bible, which became a classic. All the stories and statements of the Bible were 'absolutely errorless and binding for faith and obedience', they argued. Everything the Bible said was 'truth to the facts'. If the prophets recorded in the Bible said their words were inspired, then the Bible *was* inspired.[67] In this closed system, coherent only in its own terms, the exegete was cocooned in a circular argument. This would become the hallmark of Protestant fundamentalism.

In 1886, the revivalist preacher Dwight Lyman Moody (1837–99) founded the Moody Bible Institute in Chicago, his aim to create a cadre of scholars that would oppose the Higher Criticism which, he was convinced, would bring the nation to destruction. Similar colleges were founded by William B. Riley in Minneapolis in 1902 and by the oil magnate Lyman Stewart in Los Angeles in 1907. Surrounded now with a nimbus of evil, the Higher Criticism seemed to symbolise everything that was wrong in the modern world. 'If we have no infallible standard' in the Bible, argued the Methodist clergyman Alexander McAlister, 'all decent values would disappear'.[68] The Methodist preacher Leander W. Mitchell blamed the Higher Criticism for the drunkenness and sexual immorality now rife in the United States.[69] The Presbyterian M. B. Lambdin saw it as the cause of the rising divorce rate, graft, corruption, crime and murder.[70]

This marks the beginning of a form of religiosity known popularly as 'fundamentalism', which I have discussed at length in a previous work.[71] Coined by Protestants in the United States in the early decades of the twentieth century to distinguish themselves from 'liberal' Christians, funda-mentalism is an unsatisfactory term. The declared objective was to return to the 'fundamentals' of their faith, which they believed to be the literal interpretation of scripture together with a select group of core doctrines. Similar movements, although with very different foci, have developed in other faith traditions. Indeed, wherever a secular government has separated religion and politics, a counterculture has developed alongside it which is determined to push religion back to centre stage.

In the 1990s, at the outset of their monumental six-volume Fundamentalist Project that examined this phenomenon, Martin E. Marty and R. Scott Appleby explained that 'fundamentalisms' – be they Christian, Muslim, Jewish, Buddhist, Hindu or Confucian – all follow a similar trajectory. They are embattled spiritualities that have developed in response to a perceived crisis. They are engaged in a conflict with enemies whose secularist policies and beliefs seem inimical to religion itself. Fundamentalists do not regard this battle as a conventional political struggle, but experience it as a cosmic war between the forces of good and evil. They fear annihilation, and try to fortify their beleaguered identity by means of a selective retrieval of certain doctrines and practices of the past. Feeling profoundly threatened, they often withdraw from mainstream society to create a counterculture: in American Protestant Fundamentalism, the Bible Institutes, founded initially by Moody, Riley and Stewart, and later by Bob Jones and Jerry Falwell, were often the bastion of these separatist communities. But fundamentalists are not impractical dreamers. They have absorbed the pragmatic rationalism of modernity and, under the guidance of charismatic leaders, they refine these 'fundamentals' to create an ideology that provides the faithful with a plan of action. Eventually they fight back in an attempt to resacralise an increasingly sceptical world; this does not usually mean violence – only a tiny percentage of fundamentalists use terror tactics – but it usually takes the form of a cultural, ritualised or scholarly riposte.[72]

Every 'fundamentalist' movement, however, has a different focus. In Judaism, it has been the secular state of Israel, which fundamentalists either support or oppose. In Islam, the last of the three monotheisms to develop a 'fundamentalist' strain, it has always been sparked by an attack – ideological or physical – on the *ummah*, the Muslim community. Scripture has played a part in such movements, usually in the use of 'proof texts' to justify a course of action. But it is neither the starting point nor the principal means of expression – fundamentalists often use ritual to make their point. Yet, as we have seen, scripture was the focus of Protestant fundamentalism from the very beginning. This, perhaps, is not surprising. The Protestant Reformation had insisted on *sola scriptura*. Scripture was, therefore, the life and soul of Protestant Christianity; it was *all* they had, and when it was attacked, fundamentalists felt that their very selves were violated. Hence the extremity of their fear of the Higher Criticism.

Fundamentalisms usually begin with what is experienced as an assault – physical or ideological – by the secularist majority. Protestants established their Fundamentalist movement in 1920 but it was the famous Scopes Trial (1925) which led to their retreat from the mainstream and the creation of a counterculture. The state legislatures of Florida, Mississippi, Tennessee and Louisiana had passed laws to prohibit the teaching of evolution in the public schools. To strike a blow for free speech, the young teacher John Scopes confessed that he had broken the law when he had substituted for his school principal in a biology class. He was brought to trial in July 1925, defended by the new American Civil Liberties Union (ACLU), headed by the rationalist campaigner Clarence Darrow. The statesman William Jennings

Bryan agreed to defend the anti-evolution law and the trial became a contest between religion and science.[73] As is well known, Darrow emerged as the hero of lucid rational thought and Bryan a bumbling, incompetent anachronism. Scopes was convicted, but the ACLU paid his fine and Darrow and science were the real victors.

The press had a field day and the fundamentalists were denounced as the scourge of the nation, enemies of science and freedom, who had no place in the modern world. After this vicious media assault, the fundamentalists withdrew, creating an enclave of godliness in their own churches, broadcasting stations, publishing houses, schools, universities and Bible colleges. In the late 1970s, when their movement had gained sufficient strength, they would return to public life, launching a biblically inspired offensive to convert the nation. The ridicule of the press proved to be counterproductive. Before Scopes, evolution had not been an important issue to the fundamentalists; even Charles Hodge knew that the world had existed for far longer than the 6,000 years stated in the Bible. Very few fundamentalists had espoused 'Creation science', which argued that Genesis was scientifically sound in every single detail. But after Scopes, an unswerving biblical literalism became central to the fundamentalist mindset and Creation science would become the flagship of the movement. When they attack a faith that they deem obscurantist, critics of religion should be aware that their assault is likely to make it more extreme.

America has nevertheless remained a strongly religious nation, its evangelical strain still centred on a literal reading of the Bible. In Europe, the story was very different – and, again, I have discussed its loss of faith in an earlier work.[74] Here it was a complex process that involved not only scriptural but also political and social developments. Some Europeans, such as the British biologist Thomas H. Huxley (1825–95), regarded scientific rationalism as a new secular religion that demanded conversion and total commitment. Others, like the poet Matthew Arnold (1822–88), relinquished their faith with sorrow, feeling no Promethean defiance, no heady liberation, but hearing only the 'melancholy, long, withdrawing roar' of faith as it receded, bringing 'the eternal note of sadness in'.[75]

When the German philosopher Friedrich Nietzsche (1844–1900) considered the hearts of his contemporaries, he found that God had already died there, yet, he said, very few people were fully aware of this. In The Gay Science (1882), he told the story of a madman who ran one morning into the marketplace, crying: 'I seek God!' When the sceptical bystanders, who had lost their faith, asked him facetiously if God had run away or emigrated, he replied: 'We have killed him – you and I! We are all his murderers!'[76] The scientific and industrial revolutions had caused human beings to focus so intently on the physical and empirical world that they no longer understood the aesthetic aspects of religion which had yielded intimations of transcendence. The death of God, Nietzsche argued, was casting its first shadows over Europe. The few who could see this clearly had already become aware that 'some sun seems to have set and profound trust has been turned to doubt'.[77]

By making 'God' a purely notional truth, attainable by the rational and scientific intellect without ritual, contemplation and ethical commitment, European men and women had killed it for themselves. We might say that by their assiduous cultivation of the left hemisphere of the brain, they had lost touch with the intimations of the right. Like the Jewish Marranos who had also relied on *sola ratio*, they were beginning to experience religion as tenuous, arbitrary and lifeless and their scriptures as frankly incredible. For Karl Marx, the abolition of religion had been a project – something to be achieved in the future that would liberate human beings from the contradictions and injustices of capitalist society. Regarding himself as 'the Darwin of sociology', he had wanted to dedicate *Das Kapital* to Darwin, who, though an agnostic, was always respectful of religious faith, and courteously declined. For Nietzsche, however, the death of God had already happened. He rejected any view of the divine that tried to explain anything causally, morally or with certainty. It was now only a matter of time before 'God' would cease to be a presence in the scientific civilisation of the West. By forcing the sacred into a wholly rational mode of thought that was alien to it and by reading their scriptures as factual, Europeans had made religion unviable. In America, as we have seen, this literal reading of scripture had produced an End Time vision that, far from endorsing the rationalism of the Founders, bordered on insanity.

Nietzsche was convinced that unless a new absolute could be found to take the place of 'God', the scientific civilisation of the West would become unhinged. Not only was there no God; there was now no ordering principle. 'Where is the earth moving now?' the madman demanded. 'Do we not stray, as though through an infinite nothingness?'[78] The century that had begun in Europe with Newtonian certainty and a conviction of boundless possibility was succumbing to a nameless dread.

After completing *The Gay Science* in the summer of 1882, however, Nietzsche had a spiritual and mental crisis which he experienced as a 'revelation'. He had felt invaded by 'a feeling of freedom, of absoluteness, of power, of divinity' that had nothing to do with the conventional 'God':

> Something suddenly, with unspeakable certainty and subtlety, becomes visible, audible, something that shakes and overturns one to the depths ... an ecstasy ... a depth of happiness in which the most painful and gloomy things appear not as antitheses, but as conditioned, demanded.[79]

The result of this right-hemispheric vision of an ecstatic union of opposites was the work that he considered his masterpiece. *Thus Spoke Zarathustra* (1883–91), he believed, would become 'the Bible of the future, the highest expression of human genius which contains the destiny of humankind'.[80] The young Nietzsche, the son of a Lutheran pastor, had been a committed Christian and he had acquired an exceptional knowledge of scripture. All his books contain biblical phrases and allusions and later, when he began to attack Christianity, he would often conscientiously reread large portions of the Bible. He knew how scripture worked, therefore, and would now use the scriptural genre to demolish conventional religion.[81]

His spokesman was the Aryan prophet Zarathustra (in Greek, 'Zoroaster'), who in about 1200 BCE had experienced revelations that would eventually give birth to the Persian religion known as Zoroastrianism. Nietzsche maintained that because Zarathustra had created morality, 'the most fateful of errors', it was only right that he should be resuscitated and made to refute it.[82] But in Nietzsche's Godless scripture, Zarathustra assumed a new role. He had become identical with the Greek god Dionysus, who had inspired the art of tragic drama. Years earlier, in *The Birth of Tragedy* (1871), Nietzsche had argued that in classical Greek tragedy, the cult of Apollo, who represented clarity, control and reason, had fused with the worship of Dionysus, the god of transformation. As they watched the hero grappling with death, horror and meaninglessness, the commentary of the Chorus, which, Nietzsche believed, had been set to music and sung, had enabled the audience to achieve an *ekstasis* that affirmed life in the face of sorrow and death – an experience not unlike his own in 1882. Nietzsche blamed Socrates, who, according to Plato, had wanted to expel poets from the *polis*, for the loss of tragic insight in Greece. Socrates, he claimed, had created a culture that was too optimistic in its confidence that reason and science alone could solve the enigmas of human existence. In ancient Greece – as in post-Enlightenment Europe – logos had driven out mythos, and, as a result, God was dead and we could assuage the pain of life only in art.[83]

Nietzsche made three claims for his *Zarathustra*.[84] It was, first, a parody – a parody, some would say, of the New Testament.[85] Nietzsche was convinced that by revealing the historical implausibility of its scriptures the Higher Criticism had demolished Christianity and that its demise was only a matter of time. There are obvious allusions to the New Testament in *Zarathustra*. We see Zoroaster wandering around the world with a group of disciples in rather the same way as Jesus; one of its chapters is entitled 'The Last Supper', and another, facetiously, 'On Immaculate Perception'. But *Zarathustra* was not simply a cheap parody of the gospels: it was rather an affirmation that followed from his denial of God in *The Gay Science*. Little read in his own lifetime, Nietzsche had to be his own critic. Hence in his work we often find two voices: one that asserts and another that qualifies that assertion. This 'parody', therefore, was merely a first step that must now be deconstructed in order to achieve a new vision.[86] Christianity, Nietzsche believed, had cultivated a 'slave mentality' based on *ressentiment*, a sense of injured merit, and was motivated by a resentment of the powerful and an unrealistic desire for revenge. Because it advocated the passive endurance of suffering, Christianity, an ascetic faith, was essentially hostile to human life and must be ostracised by the strong. But Christianity had also influenced the supposedly 'secular' ideals of liberalism and socialism – equality and emancipation – which, Nietzsche was convinced, were equally damaging and must be transcended.[87]

Yet Nietzsche distinguished between institutionalised Christianity and Jesus himself, whose character, he believed, had been distorted by the early Christian writers, notably by Paul. He writes of Jesus sympathetically, rather like an older brother, arguing that he died 'too early; he himself would have recanted his teaching had he lived to my age! He was noble enough to recant!'[88] Nietzsche had no time for Jesus' undiscerning love of everybody. To love with maturity – as Jesus would have learned in time – means loving with discrimination.[89] He was therefore critical of Jesus' compassion, which he mistranslated as *Mitleid* ('pity'). If you pity someone, he had argued in *The Gay Science*, you tend to diminish their worth, because suffering is just as important to our development as happiness. We should not wish to abolish adversity:

> The entire economy of my soul and the balance affected by 'misfortune',
> the breaking open of new springs and needs, the healing of old wounds, the

shedding of entire periods of the past – terrors, deprivations, impoverish-
ments, adventures, risks and blunders – are as necessary for you as their
opposite.[90]

Nietzsche's 'parody' of Christianity, therefore, was only one part of a
dialectic, an initial exploratory offensive that nudges the Christian reader
into an uneasy reassessment of the familiar mores of Christianity, such as
compassion – and some of the modern ideas that are rooted in it – as
a preparation for his real objective, which is to provide his reader with a
'new New Testament' inspired by Dionysus. Hence, Nietzsche's second
definition: *Zarathustra*, he said, was a 'counter ideal', an alternative to the
ascetic, life-denying Christian faith.[91]

Finally, and most importantly, Nietzsche defined *Zarathustra* as a
tragedy.[92] This was not because it had an unhappy ending – it finishes on
an optimistic, triumphant note – but because it would, he hoped, give his
readers an experience akin to the Dionysian *ekstasis* in ancient Athens in
which, he believed, opposites had fused and become one. In Greek tragedy,
the audience had watched the hero undergo a profound mental and spiritual change and found that their own attitudes had undergone a similar
transformation. Nietzsche's 'new Bible', he hoped, would enable his readers
to empathise in rather the same way with Zarathustra as they watched
him accomplishing his own Dionysian conversion – on stage, as it were.
When Zarathustra marches triumphantly away into a noble future at the
end of the book, Nietzsche hoped that his readers would have an insight
into his new state of mind. They would realise that our everyday perception of joy and sorrow and life and death as opposites is illusory, because
in Dionysian *ekstasis* they merged once again into the primal holism that
had existed before Apollonian rationalism had made these artificial distinctions. They would have intimations of Nietzsche's own ecstatic vision of
the union of opposites.

But this is easier said than done. It is very difficult – indeed, almost
impossible – to welcome and affirm the joys and sorrows of life with total
equanimity. It requires what Nietzsche called 'overcoming' (*Übergang*) as
well as great courage, since the relinquishment of all our engrained values
will deeply threaten our sense of identity. This was not a matter of experiencing a fusion of joy and delight in a temporary rapture, but of holding
them together in our minds and heart in a permanent affirmation. We can
appreciate the strain that this involved by watching Zarathustra's progress:
he falls into a profound depression, becomes ill, and, on one occasion,

endures a week-long coma, as he struggles to accept that his old self must
be irrevocably broken. He describes the mental vertigo of the process as
his 'Gethsemane':

> Do you know the terror which assails him who is falling asleep?
>
> He is terrified down to his toes, because the ground seems to give way,
> and the dream begins.
>
> I tell you this in a parable. Yesterday, at the stillest hour ... my dream
> began.
>
> The hand moved, the clock of my life held its breath – I had never heard
> such stillness about me, so that my heart was terrified.

At this dark moment, the task seems beyond his strength. He weeps and
trembles like a child, but something says to him voicelessly: 'Of what
consequence are you, Zarathustra? Speak your teaching and break!'[93]

For Nietzsche, Zarathustra is a tragic hero because he has achieved this
'overcoming' and is able to say 'Yes!' joyfully to all life's experiences,
however sorrowful and desolate – a process that cannot be achieved by his
reasoning powers alone. He now sees the contradictions of life harmonising
and can hold seemingly incompatible things in a bold affirmation. He had
achieved the primal wholeness that existed before human beings learned
to analyse and make distinctions. 'My world has just become perfect,' he
cries in the penultimate chapter, 'midnight is also noonday!'

> Pain is also joy, a curse is also a blessing, the night is also a sun – be gone,
> or you will learn: a wise man is also a fool.
>
> Did you ever say Yes to one joy? O my friends, then you said Yes to *all*
> woe as well. All things are chained and entwined together, all things are in
> love.[94]

Zarathustra has no desire for the 'supernatural' Christian heaven. Instead,
he preaches what he called the 'eternal recurrence' of everything the natural
world offers – grief and pain as well as joy.

> If ever you wanted one moment twice, if ever you said: 'You please me,
> happiness, instant, moment!' then you wanted *everything* to return!
>
> You wanted everything anew, everything eternal, everything chained,
> entwined together, everything in love, O that is how you *loved* the world ...
> and you say even to woe: 'Go, but return!'[95]

Now that God is dead, Nietzsche insisted, human beings must step into the vacuum he has left by developing a superior version of their own species – the *Übermensch* or 'Superman' – who would provide the world with ultimate meaning. But this is a dangerous process. 'Man is a rope,' Zarathustra explains, 'fastened between animal and Superman – a rope over an abyss. A dangerous going-across.'[96] People must 'live dangerously'. They must rebel against the Christian 'God', who had once marked the limit of human aspiration, estranged us from our bodies and our passions, and enfeebled us with his puling ideal of compassion. There was to be no kenosis here. As an incarnation of its will to power, the *Übermensch* would force the species to evolve into a new phase when humanity would become supreme.

Even though scripture had been an aristocratic art form, it had nearly always developed a disciplined concern for the 'little people'. But Nietzsche took the aristocratic ideal to new heights, disdaining the smallness and meanness of humanity. He had no time for equality, which he dismissed as an ideal created by Christianity's embittered 'slave mentality'. Zarathustra is revolted by the pity he feels for human beings, which repeatedly impels him from his mountain solitude to preach his new gospel. Time and again, he is driven back by nausea (*Ekel*), his almost visceral horror of 'the rabble'. He understands all too well why ascetics retreated to the desert rather than 'sit around the cistern with dirty camel-drivers'.[97] When he lived among ordinary folk, Zarathustra confesses, he went through his days 'ill-humouredly ... holding my nose'.[98] In the traditional scriptures, we have seen prophets and sages descending from mountaintops to bring succour to suffering human beings; there is no such return to the market-place in *Zarathustra*. The scripture ends with a proud assertion of ego. We see Nietzsche's tragic hero leaving his unworthy companions behind and continuing his mission alone until he can find men of his own superior calibre.

'This is *my* morning, *my* day begins: *rise up now, rise up, great noontide!*'
   Thus spoke Zarathustra and left his cave, glowing and strong, like a morning sun emerging from behind dark mountains.[99]

Zarathustra would prove to be Nietzsche's most popular book. He argued that the singing of the Greek Chorus had been essential to the tragic experience, and we have seen that either music or stylised recitation was also crucial to the reception of scripture, since this gives the words an affective dimension that goes beyond the rational discourse of logos. Nietzsche, it seems, tried to replicate this experience in his purple prose. As he himself suggested: 'The whole of Zarathustra might perhaps be reckoned as music.'[100] His prose was normally beautifully disciplined and restrained but in *Zarathustra*, he deliberately cultivated a lush – and to modern tastes over-blown – poetic diction. There is no logos in *Zarathustra* – no sustained arguments and no rational explanations. But Nietzsche's first readers were transported by it – according to Carl Jung (1875–1961), even highly serious and normally sober people found it extraordinarily moving. Yet Nietzsche understood that his ornate style would not itself transform the reader. Greek drama had been a *musterion*, not unlike the Eleusinian mysteries, that had transformed initiates (*mustai*) by rigorous physical and mental disciplines. Nietzsche knew that any reader who wanted to achieve *Übergang* must go through the same gruelling regime as his Zarathustra. He could only hope that some would be inspired by his 'new New Testament' to become serious *mustai* and take humanity a step closer to its apotheosis.

Scripture, as Nietzsche was aware, is an art form, so it is not surprising that poets understood the dynamic of religion better than the Enlightenment *philosophes*. Long before Nietzsche, there had been a reaction against Enlightenment piety in the Romantic movement – and it would also have recoiled from some of Nietzsche's ideas. William Blake (1757–1827) believed that humanity had been damaged during the Age of Reason and that even religion had succumbed to a false science that alienated people from Nature and from themselves. The Enlightenment had created a God of 'fearful symmetry', like Blake's Tyger, remote from the world in 'distant deeps and skies'.[101] Newton's domineering God must undergo a kenosis, return to earth, die a symbolic death in the person of Jesus and become one with humanity.[102] The true prophet of the industrial age was the poet, not the scientist; he alone could recall human beings to the values lost in the scientific age:

> Calling the lapsèd Soul
> And weeping in the evening dew
> That might control
> The starry pole
> And fallen, fallen light renew.[103]

The 'divine image' was to be found not in Newton's distant 'Dominion' but in 'Mercy, Pity, Peace and Love'; it is found in the 'human form divine' and has a 'human heart' and 'human face'.[104]

Where Newton had recoiled from the notion of mystery in disgust, the Romantic poets revered the indefinable and recovered a sense of the transcendent. Nature was not an object to be tested, manipulated, dominated and exploited, but a source of revelation – something that the rishis of India had discovered nearly 4,000 years earlier. William Wordsworth (1770–1850) was wary of the 'meddling intellect' that 'murders to dissect', pulling reality apart in its rigorous analysis. Instead of mastering nature, the poet should cultivate a 'wise passiveness' and 'a heart that watches and receives'.[105] By carefully cultivating this attitude of silent waiting and accessing the perceptions of the right hemisphere of his brain, Wordsworth had 'learned' to look on Nature, and discover a 'presence' there – 'a sense sublime'

> Of something far more deeply interfused,
> Whose dwelling is the light of setting suns,
> And the round ocean and the living air,
> And the blue sky, and in the mind of man:
> A motion and a spirit, that impels
> All thinking things, all objects of all thought,
> And rolls through all things.[106]

This was what the Indian rishis had called *rta,* and, later, the Brahman, the Chinese Dao, the Kabbalists En Sof, Thomas Aquinas Esse Seipsum ('Being Itself')[107] and Ibn al-Arabi Mercy. Wordsworth, always careful to use language with consummate accuracy, deliberately refrained from calling this 'something' 'God', because the word had now acquired a wholly different meaning. It was not *a* being, but a reality that informed and unified the entire cosmos. This vision of the interconnection of all things brought Wordsworth an insight that was not dissimilar to that of yogins, sages and mystics – a 'serene and blessed mood', induced not by *sola ratio* but also by the body and 'the affections':

> Until, the breath of this corporeal frame
> And even the motion of our human blood
> Almost suspended, we are laid asleep
> In body, and become a living soul:
> While with an eye made quiet by the power
> Of harmony, and the deep power of joy,
> We see into the life of things.[108]

This mental attitude had to be cultivated assiduously. It meant eschewing Cartesian certainty by cultivating what Wordsworth's younger contemporary John Keats (1795–1821) called 'negative capability', achieved 'when a man is capable of being in uncertainties, Mysteries, doubts, without any irritable reaching after fact & reason'.[109] This was how the Upanishadic sages, Daoists, Confucians, Buddhists, rabbis, Sufis and Benedictine monks had read scripture in the past. Instead of seeking to control his environment by aggressive reasoning, Keats was ready to plunge into a cloud of unknowing: 'I am however young writing at random – straining at particles of light in the midst of a great darkness – without knowing the bearing of any one assertion, of any one opinion'.[110] He gleefully claimed that he had no opinions at all, because he had no identity: he seems to have achieved a measure of 'no self' (*anatta*) that eschewed what he called 'the egotistical sublime', a transcendence of self-preoccupation that was essential to true insight.[111]

The focus on rational and empirical thought in modern industrial society had altered the way European and American Christians interpreted the Bible. But scientific modernity was not confined to the West; the colonial powers would take both *sola scriptura* and *sola ratio* to other parts of the world. How would this affect other scriptural traditions?

*

The Jewish communities were probably the first to experience the effects of the Enlightenment. The Hasidim ('the Pious Ones') emerged in Poland at about the same time as the First Great Awakening gripped North America, when the poor were struggling with excessive taxation and felt abandoned by the rabbis, who had retreated into arid discussions of Torah minutiae. Popular preachers, often known as *hasidim*, took up their cause and in 1735 Israel ben Eliezer (1700–60) declared himself to be a 'master of the name' (*baal shem*), and became their rabbi. He would be known as the 'Besht', an acronym of *baal shem tov*, 'master of exceptional status'. By the end of his life, the Besht had over 40,000 followers, and by the late nineteenth century Hasidism would dominate most of the Jewish communities of Poland, the Ukraine and east Galicia, was well established in Russia and Romania, and had begun to penetrate Lithuania.[112]

The Besht claimed that he embodied the spirit of the prophet Elijah and had been instructed in the divine mysteries by Elijah's teacher, Abijah of Shiloh. The Torah, he explained, was timeless; the biblical stories were not historically accurate accounts of events of the distant past but expressed eternal, living realities in the present.[113] A Hasid had to open himself to the text, looking beyond the literal meaning of the words to the divine. Hasidim must also look through the surface of the natural world to an indwelling Presence. From the first, Hasidic prayer was wild, noisy and emotional, but unlike the First Great Awakening, there was kenosis and a joyous apprehension of the omnipresence of the divine rather than a neurotic preoccupation with personal salvation. This was a spirituality born of the right hemisphere of the brain, deeply in tune with the Other and at home with embodiment. Hasidim combined their worship with strange, vehement gestures, putting their whole selves – body and soul – into prayer. They clapped, tossed their heads, slapped the wall with their hands, and swayed back and forth, their bodily actions creating within them a new psychological awareness of the sacred and spiritual attitudes of reverence. The whole being of a Hasid should be as pliable to the divine presence as a flame responding to every gust of wind. They even turned somersaults in the synagogue, a physical subversion of the ego. 'When a man is afflicted by pride,' a Hasid explained, 'he must turn himself over.'[114]

This emotive spirituality was based on Luria's mythical account of the creation, but the Besht transformed Luria's tragic vision of divine sparks trapped in matter during the primal explosion into a joyous realisation that there was no place where God was not. The most devout Hasidim made themselves aware of their 'attachment' (*devekut*) to the divine at every moment of the day. Like Wordsworth's 'something', this 'God' was not confined to a distant heaven, like the Jesuits' 'Lord of Creation' that had so offended Fang Yizhi, but pervaded all things and was present in every activity – eating, drinking, making love, conducting business or participating in the political life of the community.[115]

By the end of the Besht's life, the European Enlightenment was just beginning to reach eastern Europe. In many ways, Hasidism was its antithesis. The Besht promoted mystical intuition rather than *sola ratio*; where the rational ideal of the Enlightenment separated religion from politics, the rational from the mystical and the emotional, the physical from the spiritual, and the human from the divine, the Hasidim cultivated a right-hemispheric vision of the connectedness of things. The Besht also rejected the egalitarianism of the Enlightenment, because he did not believe that ordinary Jews could achieve union with God directly: they would find it only in the person of the Zaddik ('a righteous man'), who had achieved a constant awareness of the sacred.[116] This was quite new in Judaism. The Hasidic

rebbe was not an embodiment of Torah like the rabbinic sages but an incarnation of the divine, functioning in the Hasidic community in rather the
same way as an avatar in India.[117] But Hasidism was democratic in its
outreach to the common people. Hasidic rebbes were not unlike the prophets
of the Second Great Awakening, who had fulminated against the theologians of Harvard and Yale. The Hasidim had declared their independence
of the learned rabbis, who had retreated from the people into their texts,
and founded their own synagogues.

Hasidism did not subscribe to *sola scriptura*. Not only was Hasidic spirituality dependent upon ritual, but the Besht insisted that prayer was more
important than Torah study – a revolutionary idea in Judaism. Hasidim had
developed their own art of reading scripture. It was said that the Besht
once visited the learned Kabbalist Dov Ber (1710–72), who would become
his successor. The two discussed a text describing angels, and the Besht
found Dov Ber's exegesis correct but felt that something was lacking. He
told him that the angels were present in the room and asked him to stand
and honour them. When Dov Ber did so, 'the whole house was suffused
with light, a fire burned all around, and they [both] sensed the presence
of the angels who had been mentioned'. 'The simple reading is as you say,'
the Besht told Dov Ber, 'but your manner of studying lacked soul.'[118] Without
ritualised bodily gestures, a purely intellectual study of the texts could not
yield a vision of the unseen but present Reality to which the written texts
could merely point.

Dov Ber would later tell his disciples that the Besht had liberated him
from purely textual study: 'The Besht taught me the language of the birds
and the trees and the holy names and formulas for uniting the holy spheres.'[119]
This enabled him to bring his insights to the common people who could
not devote their lives to Torah study like the rabbinic elite. But Dov Ber
was also able to address learned rabbis and Kabbalists, some of whom
became the Hasidic leaders of the next generation. They never forgot his
charismatic mode of study. One of them recalled:

> Several times I myself saw that when he opened his mouth to speak words
> of Torah, he looked as if he was not of this world at all and the divine
> Presence spoke out of his throat. And sometimes, even in the midst of saying
> something, in the middle of a word, he would stop and wait for a while.
> [He] said to us: 'I will teach you the way Torah is best taught, not to feel
> [conscious of] oneself at all, but to be like a listening ear that hears the world
> of sound speaking but does not speak itself.'[120]

Instead of using scripture to support his own views, Dov Ber studied Torah with Wordsworth's 'wise passiveness' and Keats's 'negative capability', approaching the text in a silent, waiting attitude that let scripture speak for itself. One day, he changed the wording of a sentence from the second book of Kings – 'And as the musician played, the hand of Yahweh was laid upon him'[121] – so that it read: 'As the musician *was played* by the hand of the Lord ...' The Presence could only be felt when the reader ceased to impose his own ideas on the text but opened himself to it, becoming a mere vessel for divine activity in the world.[122]

While the Besht led the movement, rabbinic scholars did not take it seriously, but the learned Dov Ber was a very different proposition. Elijah ben Solomon (1720–97), the head (*gaon*) of the rabbinic Academy of Vilna in Lithuania, and his supporters, known as the Misnagdim ('Opponents'), now accused the Hasidim of heresy and called for their excommunication. The Gaon was appalled by their denigration of traditional Torah study, which was the pivot of his life. He relished what he called the 'effort' of study, an intense mental activity that propelled him into an alternative state of consciousness and a mystical ascent to the divine – though he also made time for mathematics, astronomy, anatomy and foreign languages. Even though his own spirituality was not dissimilar to Hasidism, the Gaon campaigned virulently against Dov Ber and the conflict between the Hasidim and Misnagdim became almost as acrimonious as the struggle between Protestants and Catholics. The Gaon admitted that, left to itself, *sola ratio* was incapable of reaching the divine: to break through to a new mode of perception, a mystic must rely on his intuitive powers but this mystical ascent could start with a rational effort. When Jews studied modern secular subjects, they pitted themselves against the limits of their knowledge until they transcended logos by becoming aware of its limits, breaking through to a vision of a Presence immanent in all phenomena.[123] Like the Hasidim, the Gaon encountered a sacred reality in the depths of his being; he used to roll on the ground until he achieved a tranced state and dance as wildly as the common people.[124]

Eventually Hasidim and Misnagdim banded together against a more dangerous foe: the Jewish Enlightenment (Haskalah), founded by Moses Mendelssohn (1729–86). The son of a poor Torah scholar in Dessau, Germany, Mendelssohn had followed his teacher to Berlin, where he fell in love with modern secular learning, mastering German, French, English and Latin, as well as mathematics and philosophy, at prodigious speed. He longed to take part in the German Enlightenment, but was painfully aware of its disdain for Judaism. Mendelssohn wrote a riposte to the anti-Jewish polemic of the *philosophes* in his magnum opus *Jerusalem, Concerning Religious Authority and Judaism* (1783). But it is difficult to recognise the religion he described as Jewish, because he insisted that it was an entirely rational faith while ignoring almost entirely its mythical and mystical aspects. He argued that God had revealed a law rather than a set of doctrines on Sinai, which left the minds of Jews entirely free, so that Judaism was eminently suited to Enlightened modernity. This was anathema to the Hasidim, Misnagdim and the more orthodox Jews of Europe, but was extremely attractive to those who longed to discard the restrictions of the ghetto.

During the nineteenth century, however, when many German Jews assimilated with modern European culture by converting to Christianity, two related movements developed to counter this trend, both rooted in the Haskalah. One attempted a reformation to create a 'Protestant' version of Judaism. Israel Jacobson (1768–1828) founded a school in Seesen, near the Harz mountains, where students were taught secular as well as Jewish subjects, and opened a 'temple' (so called to distinguish it from the traditional synagogue) in which there was choral singing and sermons preached in German instead of Hebrew. Other temples were established in Hamburg, Leipzig, Vienna and Denmark. In the Hamburg temple, there were Protestant-style confirmation services, and the separate seating of men and women was abandoned. Reform Judaism became especially popular when it was exported to America.[125] Pragmatic, rational, liberal and humane, with little time for the mystical, it fitted comfortably into the modern world; it was ready to shed its particularism and become a universal faith.[126]

But during the 1840s, Reform began to attract scholars and rabbis who were influenced by Kant and Hegel and formed a school known as the Science of Judaism. Leopold Zunz (1794–1886), Zechariah Frankel (1801–75), Nachman Krochmal (1785–1840) and Abraham Geiger (1810–74) applied modern critical methods to Jewish scripture and modern historiography to the history of Judaism, arguing that it was not a revealed faith but had evolved slowly and was now becoming increasingly rational.[127] But these thinkers still tried to balance their innovations with traditional teaching. Krochmal and Frankel, for example, agreed that the Written Torah was revealed on Sinai, but denied the divine origin of the Oral Law, which was man-made and could, therefore, be altered to suit modern conditions. This was not cynical pragmatism. Like Reform Jews, these scholars were preoccupied with the survival of their tradition in a world that seemed bent on destroying it.

They were, however, critical of the Reform's jettisoning of ritual. Krochmal remained an observant Jew while Zunz also argued that the bodily actions and drama of ritual made sense of Jewish mythos, preventing it from degenerating into a bleak system of abstract doctrines. Frankel feared that the reformers were losing touch with emotion. *Sola ratio* was not the only path to truth, he maintained; it could not elicit the joy and the delight that traditional Judaism, at its best, had evoked in the past. The complex ritual of Yom Kippur had helped Jews cultivate a sense of awe, while the liturgical proclamation of an imminent Messianic return to Jerusalem had given them hope in tragic circumstances.[128] Reform Jews would recognise the wisdom of this critique and reinstate some of these traditional rites.

Meanwhile, traditionally minded Jews in eastern Europe felt increasingly beleaguered in a hostile world. Even after Emancipation, when they were officially liberated from legal, political and social restrictions, they continued to live as if they were still in the ghetto, immersing themselves in Torah and Talmud and shunning Gentile influence. In 1803, Rabbi Hayyim Volozhiner (1749–1821), a disciple of the Gaon of Vilna, founded the Etz Hayyim yeshiva in Volozhin, Lithuania. Similar yeshivas were founded in Mir, Telz, Slobodka, Lomza and Novogrudnok. Hitherto a yeshiva had simply consisted of a few rooms behind the synagogue, where Jews could study Torah and Talmud. But hundreds of gifted students now came from all over Europe to study with leading Talmudic experts in Volozhin. Rabbi Hayyim taught Talmud as he had learned it from the Gaon of Vilna, by analysing the text and emphasising its logical consistency, but in such an intensive way that it yielded an *ekstasis*. The learning process was itself a ritual: the rote-learning, the hours of careful preparation before class and the intensive discussion were a form of prayer. Separated from their families, students formed a quasi-monastic community, their lives wholly shaped by the yeshiva. Some were permitted to spend a little time on modern studies, but in general secular subjects were regarded as stealing time from Torah.[129]

Like the Bible Institutes in the United States, these new yeshivas were bastions of orthodoxy, a countercultural enclave that provided an alternative to modern society. The Misnagdim regarded the Jewish Enlightenment, Reform and the Science of Judaism as even more threatening than the Hasidim, because they enabled the evils of modernity to infiltrate Judaism itself. Only properly conducted Torah study could prevent the extinction of Judaism. The heads of the yeshivas exerted enormous influence over their students, demanding absolute obedience, countering the modern emphasis on autonomy and innovation by the stringent observance of the commandments. The purpose of both yeshiva and the Bible Institute was not to do battle with secular culture but to preserve the integrity of their students by steeping them in the traditions of the premodern world.

Other Jews attempted a less drastic course. In 1851, some traditionalist Jews in Frankfurt, where Reform was in the ascendant, got permission from the municipality to form a separate community and invited Samuel Raphael Hirsch (1808–88) to become their rabbi. Hirsch laid the foundations for modern neo-Orthodoxy, establishing elementary and secondary schools where students could learn both secular and Jewish subjects. Hirsch pointed out that in the past Jews had played a major role in the development of the natural sciences, especially in the Islamic world. They had nothing to fear from contact with other cultures and should embrace as many modern developments as they could, without jettisoning the past as thoroughly as the reformers.[130] Hirsch had no time for fundamentalist literalism. Students must seek out the inner meaning of the commandments by careful study and research. A law might seem irrational, but its practice could serve as a reminder of an important truth. Circumcision, for example, called to mind the importance of preserving bodily purity; while the law forbidding the mixing of meat and milk reminded Jews that the world was not theirs to treat as they pleased and that there must always be some restraint in our treatment of the divinely ordained cosmic order.

*

During the seventeenth and eighteenth centuries, the Chinese had experienced a very different 'enlightenment'. Unlike the Western *philosophes*, who wanted to free themselves from the shackles of a benighted past, the Chinese Enlightenment had consisted initially in a mystical experience of the unity of all things in the Dao, achieved by a carefully orchestrated spirituality. The Dao, of course, was not a personalised 'God' but was, rather, all that is – a productive, creative and continually developing force, which, since Mencius, the Chinese had also experienced as inherent within themselves.[131]

In the early seventeenth century, Gao Paulong, a Confucian, described his arduous path to enlightenment in his book *Kanxue Ji* ('Recollections of the Toils of Learning'). After a long period of self-cultivation and quiet-sitting, he had experienced an illumination (*wu*) that permanently transformed him. He seemed to merge with the Dao, the ultimate reality, and

found that in this return to the fundamental rhythms of life the natural
world blended with his mind to create a state of consciousness, known as
'quietude', that preceded the arousal of such emotions as anger, grief or
pleasure. In time and with practice, quietude could become habitual, experienced both in solitude and in company.[132] Gao identified it with 'reverence'
(jing), 'a state in which the mind is "without affairs" and "not set on anything"'.
Before his enlightenment, he had despised scholars who had boasted of this
experience, but now he 'regarded it as ordinary', a normal state of being.[133]
Other neo-Confucian scholars achieved this state after a long period of
studying sacred texts, experiencing an all-embracing order that was simultaneously rational, aesthetic and religious.[134]

The experience of being 'without affairs' and 'not set on anything' closely
resembles Buddhist 'emptiness' and the Cheng–Zhu goal of having 'no mind'
of one's own. This spiritual attitude, achieved by the transcendence of self,
could also pave the way for a thoroughgoing objectivity. It had contributed
to Jiao Hong's scientific study of the Classics and Fang Yizhi's exploration of
the natural world. Under the Qing dynasty, it led to the development of a
scholarly study of scripture that was not unlike the Higher Criticism
of the Bible. The Manchu Qing dynasty (1644–1911) was sympathetic to
Chinese culture and the first two-thirds of their long reign was a period of
peace and prosperity. Neo-Confucians remained at the heart of government,
but there had been a reaction against the Cheng–Zhu school, which seemed
to have become too abstract. Some scholars, therefore, developed what
they called Hanxue ('Han learning'), preferring the Han commentaries on
the Five Classics, which had been composed closer to Confucius' time than
Zhu's Four Masters. Like Jiao Hong, these 'Han exegetes' focused on textual
criticism and philology to determine the literal meaning of a text. A closely
allied movement was kaozhengxue ('evidential research' or 'empiricism'),
which was more broadly based and applied across a range of fields without
a special focus on the Han period.

Huang Zongzi (1610–95) believed that 'evidential research' represented
a return to a more genuine form of Confucianism.[135] He was convinced
that the neo-Confucian philosophical quest for an interior 'principle' was
alien to the teachings of Confucius, who had always prioritised practical
action that benefited the people. In 1692, he published an essay on the
recent consecration of a Confucian temple, asking why all the luminaries
honoured there were Cheng–Zhu scholars and mystics. He then listed
seven important junzi who had not been enshrined but who had been
'eminently devoted to the public weal'. Instead of writing commentaries

on the *Four Masters*, they had heroically dedicated their lives to public service, 'no matter what the tortures or punishments visited upon them by the ruler':

> How could the school of Confucius be so pedantic and narrow that it would be concerned with nothing but self, have nothing to do with order and disorder in the world, and be ready to cast into the ditch all those heroes of the past and present who have tried to shake the world into action?'[136]

What China needed were men who worked courageously to transform society rather than quiet-sitting sages who retreated into 'a never-never land of consciousness'.[137]

Huang epitomised the Qing focus on actualities and practicality. Instead of contemplating the past, Qing scholars were determined to live in the present. So too, of course, were the Chengs and Zhu Xi, whose *Reflections on Things at Hand* had celebrated modern sages rather than the Sage Kings of antiquity. But Huang took this a stage further in his *Ming xuean*, a survey of Ming thought, the first Chinese critical study of a single historical period. Instead of presenting Ming ideas as reflecting traditional verities, Huang discussed them as significant in themselves, tracing their development from one master to another. There was no harking back to the teachings of the ancient sages: Chinese history was no longer presented as a series of dynastic cycles or as a decline from an idealised past. The 'evidential research' of the Enlightenment not only recognised dynamic change but embraced it wholeheartedly.[138]

The Chinese were succumbing to the forward-thrusting ethos of modernity. As in Europe, the new historical writing preferred conclusions based on evidence rather than high-minded speculation, and focused on the human being as he was rather than what he might become. Consequently, there was less interest in achieving the transformation of sagehood; instead, scholars brought a more critical attitude to their study of scripture. Already in the late Ming period, Jiao Hong had focused on phonology and textual criticism, and now the scholars of 'Han learning' developed these insights and embarked on the 'Higher Criticism' of the Classics.[139] They too preferred to study the Classics rather than the *Four Masters* and their aim was rigorous scholarship instead of mystical spirituality. Their focus on philology, etymology, phonology, palaeography and close textual study became known as *paxue* ('unadorned learning') and reflected the new focus on the material and empirical.

In his definitive study of 'evidential research', Benjamin Elman explains that its goal was to discover how reliable the Classics' information about the ancient sages was; this could only be done by ascertaining exactly what they were saying in these texts. Thus, the language of the sages had to be investigated scientifically and critically.[140] 'If there is one character that is not precisely understood,' explained Dai Zhen (1723–77), a leading *Hanxue* scholar, 'the meaning of what is said necessarily falls short and the Way is lost thereby.'[141] But for Dai Zhen, Han learning was a religious as well as a historical-critical quest:

> Since the age of 17, I set my mind on hearing the Way and I believed that if I didn't seek the Way in the Six Classics, Confucius and Mencius, I would not find it; if I did not set myself the task of learning the meaning of the characters, institutions and terms of the Classics, then I would have no basis from which to understand their language. I have worked at this goal for over 30 years and thus know the source of order and disorder throughout all time.[142]

He was also anxious to redirect spirituality from abstruse metaphysical speculation to the contemplation of the physical world, which was the reality of ordinary people.[143] But Dai Zhen had not abandoned the ideal of self-transformation. His study was still informed by 'faith in the possibility of sagehood': 'The purpose of studying is to nourish a man's innate goodness to make him develop into a worthy or a sage.'[144] The new textual criticism was a spiritual as well as an intellectual quest.

But other members of the evidential movement looked askance at Dai's scholarship. As scholars increasingly turned their attention to the material world, concentrating critically and objectively on the linguistic minutiae of the scriptures, the goal of sagehood was becoming as remote as the ideal of sainthood in the West. The secularisation of consciousness had clearly begun. But it would be a mistake to equate Han learning and 'evidential research' with modern Western materialism, which would eventually leave 'God' out of the picture, because in China the material and the spiritual were never sharply distinguished. Qing study may have focused on the more material aspects of *qi*, the 'stuff of the universe', but as the American scholar Thomas Metzger points out, this was still conceived as 'a concrete reality infused with divine meaning'.[145] Professor de Bary makes a similar point, arguing that Qing study still described the 'vitalism' of the cosmos as the Way, an ordered productivity that had direction and purpose. There was, therefore, a sacred dimension in the Chinese 'investigation of things'. Later in China, these insights would be swamped by Western ideas and Chinese tradition devalued. Instead of finding the Way within themselves, like Mencius and Gao, the influence of Western materialism led some to regard Nature as a purely external reality. Like Western thinkers too, the Chinese began to regard 'enlightenment' as the liberation from an unenlightened past. But more recently, as we shall see, there has been a growing conviction that the traditional Chinese cultivation of reverence for the cosmos may prove to be what the world really needs.[146]

*

The industrialised countries of the West were eventually compelled to seek new resources and markets for their manufactured goods abroad and embark on colonialism. A new colonial power would appropriate an 'undeveloped' country, extracting raw materials to feed the industrial process, and the colony was inundated by cheap manufactured goods from the West, which ruined local businesses.[147] By the mid-nineteenth century, Britain controlled most of the Indian subcontinent, and had deposed the last Moghul emperor. The ease with which they had been so thoroughly subjugated was profoundly disturbing to the people of India, since it implied that there was something radically amiss with their social system. They had never thought of themselves as a 'nation' in the modern, European sense; instead of organised unity, they had traditionally encouraged synergy among various groups but as Westernisation took hold, their profoundly hierarchical society was required to cultivate a broad, casteless, communal identity.

The British also created 'Hinduism' in their own image and likeness, inadvertently bequeathing a legacy of sectarianism to the subcontinent. Confronted with India's bewildering social variety, they latched on to the groups that they – mistakenly – thought they understood, dividing the population into Muslims, Sikhs, Christians and 'Hindus'. The term *hindu* ('Indian') had been used by the Moghuls to refer to the indigenous peoples as distinct from the Muslim ruling class, so Buddhists, Jains and Sikhs as well as the majority population had all called themselves *hindu*.[148] But there had never been an organised Western-style 'religion' called 'Hinduism': as we have seen, people had worshipped numerous unrelated gods and engaged in devotions that had no common theological core in a 'mosaic of distinct cults, deities, sects and ideas'.[149] But now millions of Indians were lumped together into an entity that the British called 'Hinduism' which, fatefully, became twinned to the 'Indian Nation'.

As the Indian historian Romila Thapur explains, 'Hinduism' became a reality 'when there was competition for political and economic resources between various groups in a colonial situation'.[150] As Sikh, 'Hindu' and Muslim leaders vied with each other for British favour, resources and political influence, they discovered that the colonialists were more receptive if they adopted the British understanding of religion. New reform movements developed that tended to embrace contemporaneous Protestant norms in a way that inevitably distorted their own traditions. As Protestants had tried to return *ad fontes* to the early church, the Arya Samaj ('Society of Aryans'), founded in 1875 by Swami Dayananda (1824–83), tried to revive ancient Vedic orthodoxy and create an authoritative scriptural canon on the Western model.[151] Dayananda and his successors would create a network of schools and colleges in north India, and the Arya enjoyed a steady growth, with 1.5 million members in 1947.[152]

'Hindus' had long been subjected to foreign imperialism, first by the Moghuls and then by the British.[153] Since the late eighteenth century, they had also been harassed by aggressively proselytising Christian missionaries. All this contributed to the creation of a self-conscious 'Hinduism' that was clearly distinct from other 'religions'.[154] In fact, Arya Samaj's attempt to return to 'fundamentals' was, like Protestant fundamentalism, a new departure. Indians all revered the Vedas, of course, but the most ancient texts now had little meaning for most people: the hymns of the Rig Veda, for example, were chiefly experienced in mantras, divorced from their original context. The Upanishads were still widely read but had no single message. In the mid-nineteenth century, the Brahmo Samaj ('Society of Brahma'), an elite 'Hindu' movement, had developed in Calcutta to accommodate Western ideas.[155] Its founder, Rammohan Roy, believed that the Upanishads were compatible with the rational ethos of Christian Unitarianism, but the diversity of Upanishadic ideas split the movement into rival groups, each convinced it alone had the true message. When Swami Dayananda had encountered the disarray of the Brahmo Samaj, he realised that he must return *ad fontes*, to the original Vedas.[156]

Most Indians would agree that the Vedas contain all truth, but they regard this Vedic truth as a seed from which the philosophies and spiritualities that emerged later had germinated. The American scholar Brian K. Smith notes that 'the great paradox' of modern Hinduism is that 'the subject matter of the Veda was and is largely unknown by those who define themselves in relation to it ... and in many cases, appear[s] to be totally irrelevant for Hindu doctrine and practice'.[157] But Swami Dayananda encountered a teacher who gave him an entirely different perspective – a cantankerous, eighty-one-year-old guru who was a highly respected Sanskrit scholar. For Swami Virjananda, the Great Battle of the *Mahabharata* (widely thought to have occurred about 5,000 years ago) was a turning point in history. And because it marked the beginning of the Kali Yuga, the current dark age, everything written since was inherently corrupt. Scriptures composed before the Great Battle were *ars* ('of the rishis') and all later works were *anars* ('not of the rishis') and must be discarded because they led people astray.[158]

This theory provided Dayananda with both a scriptural canon and an index of Forbidden Books, but where Virjananda had simply shared his ideas with government officials, Dayananda took them to the people. Hitherto, Indian scriptures had always marched resolutely forwards, but Arya Samaj's return *ad fontes* chimed beautifully with the Protestant ideas that were now in the ascendant, providing 'Hindus' with a rational theism, a literal mindset and a canon of ancient sacred texts.[159] The first three tenets of the Arya's Ten Rules simply asserted that God was the source of all knowledge, and that knowledge was contained in the Vedic scriptures that all Aryans were required to study. Traditional Hindu ideas were all updated, reformulated rationally and literally: the *devas* were presented as wise and learned men, and the *asuras*, their divine rivals, as ignorant people.[160] Vedic references to kings and battles were interpreted as military and political directives.[161] Like the Protestant reformers, the Arya Samaj discarded the medieval 'accretions', such as *bhakti* and the ritualised worship of images, that were central to the lives of most 'Hindus' but were regarded as primitive 'idol worship' by Protestant missionaries and colonialists.

But Dayananda was not slavishly flattering his colonial masters; on the contrary, he was defiantly asserting the superiority of Indian tradition and, in the process, distorting it. He understood the traditional maxim that the Vedas contained 'all knowledge' quite literally, insisting that the Vedas were not only the first scriptures to be revealed to humanity but that 'all knowledge that is extant in the world [today] had originated in Arya Varta', the ancient Aryan heartland.[162] Vedic sacrifice, for example, had a scientific basis: when butter and ghee are thrown into the sacred fire, they 'purify the air, rain and water [and] thereby promote happiness on this earth'.[163] All the geographical and botanical references in the Vedas had universal application.[164] Arya Varta was known as the 'Golden Land' because it produced gold and precious stones. Its kings had ruled the whole world and taught Aryan wisdom to all peoples; their extraordinary science enabled them to

build the terrifying weapons described in the epics, such as the one fired
by Ashwattaman after the Great Battle. After the Great Battle, however,
all this precious knowledge was lost. It was up to the Arya Samaj to restore
this ancient glory.

The humiliation of the colonial experience had impelled Dayananda to
distort the tradition he was exalting in a way that verged on the absurd,
yet it assuaged the bruised confidence of many 'Hindus'. Dayananda was a
moderniser: he proposed ritual reforms that preserved traditional ceremonies in a simpler form that was more suitable for modern life. He also
made the scriptures available to all castes and held widely publicised purification rites for low-caste groups that would become increasingly popular
in the 1920s and 30s after his death. During the early twentieth century,
the Arya Samaj also served the needs of the Hindu diaspora who wanted
to maintain a distinctly Hindu identity. As violence between Muslims and
Hindus escalated during the 1920s, the Arya Samaj became more militant,
urging Aryans to develop the ancient virtues of the Kshatriya and founding
a military cadre, the Arya Vir Dal ('Troop of Aryan Horses'). Like its rival,
the Rashtriya Svayamsevak Singh ('National Volunteer Association'), usually
referred to as RSS, founded in 1924 by Keshar B. Hedgewar, it fell prey
to the besetting sin of modern nationalism, an intolerance of ethnic, religious and cultural minorities. In his book *Light of Truth*, Dayananda derided
Christian theology, was vitriolic in his abuse of the Prophet Muhammad,
and dismissed Guru Nanak as a well-meaning ignoramus, who had no
understanding of Vedic ritual.

In the past, Sikhs had been persecuted by the Muslim ruling class but
had always enjoyed good relations with the *hindu* majority. After Dayananda's
death, however, the Arya became even more insulting to Sikhism and regularly derided the Gurus; this, inevitably perhaps, led to an aggressive assertion of Sikh identity. By the end of the nineteenth century, there were about
one hundred radical Sikh Sabha groups all over the Punjab, dedicated to
the assertion of Sikh distinctiveness, building Sikh schools and colleges, and
producing a flood of polemical literature in a separatism that entirely
subverted Guru Nanak's original vision.[165] A Sikh fundamentalism developed
that interpreted the tradition selectively, emphasising the more martial
teachings of the Tenth Guru and ignoring the more irenic ethos of his
predecessors. A tradition originally open to all now feared Hindus, heretics,
modernisers, secularists and any form of political dominance.[166]

As we have seen earlier in the West, modern fundamentalisms are fuelled
by a fear of annihilation, a conviction that the religious and secular majority

want to eradicate the tradition of a minority.[167] The Sikh case shows that this should not be dismissed as irrational paranoia. In 1919, a British general ordered the machine-gunning of a peaceful crowd, most of them Sikhs, in the Golden Temple, killing 309 people and injuring over 1,000. After Independence in 1947, Hindu abuse escalated and Sikh peasants in the Punjab were subjected to extreme economic hardship; some, therefore, turned to extremism, demanding a separate Sikh state. In 1984, the Indian army stormed the Golden Temple to dislodge militants who had established themselves there. The temple, of course, houses the *Guru Granth Sahib*, the Sikh scripture that embodies the spirit of the Gurus, and the new vulnerability of their scripture symbolised the beleaguered Sikh identity. The rise of new elites in the Indian state fired by the new 'Hindu' nationalism meant that Sikhs who did not fall obediently into line were increasingly marginalised. As the Sikh scholar Harjot S. Oberoi has explained, they were now required 'to speak and dream through one language', the language of the 'Hindu' leaders. Older forms of Sikhism were replaced by exclusivist innovations, such as

> the demarcation of Sikh sacred space by cleansing holy shrines of Hindu icons and idols, the cultivation of Punjabi as the sacred language of the Sikhs, the foundation of cultural bodies exclusively for Sikh youth, the insertion of the anniversaries of the Sikh gurus into the ritual and sacred calendar, and most important of all, the introduction of new life-cycle rituals.[168]

Guru Nanak had had no interest in scripture, but Sikhs have now developed a deep and visceral protectiveness towards the *Guru Granth Sahib*. Like Christian fundamentalists who denounce the Higher Criticism, Sikh fundamentalists have zero tolerance for any historical-critical interpretation of their scripture. Any Sikh who dares to practise such scholarship is likely to come under fire, not only metaphorically but also literally. On 22 February 1984, Sumeet Singh, editor of the Punjab's oldest literary journal, was shot outside Amritsar for his independent reading of Sikh ideology. Singh Bhindranwale (1947–84), a major figure in Sikh fundamentalism, insistently reminded audiences to tolerate no insult to the scriptures and that they have a moral obligation to kill anyone who showed the slightest disrespect for the *Guru Granth Sahib*.[169]

From a fundamentalist perspective, because scripture is revealed it is infallible and any effort to historicise or interpret it innovatively is blasphemous. This new intransigence, which countermands centuries of

innovative interpretation, is the result of an assault that, for Sikhs, has
involved bloodshed and mass murder. Elsewhere too there were violent
clashes. On 14 February 1989, five years after the murder of Sumeet Singh,
the Iranian government issued a fatwa against the British Indian author
Salman Rushdie, who in his novel *The Satanic Verses* had created what many
Muslims regarded as a blasphemous portrait of the Prophet Muhammad
and, most dangerously, suggested that the Quran had been tainted by satanic
influence. The Iranian fatwa was condemned as un-Islamic by forty-four out
of the forty-five member countries at the Islamic Conference the following
month, but there were riots in Pakistan and in Bradford, England, where
the novel was ceremonially burned. Years of suppression and denigration
had scarred Muslim sensibilities. Dr Zaki Badawi, one of Britain's most
liberal Muslims, explained that the assault on the Quran was 'like a knife
being dug into you or being raped yourself'.[170]

But some Western secularists and liberals felt that their own most sacred
values had been violated by the Iranian fatwa. For them, humanity – not
God – was the measure of all things, and freedom of speech was a sacred
value and an inalienable right. But they tarnished their cause by denouncing
Islam in the British press as an 'evil', 'bloodthirsty' religion and Muslim
society as 'repulsive'.[171] Neither side could understand the other. The anthropologist Ernest Gellner suggested that during the modern period, an
'Enlightenment rationalist fundamentalism' has developed alongside its
religious counterpart, which refuses to take seriously the transcendence
that was hitherto a fact of human life. It permits 'no saviours, no sacred
characters or sacramental communities' and precludes 'the miraculous, the
sacred occasion, the intrusion of the Other into the Mundane'.[172]

The *Bhagavad Gita*, however, which has enjoyed a new popularity in the
modern period, challenges the radical separation of humanity and divinity,
since, in the person of Krishna, God is an aspect of the human. Indeed, the
scripture contrasts the humanisation of God with the inhumanity of war.[173]
The *Gita* has acquired its high status in India relatively recently. It is in many
respects a 'colonial text', because it spoke directly to the predicament of
the people of India during the period leading up to their struggle for independence of British colonial rule. While it functioned as a foundational text
for anti-colonial politics, it also addressed the problems of any post-colonial
society. By putting the issue of war squarely at the centre of a debate about
India's future, the *Gita* forced Hindus to face up to the unwelcome realisation that they would have to fight the British. This is not a text about the
overthrow of foreign imperialism, however: like the fratricidal war of

the *Mahabharata*, in which brothers are forced to fight brothers and friends to kill their friends and mentors, the British were not a faceless, distant enemy but were often friends and colleagues. Like the Pandavas, the people of India were coming to the end of a certain era in their history and were facing an utterly unimaginable future.

The *Gita* was also a revelation to Western people, because it challenged the Orientalist paradigm of the 'passive spirituality of the East', often patronisingly contrasted with the 'active ethos' of the Protestant, rational West.[174] It dealt squarely with the problems of violence, the individual's duty to society and its limits, and the tension between the individual and fate. It therefore challenged Locke's separation of religion and politics, and after the barbarism of the First World War, Arjuna's agonised distress at the horror of warfare seemed poignantly relevant. And yet, even though the *Gita* seemed to speak so directly to the present, nobody – Indian or British – could agree about the meaning of this scripture: it directly challenged the Enlightenment ideal of clear and distinct ideas as well as the modern Protestant understanding of scripture's incontrovertible message. Instead, like the *Mahabharata*, the *Gita* remains opaque, reminding us that a truly sacred text will probably always elude definitive interpretation.

For the German poet and critic Johann Gottfried Herder, the *Gita* proved that India was the source of true wisdom, and its concept of *dharma* reminded the philologist and statesman Wilhelm von Humboldt (1767–1835) of Kant's categorical imperative: 'Act only in accordance with that maxim through which you can, at the same time, will that it become a universal law.'[175] The American essayist Ralph Waldo Emerson (1803–82) saw the *Gita* as an essentially Buddhist poem, while the English Sanskrit scholar Ralph T. Griffith thought that it might encourage Indians to convert to Christianity. The German translator Eugene Burnouf believed that the *Gita* expressed the essence of Vedic philosophy, although the Orientalist Max Muller found it inferior to the Vedas. Sir Edward Arnold, whose translation of 'The Song Celestial' made the *Gita* widely accessible to an English-speaking audience, argued that the poem transcended sectarian divisions – but he also made it clear that in his view without Christianity the Eastern traditions were incomplete.[176]

The printing press enabled the poem to reach a wider Indian audience than ever before and it became a national symbol, read avidly by the newly literate class, who tended to interpret it allegorically. It chimed with the idea of India as the Motherland, which had been popularised by the RSS, and convinced Krishna devotees that British policy was adharmic, since in the *Gita*, Krishna, the avatar of Vishnu, explains that he descends to earth whenever *dharma* is in eclipse. Theosophists read the *Gita* as an allegory in which Arjuna's opposition to the Kauravas represented the endless battle against the lower impulses, while others interpreted it as an allegory of the ancient wisdom of India opposing British oppression, technological domination and missionary propaganda.[177]

The most momentous debate on the *Gita's* significance, however, was conducted between Mohandas (Mahatma) Gandhi (1869–1948) and the scholar and poet Aurobindo Ghose (1872–1950), who were sharply divided about the legitimacy of fighting the British. Central to Gandhi's world view was the Upanishadic insight that all beings were manifestations of the Brahman; because we all shared the same sacred core, fighting other human beings violated the metaphysical bias of the entire universe. Gandhi's refusal to obey British policy was based on the three principles of *ahimsa* (non-violence), *satyagraha* (the 'soul-force' that comes with the realisation of our divine nature) and *swaraj* ('self-rule'). He believed that Arjuna's initial reluctance to fight was not true *ahimsa*, because he still saw 'the enemy' as distinct from himself: had he realised that he and the Kauravas shared the same divine nature, he would have acquired the 'soul-force' to transform enmity into love. Aurobindo, however, argued that Krishna's validation of violence in the *Gita* simply reflected the grim facts of life; until *satyagraha* became an effective reality in the world, humans and nations would continue to fight and destroy one another. Moreover, Gandhi should be aware that his policy of abjuring violence had caused as much bloodshed as the more militant policies, because the British response to his non-violent campaigns had resulted in massive loss of life.[178]

The one thing that all these interpreters of the *Gita* had in common is the conviction that this scripture had a single meaning. The American scholar Laurie Patton, however, suggests another approach, pointing out that ever since the Rig Veda, Indian poets had never seen meaning as a question of 'either/or' but had envisaged it more inclusively as 'both/and'. Agni, for example, was *both* a *deva and* the material element of fire; soma was *both* the hallucinogenic plant *and* the divine priest. Patton suggests that we apply this approach to the *Gita*. Krishna, for example, orders Arjuna to enter the fray:

> Impartial to joy and suffering
> gain and loss, victory and defeat,
> arm yourself for the battle
> lest you fall into evil.[179]

This can certainly be read as an exhortation to fight and Gandhi himself admitted this, but argued that the verse could also be read as a spiritual struggle. Patton suggests that perhaps the reader should hold *both* interpretations simultaneously in mind, so that a person might be resolved to go into battle but, at the same time, realise that he feels ambiguous about it. For even if he refrains from violence, the desire to fight is still there, ready to erupt unless he holds it in check by constant vigilance and discipline. There is similar ambiguity in another verse that Gandhi greatly admired. It is certainly about *ahimsa*, describing a man who

> without attraction and hatred
> in self-control finds serenity.
> In serenity, all his sorrows dissolve,
> his reason becomes serene,
> his understanding sure.[180]

But this verse could also apply, Patton argues, to the self-control and discipline that any warrior must have in the heat of battle to avoid succumbing to atrocity. After all, Arjuna and Krishna are having this conversation on a real battlefield during a tragically violent war. Instead of trying to make scripture say what we want, perhaps we should look for ambiguity as being more expressive of the complexity of the human dilemma.[181]

Patton makes another important point. While the *Gita* has traditionally been read as a complex text with a simple meaning, there are real benefits to be had in interpreting it as a complex text with a complex meaning in a way that invites thoughtful discussion and debate. But to this day, Eastern traditions feel obliged to explain themselves to the modern West, which now sets the norm. When, for example, non-Western texts contain aggressive passages – as all scriptural traditions do – these scriptures tend to be understood as more intrinsically violent – or, at best, more 'primitive' – than the Judaeo-Christian scriptures of the dominant West. Even if, as is the case in 'Hinduism', there is a strong tradition of non-violence, a violent passage tends to be regarded as a 'contradiction' in an otherwise 'peaceful' tradition, rather than simply an element in the complexity of any faith, whose scriptures reflect human nature and inevitably contain both violent and irenic passages.[182]

*

The Quran is an obvious example of this bias. Ever since the Crusades, Western Christians have tended to regard it as a toxic scripture that gives Muslims a mandate to commit acts of violence in the name of religion.[183] For nearly a millennium, Islam had been a major global power, but by the beginning of the twentieth century most Muslims found themselves living under European colonial rule. Their Western rulers did not always disguise their disdain for Islamic religion and culture.[184] The shock of this sudden demotion was immense; it has been compared to the drastic effect of Darwin's evolutionary hypothesis on some forms of Christianity and has certainly deepened the hostility between Islam and the West. The Canadian scholar Wilfred Cantwell Smith pointed out that 'In the gulf between [the modern Muslim] and, for instance, the modern American, a matter of prime significance has been precisely the deep difference between a society with a memory of past greatness and a sense of present greatness.'[185] As in fundamentalist Christianity, their humiliation has driven some Muslims to cling to a more shuttered, conservative theology.

After the departure of the colonialists, many Muslim societies languished under dictatorships that were supported by various Western powers and led by army officers. Reza Khan, for example, came to power in Iran in 1921, Colonel Abd-Shishak in Syria (1949) and Jamal Abd al-Nasser in Egypt (1952). These reformers modernised their countries superficially, cruelly and often violently. In their attempt to secularise, they starved the clergy financially and systematically robbed them of any shred of power.[186] Mustafa Kemal Atatürk (1881–1938), founder of the modern republic of Turkey, summarily abolished the caliphate, which for centuries had been the chief symbol of Sunni power, closed the madrasas and forced the leaders of the Sufi Orders underground, thus depriving his people of responsible religious guidance at this crucial time. Nasser turned the *ulema* jurists into state officials who came to be despised as government lackeys. The secular modernity pioneered by the West and promoted by these ruthless Muslim leaders did not seem liberating and empowering but cruel and destructive. The Muslims' harsh introduction to modernity led to a widespread conviction that Islam was in danger of being diluted or contaminated by foreign norms. In the West, there was an engrained assumption that Islam was incompatible with modernity; it was a chronically backward religion that had never achieved a reformation.

Nevertheless, some modern Muslim thinkers have pioneered thoughtful, profound and innovative approaches to the Quran. They had learned from the rationalistic and progressive ethos of Western scholarship, which they used to promote the egalitarian and compassionate ethos of the Quran that had been diluted by faulty exegesis. Instead of composing the traditional verse-by-verse commentaries that remain popular among conservative Muslims, they tend to focus on a theme or aspect of the Quran and explore a limited number of verses in detail. They concentrate on the historical context of the original revelations to Muhammad, emphasising the fact that the Quran was embedded in a distinct social setting and a specific historical era. Many of these reforming scholars are non-Arab Muslims, hailing from Turkey, Pakistan, Tasmania, Malaysia or South Africa, and a significant number teach at universities in the United States where they enjoy greater intellectual freedom. They challenge some of the most widespread accusations hurled at Muslims today: that the Quran mandates authoritarian government, that it commands the subjugation of women, is inherently hostile to other faith traditions, and promotes violent jihad. Focusing on the explicit wording of the Quran and exploring the precise context in which a given revelation occurred, these scholars argue that in the past, Muslim jurists and theologians have often failed to grasp the full significance of their scripture.[187]

This critical approach began in the colonial period. In India, during the decline of Moghul rule, Shah Wali Allah Dihlawi (d. 1762) argued that it was imperative to abolish the widespread practice of *taqlid* ('imitation of past practice') and inaugurate, instead, a new phase of *ijtihad* ('independent judgement'). To meet the challenge of foreign rule, the Islamic legal system needed far-reaching reform. This would require a stringent review of the hadith, which claimed to record the words of the Prophet Muhammad and his Companions and had dominated Quranic interpretation since the ninth century. Far too frequently, jurists had relied on unreliable hadith that had been officially classified as *ahad*, 'weak'. A more important and trustworthy source, Dihlawi argued, was the Sunnah, the customary practice of the Prophet; by studying Muhammad's behaviour, in public and private life, Muslims could see their scripture in action. Later reformers, also struggling under colonial rule, followed Dihlawi, notably Muhammad Abdu (1849–1905), grand mufti of Egypt during the British military occupation, and his pupil, Rashid Rida (1865–1935). They too emphasised the importance of the Sunnah and strongly criticised the use of dubious hadith as proof texts. At this critical time, jurists simply could not afford to rely on hadith that contradicted the plain meaning of the Quran.

Today's reformers share this concern, asking hard questions that challenge centuries of Islamic exegesis. They too deplore the uncritical use of hadith and advocate a return to *ijtihad*. A crucial figure was Fazlur Rahman (d. 1988), the Pakistani-born professor of Islamic law at the University of Chicago, who argued that by relying on weak hadith, the medieval *ulema* had thwarted the natural development of Quranic thought. They saw Muhammad as a legalist with a juridical rather than a prophetic consciousness and depicted him 'neatly regulating in fine detail, the whole of human life – from administration to details of ritual purity'.[188] But, Rahman argued, Muhammad was primarily a moral reformer and had never issued clear legal rulings. As they struggled with the destructive effects of colonialism and its aftermath, jurists were still clinging to the past embodied in the hadith, and were losing touch with the Quran:

> Owing to the peculiar psychological complex we have developed vis-à-vis the West, we have come to defend [our] past as though it were God … almost all of it has become generally sacred to us. The greatest sensitivity surrounds the hadith, although it is generally accepted that, except for the Quran, all else is liable to the corrupting hand of history. Indeed, a critique of the hadith should not only remove a big mental block but should promote fresh thinking about Islam.[189]

To release the authentic Quranic message into the present, scholars must engage in a creative dialogue with the past. First, they must understand the specific problems to which the Quran was responding in seventh-century Arabia. This would give them a more accurate understanding of the precise Quranic response to these problems. Once they had grasped exactly what the Quran had been saying at the time of its revelation, they could restate its message in a way that spoke directly to the conditions and challenges of modernity.[190]

Like Dihlawi and Abdu, Rahman regarded the Sunnah as essential to the interpretation of the Quran but argued that an uncritical reverence for all the hadith had, over time, promoted ideas that had no scriptural basis. Indeed, the ninth-century jurist al-Shafii had gone so far as to regard the entire body of hadith as equal to the Quran; it was, he said, 'unrecited revelation' (*wahy ghayr matlu*), which differed from the recited Quran (*wahy matlu*) in form but not in substance.[191] But the very first Muslims had been more cautious. Umar, the second caliph, had deplored the irresponsible promotion of inaccurate hadith by some of the Companions; this, he foresaw, could have serious political, social and religious consequences.

He threatened Abu Huraya, a blatant self-promoter, with severe punishment if he continued to misquote the Prophet. Yet later jurists had taken Abu Huraya's hadith very seriously and frequently used them in their rulings.[192]

Rahman was not promoting *sola scriptura*, however. He never suggested that the entire hadith corpus should be jettisoned: 'If the [body of the] hadith as a whole is cast away, the basis for the historicity of the Quran is removed at a stroke.'[193] Authentic hadith were essential to his exegetical method, because they planted the Quranic message firmly in its historical context and enabled the interpreter to apply it creatively to contemporary issues. Neither Rahman nor any of the other reforming thinkers we are about to discuss had any time for the Muslims known as the *ahl al-Quran* ('Quranists') who wanted to eliminate all the hadith.[194] This movement had begun in India during the 1930s, had resurfaced briefly in the United States in the late twentieth century, and again, in a more moderate form, in Turkey in 2008. To the disappointment of some Western commentators (who blithely believed that the Quranists were about to start a Protestant-style reformation),[195] it has remained a minority group and has been firmly – and sometimes fiercely – opposed.

Rahman's contextual exegesis is well illustrated in his discussion of the Quranic revelation endorsing polygamy:

> Give orphans their property, do not replace [their] good things with bad, do not consume their property along with your own – a great sin. If you fear that you will not deal fairly with orphan girls, you may marry whichever [other] women seem good to you, two, three or four. If you fear that you cannot be equitable to them, then marry only one, or your slaves: that is more likely to make you avoid bias.[196]

Clearly the Quran is not simply catering to male lust here. Arab society in the seventh century was characterised by massive socio-economic disparity, Rahman explained, but the Quran was dealing with a new problem.[197] The wars between Mecca and Medina had resulted in a dramatic rise in the number of female orphans in the Muslim community and their guardians were greedily appropriating their property.[198] Polygamy was ineradicable in seventh-century Arabia and, in permitting Muslims only four wives, the Quran was restricting contemporary practice. But, Rahman notes, the jurists had failed to notice that this was not simply a legal ruling;

it also carried a strong ethical charge, 'a moral ideal towards which society was expected to move'.[199] The essence of this ruling, he argued, was a demand for equality. Not only did it break with tradition by insisting on the property rights of orphaned women, who had no such entitlement in pre-Islamic Arabia, it also required the husband to transcend his emotional and sexual inclinations and show no favouritism at all in any sphere of married life – an impartiality that is, Rahman argues, 'in the nature of things, impossible'.[200] In some modern Muslim-majority countries, polygamy is forbidden on religious grounds.

Other scholars have shown that for centuries Muslims had been empowered by inadequate exegesis to adopt policies that contradicted basic Islamic tenets. Their reliance on 'weak' hadith, Jamal al-Banna (d. 2013) argued, had effectually demoted the Quran to secondary status. The highly controversial decision to make apostasy a capital offence, for example, has no Quranic support. Indeed, the Quran states, in the strongest possible terms, that no human being – not even a prophet – may impose religious belief by force: 'There shall be no coercion in matters of faith.'[201] The English translation may seem rather flat but the Arabic (*la iqra fi-l din*) is emphatic, paralleling the compelling force of the Shahada, the proclamation of Muslim faith: *la ilahu illa Allah* ('No god but Allah!'). The Quran suggests that apostasy may be punishable in the next world, but never insisted on an earthly penalty.[202] The legal basis for the death penalty depends entirely on one isolated, 'weak' hadith, transmitted by Ikrima ibn Abbas, in Muhammad ibn Ismail al-Bukhari's hadith collection: 'Whoever changes his religion, put him to death.'[203] Al-Banna noted that Muslim ibn al-Hajjaj did not include it in his hadith anthology, however, because he regarded Ikrima as an unreliable transmitter.

Al-Banna believed that the demotion of the Quran began with the institution of the exegetical practice of *naskh* ('abrogation') in which certain verses were modified or deleted by a revelation that occurred later. As a result, 100–500 verses were abrogated at various times by different scholars. But all too often, an abrogation simply reflected the worldly interests of the exegete and his social and political milieu.[204] Abdulaziz Sachedina, professor of religious studies at the University of Virginia, argues that the practice of abrogation was used to dilute the religious pluralism of the Quran.[205] The Quran never states that it abrogated earlier scriptures. Indeed, it insists that religious pluralism is God's will and that instead of engaging in fruitless theological disputes, Muslims and non-Muslims alike should compete with one another in their efforts to do good in the world.[206]

Quran 2:62 states categorically that the acceptance of Islam is not essential to salvation:

> The [Muslim] believers, the Jews, the Christians, and the Sabians – all those who believe in God and the Last Day and do good – will have their rewards with their Lord. No fear for them, nor will they grieve.[207]

But those who promoted the idea that Islam had superseded the older faiths cited a hadith based on Quran 3:85: 'If anyone seeks a religion other than *islam*, it will not be accepted from him; he will be one of the losers in the hereafter.' The hadith stated that this verse had been revealed after Quran 2:62, which had therefore been abrogated, nullifying God's earlier promise. There could, therefore, be no salvation for members of the older faith traditions. As we saw earlier, when this supposedly abrogating verse had been revealed, '*islam*' was not yet the official name for Quranic religion: in its original context, therefore, the verse had simply claimed that anybody, whatever her faith tradition, who made a full 'surrender' of her life to God could achieve salvation. The Sufis would maintain this generous pluralism but the exclusive view has also put down deep roots in the Muslim psyche and is now rife throughout the Islamic world.

In the West, the Quran is often decried as chronically misogynistic and it is true that male jurists, relying on 'weak' Hadith, have for centuries foisted an aggressively patriarchal ethos on their scripture. But during the 1980s, women exegetes for the first time began to challenge this interpretation of the Quran – an extremely important development. Leila Ahmed and Fatima Mernissi have rewritten Islamic history from the women's perspective; while Aziza al-Hibri, Amina Wadud and Asma Barlas have developed a feminist hermeneutic.

Mernissi has drawn attention to an important incident which, she argues, established the validity of a woman's critique. Muhammad, as was expected of a great Arab chieftain, had more than the four wives prescribed in the Quran, but this harem was not a love nest. These marriages were politically motivated; they cemented relationships with his closest Companions and when a new tribe joined the pan-Islamic confederacy that he was building in Arabia, Muhammad would sometimes marry the sister or daughter of its chieftain. Seventh-century Arabs regarded women as an inferior species, so Muhammad's contemporaries were puzzled by his obvious respect for his wives; he regularly referred to them as his 'Companions', a title that he gave his closest male colleagues. He would often take one of them along on a military expedition and considered their advice very seriously. Umm Salamah, a sophisticated and intelligent woman, soon became the spokesperson for the women of Medina, who asked her one day why they were never mentioned in the Quran. In response, a few days later, a new revelation stated that in Islam men and women had the same status and responsibilities:

> For men and women who are devoted to God – believing men and women, obedient men and women, truthful men and women, charitable men and women, fasting men and women who remember God often – God has prepared forgiveness and a rich reward.[208]

God had, as it were, promptly answered Umm Salamah and would soon make it clear that women were among the oppressed that the Quran would vindicate.[209] Mernissi notes that this story was carefully preserved in the Islamic tradition but that by the eighth century jurists had managed to dilute this important insight and had reasserted the traditional Arab chauvinism.[210]

Like the male reformers, the new women exegetes have abandoned the traditional line-by-line commentary in favour of more holistic exegesis. Single verses, which by themselves might seem to support gender inequity, must be seen in the context of the whole. They emphasise the centrality of *tawhid* ('unity') in Islamic theology, which, al-Hibri argues, implies the metaphysical equity of all creatures. In the Quran, Satan denies this when he refuses to bow to Adam, claiming that he was created first and was, therefore, superior; a similar 'satanic logic', she points out, underlies traditional Muslim patriarchy.[211] Wadud notes that the Quran's insistence on equity was downplayed, because for centuries only men were permitted to read and recite the scripture.[212] Barlas maintains that because God is referred to as 'he' in the Quran, this cannot mean that God is male; it simply reflects the limitations of human language, because, the Quran insists, God is unlike any created being.[213]

A few days after Allah had responded so positively and promptly to Umm Salamah's question, a new surah was revealed, which was dedicated in large part to women. The Quran seemed to be firmly on the women's side: it decreed that women could no longer be bequeathed to male heirs as if they were cattle or date palms. They could themselves inherit and compete with men for a share in an estate.[214] No orphan girl could be married to her guardian against her will, as if she were simply moveable property.[215] It was traditional for the groom to present a dowry to his bride, but in practice it had belonged to her family. Now it became her inalienable property and in the event of divorce her husband could not claim it.[216] The men of the *ummah* were infuriated by these revolutionary Quranic innovations, but the Quran firmly upheld them.[217] Critics point out that women's rights were still not equal: in law, for example, the testimony of two women witnesses is equivalent to that of a single male.[218] But they should recall that Western women would not have any such legal or property rights until the nineteenth century.

Despite the intense focus on the hijab or 'the veil' today, the Quran has no interest in women's headgear. Women's clothing is discussed in only two passages.[219] In the first, the Quran urges both men and women to dress modestly in public: to 'lower their eyes', and 'guard their private parts'. Women are also instructed 'not [to] display their charms beyond what ordinarily shows'.[220] The second verse addresses a problem in Medina that was time-specific and should have no relevance today. Muhammad's enemies were attacking Muslim women when they went outside at night to relieve themselves, claiming that they had mistaken them for slave girls. The Quran, therefore, ordered women 'to make their outer garments hang low over them [*adna al-jilbab*] so as to be recognised and not insulted'.[221] Even though this verse was inspired by male depravity, Wadud notes, many Muslim men, who continue to enforce the jilbab, associate it with female weakness and immorality and ignore 'the issue of what constitutes appropriate sexual behaviour for *men*'.[222]

But one verse, which not only insists on women's submission to their husbands but also seems to sanction wife-beating, is indeed troubling: 'If you fear high-handedness [*nushuz*] from your wives, remind them [of the teachings of God], then ignore them when you go to bed, then hit [*wa-dribuhanna*] them.'[223] Male jurists have tended to overlook the inconvenient truth that later in this surah husbands are also cautioned against *nushuz*.[224] But the command to slap a 'high-handed' woman has long troubled male exegetes as well as feminist scholars, because it conflicts with the Sunnah. Everybody knew that the Prophet was revolted by the very notion of violence towards women, and so endemic was the practice that they found his attitude strange and eccentric. 'The Prophet never raised his hand against one of his wives, or against a slave, nor against any person at all,' wrote his early biographer, Muhammad ibn Sad. 'He was always against the beating of women.'[225] Some exegetes, however, find a solution to this problem in the polysemy of the Arabic language: the verbal root *DRB* in this verse can also mean: 'to have sexual relations'; 'to set an example'; or 'to depart from them or leave them alone'.[226] Muslims, we have seen, have always accepted the fact that there are 'variants' in the text. This could be one of them. This interpretation has the great advantage of being in accord with the Prophet's Sunnah, because on one occasion, Muhammad did indeed 'leave' his wives for a whole month, when they had stridently insisted, against the Quranic ethos, that he give his family the largest share of the booty captured during a raid. He eventually resolved the crisis by giving the women a choice: either they relinquish their desire 'for this present life and its finery' or he would give them all an amicable divorce.[227] The women agreed to conform to the Quranic imperative and marital relations were resumed.

This reading would conflict with centuries of Islamic tradition, but for the reforming exegetes that need not be an impediment. Khaled Abou El Fadl, professor of Islamic law at UCLA, argues that a single, uncontested interpretation of a scriptural text gives people a false sense of security in a constantly changing world. In fact, religion thrives on pluralistic readings:

> Texts that are unable to become liberated from their authors or unable to challenge the reader with levels of subtlety or tease with nuances of meaning have a nasty ... habit of becoming predictable, dull and closed. Texts that remain open stay alive, relevant and vital.[228]

Like Rahman, he criticises an uncritical reliance on hadith. Today those Muslims whom Abou El Fadl calls 'puritans' resort to this dependence on hadith, clinging to a rigid, sterile orthodoxy to compensate for 'feelings of defeatism, disempowerment, and alienation with a distinct sense of self-righteous arrogance vis-à-vis the nondescript "other", whether that "other" is the West, non-believers in general, so-called heretical Muslims, or even Muslim women'.[229] Their mistake, Abou El Fadl believes, is to exaggerate the role of the text and minimise the role of the interpreter.[230]

This emphasis on the interpreter rather than the revealed text is a hallmark of the reformers' innovative exegesis. In the past, jurists had emphasised the divine origin of the Quran but had, perhaps, failed to do justice to the human aspect of revelation. By emphasising the historical context of scripture, the reforming exegetes have redressed this imbalance. Throughout this book, we have seen that scripture is incarnational. It must enter the mind and body of the prophet or sage who receives and recites it, as well as the interpreter who explores its meaning. The Word must somehow be made flesh. The Quran, Rahman explained, is both human and divine; it is the word of God, but also the word of Muhammad.[231] The Prophet was

not just a passive recipient of lucid divine commands; his contribution to
the revelation was essential. The Quran certainly emanated from what we
call 'God', but 'it was also intimately connected with [Muhammad's] deeper
personality'.[232] In the past, exegetes described revelation as coming from
an external source, which they personified, calling it the 'Spirit' that
descended from heaven to earth, or the angel Gabriel. But that confined
the divine to a specific locality, whereas, as we have seen throughout, divinity
is omnipresent and 'rolls through all things'. The Spirit, Rahman maintained,
was also a power, faculty or agency in the Prophet's heart. Muhammad's
role was to release the Spirit by clothing it in the Arabic language so that
it could change the world.

The Iranian scholar Abdulkarim Soroush (b. 1945) also insists that while
the source of the Quran is divine, it is essential that Muslims recognise its
human dimension. Muslims can only decide which aspects of revelation are
relevant to their lives in the contemporary world if they accept that the
Quran is also a human product. Like Rahman, Soroush insists that
Muhammad had played an active role in the production of the Quran. The
revelation came to him in a formless state that transcended words and
concepts. The Prophet's role was 'to form the formless, so as to make it
accessible'. Muhammad's human personality, therefore, 'was both the recep-
tacle and the generator, both the subject and the object of his religious
revelatory experiences'. He was not simply an empty vessel for divine
speech, Soroush explains; 'revelation was under his sway, not he under the
sway of revelation'.[233] The Quran therefore, was adapted to his environment
and was shaped in significant ways by Muhammad's personal history, his
problems and his state of mind. Indeed, Soroush goes so far as to say that
if the Prophet had lived longer and experienced more events, his reactions
and responses would inevitably have grown as well ... and the Quran could
have been much lengthier than it is. There might even have been a second
volume.[234]

These views shock conservative Muslims, but ancient Islamic tradition
endorses the fact of the human input, making it clear that Muhammad had
to struggle to make sense of the revelations, which did not come to him
in a clear verbal form. His wife Aisha claimed that they consisted of an
indefinable intimation of an overwhelming but transfiguring meaning: 'The
first sign of prophethood vouchsafed to the apostle was true vision, resem-
bling the brightness of daybreak [*falaq as-subh*].'[235] The Arabic phrase
expresses the sudden transformation of the world where there is no gradual
dawn. What Muhammad experienced was a startling vision of hope, rather

than an explicit message. Putting it into words, he explained, was often agonising: 'Never once did I receive a revelation without thinking that my soul had been torn away from me.'[236] Sometimes the divine 'Voice' seemed relatively clear but it was often vague and incoherent: 'Sometimes it comes unto me like the reverberations of a bell, and that is the hardest upon me; the reverberations abate when I am aware of their message.'[237] The divine voice was not issuing clear commandments from a distant heaven; God was no clearly definable reality 'out there'. Allah was to be heard by looking within. Later, as we have seen, Sufis would experience a divine presence that was a part of themselves, assuring them: 'There is no god but thou.'

The Algerian scholar Mohammed Arkoun (d.2010) insisted that the revelation of the divine was inseparably entwined with the social, political and cultural structure of Arab society in the seventh century: 'There is no way to find the Absolute outside the social, political condition of human beings and the mediation of language.'[238] The text of the Quran is impregnated with a theological potency that is transcendent and therefore contains an abundance of meaning. New interpretations will be discovered as the text interacts with the ever-changing events of history.[239] The revelation had and has one purpose only: to change earthly reality. To achieve this, modern exegetes must first acquaint themselves with the historical situation that the Quran was addressing and then relate it practically and innovatively to their own. Their task is to translate that message creatively in a way that will change the contemporary world so that its social structure conforms to the compassion (*al-Rahman*) and mercy (*al-Rahim*) that Muslims invoke before nearly every recitation of the Quran.[240]

*

Recent terrorist attacks, however, seem to support the long-held Western view that the Quran is an essentially belligerent scripture. I have discussed the relationship between religion and violence in a recent work.[241] Here we will simply assess the extent to which the Quran has inspired these crimes. As we have seen, the Quran has no systematic teaching on the conduct of war; the 'jihad verses' are scattered randomly throughout the scripture, each in response to a specific circumstance, so, as the early exegetes realised, they were not universally applicable and, even though Muslims had been profoundly disturbed by colonialism and its aftermath, there was no instinctive recourse to violence. Neither Hasan al-Banna (1906–49), founder of the Muslim Brotherhood in Egypt, nor Abul Ala

Maududi (1903–79), who created the Jamaat al-Islami in India, would have anything to do with violent revolution or policies that inspired hatred and conflict. Their conduct in opposition, Maududi insisted, must be 'clean and commendable'.[242]

But Sayyid Qutb (1906–66) introduced a new militancy into modern Islamic discourse. He was one of 1,000 Muslim Brothers who were imprisoned by Nasser in 1954 after a failed assassination attempt, often without trial and for doing nothing more incriminating than handing out leaflets. A scholarly, sensitive man, Qutb was radicalised by the brutality of the Egyptian gaol where he wrote *Milestones*, which has been called the Bible of Muslim extremism. Qutb was a distinguished Quranic scholar yet the ideology of *Milestones* is based on the Sunnah, the practice of the Prophet Muhammad and the 'pious ancestors' (*salaf*), the first generation of Muslims, rather than the Quran. In the 'milestones' (the major turning points) of the Prophet's life, God, Qutb believed, had shown human beings how to build a properly ordered society.

First, Muhammad had formed a party (*jamaah*) of committed individuals, dedicated to the task of replacing *jahili* Mecca with a just society that recognised the absolute sovereignty of God. The second milestone was the Prophet's *hijrah* from Mecca to Medina: eventually there would have to be a complete rupture between the true Muslims, and the corrupt society in which they lived. During the third phase, Muhammad created an Islamic state in Medina, a time of brotherly affirmation and integration, in which the Muslims had prepared for the coming struggle. The fourth and final milestone was jihad, a military campaign that ended in the conquest of Mecca. But Qutb had distorted the Sunnah. By making violent jihad the climax of Muhammad's prophetic career, he had ignored Muhammad's non-violent peace initiative at Hudaybiyyah which, according to the early biographies, had been the true turning point for Islam. Unlike the early Muslim exegetes, Qutb insisted that 'jihad through the sword' was – and always would be – an essential preliminary to any other form of 'striving in the path of God'.[243]

Milestones has inspired much of the Islamic militancy that has since erupted in the Muslim world.[244] In the past, Sunni Muslims had emphasised the triumphant achievements of the *salaf*, the first Muslims. But now that the *ummah* was powerless and endangered, Salafists focused on their vulnerability during the terrifying war between Mecca and Medina. Like the beleaguered Muslim world today, the *salaf* had been surrounded by powerful enemies bent on their destruction. During the siege of Medina, they had even faced the prospect of annihilation. When modern jihadis studied the Quran, it was not the jihad verses that inspired them. They knew that most Muslims would condemn their militant activities, but drew comfort from the fact that the *salaf* had also been opposed by their fellow Muslims, who had been reluctant to fight against their kinsfolk and fellow tribesmen in Mecca. The Quran has harsh words for the *yubattianna*, who 'lagged behind' the fighters, accusing him of apathy and cowardice and even equating him with the *kufar*, the enemies of Islam.[245]

But Salafists were also inspired by the ancient Muslim practice of 'volunteering' (*tatawwa*), which has no roots in the Quran. During the early imperial period, some Muslims regarded the borders of the Umayyad and, later, the Abbasid empires as a symbol of Islamic integrity that must be defended against a hostile world.[246] During the eighth century, *ulema*, Hadith-collectors, ascetics and Quran-reciters used to assemble on these frontiers, sometimes taking part in the fighting and garrison duties, but usually supplying spiritual support to the army in prayer, fasting and study. The charter of the Palestinian organisation Hamas did not quote the jihad verses in the Quran, but urged Palestinians to become *murabitun*, 'guardians of the frontiers'.[247] Islamic Jihad, however, applied Qutb's ideas to the Palestinian tragedy, proclaiming itself to be the vanguard of a larger global struggle 'against the forces of arrogance [*jahiliyyah*]'.[248] Most recently, the *tatawwa* ideal has inspired the so-called Islamic State (IS). Created after the war following the invasion of Iraq in 2003, IS has attracted 'volunteers' from all over the world who were determined to restore the caliphate established by the *salaf* and tear down the frontiers set up by the colonialists.

The Salafi motivation of the terrorists who committed the atrocity of 11 September 2001 is evident in the extraordinary document found in the luggage of Mohamed Atta, the leader of the hijackers.[249] It issued 'Final Instructions' to the terrorists, telling them how to conduct themselves during their 'last night' on earth, when driving to the airport, when boarding the planes, and while fighting passengers and crew. As early as the second paragraph, we meet the embattled *salaf*: 'Remember the battle of the prophet ... against the infidels, as he went on building the Islamic state.'[250] The hijackers are instructed to spend their last night reading two surahs of the Quran. Surah 8 ('Battle Gains') describes the extreme vulnerability of the *salaf* at the Battle of Badr, when 'they were few, victimised in the land'[251] and had to face the powerful Meccan army with limited resources – rather as the hijackers were about to confront the immense military and economic power of the United States. Surah 9 ('Repentance') contains the famous 'Sword Verse', but the document dwells instead on the cowardice of the 'laggers' and comforts the terrorists on their last night: 'Do you prefer this present world to the life to come? How small the enjoyment of this world is, compared with the life to come.'[252]

In this document, the Quran functions as a magical talisman rather than a book of wisdom. The hijackers must whisper Quranic verses into their hands and rub its holiness into their luggage, box cutters, knives, ID and passports.[253] When they go through the security gates at the airport, they should recite a verse that had once saved the *salaf* from great danger: 'God is enough for us; he is the best protector.'[254] Even the Arabic letters of this verse had magical efficacy: they 'have no dots and this is just one of its greatnesses, for words that have dots in them carry less weight than those that do not'.[255] During the operation, the hijackers must take the *salaf* as their models: their clothes must fit snugly, like the garments of the Prophet and his Companions. When they fight the passengers, each of them must 'clench his teeth just as the *salaf* did prior to entering into battle',[256] singing songs to boost morale 'as each of the *salaf* did in the throes of battle to bring calm, tranquillity and joy to the hearts of his brothers'.[257]

Six months before the attack, two of the hijackers recorded farewell videos, which were circulated widely in the Muslim world after the atrocity. Both were members of Ziad Jarrah's team on United Airlines Flight 93, which crashed in Pennsylvania. Their messages are illustrated with footage depicting the destruction of the Twin Towers; mujahidin training in Afghanistan; piles of Muslim corpses in Chechnya; US troops attacking mosques in Kandahar; Palestinian homes being bulldozed; Palestinian children being shot by Israeli soldiers; Palestinians being arrested and dragged from their homes and lying, horribly wounded, in hospital; and US troops exercising in Saudi Arabia. The point is clear: the *ummah* is even more dangerously beleaguered today than it was in the Prophet's time. Yet again, Muslims are suffering at the hands of powerful enemies and, while most Muslims have 'stayed at home' like the 'laggers', bin Laden and his disciples, like the *salaf*, have heroically 'opened a door' and ushered in a new era.

Ahmed al-Hasnawi, a young Saudi citizen, speaks confidently and calmly. His discourse is entirely Salafi and Qutbian and strongly evokes the practice of 'volunteering'. In the past, he says, jihad was a required duty for every able-bodied Muslim if the enemy invaded the Dar al-Islam. But now, when Muslims are being attacked by Russians in Chechnya, Hindus in India, Jews in Palestine, and when Americans have even invaded Arabia, the Islamic heartland, no scholar calls for a defensive jihad, so he – Hasnawi – calls upon 'sincere *ulema*' to take up the 'forgotten duty' of jihad. Abdulaziz al-Omari was a learned Quran scholar, so his 'Last Will' is larded with Quranic quotations – but not with any of the jihad verses. Instead, he too cites passages that describe the embattled vulnerability of the *salaf*. Throughout, he dwells on the suffering of his fellow Muslims. Muslims may say that their hearts are broken by the plight of their brothers and sisters in Palestine, Chechnya, Sudan and Lebanon but they do nothing to help them. Omari keeps returning to a verse from Surah 4: 'Why should you not fight in God's cause, and for those oppressed men, women and children, who cry out: "Lord, rescue us from this town whose people are oppressors! By your grace, give us a protector and helper!"'[258] How could any Muslim turn a deaf ear to these cries for help?

There is a tragic irony here. We have seen that altruism and compassion for others is one of the chief messages of scripture; from start to finish, Omari reminds us that religion requires kenosis, an 'emptying' of self-interest. There can be no self-sacrifice like that of the martyr, who gives his life to end the suffering of others – but 9/11 resulted in the deaths of nearly 3,000 innocent people. All scripture insists that we cannot confine our benevolence to our own people; we must reach to the whole world, to the stranger – and even the enemy. In the build-up to the 2003 Iraq War, the British prime minister, Tony Blair, frequently insisted that the problem was not Western policy in the Middle East but rather a chronic tendency towards violence within the Quran. But the last messages of Hasnawi and Omari, despite their tragically and criminally shuttered vision, suggest that Western policies have in fact inspired considerable dismay in the Muslim world. We should all, perhaps, as a matter of urgency, reflect on the Prophet's last speech to the *ummah*, which ended with a quotation from the Quran in which God addresses the whole of humanity: 'O humankind, we have created you all from a single male and a single woman, and formed you into tribes and nations so that you may get to know one another.'[259]

POST-SCRIPTURE

In many ways, we seem to be losing the art of scripture in the modern world. Instead of reading it to achieve transformation, we use it to confirm our own views – either that our religion is right and that of our enemies wrong, or, in the case of sceptics, that religion is unworthy of serious consideration. Too many believers and non-believers alike now read these sacred texts in a doggedly literal manner that is quite different from the more inventive and mystical approach of premodern spirituality. Because its creation myths do not concur with recent scientific discoveries, militant atheists have condemned the Bible as a pack of lies, while Christian fundamentalists have developed a 'Creation science' claiming that the book of Genesis is scientifically sound in every detail. Jihadis cite passages from the Quran to support their acts of criminal terrorism. Religious Zionists quote 'proof texts' to assert their claim to the holy land and justify their enmity towards the Palestinians. Sikhs have been assassinated for applying modern textual criticism to the *Guru Granth Sahib*, while others quote their scriptures to assert Sikh distinctiveness in a way that directly contradicts the original vision of Guru Nanak. Not surprisingly, all this has given scripture a bad name. Our logos-driven mentality also makes it difficult for people to think in terms of conventional mythos and this makes scripture highly problematic. Many would be in tacit agreement with the character in Mrs Humphry Ward's novel *Robert Elsmere*: 'If the Gospels are not true in fact, as history, I cannot see how they are true at all, or of any value.'

This literalistic mindset subverts the traditional art of scripture. This is poignantly clear in the attempt to establish an Islamic science based on the Quran. Muslims were painfully aware that it was the Europeans' techno-logical and scientific achievements that had enabled them to colonise the world, militarily and intellectually, and they first encountered modern Western science while living under colonial rule, with all its attendant shame and humiliation. Some Muslim reformers compounded this sense of debilitating inferiority by attributing the 'backwardness' of Muslim countries to their lack of scientific knowledge, but others argued that if a scientific discovery did not accord with Quranic revelation, it could not be true.[1] Muslims know that modern rationalism, based on the principle of Cartesian doubt, diverges sharply from their traditional understanding of the Quran as God's complete and final revelation.[2] Some, therefore, have developed an Islamic version of Christian 'creation science' based on a reinterpretation of the Quranic descriptions of the wonders of creation.[3]

These are known as the 'sign [ayat] verses' because they point to the existence of the transcendent Reality that informs all things. From a Quranic perspective, the regular alternation of night and day and the movements of the sun and moon are not merely cosmic processes, but 'signs' that direct our attention to the compassionate and merciful power that arranged these cosmic laws for the benefit of human beings.

> Say: 'Just think, if God were to cast perpetual night over you until the day of Resurrection, what god other than He could bring you light? Do you not listen?' Say: 'Just think, if God were to cast perpetual day over you until the Day of Resurrection, what god other than He could give you night and day in which to rest? Do you not see? In His mercy, He has given you night and day, so that you may rest and seek His bounty and be grateful.'[4]

These verses are designed to provoke reflection – 'Just think' – and, as in other scriptures, to create an attitude of reverence towards the cosmos. They are also a call to action. In the next paragraph, Muslims are urged to 'do good to others as God has done good to you'.[5] They must be as thoughtful, generous and considerate to their fellow human beings as God has been in his arrangement of the universe. But by the end of the nineteenth century, some Muslim scholars had begun to reinterpret these and other verses to claim that the Quran had pre-empted the discoveries of Western science.

Badi al Zaman Said al-Bursi (d. 1960), for example, argued that the mystical 'Light Verse' in the Quran, which celebrates the ubiquity of the divine illumination that cannot be confined to any one religious tradition, predicted the invention of electricity and the light bulb:

> God is the Light of the heavens and earth. His Light is like this: there is a niche, and in it a lamp, the lamp inside a glass, like a glittering star, fuelled from a blessed olive tree from neither east nor west, whose oil gives light when no fire touches it – light upon light.[6]

It is painful to read this trivialisation of the Quranic message. More recently, the claim by other 'scientific' exegetes that the Quran pre-empted Big Bang theory has caused immense excitement in the Muslim world. In one of the 'sign' verses, Allah seems to be challenging modern sceptics: 'Are disbelievers not aware that the heavens and the earth used to be joined together [*ratq*] and We ripped them apart [*fatq*]?'[7] Originally, the exegetes claim, the earth and sky were joined together in 'dense fused matter' (*ratq*) but God tore them apart in an explosion (*fatq*) that created the ordered cosmos. But the Arabic verbs simply do not support this interpretation.[8] Others argue that the Quran anticipated modern embryology. The Canadian embryologist Keith Moore, for example, has been astonished by the 'accuracy' of the Quran's description of the developing human foetus:[9]

> We created man from an essence of clay, then We placed him as a drop of fluid in a safe place, then we made that drop into a clinging form, and We made that form a lump of flesh, and we made that lump into bones, and We clothed those bones with flesh, and later We make him into other forms – glory be to God, the best of creators.[10]

But, of course, the 'sign' verses are not providing Muslims with factual data; their purpose is to provoke reflection – 'Just think' – urging them to look through these natural phenomena to an ineffable, transcendent presence.

Here we have a confusion of genres. Scripture is an art form designed to achieve the moral and spiritual transformation of the individual and, if it does not inspire ethical or altruistic behaviour, it remains incomplete. The 'art' of science is quite different, because it is morally neutral. In fact, that is one of the reasons for its success. Science can say nothing about what we should do or why we should do it. It cannot and does not prescribe or even suggest how its discoveries should be applied. Science and scripture, therefore, are chalk and cheese and to apply the disciplines of one to the other can lead only to confusion.

Let us review what we have learned about the art of scripture. First, we have seen that scripture was always heard in the context of ritual, which dramatised it and enabled participants to embody it. Music, a product of the right hemisphere of the brain, stilled the analytical thinking of the left side of the brain and gave participants intimations of a more mysterious dimension of reality that transcended their mundane experience. It evoked attitudes of wonder, respect and reverence for the cosmos and other human beings. Without this liturgical context, an essential dimension of scripture is missing. Contemplating scripture outside a ritualised setting is like reading the lyrics of an aria. In India and China, elaborate ceremonial ritual gave an emotional and sensory dimension to the dry ritual science of the Brahmanas and the *Classic of Rites*. Ritual also evoked ethical attitudes of wonder, respect and reverence for the cosmos and other human beings. When Ezra introduced his *torah* to the people of Judah, he humanised it, making its novelty less disturbing, by introducing them to the ritual of Sukkoth. Without the domestic rites carefully designed by the rabbis to replace the magnificent temple liturgy, the abstruse spirituality of the Mishnah could never have taken root among the people.

From a very early date, long before they had any scriptures, the early Christians had commemorated Jesus' horrific death in a ceremonial meal. Later, the splendour of Byzantine liturgy would transform the participants' perception of both Christ and themselves. In western Europe, Benedictine monks chanted the entire Psalter, interspersed with scriptural readings, every week, an exercise that required breath control and ritualised genu-flections and bowing, physical disciplines that taught them attitudes of reverence at a level deeper than the cerebral. The haunting, repetitive cadences of the Gregorian chant also restricted and 'bound' the rational, discursive activity of the left brain so that the monks were open to the intuitive vision of the right. *Lectio divina* too was both a mental and physical rite in which the monk murmured the words and, as it were, chewed them ruminatively.

The Quran, of course, is called 'The Recitation'. From the very begin-ning, the Prophet drew on the Eastern tradition of sacred sound, and the Quran records the extraordinary effect it had on its first audiences. Quranic recitation is the major art form in the Islamic world. It evokes a state known as *huzn*, designed specifically to give audiences what Christians used to call 'the gift of tears'. It is often translated as 'sorrow', 'grief' or 'plaintiveness'. Like poetry, music, as we have seen, is intrinsically sad and linked to the passion for justice and the empathy for others that the Quran was calling for. But *huzn* also represents a more complex attitude:

> *Huzn* is the awareness of the human state vis-à-vis the Creator. With *huzn* one knows true humility, awe of the divine, human frailty and mortality. This awareness, and the emotion it stirs on the part of the reciter, is commu-nicated through the reciter's voice and artistry, heightening the listeners' sensitivity and moving them to tears.[11]

When Western people claim to have 'read' the Quran, they have, of course, experienced nothing like this.

Scripture has never yielded clear, univocal messages or lucid incontrovertible doctrines. On the contrary, before the modern era scripture was regarded as an 'indication' that could only point to the ineffable. From the rishis, through the *brahmodya* ritual, to the Upanishadic sages, the Indian expositors of scripture knew that they were trying to express 'something' that lay beyond the capacity of human language and could say only '*Neti* ... *neti*.' It was possible to grasp these truths only by the careful cultivation of a different mode of consciousness in physical exercises, rituals and complex mental disciplines. Even the Hebrew scriptures, which personified the divine, presented Yahweh as opaque, puzzling and inconsistent. It is significant that the image of God that became embedded in Jewish consciousness was Ezekiel's baffling vision of the divine *kavod* that defied all categorisation. It was this that inspired Jewish philosophers and mystics to insist that God's essential being, which Kabbalists called En Sof ('Without End'), was not even mentioned in the Bible or the Talmud. In Christianity, the Cappadocians, Denys and Thomas Aquinas all insisted that scripture could tell us nothing about what God really was. In the Quran, Allah is given ninety-nine names which Muslims recite as a mantra, but these names are contradictory, cancel one another out, and can only therefore point to a reality that lies beyond the reach of speech.

Consequently, scripture has no clear message and has nothing in common with the clear and distinct ideas that characterise *sola ratio*. Sometimes it even forces us to experience the shock of total unknowing. This was clear in the *Mahabharata*, which induces a spiritual and conceptual vertigo, but which is, significantly, one of India's most popular scriptures. Mahayana Buddhists rigorously eschewed essentialism and produced a multifarious canon that demonstrated, insistently, that all our most basic assumptions about the world were untenable. In their scriptures, Daoists inveighed against dogmatism and the lust for certainty that makes people fall in love with their own opinions, because 'The dao that can be known is not the eternal Dao'. The *Analects* left the Chinese with a deep suspicion of lucid dogmas and rigid formulations. It is impossible to find a set of tidy doctrines in the Hebrew Bible; and in the New Testament, there is not one gospel but four, each of which presents a very different picture of Jesus. The Quran too produces no clear teaching on such topics as the conduct of war, and jurists had to rely on their own 'independent reasoning' when they developed Islamic jurisprudence (*fiqh*). The Protestant reformers' discovery that they could not agree about what scripture said on such basic issues as the Eucharist split the movement into divisive sects. Yet that has not deterred later monotheists from making dogmatic and often aggressive statements about what scripture *really* means.

Scriptures could eschew such dogmatism because, until relatively recently, they were never regarded as the Last Word; as we have seen, they were always a work in progress. From as early as the Rig Veda, later texts were grafted onto older scriptures that had a very different vision because they were expressing new concerns. Scripture always drew on the past to give meaning to the present. Its message was never cast in stone. In China, Confucians read their own ideas into Confucius' words; he was the soil in which they planted their own views and reflections. In India, the Upanishadic sages radically reinterpreted the mystical experience of the ancient rishis, and new Vedantic writings continue this process to the present day. During their exile in Babylonia, an editor or group of editors completely recast the ancient traditions of Israel and Judah in a way that spoke directly to their condition and left its imprint on nearly every book of the Hebrew Bible. Later, after the catastrophic destruction of the temple, the rabbis developed the art of *midrash* that marched purposefully away from the Written Torah. They joined disparate quotations to form a *horoz* that gave the original texts an entirely different meaning, and even changed the words of scripture to give them a more compassionate significance. The authors of the New Testament ransacked the Written Torah to create their own *pesher* exegesis, reinterpreting the ancient laws and prophecies to make them predict the life, death and resurrection of Jesus. For nearly a millennium, both Eastern and Western Christians applied the four 'senses' of the Bible to every single verse of scripture, giving it a significance that would never have occurred to the original authors. While some Muslim jurists, such as Ibn Taymiyyah, tried to interpret the Quran literally, Shiis very early read their own esoteric beliefs into certain verses, and influential mystics, such as the formidable scholar Ibn al-Arabi, insisted that every time a Muslim recited a verse from the Quran it should mean something different to him.

Unlike science, scripture always had a moral dimension and was essentially a summons to compassionate, altruistic action. Its purpose was not to confirm the reader or listener in their firmly held opinions, but to transform them utterly. As Zhu Xi told his students, it was not correct to read your own ideas into the sacred texts and you should not expect to find current doctrinal teachings clearly enunciated in scripture. The art of scripture also demanded that it issued positive, practical action; otherwise it was end-stopped, its natural dynamic frustrated. In Vedic India, the action scripture inspired was a sacrificial ritual designed to support the fragile cosmic order. In China, the Mandate of Heaven insisted that the ruler deal compassionately with the 'little people'. The Confucians took this a step further and gave the Mandate global significance. The rituals that encouraged a *junzi* to behave empathically to their family members should enlarge their sympathies so that their concern radiated out in concentric circles until it embraced the entire world. Buddhists devised a form of yoga in which the practitioner extended loving sympathy to all quarters of the world, until he had achieved a state of perfect equanimity and impartiality towards all creatures. Furthermore, the Buddha sent his monks out to travel through the world to help suffering people deal with their pain. The Mahayana eventually broke with the *arahants* because they had retreated into their own inner peace and neglected this duty of compassionate action. Jains saw their rituals, which expressed their loving care and reverence for all creatures, animate or inanimate, as far more important than their canonical scriptures.

From the very beginning, the monotheistic traditions were dedicated to the ideal of social justice. The prophets of Israel denounced those rulers who enjoyed their own wealth and privilege but neglected the plight of the poor. Jesus insisted that his followers minister to the needy and the despised, feeding the hungry, caring for the sick and visiting those in prison. Paul's seven authentic letters aimed to eradicate inequality, since in Christ there was neither Jew nor Gentile, slave nor freeman, male nor female. Charity or love, he insisted, was the most essential virtue:

> If I have the gift of prophecy, understanding all the mysteries there are, and knowing everything, and if I have faith in all its fullness to move mountains, but without love, then I am nothing at all. If I give away all that I possess, piece by piece, and if I even let them take my body to burn it, but am without love, it will do me no good whatever.[12]

Later Christians who wrote in Paul's name tried to rein him in, when it became clear that Jesus was not going to return to establish a new world order any time soon. As we have seen, they turned their backs on Paul's radical views on sexual equality and urged their fellow Christians to observe the Graeco-Roman household codes, but the radical message of Christianity was never forgotten and would surface later in the work of Francis of Assisi and so-called 'heretics' like the Cathars. Scripture, insisted Augustine, teaches nothing but charity; indeed, he believed that if you lived a compassionate life dedicated to good works, you did not need scripture at all.

Finally, the Quran gave Muslims a divine mission to create a just and compassionate society in which wealth was shared fairly and the poor and vulnerable were treated with respect. Essential to the art of scripture, therefore, was what medieval European monks called *intentio*, a concentration or 'intensity' of intellect that impelled them to better the world by practical altruistic action. As Augustine famously remarked: 'I call charity a movement of the mind toward [the goal of] fruitfully enjoying God for his own sake and myself and my neighbour for God's sake.'[13] Perhaps the ideal was most memorably expressed by Zhang Zai in the 'Western Inscription': 'Show affection toward the orphan and the weak ... Even those who are tired and infirm, crippled or sick, those who have no brothers or children, wives or husbands, are all my brothers who are in distress.'

The 'principle of charity' has certainly been eroded in recent years, not only in Salafi terrorism, but also in such movements as Christian premillennialism, which, exploiting the noxious *Schadenfreude* of the book of Revelation, looks forward to an End Time scenario in which born-again Christians will relish the torments of their enemies from the safe vantage point of heaven. The early modern attempt to return 'to the wellsprings' (*ad fontes*) of the faith has led to a suspicion of the progressive inventiveness of the traditional art of scripture and inspired a perverse biblical literalism. The Reconstruction Movement, for example, founded in the 1980s by the Texan businessman Gary North, would implement every single law of the Bible, reintroducing slavery, executing homosexuals and stoning disobedient children.[14] This slavish return to the past is also evident in the Wahhabi ideology of Saudi Arabia, which has not only revived seventh-century Islamic punishments, but has condoned the persecution of Shiis and Sufis because they developed after the Prophet's lifetime.[15] Such practices, not surprisingly, have given both religion and scripture a bad name.

But just as worrying is a privatisation of faith that completely overturns the dynamic *intentio* of the scriptural genre. Secularisation – the separation of religion and politics – could have benefited religion by liberating it from the inherent injustice of the state, but it has not inspired a prophetic critique of society. Reducing religion to a 'private search' seems to have subjectivised and even trivialised it. The art of scripture was designed to help human beings to achieve radical spiritual transformation. People used to aspire to sagehood, Buddhahood or deification; now, however, we simply diet, have a makeover or go shopping. In the consumer society, one sociologist has remarked, 'We create ourselves through things. And we change ourselves by changing our things.'[16] Instead of extirpating egotism from the psyche, yoga has become an aerobic exercise or a means of easing personal tension and improving physical flexibility. Mindfulness, designed to teach Buddhists *anatta* ('no self') – that the 'self' we prize so dearly is illusory and non-existent – is now used to help people feel more centred and comfortable in themselves. The old scriptural ideal of kenosis seems in abeyance. Extensive interviews conducted in 2002–03 have found that the predomin-ant faith of teenagers and many of their parents in the United States is something that sociologists call 'moralistic therapeutic deism'. The purpose of religion is to make one 'feel good and happy about oneself and one's life' and God's 'job is to solve our problems and make people feel good'. God is a kind of 'cosmic therapist': always on call, he sorts out any prob-lems, and helps people to feel better about themselves.'[17] The stern Christ of the gospels has been replaced by a Jesus who has become 'my personal saviour' – a kind of personal trainer, focused on my individual well-being.

As the British psychiatrist Iain McGilchrist has shown in his seminal book *The Master and his Emissary: The Divided Brain and the Making of the Western World* (2009), the modern West has cultivated the rational activities of the left hemisphere of the brain so assiduously that the important insights of the right hemisphere have been marginalised.[18] Consequently, the transcend-ence that was essential to the art of scripture is no longer sought in the traditional kenotic disciplines but is sometimes reduced to a little mild uplift or an undisciplined frenzy centred, like the hysterical piety of the First Great Awakening, on *me*. Crucial to the traditional approach to scrip-ture was the requirement of the altruism and compassion rooted in the right hemisphere. These are qualities that are sorely needed in our world today.

At the root of many of our problems, global and national, is an inequality that, for all our good intentions, modern society has been unable to assuage. This has been evident in the horrific spectacle of thousands of migrants travelling in flimsy, inadequate boats from Africa and the Middle East and literally dying to get into Europe. In London in June 2017, seventy-two people, many of them Muslims, were burned to death in Grenfell Tower, a local-authority apartment block, because the Council of Kensington and Chelsea, the richest borough in the city, had encased the building in cheap but flammable cladding and failed to provide adequate fire-safety equipment. In the United States, the richest country in the world, a

THE LOST ART OF SCRIPTURE

disturbing number of people still cannot get adequate healthcare. In agrarian society, the aristocracy, as we have seen, generally regarded their peasants as an inferior species, but at least they saw them working in their fields. But in the modern West, most of us never see the labourers who manufacture the goods we are pressured to buy, and who are slaving in substandard conditions for low wages in distant impoverished countries.[19] We have become adept in blocking off such inconvenient truths and no longer allow ourselves to feel moral responsibility for others. This attitude has led to the greatest waning of political engagement and concern for social equity since the 1960s.[20] Television presenters now seem to be required to warn viewers that spectacles on the evening news may be distressing, giving them the chance to close their eyes or switch to another channel lest they see yet more disturbing footage from war-torn Syria or Yemen. We have become expert in refusing to allow the suffering of the world to impinge on our cocooned existence.

Social justice was crucial to the monotheistic scriptures, and, like all scriptures, they insisted that compassion cannot be confined to one's own group. you had to have what Mozi had called *jian ai*, 'concern for everybody': you must love the stranger, the foreigner, even the enemy, and reach out to all tribes and nations. We have now created a global market that has made us more interdependent than ever before, yet people are retreating into national ghettoes and closing their eyes to the problems of the wider world. This was evident in the Brexit vote in the United Kingdom; in the first week after the 2016 vote, hate crimes against foreigners increased in London by forty-eight per cent. It was also evident in the 2017 inauguration speech of President Trump, when he vowed to put 'America First'. When the Berlin Wall fell in 1989, people cheered and danced in the street, but during his election campaign, people were cheering at the prospect of a new wall separating Mexico from the United States.

It seems that *sola ratio* cannot solve these problems: we have never found a purely rational justification for human rights. Despite its extraordinary social and cultural achievements, the twentieth century saw one mass slaughter after another: from the Armenian genocide during the First World War, to the Nazi Holocaust, to the massacres in Bosnia. In the West, we pride ourselves on our humanity, but during the wars in Iraq and Afghanistan, although we quite rightly mourned our own soldiers who died in the conflict, there was no sustained outcry about the unacceptably high civilian casualties – ordinary people who were simply in the wrong place at the wrong time. We thus gave the impression that we consider some lives to be more valuable than others. Given the rising tide of violence and terrorism, which indicates that the state has lost the monopoly of violence, this attitude is no longer sustainable.

The fact that in all the traditions we have considered, despite their striking and interesting differences, the art of scripture has been so similar suggests that it tells us something important about the human condition. None of the scriptural traditions we have considered could eradicate the systemic violence of the agrarian state, but they offered an alternative ideal, acting as a continual 'reminder' (*dhikr*) of what should be done. The idea of compassion is built into our neurology but the scriptures we have studied were aware that such attitudes as reverence for others and respect even for the stranger or the enemy were not easily acquired; they had to be cultivated assiduously by the rituals and practices that we have considered in this book. They all insisted, in their different ways, on the divine core of every single human being and claimed that even the man in the street could achieve 'deification' or become a sage like Yao and Shun. If a secular ideology cannot provide a rationale for human rights, the scriptural ideal needs urgently to be restated in a way that speaks to the modern world. In the past, scripture did not slavishly return *ad fontes* but always moved forward creatively to address new challenges. Unless our traditions can meet this urgent need, we are rendering our scriptures irrelevant – unable to speak to the major issues of the day.

Distinguished theologians have of course tried to address these issues. The Jewish philosopher Martin Buber (1878–1965) had been profoundly influenced by the spirituality and rituals of Hasidism and his theological writings always emphasised the immediacy of the divine presence in scripture.[21] He insisted that the Bible was really a live voice rather than a book. That is why for centuries Jews had called scripture *miqra* (a 'calling out'). The exegete's task, therefore, was to penetrate the written text of the Bible and attend to what Buber called its 'spokenness' (*Gesprochenheit*); after all, the Bible consisted of a succession of human encounters with the divine. When God called Abraham, Moses or one of the prophets, they regularly replied '*Hinneni!*' ('Here I am!'), declaring that they were fully present, ready and attentive. Readers today must be similarly focused, paying close attention to the recurrence of words and phrases and be alert to the rhythms of the divine speech. In this way, they too would become aware of the presence that reveals itself to human beings in new ways at every moment. Buber rejected the idea that the divine revelation had occurred once and for all in the distant past or was simply imparting theoretical doctrines. When speaking from the Burning Bush, God had revealed the divine name:

ehyeh asher ehyeh: he was One 'Who would be there as He would be there'. The Sinai revelation too, Buber insisted, had been a disclosure of the divine presence rather than a law.

After the Holocaust, Buber urged Jews to make themselves persistently aware of the meaning of this Presence as it was recorded in the Bible, so that, even after such horror, they might once again recognise the God that was the source of all – of evil as well as good. Such a God could not be known cognitively in the manner of the brain's left hemisphere; this perception requires the holistic vision of the right in which good and evil may be fused in some indescribable way. Buber distinguished what he called biblical humanism from its modern Western counterpart: it did not attempt 'to raise the individual above the problems of the moment'. Instead, it sought 'to train him to stand firm in them – to prove himself in them'. Jews, he insisted, must not try to 'escape from them into a world of logos, of perfected form!'[22]

Buber pointed out that during their years in the wilderness, the tension between Moses and his people, who still yearned for the fleshpots of Egypt, was rooted in their desire for a more controllable God. While 'Israel' served the God of an open future, 'Egypt' was more conservative, worshipping idols that were created in the image and likeness of human beings. Scripture did not provide dogmatic certainty but, during a period of such tragic horror, it could enable readers to acquire a new understanding of God's presence in history and inspire a scholarship that was more involved in the tasks and challenges of the time. Buber was convinced that the struggle to discover the divine in the terrors of history would lead to personal transformation. Like all great *midrash*, his exegesis led his readers beyond the text and into life's dark enigmas. As an old rabbinic maxim has it: 'The abstract midrashic study of texts is not the main thing, but rather the transformation of these texts, through *midrash*, into sources of power for the renewal of personal and interpersonal life.'[23]

Hans Frei (1922–88), a convert from Judaism who became an Episcopalian priest and professor of theology at Yale, pointed out that in the pre-critical world, even though the scriptures were seen – in the premodern sense – as historical, readers had always reached beyond the texts to address the issues of the day.[24] Origen, Augustine and Thomas Aquinas had assessed current events as either negatively or positively reflecting patterns established in scripture. But during the Enlightenment, the biblical narratives began to be read as history in the modern sense. People forgot that they were written as stories that were merely 'history-like' and began to regard them as wholly factual accounts and, therefore, for some they became incredible. But, Frei argued, the person of Jesus should establish the norm by which Christians judge the world and current events. He was certainly a historical figure, yet he did not have religious value simply because he had existed once upon a time; he became factual only when incarnated in our daily lives.

Christians, therefore, had a twofold task. They had to read the gospels and their history-like stories with all the critical, literary and historical acumen that they could muster. They also had to read and interpret their own times with all the historical, sociological and cultural sensibility at their disposal. Like Buber, Frei believed that the Bible should be read in conjunction with a critical interpretation of current events. This should not be a complicated, abstrusely hermeneutical discipline. It simply meant that the Bible and the newspaper should, as it were, lie side by side.

Politics and the Bible should coexist in a symbiotic relationship, Frei argued, because it would prevent scriptures from becoming a convenient instrument for the clerical and political establishments. Instead of backing up their claims, scripture should call the establishment to account because the gospels were essentially subversive. Jesus' teachings had inspired hopes and expectations in the crowds who followed him, which were then smashed but reconstituted by his resurrection. The gospels' dissident ideas – about God, justice, equity, compassion and suffering – must be brought to bear on our mundane circumstances. This, of course, was not achievable in a single, superficial reading; it could only be the result of a continuous process in which the readers daily transformed their understanding of themselves and the world in which they lived – and acted accordingly.

The American theologian George Lindbeck (1923–2018) came to a similar conclusion.[25] In the monotheistic traditions – the 'religions of the Book' – the sacred text is paradigmatic but, he argued, this is only a problem if we distinguish it radically from other literary classics. Since the printing revolution and the spread of literacy, our inner world has been created by fragments of many different texts, which co-inhere in our minds, one qualifying another. Our moral universe is, therefore, shaped by *King Lear*, *Middlemarch* and *War and Peace* as well as by the Bible. These classics also inform our imaginations and the way we experience the world, so, whatever our faith, we have a multi-textual perspective on reality. But for those who truly prize their sacred texts, the Bible or the Quran supply an overall and authoritative interpretive framework. Augustine, for example, struggled (not always successfully) to encompass the writings of Plato and such political disasters as the Fall of Rome within a biblical perspective. Thomas

Aquinas attempted something similar with Aristotelianism, arguing that the task of the interpreter was to extend the meaning of scripture so that it embraced the whole of reality.[26] There were similar projects in Islam, Buddhism and the Hindu traditions.

Because of its distinctive tradition of biblical typology, Christianity went further. Not only did Christians attempt to incorporate the Hebrew scriptures into the New Testament, but they also extended it to cover current developments. King David not only became a type of Christ but was also regarded as a prototype of Charlemagne, who, in turn, became a model for such future European kings as Charles V. So instead of translating scriptural teachings into extra-scriptural realities, theology reinterprets reality according to scriptural categories. But in the West, there had been a progressive move away from allegorising and a greater reliance on the literal sense of the Bible as well as an emphasis on intertextuality – one passage of scripture being interpreted by other biblical passages. As the ethos of the Enlightenment progressed, the old typological exegesis collapsed under the increasing influence of rationalistic, scientific, Pietistic and the historical-critical methods, so scripture was no longer the lens through which theologians interpreted their world. Instead of the Bible illuminating the world, the world explained the Bible. Scripture had become itself the focus of study and traditional interpretive methods had been replaced by exegesis that prioritised facticity. This has led not only to the unhealthy literalism of fundamentalism but also to widespread scepticism.

Instead, Lindbeck concluded, the Bible should be read in a literary manner, so each text must be interpreted in a way that is consistent with its genre. The first chapter of Genesis, for example, should not be read as if it were a scientific account of the origins of life; Leviticus, a legal text, should not be given a wholly mystical interpretation; and the gospel of John made no pretence of recounting veridical history. Christians should not model themselves on the Christ reconstructed by the historical-critical method but rather on Jesus as he is presented in the distinctive genre of each gospel. The entire Bible is brought together by what we call 'God' but it never attempts a metaphysical description of God's essence, in the way that some modern theology has done. The Bible, as Frei had explained, can be read as 'history-like' even if it does not attempt 'likely history'.

Our reading of scripture, Lindbeck argued, must be innovative. In the past, as we have seen, scriptures were altered and reinterpreted quite dramatically to meet changing conditions. Lindbeck was convinced that we should continue this tradition, but this requires intellectual skills that go against the grain of the modern academic reverence for the integrity of the original text. Yet unless scripture is made to reach out creatively to meet our current predicaments, it will fail the test of our time. Hard questions must be asked. How does the traditional Christian way of viewing the 'Old Testament' as merely ancillary to the New affect Jewish–Christian relations? How does the claim that Christ is God's ultimate revelation impede Christians' understanding of the Quran? What does Sinai or Calvary have to say in the face of the Holocaust or the Armenian and Bosnian massacres? How can scripturalists incarnate biblical norms into the modern world, as they did in the past? 'A condition for the vitality of these traditions', Lindbeck concluded, 'is that they redescribe in their own distinctive idioms the new social and intellectual worlds in which adherents actually live and into which humanity as a whole is now moving.'[27]

The German novelist Thomas Mann (1875–1955) agreed that scripture must be made to address the contemporary world. His own response to the rise of Hitler and the Second World War was a series of four novels based on the biblical story of Joseph, the great-grandson of Abraham, published between 1934 and 1944. He wrote *The Tales of Jacob* and much of *The Young Joseph* in Germany, and *Joseph in Egypt* in Switzerland and *Joseph the Provider* in exile in California. Mann knew that religion was an art form and he presents Joseph as an artist who was deeply religious but also politically and socially engaged. In a lecture delivered in the Library of Congress in Washington shortly before the end of the war, Mann argued that while it had once been feasible to separate the 'purely aesthetic', the 'purely philosophical' and the 'purely religious' spheres from political life, this was no longer possible, since, after the horrifying conflicts of the last fifty years, humanity was yearning for 'a world of totality, of spiritual unity, and collective responsibility'. The world, he was convinced, 'wants to become *one*, all the way, in practical reality down to economic matters'.[28]

Joseph's story is one of the better-known tales of the Bible, if only because of the famous musical. In the book of Genesis, the young Joseph, the child of Jacob's beloved wife Rachel, was his father's favourite and was fiercely resented by the ten sons born to Jacob's less-loved wife Leah and his concubines. Joseph exacerbates the situation by tactlessly bragging about his dreams of future greatness, and his brothers resolve to get rid of him. While tending their flocks far from home, they tear off Joseph's famous robe of many colours, throw him into a pit and abandon him, telling the distraught Jacob that his beloved son had been killed by a wild beast.[29]

Reuven, Jacob's eldest son, goes back to rescue Joseph but the pit is empty, because he had been picked up by Arab merchants and taken to Egypt, where he was sold to Potiphar, one of Pharaoh's officials. Thanks to his natural charisma, Joseph rises to a prominent position in the household and resists the blandishments of Potiphar's wife, who has him thrown into prison. There too he gains the confidence of his warders and wins his freedom by his skilful interpretation of Pharaoh's dreams. On his release, he becomes grand vizier of Egypt after finding a canny solution to the problem of Egypt's impending famine. Years later, he meets his brothers again when famine forces them to buy grain in Egypt and adroitly masterminds a reconciliation.

While some theologians and fundamentalists were reading the Bible with an unparalleled literalism, Mann, the artist, understood its mythical appeal. At the various stages of life, he believed, one has different foci and, with advancing age, 'the human, eternally recurring, timeless – in short, the mythical – steps into the foreground'.[30] His celebrated novel *The Magic Mountain* (1924), set in a Swiss sanatorium, was, he realised, a modern version of the archetypal myth of the heroic quest.[31] Hans Castorp, the novel's hero, is really seeking the mythical Holy Grail, symbol of the 'knowledge, wisdom, and consecration' that gives life meaning; and the sanatorium was 'a shrine of initiatory rites, a place of adventurous investigation into the mystery of life'. But while the traditionally mythical hero undergoes his ordeal to benefit society, Castorp was engaged in a solipsistic, parasitic and ultimately pointless quest.[32] Mann also saw the biblical story of Joseph as a myth, one that reflected contemporary concerns. The monotheistic God had always manifested itself in historical events, so for Mann – as for Buber, Frei and Lindbeck, as well as for Fazlur Rahman or Khaled Abou El Fadl – 'religiousness' demanded an acute attentiveness to the changes taking place in society because 'concern with God' was not a private search for the divine but rather an 'intelligent listening to what the world spirit wants'.[33]

At this date, however, myth was not only regarded as merely fictitious but had become deeply suspect since Alfred Rosenberg's *The Myth of the Twentieth Century* (1930) had expounded the extreme Nazi doctrines that he later put into practice in eastern Europe. Again, while Mann was writing his tetralogy, leading Christian theologians were attempting to purge scripture of myth: in his *New Testament and Mythology* (1941), Rudolf Bultmann had proposed the demythologisation of scripture, arguing that it was impossible for people who used electric lights and made use of modern medicine to believe the myths of a bygone world. Mann had been inspired and intrigued by Sigmund Freud's creative use of mythology in the new science of psychoanalysis but in 1939, Freud published *Moses and Monotheism*, a retelling of the biblical story of the Exodus, which, like Mann's tetralogy, was also set partly in ancient Egypt. Freud had controversially suggested that Moses had not been of Hebraic descent but had been an Egyptian follower of Pharaoh Amenhotep IV, known as Akhenaton (*c.* 1352–1338 BCE), who had tried to impose the monotheistic cult of the sun god Aton-Re as the sole religion of Egypt. After Akhenaton's death, according to Freud, Moses had led a small band of followers into the desert, but they had rebelled and murdered him, passing on the inherited guilt of their 'original sin' to future monotheists.

Mann's myth is more positive. In the third volume of his tetralogy, he has Joseph arrive in Egypt during the reign of Akhenaton, a period of violent religious and political conflict since there was strong resistance to Pharaoh's religious reforms. Mann depicted the opposition to Akhenaton as the mirror image of the Nazi movement. Like the Germany of his day, Egypt is presented as simultaneously progressive and deeply reactionary. The theology of Bechnechous, the high priest who leads the opposition, is so conservative that it borders on the archaic. He even wears a High Frankish costume and a tiger skin, combining his fanatical adulation of past glory with an insatiable lust for power. Like the Nazis, he clings to a romantic vision of a past that is no longer viable and his ideology springs from a passionate nationalism that is imbued with an overt racism. He demands an unquestioning submission to the rituals of the old cults but deliberately ignores their moral ethos. Bechnechous is the aristocratic version of this pernicious nationalism. Instead of listening to the 'world spirit', his aim is a forcible restoration of the past. The dwarf Duda represents the populist strain of fascism, voicing the same ideas but more crudely – insisting, for example, that Joseph eats separately from Potiphar's Egyptian servants. Recent research has revealed how closely Mann's novel corresponds to the Nazi reaction against the Weimar Republic.[34]

But while Mann was critiquing the politics of his time, the theme of personal transformation is also crucial to the Joseph novels, which trace Joseph's transition from an archaic consciousness to a modern sense of self. The fictional narrator of the tetralogy, who comments throughout on the action, explains that in ancient societies ruled by mythos, a person's individuality was submerged in the collective. Instead of striking out for themselves, people sought to repeat mythical history and defined themselves entirely by the mythical role allotted to them. We are introduced to this archaic mentality in Eliezer, the young Joseph's teacher, who, when recounting the deeds of Abraham in the distant past, speaks quite unself-consciously in the first-person singular, presenting himself as an active participant in these stories, which were a present, living reality to him rather than remote historical events. As he listens to Eliezer's tales, Joseph realises that the old man lacked a defined sense of self:

> In short, he was an institution ... and when the young Joseph sat at the lesson hour ... and the boy ... gazed into the face of his old teacher who 'looked like' Abraham and knew how to say 'I' in so ample and majestic a way, strange thoughts and feelings must have flashed through that young mind ... His lovely and well-favoured eyes were fixed on the figure of the narrator; but he looked through him into an endless perspective of Eliezer-figures, who all said 'I' through the mouth of the present manifestation ... and the succession of identities lost itself not in darkness but in light. [35]

At this earlier stage of human development, it seems, men and women had not yet developed the analytical skills of the left hemisphere fully and enjoyed a holistic, mythical outlook in which events in the past still happened *all the time*. The novel requires us to enter into these past modes of thought and in *The Tales of Jacob*, the first volume of the tetralogy, Mann shows how this archaic ethos had operated in the lives of Abraham, Isaac, Esau, Jacob and his uncle Laban, in all of whom the self is relativised by the multiple identity of the mythical consciousness. [36]

The young Joseph certainly shares this mentality but he is also an artist in the making, as we see in the elaborate stories he tells his brothers. But when he is forcibly expelled from the collective, he is brutally propelled into a sudden awakening and, for the first time, as he sits abandoned in the pit, speaks of himself as 'I'. As he travels with the Arabs to Egypt, he starts to feel 'newborn' and we see him falling prey to a worrying self-inflation, comparing himself to such gods as Osiris/Adonis, the Egyptian lord of the underworld. Increasingly, he glories in his romantic role, casting himself as the mythical hero of unfolding events. To Potiphar he presents himself with charming self-importance as a saviour figure – and in this scene the narrator even compares him to Christ. This incipient narcissism is dangerous and Joseph is clearly heading for a fall. His ego is flattered by the advances of Mut-em-emenet, Potiphar's wife, and he arrogantly ignores the advice of the wise dwarf Gottlieb, who warns him that even the great Gilgamesh could not withstand the blandishments of the goddess Ishtar. Obstinately, Joseph, still in saviour-mode, goes out of his way to meet Mut so that he can guide her back to the right path. But his body responds to her sexually and his virtue is saved only at the eleventh hour when

> He saw his father's face ... Not an image of settled and personal lineaments which he saw somewhere in the room. Rather he saw it in his mind's eye – the Father's in a broad and general sense.[37]

Unlike the father figure in Freudian psychology, Jacob is not a castrating tyrant but the compassionate redeemer of Joseph's identity and an essential part of himself.[38] The developing ego cannot cast aside the cultural legacy of mythos, symbolised by Jacob, which is deeply rooted in the human personality.

Joseph has learned his lesson. He suffers a second symbolic death by being thrown into an Egyptian gaol but he no longer presents himself as the invincible saviour nor does he cast himself in archetypal roles that make him out to be more than he seems. He has undergone a kenosis. Joseph is still the artist – as is evident in his creative interpretation of Pharaoh's dreams which secures his release – but, as grand vizier of Egypt, he merges mythos and logos, becoming a skilled economist and regaining his equilibrium in social responsibility. He can assimilate with Egyptian culture, while maintaining his Hebraic mythical inheritance. He marries an Egyptian woman, and even becomes a priest of Aton-Re, justifying this to himself by emphasising the universal nature of Jewish monotheism – his God is present in all gods – rather than its exclusivity.

Mann tells many stories in the tetralogy, but there are no stories about God, because, as the narrator makes clear, God is not a being:[39] God was in the fire, but was not the fire; 'He was the space in which the world existed; but the world was not the space in which he existed.'[40] He was immanent and transcendent, defying human categorisation. Abraham, we are told, had discovered God by becoming increasingly aware of the limitations of traditional deities, and insisting that he would serve only the highest. So, as the narrator explains, Abraham had invented the human idea of God, which could never measure up to the reality itself:

> in a way, Abraham was God's father. He had perceived and thought him into being. The mighty properties which he ascribed to him were probably God's original possession, Abraham was not their creator, but was he not so after all in a certain sense, when he recognised them, preached them, and by thinking made them real?[41]

We have seen that theologians and philosophers had long insisted that our idea of God is entirely distinct from and bears little relation to the unknowable reality itself. We only know the 'God' we have created for ourselves and should remind ourselves that what we call 'God' is always greater than we can conceive. Mann depicts God as part of a profound dimension of the human personality.[42] 'The mighty properties were indeed something outside of Abraham, but at the same time they were also in him and of him. The power of his own soul was at certain moments scarcely distinguishable from them.'[43] Our brains, as we now know, can present us with only a representation of the reality that surrounds us – not the reality itself – and that includes the divine. As Bede Griffiths put it, the human being is a microcosm in which the macrocosm is present as a hologram. Mann, the novelist, had understood what many contemporary theologians seemed to have forgotten. Abraham, the narrator explains to the reader, had done a good deed – to God, to himself and to those who listened to him. He had 'made ready the way of realisation of Him in the mind of man ... He had thought Him into being in the human mind.'[44]

In 1944, Mann was convinced that after the tragedies they had witnessed, people were yearning for wholeness – a unity that he depicts in the reconciliation between Joseph and his brothers. Here he follows the biblical story quite closely, but he carefully presents Joseph as an artist, who is self-consciously conducting a psychodrama of his own making, putting his bewildered and terrified brothers, who have not recognised their little brother in the formidable grand vizier, through a series of ordeals. They are thrown into prison; some are made hostages, forced to travel back and forth between Canaan and Egypt, and accused of theft. This is a ritualised *musterion*, like the Eleusinian mysteries that propelled initiates, the *mustai*, into a different mode of thought and insight. Joseph is creating a ritualised drama designed to make his brothers fully aware of their crimes and thus achieve a new state of mind, its purpose a profound and lasting transformation. Joseph repeatedly presents himself to the reader as a 'poet', designing and carefully choreographing the drama down to the last detail, even involving servants in the sacred game, until the final act, the 'transformation scene' when he reveals his identity to the astonished *mustai*.

In the biblical story, when Joseph's brothers finally realise who he is, they are dumbfounded. There are no cries of joy, recognition and relief. The brothers' stunned silence, in a biblical narrative in which dialogue has been unusually important, is significant. The authors of Genesis leave us with the distinct impression that the reconciliation was one-sided. The family is ostensibly reunited and Jacob is persuaded to settle in Egypt, but when their father dies seventeen years later, the brothers are still afraid: 'What if Joseph still bears a grudge against us and pays us back in full for all the wrong we did to him?'[45] The same is true in the Joseph novels. Mann was a realist. The 'world soul' might be longing for peace as the war neared its end, but he knew that after decades of terror, hatred and mass death, reconciliation would be hard to achieve.

In his tetralogy, Jacob, on his deathbed, blesses each of his sons. Again, as in Genesis, despite Jacob's love for Joseph, he appoints his son Judah as his heir and the leader of the Chosen People: Mann's readers know that one of Judah's descendants will be King David, the ancestor of Jesus. Joseph, however, remains Jacob's favourite, although he acknowledges that Joseph's artistic gifts are not of the highest order: 'It is a charming blessing but not the highest, the sternest ... Play and playing it was, familiar, friendly, appealingness, approaching salvation yet not quite seriously a calling or a gift.' But Jacob's words, when he blesses Joseph, evoke the unification that Mann desires for the world: 'Be blessed as you are blessed, with the blessing of heaven above, blessings of the deep that lieth under, with blessings gushing from the breast of heaven and the womb of earth!'[46] This deliberately refers back to the opening of the tetralogy, when, discussing an ancient Gnostic myth of the fall of humanity, the narrator concludes that redemption might lie in the interpenetration of heaven and earth, the sanctification of each by the other.[47] At the end of the tetralogy, it is Joseph the artist who embodies this blessing. Joseph was not only Jacob's favourite but Mann's too, because he was convinced that only in the medium of art could religion – defined by Mann as a sensitive and empathic concern for the state of the world – be revealed and accepted as the basis of culture.[48]

As in Genesis, after Jacob's death Joseph's brothers are still wary of him but Joseph explains that they have all – himself as well as his brothers – simply been taking part in 'God's play', each with his own allotted role in the unfolding myth. Now they must look to the future: 'Thus he spoke to them and they laughed and wept together and stretched out their hands as he stood among them and touched him, and he too caressed them with his hands.'[49] The tetralogy ends with a hopeful human image of the ultimate reconciliation, but, as we know to our cost today, Mann's hopes for world unity were not fulfilled.

More recently, the Israeli novelist David Grossman has made a scripture which, at first sight, seems somewhat unpromising and speaks to some of the seemingly intractable conflicts of our own time in his novella *Lion's Honey:*

The Myth of Samson (2005). Set in the very early years of Israelite history when the tribes were still living in the Canaanite highlands, Samson's story occupies merely three chapters of the book of Judges. He is divinely and miraculously conceived by a barren woman to save the Israelites from the Philistines, who are mercilessly harrying their settlements with their advanced weaponry. A Nazirite from birth – vowed to abstain from wine and from cutting his hair – Samson is a man of immense physical strength and he does indeed inflict severe casualties on the Philistines while, at the same time, being mysteriously drawn to them. He even seeks out Philistine women rather than settling down with a nice Israelite girl. One of these women is the famous temptress Delilah, who cuts his hair, on which his strength depends, while he is asleep. The Philistines bind the now weakened Samson, blind him and set him to work in a mill in Gaza, but, when his hair has grown back, he pulls down the temple of their god Dagon, when it is crowded with Philistine chieftains, by leaning on its supporting pillars, crying: '"May I die with the Philistines!" He thrust now in all his might and the building fell on all the people there. Those he killed at his death outnumbered those he had killed in his life.'[50]

Samson is an unattractive and unlikely hero. His actions appear arbitrary, remain unexplained, and he himself seems all brawn, no brain, and almost autistic. Yet, with consummate skill, Grossman transforms him into a tragic hero of exceptional pathos – far more successfully than Milton in *Samson Agonistes*. A truly skilled midrashist, Grossman interrogates nearly every single verse of the terse biblical account, reading between the lines, just like the rabbis. He explores in intimate and sympathetic detail the terror of Samson's bewildered parents when his birth is announced by a somewhat rebarbative 'angel of the Lord', concluding with the piercing insight that maybe their fear 'is also a fear of the unborn child, their child for whom they had waited and prayed, who even now is surrounded not only by amniotic fluid, but by an impenetrable membrane of enigma and menace'.[51]

This is the tragedy of a man who – and Grossman does not let God off the hook here – simply did not have the stature to fulfil the task for which he was created. Grossman notes that the Bible tells us nothing about Samson's inner world, about his education, or the 'utter loneliness'[52] of a man who is set apart from his peers by his sheer bulk and strength and regarded even by his parents as a frightening mystery. He grows up in a lonely vacuum, forming an identity that is 'elusive, defying definition, filled with contradiction, legendary, miraculous'. And that, Grossman suggests, is perhaps why he goes womanising in Gaza again and again, 'to rub up against another being that is utterly foreign'.[53]

Grossman cites others who have been intrigued by the enigma of Samson, who has fascinated painters (Rembrandt, Doré and Van Dyck), writers (Josephus, Jabotinsky and Rilke) and psychiatrists. But this is not merely an exploration of the past; Grossman shows how this ancient scripture still speaks directly to our own world. He notes, for example, the ambivalent image of Samson in Jewish tradition, which has sometimes condemned him for his aggression, clownish behaviour and his relations with *goyische* women, but has also revered him as a national hero. Perhaps, Grossman wonders, this is because Samson proleptically expresses qualities that are quintessentially Jewish, the result of years of ostracisation and persecution: 'loneliness and isolation, his strong need to preserve his separateness and mystery, yet also his limitless desire to mix and assimilate with Gentiles'.[54] For centuries of imposed weakness, Jews have also taken pride in Samson's physical strength, his bravery and virility, as well as 'his ability to apply force without any restraints or moral inhibitions'.[55] Grossman, however, also wonders whether there is 'a certain problematic quality for Israeli sovereignty that is also embodied in Samson's relationship to his own power', and suggests that 'Israel's considerable military strength is an asset that becomes a liability ... which has not really been internalised in the Israeli consciousness.'[56] This, Grossman suggests, can lead not only to making power an end in itself but also 'to a tendency to turn almost automatically to the use of force instead of weighing other means of action' – all very 'Samsonic' modes of behaviour.[57]

When contemplating Samson's heroic death, Grossman notes finally that 'in the echo chamber of our own time and place there is no escaping the thought that Samson was, in a sense, the first suicide-killer'. Although his circumstances seem to be different from those inspired to commit terrorist atrocities today, Grossman concludes, 'it may be that the act itself established in human consciousness a mode of murder and revenge directed at innocent victims, which has been perfected in recent years'.[58] Clearly too, Samson's personal history of ostracisation, living in a deeply threatened society, humiliation, his virtual castration, desire for revenge, torture and enslavement – all ending in mass slaughter – has a direct bearing on one of the gravest predicaments of our time.

But Grossman's *midrash* is also especially relevant to the issue that has preoccupied us throughout this book – the art of scriptural interpretation. There is one very odd story, which strikes many readers as a curious irrelevance. Samson has fallen for his first Philistine woman and sets out, with his parents, to arrange their marriage. But as he reaches the vineyards of Timna, a young lion comes roaring towards him. Empowered by the spirit of Yahweh, Samson simply tears the lion to pieces with his bare hands and goes on to woo the lady. About a year later,[59] returning to Timna for his wedding, he makes a detour to investigate the lion's carcase – only to discover that a swarm of bees have made their hive in the skeleton, which is oozing with honey. Heedless of the bees, Samson grabs the honey with both hands but, instead of going on to Timna, he returns to his parents' home, eating as he walks, and shares the honey with them, before going on to his wedding. There is, Grossman comments, an astonishing poignancy in the contrast between Samson's massive physique and his childlike soul: 'He walks and eats, walks and licks, till he gets home to mum and dad, and gives them the honey, "and they ate it", apparently straight from their hands.' But, Grossman believes, something happened to Samson when he found that honey: the strange sight was 'a private revelation ... a new, almost prophetic intuition'. He 'suddenly discovers the way in which an *artist* looks at the world'.[60]

Clearly Samson does not conform to the conventional view of the sensitive artist, but Grossman suggests that when he looked at the dead lion's remains and tasted the honey, linking these sensations with his feelings about the woman he was about to marry, something was, perhaps, born within him: 'Something connected in an altogether new way with perception, with a way of looking at reality, indeed something akin to a world view.'[61] He realised that he himself, in killing the lion, had – however inadvertently – created this extraordinary phenomenon: the lion's bleached and blackened bones, the oozing honey, and the continuous buzzing of the bees. Through his strength, he had created this 'powerful sight, oddly beautiful, utterly unique, and that also radiates a sense of a deep, hidden symbolic meaning'.[62] And, perhaps, when he rushed home to his parents, with his hands dripping with honey, he was saying, in effect: 'Just once, look deep inside me, and you will finally see that "out of the strong came something sweet".'[63] Later, during the wedding, Samson challenges his 'companions' – possibly bodyguards assigned to him by the understandably suspicious Philistines – to decipher this riddle:

> Out of the eater came what is eaten
> and out of the strong came what is sweet.[64]

From this time, having discovered his artistic soul, Grossman points out, nearly everything Samson says is poetic. His 'companions' bully his new wife, forcing her to wheedle the solution out of Samson, and when she does so, they belittle the riddle – pouring scorn on Samson's transformative vision. In revenge, the punishment Samson devises for them is an intricate work of art, which in the art world of today would be called a 'perform-ance', which, again, is profoundly symbolic. He catches no fewer than 300 foxes, ties them in pairs, and then fastens lighted torches between them, before sending them out into the Philistines' fields.[65] As Grossman explains, this extraordinarily complex feat displays Samson's new 'artistic need to draw upon something private and singular in all he does'; it expresses 'his doubleness, the fire raging within him, the powerful urges that tear him to shreds, the pairs of conflicting forces warring in him always ... the super-muscled frame and artistic-spiritual heart'.[66]

Perhaps only an artist could perceive the artistic nature of Samson's story and discern this poignancy in a scripture that, on first reading, seems to lack any sense of the interior life. Such artistry is required of every exegete, who must delve through the surface of the text to discover the 'lion's honey' within, finding something new and undiscovered by the myriads of interpreters who had previously studied a text that speaks not only to his or her interior needs but also addresses the dilemmas of society. Ibn Arabi, it will be recalled, said that every time one reads a scriptural text it should mean something different. It is possible, perhaps, to see Samson's vision of the lion's honey as the product of the right hemisphere of the brain that is alert to the underlying unity of all things, the *coinci-dentia oppositorum*. Perhaps he sees the co-inherence of life and death in the humming vitality and busy productivity of the bees who inhabit the lion's skeleton, as well as the convergence of violence and sweetness. His immediate response is to plunge deeply into the lion's carcase to extract this deliciousness, make it a part of himself and share it with others. Exegesis cannot remain on the surface of the text, content with its literal meaning; exegetes may be stung if their interpretations clash with settled orthodoxy, established custom or with the interests of the rich and powerful. Finally, interpreters of scripture cannot hug their discoveries to nurture a privatised faith: they must impart it to others and make it speak to the issues of the day.

Both Mann and Grossman made ancient scriptural stories speak to the political issues of the day: their focus was society. But we have seen that from the very beginning another major scriptural preoccupation was the state of the cosmos. In 2017, we learned that carbon levels were at their highest since records began, and as I write this in the summer of 2018,

Europe has suffered a heatwave in which temperatures reached unprecedented levels, resulting in flash-flooding as well as forest fires in Norway,
in the Arctic Circle. Exegetes should surely be addressing this problem.

Confucianism has suffered greatly from the onslaught of secular
modernity.[67] The eminent sinologist Joseph Levenson regarded it as moribund, chronically feudal and hopelessly anachronistic. But this judgement
was premature. Since the 1920s, a group who call themselves the 'New
Confucians' have engaged in a hermeneutic retrieval, a systematic
reappraisal of their texts. These scholars were heirs of the European
Enlightenment and brought the insights of Plato, Descartes, Leibniz, Kant,
Hegel, Dewey and Derrida to their exegesis, transforming the tradition
in a way that could speak to the modern world. They understood, for
example, that they must take feminist and Marxist critiques of Confucianism
on board. During the last thirty years, three leading thinkers – Qian Mu,
Tang Junyi and Feng Yulan – have decided that the most significant contribution to the modern world that Confucianism can make is its ideal of
the 'unity of Heaven and humanity' (*tianrenheyi*).[68] Rejecting Mao Zedong's
insistence on the human ability to control nature, Feng drew attention to
the relevance of Zhang Zai's 'Western Inscription', while Tang pointed
out that the Confucian ideal of *ren* entailed a warm heart as well as a
rational mind. They all agreed that the modern obsession with power and
mastery of the environment has made modern human beings impervious
to ecological concerns.

This is entirely the kind of creative revision of sacred texts that all religious people can and should be making in this time of ecological and social
crisis. Citing the *Doctrine of the Mean*, the New Confucians point out that
human beings have evolved from 'Heaven', and are imbued with the same
vital energy as stones, plants and animals:

> The heaven now before us is only this bright, shining mass; but when viewed in
> its unlimited extent, the sun, moon, stars and constellations are suspended
> in it and all things are covered by it. The earth before us is but a handful of
> soil; but in its breadth and depth, it sustains mountains like Hua and Yüeh
> without feeling their weight, contains the rivers and seas without letting
> them leak away and sustains all things. The mountain before us is only a
> fistful of straw; but in all the vastness of its size, grass and trees grow upon
> it, birds and beasts dwell in it, and stores of precious things [minerals] are
> discovered in it. The water before us is but a spoonful of liquid, but in

all its unfathomable depth, the monsters, dragons, fishes, and turtles are produced in them, and wealth becomes abundant because of it.[69]

But this requires more than a notional assent. The New Confucians insist that to overcome our modern habit of regarding the earth as a mere commodity will require self-knowledge, introspection and deep reflection. They are in full agreement with the Earth Charter, a declaration of values for the twenty-first century by an independent, international body, which was launched on 29 June 2000. It states that we can achieve a just, sustainable and peaceful global society, only if we 'care for the community of life with understanding, compassion, and love' – virtues that require the intensive self-cultivation produced in part by the art of scripture.

The synchronicity of environmental and religious thought was also clear at the Global Forum Conference in Moscow (1990), during which scientists challenged religious leaders to reconsider the relationship of humanity with the earth:

> As scientists, many of us have had profound experiences of awe and reverence before the universe. We understand that what is regarded as sacred is more likely to be treated with care and respect. Our planetary home should be so regarded. Efforts to safeguard and cherish the environment need to be infused with a vision of the sacred.[70]

Instead of using the 'sign' verses of the Quran to prove that they pre-empt the discoveries of modern science, Muslim exegetes could demonstrate how they speak of the sacrality of the natural world. In the same way, Hindu scholars could bring to the fore the Vedic reverence and concern for the cosmos and search for new ways of putting Prajapati's broken world together again. And we can all learn from the Jains' vision of a world in pain. In Genesis, Elohim places a clear limit on humanity's freedom to exploit the planet. When Adam transgresses this limit, and eats the forbidden fruit, the productive earth is blighted by thorns and thistles and from being the master of the Garden, Adam becomes the earth's slave.

Religion is often regarded as irrelevant to modern concerns. But whatever our 'beliefs', it is essential for human survival that we find a way to rediscover the sacrality of each human being and resacralise our world. Perhaps we should end with an ancient text that considers what will happen when the world 'grows old' and an awareness of this ubiquitous holiness is no longer observed, interpreted and animated by the ritualised language that helps to create that sense of sacrality within us:

> This totality, so good that there neither ever was, nor is, nor shall be anything better, will be in danger of perishing; men will regard it as a burden and will despise it ... No one will lift up his eyes to heaven. The pious will be thought mad, the godless wise and the wicked good. The gods will take leave of men – O painful leave-taking ...
>
> In those days, the earth will no longer be firm, the sea will cease to be navigable, the heavens will no longer hold the stars in their course; every godly voice will inevitably fall silent. The fruits of the earth will rot, the soil will be barren, and the air itself will be stale and heavy. That will be the old age of the world: the absence of religion [*irreligio*], order [*inordinatio*], and understanding [*inrationabilitas*].[71]

ACKNOWLEDGEMENTS

As always, I could not have written this book without the help of so many people. First, my agents: Felicity Bryan (to whom this book is dedicated), Peter Ginsberg and Andrew Nurnberg, who all took me on with great faith and courage at the nadir of my career and have given me indispensable and affectionate support now for over thirty years. Also, many, many thanks to Michele Topham and Carole Robinson in Felicity Bryan's office for the never-failing kindness, friendship and practical help and advice.

I am particularly grateful this time to my editors: Stuart Williams and – most especially – Jörg Hensgen at the Bodley Head and Dan Frank at Knopf for their enthusiasm, encouragement and truly inspiring suggestions, which made the editing process not only exciting but almost as revelatory as scripture itself. Also crucial has been the meticulous work and encouraging comments of David Milner, the copy editor; Alison Rae's careful proof-reading; Vicki Robinson's excellent index; and the superb cover by Luke Bird, Julia Connolly and Lily Richards – this is the first book I have ever seen that is as handsome without its cover as it is with it!

Finally, many thanks to my publicist Joe Pickering for promoting the book so assiduously and considerately, and to Nancy Roberts, my assistant, who has ensured that this time I have had the time to research and write by dealing so firmly with my copious correspondence.

GLOSSARY

A Note on Chinese terms: Chinese language is not based on an alphabet, which consists of letters that have no intrinsic meaning. A Chinese character gives an indication of sound, but also provides an indication of meaning. Readers, therefore, will find that when transliterated, some words, such as *shi* or *wu*, appear to have several, divergent meanings.

Abidharma (Sanskrit): the third and final section of the Buddhist canon, focusing chiefly on philosophical and psychological issues, which achieved its final form during the first century BCE but is regarded by *Theravadin* Buddhists as teachings which the Buddha imparted to his disciple Sariputta during the monks' annual retreat in the monsoon months.

Ad fontes (Latin): a return 'to the wellsprings' of the faith to recover its original spirit and initiate a reform. Luther, for example, attacked the medieval scholastic theologians to restore the 'pure Christianity' of the Bible and the early Fathers of the church.

Adharma (Sanskrit): a catastrophic neglect of *dharma*, the moral and spiritual duties pertaining to each of the four classes of Vedic society that were essential to the well-being of the community.

Aggada, plural *aggadot* (Hebrew): stories and legends that illuminate the teachings and rulings of the rabbis.

Ahimsa (Sanskrit): literally, 'no harm' or 'harmlessness'; non-violence.

Ahlal-Beit (Arabic): 'the People of the House', i.e. the Prophet Muhammad's family.

Ahlal-kitab (Arabic): 'the people of the book' or 'the people of scripture', the Quranic term for Jews and Christians who had received prior revelations from God. After the Prophet's death, Zoroastrians, Buddhists and Hindus would be included in this category.

Akusala (Pali): 'unhelpful' activities such as violence, stealing, lying, intoxication and sex that were forbidden to Indian renouncers seeking enlightenment. The Buddha would take this a step further, cultivating the positive and 'helpful' (*kusala*) attitudes that were the opposite of these restraints. *Ahimsa*, for example, was not sufficient for the attainment of enlightenment; one must also behave gently and kindly to everything and everybody.

Alam al-mithal (Arabic): 'the world of pure images', a term coined by Iranian Muslim mystics to refer to the psychological state that exists between the realm of sense perception and that of rational abstraction – the world of the imagination or the subconscious, which was regarded as an essential part of our humanity.

Allegoria (Greek): a narrative that expresses abstract ideas in concrete events or imagery. Greek theorists allegorised the Homeric epics to give them a different significance, and Jewish and Christian exegetes applied this practice, in different ways, to the Bible. It is the highest of the three *Senses of scripture* developed by Origen.

Anatta (Pali): literally, 'no self'. The Buddha's doctrine that denies the existence of a constant, stable and discrete personality.

Annals: see *Spring and Autumn Annals*.

Apocalupsis (Greek): literally, an 'unveiling', translated into Latin as *revelatio*, a 'revelation' that unveils a hitherto unperceived eternal truth that has suddenly become clear.

Apophatic (Greek derivation): 'speechless', 'wordless', 'silent'; a theology that emphasises the ineffability of the divine.

Arahant (Sanskrit): an 'accomplished one', a 'worthy'. A Buddhist monk who has attained *nirvana*.

Asura (Sanskrit): a demon; *asuras* were primordial deities who had become demonic and were engaged in ceaseless conflict with the *devas*.

Atman (Sanskrit): the real or true Self, defined in the *Upanishads* as the vital force that is present and active at the deepest core of every form of life and is identical with the *Brahman*.

AUM (Sanskrit): the most sacred syllable in the Hindu tradition, regarded as the essence of all things, sacred and profane, and as the 'seed' of all *mantras*. It is experienced in the 'reverberation' of the chant and the ensuing silence that expresses the attainment of the ineffable *Brahman/atman*.

Ayah, plural *ayat* (Arabic): a 'sign' of the presence and power of God in the natural world and in miraculous events. The greatest 'sign' of the divine presence is the *Quran*; consequently, each one of its verses is known as an *ayah*.

Bandhu (Sanskrit): the 'connection', 'counterpart' or 'correspondence' between heavenly and earthly realities. In the ritual science of the *Brahmanas*, participants made themselves aware that every single liturgical action, implement or *mantra* in the sacrificial rite was linked with a cosmic reality, so that gods were yoked with humans, animals, plants and ritual utensils.

Baqa (Arabic): 'revival', the climactic experience of Sufi mysticism; the realisation that God is all.

Batin (Arabic): the 'hidden' wisdom that is present in each verse of the Quran and is discovered in the spiritual exegesis of *Sufis* and *Shiis*.

Bavli (Hebrew): the Babylonian Talmud, completed *c.*500 CE.

Bhakti (Sanskrit): 'devotion'. A Hindu spirituality that focuses on the love for and adoration of a deity – Vishnu, Shiva or Devi – who has been selected by the *bhakta* ('devotee') as their chosen manifestation of the wholly transcendent divine.

Bhugu, plural *bhgavas* (Sanskrit): a 'flawed' *Brahmin*, who did not observe the *dharma* of his class but married *Kshatriya* women, engaged in black magic and specialised in the martial arts instead of observing *ahimsa*. Nearly all the Brahmins in the *Mahabharata* are *bhgavas*.

Bin (Chinese): the 'hosting' ritual in which the *Shang* and *Zhou* royal families ceremonially entertained the gods, spirits and their deceased ancestors in an elaborate feast. Younger members of the royal family, representing their deceased relatives, were believed to be possessed by their spirits during the rite.

Bodhisattva (Sanskrit): an 'enlightenment being'. In *Theravada* Buddhism, this title refers only to the historical *Buddhas* before they attained *nirvana* in their previous lives; in *Mahayana* Buddhism, the title is applied to any compassionate being who has vowed to attain enlightenment and become a Buddha with the aim of helping others gain release from the pain and sorrow of life.

Brahman (Sanskrit): the word derives from the root *BRMH* (to grow, increase). It was first used of a 'verbal formula' that the *rishi* felt swelling up from the depths of his being that had sacred power and was used in Vedic ritual. Later, it was applied to the *Brahmins*, who controlled the ritual. Finally, it came to mean the impersonal source of power, 'the All', the essence of existence, the foundation of all that exists, and the force that holds the cosmos together and enables it and its elements to grow and thrive.

Brahmana (Sanskrit): an 'explanation of the sacred power' (*Brahman*) contained in the *mantras* which were chanted during the sacrificial ritual. More specifically, it came to refer to a genre of texts, dated between 1000 and 800 BCE, that defined and explained Vedic ritual science and the myths and philosophical speculations on which it was based.

Brahmin (Sanskrit): a member of the priestly class, the highest class in Vedic society.

Brahmodya (Sanskrit): a ritualised contest developed in India in the tenth century BCE; contestants tried to find a verbal formula that defined the ineffable reality of the *Brahman* by posing one unanswerable question after another until they were reduced to speechless awe – and in that silence, the Brahman was present.

Buddha (Sanskrit): an 'enlightened one' who has 'awoken' to the truth of *nirvana*. In *Theravada* Buddhism, the term is usually applied to Gotama Buddha (d. *c.*400 BCE). In *Mahayana* Buddhism, the idea of Buddhahood has become a universal principle, since all beings have an inherent 'Buddha-nature' and therefore have the potential to attain enlightenment.

Buddhanasmrti (Sanskrit): 'recollection of the Buddha', a meditative practice in both *Theravada* and *Mahayana* Buddhism, in which practitioners call to mind the qualities and physical features of the *Buddha* in such detail that they enter a different state of consciousness, feel that they are in his presence, and have reached the plane of Buddhahood. Many of the Mahayana scriptures are the result of these meditative experiences.

Buddhavacana (Sanskrit): the 'Word of the Buddha', a term used of the Buddhist scriptures, even though large portions of the *Abidharma* in the *Pali Canon* and the multifarious *Mahayana* scriptures were composed long after the time of Gotama Buddha. But since the word 'Buddha' simply means the 'Enlightened One', *Buddhavacana* can simply mean 'enlightened teachings' imparted by the *arahants* and *bodhisattvas*.

Canon (derived from the Greek *kanon*, 'rule'): a collection of scriptures that have authority in a religious tradition. In Judaism, Christianity and Islam, texts have canonical status because they are believed to have been inspired or revealed – in some sense – by God. The term 'canon' is often applied to collections of authoritative sacred texts in other traditions, although they are not regarded as revealed in this way. The Vedic scriptures are eternal (see *Veda*; *Shruti*; *Smrti*) and the Buddhist scriptures record the teachings of the *Buddha* (but see *Buddhavacana*), who attained *nirvana* by his own efforts so they are not divinely inspired.

Chan (a Chinese version of the Sanskrit *dhyana*, 'meditation' – *chan* was translated into Japanese as *zenno* and, hence, *Zen*): this Buddhist tradition, developed in China, does not rely on scripture but rather on a direct transmission 'not founded on words and letters' from an already-enlightened person. Unlike Indian Buddhism, enlightenment does not require a conscious effort because *nirvana* is inherent in our human nature.

Cheng (Chinese): 'authenticity', 'sincerity'; the process of becoming one's complete self; an active force that enables us not only to perfect ourselves but at the same time to perfect others and transform the world.

Christos (Greek): a person anointed for a special task; in the New Testament, when applied to Jesus of Nazareth, it was a translation of the Hebrew *messhiah*.

Converso (Spanish): 'convert'; a Jew who was forced to convert to Christianity by the Inquisition.

Cuius regio, eius religio (Latin): 'he who controls the region controls its religion'. The practical outcome of the Wars of Religion in sixteenth- and seventeenth-century Europe, which entitled the ruler to decide the official religion of his country.

Dao (Chinese): 'the Way'; the correct course or path. The object of much Chinese ritual and morality was to ensure that human affairs were aligned with the Way of Heaven (see *Tian*), the Way things ought to be. In Confucianism, the pictograph suggests 'teaching'. In Daoism, the Dao becomes the ultimate, ineffable reality, the mysterious source of being, the unproduced producer of all that exists, which guarantees the safety and order of our world.

Dar al-Islam (Arabic): 'the Abode of Islam'. A key term in the imperial ideology of the Abbasid empire, formulated by Muhammad Idris al-Shafii (d.820), which divided humanity into the Dar al-Islam and the Dar al-Harb ('the Abode of War'). There could be no permanent peace between the two, since the Muslim **ummah**, which was only one of many divinely guided communities, had a God-given mission to extend its political rule by force to liberate human beings from the tyranny of an ungodly state. This became the classical doctrine of **jihad**, but it had no basis in the **Quran**. Rather, it was a typical premodern imperial ideology.

Dasas (Sanskrit): 'barbarians'. The Vedic term for the indigenous peoples of India.

De (Chinese): 'power', 'virtue'. An efficacy that was intellectual, moral and even physical, derived from the alignment of human behaviour with the **Dao** of Heaven. A king or prince who ruled with *Daode* ('the power of the Way') had a moral potency that was almost magically effective. The ancient Sage Kings **Yao** and **Shun** were said to have brought order and peace to the world not by vigorous policies but by 'doing nothing' (**wu-wei**), because they were aligned with the heavenly Way things ought to be.

Deva (Sanskrit): 'the shining one'. To translate this as 'god' is misleading, since anything – a mountain, a river, the hallucinogenic plant soma or a human teacher – that reflected the luminous mystery of the **Brahman** was, and still is, revered as a *deva* in India. The Aryans expressed their sense of affinity with these natural forces by giving them human characteristics.

Devekut (Hebrew): 'concentration'; a union with God achieved through meditative techniques.

Devi (Sanskrit): the Mother Goddess in India.

Dharma (Sanskrit): a complex word. Originally, it referred to the natural condition of things, their essence, and the fundamental law of their existence. Later it was used to define the laws and duties of each class of Vedic society. Eventually, it referred to religious truth, describing the sacred teachings of a tradition.

Dhi (Sanskrit): the 'inner vision' achieved by the *rishis*.

Dhikr (Arabic): 'remembrance', 'reminder'. One of the core concepts of the **Quran**, which presents itself as a reminder of the duties and responsibilities of human beings, who are often forgetful of matters of ultimate concern. In **Sufism**, the ritualised recitation of the name of God in a communal *dhikr*, accompanied by breathing, repetition of certain phrases, and stylised movements, is a deeply experienced remembrance of Allah and these sacred duties.

Dhimmi (Arabic): a 'protected subject' in the Islamic empire, where Islam was the religion of the Muslim ruling class, but, as was standard in premodern empires, the *dhimmis* – Jews, Christians, Zoroastrians, Hindus, etc. – were permitted to practise their faith, enjoyed a measure of self-government, but paid a tax in return for military protection.

Din (Arabic): 'way of life', 'customary practice and duty'. It is often translated as 'religion' but, like most premodern traditions, the **Quran** does not regard 'religion' as a separate activity, distinct from a secular realm. *Din* is, rather, an entire way of life. The Day of Judgement is called *yawm al-din* in the Quran, a 'moment of truth' that can occur whenever an individual fully realises what is truly important.

Disciplina (Latin): the daily rituals of the Benedictine Rule, which were carefully designed to restructure the emotional life of the monks; the habitual physical movements required by the Rule enabled them to cultivate interior attitudes of reverence and humility.

Dogma (Greek and Latin): Greek-speaking Christians distinguished between the dogma and the **kerygma** of the church. Dogma represented the deeper meaning of religious truth, which could not be expressed verbally but could only be intuited by the symbolic gestures of the liturgy and in silent, *apophatic* contemplation. The dogma of Christianity was comprehensible only after years of spiritual and liturgical practice. In the West, dogma has come to mean a body of opinion categorically and authoritatively stated.

Dukkha (Sanskrit): often translated simply as 'suffering', it should also be rendered as 'awry', 'unsatisfactory'. In Buddhism, the first noble truth is the acknowledgement that life is essentially flawed and the goal is to liberate oneself from pain by achieving *nirvana*.

Ekstasis (Greek): 'ecstasy'. Literally, it means 'stepping out', going beyond the self and transcending normal experience.

Elohim (Hebrew): often translated as 'God', it more accurately sums up everything that the divine means to human beings.

Emptiness (in Sanskrit, *sunyata*): a central concept in **Mahayana** Buddhism that took the **Buddha**'s teaching of **anatta** ('no self') to its logical conclusion, denying that anything had substantive existence.

Everything – even the *nirvana* to which all Buddhists aspired – was essentially illusory, which required the ultimate renunciation since the quest for enlightenment could degenerate into a desire for the affirmation and glorification of the self.

Energeiai (Greek): the 'activities' of God that are entirely distinct from God's essence (*ousia*), which, like **En Sof**, is eternally unknowable to human beings. We can glimpse the otherwise inaccessible divine only by God's 'manifestations' in the world.

En Sof (Hebrew): 'Without End'. In **Kabbalah**, En Sof represents the eternally hidden essence of God, which is unknowable, inconceivable and impersonal. En Sof is not even mentioned in the Bible or the Talmud, since it cannot be the subject of revelation to humanity.

Evil inclination (in Hebrew, *yetzer hara*): the rabbis taught that the *yetzer hara* was essential to our humanity. God had pronounced it 'very good' when he created it, because it was inextricably combined with some of our most creative achievements.

Ex nihilo (Latin): 'out of nothing'. The doctrine that God had created the world 'out of nothing' was affirmed for the very first time at the Council of Nicaea in 325 CE. Hitherto the world was thought to have emanated eternally from the Godhead.

Falsafah (Arabic): 'philosophy'; the attempt by Muslim *faylasufs* ('philosophers') to interpret the **Quran** according to Aristotelian science, but it was also an entire way of life or *din*, because these Muslims attempted to order their lives in accordance with the rational laws that governed the cosmos.

Fana (Arabic): 'annihilation', 'dissolution'. The state of perfection achieved by **Sufi** mystics when they realise that God is 'all in all' and that they are nothing at all, that they possess nothing, and are not possessed by anything but God. It is 'to die before one dies' and enter the state of *baqa*.

Fatwa (Arabic): a legal opinion given by a qualified Muslim official concerning a point of Islamic law which has inspired a certain doubt or where there is no clear ruling in existence. A fatwa can be contested by recourse to existing precedent since it is not regarded as an infallible or permanent pronouncement.

Fiqh (Arabic): 'intelligence', 'knowledge' of God's law; a term used of Islamic jurisprudence.

Four Masters: a group of texts that formed the syllabus of Zhu Xi's reform of Confucian studies during the Song period and had to be read in a certain order: the *Great Learning*, the *Analects*, the *Mencius* and the *Doctrine of the Mean*.

Gemara (Hebrew): the 'completion'; the rabbinical discussions of the *Mishnah* recorded in the Jerusalem and Babylonian Talmuds.

Gewu (Chinese): the 'investigation of things' recommended in the *Great Learning* as essential for the enlightenment of the individual and the rectification of the world. Some Chinese philosophers made it an interior search for *li*, a divine 'principle' in the human mind, while others focused on the investigation of physical and empirical phenomena.

Ghazi states: after the Mongol invasions of the thirteenth century, states on the fringes of territory under Mongol control were ruled by Muslim chieftains who tended towards *ghuluww* ('exaggerated') interpretations of Shii ideology.

Ghazu (Arabic): the 'acquisition raid' that was routinely practised in pre-Islamic Arabia as a means of redistributing chronically scarce resources and was conducted almost as a national sport. Tribesmen would attack another tribe, carrying off camels, cattle and food, but were careful to avoid a vendetta by not killing a human being. The Prophet Muhammad resorted to this practice after the *Hijrah* to prevent the Meccan emigrants from being an economic drain on the community of Medina.

Ghuluww (Arabic): 'extreme'; the radical ideology developed in *Ghazi states* by Shii theorists known retrospectively as the *ghulat*, the 'exaggerators'. Influenced by Christian, Jewish and Zoroastrian mythology, they revered Ali as an incarnation of the divine, and believed that their leaders had not died but were in hiding ('occultation') and would return to lead their followers to victory. Others were fascinated by the idea of a Holy Spirit descending into a human being and imparting divine wisdom to him.

Glossa Ordinaria (Latin): a synthesis of patristic and Carolingian exegesis on the entire Bible, compiled initially by French scholars during the twelfth century, which rapidly became a standard tool in the universities. A 'gloss', a brief clarification, was inserted between the lines of the biblical text and a longer explanation inscribed in the margins.

Golah (Hebrew): The community of Hebrew exiles who were deported to Babylonia during the early sixth century BCE.

Golden Rule: a maxim developed in nearly every religious tradition as the epitome of all ethical action, expressed either negatively: 'Never treat others as you would not wish to be treated yourself', or positively: 'Always treat others as you would wish to be treated yourself.'

Gongyang (Chinese): a commentary on the *Spring and Autumn Annals* composed and transmitted orally from the fourth century BCE.

Goyi (Chinese): 'interpretation by analogy'. An exegetical method developed while Buddhist texts were being translated into Chinese during the fourth and third centuries BCE, which elucidated Buddhist ideas by identifying them with Daoist philosophical categories.

Guliang (Chinese): a commentary on the *Spring and Autumn Annals*, composed and transmitted orally from the fourth century BCE.

Guru (Sanskrit): A Hindu teacher who is regarded as a channel for divine wisdom and conveys the reality of sacred truth by example as well as by discursive instruction. In Sikhism, the term was first used of Guru Nanak and his nine successors and was later applied to the Spirit which had inspired the Ten Gurus, all of whom had manifested the same divine light. It is now enshrined in the *Adi Granth*, the Sikh scripture, in the Golden Temple in Amritsar.

Gymnasium (Greek): an educational institution for the enculturation of Greek youth and elite members of the native communities in Greek colonies. Students memorised the Homeric epics but the chief emphasis was on the physical education that enabled students to achieve the mastery and development of the body.

Hadith (Arabic): 'narratives', 'news' or 'reports'; traditions preserving the words, maxims and accounts of the deeds and customary practice of the Prophet Muhammad and his Companions. In English, the term Hadith is used as a collective noun for 'narratives' as well as for a single tradition. A hadith consists of two parts: the *matn* (the text) and the *isnad*, the chain of its transmitters that determines its reliability. The most prestigious anthologies are those collected by Muhammad ibn Ismail al-Bukhari and Muslim ibn al-Hajjaj during the ninth century.

Halakha (Hebrew): derived from the Hebrew *halak*, 'he went', the term refers either to a singular law or to the entire Jewish legal system, which is traditionally believed to go back to Moses. It is composed of the Written Law (the Hebrew Bible) and the Oral Law developed by the rabbis and preserved in the *Mishnah* and the Talmuds.

Hanifiyyah (Arabic): the monotheistic faith practised by some Arabs in the pre-Islamic period. In the *Quran*, the term is used of the 'pure religion' of Abraham who had lived long before the *Torah* and the Gospel and thus before the faith had split into competing sects.

Haram (Arabic): things that are 'forbidden' or 'prohibited' in the *Quran*; it is also applied to a sacred enclave, such as Mecca, whose sanctity prohibits certain activities (in the case of Mecca, violence) and is set apart for worship and pilgrimage.

Harb (Arabic): 'fighting', 'warfare', a word that appears only four times in the *Quran*.

Heaven: see *Tian*.

Hesed (Hebrew): often translated as 'love', its basic meaning is 'loyalty'.

Hexagram (in Chinese, *gua*): in the *Yijing*, a hexagram is a figure consisting of six horizontal lines, which are either solid (*yang*) or broken (*yin*); they are formed by combining the original eight *trigrams* in sixty-four different combinations. The symbolism of the *Yijing* derives from an ancient form of divination that took the practice of the casting of yarrow stalks. The hexagrams may have originated in the patterns formed when the stalks were thrown. Over time, each hexagram was accompanied by a cryptic line-statement (now virtually indecipherable), and each line in the hexagram has a similar description.

Hijrah (Arabic): the migration of the first Muslim community from Mecca to Medina in 622 CE.

Hilm (Arabic): 'mercy', 'forbearance'; a key term in the early surahs of the *Quran*.

Holy: see *Qaddosh*.

Homoousios (Greek): 'of one substance'. The term in the Nicene Creed (325) that expressed the relation of the divinity shared by the Father and the Son and opposed the Arian belief that the Son had been created by the Father. It was used again in the Council of Chalcedon (451) to express the relationship of Christ to his human nature and during the fourth century, it was extended to the Holy Spirit's relation with Father and Son.

Horoz (Hebrew): a 'chain' created by rabbinic and early Christian exegetes that linked disparate scriptural verses together, thus giving them an entirely new meaning.

Hudaybiyyah (Arabic): refers to the treaty made between the Prophet Muhammad and the **Quraysh** at the Well of Hudaybiyyah in Mecca in 628. Accompanied by 1,000 Muslim pilgrims, Muhammad risked his life by entering the **Haram** virtually unarmed at the height of the war between Mecca and Medina. He dismayed his companions by agreeing to all the demands of the Quraysh, calmly relinquishing many of the advantages the Muslims had gained during the war. But the **Quran** declared that Hudaybiyyah was a 'manifest victory' (48:1–13) and two years later the Meccans voluntarily opened their city gates to admit the Muslim army.

Hypostasis, plural *hypostases* (Greek): 'individual reality', 'person'; a term used in the formulation of the Christian doctrine of the Trinity as 'three *hypostases* and one *ousia*'.

Ijtihad (Arabic): the 'independent reasoning' by a properly trained expert that leads to a judgement on a legal or theological issue that involves a new interpretation of the **Quran** and the **Sunnah** (instead of simply following the established norm) to resolve a new problem faced by the community.

Ilm (Arabic): the 'esoteric' knowledge of the **Quran** that, according to the **Shiah**, Muhammad had imparted to Ali, his only surviving male relative, who transmitted it to his own sons, Hasan and Husain, the Second and Third Shii **Imams** respectively; thereafter, it was transmitted to Husain's descendants. There is, however, a dispute among Shiis about whether the line ended with the Seventh or the Twelfth Imam (see **Ismailis** and **Twelver Shiism**).

Imam (Arabic): the 'leader' of Muslim congregational prayer, who can be any man of good standing but who is usually theologically educated. In the **Shiah**, however, the imam became an alternative to the Sunni caliph, who was regarded by most Muslims as the rightful leader of the entire **ummah**. Shiis contended that only a descendant of the Prophet Muhammad through the line of Ali ibn Abi Talib, his cousin and son-in-law, had the esoteric knowledge (**ilm**) of the **Quran** that would enable him to interpret scripture creatively and infallibly to meet new challenges.

Intentio (Latin): the 'concentration' of **Lectio divina** in which the exegete focuses energetically on every single word of scripture to find fresh meanings. *Intentio* also requires a turning away from self to others and a firm resolve to work energetically for a more compassionate world.

Islam (Arabic): the 'surrender' of the ego in the service of God and others that is required by the **Quran** and is epitomised in the prostrations of Muslim prayer.

Ismailis: the Sixth **Imam**, Jafar al-Sadiq (d.765), imparted the esoteric **ilm** of the **Quran** to his oldest son, Ismail, who died before his father. Ismailis believe that the line ended with him. They developed their own mystical and metaphysical traditions. **Twelver Shiis**, however, believe that after Ismail's death, the succession passed to Jafar's second son, Musa al-Kazim.

Istighna (Arabic): 'pride'; haughty self-reliance, aggressive independence and self-sufficiency.

Jahiliyyah (Arabic): often mistranslated as 'the Time of Ignorance' and applied to the pre-Islamic period in Arabia. But it is clear in the Muslim sources that the primary meaning of *jahiliyyah* is violent and explosive irascibility, arrogance and tribal chauvinism.

Jatarka (Pali): 'birth stories'. A history of the previous lives of the **Buddha**, all of which exemplify a positive quality of the Buddha in his multitude of existences as a **bodhisattva**.

Jian ai (Chinese): the chief virtue of the **Mohist** school, often translated as 'universal love' but more accurately rendered: 'concern for everybody'; a principled impartiality.

Jihad (Arabic): 'struggle', 'effort', 'endeavour'. It does not mean 'holy war'. The word occurs only forty-one times in the **Quran** and in only ten of those instances does it refer unequivocally to warfare. Almsgiving, when you have little yourself, is also a jihad. The word jihad occurs most frequently with the phrase *fi sabil Allah* ('in the path of God'), when it demands a non-retaliatory and non-violent response to the persecution of the **Quraysh** during the early phase of the Prophet's career.

Jina (Sanskrit): a spiritual 'conqueror' who had achieved enlightenment by a relentless cultivation of **ahimsa**.

Jing (Chinese): (1) a 'classic'; a work of unique spiritual importance that gives the reader intimations of the transcendent and expresses a universal truth. Originally *jing* was a term used in weaving: it was the warp that strengthened the structure of the fabric in rather the same way as a literary classic could support society. (2) a spiritual attitude cultivated assiduously by the neo-Confucians: a sense of deep awe and reverence which results from the practice of *gewu* and *jingzuo*.

Jingzuo (Chinese): 'quiet-sitting', a Chinese adaptation of yoga which involved sitting quietly, in a relaxed state, and cultivating the interior attentiveness of *jing*.

Jiva (Sanskrit): 'soul'; a living entity that was luminous and intelligent. Jains believe that every single creature – humans, plants, animals, trees and even stones – has a *jiva* that can experience pain and fear and must therefore be protected and respected.

Junzi (Chinese): originally an 'aristocrat' or 'gentleman'; Confucius democratised the term so that it could apply to anyone who assiduously cultivated *ren* and became a profound or superior human being.

Kabah (Arabic): 'cube'; the cube-shaped shrine of great antiquity in the heart of the Meccan *Haram*. Local tradition claimed that it had been built by Adam to mark the centre of the world and was rebuilt later by Abraham when he visited his son Ishmael in the Arabian wilderness. By Muhammad's time, it had become a place of pilgrimage for all Arabs, pagan as well as Christian. In 630, Muhammad dedicated the Kabah to Allah (*Quran* 2:125; 22:126). It marks the most sacred place in the Muslim world.

Kabbalah (Hebrew): 'inherited tradition'; an immensely influential Jewish mystical spirituality, which developed in Spain during the medieval period and was practised by Jewish *faylasufs* as well as mystics. In *Kabbalah*, the mystic descends ever deeper into the scriptural text, uncovering layer after layer of mystical meaning and discovers that this descent is in fact an ascent to the ineffable source of being.

Kafir (Arabic): often translated as 'unbeliever' but more accurately it refers to a person who rudely spurns something offered with great kindness, aggressively rejecting Allah and refusing to acknowledge his or her dependence on the Creator.

Karbala: a plain outside Kufah in Iraq where the Prophet Muhammad's grandson Husain, his family and supporters were massacred by Umayyad troops in 680. All Muslims lament this tragedy, but for the Shiah it symbolises the chronic injustice of life and the apparent incompatibility of the religious imperative and the harsh world of politics.

Karma (Sanskrit): 'actions'; the term refers to the law of consequence which inspired the doctrine of reincarnation and rebirth in Indian religion. Initially, it was thought that an accumulation of ritual actions would result after death in rebirth in the world of the gods; later, the term was generalised to all actions, sacred and secular, physical and mental. Every action has a consequence: good acts will result in a positive rebirth; bad actions in a negative reincarnation. The aim is to liberate yourself entirely from *samsara*, the relentless cycle of rebirth and redeath.

Kavod (Hebrew): the 'glory' of Yahweh; a luminous afterglow or reflection of the divine which could be traumatic and bewildering as well as affirmative. Since God itself is inaccessible to humanity, the 'glory' is the closest we get.

Kenosis (Greek): the 'emptying' of mind and heart so that they became free of self-preoccupation; the transcendence of egotism that is essential to spiritual progress in all traditions.

Kerygma (Greek): the public, readily explicable and overt message of the Gospel – not to be confused with *dogma*, which cannot be expressed verbally or with clarity.

Kevala (Sanskrit): 'omniscience'. In Jainism, the enlightenment achieved by *ahimsa* enables the saint to ascend to the summit of the universe, where having shed all addiction to ego and self, he is separate from all other beings, unlimited and complete.

Krishna: a composite figure in the Hindu traditions; he appears first as a character in the *Mahabharata* but in the *Bhagavad Gita* he is revealed as the avatar of Vishnu and the object of *bhakti*. His transformation seems to express a longing for a personal and emotional rather than an austerely philosophical focus for religious devotion.

Kshatriya (Sanskrit): an 'empowered one'. A member of the warrior class in Vedic society, who is responsible for the military defence, political expansion and enrichment of the community.

Kusala (Sanskrit): 'helpful', 'wholesome'. The positive attitudes and actions that are conducive to enlightenment; cf. *akusala*.

Lakshanas (Sanskrit): the five 'topics' of the *Puranas*, which establish the world view of the story: creation, the genealogy of gods and *rishis*; the reigns of the Manus (the semi-divine patriarchs who ruled the world in ancient times); the destruction and recreation of the worlds; and the history of humanity.

Lectio divina (Latin): 'holy reading'. An essential practice of the Benedictine Order in which monks 'ruminated' on the scriptures; unlike exegesis, which determined the meaning of the sacred text, it was designed to cultivate an attitude of prayer and an apprehension of the divine presence.

Legalism (in Chinese, Fajia): often translated as 'School of Law'. The term *fa* was used to describe a tool, such as a carpenter's square, that reshaped raw materials and made them conform to a fixed pattern. Legalists wanted to impose a pragmatic polity, backed up by draconian punishments and a rigorous penal code, which would work automatically and impartially. Where Confucians believed that only a Sage King could reform society, the Legalists considered the morality of the ruler to be an irrelevance.

Li (Chinese): (1) the ritual code of 'appropriate behaviour' that regulated the life of the *junzi*; the physical rites that were designed to cultivate interior attitudes of *kenosis* (selflessness) and *rang* ('yielding'). (2) 'principle': neo-Confucians were committed to discovering the ultimate reality that lay at the heart of all things and was immanent in the human mind.

Liqi fenshu (Chinese): 'the unity of principle and the diversity of its particularisation'. While the divine principle (*li*) itself was essentially identical, its discovery in the mind would be experienced differently in every case, since it was filtered through the unique circumstances, responsibilities and duties of the individual.

Logos (Greek): (1) 'reason'. The rational, pragmatic and analytical activity of the left hemisphere of the brain which enables human beings to function practically in the world. To be effective, logos must relate accurately to facts and correspond to external realities; we rely on logos when we want to get something done or persuade people to adopt a policy or a course of action. Unlike *mythos*, logos is future-oriented, intent on achieving greater control of our environment and inventing something new. (2) 'word'. In early Christianity, Logos became a title of Christ, based on the popular Stoic idea of the logos or 'universal reason' that permeated the world order, and also on the Hebrew conception of God's Word or *Wisdom*. The Prologue to John's gospel describes Jesus as the incarnate Logos of God.

Mahayana (Sanskrit): believed by most Buddhists to be the 'Greater Vehicle' of Buddhist teachings as opposed to the Hinayana ('Lesser Vehicle) of the **Theravada**. The difference is that while the Theravadins' final goal is the attainment of **nirvana** and the relinquishment of **samsara**, the Mahayana emphasises compassion. Instead of leaving the world after their enlighten-ment, the **bodhisattva**, the ideal practitioner in the Mahayana, remains at large to help all sentient beings find release from the **dukkha** of life.

Mantra (Sanskrit): 'instrument of thought'. A verse, syllable or series of syllables believed to be of divine origin that is used in ritual or meditation. Because sound was sacred in ancient India, a mantra was itself a **deva**; it derived its power from the primordial sound that was the source of creation (cf. **Vac**). When chanted repetitively, the sonoral vibrations within the worshipper have transformative power: a *bhakta*, for example, becomes one with his *deva* and with the **guru**, who imparted it to him. We might say that the monotony of the exercise numbs the analytical activities of the left hemisphere and enhances a right-brain awareness of the essential unity of all things.

Marranos (Spanish): 'pigs'. A term derisively applied to those Spanish Jews who were forcibly converted to Christianity and to their descendants; the **conversos** defiantly adopted it as a badge of pride.

Memoria (Latin): 'memory', but in medieval Europe, this was not just a retrospective mental activity; it also implied creativity and invention in pursuit of self-transformation.

Messhiah (Hebrew): one who is ritually 'anointed' for a special task. See **Christos**. Originally the term applied to anyone who was given a divine mandate, such as the king who was anointed at his coronation and became a 'son of God'. In the first century CE, some Jews hoped for a divinely appointed *messhiah* to liberate Israel from imperial oppression. The Christians believed that Jesus was this messiah.

Metaphor: derived from the Greek *meta* ('across') and *pherein* ('to carry'), a metaphor carries speaker and audience across an implied gap, uniting things that seem disparate. It is the language of the right hemisphere of the brain, pointing to the underlying unity of reality, and is therefore the language of both poetry and religion.

Midrash (Hebrew): derived from the verb *darash*, 'to investigate', 'to seek out'. After the loss of the temple, it was the name given to the exegesis pioneered by the rabbis, which implied that the meaning of the scriptural text was not immediately self-evident. Midrash was a search for something fresh, since the old rites and meanings no longer applied in the broken Jewish world.

Min (Chinese): 'the little people', i.e. the peasant class in premodern agrarian society who were reduced to serfdom and regarded as scarcely human.

Mishnah (Hebrew): 'learning by repetition'. Originally, the term applied to the oral legislation developed in the late first and second centuries CE by the early rabbis, who were known as the *tannaim*, the 'repeaters'. Eventually, this oral material was redacted and compiled in written form by Judah ha-Nasi, who arranged it in six *sedarim* ('orders'). This written text formed the basis of the two Talmuds, the **Bavli** and the **Yerushalmi**.

Mitzvah (Hebrew): a commandment, ritual duty or good deed.

Mohism: the Chinese philosophical school founded by Master Mo (c.480–390 BCE) whose ethos was fiercely egalitarian and opposed to the aristocratic philosophy of Confucius. See *jian ai*. Members intervened to stop wars and defend cities in the more vulnerable states during the Warring States period.

Moksha (Sanskrit): 'liberation' from the ceaseless cycle of redeath and rebirth of *samsara* and the consequent awakening to one's true self.

Muslim (Arabic): a man or woman who makes the act of existential surrender (*islam*) to God, as enjoined by the **Quran**.

Mustai (Greek): 'initiates'; people who undergo the intense psychodrama of a Greek *musterion*, which gives them an intense, personal and often indelible experience of the divine.

Musterion (Greek): 'mystery'; derived from the verb *muein* ('to close the eyes or the mouth'), referring to an obscure experience, hidden from ordinary sight that lies beyond the world of *logos* and definition. *Musterion* was also linked with the related verb *myein* ('to initiate') and *myesis* ('initiation'). Hence the Mystery cults that developed in the Greek world during the sixth century BCE, notably at Eleusis, which gave participants an overwhelming experience of the sacred. Christians later applied the word to the initiations of baptism and the Eucharist. Origen saw exegesis as a *musterion*, a transformative, initiatory process.

Mysticism (English, but also derived from *muein* and *myein* – see *musterion*): a quest for transcendence that lies beyond the reach of speech, sight and ordinary categories of thought by means of physical, mental and spiritual exercises and disciplines. All religious traditions, theistic and non-theistic, have developed a mystical tradition that apprehends a reality that lies beyond the spatio-temporal realm but also within the self.

Mythos (Greek): 'myth'. A story that was not intended to be factual or historical but which rather expressed the meaning of an event or narrative and expressed its timeless, eternal dimension. It was an occurrence that in some sense had happened once, but which also happens all the time. Myth can also be regarded as an early form of psychology, describing the labyrinthine and obscure world of the psyche: *mythos* is also related to the verbs *muein* and *myein* (see ***musterion***), referring to experiences and convictions that cannot be easily expressed verbally, which elude the clarity of ***logos***, and are different from the discourse and thought habits of practical, everyday reality.

Nirvana (Sanskrit): 'extinction', 'blowing out'; the extinction of the ego in Buddhism that brings enlightenment and liberation from pain and suffering. It is experienced as a sacred haven of peace in the depths of the self, an indefinable reality, because it corresponds to no concept and is incomprehensible to those still mired in selfishness and egotism.

Occultation (in Arabic, *ghaybah*): by the ninth century, the Abbasid dynasty was declining and the caliphs felt that in these uncertain times they could not permit the Shii ***imams***, who tacitly threw the legitimacy of the caliphate into question, to remain at large. The Eleventh Imam died (probably poisoned) in prison and it was said that the Twelfth had gone into hiding to save his life; by 934, when he could no longer feasibly be alive, the Shii community received a message: the imam had been miraculously concealed by God. He was still the infallible guide of the Shiah and would return shortly before the Last Judgement to inaugurate a rule of justice. The ***mythos*** of his occultation expressed the sense of the sacred as elusive but tantalisingly absent, present in the world but not of it.

Oral Torah: in the third century, the rabbis concluded that the oral traditions that they had been developing since the destruction of the temple (see ***midrash***; ***mishnah***) were a continuation of the revelatory process that had begun on Sinai: 'Two *torahs* were given to Israel. One by mouth, the other by script' (*Sifre* on Deuteronomy, 351). Revelation was not confined to the distant past; it was a process that continued every time a Jew studied the sacred texts of the past with his teacher.

Ousia (Greek): 'essence', 'that which makes a thing what it is'; a person or object seen from within. The Greek Fathers of the church maintained that when applied to what we call 'God', the term denotes the divine essence, nature or substance that will always elude human understanding or experience. We could glimpse the divine only partially through God's *hypostases*.

Pali Canon: the earliest Buddhist scriptures, composed in Pali, the north Indian dialect probably spoken by the **Buddha**; their transmission began shortly after the Buddha's death but the canon continued to develop until the first century BCE (see **Abidharma**; **Buddhavacana**). The canon is often called the Tripitaka ('Three Baskets') because the original manuscripts were kept in three different containers: Vinaya ('Monastic Discipline'); Sutta ('Discourses of the Buddha'); and the Parivara, which later developed into the Abidharma ('Further Teachings').

Pardes (Persian): 'garden', 'orchard', perhaps underlying the Greek *paradeisos*. During the thirteenth century, the Spanish Jewish mystics who developed the **Kabbalah** read the word as an acronym of the four major methods of biblical interpretation: *peshat* (literal), *remez* (allegorical), *darash* (moral) and *sod* (esoteric or mystical).

Pentateuch (Greek derivation): the first five books of the Hebrew Bible: Genesis, Exodus, Leviticus, Numbers and Deuteronomy.

Pesher (Hebrew): 'deciphering'; a form of exegesis used by the Qumran sectarians and the early Christians, who read the Hebrew Bible as a code and claimed that the ancient biblical stories and prophecies had predicted the activities of their own communities in the Last Days.

Pharisee: the origins of this Jewish sect are obscure. It seems that Pharisees were originally scribes, who were expert in the 'traditions of the elders' (Josephus). In the gospels, they appear to have acted as **Retainers** of the Jewish priestly aristocracy who ruled the province of Judea under the Romans.

Philosophia (Greek): 'the love of Wisdom'. In ancient Greece, *philosophia* was not simply an abstract cerebral discipline, but was also an initiation (*myesis*) into a new vision of live that had to be expressed practically in daily life.

Pillars of Islam (in Arabic, Arkan al-Din): the five obligatory practices of Islam – the **Shahada** (profession of faith), Salat (formal prayer), Zakat (tithe for the poor), Hajj (pilgrimage to Mecca) and Sawm (the Ramadan fast), all rooted in the **Quran**.

Pirke Avot (Hebrew): 'the Sayings of the Fathers'; a greatly loved text, composed in about 220 CE, which traces the rabbinical movement back to

Hillel and Shammai and preserves maxims that describe the spiritual benefits of **Torah** study.

Polis, plural *poleis* (Greek): a democratic Greek city state.

Postillae (Latin): line-by-line commentaries composed by the Franciscans during the thirteenth century which developed the **Glossa Ordinaria**, taking medieval Christian exegesis to a more philosophical level.

Prajapati (Sanskrit): 'the All'; a *deva* who personifies the **Brahman** in the late hymns of the Rig Veda. Later, in the **Brahmanas**, he appears as the Creator God and merged with **Purusha**.

Principle of accommodation: this exegetical principle was developed by Augustine, affirmed by Calvin, and was followed in the West until the early modern period. Augustine argued that biblical cosmology had long been superseded. God had adapted revelation to the world view of ancient Israel so that they could understand it. God was instructing the Israelites in morality and theology, not science, so it was essential that current scientific advance be respected or scripture would fall into disrepute.

Prophet (Greek derivation, *pro* = 'for', *fetes* = 'speaker'): 'one who speaks for another' (i.e. a deity), not, as in current parlance, one who predicts the future. Throughout the ancient Near East, prophets were cultic functionaries who made known what was otherwise unknowable; most of the Hebrew prophets were probably cultic figures: some had visions of God in a temple setting. Later, Muhammad would claim that his revelation was substantially the same as that of previous prophets, but that the message had been corrupted over time. He was, therefore, the 'Seal of the Prophets' who had restored the original divine message.

Psyche (Greek): in Greek psychology, *psyche* represents the natural powers of the mind and heart and was regarded as distinct from *pneuma*, the soul.

Purana (Sanskrit): 'ancient tale'. Puranas are considered **smrti**, though some Puranas claimed that the genre preceded the **Vedas**. They were probably compiled between 500 and 1500 CE, though they include much earlier material. They may have originated in texts that imparted Vedic truth to women and to the **Shudras** who were barred from the Vedas but later they became associated with the **bhakti** cults of Vishnu/Krishna and Shiva. Each Purana is supposed to expound the **lakshanas**; they are presented as revelations and cast in a dialogue form and emphasise the importance of loving devotion (*bhakti*); Hindu reformers have attacked Puranic theology but it remains the dominant form of Indian spirituality.

Purusha (Sanskrit): 'man' / 'person', who is presented in the famous *Purusha Hymn* (RV 10.90) as the primordial Person who voluntarily allowed the gods to sacrifice him; the entire cosmos was formed from his dismembered body. His sacrifice became the model for all Vedic sacrifice, generating the Vedic hymns and meters and the socio-economic classes of Aryan society. In the **Brahmanas**, Purusha has been merged with the figure of **Prajapati**.

'Q' (from the German *Quelle*, 'source'): a symbol used by scholars to represent a hypothetical document which has not survived but which seems to have been an anthology of Jesus' sayings, compiled, perhaps, during the 50s CE, that was used as a source by the evangelists known as Matthew and Luke.

Qaddosh (Hebrew): usually translated as 'holy', a more literal meaning is 'separate', 'other'; it expresses the absolute transcendence of the divine.

Qibla (Arabic): the 'direction' of prayer. After the migratory **hijrah**, Muhammad received a revelation commanding Muslims to pray facing the **Kabah** in Mecca instead of Jerusalem, as had been customary hitherto. This gesture symbolised their desire to return to the **hanifiyyah**, the pure religion of Abraham, who had rebuilt the Kabah long before the original monotheistic faith had split into the rival sects of Judaism and Christianity. Muslims, therefore, turn towards Mecca when performing the canonical prayers (*salat*) and in the mosque the *qibla* is marked by the *mihrab*.

Quran (Arabic): 'recitation'. The word may have derived from the Syrian *qeryana*, 'scripture reading', but in the Quran, the word *quran* means primarily the activity of reciting which was essential to the Islamic scriptural experience and would develop into a fine art. The Quran is thought to have been taken from the *Umm al-Kitab*, the pre-existing scripture that exists eternally in heaven. In its final form, the Quran consists of 114 surahs or chapters, roughly arranged in decreasing order of length. In general, the earlier surahs are the shorter ones and, therefore, found at the end of the scripture.

Quraysh: the tribe of Muhammad which had made Mecca a centre of trade and pilgrimage. After the **hijrah**, the Quraysh who remained in Mecca were determined to wipe out the **ummah** but after the cessation of hostilities most accepted **Islam**.

Rang (Chinese): 'yielding'. An attitude cultivated by the *li*, the rites: instead of competing aggressively for status, the *junzi* should defer to others in the spirit of **kenosis**.

Religio (Latin): 'bonding', 'reverence'. In the premodern world, the word religion did not indicate a system of obligatory beliefs and practices separate from all 'secular' activities. Words that we now translate as 'religion' in other languages, such as the Arabic *din*, invariably refer to something vaguer and more encompassing – to a whole way of life. Our modern Western notion of 'religion' dates only from the seventeenth and eighteenth centuries. The Latin word *religio* had imprecise connotations of obligation, which could be legal or professional as well as a duty to the gods. For Christian theologians, *religio* came to mean an attitude of reverence towards God and the universe; for Augustine, it meant the bond that unites us to the divine and to one another; and in medieval Europe, *religio* came to refer to the monastic life and distinguished the monk from the 'secular' priest who lived and worked in the 'world' (*saeculum*).

Ren (Chinese): originally, 'human being'. Confucius gave the word new meaning but refused to define it, because it transcended any of the intellectual categories of his time, but it retained connotations of 'humanity', implying human-heartedness, compassion, love or altruism, and was a product of the *li*, the rites of courtesy and consideration. *Ren* endowed the individual with equanimity, equilibrium and serenity. Mencius narrowed the term to 'benevolence' and made it one of his four cardinal virtues.

Retainers: in the premodern agrarian state, a small aristocracy was served by a class of retainers who functioned as military officers, domestics, scribes, lawyers, priests, etc. supporting the ruling class and conveying its ideology to the people.

Rishi (Sanskrit): 'seer'; the rishis were the visionary authors of the Vedic hymns, which they both 'heard' and 'saw' in some unfathomable way in the depths of their being. The first rishis were the ancestors of seven great ancient families in the Aryan community and were thought to have had supernatural powers.

Ritual (derived from the Latin *ritus*, 'structure', 'ceremony'): inseparable from **mythos** and, in the premodern world, from the performance of scripture. It has been variously defined as a form of play; as a means of expressing and endorsing the collective consciousness or achieving release from tension. The definition of Professor Jonathan Smith is particularly helpful: 'Ritual is a means of performing the way things ought to be in conscious tension with the way things are in such a way that this ritualised perfection is recollected in the ordinary, uncontrolled, course of things.'

Rta (Sanskrit): 'fixed order', 'rule'. The fundamental order and balance that ancient Aryans observed in the universe, which had to be sustained through sacrificial *ritual*. *Devas*, such as Varuna or Mitra, were 'guardians' of *rta*, not its controller or creator. More fundamental than the gods, *rta* anticipates such other impersonal forces in Hindu religion as *karma*, *dharma* and *Brahman*.

Ru (Chinese): 'ritualists', the 'literati'. The term referred chiefly to adherents of the tradition that is called 'Confucianism' in the West.

Sabr (Arabic): 'patience', 'forbearance', 'fortitude'.

Sacrament (derived from the Latin *sacramentum*, 'oath'): used to translate the Greek *musterion* in the Latin New Testament. Augustine defined the way the word has been understood in Western Christianity: 'the visible form of invisible grace'; by the twelfth century the term was used of such sacraments as baptism or the Eucharist, in which meaning is expressed in physical, non-verbal symbols, such as water, chrism, bread and wine. In this sense it is applied to similar rites in non-Christian religions.

Sama (Arabic): 'hearing', 'listening'. A *Sufi* practice of making or listening to music that elicits a heightened emotional state and can segue into trance, generating a sense of the divine presence.

Samsara (Sanskrit): 'keeping going'. The inexorable cycle of death and rebirth, which propelled beings from one life to the next, according to the *karma* they had accumulated. The word was also applied to the restlessness and transience of the human condition.

Sangha (Sanskrit): originally, the tribal assembly of the Aryan clans. By extension, it was applied to the religious orders of such renouncers as the Buddhists.

Sefer (Hebrew): 'scroll', particularly the Sefer Torah discovered in the Jerusalem Temple in 622 during the reign of Josiah.

Sefirah (Hebrew): 'numeration'. A term applied in *Kabbalah* to the ten emanations that emerge from *En Sof*. Each *sefirah* points to a different aspect of God's creative nature as it becomes manifest in the Chain of Being.

Together they form a dynamic unit, sometimes portrayed as a tree, in which God's activity is revealed. It was an attempt to explain how the utterly ineffable and transcendent God can interact with the frail, physical world.

Senses of scripture: a Christian form of biblical interpretation pioneered by Origen in which exegetes make a spiritual ascent to the divine. First, they studied the *literal* sense of a text; next they applied it to their own lives and situation in the *moral* sense, later called the *topological* sense. Finally, the most advanced exegetes engaged in intensive meditation to attain the *spiritual* sense by means of **allegoria**. Without allegory, Origen was convinced, the Bible made no sense at all. Origen's exegesis was brought to the West where a fourth sense was added: the *anagogical* or mystical sense which revealed a text's eschatological significance. In western Europe, this remained the principal way of reading the Bible until the Reformation.

Shahada (Arabic): 'witness', the first **Pillar of Islam**; a profession of faith: 'I bear witness that there is no god but Allah and Muhammad is his prophet.' It proclaims the uniqueness of Allah and the centrality of Muhammad's prophecy.

Shang: the first historical Chinese dynasty (*c.* 1600–1045 BCE).

Shekhinah (Hebrew): 'dwelling'; from the Hebrew *shakan*, 'to pitch one's tent'. The divine 'Presence' that dwelt in the Holy of Holies in the Jerusalem temple; identified with the glory (**kavod**) of God glimpsed by the **prophets**; after the destruction of the temple, the rabbis taught Jews to experience the Shekhinah when they engaged in **midrash** together. Jewish Christians also experienced the Shekhinah, which they identified with the person of Jesus, when they studied the Hebrew scriptures together or celebrated the Eucharist. Kabbalists maintained that the Shekhinah, the tenth and final **sefirah**, represented the feminine principle in the Godhead.

Shen (Chinese): the divine potential that exists in every human being.

Shi (Chinese): see **Retainers**.

Shiah (Arabic): 'party'; the Shiah i-Ali, 'the Partisans of Ali', were convinced that Ali was Muhammad's legitimate successor (*khalifa*) so they did not accept the caliphate of the first three *rashidun* ('rightly guided') caliphs accepted by most Muslims: Abu Bakr, Umar and Uthman. They also believed that Ali's sons, Hasan and Husain, were cheated of their right to succeed. See **imam, ilm, Ismailis, occultation, Twelver Shiism**.

Shiva (Sanskrit): 'auspicious'; he is a *deva* mentioned only fleetingly in the **Vedas** but his cult may have roots in the pre-Vedic period, his influence evolving very gradually. A great yogin and ascetic, he is associated with generation and destruction and is one of the *devas* revered in **bhakti**.

Shruti (Sanskrit): 'that which is heard'; the sacred and eternal truth 'heard' and 'seen' by the **rishis** in the mythical past and in historical time transmitted by the **Brahmins**. It therefore signifies the revealed corpus of Hindu scripture. Synonymous with the **Veda**, *shruti* concludes with the **Upanishads**.

Shu (Chinese): 'reciprocity', the attitude summed up in the **Golden Rule**; a Confucian virtue and an important component of **ren**.

Shudra (Sanskrit): 'servants'; the lowest of the four classes of Vedic society.

Shun: the second virtuous Sage King of the Xia dynasty. The son of a poor man, who mistreated him, he succeeded **Yao**, who chose him as his heir because his own son was cruel and irascible.

Smrti (Sanskrit): 'recollection', 'that which is remembered'; post-Vedic Hindu scripture, regarded as secondary and subservient to **shruti**, which it 'remembers' and develops orally. It is sacred and of divine origin but an indirect form of revelation. *Smrti* consists of the **sutras**, the law codes, the *Mahabharata*, the *Ramayana* and the **Puranas**.

Sola ratio (Latin): 'by reason alone'; the Enlightenment conviction that reasoning or **logos** is the sole path to truth.

Sola scriptura (Latin): 'by scripture alone'; the Protestant belief that the truths of Christian faith and practice can and must be established only by scripture, without additions from sacred tradition (a Western equivalent of the Indian **smrti**).

Spring and Autumn Annals (in Chinese, Chunqiu): in ancient times, this terse chronicle had functioned as the Temple Annals of the principality of Lu; ritualists had recorded important events – battles, famines, natural disasters – and reported these happenings daily to the ancestors. These annals are our main source for the period 722–481 BCE, which is therefore known as 'Springs and Autumns' (the seasons listed in the headings of each section). Thanks to the commentaries transmitted in the fourth century BCE (the **Gongyang**, **Guliang** and **Zuozhuan**), it became one of the Chinese Classics.

Sufi, Sufism: Arabic derivation, *tasawwuf*, the simple woollen garment worn by the Prophet Muhammad and adopted by the early Sufis to differentiate themselves from the luxury of the imperial court; it became the term for the mystical tradition of *Islam*.

Sukkoth (Hebrew): 'booths'. The autumn festival celebrated after the harvest which was inaugurated by Ezra, adapted from an older temple ritual. In the new rite, Israelites were commanded to build shelters from 'palm branches, boughs of leafy trees and willows from the river bank' and live in them for seven days in memory of their ancestors' nomadic existence after the Exodus from Egypt (Leviticus 23:39–43).

Sunnah (Arabic): 'custom', 'customary practice' based on the way the Prophet Muhammad and his Companions (*sahaba*) lived and behaved as recorded in the *Quran* and the *Hadith*. By imitating their external practices, Muslims hope to gain their interior disposition. The Sunnah is, therefore, one of the important sources of *fiqh*. Those Muslims who adhere to the Quran and the Sunnah are known as **Sunnis**. *Shiis* also observe most of the Sunnah, but emphasise the role and practice of the Shii *imams*.

Sutra (Sanskrit): 'thread'. In Hinduism, sutra literature, written in elliptic, condensed prose, deals with the performance of sacrifices, household rites, or rituals and *mantras* practised in the household of a *guru* or an *ashram*. In Buddhism, sutras (Pali: *sutta*) are collections of the *Buddha*'s teachings (see *Pali Canon*). In the *Mahayana*, additional sutras (e.g. the *Lotus Sutra*) have been preserved; written originally in Sanskrit, some survive only in Chinese or Tibetan translation.

Tanakh (Hebrew): the Hebrew Bible. An acronym – **T**orah (Pentateuch), **N**eviim (Prophets) and **K**etuvim (Writings).

Tanna, plural *tannaim* (Hebrew): 'reciter'. The early rabbis who composed the *Mishnah* at Yavne, who transmitted and developed their teachings orally.

Tapas (Sanskrit): 'heat'. In Indian religion, asceticism – a disciplined spiritual and physical exercise – is perceived as emitting a force of creative heat that enables the practitioner to acquire spiritual power and gain *moksha*. *Prajapati* brought the cosmos into being by heating himself ascetically; the fire sacrifice also created *tapas*, and the patron would sit, sweating, near Agni, the sacred fire, at the beginning of the ritual.

Tariqa (Arabic): 'path', 'way'. A term used by *Sufis* to classify the various Sufi orders that provide adherents with a path to holiness as well as the systems, rules and rituals that enable practitioners to achieve *fana* and *baqa*.

Tathagata (Pali): the title which the **Buddha** is said to have chosen for himself: 'Thus gone'; having attained *nirvana*, his ego – his selfhood – had been extinguished.

Tawil (Arabic): a commentary on the **Quran** which employed allegorical exegesis.

Theologia (Latin): 'discourse about God'. A more philosophical approach to the divine than the traditional scriptural approach; it was pioneered in the West by the French philosopher Peter Abelard (1079–1142).

Theoria (Greek): 'contemplation'; in the modern West, 'theory' has become a mental construct or hypothesis.

Theosis (Greek): 'deification'; the participation in the divine that, for Eastern Christians, is the goal of human existence. Human beings are called to participate in the deified humanity of Christ, becoming, like him, 'whole man, soul and body, by nature, and becoming whole God, soul and body by grace' (Maximus the Confessor, c.580–662).

Theravada (Pali): the Teaching of the 'Elders' of the Buddhist Order (**Sangha**). An early form of Buddhism based on the **Pali Canon** in contrast with the **Mahayana**, who developed their own scriptural canon.

Tian (Chinese): 'Heaven'. Originally, the high god of the Zhou dynasty. Although Heaven had humanlike characteristics, the title referred to an all-encompassing reality rather than a personalised God; Tian can also be translated as 'Nature', the supreme source of power and order, and from a very early date it was also associated with human morality. To live in accordance with the Way (**Dao**) of Heaven, therefore, was the goal of life. While Tian was the embodiment of *yang*, Earth was the embodiment of *yin*. Humanity formed a sacred triad with Heaven-and-Earth.

Tianli (Chinese): a neo-Confucian term for the 'principle' (*li*) of Heaven which is present in the human mind.

Tikkun (Hebrew): in the **Kabbalah** of Isaac Luria, *tikkun* is the 'restoration' of the **Shekhinah** to the Godhead, which devotees can bring about by their ritual and ethical practice, that will repair the fractured cosmos.

Torah (Hebrew): initially simply 'teaching'; in the **Tanakh**, the term Torah became synonymous with the **Pentateuch**; and in rabbinic Judaism a distinction was made between the Written Torah (the Hebrew Bible) and the **Oral Torah**. Jewish speculation later gave the Torah a cosmic dimension so that it was equated with the figure of *Wisdom* in the book of Proverbs, God's 'master craftsman' during the creation.

Trigram (in Chinese, *gua*): the trigram is a three-lined symbol, consisting of three parallel lines, which are either all solid (*yang*), or broken (*yin*), or combinations; they functioned in an ancient form of divination, whose origins are obscure to us (see *hexagram*). Over time, the discovery of the trigrams was attributed to the ancient Sage King Fu Xi, who saw these images in the heavens and linked them with patterns he observed on earth. During the third and second centuries BCE, the *Yijing* was transformed by ten learned commentaries into a wisdom text that outlined the relationship of the sacred triad of Heaven, Earth and Humanity. Each trigram reflected the dynamic interaction of these forces.

Twelver Shiism: the largest group of the *Shiah*, which accepts the legitimacy of all twelve of the *imams* descended from Ali.

Ummah (Arabic): the 'community' of Muslims. The *Quran* called Muhammad to create a united *ummah*, which reflected the unity of God, out of the disunited, warring tribes of Arabia.

Upanishad (Sanskrit): 'esoteric teaching', derived from *upa-ni-shad*: 'to sit close by', alluding to the proximity necessary for the transmission of such knowledge; an alternative translation and etymology is 'connection'; these new scriptures were developing the ritual science of *bandhus*. These mystical texts complete the Vedic corpus, which is why they are called *Vedanta*: 'the end of the Veda'.

Upaya (Sanskrit): 'skill in means'; the adaptation of Buddhist teaching to the circumstances, needs and spiritual attainments of the audience. This is especially important in *Mahayana* Buddhism. It is rooted in the idea that the *Buddha*'s teachings are provisional and may vary: what is appropriate for one time or group may not be appropriate or helpful (*kusala*) for another.

Vac (Sanskrit): 'Speech', the Hindu *deva* that manifested speech acquired special prominence in early Vedic times because of the emphasis on the eternally sacred sound heard by the *rishis*. Vac is not unlike the *Word/Wisdom/ Logos* of the Hebrew and Christian traditions as a source of creation. As sacred sound, Vac is also the 'mother' of the *Veda* and of all sacred *mantras*.

Vaishya (Sanskrit): 'clansman'; the third class of Vedic society, whose function was to create the wealth of the community, first by stock-breeding and farming, and later by trade and commerce.

Veda (Sanskrit): 'knowledge'. The four collections (*samhitas*) that form the core of Hindu scripture: the Rig Veda, Sama Veda, Yajur Veda and Atharva Veda which together comprise the basis of revealed (*shruti*) scripture. The **Brahmanas** provide prose explanations of the **mantras** in the core texts, and the **Upanishads** complete the Vedic corpus.

Vinaya (Pali): 'that which separates'; the rules that govern the Buddhist monastic Order.

Vulgate (Latin derivation): 'vernacular'. Jerome's Latin translation of the Hebrew scriptures and the Greek New Testament.

Wen (Chinese): the routinised civil order of the imperial government in China, supported by the Confucian officials, ideally based on benevolence (*ren*), culture and rational persuasion.

Wisdom (in Hebrew, *hokhmah*, 'discrimination'): expressive of the ethical quality of life, it produced a distinctive form of literature in the ancient Near East and thus became a distinct cultural tradition within Judaism. Wisdom was regarded as a divine gift, was personified as a co-worker with Yahweh in the creation of the world (Proverbs 8); it was identical with the divine Word or **Logos** that brought the world into being (Genesis 1). Early Christians saw Jesus as the incarnation of this creative Logos (John 1).

Wu (Chinese): the military order of the Chinese imperial government.

Wu-wei (Chinese): 'doing nothing'. The mode of action of Daoism, which did not mean total inactivity; rather it restricted activity to what is necessary and avoided extremity. This restraint allowed the **Dao** to run its natural course without human interference: 'In the pursuit of the Way one does less every day ... It is always through not meddling that the empire is won' (*Dao De Jing*, 48; Lao translation).

Xie (Chinese): 'learning' which, in Confucianism, was a communal activity, inseparable from moral self-cultivation.

Yangists: followers of Master Yang (dates uncertain) who renounced society during the dangerous Warring States period to preserve his life, which he regarded as the most sacred commodity.

Yao: the first Sage King of the Xia dynasty, who is said to have brought peace to the world simply by cultivating his humanity (*ren*).

Yerushalmi (Hebrew): the Jerusalem Talmud.

Yi (Chinese): 'righteousness', 'ethical conduct' that is just, correct and accords with customary moral principles. Rooted in early Confucian thought, *yi* includes the intention that inspires correct behaviour as well as good deeds.

Yielding: see *rang*.

Yijing (Chinese): the 'Classic of Changes', which developed from an ancient system of divination based on the casting of yarrow stalks. No clear philosophical conclusions can be drawn from the ancient 'line-statements' that traditionally accompanied the sixty-four *hexagrams*. But during the third and second centuries BCE, commentaries on these statements (ascribed to Confucius and known as the 'Wings') developed a positive, rationalised account of a well-ordered universe, in which there is constant change and which produces only what is good (see *yin* and *yang*).

Yin and **yang** (Chinese): the two polar extremes of the infinite *Dao* from whose fluctuation and interaction the ever-changing universe in all its multiple forms has emerged. In Chinese cosmology, the five elements derive from their intermingling, as have the processes of history and time. Hence, the yin/yang opposition lies at the heart of ancient Chinese divination (see *hexagrams* and *trigrams*), which was an attempt to create a proto-science to account for the process of change. Even though they are the source of all opposition, each contains the seed of the other and the two are interdependent. Yin represents the female aspect of reality; it is yielding, reflective, giving rise to the moon, water, clouds and even numbers. Its season is winter; its activity interior and conducted in dark, enclosed places. The yang is the source of the masculine; it is hard, associated with the sun and odd numbers, and is active in summer and daylight; an external, outgoing power with abundant output.

Yoga (Sanskrit): the 'yoking' of the powers of the mind in a meditative discipline designed to eliminate the egotism that holds us back from *moksha* and *nirvana*.

Yu: a hero of the mythical Xia period, who designed a technology that controlled the flood waters that devastated the Great Plain.

Yu-wei (Chinese): disciplined, purposeful action.

Zhou: the dynasty that ruled China from 1044, after defeating the *Shang* until the First Qin Emperor united China at the end of the Warring States period in 221 BCE.

Zimzum (Hebrew): in Lurianic *Kabbalah*, the kenotic (see *kenosis*) 'withdrawal' of *En Sof* into itself to make a space for the world.

Zuozhuan (Chinese): a fourth-century BCE commentary on the *Spring and Autumn Annals* that may originally have been an historical account of the Spring and Autumn period but which later, when hermeneutics became prestigious, was adapted to fit around the events recorded in the *Annals*.

SELECT BIBLIOGRAPHY

ABDEL-HALEEM, M. A. S., trans., *The Qur'an: A New Translation* (Oxford, 2004)

ABOU EL FADL, Khaled, *And God Knows the Soldiers: The Authoritative and Authoritarian in Islamic Discourses* (Lanham, 2001)

    The Great Theft: Wrestling Islam from the Extremists (New York, 2007)

AESCHYLUS, *The Oresteia*, trans. Robert Fagles (London, 1966)

    Prometheus Bound and Other Plays, trans. Philip Vellacott (London, 1991)

AFSARUDDIN, Asma, *Striving in the Path of God: Jihad and Martyrdom in Islamic Thought* (Oxford, 2013)

    Contemporary Issues in Islam (Edinburgh, 2015)

AHLSTRÖM, Gösta W., *The History of Ancient Palestine* (Minneapolis, 1993)

AITKEN, Ellen, *Jesus' Death in Early Christian Memory: The Poetics of the Passion* (Fribourg, 2004)

AKENSON, Donald Harman, *Surpassing Wonder: The Invention of the Bible and the Talmuds* (New York, 1998)

ALON, Gedaliah, *The Jews in their Land in the Talmudic Age (70–640 CE)*, trans. Gershon Levi (Cambridge, MA, 1989)

ALPER, Harvey P., ed., *Understanding Mantras* (Delhi, 2012 edn)

ALTER, Robert and Frank KERMODE, eds., *The Literary Guide to the Bible* (London, 1987)

AQUINAS, Thomas, *Thomas Aquinas, Summa Theologiae: A Concise Translation*, ed. and trans. Timothy McDermott (London, 1989)

    Thomas Aquinas: Selected Writings, ed. and trans. Ralph McInerny (Harmondsworth, 1998)

ASAD, Talal, *Genealogies of Religion: Discipline and Reasons of Power in Christianity and Islam* (Baltimore, MD, 1993)

ASLAN, Reza, *No God but God: The Origins, Evolution and Future of Islam* (London, 2005)

ASSMANN, Jan, *Religion and Cultural Memory*, trans. Rodney Livingstone (Stanford, 2006)

Cultural Memory and Early Civilization: Writing, Remembrance and Political Imagination (Cambridge, 2011)

ATHANASIUS, *Life of St Anthony of Egypt*, ed. and trans. Philip Schaff and Henry Wace, n.p., n.d.

AUERBACH, Erich, *Mimesis: The Representation of Reality in Western Literature*, trans. Willard Trask (Princeton, 1953)

AUGUSTINE, *The Confessions*, trans. Philip Barton (London, 2001)
  On Christian Doctrine, trans. D. R. Robinson (Indianapolis, 1958)
  City of God, trans. Henry Bettenson (London, 1972)

AUNE, David E., *The Cultic Setting of Realized Eschatology in Early Christianity* (Leiden, 1972)

AWN, Peter, 'Classical Sufi Approaches to Scripture', in Steven T. Katz, ed., *Mysticism and Sacred Scripture* (Oxford, 2000)

AYOUB, Mahmoud, *The Qur'ān and Its Interpreters* (Albany, 1984)
  'The Speaking Qur'ān and the Silent Qur'ān: A Study of the Principles and Development of Imāmī Shī'ī tafsīr', in Andrew Rippin, ed., *Approaches to the History of the Interpretation of the Qur'ān* (Oxford, 1988)

BAINTON, Roland H., *Here I Stand: A Life of Martin Luther* (New York, 1950)

BAMMEL, F. and C. F. D. MOULE, eds., *Jesus and the Politics of His Day* (Cambridge, 1981)

BAMYEH, Mohammed A., *The Social Origins of Islam: Mind, Economy, Discourse* (Minneapolis, 1999)

BARNARD, John H., ed. and trans., *The Pilgrimage of St Sylvia of Aquitania to the Holy Places* (London, 1971)

BARR, David, *The Reality of Apocalypse: Rhetoric and Politics in the Book of Revelation* (Atlanta, 2006)

BAUMAN, Zygmunt, *Does Ethics Have a Chance in a World of Consumers?* (Cambridge, MA, 2008)

BAYLY, C. A., 'India, the *Bhagavad Gita* and the World', in Kapila Shruti and Faisal Devji, eds., *Political Thought in Action: The Bhagavad Gita and Modern India* (Cambridge, 2013)

BECKMAN, Gary and Theodore J. LEWIS, eds., *Texts, Artifact, and Image: Revealing Ancient Israelite Religion* (Providence, 2006)

BELL, Catherine, *Ritual Theory, Ritual Practice* (Oxford, 1992, 2009)

BERLINERBLAU, Jacques, *The Secular Bible: Why Nonbelievers Must Take Religion Seriously* (Cambridge, 2005)

BERRY, Thomas, 'Individualism and Holism in Chinese Tradition: The Religious-Cultural Context', in Tu Weiming and Mary Evelyn Tucker, eds., *Confucian Spirituality I* (New York, 2003).

BEYER, Stephan, *The Buddhist Experience: Sources and Interpretations* (Belmont, 1974)

BIARDEAU, Madeleine, 'The Salvation of the king in the *Mahabharata*', *Contributions to Indian Sociology, New Series*, 15:1–2 (1981)

BICKERMAN, Elias J., *From Ezra to the Last of the Maccabees* (New York, 1962)
> *The Jews in the Greek Age* (Cambridge, MA, 1990)

BLAKE, William, *A Selection of Poems and Letters*, ed. J. Bronowski (London, 1958)

BLOCH, Ruth H., *Visionary Republic: Millennial Themes in American Thought, 1756–1800* (Cambridge, 1985)

BONAVENTURE, *The Works of Saint Bonaventure*, 2 vols., ed. and trans. Philotheus Boehner and M. Frances Laughlin (New York, 1958)

BONNER, Michael, *Jihad in Islamic History* (Princeton, 2006)

BOODBERG, Peter, 'The Semasiology of Some Primary Confucian Concepts', *Philosophy East and West*, 2, No. 4 (October 1953)

BOSSY, John, *Christianity in the West, 1400 to 1700* (Oxford, 1985)
> 'The Counter-Reformation and the People of Catholic Europe', *Past and Present*, 47 (May 1970)

BOTHA, Pieter J. J., *Orality and Literacy in Early Christianity* (Eugene, 2012)

BOURDIEU, Pierre, *Outline of a Theory of Practice*, trans. Richard Nice (Cambridge, 1977)

BOUSTAN, Ra'anan S., Alex P. JASSEN and Calvin J. ROETZEL, eds., *Violence, Scripture and Textual Practice in Early Judaism and Christianity* (Leiden, 2010)

BOYER, Paul, *When Time Shall Be No More: Prophecy and Belief in Modern American Culture* (Cambridge, MA, 1992)

BOYNTON, Susan and Diane J. REILLY, eds., *The Practice of the Bible in the Middle Ages: Production, Reception, and Performance in Western Christianity* (New York, 2011)

BRAKKE, David, *Athanasius and Asceticism* (Baltimore, 1995)

BRAKKE, David, Michael L. SATLOW and Steven WEITZMAN, eds., *Religion and the Self in Antiquity* (Bloomington, 2005)

BROCKINGTON, John L., *The Sanskrit Epics* (Leiden, 1998)

BROKAW, Cynthia, 'Tai Chen and Learning in the Confucian Tradition', in Benjamin A. Elman and Alexander Woodside, eds., *Education and Society in Late Imperial China, 1600–1900* (Berkeley, 1994)

BROWN, C. Mackenzie, 'The Origin and Transmission of the Two Bhagavata Puranas: A Canonical and Theological Dilemma', *Journal of the American Academy of Religion*, 51 (1983)
> 'Purana as Scripture: From Sound to Image of the Holy Word', *History of Religions* (August 1986)

BROWN, Daniel, *Rethinking Tradition in Modern Islamic Thought* (Cambridge, 1996)

BROWN, Peter, *Society and the Holy in Late Antiquity* (Berkeley, 1982)
> *The Body and Society: Men, Women and Sexual Renunciation in Early Christianity* (London, 1988)
> *The Rise of Western Christendom: Triumph and Diversity, AD 200–1000* (Oxford, 1996)

BUBER, Martin, *On Judaism*, ed. Nahum Glatzer (New York, 1967)
> *Moses, the Revelation and the Covenant*, with Introduction by Michael Fishbane (New York, 1988 edn)
> *On the Bible: Eighteen Studies* (Syracuse, 2000)

BUCKLEY, Michael J., *At the Origins of Modern Atheism* (New Haven, 1987)

BRUNS, Gerald L., 'Midrash and Allegory: The Beginnings of Scriptural Interpretation', in Robert Alter and Frank Kermode, eds., *The Literary Guide to the Bible* (London, 1987)

BUDDHAGHOSA, *The Path of Purification (Visuddhimagga)*, trans. Bhikku Nanamoli (Kandy, 1975)

BULTMANN, Rudolf, *Kerygma and Myth*, Vol. I, ed. H. W. Bartsch (London, 1957)
> *Jesus Christ and Mythology* (New York, 1958)

BURKE, Jason, *The New Threat from Islamic Militancy* (London, 2015)

BURTON, John, *The Collection of the Qur'ān* (Cambridge, 1977)

BUTTERWORTH, G. W., trans., *Origen: On First Principles* (Gloucester, MA, 1973)

CALVIN, John, *Institutes of the Christian Religion*, 1536 edn, trans. Ford Lewis (Grand Rapids, 1975)

CAMERON, Euan, *The European Reformation*, 2nd edn (Oxford, 2012)

CAMPBELL, Joseph, *The Hero with a Thousand Faces* (Princeton, 1949)
> *Oriental Mythology: The Masks of God* (New York, 1982)

CARPENTER, David, 'The Mastery of Speech, Canonicity and Control in the Vedas', in Lorie, L. Patton, ed., *Authority, Anxiety and Canon: Essays in Vedic Interpretation* (Albany, 1994)

CARR, David M., *Writing on the Tablet of the Heart: Origins of Scripture and Literature* (Oxford, 2005)
> *Holy Resilience: The Bible's Traumatic Origins* (New Haven, 2014)

CARRUTHERS, Mary J., *The Book of Memory: A Study of Memory in Medieval Culture* (Cambridge, 1990)

    The Craft of Thought: Meditation, Rhetoric, and the Making of Images, 400–1200 (Cambridge, 1998)

CHAN, Wing-tsit, ed. and trans., *A Source Book in Chinese Philosophy* (Princeton, 1969)

    ed. and trans., *Reflections on Things at Hand: The Neo-Confucian Anthology Compiled by Chu Hsi and Lu Tsu-chien* (New York, 1967)

    'Chu Hsi's Completion of Neo-Confucianism', in Françoise Aubin, ed., *Song Studies: In Memoriam Etienne Balazs*, 11.1 (1973)

CHANG, Garma C. C., ed., *A Treasury of Mahayana Sutras* (University Park, 1983)

CHANG, Kwang-chih, *Shang Civilization* (New Haven, 1980)

CHARLESWORTH, James H., ed., *The Old Testament Pseudepigrapha*, 2 vols. (Peabody, 1983)

CHELKOWSKI, Peter J., ed., *Ta'ziyeh: Ritual and Drama in Iran* (New York, 1979)

CH'IEN, Edward T., 'Chiao Hung and the Revolt against Ch'eng-Chu Orthodoxy', in Wm. Theodore de Bary, ed., *The Unfolding of Neo-Confucianism* (New York, 1975)

CHITTICK, William C., ed. and trans., *The Sufi Path of Knowledge: Ibn al-'Arabi's Metaphysics of Imagination* (Albany, 1994)

    Imaginal Worlds: Ibn al-'Arabi and the Problem of Religious Diversity (Albany, 1994)

CHODKIEWICZ, Michel, *An Ocean Without Shore: Ibn al-'Arabi, the Book and the Law* (Albany, 1993)

CLIFFORD, Richard R., *The Cosmic Mountain in Canaan and the Old Testament* (Cambridge, MA, 1972)

COBURN, Thomas B., 'Scripture in India: Towards a Typology of the Word in Hindu Life', in Miriam Levering, ed., *Rethinking Scripture: Essays from a Comparative Perspective* (Albany, 1989)

COCHELIN, Isabelle, 'When Monks Were the Book: The Bible and Monasticism(6th–11th Centuries)', in Susan Boynton and Diane J. Reilly, eds., *The Practice of the Bible in the Middle Ages: Production, Reception, and Performance in Western Christianity* (New York, 2011)

COHEN, Abraham, *The Teachings of Maimonides* (London, 1927)

COHEN, Boaz, ed., *Everyman's Talmud* (New York, 1975)

COHN, Norman, *The Pursuit of the Millennium: Revolutionary Millenarians and Mystical Anarchists in the Middle Ages* (London, 1984 edn)

COLE, W. Owen, *The Guru in Sikhism* (London, 1982)

COLLINS, Steven, *Selfless Persons: Imagery and Thought in Theravada Buddhism* (Cambridge, 1992)

'On the Very Idea of the Pali Canon', *Journal of the Pali Text Society*, 15 (1960)

COLLINS, John J. and Michael FISHBANE, eds., *Death, Ecstasy and Other Worldly Journeys* (Albany, 1995)

CONZE, Edward, *Buddhist Scriptures* (London, 1959)

   The Prajnaparamita Literature (Gravenhage, 1960)

   trans., *Selected Sayings from the Perfection of Wisdom* (London, 1968)

   trans., *The Perfection of Wisdom in Eight Thousand Lines and its Verse Summary* (Bolinas, 1973)

CONZE, Edward, I. B. HORNER, D. SNELLGROVE and A. WALEY, eds., *Buddhist Texts Through the Ages* (New York, 1964)

CORBIN, Henry, *Spiritual Body and Celestial Earth: From Mazdean Iran to Shī'īte Iran*, trans. Nancy Pearson (Princeton, 1977)

   History of Islamic Philosophy, trans. Liadain Sherrard and Philip Sherrard (London, 1993)

COWARD, Harold, *Sacred Word and Sacred Text: Scripture in World Religions* (Delhi, 1988).

   ed., *Experiencing Scripture in World Religions* (Eugene, 2000)

COWARD, Harold and Krishna SIVARAMAN, eds., *Revelation in Indian Thought: A Festschrift in Honour of Professor T. R. V. Murti* (Emeryville, 1977)

CRECELIUS, Daniel, 'Non-Ideological Response of the *Ulema* to Modernization', in Nikki R. Keddie, ed., *Scholars, Saints and Sufis: Muslim Religious Institutions in the Middle East since 1500* (Berkeley, 1972)

CROOKE, Alastair, *Resistance: The Essence of the Islamist Revolution* (London, 2009)

CROSS, Frank Moore, *Canaanite Myth and Hebrew Epic: Essays in the History of the Religion of Israel* (Cambridge, MA, 1973)

   From Epic to Canon: History and Literature in Ancient Israel (Baltimore, 1998)

CROSSAN, John Dominic, *Jesus: A Revolutionary Biography* (San Francisco, 1987)

DAMROSCH, David, *The Narrative Covenant: Transformations of Genre in the Growth of Biblical Literature* (San Francisco, 1987)

   'Leviticus', in Robert Alter and Frank Kermode, eds., *The Literary Guide to the Bible* (London, 1987)

DANIELSON, Dennis, ed., *The Cambridge Companion to Milton*, 2nd edn (Cambridge, 1999)

DE BARY, Wm. Theodore, *Self and Society in Ming Thought* (New York, 1970)

   ed., *The Buddhist Tradition in India, China and Japan* (New York, 1969) ed., *The Unfolding of Neo-Confucianism* (New York, 1975)

Learning for One's Self: Essays on the Individual in Neo-Confucian Thought (New York, 1991)

'Zhu Xi's Neo-Confucian Spirituality', in Tu Weiming and Mary Evelyn Tucker, eds., *Confucian Spirituality*, vol. II (New York, 2004)

DE BARY, Wm. Theodore and Irene BLOOM, eds., *Sources of Chinese Tradition: From Earliest Times to 1600*, 2nd edn (New York, 1999)

eds., *Eastern Canons: Approaches to the Asian Classics* (New York, 1990)

DE BARY, Wm. Theodore, Wing-tsit CHAN and Burton WATSON, eds., *Sources of Chinese Tradition* (New York, 1960)

DELONG-BAS, Natana J., *Wahhabi Islam: From Revival and Reform to Global Jihad* (Cairo, 2005)

DENNY, Frederick M. and Rodney L. TAYLOR, eds., *The Holy Book in Comparative Perspective* (Columbia, 1993)

DENYS the Areopagite, *Pseudo-Dionysius: The Complete Works*, ed. and trans. Colm Luibheid and Paul Rorem (Mahwah, 1967)

DEOL, Jeevan, 'Text and Lineage in Early Sikh History: Issues in the Study of the *Adi Granth*', *Bulletin of the School of Oriental and African Studies*, 64.1 (2001)

DESCARTES, René, *Descartes: Key Philosophical Writings*, trans. Elizabeth S. Haldane and G. R. T. Ross, ed. Enrique Chávez-Arvizo (Ware, 1997)

Discourse on Method, Optics, Geometry, and Meteorology, trans. Paul J. Olscamp (Indianapolis, 1965)

DEVER, William G., *What Did the Biblical Writers Know and When Did They Know It? What Archaeology Can Tell Us About the Reality of Ancient Israel* (Grand Rapids, 2001)

DEWEY, Arthur J., *Inventing the Passion: How the Death of Jesus Was Remembered* (Salem, 2017)

DEWEY, Joanna, *The Oral Ethos of the Early Church: Speaking, Writing, and the Gospel of Mark* (Eugene, 2013)

DINUR, Benzion, 'The Origins of Hasidism and Its Social and Messianic Foundations', in Gershon David Hundert, ed., *Essential Papers on Hasidism: Origins to Present* (New York, 1991)

'The Messianic-Prophetic Role of the Baal Shem Tov (Besht)', in Marc Saperstein, ed., *Essential Papers on Messianic Movements and Personalities in Jewish History* (New York, 1992)

DONIGER, Wendy, ed., *Hindu Myths: A Sourcebook translated from the Sanskrit* (London, 1979)

ed., *The Critical Study of Sacred Texts* (Berkeley, 1979)

ed. and trans., *The Rig Veda: An Anthology* (London, 1981)

trans., *The Rig Veda* (London, 1982)

ed., *Purana Perennis: Reciprocity and Transformation in Hindu and Jaina Texts* (Albany, 1993)

The Hindus: An Alternative History (Oxford, 2009)

DONNER, Frederick M., *Narratives of Islamic Origins: The Beginnings of Islamic Historical Writing* (Princeton, 1998)

DUBNOW, Simon, 'The Maggid of Miedzyrzecz, His Associates and the Center in Volhynia (1760–1772)', in Gershom David Hundert, ed., *Essential Papers on Hasidism: Origins to Present* (New York, 1991)

DUDERIJA, Adis, 'Evolution in the Concept of Sunnah During the First Four Generations of Muslims in Relation to the Development of the Concept of an Authentic Hadith as Based on Recent Western Scholarship', *Arab Law Quarterly*, 26 (2012)

DUNDAS, Paul, *The Jains*, 2nd edn (London, 2001)

'Somnolent Sutras: Scriptural Commentary in Svetambara Jainism', *Journal of Indian Philosophy*, 224, No. 1 (March 1996)

DUNN, James D. G., *The Cambridge Companion to St Paul* (Cambridge, 1969)

DUPRÉ, Louis, 'The Mystical Experience of the Self and Its Philosophical Significance', in Richard Woods, ed., *Understanding Mysticism* (Garden City, 1980)

DUPRÉ, Louis and Don E. Saliers, eds., *Christian Spirituality, vol. III: Post Reformation and Modern* (New York, 1989)

DUSENBERY, Verne A., 'The Word as Guru: Sikh Scripture and the Translation Controversy', *History of Religions*, Vol. 31.4 (May 1992)

EARL, James W., *Beginning the Mahabharata: A Reader's Guide to the Frame Stories* (Woodland Hills, 2011)

ECK, Diana L., *Darśan: Seeing the Divine Image in India* (New York, 1998)

EISENSTADT, S. N., ed., *The Origins and Diversity of Axial Age Civilizations* (Albany, 1986)

ELIADE, Mircea, *Yoga, Immortality and Freedom*, trans. Willard J. Trask (London, 1958)

ELIOR, Rachel, 'HaBaD: The Contemplative Ascent to God', in Arthur Green, ed., *Jewish Spirituality*, vol. II (London, 1988)

ELIZARENKOVA, Tatyana J., *Language and Style of the Vedic Ṛṣis* (Albany, 1995)

ELMAN, Benjamin A., *From Philosophy to Philology: Intellectual and Social Aspects of Change in Late Imperial China* (Cambridge, MA, 1984) with Alexander Woodside, eds., *Education and Society in Late Imperial China, 1600–1900* (Berkeley, 1994)

ELVIN, Mark, *Another History: Essays on China from a European Perspective* (Canberra, 1996)

'Was There a Transcendental Breakthrough in China?', in S. N. Eisenstadt, ed., *The Origins and Diversity of Axial Age Civilizations* (Albany, 1986)

EMBREE, Ainslie T., ed., *Sources of Indian Tradition, Volume One: From the Beginning to 1800,* 2nd edn (New York, 1998)

ESPOSITO, John L., ed., *Voices of Resurgent Islam* (New York, 1983)

Unholy War: Terror in the Name of Islam (Oxford, 2002)

with Dalia Mogahed, *Who Speaks for Islam? What a Billion Muslims Really Think* (New York, 2007)

ETTINGER, Shmuel, 'The Hasidic Movement – Reality and Ideals', in Gershom David Hundert, ed., *Essential Papers on Hasidism: Origins to Present* (New York, 1991)

EVANS, G. R., *The Language and Logic of the Bible: The Earlier Middle Ages* (Cambridge, 1984)

FAIRBANK, John King and Merle GOLDMAN, *China: A New History*, 2nd edn (Cambridge, MA, 2006)

FENSHAM, F. Charles, 'Widow, Orphan and the Poor in Ancient Near Eastern Literature', in Frederick E. Greenspahn, ed., *Essential Papers on Israel and the Ancient Near East* (New York, 1991)

FINDLY, Ellison Banks, 'Mantra Kavisasta: Speech as Performative in the RgVeda', in Harvey P. Alper, ed., *Understanding Mantras* (Delhi, 2012 edn)

FINGARETTE, Herbert, *Confucius: The Secular as Sacred* (New York, 1972)

FINKELSTEIN, Israel and Neil Asher SILBERMAN, *The Bible Unearthed: Archaeology's New Vision of Ancient Israel and the Origins of Its Sacred Texts* (New York, 2001)

FIRESTONE, Reuven, *Jihad: The Origin of Holy War in Islam* (New York, 1999)

Holy War in Judaism: The Fall and Rise of a Controversial Idea (Oxford, 1999)

FISCHER, Michael, *Iran: From Religious Dispute to Revolution* (Cambridge, MA and London, 1980)

FISHBANE, Michael, *Text and Texture: Close Readings of Selected Biblical Texts* (New York, 1979)

Biblical Interpretation in Ancient Israel (Oxford, 1985)

The Garments of Torah: Essays in Biblical Hermeneutics (Bloomington, 1989)

The Exegetical Imagination: On Jewish Thought and Theology (Cambridge, MA, 1998)

with John J. Collins, eds., *Death, Ecstasy, and Other Worldly Journeys* (Albany, 1995)

FITZGERALD, Allen D., ed., *Augustine Through the Ages: An Encyclopedia* (Grand Rapids, 1999)

FLOOD, Gavin, *An Introduction to Hinduism* (Cambridge, 1996)

The Ascetic Self: Subjectivity, Memory and Tradition (Cambridge, 2004)

ed., *The Blackwell Companion to Hinduism* (Oxford, 2003)

FOLEY, John Miles, *How to Read an Oral Poem* (Urbana, 2002)

FOLKERT, Kendall W., 'The "Canons" of "Scripture"', in Miriam Levering, ed., *Rethinking Scripture: Essays from a Comparative Perspective* (Albany, 1989)

FORD, Amanda, *Retail Therapy: Life Lessons Learned While Shopping* (York Beach, 2002)

FOX, Everett, trans., *The Five Books of Moses* (New York, 1990)

The Early Prophets: Joshua, Judges, Samuel, and Kings (New York, 2014)

FREDRIKSEN, Paula and Adele REINHARTZ, eds., *Jesus, Judaism, and Christian Anti-Judaism: Reading the New Testament after the Holocaust* (Louisville, 2002)

FREI, Hans, *The Eclipse of Biblical Narrative: A Study in Eighteenth and Nineteenth Century Hermeneutics* (New Haven, 1974)

FRIEDMAN, Menachem, 'Habad as Messianic Fundamentalism: From Local Particularism to Universal Jewish Mission', in Martin E. Marty and R. Scott Appleby, eds., *Accounting for Fundamentalisms: The Dynamic Character of Movements* (Chicago, 1994)

FRIEDMAN, Richard Elliott, *Who Wrote the Bible?* (San Francisco, 1987)

FRYKENBERG, Robert E., 'Hindu Fundamentalism and the Structural Stability of India', in Martin E. Marty and R. Scott Appleby, eds., *Fundamentalisms and the State* (Chicago, 1993)

FULLER, Robert C., *Naming the Antichrist: The History of an American Obsession* (Oxford, 1995)

FUNG Yu-lan, *A Short History of Chinese Philosophy*, ed. Derk Bodde (New York, 1976)

FUNKENSTEIN, Amos, *Theology and the Scientific Imagination: From the Middle Ages to the Seventeenth Century* (Princeton, 1986)

FUTRELL, Alison, *Blood in the Arena: The Spectacle of Roman Power* (Austin, 1997)

GALLAGHER, Shaun, *How the Body Shapes the Mind* (Oxford, 2005)

GARDNER, Daniel K., ed. and trans., *Learning to Be a Sage: Selections from the Conversations of Master Chu, Arranged Topically* (Berkeley, Los Angeles and Oxford, 1990)

    ed. and trans., *The Four Books: The Basic Teachings of the Later Confucian Tradition* (Indianapolis, 2001)

        'Attentiveness and Meditative Reading in Cheng–Zhu Confucianism', in Tu Weiming and Mary Evelyn Tucker, eds., *Confucian Spirituality*, vol. II (New York, 2004)

GÄTJE, Helmut, *The Qur'ān and Its Exegesis: Selected Texts with Classical and Modern Muslim Interpretations*, ed. and trans. Alford T. Welch (Oxford, 2008 edn)

GAUKROGER, S., *The Emergence of a Scientific Culture: Science and the Shaping of Modernity, 1210–1685* (Oxford, 2006)

GELLNER, Ernest, *Postmodernism, Reason and Religion* (London, 1992)

GEMES, Ken and John RICHARDSON, eds., *The Oxford Handbook of Nietzsche* (Oxford, 2013)

GERNET, Jacques, *Ancient China: From the Beginnings to the Empire*, trans. Raymond Rudorff (London, 1968)

    A History of Chinese Civilization, trans. J. R. Foster and Charles Hartman, 2nd edn (Cambridge, 1996)

GETHIN, Rupert, *The Foundations of Buddhism* (Oxford, 1996)

GHOSE, Aurobindo, *The Secret of the Veda* (Pondicherry, 1971)

    Essays on the Gita (Pondicherry, 1972)

GIMELLO, Robert M., 'The Civil Status of Li in Classical Confucianism', *Philosophy East and West*, 22 (1972)

GOLD, Daniel, 'Organized Hinduisms: From Vedic Truth to Hindu Nation', in Martin E. Marty and R. Scott Appleby, eds., *Fundamentalisms Observed* (Chicago, 1991)

GOMBRICH, Richard F., *How Buddhism Began: The Conditioned Genesis of the Early Teachings* (London, 1996)

    Theravada Buddhism: A Social History from Ancient Benares to Modern Colombo, 2nd edn (London, 2008)

GONDA, Jan, *Notes on Brahman* (Utrecht, 1950)

    'The Vedic Concept of Amhas', *Indo-Iranian Journal*, 1 (1957)

    'The Indian Mantra', *Oriens*, 16 (1964)

    Vedic Literature (Wiesbaden, 1975)

    The Vision of the Vedic Poets (New Delhi, 1984)

    Change and Continuity in Indian Religion (The Hague, 1985)

GOODY, Jack, *The Interface Between the Written and the Oral* (Oxford, 1979)

GORFINKLE, Joseph I., trans., *Pirke Avot: Traditional Text; Sayings of the Jewish Fathers* (New York, 2013)

GOTTWALD, Norman K., *The Hebrew Bible in Its Social World and Ours* (Atlanta, 1993)

    The Politics of Ancient Israel (Louisville, 2001)

GRAHAM, A. C., *Disputers of the Tao: Philosophical Argument in Ancient China* (La Salle, 1989)

    Divisions in Early Mohism Reflected in the Core Chapters of Mo-tzu (Singapore, 1985)

    Two Chinese Philosophers: The Metaphysics of the Brothers Ch'eng (La Salle, 1992)

GRAHAM, William A., *Divine Word and Prophetic Word in Early Islam: A Reconsideration of the Sources, with Special Reference to the Divine Saying or Hadith Qudsī* (The Hague, 1977)

    Beyond the Written Word: Oral Aspects of Scripture in the History of Religion (Cambridge, 1987)

GRANET, Marcel, *Chinese Civilization*, trans. Kathleen Innes and Mabel Brailsford (London and New York, 1951)

    The Religion of the Chinese People, ed. and trans. Maurice Freedman (Oxford, 1975)

GREEN, Arthur, ed., *Jewish Spirituality*, 2 vols. (New York, 1986, 1988)

GREENBERG, Moshe, 'The Stabilization of the Text of the Hebrew Bible', *Journal of the American Oriental Society*, 76 (1971)

GREENSPAHN, Frederick E., *Essential Papers on Israel and the Ancient Near East* (New York, 1991)

GREGORY, Brad S., *The Unintended Reformation: How a Religious Revolution Secularized Society* (Cambridge, MA, 2012)

GRIFFITH, Ralph T. H., trans., *The Rig Veda* (New York, 1992)

GRIFFITHS, Bede, *A New Vision of Reality: Western Science, Eastern Mysticism and Christian Faith*, ed. Felicity Edwards (London, 1992 edn)

GROSSMAN, David, *Lion's Honey: The Myth of Samson*, trans. Stuart Schoffman (Edinburgh, 2006)

GÜTTMANN, Julius, *Philosophies of Judaism: The History of Jewish Philosophy from Biblical Times to Franz Rosenzweig* (London, 1964)

HADOT, Pierre, *Philosophy as a Way of Life*, ed. Arnold I. Davidson, trans. Michael Chase (Oxford, 1995)

HALBERTAL, Moshe, *People of the Book: Canon, Meaning and Authority* (Cambridge, MA, 1997)

HALBFASS, Wilhelm, *Tradition and Reflection: Explorations in Indian Thought* (Albany, 1991)

HALBWACHS, Maurice, *On Collective Memory* (Chicago, 1992)

HARDY, Friedhelm, 'Information and Transformation: The Two Faces of Puranas', in Wendy Doniger, ed., *Purana Perennis: Reciprocity and Transformation in Hindu and Jaina Texts* (Albany, 1993)

HARRIS, William, *Ancient Literacy* (Cambridge, MA, 1989)

HARRISON, Paul M., 'Buddhanusmrti in the Pratyutpanna-buddha-sammukhavasthita-samadhi-sutra', *Journal of Indian Philosophy*, 9 (1978)

HARTWICH, Wolf-Daniel, 'Religion and Culture: Joseph and his Brothers', trans. Ritchie Robertson, in Robertson, ed., *The Cambridge Companion to Thomas Mann* (Cambridge, 2002)

HARVEY, Susan Ashbrook, *Scenting Salvation: Ancient Christianity and the Olfactory Imagination* (Berkeley, 2006)
> 'Locating the Sensing Body: Perception and Religious Identity in Late Antiquity', in David Brakke, Michael L. Satlow and Steven Weitzman, eds., *Religion and the Self in Antiquity* (Bloomington, 2005)

HATCH, Nathan, *The Democratization of American Christianity* (New Haven, 1989)

HAVELOCK, Eric A., *Preface to Plato* (Cambridge, 1963)

HAZONY, Yoram, *The Philosophy of Hebrew Scripture* (Cambridge, 2012)

HECK, Paul L., '"Jihad" Revisited', *Journal of Religious Ethics*, 32, 1 (2004)

HEESTERMAN, J. C., *The Inner Conflict of Tradition: Essays in Indian Ritual, Kinship and Society* (Chicago, 1985)
> *The Broken World of Sacrifice: An Essay in Ancient Indian Ritual* (Chicago, 1993)
> 'Ritual, Revelation and the Axial Age', in S. N. Eisenstadt, ed., *The Origins and Diversity of Axial Age Civilizations* (Albany, 1986)

HEILMAN, Samuel C. and Menachem FRIEDMAN, 'Religious Fundamentalism and Religious Jews: The Case of the Haredim', in Martin E. Marty and R. Scott Appleby, eds., *Fundamentalisms Observed* (Chicago, 1991)

HEIMERT, Alan, *Religion and the American Mind: From the Great Awakening to the Revolution* (Cambridge, MA, 1968)

HENDERSON, John B., *Scripture, Canon and Commentary: A Comparison of Confucian and Western Exegesis* (Princeton, 1991)

HENGEL, Martin, *Judaism and Hellenism: Studies in Their Encounter in Palestine During the Early Hellenistic Period*, trans. John Bowden, 2 vols. (London, 1974)
> *Crucifixion in the Ancient World and the Folly of the Message of the Cross*, trans. John Bowden (London, 1977)

Between Jesus and Paul: Studies in the Earliest History of Christianity, trans. John Bowden (Philadelphia, 1983)

The Pre-Christian Paul, trans. John Bowden (Philadelphia, 1991)

The Charismatic Leader and His Followers, trans. James Greig, 2nd edn (Eugene, 2005)

HERVIEU-LÉGER, Danièle, *Religion as a Chain of Memory*, trans. Simon Lee (New Brunswick, 1993)

HEZSER, Catherine, *Jewish Literacy in Roman Palestine* (Tübingen, 2001)

HILLENBRAND, Carole, *The Crusades: Islamic Perspectives* (Edinburgh, 1999)

HILTEBEITEL, Alf, *The Ritual of Battle: Krishna in the Mahābhārata* (Ithaca, 1976)

Rethinking the Mahābhārata: A Reader's Guide to the Education of the Dharma King (Chicago, 2001)

Dharma (Honolulu, 2010)

HOBBES, Thomas, *Leviathan*, ed. Richard Tuck (Cambridge, 1991)

HODGE, Charles, *What Is Darwinism?* (Princeton, 1974)

HODGSON, Marshall G. S., *The Venture of Islam: Conscience and History in a World Civilization*, 3 vols. (Chicago, 1974)

HOLCOMB, Justin S., ed., *Christian Theologies of Scripture: A Comparative Introduction* (New York, 2006)

HOLDREGE, Barbara A., *Veda and Torah: Transcending the Textuality of Scripture* (Albany, 1996)

HOPKINS, D. H., *The Highlands of Canaan* (Sheffield, 1985)

HOPKINS, Thomas J., *The Hindu Religious Tradition* (Belmont, 1971)

HORSLEY, Richard A., *Jesus and the Spiral of Violence: Popular Jewish Resistance in Roman Palestine* (Minneapolis, 1993)

Text and Tradition in Performance and Writing (Eugene, 2013)

ed., *Oral Performance, Popular Tradition, and Hidden Transcript in Q* (Atlanta, 2006)

HUDSON, Emily T., *Disorienting Dharma: Ethics and the Aesthetics of Suffering in the Mahābhārata* (Oxford, 2013)

HUME, David, *Of the Standard of Taste and Other Essays*, ed. John W. Lenz (Indianapolis, 1961)

A Treatise on Human Nature, eds. L. A. Selby-Bigge and P. H. Nidditch (Oxford, 1978)

HUNDERT, Gershon David, ed., *Essential Papers on Hasidism: Origins to Present* (New York, 1991)

HURTADO, Larry W., *One God, One Lord: Early Christian Devotion and Ancient Jewish Monotheism*, 2nd edn (London, 1998)

Lord Jesus Christ: Devotion to Jesus in Earliest Christianity (Grand Rapids, 2003)

How on Earth Did Jesus Become a God? Historical Questions about Earliest Devotion to Jesus (Grand Rapids, 2005)

IBN ISHAQ, Muhammad, *The Life of Muhammad: A Translation of Ibn Ishaq's Sirat Rasul Allah*, trans. Alfred Guillaume (Oxford, 1955)

IQBAL, Muzaffar, 'Scientific Commentary on the Qur'an', in S. H. Nasr, ed., *The Study Qur'an: A New Translation and Commentary* (New York, 2015)

IRENAEUS, *The Works of Irenaeus,* eds. and trans. Alexander Roberts and W. H. Rambant (Edinburgh, 1884)

IZUTSU, Toshihiko, *God and Man in the Koran: Semantics of the Koranic Weltanschauung* (Tokyo, 1964)

Ethico-Religious Concepts in the Qur'ān (Montreal, 2002)

JAFFEE, Martin S., *Torah in the Mouth: Writing and Oral Tradition in Palestinian Judaism 200 BCE–400 CE* (Oxford, 2001)

JAMES, William, *The Varieties of Religious Experience: A Study in Human Nature* (London, 1982 edn)

JEFFERSON, Thomas, *The Life and Selected Writings of Thomas Jefferson,* eds. Adrienne Koch and William Peden (New York, 1998)

The Writings of Thomas Jefferson, Vol. XI, eds. A. A. Lipscomb and E. E. Burgh (Washington DC, 1911)

JOHN of the Cross, *The Complete Works of John of the Cross*, trans. E. Allison Peers (London, 1953)

JOHNSON, James William, *The Formation of English Neo-Classical Thought* (Princeton, 1970)

JOHNSON, Luke Timothy, 'The New Testament's Anti-Jewish Slander and the Conventions of Ancient Polemic', *Journal of Biblical Literature*, 108 (1989)

JOHNSON, Mark, *The Meaning of the Body: Aesthetics of Human Understanding* (Chicago, 2007)

JOHNSON, Paul, *A History of the Jews* (London, 1987)

JOHNSTON, William, *Silent Music: The Science of Meditation* (London, 1977 edn)

JORDENS, J. T. F., *Dayananda Sarasvati: His Life and Ideas* (Delhi, 1978)

JOSEPHUS, Flavius, *The Antiquities of the Jews*, trans. William Whiston (Marston Gale, n.d.)

The Jewish War, trans. G. A. Williamson (Harmondsworth, 1967)

Against Apion, trans. H. St J. Thackeray, Loeb Classical Library, No. 186 (London, 1926)

JUERGENSMEYER, Mark and N. Gerald BARRIER, eds., *Sikh Studies: Comparative Perspectives on a Changing Tradition* (Berkeley, 1979)

KAISER, Christopher Barina, *Seeing the Lord's Glory: Kyriocentric Visions and the Dilemma of Early Christology* (Minneapolis, 2014)

KANT, Immanuel, *On History*, ed. Lewis White Beck (Indianapolis, 1963)

KAPILA, Shruti and Faisal DEVJI, *Political Thought in Action: The Bhagavad Gita and Modern India* (Cambridge, 2013)

KARLGREN, Bernhard, trans., *The Book of Odes* (Stockholm, 1950)

KATZ, Steven T., ed., *Mysticism and Sacred Scripture* (Oxford, 2000)

KAUTSKY, John, H., *The Political Consequences of Modernization* (New York, 1972)

    The Politics of Aristocratic Empires, 2nd edn (New Brunswick, 1997)

KEATS, John, *The Letters of John Keats*, ed. H. E. Rollins (Cambridge, MA, 1958)

KEDDIE, Nikki R., ed., *Scholars, Saints and Sufis: Muslim Religious Institutions in the Middle East Since 1500* (Berkeley, 1972)

    ed., *Religion and Politics in Iran: Shi'ism from Quietism to Revolution* (New Haven, 1974)

KEIGHTLEY, David N., 'The Religious Commitment: Shang Theology and the Genesis of Chinese Political Culture', *History of Religions*, 17, 3/4 (February–May 1978)

    'Late Shang Divination: The Magico-Religious Legacy', in Henry Rosemont, ed., *Explorations in Early Chinese Cosmology* (Chico, 1984)

    'Shamanism, Death and the Ancestors: Religious Mediation in Neolithic and Shang China (*c.*5000–1000 BC)', *Asiatische Studien* 52, 3 (1998)

KEPEL, Gilles, *The Prophet and Pharaoh: Muslim Extremism in Egypt*, trans. Jon Rothschild (London, 1985)

    Jihad: The Trail of Political Islam, trans. Antony F. Roberts, 4th edn (London, 2009)

KINSLEY, David R., *The Sword and the Flute: Kali and Krsna: Dark Visions of the Terrible and the Sublime in Hindu Mythology*, 2nd edn (Berkeley, 2000)

KLOSTERMAIER, Klaus K., *A Survey of Hinduism*, 2nd edn (Albany, 1994)

    Hinduism: A Short History (Oxford, 2000)

KOPF, David, *The Brahmo Samaj and the Shaping of the Modern Indian Mind* (Princeton, 1979)

KRAELING, Emil G., *The Old Testament Since the Reformation* (London, 1955)

KRAEMER, David, *The Mind of the Talmud: An Intellectual History of the Bavli* (New York, 1990)

KRAMER, Samuel N., *Sumerian Mythology: A Study of Spiritual and Literary Achievement in the Third Millennium BC* (Philadelphia, 1944)

KRAUSS, Hans-Joachim, *Worship in Israel: A Cultic History of the Old Testament* (Oxford, 1966)

KUGEL, James L., *The Bible As It Was* (Cambridge, MA, 1997)

LAJPAT RAI, Lala, *The Arya Samaj: An Account of Its Origin, Doctrines and Activities, with a Biographical Sketch of the Founder* (London, 1915)

LAKOFF, George and Mark JOHNSON, *Philosophy in the Flesh: The Embodied Mind and Its Challenge to Western Thought* (New York, 1999)

LAL, Ramji, ed., *Communal Problems in India — A Symposium* (Gwalior, 1988)

LAMBERT, W. G., *Babylonian Wisdom Literature* (London, 1960)

LaMOTTE, Etienne, 'La critique d'interprétation dans le bouddhisme', *Annuaire de l'Institut de philologie et histoire orientales et slaves*, Brussels, no. 9 (1949)

> *Histoire du Bouddhisme indien* (Louvain, 1958)

LANG, Jeffrey D., 'Religion and Violence in Hindu Traditions', in Richard Murphy, ed., *The Blackwell Companion to Religion and Violence* (Chichester, 2011)

LAU, D. C., ed. and trans., *Lao-tzu: Tao Te Ching* (London, 1963)

> ed. and trans., *Mencius* (London, 1970)

> ed. and trans., *Confucius: The Analects (Lun yu)* (London, 1979)

LEGGE, James, trans. *The She King, or, The Book of Poetry* (Oxford, 1893)

> trans., *Li Ji: The Book of Rites*, ed. Dai Sheng (Beijing, 2013)

LIENHARD, Marc, 'Luther and the Beginnings of the Reformation', in Jill Raitt, Bernard McGinn and John Meyendorff, eds., *Christian Spirituality*, vol. II: *High Middle Ages and Reformation* (New York, 1988)

LENSKI, Gerhard E., *Power and Privilege: A Theory of Social Stratification* (Chapel Hill, 1966)

LEVERING, Miriam, ed., *Rethinking Scripture: Essays from a Comparative Perspective* (Albany, 1989)

LEWIS, Mark Edward, *Writing and Authority in Early China* (Albany, 1999)

LIGHT, Laura, 'The Bible and the Individual: The Thirteenth-Century Paris Bible', in Susan Boynton and Diane J. Reilly, eds., *The Practice of the Bible in the Middle Ages: Production, Reception, and Performance in Western Christianity* (New York, 2011)

LINCOLN, Bruce, *Holy Terrors: Thinking about Religion after September 11*, 2nd edn (Chicago, 2006)

LINDBERG, David C. and Ronald L. NUMBERS, eds., *God and Nature: Historical Essays on the Encounter between Christianity and Science* (Berkeley, 1986)

LOCKE, John, *A Letter Concerning Toleration* (Indianapolis, 1955)

    An Essay Concerning Human Understanding (Oxford, 1975)

    Two Treatises of Government, ed. Peter Laslett (Cambridge, 1988)

LOEWE, Michael, *Faith, Myth and Reason in Han China* (Indianapolis, 2005)

LOEWE, Michael and Edward L. SHAUGHNESSY, eds., *The Cambridge History of Ancient China: From the Origins of Civilization to 221 BC* (Cambridge, 1999)

LOPEZ, Donald S., ed., *Buddhist Hermeneutics* (Honolulu, 1992)

    ed., *Buddhist Scriptures* (London, 2004)

LORD, A. B., *The Singer of Tales* (Cambridge, MA, 1960)

LOSSKY, Vladimir, *The Mystical Theology of the Eastern Church* (London, 1957)

    'Theology and Mysticism in the Traditions of the Eastern Church', in Richard Woods, ed., *Understanding Mysticism* (Garden City, 1980)

LOUTH, Andrew, *Discerning the Mystery: An Essay on the Nature of Theology* (Oxford, 1983)

    The Origins of the Christian Mystical Tradition: From Plato to Denys (Oxford, 1981)

    Maximus the Confessor (London, 1996)

LOVELACE, R. C., 'Puritan Spirituality: The Search for a Rightly Reformed Church', in Louis Dupré and Don E. Saliers, eds., *Christian Spirituality*, vol. III: *Post Reformation and Modern* (New York, 1989)

LUTHER, Martin, *Luther's Works*, ed. Jaroslav Pelikan and Helmut T. Lehmann, 55 vols. (Philadelphia, 1955–86)

MADAN, T. N., 'The Double-Edged Sword: Fundamentalism and the Sikh Religious Tradition', in Martin E. Marty and R. Scott Appleby, eds., *Fundamentalisms Observed* (Chicago, 1991)

MAGNUS, Bernd and Kathleen M. HIGGINS, eds., *The Cambridge Companion to Nietzsche* (Cambridge, 1996)

MAHONY, William K., *The Artful Universe: An Introduction to the Vedic Religious Imagination* (Albany, 1998)

MANDAIR, Arvind-Pal Singh, 'Sikh Philosophy', in Pashaura Singh and Louis E. Fenech, eds., *The Oxford Handbook of Sikh Studies* (Oxford, 2014)

McAULIFFE, Jane Dammen, ed., *The Cambridge Companion to the Qur'ān* (Cambridge, 2006)

    ed., *Encyclopaedia of the Qur'ān*, 5 vols. (Leiden, 2001–06)

McGILCHRIST, Iain, *The Master and his Emissary: The Divided Brain and the Making of the Western World* (New Haven and London, 2009)

McGRATH, Alister, E., *Reformation Thought: An Introduction*, 4th edn (Oxford, 2012)

    A Life of John Calvin: A Study in the Shaping of Western Culture (Oxford, 1990)

McLEOD, W. H., *The Evolution of the Sikh Community: Five Essays* (Oxford, 1976)

McNEILL, D., *Hand and Mind: What Gestures Reveal About Thought* (Chicago, 1992)

McVEY, Kathleen, *Ephrem the Syrian: Hymns 259–468* (Mahwah, 1989)

MANGUEL, Alberto, *A History of Reading* (London, 1996)

MANN, Gurinder Singh, *The Making of Sikh Scriptures* (Oxford, 2001)

MANN, Thomas, *Joseph and His Brothers*, trans. H. T. Lowe-Porter (London, 1978)

    'The Joseph Novels', in Charles Neider, ed., *The Stature of Thomas Mann* (New York, 1947)

    The Magic Mountain, trans. H. T. Lowe-Porter (London, 1999 edn)

    'The Making of *The Magic Mountain*', in *The Magic Mountain*, trans. H. T. Lowe-Porter (London, 1999)

MARSDEN, George M., *Fundamentalism and American Culture: The Shaping of Twentieth Century Evangelicalism, 1870–1925* (New York, 1980)

MARTY, Martin E. and R. Scott APPLEBY, eds., *Fundamentalisms Observed* (Chicago, 1991)

    Fundamentalisms and Society: Reclaiming the Sciences, the Family, and Education (Chicago, 1993)

    Fundamentalisms and the State: Remaking Polities, Economies, and Militance (Chicago, 1993)

    Accounting for Fundamentalisms: The Dynamic Character of Movements (Chicago, 1994)

    Fundamentalisms Comprehended (Chicago, 1995)

MASPERO, Henri, *China in Antiquity*, trans. Frank A. Kierman Jr., 2nd edn (Folkestone, 1978)

MATCHETT, Freda, *Kṛṣṇa: Lord or Avatāra? The Relationship between Kṛṣṇa and Viśnu* (Richmond, 2001)

METZGER, Thomas, *Escape from Predicament: Neo-Confucianism and China's Evolving Political Culture* (New York, 1977)

MEYENDORFF, John, *Byzantine Theology: Historical Trends and Doctrinal Themes* (New York, 1974)

    Christ in Eastern Christian Thought, trans. Fr Yves Dubois (Baltimore, 1975)

MIGNE, Jean-Paul, ed., *Patrologia Latina*, 217 vols. (Paris, 1841–55)

    ed., *Patrologia Graeca*, 161 vols. (Paris, 1857–66)

MILLER, Barbara Stoler, trans., *The Bhagavad-Gita: Krishna's Counsel in Time of War* (New York, 1986)

MILLER, Robert D. II, SFO, *Oral Tradition in Ancient Israel* (Eugene, 2011)

MILTON, John, *The Poetical Works of John Milton, Vol. I, Paradise Lost*, ed. Helen
    Darbishire (Oxford, 1952)

    Complete Prose Works of John Milton, 8 vols., ed. Don M. Wolfe (New
        Haven, 1953–82)

    The Complete Poetry and Essential Prose of John Milton, eds. William
        Kerrigan, John Rumrich and Stephen M. Fallon (New York, 2007)

MINFORD, John, trans., *I Ching (Yijing): The Book of Change* (London, 2004)

MITCHELL, Richard P., *The Society of the Muslim Brothers* (New York, 1969)

MOMEN, Moojan, *An Introduction to Shi'i Islam: The History and Doctrines of
    Twelver Shi'ism* (Oxford, 1985)

MONTEFIORE, C. G. and H. LOEWE, eds., *A Rabbinic Anthology* (New
    York, 1974)

MOORE, Charles A., ed., *The Chinese Mind* (Honolulu, 1967)

MURPHY, Andrew R., ed., *The Blackwell Companion to Religion and Violence*
    (Chichester, 2011)

NANAMOLI, Bhikku, ed. and trans., *The Life of the Buddha, According to the
    Pali Canon* (Kandy, 1992 edn)

NASR, Sayyed Hossein, *Ideas and Realities of Islam* (London 1971)

    ed., *Islamic Spirituality: Foundations* (New York, 1987)

NASR, Sayyed Hossein, with C. K. DAGLI, M. M. DAKANI, J. E. B.
    LUMBARD and M. RUSTOM, *The Study Quran: A New Translation and
    Commentary* (New York, 2015)

NEIDER, Charles, ed., *The Stature of Thomas Mann* (New York, 1947)

NELSON, Kristina, *The Art of Reciting the Qur'an* (Cairo, 2001)

NEUSNER, Jacob, *The Ecology of Religion: From Writing to Religion in the
    Study of Judaism* (Nashville, 1989)

    Judaism: The Evidence of the Mishnah (New York, 1998)

    Medium and Message in Judaism (Atlanta, 1989)

    'The Use of the Mishnah for the History of Judaism prior to the time
        of the Mishnah', *Journal for the Study of Judaism*, 11 (December 1980)

    'The Mishnah in Philosophical Context and Out of Canonical Bounds',
        Journal of Biblical Literature 11 (Summer 1993)

NEWTON, Sir Isaac, *Sir Isaac Newton's Mathematical Principles of Natural
    Philosophy and His System of the World*, trans. Andrew Motte; rev. Florian
    Cajori (Berkeley, 1962)

    The Correspondence of Isaac Newton, 7 vols., eds. H. W. Turnbull, J. F.
        Scott, A. R. Hill and L. Tilling (Cambridge, 1954–77)

NIDITCH, Susan, *Oral World and Written Word: Ancient Israelite Literature*
    (Louisville, 1996)

NIETZSCHE, Friedrich, *Thus Spoke Zarathustra*, trans. R. J. Hollingdale (London, 1961)

    On the Genealogy of Morals, trans. Walter Kaufman and R. J. Hollingdale (New York, 1967)

    Ecce Homo: How One Becomes What One Is, trans. R. J. Hollingdale (London, 1979)

    The Birth of Tragedy, trans. Shaun Whiteside, ed. Michael Tanner (London, 1993)

    The Genealogy of Memory, trans. C. Diethe (Cambridge, 1994)

NOLL, Mark A., ed., *Religion and American Politics: From the Colonial Period to the 1980s* (Oxford, 1990)

NOLTE, Charlotte, *Being and Meaning in Thomas Mann's Joseph Novels* (London, 1996)

NORTH, Gary, *In the Shadow of Plenty: The Biblical Blueprint for Welfare* (Fort Worth, 1986)

    The Sinai Strategy: Economics and the Ten Commandments (Tyler, 1986)

NOTH, Martin, *The Laws of the Pentateuch and Other Studies* (Edinburgh, 1966)

    The Deuteronomistic History (Sheffield, 1981)

OBEROI, Harjot, 'From Ritual to Counter-Ritual: Rethinking the Hindu–Sikh Question, 1884–1915', in Joseph T. O'Connell, ed., *Sikh History and Religion in the Twentieth Century* (Toronto, 1988)

    'Sikh Fundamentalism: Translating History into Theory', in Martin E. Marty and R. Scott Appleby, eds., *Fundamentalisms and the State: Remaking Polities, Economies, and Militance* (Chicago, 1993)

OCHS, Peter, ed., *The Return to Scripture in Judaism and Christianity: Essays in Postcritical Scriptural Interpretation* (Eugene, 1993)

O'FLAHERTY, Wendy (see also Wendy DONIGER), ed., *The Critical Study of Sacred Texts* (Berkeley, 1979)

OLIVELLE, Patrick, ed. and trans., *Samnyasa Upanisads: Hindu Scriptures on Asceticism and Renunciation* (Oxford, 1992)

    ed. and trans., *Upanisads* (Oxford, 1996)

    'The Renouncer Tradition', in Gavin Flood, ed., *The Blackwell Companion to Hinduism* (Oxford, 2003)

OLLENBURGER, Ben C., *Zion: The City of the Great King: A Theological Symbol of the Jerusalem Cult* (Sheffield, 1987)

ONG, Walter J., *Orality and Literacy: The Technologizing of the Word* (London, 1982)

ORIGEN, *Origen: Contra Celsum*, ed. and trans. Henry Chadwick (Cambridge, 1965)

Origen: On First Principles, trans. G. W. Butterworth (New York, 1966)

Origen: The Song of Songs: Commentary and Homilies, trans. J. P. Lawson (New York, 1956)

ORNSTEIN, Robert E., 'Two Sides of the Brain', in Richard Woods, ed., *Understanding Mysticism* (Garden City, 1980)

OTTO, Rudolf, *The Idea of the Holy: An Inquiry into the Non-Rational Factor in the Idea of the Divine and Its Relation to the Rational*, trans. John W. Harvey (Oxford, London and New York, 1958)

PADOUX, André, 'Mantras – What Are They?', in Harvey P. Alper, ed., *Understanding Mantras* (Delhi, 2012 edn)

PALMER, Martin, trans., with Jay RAMSAY and Victoria FINLAY, *The Most Venerable Book* [Shang Shu] (London, 2014)

trans., with Elizabeth BREUILLY, *The Book of Chuang Tzu* (London, 1996)

PANKSEPP, J., *Affective Neuroscience: The Foundations of Human and Animal Emotions* (Oxford, 1998)

PATTON, Lorie L., ed., *Authority, Anxiety and Canon: Essays in Vedic Interpretation* (Albany, 1994)

'The Failure of Allegory: Notes on Textual Violence in the *Bhagavad Gita*', in John Renard, ed., *Fighting Words: Religion, Violence and the Interpretation of Sacred Texts* (Berkeley, 2012)

PELIKAN, Jaroslav, *The Christian Tradition: A History of the Development of Doctrine*, 5 vols. (Chicago, 1971–89)

Whose Bible Is It? A History of the Scriptures Through the Ages (New York, 2005)

ed., *The World Treasury of Modern Religious Thought* (Boston, MA, 1990)

PETERSON, Willard J., 'Fang-chih: Western Learning and the "Investigation of Things"', in Wm. Theodore de Bary, ed., *The Unfolding of Neo-Confucianism* (New York, 1975)

PHILO, *Philo in Ten Volumes*, ed. and trans. F. H. Colson and G. H. Whitaker (Cambridge, MA, 1950)

PLATO, *Complete Works*, ed. John M. Cooper (Indianapolis, 1997)

PORTER, J. M., ed., *Luther: Selected Political Writings* (Eugene, 2003)

PORTER, Roy, 'The Scientific Revolution and Universities', in Hilde de Ridder-Symoens, ed., *Universities in Early Modern Europe (1500–1800)* (Cambridge, 1986)

POWERS, John, *A Bull of a Man: Images of Masculinity, Sex and the Body in Indian Buddhism* (Cambridge, 2009)

PUETT, Michael J., *To Become a God: Cosmology, Sacrifice and Self-Divinization in Early China* (Cambridge, MA, 2002)

QUEEN, Sarah A., *From Chronicle to Canon: The Hermeneutics of the Spring and Autumn According to Tung Chung-shu* (Cambridge, 1996)
  trans., with John A. MAJOR, *Luxuriant Gems of the Spring and Autumn* (New York, 2016)
QUTB, Said, *This Religion of Islam* (Gary, n.d.)
  Milestones (Delhi, 1998)
RAHMAN, Fazlur, *The Philosophy of Mulla Sadra* (Albany, 1973)
  Islam (Chicago, 1979)
  Major Themes of the Qur'an, 2nd edn (Chicago, 2009 edn)
  'Sunnah and Hadith', *Islamic Studies*, I (1962)
RAITT, Jill, ed., with Bernard MCGINN and John MEYENDORFF, *Christian Spirituality*, vol. II: *High Middle Ages and Reformation* (New York, 1988)
RENARD, John, ed., *Fighting Words: Religion, Violence and the Interpretation of Sacred Texts* (Berkeley, 2012)
RENOU, Louis, *Religions of Ancient India* (London, 1953)
  'Sur la notion de *brahman*', *Journal Asiatique*, 237 (1949)
RHYS DAVIDS, T. W., *Dialogues of the Buddha*, 2 vols. (London, 1899)
RIPPIN, Andrew, ed., *Approaches to the History of the Interpretation of the Qur'ān* (Oxford, 1988)
  ed., *The Blackwell Companion to the Qur'ān* (Oxford, 2006)
ROBERTSON, Ritchie, ed., *The Cambridge Companion to Thomas Mann* (Cambridge, 2002)
ROUSSEAU, Jean-Jacques, *Discourse on the Origin of Inequality*, ed. Greg Boroson (Minneola, 2004)
RUDAVSKY, David, *Modern Jewish Religious Movements: A History of Emancipation and Adjustment*, rev. edn (New York, 1967)
RUMI, Jalal ad-Din, *The Masnavi*, trans. Jawid Mojaddedi, 3 vols. (Oxford, 2004, 2007, 2013)
RUTHVEN, Malise, *A Satanic Affair: Salman Rushdie and the Rage of Islam* (London, 1990)
SACHEDINA, Abdulaziz Abdulhussein, *Islamic Messianism: The Idea of the Mahdi in Twelver Shi'ism* (Albany, 1981)
SACKS, Jonathan, *The Dignity of Difference: How to Avoid the Clash of Civilizations*, rev. edn (London, 2003)
SAEED, Abdullah, *Reading the Qur'an in the Twenty-First Century: A Contextualist Approach* (London, 2014)
SAID, Labib as-, *The Recited Koran: A History of the First Recorded Version* (Princeton, 1975)

SÁNCHEZ, Francisco, *Opera Philosophica*, ed. Joachim de Carvalho (Coimbra, 1955)

SANDS, Kristin Zahra, *Sufi Commentaries on the Qur'an in Classical Islam* (London, 2006)

SAPERSTEIN, Marc, ed., *Essential Papers on Messianic Movements and Personalities in Jewish History* (London, 1992)

SARASWATI, Swami Dayananda, *Light of Truth, or, An English Translation of the Stayarth Prakaś*, trans. Dr Chiranjiva Bharaddvaja (New Delhi, 1975)

SARTRE, Jean-Paul, *The Imaginary: A Phenomenological Psychology of the Imagination*, trans. Kenneth Williford and David Rudrauf (London, 2012)

SCHIMMEL, Annemarie, *Deciphering the Signs of God: A Phenomenological Approach to Islam* (Edinburgh, 1994)

SCHNIEDEWIND, William M., *How the Bible Became a Book* (Cambridge, 2004)

SCHOLEM, Gershom, *Major Trends in Jewish Mysticism* (New York, 1955 edn)
    ed., *Zohar: The Book of Splendor: Basic Readings from the Kabbalah* (New York, 1959)
    On the Kabbalah and Its Symbolism, trans. Ralph Manheim (New York, 1965)
    The Messianic Idea in Judaism and Other Essays on Jewish Spirituality (New York, 1971)

SCHWARTZ, Benjamin I., *The World of Thought in Ancient China* (Cambridge, MA, 1985)

SCHWARTZ, Louis, ed., *The Cambridge Companion to Paradise Lost* (Cambridge, 2014)

SCHWARTZ, Seth, *Imperialism and Jewish Society, 200 BCE to 640 CE* (Princeton, 2001)
    'Language, Power and Identity in Ancient Palestine', *Past and Present*, 148 (1995)

SEGAL, Charles, 'Catharsis, Audience and Closure in Greek Tragedy', in M. S. Silk, ed., *Tragedy and the Tragic: Greek Theatre and Beyond* (Oxford, 1996)

SEGAL, M. H., 'The Promulgation of the Authoritative Text of the Hebrew Bible', *Journal of Biblical Literature*, 72 (1963)

SELENGUT, Charles, 'By Torah Alone: Yeshiva Fundamentalism in Jewish Life', in Martin E. Marty and R. Scott Appleby, eds., *Accounting for Fundamentalisms: The Dynamic Character of Movements* (Chicago, 1994)

SELLS, Michael, ed. and trans., *Early Islamic Mysticism: Sufi, Qur'ān, Mi'rāj, Poetic and Theological Writings* (New York, 1996)
    ed. and trans., *Approaching the Qur'an: The Earliest Revelations* (Ashland, 1999)

'Sound, Spirit and Gender in Surāt al-Qadra', *Journal of the American Oriental Society*, 3, 2 (April/May 1991)

'Sound and Meaning in Surāt al-Qari'a', *Arabica*, 40, 3 (1993)

SELORAN, Thomas W., 'Forming One Body: The Cheng Brothers and Their Circle', in Tu Weiming and Mary Evelyn Tucker, eds., *Confucian Spirituality*, vol. II (New York, 2004)

SHACKLE, Christopher, 'Repackaging the Ineffable: Changing Styles of Sikh Scriptural Commentary', *Bulletin of the School of Oriental and African Studies*, 71, 2 (2008)

SHACKLE, Christopher and Arvind-Pal Singh MANDAIR, eds. and trans., *Teachings of the Sikh Gurus: Selections from the Sikh Scriptures* (Oxford and New York, 2005)

SHAUGHNESSY, Edward L., *Before Confucius: Studies in the Creation of the Chinese Classics* (Albany, 1997)

'Western Zhou History', in Michael Loewe and Edward L. Shaughnessy, eds., *The Cambridge History of Ancient China: From the Origins of Civilization to 221 BCE* (Cambridge, 1999)

SHEA, William M. and Peter A. HUFF, eds., *Knowledge and Belief in America: Enlightenment Traditions and Modern Religious Thought* (New York, 1995)

SHEEHAN, Jonathan, *The Enlightenment Bible: Translation, Scholarship, Culture* (Princeton, 2005)

SHULMAN, David, 'Toward a Historical Poetics of the Sanskrit Epics', *International Folklore Review*, 8 (1991)

SILK, M. S., ed., *Tragedy and the Tragic: Greek Theatre and Beyond* (Oxford, 1996)

SINGER, Milton, ed., *Krishna: Myths, Rites and Attitudes* (Honolulu, 1966)

SINGH, Pashaura, *The Guru Granth Sahib: Canon, Meaning and Authority* (New Delhi, 2000)

Life and Work of Guru Arjan: History, Memory and Biography in the Sikh Tradition (New Delhi, 2006)

'Competing Views of Canon Formation in the Sikh Tradition: A Focus on Recent Controversy', *Religious Studies Review*, 28, 1 (2002)

'Scripture as Guru in the Sikh Tradition', *Religion Compass*, 2/4 (2008)

'An Overview of Sikh History', in Pashaura Singh and Louis E. Fenech, eds., *The Oxford Handbook of Sikh Studies* (Oxford, 2014)

SINGH, Pashaura and Louis E. FENECH, eds., *The Oxford Handbook of Sikh Studies* (Oxford, 2014)

SLINGERLAND, Edward, trans., *Confucius: Analects, with Selections from Traditional Commentaries* (Indianapolis, 2003)

SLOEK, Johannes, *Devotional Language*, trans. Henrik Mossin (Berlin, 1996)

SMALLEY, Beryl, *The Study of the Bible in the Middle Ages* (Oxford, 1941)

    Studies in Medieval Thought and Learning (Oxford, 1979)

SMITH, Brian K., *Reflections on Resemblance, Ritual and Religion* (Oxford, 1992)

SMITH, Christian and Melinda Lundquist DENTON, *Soul Searching: The Religious and Spiritual Lives of American Teenagers* (New York, 2005)

SMITH, Frederick M., 'Puraveda', in Lorie L. Patton, ed., *Authority, Anxiety, and Canon: Essays in Vedic Interpretation* (Albany, 1994)

SMITH, John D., ed. and trans., *The Mahabharata: An Abridged Translation* (London, 2009)

    'The Two Sanskrit Epics', in A. T. Hatto, ed., *Traditions of Heroic and Epic Poetry* (London, 1981)

SMITH, Jonathan Z., *Map Is Not Territory: Studies in the History of Religions* (Chicago, 1978)

    Imagining Religion: From Babylon to Jonestown (Chicago, 1982)

SMITH, Kidder, '*Zhou yi* Interpretation from Accounts in the *Zuozhuan*', *Harvard Journal of Asiatic Studies*, 48 (1989)

    'The Difficulty of the *Yijing*', *Chinese Literature: Essays, Articles, Reviews (CLEAR)*, 15 (December 1993)

SMITH, Mark S., *The Early History of God: Yahweh and the Other Deities in Ancient Israel* (San Francisco, 1987)

    The Origins of Biblical Monotheism: Israel's Polytheistic Background and the Ugaritic Texts (New York, 2001)

SMITH, Wilfred Cantwell, *Islam in Modern History* (Princeton, 1957)

    The Meaning and End of Religion: A New Approach to the Religious Traditions of Mankind (New York, 1962)

    Belief and History (Charlottesville, 1985)

    Faith and Belief: The Difference Between Them (Princeton, 1987)

    What Is Scripture? A Comparative Approach (London, 1993)

SPELLBERG, Denise A., *Thomas Jefferson's Qur'an: Islam and the Founders* (New York, 2013)

SPERLING, David S., *The Original Torah: The Political Intent of the Bible's Writers* (New York, 1998)

SPILKA, B., with R. W. HEAD, B. HUNDSBERGER and R. GORSUCH, *The Psychology of Religion*, 3rd edn (Guilford, NY, 2003)

SPINOZA, Benedict de, *Tractatus Thelogico-Politicus*, trans. R. H. M. Elwes (London, 1895)

STAAL, Frits, 'Oriental Ideas on the Origin of Language', *Journal of the American Oriental Society*, 99 (1979)

 'Vedic Mantras', in Harvey P. Alper, ed., *Understanding Mantras* (Delhi, 2012 edn)

STEINER, George, *Real Presences: Is There Anything in What We Say?* (Cambridge, 2004)

STEVENSON, Margaret Sinclair, *The Heart of Jainism* (London, 1915)

STORR, Anthony, *Music and the Mind* (London, 1992)

STRENG, Frederick J., *Understanding Religious Life*, 3rd edn (Belmont, 1985)

TABARI, Abu Jafar Muhammad ibn Jarir al-, *The Commentary on the Qur'ān*, trans. and abridged J. Cooper (Oxford, 1987)

TAGORE, G. V., *The Bhagavata Purana* (Delhi, 1979)

TAYLOR, Rodney L., *The Confucian Way of Contemplation: Okada Takehiko and the Tradition of Quiet-Sitting* (Columbia, 1988)

 The Religious Dimensions of Confucianism (Albany, 1990)

 'Confucian Spirituality and Qing Thought', in Tu Weiming and Mary Evelyn Tucker, eds., *Confucian Spirituality,* vol. II (New York, 2004)

TERESA of Avila, *The Interior Castle*, trans. E. Allison Peers (New York, 1964)

THAPAR, Romila, *Aśoka and the Decline of the Mauryas* (Oxford, 1961)

 Early India: From the Origins to AD 1300 (Berkeley, 2002)

 'Genealogical Patterns as Perceptions of the Past', *Studies in History*, 7, 1 (1991)

 'Historical Realities', in Ramji Lal, ed., *Communal Problems in India – A Symposium* (Gwalior, 1988)

THOMAS, Rosalind, *Literacy and Orality in Ancient Greece* (Cambridge, 1992)

THURMAN, Robert A. F., trans., *The Holy Teaching of Vimalakirti* (University Park, 1976)

 'Buddhist Hermeneutics', *Journal of the American Academy of Religion*, 46, 1 (January 1978)

 'The Teaching of Vimalakirti', in Wm. Theodore de Bary and Irene Bloom, eds., *Eastern Canons: Approaches to the Asian Classics* (New York, 1990)

TIBI, Bassam, 'The Worldview of Sunni Arab Fundamentalists: Attitudes toward Modern Science and Technology', in Martin E. Marty and R. Scott Appleby, eds., *Fundamentalisms and Society: Reclaiming the Sciences, the Family, and Education* (Chicago, 1993)

TOULMIN, Stephen, *Cosmopolis: The Hidden Agenda of Modernity* (Chicago, 1990)

TRIMBLE, Michael R., *The Soul in the Brain: The Cerebral Basis of Language, Art, and Belief* (Baltimore, 2007)

TSUKAMOTO, Z., *A History of Early Chinese Buddhism*, trans. L. Hurvitz (Tokyo, 1985)

TU Weiming, *Confucian Thought: Selfhood as Creative Transformation* (Albany, 1985)

    Way, Learning and Politics: Essays on the Confucian Intellectual (Albany, 1993)

    'Toward a Third Epoch of Confucianism: A Background Understanding', in Irene Eber, ed., *Confucianism: The Dynamics of Tradition* (New York, 1986)

    'The Confucian Sage: Exemplar of Personal Knowledge', in John Stratton Hawley, ed., *Saints and Virtues* (Berkeley, 1987)

    'The Search for Roots in Industrial East Asia: The Case of Confucian Revival', in Martin E. Marty and R. Scott Appleby, eds., *Fundamentalisms Observed* (Chicago, 1991)

    'Perceptions of Learning (*Hsüeh*) in Early Ch'ing Thought', in Tu Weiming, ed., *Way, Learning and Politics: Essays on the Confucian Intellectual* (Albany, 1993)

    'The Ecological Turn in New Confucian Humanism: Implications for China and the World', in Tu Weiming and Mary Evelyn Tucker, eds., *Confucian Spirituality*, vol. II (New York, 2004)

TU Weiming and Mary Evelyn TUCKER, eds., *Confucian Spirituality*, 2 vols. (New York, 2003, 2004)

TURNER, Denys, *The Darkness of God: Negativity in Christian Mysticism* (Cambridge, 1995)

    Faith, Reason and the Existence of God (Cambridge, 2004)

TURNER, Denys and Oliver DAVIES, eds., *Silence and the Word: Negative Theology and Incarnation* (Cambridge, 2002)

TURNER, James, *Without God, Without Creed: The Origins of Unbelief in America* (Baltimore, MD, 1985)

TWITCHELL, James, 'Two Cheers for Materialism', in Juliet B. Schor and Douglas B. Holt, eds., *The Consumer Society Reader* (New York, 2000)

ULRICH, Eugene, *The Dead Sea Scrolls and the Origins of the Bible* (Grand Rapids, 1999)

VAN BUITENEN, J. A. B., ed. and trans., *The Mahabharata*, 5 vols (Chicago, 1973–81)

VAN LANCKER, Diana, 'Personal Relevance and the Human Right Hemisphere', *Brain and Cognition*, 17 (1991)

VAN LIERE, Frans, *An Introduction to the Medieval Bible* (Cambridge, 2014)

VAN NORDEN, Bryan W., ed., *Confucius and the Analects: New Essays* (Oxford, 2002)

VAN SETERS, John, *In Search of History: Historiography in the Ancient World and the Origins of Biblical History* (New Haven, 1983)

VERMES, Geza, ed. and trans., *The Complete Dead Sea Scrolls in English* (London, 1997)

VON RAD, Gerard, *The Problem of the Hexateuch and Other Essays*, trans. E. W. Trueman (Edinburgh, 1966 edn)

VON TEVENAR, Gudrun, 'Zarathustra: "That Malicious Dionysian"', in Ken Gemes and John Richardson, eds., *The Oxford Handbook of Nietzsche* (Oxford, 2013)

WALEY, Arthur, trans., *The Book of Songs* (London, 1937)
        trans., *The Analects of Confucius* (New York, 1992 edn)

WARD, Benedicta, ed. and trans., *The Prayers and Meditations of St Anselm and the Proslogion* (London, 1973)

WARD, Mrs Humphrey, *Robert Elsmere* (Lincoln, NB, 1969 edn)

WARFIELD, B. B., *The Inspiration and Authority of the Bible* (Philadelphia, 1948 edn)

WATSON, Burton, ed. and trans., *Records of the Grand Historian* (New York, 1961)
        ed. and trans., *Han Fei Tzu: Basic Writings* (New York, 1964)
        ed. and trans., *Xunzi: Basic Writings* (New York, 2003)
        ed. and trans., *Mozi: Basic Writings* (New York, 2003)

WATT, W. Montgomery, *Muhammad's Mecca: History and the Qur'an* (Edinburgh, 1988)

WEBER, Max, *The Religion of China*, trans. H. Gerth (New York, 1951)
        The Protestant Ethic and the Spirit of Capitalism and Other Writings, ed. and trans. Peter Baehr and Gordon C. Wells (Harmondsworth, 2005)

WEINFELD, Moshe, *Deuteronomy and the Deuteronomic School* (Oxford, 1972)

WHITAKER, Jarrod L., *Strong Arms and Drinking Strength: Masculinity, Violence and the Body in Ancient India* (Oxford, 2011)

WHYBRAY, R. N., *The Making of the Pentateuch: A Methodological Study* (Sheffield, 1987)

WILLIAMS, Paul, *Mahayana Buddhism: The Doctrinal Foundations* (London, 1989)

WILLIAMS, Rowan, *Arius: Heresy and Tradition* (London, 1987)

WILSON, Stephen G., *Related Strangers: Jews and Christians, 70–170 CE* (Minneapolis, 1995)

WIRT, Sherwood Eliot, ed., *Spiritual Awakening: Classic Writings of the Eighteenth Century to Inspire and Help the Twentieth Century Reader* (Tring, 1988)

WOODS, Richard, ed., *Understanding Mysticism* (Garden City, 1980)

YAO, Xinzhong, *An Introduction to Confucianism* (Cambridge, 2000)

YATES, Frances A., *The Art of Memory* (London, 1966)

YOVEL, Yirmiyahu, *Spinoza and Other Heretics,* vol. I: *The Marrano of Reason* (Princeton, 1989)

ZHU Xi, *Chu-tsu yü-lei,* ed. Li Cheng-to (Peking, 1986)
> *Learning to be a Sage: Selections from the 'Conversations of Master Chu',* *Arranged Topically,* trans. and commentary Daniel K. Gardner (Berkeley, 1990)

ZÜRCHER, E., *The Buddhist Conquest of China: The Spread and Adaptation of Buddhism in Early Medieval China* (Leiden, 1959)

NOTES

Full bibliographic details of abbreviated entries are given in the Select Bibliography.

Introduction

1. Sartre. • 2. Trimble, 204–05; Spilka et al., 150, 209. • 3. Griffiths, 31. Griffiths' emphasis. • 4. Van Lancker; McGilchrist, 40–54; Ornstein. • 5. McGilchrist, 78–93. • 6. James. • 7. Steiner, 217. • 8. Streng, 2. Streng's emphasis. • 9. Ibid., 3. • 10. William Wordsworth, 'Lines Composed a Few Miles Above Tintern Abbey, on Revisiting the Banks of the Wye During a Tour, July 13, 1798', lines 39–42. • 11. Ibid., lines 88–89. • 12. Kautsky, *Aristocratic Empires*. • 13. Mark Johnson, *The Body in the Mind: The Bodily Basis of Meaning, Imagination, and Reason* (Chicago, 1987). • 14. Sloek, 53–96.

PART ONE: COSMOS AND SOCIETY

1. Israel: Remembering in Order to Belong

1. Genesis 2:9. Unless otherwise stated, all quotations from the Hebrew Bible and the New Testament are taken from *The Jerusalem Bible* (London, 1966). • 2. Genesis 2:17. • 3. Carr, *Tablet of the Heart*, 60–61. • 4. Lenski, 227–28; A. L. Oppenheim, *Ancient Mesopotamia: Portrait of a Dead Civilization* (Chicago, 1977), 88–89. • 5. Kramer, 118. • 6. Gottwald, *Politics of Ancient Israel*, 118–19. • 7. Genesis 3:1–7. • 8. Quoted in Carr, *Tablet of the Heart*, 17. • 9. Genesis 3:21. • 10. Genesis 3:1. • 11. Weinfeld, 59–157. • 12. Fensham, 176–82. • 13. Lambert, 134–35. • 14. Assmann, *Cultural Memory and Early Civilization*, 208–12, 231. • 15. Jan Assmann, 'Remembering in Order to Belong: Writing, Memory, and Identity', in Assmann, *Religion and Cultural Memory*, 86–95. • 16. Carr, *Tablet of the Heart*, 11–12. • 17. Ibid., 4–6; Thomas, 91–92. • 18. William A. Graham, *Beyond the Written Word*, 60. • 19. Carr, *Tablet of the Heart*, 8, 6–11. • 20. Ibid., 31. • 21. Harris, 12–20. • 22. Carr, *Tablet of the Heart*, 11. • 23. Ibid., 32. • 24. Ibid., 32–36. • 25. Proverbs

22:17–19, 22–24. • 26. Finkelstein and Silberman, 89–92. • 27. D. H. Hopkins.
• 28. Kautsky, *Aristocratic Empires*, 275. • 29. Joshua 9:15; 1 Samuel 27:10, 30:23;
2 Samuel 21; Judges 1:16, 4:11. • 30. Cross, *Canaanite Myth*, 52. • 31. Genesis 4.
• 32. Finkelstein and Silberman, 103–07; Dever, 110–18. • 33. Deuteronomy
32:8–9. • 34. Mark S. Smith, *Origins of Biblical Monotheism*, 93–96. • 35. Psalms
82:2–5. • 36. Leviticus 25:23–28, 35–55; Deuteronomy 24:19–22; Gottwald,
Hebrew Bible, 162. • 37. Psalms 89:10–13; 93:1–4; Job 7:12; 9:8; 26:12; 40:15–24.
• 38. Deuteronomy 33:2; cf. Exodus 15:1–8; Habakkuk 3:3–15. • 39. Cross, *From
Epic to Canon*, 24–40. • 40. Exodus 15:8, 10. • 41. Exodus 15:16–18. • 42. Exodus
15:14–15. • 43. Cross, *From Epic to Canon*, 47. • 44. Genesis 28:10–19. • 45.
Genesis 32:23–32. • 46. Gottwald, *Politics of Ancient Israel*, 177–79. • 47. 1 Kings
7:15–26. • 48. Dever, 267–69. • 49. 2 Samuel 8:17; 20:25; 1 Kings 4:3. • 50. 1
Kings 4:3. • 51. Proverbs 22:17–19; adapted Carr, *Tablet of the Heart*, 126. • 52.
Proverbs 2:2; Psalms 788:1; 1 Kings 3:9; Proverbs 3:3, cf. 6:21. • 53. Proverbs
13:24; 22:15; 26:3; 29:17. • 54. Proverbs 5:12–14. • 55. Carr, *Tablet of the Heart*,
127–31. • 56. Psalms 110:1. • 57. Psalms 2:7. • 58. Deuteronomy 31:19–22; 32:1.
• 59. Exodus 31:18; 32:16. • 60. Niditch, 79–80. • 61. Isaiah 4:3; Deuteronomy
12:1; Exodus 32:32; Psalms 69:28; 139:6. • 62. 2 Samuel 7:9–10. • 63. Clifford,
57–68; cf. Psalm 47. • 64. Ibid., 68. • 65. Clifford, *passim*; R. E. Clements, *God
and Temple* (Oxford, 1965), 47; Kraus, 201–04. • 66. Psalms 72:7. • 67. Psalms
46:5–9; 48:12–13. • 68 Dar as-Sharrukun Cylinder, trans. Schniedewind, 65. •
69. Ibid., 65–66. • 70. Niditch, 339–77. • 71. Deuteronomy 17:9–12; 31:2–13;
Numbers 5:23; Hosea 4:6. • 72. 1 Chronicles 25:2–6; 2 Chronicles 5:12. • 73.
Psalms 1:2; Carr, *Tablet of the Heart*, 152–53. • 74. 2 Kings 2:1–18; 4:38. • 75. Isaiah
29:13–14. • 76. Isaiah 8:16; 30:8; Jeremiah 36:1–3; Habakkuk 2:2–3. • 77. Carr,
Tablet of the Heart, 143–44. • 78. Amos 7:14. • 79. Finkelstein and Silberman,
206–12. • 80. Amos 2:6–7. • 81. Amos 5:21–24. • 82. Amos 1:3; 2:3; 6:14;
2:4–16. • 83. Amos 7:17. • 84. A. Kirk Grayson, 'Assyrian Rule of Conquered
Territory in Ancient Western Asia', in Jack Sasson, ed., *Civilizations of the Near East*
(New York, 1995), 959–68. • 85. Amos 3:8. • 86. Amos 7:15. • 87. Amos 9:1. •
88. Jeremiah 1:9. • 89. Jeremiah 29:7, 9. • 90. Hosea 1:2; Abraham Heschel, *The
Prophets*, 2 vols. (New York, 1962), I, 52–57. • 91. Hosea 3:1–5. • 92. Hosea 14:1.
• 93. Carr, *Holy Resilience*, 25. • 94. Hosea 6:6; my emendation. • 95. Carr, *Holy
Resilience*, 25, 35–36. • 96. Hosea 12:3–5. • 97. Hosea 12:13. • 98. Hosea 11:4.
• 99. Hosea 11:5 • 100. Isaiah 6. • 101. Isaiah 2:2–3. • 102. Isaiah 7:14; the
Septuagint, the Greek translation of the Hebrew Bible, would translate *alma* as
parthenos ('virgin'). • 103. Isaiah 9:1. • 104. Isaiah 9:5. • 105. Isaiah 9:6. • 106. 2
Kings 21:1–18; 2 Chronicles 33:1–10. • 107. Ahlström, 734. • 108. Richard Eliot
Friedman, 87–88. • 109. 2 Kings 22. • 110. Deuteronomy 27. • 111. Deuteronomy
17:14–20. • 112. 2 Kings 22:11. • 113. 2 Kings 23:4–20. • 114. Jan Assmann,
'What is "Cultural Memory"?', in Assmann, *Religion and Cultural Memory*, 3. • 115.
Bernard M. Levinson, *Deuteronomy and the Hermeneutics of Legal Innovation* (Oxford,

1997), 148–49. • 116. Deuteronomy 11:21; 12:5. • 117. Deuteronomy 17:18–20. • 118. Jeremiah 44:15–19; Ezekiel 8. • 119. Deuteronomy 7:22–26. • 120. Carr, *Tablet of the Heart*, 134–46. • 121. Deuteronomy 4:4–9, 44. • 122. Niditch, 100. • 123. Deuteronomy 6:4–9. • 124. Joshua 1:8. • 125. Jan Assmann, 'What is "Cultural Memory"?', in Assmann, *Religion and Cultural Memory*, 19–20. • 126. Deuteronomy 8:3. • 127. Deuteronomy 6:10–12. • 128. Assmann, *Cultural Memory*, 191–93. • 129. Jeremiah 36:29. • 130. Niditch, 104–05.

2. *India: Sound and Silence*

1. Edwin Bryant, *The Quest for the Origins of Vedic Culture: The Indo-Aryan Debate* (Oxford, 2001); S. C. Kak, 'On the Chronology of Ancient India', *Indian Journal of History and Science*, 22, 3 (1987); Colin Renfrew, *Archaeology and Language: The Puzzle of Indo-European Origins* (London, 1987). • 2. Holdrege, 229–30. • 3. Klostermaier, *Survey of Hinduism*, 68. • 4. Aitereya Aranyaka, 5.5.3, trans. J. G. Staal, 'The Concept of Scripture in Indian Tradition', in Juergensmeyer and Barrier, eds., 122–23; Coburn, 104. • 5. Wilfred Cantwell Smith, *What Is Scripture?*, 139. • 6. Carpenter, 20. • 7. Brian K. Smith, 20–26. • 8. Kautsky, *Aristocratic Empires*. • 9. Doniger, *The Hindus*, 114. • 10. Whitaker, 24–28. • 11. Rig Veda (RV) 4.22.9; 8.100.1. • 12. RV 4.1.15. • 13. RV 1.166.7; 6.66.10. • 14. RV 9.111.3; 8.66.9; 2.25.24. • 15. Renou, *Religions of Ancient India*, 65–66. • 16. Ibid., 19. • 17. RV 10.4.3–5. • 18. RV 3.7.2; 8.18.10; 8.91.5–6. • 19. Mahony, 11–13. • 20. RV 10.90; 1.164.41. • 21. Heesterman, 'Ritual, Revelation and the Axial Age', 403. • 22. Heesterman, *Broken World*, 126. • 23. Klostermaier, *Survey of Hinduism*, 130. • 24. Griffiths, 58–59. • 25. Elizarenkova, 19. • 26. RV 8.48.3, 11; trans. Doniger. • 27. RV 3.59.1. • 28. RV 8.48.9; 3.5.3; 1.26.2–4; trans. Doniger. • 29. RV 1.164.46; trans. Doniger. • 30. RV 1.11.9; 5.41.17; 6.74.2; Mahony, 102–04. • 31. RV 10.125.1, 7–8; trans. Doniger. The Ashvins were divine twins, the sacred guardians of fertility. • 32. John 1:1–2. • 33. Sloek, 63–67. • 34. Wilfred Cantwell Smith, *What Is Scripture?*, 234. • 35. Johannes Ruysbroek, *De Spiegel dar Ensige Sulichpichest*, quoted in Dupré, 454; my emphasis. • 36. Johnston, 33, 55–57. • 37. RV 6.9.6; trans. Doniger. • 38. RV 1.139.2; trans. Gonda, *Vision*, 69; cf. 1.18.5; 1.139.2; 1.22. • 39. Elizarenkova, 16–17. • 40. Gonda, 'The Indian Mantra'. • 41. Michael Witzel, 'Vedas and Upanisads', in Flood, ed., *Blackwell Companion to Hinduism*, 69, 71; Holdrege, 278; Gonda, *Vision*, 39, 42–50. • 42. RV 5.29.15; trans. Griffith. • 43. Mahony, 216–18. • 44. Elizarenkova, 15–16. • 45. Gonda, *Vision*, 27–34, 56–57. • 46. Wilfred Cantwell Smith, *What Is Scripture?*, 138. • 47. RV 4.13.2–3. • 48. RV 6.70.1. • 49. Elizarenkova, 17–18. • 50. RV 10.54.2. • 51. Renou, *Religions of Ancient India*, 5, 11. • 52. Elizarenkova, 26–28. • 53. RV 7.23. • 54. Findly, 32–44. • 55. RV 6.9.1; trans. Findly. • 56. RV 6.9.3; trans. Findly; my emphasis. • 57. Ibid. • 58. RV 3.53.15–16. • 59. RV 10.71.1–2; trans. Doniger. • 60. Ibid., v. 4.

• 61. Ibid., v. 5. • 62. Ibid., v. 6. • 63. Gonda, *Change and Continuity*, 200. • 64. Renou, 'Sur la notion de *brahman*'. • 65. Heesterman, *Inner Conflict*, 70–72, 73. • 66. RV 10.129.6–7; trans. Doniger. • 67. Flood, *Introduction to Hinduism*, 39; Klostermaier, *Survey of Hinduism*, 68; Jan Gonda, *Samhitas and Brahmanas* (Wiesbaden, 1974) • 68. Klostermaier, *Survey of Hinduism*, 68. • 69. Flood, *Introduction to Hinduism*, 37. • 70. Mahony, 121. • 71. Kaushitiki Brahmana (KB) 6.11; Heesterman, *Broken World*, 150. • 72. Padoux, 297–98. • 73. The patron was usually accompanied by his wife, though the texts focus on the activity of the husband. • 74. Thomas J. Hopkins, 31–32. • 75. Brian K. Smith, 30–34, 72–82; Renou, *Religions of Ancient India*, 18. • 76. Shatapatha Brahmana (SB) 1.8.1.4; trans. Heesterman, *Broken World*, 57. • 77. SB 11.2.2.5; trans. Brian K. Smith, 103. • 78. Taittiriya Brahmana (TB) 1.5.9.4; trans. Brian K. Smith, 103. • 79. Aitereya Brahmana (AB) 4.21. • 80. Thomas J. Hopkins, 34. • 81. RV 121; trans. Doniger. • 82. Albert Einstein, 'Strange Is Our Situation Here on Earth', in Pelikan, ed., *The World Treasury of Modern Religious Thought*, 225. • 83. Quoted in Huston Smith, *Beyond the Post-Modern Mind*, rev. edn (Wheaton, 1989), 8. • 84. RV 10.9.12–14; trans. Doniger. • 85. Ibid., 9; trans. Doniger. • 86. Colossians 1:15–20. • 87. AB 5.32; trans. Brian K. Smith, 57. • 88. TB 1.23.8; trans. Brian K. Smith, 58. • 89. Jaminiya Brahmana (JB) 1.111; TB 1.1.3.5; q.7.1.4. • 90. Pancavimsa Brahmana (PB) 24.11.2. • 91. SB 6.1.2.17; trans. Brian K. Smith, 65. • 92. SB 11.1.6.3. • 93. PB 7.5.1; JB 1.116, 117, 128. • 94. AB 5.32; KB 7.10. • 95. Holdrege, 46–60. • 96. Gonda, 'The Indian Mantra'; Findly, 15–44; Holdrege, 237–38. • 97. Gonda, *Vision*, 63–4. • 98. Harvey P. Alper, 'Introduction', in Alper, ed., 3–4. • 99. Staal, 'Vedic Mantras', in Alper, ed., 73–81. • 100. Staal, 'Oriental Ideas'. • 101. Coburn. • 102. Iamblichus, *De Mysteriis* 6.6, 7. 4; Jan Assmann 'Text and Ritual: The Meaning of the Media for the History of Religions', in Assmann, *Religion and Cultural Memory*, 131–33. • 103. Johnston, 56–69. • 104. Gonda, *Vision*, 63–64. • 105. Ibid., 318–48. • 106. Jan Assmann, 'Cultural Texts Suspended Between Writing and Speech', in Assmann, *Religion and Cultural Memory*, 109. • 107. SB 5.1.3.11; trans. Mahony, 132. • 108. SB 7.1.2.9–11; trans. Mahony, 135. • 109. SB 1.2.5.14; trans. Mahony, 135. • 110. Apostramba Shantra Sutra 15.1.16.10. • 111. SB 7.1.2.11; trans. Mahony, 135. • 112. Brian K. Smith, 65. • 113. SB 7.1.2.7–8; trans. Mahony, 134.

3. China: The Primacy of Ritual

1. Gernet, *Ancient China*, 37–65; Gernet, *History*, 39–40; de Bary and Bloom, *Sources*, 3–25. • 2. Fairbank and Goldman, 45. • 3. K. C. Chang, *Art, Myth and Ritual: The Path to Political Authority in Ancient China* (Cambridge, MA, 1985), 42–44. • 4. *Jiaguwen heiji* (HJ) 24146, and 24140, in de Bary and Bloom, *Sources*, 6. • 5. HJ 13636, in de Bary and Bloom, *Sources*, 8. • 6. Gernet, *History*, 45–47. • 7. HJ 6047, in de Bary

and Bloom, *Sources*, 18. • 8. Mark Edward Lewis, *Writing and Authority in Early China* (Albany, NY, 1999), 14–15. • 9. David H. Keightley, 'The Religious Commitment: Shang Theology and the Genesis of Chinese Political Culture', *History of Religions*, 17, 3/4 (Feb.–May 1978) • 10. Michael J. Puett, *To Become a God: Cosmology, Sacrifice, and Self-Divinization in Early China* (Cambridge, MA, 2002), 44. • 11. HJ 10124; de Bary and Bloom, *Sources*, 12. • 12. HJ 39912; de Bary and Bloom, *Sources*, 12. • 13. Gernet, *History*, 51–52. • 14. Ibid., 85; de Bary and Bloom, *Sources*, 24–25. • 15. Wilfred Cantwell Smith, *What Is Scripture?*, 176–180. • 16. Quotations from the *Yijing* are from Minford. Interpretation in Palmer et al., xl–xlv. • 17. Yao, 49. • 18. 'The Shao Announcement', *Shujing*, trans. de Bary and Bloom, *Sources*, 37–38. Some scholars argue that this speech was given by the duke of Shao, but like many others, de Bary and Bloom assign it to the duke of Zhou. • 19. 'The Counsel of Gaoyao', *Shujing*, 4; trans. Palmer et al., 21. • 20. For example, Chan, *passim*. • 21. Benjamin I. Schwartz, 53. • 22. C. Lévi-Strauss, *The Savage Mind* (Oxford, 1966), 233–34. • 23. Assmann, *Cultural Memory*, 2–61. • 24. Jan Assmann, 'Text and Ritual: The Meaning of the Media for the History of Religion', in Assman, *Religion and Cultural Memory*, 125. • 25. In ancient China, musicians were usually blind. • 26. Ode 271 in the standard Mao edition. Unless otherwise stated, all translations from the *Odes* are taken from Waley, *Book of Songs*. • 27. Mao 267. • 28. *Liji Zhengshu*, 11.21.a–b; Maspero, 149–157; Edward L. Shaughnessy, 'From Liturgy to Literature: The Ritual Contexts of the Earliest Poems in the *Book of Poetry*', in Shaughnessy, *Before Confucius*, 166–69. • 29. Ode 295: 'Martial'. • 30. *Zuozhuan*, 12; trans. Shaughnessy, 'From Liturgy to Literature', 167. My emphasis. • 31. Chow Tse-tung, 'The Early History of the Chinese Word *Shih* (Poetry)', in Wen-lin, ed., *Studies in the Chinese Humanities* (Madison, 1968), 151–209. • 32. Steven Mithen, *The Singing Neanderthals: The Origin of Music, Language, Mind and Body* (Cambridge, MA, 2007). • 33. Storr, 24. • 34. I. A. Richards, *Principles of Literary Criticism* (London, 1976), 103, 112. • 35. *Documents* 50–51; Shaughnessy, 'From Liturgy to Literature', 169–74. • 36. Ibid. • 37. Mao 286. • 38. Mao 288. • 39. Ibid. • 40. Mark Johnson, 19. • 41. Flood, *Ascetic Self*, 218–25. • 42. Mao 209. • 43. Ibid. • 44. Benjamin I. Schwartz, 48–49. • 45. Jessica Rawson, 'Statesmen or Barbarians? The Western Zhou as Seen through their Bronzes', *Proceedings of the British Academy*, 75 (1989); Shaughnessy, 'Western Zhou History', 332–33; Shaughnessy, 'From Liturgy to Literature', 183–87. • 46. Mao 280. • 47. Mao 282. • 48. Ibid. • 49. Mao 214, trans. Karlgren. • 50. Gernet, *History*, 53. • 51. Ibid., 84. • 52. Elvin, 'Was There a Transcendental Breakthrough in China?', 229–331. • 53. Huston Smith, *The World's Religions: Our Great Wisdom Traditions* (San Francisco, 1991), 161–62. • 54. Gernet, *History*, 58–64; Granet, *Religion*. • 55. Gernet, *Ancient China*, 71–75; remarks by Jacques Gernet, reported in Jean-Pierre Vernant, *Myth and Society in Ancient Greece*, trans. Janet Lloyd, 3rd edn (New York, 1996), 80–82. • 56. Granet, *Chinese Civilization*, 258–60, 284–357; Granet, *Religion*, 97–100. • 57. *Liji* 1.96. Unless otherwise stated, quotations from the *Liji* are from *Li Ji/The Book of*

Rites, ed. Dai Sheng. • 58. Ibid., 1.104. • 59. Ibid., 1.704. • 60. Ibid., 1.685. • 61. Ibid., 1.715, 719. • 62. Ibid., 1.720. • 63. Fung, 32–37. • 64. Canon of Yao, *Shujing*, trans. de Bary and Bloom, *Sources*, 29. • 65. Canon of Yao, trans. Palmer et al., 5. • 66. Canon of Shun; trans. Palmer et al., ibid. • 67. Canon of Shun, 9–10; trans. Palmer et al., ibid. • 68. *Liji* 2.636. • 69. Ibid., 2.359. • 70. Flood, *Ascetic Self*, 226–27. • 71. McNeil, 245. • 72. Gallagher; Mark Johnson, *The Body in the Mind: The Bodily Basis of Meaning, Imagination and Reason* (Chicago, 1987); Maxine Sheets-Johnstone, *The Primacy of Movement* (Amsterdam, 1999). • 73. Granet, *Chinese Civilization*, 328–43. • 74. McGilchrist, 363. • 75. Gernet, *Ancient China*, 75. • 76. Granet, *Chinese Civilization*, 261–79; cf. my own *Fields of Blood: Religion and the History of Violence* (London, 2014), 86–87. • 77. Kidder Smith. • 78. Lewis, 155–56; cf. *Zuozhuan*, Xiang, 29. • 79. Lewis, 163. • 80. Ibid., 148, 158. • 81. Ibid., 159–63. • 82. Mao 181; *Zuozhuan*, Xiang, 16. • 83. *Zuozhuan*, Wen, 4. • 84. *Zuozhuan*, Xiang, 9, trans. Lewis, 246–48; Kidder Smith. • 85. *Zuozhuan*, Xi, 15; trans. Lewis.

PART TWO: MYTHOS

4. New Story; New Self

1. Ezekiel 1:4–23. • 2. Ezekiel 2:10–15. • 3. Otto, 31. • 4. 2 Kings 25:27–30. • 5. Jonathan Z. Smith, 'Earth and Gods', in Jonathan Z. Smith, *Map Is Not Territory*, 119. • 6. Carole Beebe Tarantelli, 'Life Within Death: Toward a Metapsychology of Catastrophic Psychic Trauma', *International Journal of Psychoanalysis*, 84 (2003). • 7. Cathy Carruth, *Trauma: Explorations in Memory* (Baltimore, 1995), 153. • 8. Carr, *Holy Resilience*, 5. • 9. Aeschylus, *Agamemnon*, 176–82, in Aeschylus, *Oresteia*. • 10. Carr, *Holy Resilience*, 76. • 11. Ezekiel 4:1–11. • 12. Ezekiel 24:15–24. • 13. Hazony, 39–40. • 14. Psalm 137. • 15. Akenson, 25–29; Gerhad von Rad, 'The Form-Critical Problem of the Hexateuch', in von Rad; Noth, *Deuteronomic History*. • 16. Akenson, 47–58; Hazony, 43–5. • 17. Hazony, 43–45. • 18. Carr, *Holy Resilience*, 91–120. • 19. Ezekiel 33:24. • 20. Halbertal, 42. • 21. Genesis 12:1–2. • 22. Jeremiah 24:8. • 23. Genesis 12:3. • 24. Genesis 15:18. • 25. Genesis 12:10–20; 15:2; 17:17. • 26. Genesis 22:2. • 27. Genesis 20:1–18. • 28. Carr, *Holy Resilience*, 107–16. • 29. Exodus 4:24. • 30. Genesis 32:30; in Fox, *Five Books*. • 31. Genesis 25:20–28. • 32. Genesis 32:29–30. • 33. Exodus 3:14. • 34. Exodus 4:10; trans. Fox, *Five Books*. • 35. Exodus 4:14. • 36. Exodus 32:1–10. • 37. Jeremiah 28. • 38. Exodus 23:14–17. • 39. Exodus 12:25–27. • 40. Exodus 14:11; 16:3; 17:3; 32:9; 38:3. • 41. Lengthy description of the Tabernacle in Exodus 25–40. • 42. Leviticus 26:12; trans. Cross, *Canaanite Myth*, 298. • 43. Cross, *Canaanite Myth*, 298–300. • 44. Damrosch, 'Leviticus'. • 45. Leviticus 25. • 46. Leviticus 19:34. • 47. 'Second Isaiah' is so called because his oracles were included in the same

scroll as those of Isaiah of Jerusalem. • 48. Isaiah 45:1 • 49. Isaiah 53:2–3. • 50. Isaiah 52:13–15; 53:4–5. • 51. Isaiah 40:5. • 52. It is very difficult to date this period, and scholars date the missions of Ezra and Nehemiah differently. Ahlström, 880–83; Bickerman, *Jews in the Greek Age*, 29–32. • 53. Ezra 7:6; trans. Michael Fishbane, 'From Scribalism to Rabbinism: Perspectives on the Emergence of Classical Judaism', in Fishbane, *Garments of Torah*, 65. • 54. 1 Kings 22:8. • 55. Ezra 7:6–9; trans. Fishbane, 'From Scribalism to Rabbinism', in Fishbane, *Garments of Torah*, 65; cf. Ezekiel 1:3. • 56. Nehemiah 8:8. • 57. Nehemiah 8:7. • 58. Nehemiah 8:9–12. • 59. Nehemiah 8:17. • 60. Nehemiah 8:16–17. • 61. Bruns, 626–27. • 62. T. Bab Metziah 5:8; 4 Ezra 14:37–48. • 63. Lewis, 53–56. • 64. For example, *Analects* 3.8; 4.15. • 65. *Analects* 2.5–8. • 66. Lewis, 54–59, 83. • 67. *Analects* 1.1; trans. Slingerland. • 68. *Analects* 6.3. • 69. *Analects* 2.18. • 70. *Analects* 5.27. • 71. *Analects* 1.4. • 72. The last text, *Music*, has not survived, but it was closely related to *Odes*, which were, of course, sung. • 73. *Analects* 6.30; trans. Tu, *Confucian Thought*, 68. • 74. Tu, *Confucian Thought*, 113–16. • 75. *Analects* 12.3. • 76. *Analects* 12.1; trans. Benjamin I. Schwartz, 77. • 77. *Analects* 12.2; trans. Lau. • 78. Ibid. • 79. *Analects* 15.24; trans. Slingerland. • 80. *Analects* 4.15; trans. Lau. • 81. *Analects* 15.23; trans. Waley. • 82. *Analects* 9.11; trans. Slingerland. • 83. *Analects* 2.4. • 84. *Analects* 7.1; trans. Slingerland. • 85. *Analects* 3.8. • 86. Benjamin I. Schwartz, 62–66. • 87. Lewis, 85–87. • 88. *Analects* 12.3; trans. Slingerland. Similar sentiments about speech can be found in *Analects* 1.3; 5.5; 2.5, 25; 15.11; 16.4. • 89. *Analects* 1.12–14. • 90. *Analects* 2.5–8. • 91. *Analects* 17.19; trans. Lau. This is a late chapter but contains earlier material so may be Confucius' *ipsissima verba*. Robert Eno, *The Confucian Creation of Heaven: Philosophy and the Defence of Ritual Mastery*, 2 vols. (Albany, 1990), 242, note 6. • 92. *Analects* 8.19. • 93. Tu, *Confucian Thought*, 115–16. • 94. *Chandogya Upanishad* (CU) 3.5.4; unless otherwise stated, all translations of the Upanishads are from Olivelle, *Upanisads*. • 95. M. Witzel, 'Vedas and Upanisads', in Flood, ed., *Blackwell Companion to Hinduism*, 85–86. • 96. Olivelle, *Upanisads*, xxxiv–xxxvi. • 97. Ibid., lii. • 98. *Brhadaranyaka Upanishad* (BU) 1.1.1. • 99. CU 1.1.2. • 100. Mahony, 152–53; Coward, *Sacred Word*, 123–24; Flood, *Introduction to Hinduism*, 83–84. • 101. Ghose, *Secret of the Veda*, 12. • 102. RV 10.168.4; trans. Griffiths. • 103. RV 3.54.8; trans. Griffiths. • 104. BU 1.5.3. • 105. Klostermaier, *Survey of Hinduism*, 200–01. Some of the early Upanishadic mystics were women. • 106. BU 2.5.19. • 107. BU 3.4. • 108. BU 4.5.15. • 109. Dupré, 459–62. • 110. Meister Eckhart, Sermon: 'Qui audit me, non confundetur', in *Meister Eckhart*, ed. and trans. Raymond Bernard Blackney (New York, 1957), 205. • 111. BU 4.4.5–7. • 112. Klostermaier, *Survey of Hinduism*, 200–03. • 113. Heesterman, *Broken World*, 164–74; Gonda, *Change and Continuity*, 228–35, 285–94. • 114. Coward, *Sacred Word*, 126. • 115. CU 8.1.1–6; 8.3.3–5. • 116. BU 4.4.23–25 • 117. CU 6.7. • 118. CU 6.8.7. My emphasis. • 119. CU 6.10. My emphasis. • 120. Holdrege, 346–52. • 121. BU 6.2.15. • 122. BU 2.5.19. • 123. *Aitereya Upanishad* 3.1.13. • 124. *Mandukya Upanishad* 3.1.7. • 125. BU 2.4.4–5.

5. Empathy

1. A. C. Graham, *Disputers*, 54–62; Benjamin I. Schwartz, 137–57; Fung, 50–52; Lewis, 59–60. • 2. A. C. Graham, *Divisions*. • 3. *Mozi* 26.4. • 4. *Mozi* 3.25. • 5. Mao 24; trans. Watson. • 6. *Mozi* 3.31; trans. Watson, *Mozi*, 101. • 7. Lewis, 112–13. • 8. *Mozi* 1.26; trans. Watson, *Mozi*, 92. • 9. Graham, *Disputers of the Tao*, 41. • 10. *Mozi* 3.16; trans. Fung, 55. • 11. *Mozi* 3.16; trans. Watson, *Mozi*, 46. • 12. Ibid. • 13. Watson, *Mozi*, 48; these lines are not found in the extant *Odes*, but appear in the *Hongfang* section of *Documents*. • 14. Gernet, *Ancient China*, 67–81; Gernet, *History*, 89–114. • 15. A. C. Graham, *Disputers*, 299–399. • 16. Ibid., 64–74. • 17. *Analects* 14.37, 39. • 18. *Mencius* 3B.9. Unless otherwise stated, all quotations from the *Mencius* are from Lau, *Mencius*. • 19. Ibid., 7A.26 • 20. *Lu-shi Chunqiu*, 17.7; *Hanfeizi*, 50; *Huainanzi*, 13; Fung, 60–62. • 21. *Laozi*, 13; *Zhuangzi*, 3. • 22. A. C. Graham, *Disputers*, 300. • 23. *Shangiunshu*, 20; trans. Benjamin I. Schwartz, 328. • 24. A. C. Graham, *Disputers*, 111–32; Benjamin I. Schwartz, 255–90; Fung, 68–69; Tu, *Confucian Thought*, 61–109. • 25. *Mencius* 2A.1. • 26. Benjamin I. Schwartz, 255. • 27. *Mencius* 3A.4. • 28. *Mencius* 3B.9. • 29. *Mencius* 2A.6. • 30. Ibid. • 31. *Mencius* 7A.13. • 32. *Mencius* 6B.2. My emphasis. • 33. *Mencius* 7A.4; modified by Tu, *Confucian Thought*, 61. • 34. *Mencius* 6A.11. • 35. Tu, *Confucian Thought*, 96. • 36. *Mencius* 7A.16. • 37. *Mencius* 7A.21. • 38. *Mencius* 7A.40; cf. 4B.22. • 39. *Mencius* 7B.26. • 40. *Mencius* 3B.9. • 41. Queen, 16–21. • 42. *Mencius* 3B.9. • 43. Thomas J. Hopkins, 50–51. • 44. Gonda, *Change and Continuity*, 380–84. • 45. Ibid., 381–82; Olivelle, 'The Renouncer Tradition', 281–82. • 46. Dundas, *Jains*; Steven Collins, 48–49, 64; Flood, *Introduction to Hinduism*, 87–88; Heesterman, *Inner Conflict*. • 47. Dundas, *Jains*, 22–44; Stevenson, 8–55. • 48. Dundas, *Jains*, 27; Thomas J. Hopkins, 54–55. • 49. Acaranga Sutra (AS) 1.4.1.1–2; trans. Dundas, *Jains*, 41–42. • 50. Dundas, *Jains*, 43–44. • 51. AS 1.5.6.3–4; trans. Dundas, *Jains*, 43. • 52. Stevenson, 5–6. • 53. Dundas, *Jains*, 234–35. • 54. AS 1.2.3. • 55. Dundas, *Jains*, 171–72. • 56. Ibid., 60–62; Dundas, 'Somnolent Sutras'. • 57. Stevenson, 16. • 58. AvNiry 92; trans. Dundas, *Jains*, 61. • 59. Dundas, 'Somnolent Scriptures'. • 60. Dundas, *Jains*, 167. • 61. Dundas, 'Somnolent Scriptures'. • 62. Folkert, 175–76. • 63. Eliade, 53–84. • 64. Campbell, *Oriental Mythology*, 263. • 65. Vinaya Mahavagga 1.4. I have consulted many translations of the Buddhist scriptures, but have paraphrased them, producing my own version to make them more accessible to a Western reader. • 66. Ibid., 1.11. • 67. Samyutta Nikaya (SN) 3.120. • 68. Wilfred Cantwell Smith, *What Is Scripture?*, 166. • 69. Louis R. Lancaster, 'Buddhist Literature: Its Canons, Scribes and Editors', in O'Flaherty, ed., 217; Coward, *Sacred Word*, 141–42. • 70. Wilfred Cantwell Smith, *What Is Scripture?*, 169–71. • 71. Digha Nikaya (DN) 16; Anguttara Nikaya (AN) 76. • 72. AN 7.9.2. • 73. Coward, *Sacred Word*, 151. • 74. Vinaya Mahavagga 1.21; SN 35.28. • 75. AN 6.63. • 76. Gombrich, *Theravada Buddhism*, 14–17. • 77. Majjima Nikaya (MN)1; SN 22.59. • 78. Vinaya Mahavagga 1.6. • 79. Gombrich, *Theravada Buddhism*, 59–61.

• 80. DN 9. • 81. Gombrich, *Theravada Buddhism*, 17–20; T. W. Rhys Davids, 'Introduction to the Kassapa-Sihananda Sutta', in Rhys Davids, II, 206–07. • 82. Gethin, 44. • 83. Flood, *Ascetic Self*, 119–38. • 84. Powers, 120–24. • 85. SN 4.211–13; MN 1.181; DN 1.70–71; trans. Powers, 121. • 86. Walter Burkert, *Greek Religion*, trans. John Raffan (Cambridge, MA, 1985), 114, 152; Seth L. Schein, *The Mortal Hero: An Introduction to Homer's Iliad* (Berkeley, 1984), 57–58. • 87. Charles Segal, 149–66. • 88. Aeschylus, *Agamemnon*, 176–84, in Aeschylus, *Oresteia*. • 89. Aeschylus, *The Persians*, 179–184, in Aeschylus, *Prometheus Bound and Other Plays*. • 90. Burkert, *Greek Religion*, 65–67; Roland Parker, *Athenian Religion: A History* (Oxford, 1996), 34–41. • 91. Jean-Pierre Vernant, 'The Historical Moment of Tragedy', in Jean-Pierre Vernant and Pierre Vidal-Naquet, *Myth and Tragedy in Ancient Greece*, trans. Janet Lloyd (New York, 1990), 7–26. • 92. Jean-Pierre Vernant, 'Tensions and Ambiguities in Greek Tragedy', in Vernant and Vidal-Naquet, op. cit., 34–35. • 93. Jean-Pierre Vernant, 'Oedipus without the Complex', in Vernant and Vidal-Naquet, op. cit., 88–89. • 94. Jean-Pierre Vernant, 'Intimations of the Will in Greek Tragedy', in Vernant and Vidal-Naquet, op. cit., 49–84. • 95. Louis Gernet, *Récherches sur de dévelopment de la pensée juridique et morale en Gréce* (Paris, 1917), 305. • 96. André Rivier, 'Remarques sur le "nécessaire" et la "nécessité" chez Eschyle', *Revue des Études Greques*, 81 (1968). • 97. Vernant, 'Tensions and Ambiguities', 29–48. • 98. Vernant, 'Historical Moment', 27–28. • 99. Sophocles, *King Oedipus* (KO) 1082. Unless otherwise stated all quotations are taken from *The Three Theban Plays: Antigone, Oedipus the King, Oedipus at Colonus*, trans. Robert Fagles (New York, 1982). • 100. Homer, *Odyssey*, XI, 275–76. • 101. KO 135. • 102. KO 112, 362, 450, 688, 659. • 103. KO 1293, 1387–88, 1395. • 104. KO 33, 1433. • 105. KO 58–59, 84, 105, 397. • 106. Jean-Pierre Vernant, 'Ambiguity and Reversal: On the Enigmatic Structure of Oedipus Rex', in Vernant and Vidal-Naquet, op. cit., 124. • 107. KO 469, 479. • 108. KO 1255, 1265. • 109. KO 1451. • 110. KO 131–41. • 111. KO 551. • 112. Vernant, 'Ambiguity and Reversal', 117 • 113. KO 816, 818. • 114. KO 1230–31. • 115. KO 1298–302 • 116. KO 1311. • 117. KO 1329–32. • 118. KO 125–96. • 119. KO 1320–23. • 120. Charles Segal, 166–68; Claude Calame, 'Vision, Blindness and Mask: The Radicalization of the Emotions', in Silk, ed., 19–31; Richard Buxton, 'What Can You Rely On in *Oedipus Rex*?', in Silk, ed., 38–49. • 121. KO 127, 1312, 1299, 1321. • 122. Plato, 'Apology', trans. G. M. A. Grube, in John M. Cooper, ed., *Plato: Complete Works* (Indianapolis, 1997), 40–41.

6. Unknowing

1. Thapar, *Early India*, 174–78. • 2. Thapar, 'Genealogical Patterns'. • 3. H. H. Wilson, trans., *The Vishnu Purana* (Calcutta, 1840, 1972), 374. • 4. Major Rock Edict, in Thapar, *Aśoka*, 254. • 5. B. B. Lai, 'Mahabharata and Archaeology',

in S. P. Gupta and K. S. Ramachandran, eds., *Mahabharata: Myth and Reality* (New Delhi, 1985), 57–59; John Keay, *India: A History* (New York, 2000), 42. • 6. Doniger, *The Hindus*, 254. • 7. Barbara Stoler Miller, 'The Mahabharata as Theatre', in de Bary and Bloom, *Eastern Canons*, 136–37. • 8. John D. Smith, 'The Two Sanskrit Epics', 48. • 9. Brockington, 246–45; Thomas J. Hopkins, 88–89. • 10. Hiltebeitel, *Rethinking the Mahabharata*, 18–29; Brockington, 20–21. • 11.Earl, *Beginning the Mahabharata*, 13–20. • 12. *Mahabharata* 1.1.1–26. • 13. Hiltebeitel, *Rethinking the Mahabharata*, 112–15; Earl, 11. • 14. Hiltebeitel, *Rethinking the Mahabharata*, 114–15; Earl, 26–35. • 15. Van Buitenen, II, 29; cf. Hudson, 22–23. • 16. Hiltebeitel, *Rethinking the Mahabharata*, 316. • 17. Ibid., 72; Shulman. • 18. Shulman. • 19. Hudson, 30–31. • 20. Hiltebeitel, *Rethinking the Mahabharata*, 177–214. • 21. *Mahabharata* 6.44.34–38; trans. Hudson, 172. • 22. *Mahabharata* 19.3.33, in John D. Smith, *The Mahabharata*. • 23. *Mahabharata* 5.36.42–45; trans. van Buitenen, vol. III. • 24. Hudson, 95–96. • 25. *Mahabharata* 5.46–66; 5.70.46–66; 7.70.74; trans. van Buitenen. • 26. Hudson, 74–105. • 27. *Mahabharata* 2.60.5; trans. van Buitenen. • 28. *Mahabharata* 2.27.9; trans. van Buitenen; modified. • 29. *Mahabharata* 7.164.100; trans. John D. Smith. • 30. *Mahabharata* 7.164. • 31. *Mahabharata* 11.26. • 32. Hudson, 206–16. • 33. *Mahabharata* 17.3.20; trans. John D. Smith. • 34. *Mahabharata* 18.1.6; trans. John D. Smith. • 35. *Mahabharata* 18.3.10; trans. John D. Smith. • 36. Michael La Fargue, *Tao and Method: A Reasoned Approach to the Tao Te Jing* (Albany, 1994). • 37. Lewis, 297–300. • 38. *Daodejing* 1. Unless otherwise stated, all quotations from the *Daodejing* are taken from Lau, *Lao-tzu: Tao Te Ching*. • 39. *Daodejing* 25. • 40. Fung, 95–96. • 41. *Daodejing* 3. • 42. A. C. Graham, *Disputers*, 220–30. • 43. Fung, 97. • 44. *Daodejing* 40. • 45. *Daodejing* 23. • 46. *Daodejing* 9. • 47. *Daodejing* 29. • 48. *Daodejing* 7. • 49. *Daodejing* 22. • 50. *Daodejing* 13; trans. de Bary and Bloom, *Sources*, 83–84. • 51. A. C. Graham, *Disputers*, 172–203; Benjamin I. Schwartz, 213–36; Fung, 104–17. • 52. *The Book of Zhuangzi*, 20.61–68. • 53. *Zhuangzi* 18.15–19. Unless otherwise stated, quotations from the *Zhuangzi* are from Palmer and Breuilly. • 54. *Zhuangzi* 2.78–80. • 55. *Zhuangzi* 6.93; trans. and ed. David Hinton, *Chuang Tzu: The Inner Chapters* (Washington DC, 1998); modified. • 56. *Zhuangzi* 2.50–53. • 57. *Zhuangzi* 6.31. • 58. *Zhuangzi* 1.21. • 59. *Zhuangzi* 6.11. • 60. There were originally six Classics, but in the turmoil during and following the late Warring States period, the 'Classic of Music' was lost. • 61. Xunzi, 'Encouraging Learning'; trans. Burton Watson, *Hsun Tsu: Basic Writings* (New York, 1963), 19. • 62. Xunzi, 'Man's Nature is Evil', in Watson, *Hsun Tsu*, 166. • 63. Xunzi, 'A Discussion of Rites', in Watson, *Hsun Tsu*, 93. • 64. Xunzi, 'Encouraging Learning', in Watson, *Hsun Tsu*, 19–20. Note that the *Yijing* ('Changes') has not yet become one of the classical scriptures. • 65. Ibid., 21. • 66. Ibid., 20. • 67. Ibid. • 68. Ibid., 21, 28–30. • 69. Xunzi, 'A Discussion of Rites', in Watson, *Hsun Tsu*, 100. • 70. Xunzi, 'Encouraging Learning', in Watson, *Hsun Tsu*, 21. • 71. Ibid., 20–21. • 72. Xunzi, 'Dispelling Obsession', in Watson, *Hsun Tsu*, 127–28. • 73. Ibid., 129. • 74. Ibid. • 75. Chan, *Source Book*, 262–65. • 76. Appendix 1.4 in ibid., 265. • 77. Ibid. • 78. Great Appendix 1.5; Z. N. Sung, ed. and trans., *The Text of the Yi King* (New York, 1969), 279. • 79. *Zhou yi Zheng yi* ('The Great Tradition'), 8, trans. Lewis, 197. • 80. Ibid., 198 • 81. Lewis, 195–98. • 82. Queen, 115. Queen also names two other traditions: the Zou and the Jia, both of which declined due to lack of transmitters or loss of texts. • 83. Henderson, 64. • 84. David Keightley, 'Late Shang Divination', 23. • 85. Henderson, 75; Loewe, *Faith*, 186. • 86. Henderson, 88. • 87. Commentary to Duke Ai, 41; trans. Queen, 122. • 88. Queen, 119–22; Lewis, 130–32. • 89. Zhang 4; trans. Lewis. • 90. Chan, *Source Book*, 262–70; Queen, 125, 230–32; Lewis, 139–44. • 91. Carr, *Tablet of the Heart*, 178–86. • 92. Ibid., 199–200. • 93. Ibid., 207–12; Richard A. Horsley, 'The Origins of Hebrew Scripture Under Imperial Rule: Oral-Written Scribal Cultivation of Torah – Not "Re-Written Bible"' and 'Oral Composition-and-Performance of the Instructional Speeches of Ben Sirah', in Horsley, *Text and Tradition*. • 94. Ben Sira 24.33–34; this book is often titled 'Ecclesiasticus'• 95. Holdrege, 136. • 96. Ben Sira 24.33. • 97. Ibid., 24.3, 8, 28–30. • 98. Holdrege, 133. • 99. Proverbs 8.22, 30–31.

7. Canon

1. Lewis, 61–62. • 2. Sima Qian, *Shiji*, in *Records of the Grand Historian*, ed. and trans. Burton Watson (New York, 1961), 6.239; Fairbank and Goldman, 56. • 3. Lewis, 339–40; Henderson, 40. • 4. Benjamin I. Schwartz, 237–53. • 5. Liu Xin, *Hanshu* ('History of the Former Han'), 130, in A. C. Graham, *Disputers*, 379–80. • 6. *Hanfeizi* 5, in Watson, *Han Fei Tzu*. • 7. Loewe, *Faith*, 6–7. • 8. Fingarette. • 9. Sima Qian, *Shiji*, 8.1, cited by Fung, 215. • 10. A. C. Graham, *Disputers*, 313–77; Benjamin I. Schwartz, 383–406. • 11. Henderson, 40–43. • 12. Queen, 4–10, 20–36, 111–12, 227–40. • 13. Queen and Major, 8/12a/1/19–12a.3.15. • 14. Ibid., 11/66/3/1–1b.7.1. • 15. *Shiji*, 121; Lewis, 348. • 16. Lewis, 349–50. • 17. Loewe, *Faith*, 182–83. • 18. Ibid., 12–15. • 19. Lewis, 218–35. • 20. *Shiji*, 47; trans. Lewis, 234. • 21. Ibid., 237. • 22. Benjamin I. Schwartz, 383–404. • 23. LaMotte, 'La critique d'interpretation dans le bouddhisme'. My emphasis. • 24. A. L. Basham, 'Ashoka and Buddhism: A Re-examination', *Journal of the International Association of Buddhist Studies*, 5, 1 (1982). • 25. LaMotte, *Histoire du Bouddhisme indien*, 300. • 26. Paul Williams, 4. • 27. Majjima Nikaya, 143. • 28. Paul Williams, 9. • 29. Ibid., 19–20, 25–28, 168–70. • 30. Lopez, *Buddhist Hermeneutics*, 47. • 31. Paul Williams, 3. • 32. Coward, *Sacred Word*, 160. • 33. Ibid., 219–20. • 34. Ibid., 217–22. • 35. Sutta Nipata, 1147; trans. Paul Williams. • 36. Buddhaghosa, *The Path of Purification* (*Visuddhimagga*), trans. Bhikku Nanamoli (Kandy, 1975), 230. • 37. *Satashakti Prajnaparamiter*; trans. from the Chinese in Garma C. C. Chang, 110; my emphasis. • 38. Paul Williams, 29. • 39. Ibid., 40–74. • 40. Stephen Beyer, *The Buddhist Experience: Sources and Interpretations* (Belmont, CA, 1974), 340. • 41. Conze,

Perfection of Wisdom, 300. • 42. Ibid., 9–10. • 43. Ibid., 9, 84. • 44. Ibid., 99. • 45. Ibid., 238–39. • 46. Ibid., 25. • 47. Paul Williams, 141–52; Wing-tsit Chan, 'The *Lotus Sutra*', in de Bary and Bloom, *Eastern Canons*; translated text of the *Lotus Sutra* in Chang, *A Treasury of Mahayana Sutras*. • 48. *Lotus Sutra*, Chapter 5. • 49. Ibid., Chapter 7. • 50. Ibid., Chapter 16. • 51. Trans. Chang, *A Treasury of Mahayana Sutras*, 174. • 52. *Lotus Sutra*, Chapter 14. • 53. Paul Williams, 152. • 54. Thurman, *Holy Teaching*; Thurman, 'The Teaching of Vimilakirti'. • 55. *Ekakshariprajnaparamita* ('The Perfection of Wisdom in a Single Letter'). • 56. Lopez, *Buddhist Hermeneutics*, 47–48. • 57. Nagarjuna, *Mulamadhhyamaka-kavita*, 23–24; trans. Lopez, *Buddhist Hermeneutics*, 48. • 58. Ibid. • 59. Preface to Ben Sira ('Ecclesiasticus'); my emphasis. • 60. Ben Sira 24.32–34. • 61. Carr, *Holy Resilience*, 142–43. • 62. Hengel, *Judaism and Hellenism*, I, 294–300; Bickerman, *From Ezra to the Last of the Maccabees*, 286–89; *The Jews in the Greek Age*, 294–96. • 63. Carr, *Tablet of the Heart*, 200; Shaye Cohen, *The Beginnings of Jewishness: Boundaries, Varieties, Uncertainties* (Berkeley, 1999), 132–35. • 64. M. H. Segal; Greenberg, 'The Stabilization of the Text of the Hebrew Bible', 76; Carr, *Holy Resilience*, 146–55. • 65. Kugel, 3. • 66. Genesis 5:21–24. • 67. 1 Enoch, Chapters 12–16. • 68. 1 Enoch 15:1; trans. E. Isaac in Charlesworth. • 69. Weinfeld, 200–01. • 70. Daniel 7:9–10. • 71. Daniel 7:13–14. • 72. Philo 6.476. • 73. 1 Maccabees 3:46–66. • 74. 2 Maccabees 15:9. • 75. 1 Maccabees 9:27; cf. 4:44–46, 14:41. • 76. Richard A. Horsley, 'The Origins of the Hebrew Scripture Under Imperial Rule' and 'Contesting Authority: Popular vs. Scribal Tradition in Continuing Performance', in Horsley, *Text and Tradition*; Carr, *Tablet of the Heart*, 215–39; Jaffee, 31–37. • 77. Alex P. Jassen, 'The Dead Sea Scrolls and Violence: Sectarian Formation and Eschatological Imagination', in Boustan et al., eds. • 78. Qumran Community Rule (1QS.6.45), in Vermes. • 79. Jaffee, 37. • 80. Seth Schwartz, *Imperialism*, 40–47. • 81. Josephus, *Antiquities*, 13.288–98, 408–10. • 82. Jaffee, 38–61. • 83. Josephus, *Against Apion*, 1.38; trans. Thackeray, Loeb Classical Library. • 84. Josephus, *Jewish War*, 2.260–62.

8. Midrash

1. Firestone, *Holy War*, 46–47. • 2. Akenson, 319–25. • 3. Jaffee, 1–10. • 4. Ibid., 83. • 5. Psalm 22:14. • 6. *M. Yadayin* 4.3, trans. Jaffee, 80. • 7. Ibid., 80–81; Akenson, 315–17; Neusner, 'The Use of the Mishnah'. • 8. *Pesikta Rabbati* 3.2, in William G. Braude, ed. and trans., *Pesikta Rabbati Discourses for Feasts, Fasts and Special Sabbaths,* 2 vols. (New Haven, 1988). • 9. Halbertal, 45–46, 50–54. • 10. B. Gittin 66; B. Baba Metzia 36a. • 11. *Pesikta Rabbati* 21; *M. Tehilim* 12.4; trans. Halbertal, 53–54. • 12. Akenson, 319–21; Neusner, *Judaism*, 48–121. • 13. *M. Middoth* 5.4; 2.5. • 14. *M. Tamid* 1.2. • 15. B. Menahoth 29b. • 16. *Sifre* on Leviticus 13:47. • 17. Jaffee, 100–02. • 18. Bruns, 'Midrash and Allegory', 634. • 19. Neusner, *Medium and Message*, 3; 'Mishnah in Philosophical Context'; Akenson, 305–20. • 20. Neusner,

Evidence of the Mishnah, 229. • 21. M. *Pirke Avot* 3.3.7; trans. Gorfinkle. • 22. M. *Pirke Avot* 6.1; trans. Fishbane, *Garments of Torah*, 77. • 23. M. *Song of Songs Rabbah* 1.102; trans. Bruns, 'Midrash and Allegory', 627. • 24. Fishbane, *Garments of Torah*, 22. • 25. Deuteronomy 21.23. • 26. M. *Sanhedrin* 6.4–5; trans. Fishbane, *Garments of Torah*, 30. • 27. M. *Pirke Avot*; trans. Gorfinkle. • 28. Psalm 89.2; *Avot de R. Nathan*; trans. Montefiore and Loewe. • 29. *Sifre* on Deuteronomy, 306; trans. Jaffee, 90. • 30. *Sifre* on Deuteronomy, 351; trans. Jaffee, 90. • 31. Braude, trans., *Pesikta Rabbati*, 2.2 • 32. Richard A. Horsley, 'Contesting Authority: Popular vs. Scribal Tradition in Continuing Performance', in Horsley, *Text and Tradition*, 102–105, 113–16. • 33. Josephus, *Antiquities of the Jews*, 18.36–38; A. N. Sherman White, *Roman Laws and Roman Society in the New Testament* (Oxford, 1963), 139. • 34. Mark 1:15. • 35. Luke 6:20–38; Matthew 20:16; Horsley, *Spiral of Violence*, 167–68. • 36. Matthew 25:34–40. • 37. Mark 12:13–17. • 38. Horsley, *Spiral of Violence*, 306–16; F. F. Bruce, 'Render to Caesar', in Bammel and Moule, eds., 258. • 39. Matthew 21:12–13. • 40. Horsley, *Spiral of Violence*, 286–89; Sean Frayne, *Galilee: From Alexander the Great to Hadrian, 323 BCE to 135 CE: A Study of Second Temple Judaism* (Notre Dame, 1980), 283–86. • 41. Josephus, *Jewish War*, 2.75; Hengel, *Crucifixion*, 76. • 42. Crossan, 163. • 43. 1 Corinthians 15:3–4; my emphasis. • 44. Psalm 110:1. • 45. Psalm 2:7. • • 46. Psalm 8:5–6. • 47. Daniel 7:13–14. • 48. Martin Hengel, 'Christology and New Testament Chronology' and '"Christos" in Paul', in Hengel, *Between Jesus and Paul*. • 49. Joel 2:28–29. • 50. 1 Corinthians 11:23–26. • 51. Galatians 3:27–28. • 52. Arthur J. Dewey, 49–61. • 53. Joanna Dewey, 'Our Text of Mark: How Similar to First Century Versions?', in Joanna Dewey, 176–78; Pieter J. J. Botha, 'Mark's Story as Oral Traditional Literature', in Botha, 166–68. • 54. Mark 8:31–33; 9:30–32; 10:32–34. • 55. Josephus, *Jewish War*, 5.449–51. • 56. Arthur J. Dewey, 79–81. • • 57. Psalm 22:6–8. • 58. Mark 15:31. • 59. Mark 15:2–4; Psalm 22:18. • 60. Psalm 22:1. • 61. Mark 14:18; Psalm 41:9. • 62. Mark 14:34; Psalm 42:6, 11; 43:5. • 63. Mark 15:36; Psalm 69:21. • 64. Mark 15:37. • 65. Mark 8:34–36; Matthew 16:24–25; Luke 9:23–34. • 66. Mark 13:9–10; 13. • 67. Mark 13:24–27. • 68. Matthew 1:23. • 69. Micah 5:1; Matthew 2:6. • 70. Matthew 5:33. • 71. Exodus 20:7; Matthew 5:38–39. • 72. Leviticus 19:18; Matthew 5:44. • 73. Matthew 5:20. • 74. Luke 1:46–56; passages cited from the Hebrew Bible are: 1 Samuel 1:1; Psalm 103:17; Psalm 111:9; Job 5:11; 12:19; Psalm 98:3; Psalm 107:9; Isaiah 41:8–9. • 75. Luke 24:15–27. • 76. Luke 24:32. • 77. Matthew 17:2. • 78. Matthew 17:5. • 79. Hurtado, *How on Earth*, 200. • 80. Hurtado, *Lord Jesus Christ*, 383–89. • 81. John 1:1–3. • 82. John 1:14. • 83. Aune. • 84. 1 Corinthians 12:4–11. • 85. Isaiah 53:3; 49:13. • 86. Philippians 2:6–7. • 87. Philippians 2:9–11. • 88. Philippians 2:3–5. • 89. Romans 13:1–2, 4. • 90. Richard A. Horsley and Neil Asher Silberman, *The Message and the Kingdom* (Minneapolis, 1997), 191; Neil Elliott, 'Romans 13:1–7 in the Context of Imperial Propaganda', in Richard A. Horsley, ed., *Paul and Empire: Religion and Power in Roman Imperial Society* (Harrisburg, 1997); Neil Elliott, 'Paul and the Politics of Empire', in Richard A. Horsley, ed., *Paul and Politics: Ekklesia, Israel, Imperium, Interpretation* (Harrisburg, 2000). The same policy probably explains Paul's apparent acceptance of the institution of slavery in the Epistle to Philemon. • 91. Romans 13:9–10. • 92. Scholars agree that Paul's authentic letters are 1 and 2 Corinthians; Romans; Philippians; Galatians; 1 Thessalonians; and Philemon. • 93. Ephesians 1:11, 21; Colossians 3:18–25; cf. 1 Peter 2:18–3:7; James D. G. Dunn, 'The Household Rules in the New Testament', in Stephen C. Barton, ed., *The Family in Theological Perspective* (Edinburgh, 1996). • 94. 1 Timothy 2:9–15; cf. Titus 2:3–5; Arland J. Hultgren, 'The Pastoral Epistles', in Dunn, ed.; Calvin J. Retzel, 'Paul in the Second Century', in Dunn, ed.; Dunn, 'Household Rules'; Ernst Käsemann, 'Paul and Early Catholicism', in Ernst Käsemann, *New Testament Questions of Today* (Philadelphia, 1969), 249. • 95. Leo D. Lefebure, 'Violence in the New Testament and the History of Interpretation', in Renard, ed., 75–100. • 96. Matthew 12:33; 15:3–9; 16:5–12; 23:16; Mark 7:1–8. • 97. Matthew 27:25. • 98. Lefebure, 'Violence in the New Testament', in Renard, 77–81. • 99. Luke Timothy Johnson. • 100. Amy-Jill Levine, 'Matthew, Mark and Luke; Good News or Bad?', in Fredriksen and Reinhartz, eds., 78. • 101. John 10:30; 5:30; 8:16, 33–58; 5:18; 6:38; 8:26; 10:18. • 102. John 8:33–58. • 103. Hurtado, *Lord Jesus Christ*, 402–07. • 104. 1 John 3:10–24; 4.7; cf. Gospel of John 15:12–13, 18–27. • 105. Gospel of John 6:60–66; cf. 1 John 4:5–6. • 106. Kimberly B. Stratton, 'The Eschatological Arena: Reinscribing Roman Violence in Fantasies of the End Times', in Boustan et al., eds., 45–76; Barr, 208; Futrell. • 107. *Pesikta de R. Kahane*, 283; trans. Stratton, 'Eschatological Arena', 58. • 108. Revelation 14:10–11. • 109. John 1:30. • 110. Revelation 19:11–16. • 111. Sacks, 207–08. • 112. *Bhagavad Gita* 1.25. All quotations are taken from Barbara Stoler Miller. • 113. Ibid., 1.39. • 114. Ibid., 7.1, 5. • 115. Ibid., 7.6–7. • 116. Ibid., 10.34–35. • 117. Ibid., 11.6. • 118. Ibid., 11.14. • 119. Ibid., 4.6–7. • 120. Ibid., 11.55. • 121. Ibid., 9.32. • 122. Ibid., 13.7. • 123. Ibid., 13.6–9.

9. Embodiment

1. Origen, *On First Principles*, 1.3.8. • 2. Origen, *Dialogue with Heraclides*, 150, in H. E. Chadwick, ed. and trans., *Alexandrian Christianity* (London, 1954), 446. • 3. Origen, *On First Principles*, 4.2.7. • 4. Ibid., 4.1.6. • 5. Origen, 'Commentary on the Song of Songs', in *Origen: The Song of Songs Commentary and Homilies*, 61. • 6. Origen, 'Commentary on John'; R. R. Reno, trans., 'Origen', in Holcomb, ed., 28. • 7. Hadot. • 8. James B. Rives, *Religion in the Roman Empire* (Oxford, 2007), 207–08. • 9. Pelikan, *Christian Tradition*, I, 194–210; Robert C. Gregg and Dennis E. Groh, *Early Arianism – A View of Salvation* (London, 1981), 146–56; Rowan Williams; Louth, *Origins*, 76–77. • 10. Proverbs 8:22. • 11. Arius, Epistle to Alexander, 2; Pelikan, *Christian Tradition*, I, 194. • 12. Rowan Williams, 96. • 13. Psalm 45:7. • 14. Philippians 2:9–10. • 15. Arius, Epistle to Alexander; Pelikan, *Christian Tradition*, I, 194. • 16. Rowan Williams, 111–12. • 17. Matthew 19:21. • 18. Acts of the

Apostles 4:32, 34–35. • 19. Rowan Williams, 85–91. • 20. The 'Nicene Creed' in use today was in fact created at the Council of Constantinople in 380. • 21. Athanasius, *Against the Aryans*, 2.23–34. • 22. Pelikan, *Christian Tradition*, I, 203–05. • 23. Athanasius, *On the Incarnation*, 54, trans. Andrew Louth, *The Origins of Christian Mysticism: From Plato to Denys* (Oxford, 1981), 78. • 24. Harvey, *Scenting Salvation*, 58–59. • 25. Philip Schaff and Henry Ware, eds. and trans., *Life of St Anthony of Egypt by St Athanasius of Alexandria*, n.d.; n.p. Paragraph 18. • 26. Peter Brown, *Body and Society*, 236. • 27. Hymn 35.2 in McVey. • 28. Ephrem, *De Nativitate*, 4.144–45; trans. Harvey, 'Locating the Sensing Body', 157. • 29. Harvey, 'Locating the Sensing Body', 146. • 30. Lossky, 'Theology and Mysticism', 170. • 31. Maximus, *Ambigua*, 42; trans. Meyendorff, *Byzantine Theology*, 164; modified (Meyendorff translates *anthropos* as 'man'). • 32. Maximus, *Ambigua*, 5. • 33. Gregory of Nyssa, *That There Are Not Three Gods*, 42–43; trans. Pelikan, *Christian Tradition*, I, 222. • 34. Definition in the *Oxford Dictionary*. • 35. Basil, *On the Holy Spirit*, 28.66. • 36. Walter Burkert, *Ancient Mystery Cults* (Cambridge, MA, 1986), 7–9. • 37. Gregory of Nyssa, *That There Are Not Three Gods*. • 38. Gregory of Nazianzus, *Oratio*, 40, 41; trans. Lossky, *Mystical Theology*, 45–46. • 39. Rowan Williams, 236. • 40. Psalm 118:22. • 41. *The Breviary or Short Description of Jerusalem*, trans. Aubrey Stewart, with notes by C. W. Wilson (London, 1890), 14–15. • 42. Carruthers, *Craft of Thought*, 42–44. • 43. Jerome, Epistle 46:5; Migne, *Patrologia Latina* 22.486; cf. John 20:5–12. • 44. Barnard. • 45. Smalley, *Study of the Bible*, 8–9. • 46. Ibid., 11. • 47. Augustine, *On Christian Doctrine*, 30. • 48. Bruns, 635–36. • 49. Matthew 13:38. • 50. Alexander Roberts and W. H. Rambant, eds. and trans., *The Writings of Irenaeus* (Edinburgh, 1884), 461; modified. • 51. Augustine, 'On Psalm 98.1', in Michael Cameron, 'Enerrationes in Psalmos', in Fitzgerald, ed., 292. • 52. Augustine, *On Christian Doctrine*, 30. • 53. Ibid., 88. • 54. Pamela Bright, 'Augustine', in Holcomb, ed., 42–50. • 55. Augustine, *The Confessions*, 13.15.18. • 56. Augustine, *On the Psalms*, 103.4.1. • 57. Ibid., 12.35.33. • 58. Ibid., 12.25.34. • 59. Ibid. • 60. Ibid., 13.15.18. • 61. Psalm 103:2. • 62. Augustine, *The Literal Sense of Genesis*, 1.18, 19, 21. • 63. Augustine, *City of God*, 12.14. My emphasis • 64. Ibid. • 65. Maximus, *On the Ascetical Life*, in Migne, *Patrologia Graeca*. 90.905A; 953B. • 66. Romans 5:12. • 67. Theodoret, in Migne, *Patrologia Graeca* 83.512; Meyendorff, *Byzantine Theology*, 143–49. • 68. Genesis 6:1, 5–16. • 69. Genesis 1:31; my emphasis. • 70. Genesis Rabbah, Bereshit 9:7. • 71. Michael Avi-Yonah, *The Jews of Palestine: A Political History from the Bar Kokhbah War to the Arab Conquest* (Oxford, 1976), 160–76. • 72. *Y. Peah* 2.6, 17a; trans. Jaffee, 143. • 73. Ibid., 2:6. • 74. Deuteronomy 9:10; trans. Jaffee, 149. • 75. *Y. Peah* 2.6, 17a; trans. Jaffee, 143. • 76. Cf. Song of Songs, 7:10. • 77. Psalm 39:7; *Y. Sheqalim* 2.7; 47a.6–8; trans. Jaffee. • 78. Jaffee, 150–52. • 79. *B. Baba Batria* 12a. • 80. *B. Baba Metzia* 49b; Deuteronomy 39:12; Cohen, 40–41. • 81. Akenson, 379. • 82. Paul Williams, 118–19. • 83. David W. Chappell, 'Hermeneutic Phases in Chinese Buddhism', in Lopez, eds., *Buddhist Hermeneutics*, 1775–184. • 84. Fung, 246–54. • 85. Sengzhou, 'The Treasure House', 3, in Fung, 252. There are doubts about the authenticity of this essay. • 86. Quran 50:15.

10. Recitation and Intentio

1. Genesis 21:8–21. • 2. Quran 10:22–24; 2:61; 39:38. • 3. Bamyeh, 38. • 4. Ibid., 25–27. • 5. Ibid., 79–80. • 6. For example, Quran 56:78; 43:1–4. • 7. Gätje, 2. • 8. Frederick M. Denny, 'Islam: Qur'an and Hadith', in Denny and Taylor, eds., 87–88. • 9. It is, therefore, inaccurate simply to translate *jahiliyyah* as 'ignorance'; Izutsu, *Ethico-Religious Concepts*, 28–45. • 10. Michael Sells, *Approaching the Quran*, xvi. • 11. Izutsu, *God and Man in the Koran*, 148. • 12. Surah 96:1, 6–8; trans. Sells, *Approaching the Quran*. • 13. Ibid., 21. • 14. William A. Graham, *Beyond the Written Word*; Nelson, 3; Wilfred Cantwell Smith, *What Is Scripture?*, 52. • 15. Quran 3:84–85; trans. Abdel-Haleem. • 16. Quran 5:48; trans. Abdel-Haleem. • 17. Quran 5:35; trans. Abdel-Haleem. • 18. Quran 113:1; trans. Sells, *Approaching the Quran*; Bamyeh, 123–29. • 19. Sells, *Approaching the Quran*, xliii. • 20. Quran 99:6–9; trans. Sells, *Approaching the Quran*. • 21. Quran 90:13–16; trans. Sells, *Approaching the Quran*. • 22. Quran 81:36; trans. Sells, *Approaching the Quran*. • 23. Quran 88:20; trans. Sells, *Approaching the Quran*. • 24. Izutsu, *Ethico-Religious Concepts*, 66. • 25. Quran 15:94–96; 21:36; 18:106; 40:4–5; 68:56; 22:8–9. • 26. Quran 107:1–3, 6–7; trans. Sells, *Approaching the Quran*. • 27. Izutsu, *Ethico-Religious Concepts*, 28. • 28. Quran 2:144. • 29. Quran 6:35. • 30. Quran 5:73. • 31. Quran 2:116; 19:88–92; 10:68; 5:73–77, 116–118. • 32. Watt, 101–06. • 33. Quran 33:10–11; trans. Abdel-Haleem. • 34. Hodgson, I, 367. • 35. Quran 75:16–18; trans. Abdel-Haleem. • 36. Quran 7:205. • 37. Quran 19:58; 39:23; 5:83; trans. Abdel-Haleem. • 38. Ibn Ishaq, 158. • 39. Gorgias, *Encomium*, 9, in McGilchrist, 73. • 40. Suzanne Langer, *Philosophy in a New Key: A Study in the Symbolism of Reason, Rite and Art* (Cambridge, MA, 1942), 222. • 41. McGilchrist, 73–74. • 42. William A. Graham, *Beyond the Written Word*, 85–88, 110–114; Nelson, 3–13; Wilfred Cantwell Smith, *What Is Scripture?*, 69–74. • 43. Denny, 'Islam: Qur'an and Hadith', 90–91. • 44. Coward, *Sacred Word*, 81. • 45. Sells, *Early Islamic Mysticism*, 11–17. • 46. The Greek form of Zarathustra's name was Zoroaster. • 47. Denny, 'Islam: Qur'an and Hadith', 92–93; Coward, *Sacred Word*, 53; Gätje, 24–25. • 48. Gätje, 28–30; Coward, *Sacred Word*, 93–94; Donner, 32, 47. • 49. William A. Graham and David Kermani, 'Recitation and Aesthetic Reception', in McAuliffe, ed., *Cambridge Companion to the Qur'an*, 117–18. • 50. Bonner, 119–120. • 51. Quran 5:32–34; trans. Abdel-Haleem. • 52. Quran 5:39; trans. Abdel-Haleem. • 53. Quran 8:61–62; trans. Abdel-Haleem. • 54. In English, it is customary to use the singular term Hadith as a collective noun, referring to 'reports' in the plural as well as a single 'report'. • 55. Denny, 'Islam: Qur'an and Hadith', 97–103; Coward, *Sacred Word*, 94–95; Saeed, 76–78; Hodgson, I, 63–65. • 56. Awn, 143. • 57. Wilfred Cantwell Smith, *What Is Scripture?*, 46. • 58. Bonner, 21–22; Heck. • 59. Quran 2:279. • 60. Afsaruddin, *Striving in the Path of God*, 1–3, 269–71. • 61. Quran 3:200; trans. Abdel-Haleem. • 62. Afsaruddin, *Striving in the Path of God*, 271. • 63. Quran 22:39–40; trans. Abdel-Haleem. • 64. Quran 22:46; trans.

Abdel-Haleem. • 65. Afsaruddin, *Striving in the Path of God*, 43–44. • 66. Quran 2:190; trans. Afsaruddin. Abdel-Haleem translates: 'Do not overstep the limits', and explains that the phrase *la ta'tadu* is so general that commentators have agreed that it includes prohibition of starting hostilities, fighting non-combatants, disproportionate response to aggression. • 67. Quran 2:191–93; trans. Abdel-Haleem. • 68. Quran 2:216; trans. Abdel-Haleem. • 69. Quran 9:5; trans. Abdel-Haleem. • 70. Afsaruddin, *Striving in the Path of God*, 276. • 71. Quran 9.5; trans. Abdel-Haleem. • 72. Afsaruddin, *Striving in the Path of God*, 25–29. • 73. Bonner, 46–54; David Cook, *Understanding Jihad* (Berkeley, 2005), 13–19; Firestone, *Jihad*, 93–99. • 74. Muhammad ibn Isa al-Tirmidhi, Al-jami al-sahih; cited in David Cook, 'Jihad and Martyrdom in Islamic History', in Murphy, ed., 283–84. • 75. Bonner, 92–93. • 76. Afsaruddin, *Striving in the Path of God*, 270. • 77. Klostermaier, *Survey of Hinduism*, 221–22. • 78. Ibid., 94–96; Klostermaier, *Hinduism: A Short History*, 57–63. • 79. *Bhagavata Purana* (BP) 2.92.32; trans. C. Mackenzie Brown, 'Origin and Transmission'. • 80. *Devi Bhagavata Purana* (DBP) 1.14.52; trans. C. Mackenzie Brown, 'Origin and Transmission'. • 81. Matchett, 3. • 82. David Shulman, 'Remaking a Purana: The Rescue of Gajendra in Potena's Telegu *Mahabhagavatamu*', in Doniger, ed., *Purana Perennis*, 124. • 83. Klostermaier, *Survey of Hinduism*, 57. • 84. C. Mackenzie Brown, 'Origin and Transmission', 51. • 85. Hardy, 159–61, 182. • 86. C. Mackenzie Brown, 'Purana as Scripture'. • 87. DBP 12.14.15. • 88. C. Mackenzie Brown, 'Purana as Scripture'. • 89. BP 195.56–65; trans. Tagore. • 90. Shulman, 'Remaking a Purana', 123. • 91. Telegu version of the BG, quoted by Velcheru Narayana Roy, 'Purana as Brahminic Ideology', in Doniger, ed., *Purana Perennis*, 98–99. • 92. J. A. B. van Buitenen, 'On the Archaism of the *Bhagavata Purana*', in Singer, ed., 31. • 93. BP 9.14.48; in Halbfass, 4. • 94. BP 1.4.14–1.5.49; 1.7.3–8. • 95. Frederick M. Smith, 115–21. • 96. BP 6.4.46. • 97. BP 10.3.9–16. • 98. BP 10.3.19, 24. • 99. BP 10.1–23; 7.4–5, 15. • 100. BP 10.8.29–36. • 101. BP 10.42.22. • 102. BP 10.41.24–31. • 103. BP 10.22. • 104. BP 10.29.1. • 105. Kinsley, 13–65. • 106. *Daxue*, 'Great Learning'; trans. de Bary, in de Bary and Bloom, eds., *Sources*, 330. • 107. Fung, 181. • 108. Berry, 47. • 109. 'Great Learning'; trans. de Bary, in de Bary and Bloom, eds., *Sources*, 330. • 110. Ibid., 331. • 111. Chan, *Source Book*, 95–114; Fung, 166–77; Benjamin I. Schwartz, 405–06; Gardner, *Four Books*, 107–29. • 112. *Doctrine of the Mean*, 1; trans. Chan, *Source Book*, 98. • 113. *Doctrine of the Mean*, 1, 30; trans. Chan, *Source Book*, 112. • 114. *Doctrine of the Mean*, 1, 12; trans. Chan, *Source Book*, 98, 100. • 115. *Doctrine of the Mean*, 1, 20; trans. Chan, *Source Book*, 106. • 116. *Doctrine of the Mean*, 1, 20; trans. Chan, *Source Book*, 107. • 117. Ibid. • 118. *Doctrine of the Mean*, 1, 25; trans. Chan, *Source Book*, 108. • 119. Ibid. • 120. Zhou Dunyi, 'Penetrating the Book of Changes', 30; trans. Chan, *Source Book*, 477. • 121. Zhou Dunyi, 'Penetrating the Book of Changes', 39.2; trans. Chan, *Source Book*, 479. • 122. Zhang Zai, 'Ximing' ('Western Inscription'); trans. Wing-tsit Chan, in de Bary and Bloom, eds., *Sources*, 683–84. • 123. Chan, *Reflections*, 14.6a. • 124. *Yi chuan wenji*

('Collection of works by Cheng Yi'), 7.6a. • 125. Xi Zhu, *Literary Remains of the Two Chengs*, 2a; trans. de Bary, *Learning for One's Self*, 283. • 126. Cheng Yi, *Er-Cheng chuanshu*, 7.6b, in Wm. Theodore de Bary, *Neo-Confucian Orthodoxy and the Learning of the Mind and Heart* (New York, 1981), 4. • 127. Zhu Xi, *Reflections*, 2.16; trans. Wm. Theodore de Bary, 'Neo-Confucian Cultivation and the Seventeenth Century Enlightenment', in de Bary, ed., *Unfolding of Neo-Confucianism*. • 128. Memorial of Zhu Zang to Song Emperor Gaozong (r. 1127–62) in 1136 CE, in Seloran, 56. • 129. *Documents*, 4.8b; trans. Gardner, 'Attentiveness and Meditative Reading', 99. • 130. *Doctrine of the Mean*, 1; trans. Chan, *Source Book*, 98. • 131. Cheng Yi, *Er-Cheng Yishu*, 223.9, in Gardner, 'Attentiveness', 103. • 132. Cheng Ye, *Er Cheng Yishi*, 188.31; Gardner, ibid. • 133. Ibid. • 134. Cheng Hao, *Shi ren pian*, in Chan, *Source Book*, 523–24. • 135. Trans. A. C. Graham, *Two Chinese Philosophers*, 98. • 136. Zhu Xi, *Reflections*, 2.2a; trans. Chan, *Reflections*, 40. • 137. De Bary, 'Neo-Confucian Cultivation', 165–66. • 138. Cheng Yi, *Er-Cheng Yishu*, 209.7; trans. A. C. Graham, *Two Chinese Philosophers*, 76. • 139. Zhu Xi, *Reflections*, 3.31; trans. Chan, *Reflections*, 93. • 140. Seloran, 59–68. • 141. Zhu Xi, *Reflections*, 3.44; trans. Chan, *Reflections*, 105. • 142. Cheng Yi, *Er-Cheng Yishu*, 22a, 279; trans. Chan, *Reflections*, 103. • 143. Cheng Yi, *Er-Cheng Yishu*, 3.30; trans. Chan, *Reflections*, 100. • 144. Cheng Yi, *Er-Cheng Yishu*, 3.2; trans. Chan, *Reflections*, 92. • 145. De Bary, 'Neo-Confucian Cultivation', 171–74. • 146. Zhu Xi, *Reflections* 14.21; trans. Chan, *Reflections*, 304. • 147. Zhu Xi, *Reflections* 14.2b; trans. Chan, *Reflections*, 299. • 148. Zhu Xi, *Reflections* 14.5a; trans. Chan, *Reflections*, 305–06. • 149. Carruthers, *Book of Memory*; *Craft of Thought*. • 150. 1 Corinthians 3:10–13. • 151. 1 Corinthians 3:16; my emphasis. • 152. Gregory, *Moralia in Job*, 'Prologue'; trans. Carruthers, *Craft of Thought*, 18. • 153. Gregory, *Moralia in Job*, 'Prologue', 1.33; trans. Carruthers, *Craft of Thought*, 19. • 154. Gregory, *Moralia in Job*, 'Prologue', 2.1–5; Augustine, *On the Psalms*, 103; trans. Carruthers, *Craft of Thought*, 210. • 155. Peter Chrysologus, Sermon 98.22–23; cf. Luke 13:18–19; in Carruthers, *Craft of Thought*, 64. • 156. Talal Asad, 'On Discipline and Humility in Medieval Christian Monasticism', in Asad, *Genealogies of Religion*, 148. • 157. Light, 'The Bible and the Individual', 228–30. • 158. Richard Gyug, 'Early Medieval Bibles, Biblical Books, and the Monastic Liturgy in the Beneventan Region', in Boynton and Reilly, eds., 36–37. • 159. Christopher A. Jones, ed. and trans., *Aelfric's Letter to the Monks of Eynsham* (Cambridge, 1998). • 160. Benedict, Rule, 19.1–7. • 161. Ibid., 43. • 162. Isabelle Cochelin, 'When Monks Were the Book: The Bible and Monasticism (6th–11th Centuries)', in Boynton and Reilly, eds., 61–73. • 163. Johnston, 59. • 164. *The Monastic Agreement of the Monks and Nuns of the English Nation*, trans. Thomas Symons (London, 1953), 37. • 165. Cochalan, 'When Monks Were the Book', 67. • 166. Rule 53.12–15. • 167. Flood, *Ascetic Self*, 164–72. • 168. Ewart Cousins, 'The Humanity and Passion of Christ', in Raitt et al., eds., 377–83. • 169. Carruthers, *Book of Memory*, 183–84, 285. • 170. Gregory, *Regula Pastoralis*, 3.12. • 171. Hugh of Fouilloy, *De claustro animi*, 4.33; Migne, *Patrologia Latina* 176.1171D. • 172. Song of Songs 2:10; 1 Kings 19:12. • 173. Carruthers, *Book of*

Memory, 215–16. • 174. Augustine, *The Confessions*, 6.3.3; trans. Carruthers, *Book of Memory*, 215. • 175. Augustine, *De Doctrina Christiana*, 3.10.37, in R. P. H. Green, trans., *Saint Augustine: On Christian Teaching* (Oxford, 2008); Carruthers, *Book of Memory*, 15–16 • 176. Hugh, *De modo dicendi* 8; Migne, *Patrologia Latina* 176.879; Carruthers, *Craft of Thought*, 99. • 177. Hugh, 'The Three Best Memory-Aids for Learning History', in Carruthers, *Book of Memory*, Appendix A, 339–44; ibid., 89–90. • 178. Smalley, *Study of the Bible*, 121–27; Pelikan, *Whose Bible Is It?*, 106. • 179. Smalley, *Study of the Bible*, 86–154; Van Liere, 133–34. • 180. *Proslogion* 2.161; my translation. • 181. Evans, 17–23. • 182. *Proslogion* 1:86–89; 91–95, in Benedicta Ward.

11. Ineffability

1. Norman Cohn, 87–88. • 2. Georges Duby, *The Chivalrous Society* (London, 1977), 9–11. • 3. R. I. Moore, *The Formation of a Persecuting Society: Power and Deviance in Western Europe 950–1250* (Oxford, 1987), 105–06. • 4. Quoted and translated in Carruthers, *Book of Memory*, 217. • 5. 2 Corinthians 13; Mark 13:21. • 6. Gregory, 312–14. • 7. Van Liere, 98–103. • 8. Gregory, 315–16. • 9. *Summa Theologiae*, 8.46.2, in Thomas Aquinas, *Summa Theologiae: A Concise Translation*, ed. and trans. Timothy McDermott (London, 1989). • 10. Aquinas, *Summa contra Gentiles*, 1.5.3, in Thomas Aquinas, *Selected Writings*, ed. and trans. R. McInerny (Harmondsworth, UK, 1998). • 11. Ephesians 1:21; Aquinas, *Commentary on St Paul's Epistle to the Ephesians*, trans. M. L. Lamb (Albany, 1966), 73–79. • 12. Denys Turner, *Faith, Reason and the Existence of God*; Denys Turner, 'Apophatism, Idolatry and the Claims of Reason', in Turner and Davies, eds., *Silence and the Word*, 23–34; Pelikan, *Christian Tradition*, 3.78–79. • 13. Carruthers, *Craft of Thought*, 99–100; *Book of Memory*, 216. • 14. Acts 17:34. • 15. Denys, *The Divine Names* (DN), 596A. • 16. Denys, Epistle 9, 1104D–1105B, in *Pseudo-Dionysius*. • 17. Denys, *Mystical Theology*, 1033B. • 18. Ibid., 1048A. • 19. DN 872; trans. Luibheid and Rorem; my emphases. • 20. Bonaventure, *Journey of the Mind to God*, 6.3; all quotations are taken from Boehner and Laughlin. • 21. Ibid., 6.7. • 22. John 13:1. • 23. Bonaventure, *Journey of the Mind to God*, 7.6. • 24. Edward Grant, 'Science and Theology in the Middle Ages', in Lindberg and Numbers, eds., 61. • 25. Herbert McCabe, Appendix 3 to vol. III of the Blackfriars edition of Brian Davies, *The Thought of Thomas Aquinas* (Oxford, 1992), 41. • 26. Gregory, 317. • 27. Roy Porter, 531–62. • 28. Corbin, *Spiritual Body*, 51. • 29. Mahmoud Ayoub, 'The Speaking Qur'an and the Silent Qur'an: A Study of the Principles and Development of Imami Shi'is Tafsir', in Rippin, ed., *Approaches*, 181. • 30. Corbin, *History of Islamic Philosophy*, 45. • 31. Diana Steigerwald, 'Twelver Shi'i *Ta'wil*', in Rippin, ed., *Blackwell Companion*, 374–76. See Quran 11:73; 21:73. • 32. Quran 24:35–36; trans. Abdel-Haleem. • 33. S. H. Nasr, *Ideals and Realities of Islam* (London, 1971), 59. • 34. Quran 17:1. • 35. Hodgson, I, 404–05. • 36. Quran 3:7; trans. Abdel-Haleem. • 37. Hodgson, I, 402–03; Sands, 7–8. • 38. Abu Talib al-Makki, *Qut al-qulab*, in Sands, 31. •

39. Ibid., 32. • 40. Tabari, *Jami al-bayan*, 3.175. • 41. Ar-Razi, *Al-Tafsir al-Kabir*, 2.88; 4.155. • 42. *Masnawi* simply means 'poem in rhyming couplets'. • 43. Jawid Mojaddedi, 'Rumi', in Rippin, ed., *Blackwell Companion*, 364–67. • 44. Attributed to the fifteenth-century poet and mystic Abd al-Rahman Jami; Mojaddedi, 'Rumi', in Rippin, ed., *Blackwell Companion*, 362, 371. • 45. *Masnawi*, 3.4248–50; all translations from the *Masnawi* are taken from Mojaddedi, *Masnawi*. • 46. Ibn al-Arabi, *Al Futuhat al-Makkiya* ('The Meccan Openings'), 4.367.3. • 47. Ibid., 3.128–29. • 48. Ibid, 3.93–94; trans. Chodkiewicz, 25–26. • 49. Quran 20:133; 53:36; 87:18. • 50. *Al-Futuhat*, 4.367, 3; trans. Chittick, *Sufi Path*. • 51. Ibid., 2.119.24. • 52. Quran 10:24; trans. Abdel-Haleem. • 53. *Al Futuhat*, 3.71.4. • 54. Ibid., 2.581.11; trans. Chittick, *Sufi Path*. • 55. Chodkiewicz, 19–31. • 56. Ibid., 193. • 57. Quran 107; trans. Abdel-Haleem. • 58. Chittick, 'Hermeneutics of Mercy', in *Sufi Path of Knowledge*, 153–67. • 59. Reynold A. Nicholson, ed. and trans., *Eastern Poetry and Prose* (Cambridge, 1922), 148. • 60. Robert the Monk, *Historia Iherosolimitana; Recueil des historians des croisades, ed. Academie des Inscriptions et Belles Lettre*s (1841–1900), III, 741. • 61. Fulcher of Chartres, *A History of the Expedition to Jerusalem, 1098–1127,* ed. and trans. Frances Rita Ryan (Knoxville, 1969), 60–67; Jonathan Riley-Smith, *The First Crusade and the Idea of Crusading* (London, 1986), 143. • 62. Hillenbrand, 75–81; Bonner, 137–40. • 63. Quran 2:190–94. • 64. Afsaruddin, *Striving in the Path of God*, 42–99. • 65. B. *Sukkot* 28a. • 66. *M. Avot* 3.2; *Pesikta de R. Kahana* 15.9. • 67. Holdrege, 179–95, 254–60, 359–74. • 68. Genesis 1:26; trans. Holdrege. • 69. *Pirke de R. Eliezer* 99, 44a; *M. Avot* 5.6. This discourse was attributed to the Yavne sage Rabbi Eliezer ben Hyrcanus. • 70. B. *Eruvim* 13a. • 71. Henry Malter, *Saadia Gaon: His Life and Work* (Philadelphia, 1942). • 72. Abraham Cohen; David Yellin and Israel Abraham, *Maimonides* (London, 1927); Halbertal, 34–40; 54–62. • 73. Maimonides, *The Guide of the Perplexed*, trans. S. Pines (Chicago, 1974), 6–7. • 74. Ibid., 8. • 75. J. Abelson, *The Immanence of God in Rabbinic Literature* (London, 1912), 257. • 76. Julius Guttmann, *Philosophies of Judaism: The History of Jewish Philosophy from Biblical Times to Franz Rosensweig*, trans. David W. Silverman (London, 1914), 179. • 77. I. Tweksy, *Introduction to the Code of Maimonides (Mishneh Torah)* (New Haven, 1980), 62–74. • 78. Moshe Idel, 'PaRDeS: Some Reflections on Kabbalistic Hermeneutics', in Fishbane and Collins, eds., 251–56; Fishbane, *Garments of Torah*, 113–120. • 79. Scholem, *Major Trends*, 1–79, 119–243; Fishbane, *Exegetical Imagination*; Fishbane, *Garments of Torah*, 34–63. • 80. Scholem, ed., *Zohar*, 87–91, 211–12. • 81. Gershom Scholem, 'The Meaning of the Torah in Jewish Mysticism', in Scholem, *On the Kabbalah*, 44. • 82. Gershom Scholem, 'On the Ritual of the Kabbalists', in Scholem, *On the Kabbalah*, 126. • 83. Gershom Scholem, 'General Characteristics of Jewish Mysticism', in Woods, ed., 158–59. • 84. Fishbane, *Exegetical Imagination*, 100, 101. • 85. *Zohar* II.94B, in Scholem, eds., *Zohar*, 90. • 86. Ibid. • 87. Ibid., 22. • 88. *Zohar* II.182a. • 89. Zhu Xi, Preface to the *Zhongyong zhangju*; trans. de Bary, *Neo-Confucian Orthodoxy*, 5–6. • 90. Taylor, *Religious Dimensions*, 79–80. • 91. De Bary, 'Zhu Xi's Neo-Confucian Spirituality', in Tu and Tucker, eds., II, 72–95. • 92. Zhu Zi, *Ren Shu*, adapted by

de Bary, 'Zhu Xi's Neo-Confucian Spirituality', in Tu and Tucker, eds., II, 93, from Chan, *Source Book*, 596. • 93. Ibid. • 94. Zhu Xi, *Yenping dawen*, 3. • 95. De Bary, 'Zhu Xi's Neo-Confucian Spirituality', in Tu and Tucker, eds., II, 86–87. • 96. Henderson, 50–52. • 97. Chan, *Reflections*, 102. • 98. Wm. Theodore de Bary, 'Introduction', in de Bary, ed., *Unfolding of Neo-Confucianism*, 10. • 99. Gardner, *Learning to be a Sage*, 10–22. • 100. Denis Twitchett, *Printing and Publishing in Medieval China* (New York, 1983), 23–81; L. C. Goodrich, 'The Development of Printing in China', *Journal of the Hong Kong Branch of the Royal Asiatic Society*, 3 (1963). • 101. John W. Chaffee, 'Chu Hsi and the Revival of the White Deer Grotto Academy', 1179–81, *T'oung Pao*, 71 (1985). • 102. Zhu Xi, *Huian xiansheng yu lei* (YL), 197.10, in Gardner, 'Attentiveness', 109. • 103. Zhu Xi, YL 4.33; trans. Gardner, *Learning to be a Sage*, 42. • 104. YL 4.32; trans. Gardner, *Learning to be a Sage*, 42. • 105. YL 16.46.45. • 106. YL 169.14. • 107. YL 162.9; trans. Gardner, 'Attentiveness', 112. • 108. YL 5.31; trans. Gardner, *Learning to be a Sage*, 46. • 109. YL 5.36; trans. Gardner, *Learning to be a Sage*, 46. • 110. YL 5.34; trans. Gardner, *Learning to be a Sage*, 48. • 111. YL 6.46. • 112. YL 4.31; trans. Gardner, *Learning to be a Sage*, 54. • 113. YL 3.28; trans. Gardner, 'Attentiveness', 114. • 114. Cole, 15. • 115. *Adi Granth* (AG) 150; trans. Singh, 'An Overview of Sikh History', 21. • 116. AG 722.

PART THREE: LOGOS

12. Sola Scriptura

1. Quoted in Marvin B. Becker, *Florence in Transition: Studies in the Rise of the Territorial State* (Baltimore, 1968), 6. • 2. Quoted in Charles Trinkhaus, *The Poet as Philosopher: Petrarch and the Formation of Renaissance Consciousness* (New Haven, 1979), 126. • 3. Letter to his brother Gherado, 2 December 1348, in David Thompson, ed., *Petrarch: A Humanist among Princes: An Anthology of Petrarch's Letters and Translations from his Works* (New York, 1971), 90. • 4. McGrath, *Reformation Thought*, 32–34. • 5. Ibid., 37–39. • 6. Hodgson, III, 179–95. • 7. I have discussed this in detail in *The Battle for God: A History of Fundamentalism* (London, 2000), *passim*. • 8. Gregory, 84–87. • 9. Richard Marius, *Martin Luther: The Christian between God and Death* (Cambridge, MA, 1999), 73–74, 213–15, 486–87. • 10. Psalm 71:2. • 11. Lienhard, 'Luther and the Beginnings of the Reformation', 22. • 12. Romans 1:16–17; Habakkuk 2:4; my emphasis. • 13. McGrath, *Reformation Thought*, 74. • 14. Luther, *Luther's Works* (LW), 25.188–89. • 15. LW 10.239. • 16. Scott H. Hendrix, *Luther and the Papacy: Stages in a Reformation Conflict* (Philadelphia, 1981), 83; Bainton, 90. • 17. Norman Cohn, 107–16. • 18. Cameron, 169–70. • 19. Zwingli, *On the Clarity and Certainty of the Word of God* (1522), in McGrath, *Reformation Thought*, 107. • 20. Zwingli, *On the Clarity and Certainty of the Word of God*, in Gregory, 87. • 21. During the Second Zurich Disputation (1523). *Corpus Reformatum* (CR), Vol. 88, 24–25, in Gregory, 87. • 22. Matthew 26:26. • 23. McGrath, *Reformation Thought*, 105–07;

my emphasis. • 24. McGilchrist, 314–23. • 25. Ibid., 117–18. • 26. Ibid., 180. • 27. Gregory, 88–89. • 28. Ibid., 98. • 29. Philip S. Watson, *Let God be God! An Interpretation of the Theology of Martin Luther* (Philadelphia, 1947), 149. • 30. James 2:14–16. • 31. McGrath, *Reformation Thought*, 110. • 32. Martin Luther, 'Admonition to Peace: A Reply to the Twelve Articles of the Peasants in Swabia', trans. J. J. Schindel, rev. Walther I. Brandt, in J. M. Porter, ed., 78. • 33. Martin Luther, 'Against the Robbing and Murdering Hordes of the Peasants', trans. Charles M. Jacobs, rev. Robert C. Schultz, in J. M. Porter, ed., 86. • 34. Martin Luther, 'Temporal Authority: To What Extent It Should be Obeyed', trans. J. J. Schindel, rev. Walther I. Brandt, in J. M. Porter, ed., 54. • 35. McGrath, *Reformation Thought*, 107–11. • 36. Calvin, Preface; trans. McGrath, *Reformation Thought*, 108. • 37 McGrath, *A Life of John Calvin*, 131. • 38. Kraeling, 21–22; Randall C. Zachman, 'John Calvin', in Holcomb, ed., 117–29. • 39. John Bossy, 'Counter-Reformation'. • 40. James Turner, 10–11, 19–20. • 41. Richard Tarnas, *The Passion of the Western Mind: Understanding the Ideas That Have Shaped Our World View* (London, 1991), 242. • 42. John of the Cross, *The Dark Night of the Soul*, 1.9.7, in E. Allison Peers, trans., *The Complete Works of John of the Cross* (London, 1953); my emphasis. • 43. Teresa, *Relations*, 5, in E. Allison Peers, ed. and trans., *The Complete Works of St Teresa*, 3 vols. (New York, 1957), I.328. • 44. Teresa, *The Interior Castle*, 4., trans. E. Allison Peers (New York, 1964). • 45. Quoted in Dupré, 458. • 46. William T. Cavanaugh, *The Myth of Religious Violence* (Oxford, 2009), 142–55; and my own *Fields of Blood: Religion and the History of Violence* (London, 2014), 225–32. • 47. Geoffrey Parker, *The Thirty Years War* (London, 1984). • 48. Buckley, 85–87. • 49. Descartes, *Discourse on Method*, 4.32. Unless otherwise stated, quotations from Descartes' work are taken from *Descartes: Key Philosophical Writings*. • 50. Descartes, *Meditations*, 5.67. • 51. Descartes, *Discourse on Method*, 3.37. • 52. Ibid., 3.11–19. • 53. McGilchrist, 332–33; Louis Sass, *Madness and Modernism: Insanity in the Light of Modern Art, Literature and Thought* (Cambridge, MA, 1992). • 54. Descartes, *Meditations*, 2.32. • 55. Ibid., 6.76. • 56. Ibid., 2.81. • 57. 1 Corinthians 1:24. • 58. Milton, *De Doctrina Christiana* (DDC), 6.213. Unless otherwise stated, quotations from Milton's prose writings have been taken from *Complete Prose Works of John Milton*, ed. Wolfe. • 59. Milton, *Areopagitica*, 2.549, 516. • 60. Milton, *The Ready and Easy Way to Establish a Free Commonwealth*, 7.443. • 61. Milton, *Paradise Lost* (PL), *The Poetical Works of John Milton, Vol. I, Paradise Lost*, ed. Darbishire, 1.1–4. • 62. Ibid. • 63. Lovelace, 313. • 64. DDC 955. • 65. Job 41:1; Isaiah 14:12; Ezekiel 28. • 66. John Carey, 'Milton's Satan', in Danielson, ed., 161–71. • 67. PL 9.473. • 68. PL 2.125–26. • 69. PL 4.75–78. • 70. PL 5.785–86, 794–97. • 71. Milton, *Areopagitica*, 2.524. • 72. PL 4.433–35. • 73. PL 5.860. • 74. William Shullenberger, 'Imagining Eden', in Louis Schwartz, ed., 134–36. • 75. PL 9.782–84. • 76. PL 12.586–87. • 77. Gregory Chaplin, 'Beyond Sacrifice: Milton and the Atonement', *PMLA*, 125 (2010). • 78. PL 11.496. • 79. Kathleen Swain, *Before and After the Fall: Contrasting Modes in 'Paradise Lost'* (Amherst, 1992), 236. • 80. PL 12.561–64. •

81. Shullenberger, 'Imagining Eden', 136; Mary C. Fenton, 'Regeneration in Books 11 and 12', in Louis Schwartz, ed., 190. • 82. PL 12.582–83. • 83. PL 3.95–99. • 84. PL 3.117–23. • 85. PL 2.558–59, 565. • 86. Paul Johnson, 229; Yovel, 17–18. • 87. Introduction, *Shulkhan Arukh*; trans. Halbertal, 76. • 88. Introduction, *Torat Hatat* (Cracow, 1569); trans. Halbertal, note 52. • 89. Quoted in *Responsa Roma* (Jerusalem, 1971); trans. Halbertal, 78. • 90. Halbertal, 78–79. • 91. Ibid., 80–81. • 92. J. Elboim, *Petichut ve-Histagrut* (Jerusalem, 1990); trans. Halbertal, 99. • 93. R. Shlomo b. Mordechai, *Mizbach ha-Zehav* 12a (Basel, 1604); trans. Halbertal, ibid. • 94. Karo, *Magid Mesharim* 40a–b; trans. Halbertal, 123. • 95. Scholem, *Major Trends*, 246–49. • 96. Scholem, *Messianic Idea*, 43–48. • 97. Gershom Scholem, *Sabbetai Sevi: The Mystical Messiah* (London, 1973), 37–42. • 98. Ibid., 23–35. • 99. R. J. Werblowsky, 'The Safed Revival and Its Aftermath', in Green, ed., 2.15–19, 21–24; Lawrence Fine, 'The Contemplative Practice of Yehudin in Lurianic Kabbalah', in Green, ed., 1.73–8, 89–90; Louis Jacobs, 'The Uplifting of the Sparks in Later Jewish Mysticism', in Green, ed., 2.108–11; Scholem, *On the Kabbalah*, 150. • 100. John Voll, 'Renewal and Reform in Islamic History', in Esposito, ed. • 101. Momen, 114–16. • 102. Magel Baklash, 'Taziyeh and Its Philosophy', in Chelkowski, ed., 105. • 103. Mary Hegland, 'Two Images of Husain: Accommodations and Revolution in an Iranian Village', in Keddie, ed., *Religion and Politics*, 221–25. • 104. Momen, 117–18. • 105. Nikki R. Keddie, '*Ulema*'s Power in Modern Iran', in Keddie, ed., *Scholars, Saints and Sufis*, 223. • 106. Hodgson, III, 42–46; Mangol Bayat, *Mysticism and Dissent: Socio-Religious Thought in Qajar Iran* (Syracuse, 1982), 28–47. • 107. Rahman, *Philosophy of Mulla Sadra*, 12, 36–37, 115, 117, 206. • 108. Fischer, 239–42. • 109. Delong-Bas, 8–14. • 110. Ibid., 14–40. • 111. Ibid., 194–200. • 112. Ibid., 212–34. • 113. McLeod, 60. • 114. In this account, I am much indebted to the essay by Arvind-pal Singh Mandair, 'Sikh Philosophy', in Singh and Fenech, eds., 298–316. • 115. *Adi Granth* (AG) 4.3. Unless otherwise stated, quotations from the Sikh scriptures are from Shackle and Mandair. • 116. AG 1.1. • 117. AG 4.6. • 118. AG 8.9. • 119. Interview with Harold Coward in Calgary, 1985. • 120. Cole, 89. • 121. AG 683.3, quoted in W. Owen Cole and Piara Singh Samdhi, *The Sikhs: Their Religious Beliefs and Practices* (New Delhi, 1978), 55. • 122. Coward, *Sacred Word*, 131–33. • 123. Harjot Oberoi, 'Sikhism', in Coward, ed., *Experiencing Scripture*, 135. • 124. De Bary, 'Introduction', 4–5; 'Neo-Confucian Cultivation', in de Bary, ed., *Unfolding of Neo-Confucianism*, 141–44, 153–90. • 125. *Doctrine of the Mean*, 1, 20; trans. Chan, *Source Book*, 107. • 126. Zhu Xi, *Zhongyong huowen*, 20, 105b–196a; trans. Chan, *Reflections*, 69. • 127. Edward T. Ch'ien, 'Chiao Hung and the Revolt against Ch'eng-Chu Orthodoxy', in de Bary, ed., *Unfolding of Neo-Confucianism*, 276–96. All quotations from Jiao's writings are taken from this article. • 128. Jiao Hong, *Danyuan*, 22.36. • 129. Jiao Hong, *Jinling Congshu*, Preface, 1a. • 130. *Danyuan*, 12.18a. • 131. Jiao Hong, *Bizheng xi*, 2.169. • 132. *Danyuan ji*, 22.3b. • 133. *Bizheng xi*, 1.27. • 134. Ibid. • 135. Jiao Hong, *Jingli zhi*, 2.20. • 136. Peterson, 370–401. All quotations from Fang's work are taken from this article. •

137. *Great Learning* 3; trans. A. C. Graham, *Two Chinese Philosophers*, 74; my emphasis.
• 138. Ibid., 79. • 139. Fang Yizhen, *Wu li xiao*, 1a. • 140. Ibid. • 141. Ibid. • 142.
Ibid., 7b. • 143. Fang Yizhen, *Xiyu xin bi*, 24b–25a. • 144. Fang Yizhen, *Wu li xiao*,
1.25a. • 145. Ibid., 1.6. • 146. Ibid., 12a. • 147. Ibid., 1.22b.

13. Sola Ratio

1. Yovel, 19–24. • 2. Ibid., 75–76. • 3. José Faur, 'Sanchez' Critique of *Authoritas:
Converso* Scepticism and the Emergence of Radical Hermeneutics', in Ochs, ed. •
4. Sanchez, 'Quod Nihil Scitur', in ibid., 263–64. • 5. Yovel, 42–51, 57–63.
• 6. Ibid., 4–13, 172–74. • 7. Faur, 'Sanchez' Critique', 268. • 8. Spinoza, 119. •
9. Ibid., 91. • 10. Ibid., 99. • 11. Newton, *Mathematical Principles*, 544. • 12. Ibid.,
546. • 13. Isaac Newton, Yehuda MS. 41, fol. 7, Jewish National University Library,
Jerusalem; Richard S. Westfall, 'The Rise of Science and the Decline of Orthodox
Christianity: A Study of Kepler, Descartes and Newton', in Lindberg and Numbers,
eds., 232–33. The original manuscript shows that Newton decided, as an after-
thought, to insert 'with out revelation' between the lines, after 'knowledge of a
deity'. • 14. Isaac Newton, MS William Andreas Clark Memorial Library, UCLA,
Los Angeles; Westfall, 'Rise of Science', 231. • 15. Newton, Yehuda MS. 41, fol.
6; Westfall, 'Rise of Science', 230. • 16. Newton, Yehuda MSS. 1.4, fol. 50, and
2, fol. 7; Westfall, 'Rise of Science', 231–32. • 17. Wilfred Cantwell Smith, *Belief
and History*; *Faith and Belief*; and my own *The Case for God* (London, 2009). • 18.
Newton to Bentley, 1691, in Newton, *Correspondence*, 3.233. • 19. Ibid., 3.324,
326. • 20. Funkenstein, 357–60. • 21. Locke, *An Essay Concerning Human
Understanding*, 4.18.3. • 22. Locke, *A Letter Concerning Toleration*, 31, 27. • 23. Frei,
109. • 24. Ibid., 115. • 25. Ibid., 85–92. • 26. Ibid., 161–62. • 27. David Hume,
'Of the Study of History', in Hume, *Of the Standard of Taste*, 96. • 28. James William
Johnson, 43–45. • 29. Frei, 157–60; Sheehan, 54–84, 95–136. • 30. Sheehan,
28–44. • 31. Frei, 136–56. • 32. Johann Gottfried Herder, *Briefe das Studium der
Theologie betreffend*; Letter no. 2; trans. Frei, 185. • 33. Gregory, 377–80. • 34.
Locke, *Two Treatises of Government*, 1.2.4. • 35. Hobbes, 1.13.61–63. • 36. Rousseau,
Section 1. • 37. Hatch, 22. • 38. Kant, 3. • 39. Bauman, 111. • 40. Thomas Jefferson
to Peter Carr, 10 August 1787, *Life and Selected Writings*, 400. • 41. Ibid.; Spellberg,
231–32. • 42. Spellberg, 235. • 43. Locke, *A Letter Concerning Toleration*, 17. • 44.
Jefferson, *Writings of Thomas Jefferson*, XI.428. • 45. Locke, *A Letter Concerning
Toleration*, 15. • 46. Locke, *Two Treatises of Government*, 'Second Treatise', 5.24;
5.120–21; 5.3. • 47. Hatch, 9. • 48. I have discussed this in *The Battle for God: A
History of Fundamentalism* (London, 2000). • 49. Heimert, 43. • 50. Bloch, 14–15.
• 51. Jonathan Edwards, 'A Faithful Narrative of the Surprizing Work of God in
Northampton', in Sherwood Elio Witt, ed., *Spiritual Awakening: Classic Writings of
the Eighteenth Century to Inspire and Help the Twentieth Century Reader* (Tring, 1988),

110–13. • 52. Hatch, 68–157. • 53. Daniel Walker Howe, 'Religion and Politics in the Antebellum North', in Noll, ed., 132–33; George Marsden, 'Afterword', in ibid., 382–83. • 54. Mark A. Noll, 'The Rise and Long Life of the Protestant Enlightenment in America', in Shea and Huff, eds. • 55. Boyer, 87–90; Marsden, 50–55; Charles B. Strozier, *Apocalypse: On the Psychology of Fundamentalism* (Boston, MA, 1994), 183–85. • 56. 2 Thessalonians 2:3–8. This was not written by Paul but is a Deutero-Pauline epistle. • 57. Boyer, 83–85. • 58. 1 Thessalonians 4:16. • 59. Marsden, 57–63. • 60. Ibid., 14–17; Nancy Ammerman, 'North American Protestant Fundamentalism', in Marty and Appleby, eds., *Fundamentalisms Observed*, 8–12. • 61. Pierson, *Many Infallible Proofs* (1895), quoted in Marsden, 55. • 62. Sloek, 83. • 63. Hodge, 142. • 64. James R. Moore, 'Geologists and Interpreters of Genesis in the Nineteenth Century', in Lindberg and Numbers, eds., 329–34. • 65. Mrs Humphrey Ward, 414. • 66. Marsden, 110–15. • 67. Archibald Hodge and Benjamin Warfield, 'Inspiration', *Princeton Review*, 2 (11 April 1881). • 68. *New York Times*, 5 April 1894. • 69. *New York Times*, 5 April 1899. • 70. *Union Seminary Magazine*, 19 (1907–08). • 71. Armstrong, *Battle for God*. • 72. Martin E. Marty and R. Scott Appleby, 'Conclusion: An Interim Report on a Hypothetical Family', in Marty and Appleby, eds., *Fundamentalisms Observed*, 814–42. • 73. Armstrong, *Battle for God*, 176–78; *Case for God*, 272–74. • 74. Armstrong, *Case for God*, 217–315. • 75. Matthew Arnold, 'Dover Beach', lines 25, 14, in *Arnold: Poetical Works*, eds. C. B. Tinker and H. F. Lowry (Oxford, 1945). • 76. Nietzsche, *The Gay Science* (GS), trans. Walter Kaufman (New York, 1974), 181. • 77. Ibid., 279. • 78. Ibid., 181. • 79. Nietzsche, *Ecce Homo* (EH), 102–03. • 80. Friedrich Nietzsche, *Kritische Studienausgabe in 15 Einzelbänden*, ed. G. Colli and M. Montinari (Berlin, 1988), vol. 15, 88. • 81. Jörg Salaquarda, 'Nietzsche and the Judaeo-Christian Tradition', in Magnus and Higgins, eds., 94. • 82. EH, 128. • 83. Trimble, 194–96. • 84. Von Tevenar, 272–95. • 85. GS, Preface, 1. • 86. R. J. Hollingdale, 'Introduction', in Nietzsche, *Thus Spoke Zarathustra: A Book for Everyone and No One* (TSZ), 16. All quotations, unless otherwise stated, are taken from this translation. • 87. Salaquarda, 'Nietzsche and the Judaeo-Christian Tradition', 90–104. • 88. TSZ, 98–99. • 89. Christopher Janaway, '*The Gay Science*', in Gemes and Richardson, eds., 258–60. • 90. GS, 338. • 91. Nietzsche, *On the Genealogy of Morals*, 2.25. • 92. GS, 342. • 93. TSZ, 167. • 94. Ibid., 331–32. • 95. Ibid., 332; translator's emphasis. • 96. Ibid., 43. • 97. Ibid., 121. • 98. Ibid. • 99. Ibid., 336; translator's emphasis. • 100. EH, 99. • 101. Blake, 'The Tyger', lines 4–5. • 102. Blake, *Jerusalem*, 33: lines 1–24; 96: lines 23–28. • 103. Blake, 'Introduction', *Songs of Experience*, lines 6–10. • 104. Blake, 'The Divine Image'. • 105. Wordsworth, 'Expostulation and Reply' and 'The Tables Turned', in *Wordsworth: Poetical Works*, ed. Thomas Hutchinson; rev. Ernest de Selincourt (Oxford, 1904). • 106. Wordsworth, 'Lines Composed a Few Miles Above Tintern Abbey on Revisiting the Banks of the Wye During a Tour, July 13, 1798', lines 37–49. • 107. Aquinas, *Summa Theologiae*, 1a.q.3.1–5, 14–15. • 108. Wordsworth, 'Tintern Abbey', 37–49. • 109. John Keats to George and Georgiana

Keats, 21 December 1817, *Letters of John Keats*. • 110. John Keats to George and Georgiana Keats, 19 March 1819, *Letters of John Keats*. • 111. Keats to Richard Woodhouse, 27 October 1818, *Letters of John Keats*. • 112. Benzion Dinur, 'The Origins of Hasidism and Its Social and Messianic Foundations', in Hundert, ed., 86–161; Simon Dubnow, 'The Maggid of Miedzyryrzecz, His Associates and the Center in Volhynia', in Hundert, ed., 58. • 113. Benjamin Dinur, 'The Messianic-Prophetic Role of the Baal Shem Tov', in Saperstein, ed., 378–80. • 114. Shmuel Ettinger, 'The Hasidic Movement: Reality and Ideals', in Hundert, ed., 257. • 115. Gershom Scholem, 'The Neutralization of Messianism in Early Hasidism' in Scholem, *Messianic Idea*, 189–200; '"Devekut" or Communion with God', in ibid., 203–37; Louis Jacobs, 'The Uplifting of the Sparks in Later Jewish Mysticism', in Green, ed., 2.116–25; Louis Jacobs, 'Hasidic Prayer', in Hundert, ed., 330–48. • 116. Scholem, 'Neutralization of Messianism', 196–98. • 117. Scholem, *Major Trends*, 334. • 118. Dubnow, 61. • 119. Ibid., 62. • 120. Ibid., 65. • 121. 2 Kings 3:25. • 122. Dubnow, 65; my emphasis. • 123. Rachel Eliot, 'HaBaD: The Contemplative Ascent to God', in Green, ed., 2.158–203. • 124. Jacobs, 'Hasidic Prayer', 340. • 125. Rudavsky, 157–64, 286–87. • 126. Ibid., 290. • 127. Güttmann, 308–51. • 128. Rudavsky, 188, 194–95, 201–04. • 129. Samuel C. Heilman and Menachem Friedman, 'Religious Fundamentalism and Religious Jews', in Marty and Appleby, eds., *Fundamentalisms Observed*, 211–15; Charles Selengut, 'By Torah Alone: Yeshiva Fundamentalism in Jewish Life', in Marty and Appleby, eds., *Accounting for Fundamentalisms*, 239–41; Menachem Friedman, 'Habad as Messianic Fundamentalism', in ibid., 201. • 130. Rudavsky, 219–43. • 131. De Bary, 'Introduction', in de Bary, ed., *Unfolding of Neo-Confucianism*, 32. • 132. Taylor, *Religious Dimensions*, 58. • 133. Heinrich Bosch, 'The Tung-Lin Academy and Its Political and Philosophical Significance', MS. XIV (1949–55), 119–29. • 134. De Bary, 'Neo-Confucian Cultivation', in de Bary, ed., *Unfolding of Neo-Confucianism*, 182–83. • 135. Ibid., 191–94. • 136. Ibid., 193–94. • 137. Ibid., 203–04. • 138. Ibid., 197–98. • 139. Taylor, 'Confucian Spirituality and Qing Thought', II.163–209. • 140. Elman, 28. • 141. Quoted in Cynthia Brokaw, 'Tai Chen and Learning in the Confucian Tradition', in Elman and Woodside, eds., 290. • 142. Ibid., 271. • 143. Tu, 'Perceptions of Learning', 120. • 144. Brokaw, 279–80. • 145. Metzger, 163. • 146. De Bary, 'Introduction', 32. • 147. Kautsky, *Political Consequences of Modernization*, 60–61. • 148. Wilfred Cantwell Smith, *Meaning and End of Religion*, 61–62. • 149. Thapar, 'Historical Realities'. • 150. Ibid., 83. • 151. Daniel Gold, 'Organized Hinduisms: From Vedic Truth to Hindu Nation', in Marty and Appleby, eds., *Fundamentalisms*, 533–77. • 152. Kenneth W. Jones, 'The Arya Samaj in British India, 1874–1947', in Robert D. Baird, ed., *Religion in Modern India* (New Delhi, 1981), 36–39. • 153. Gold, 'Organized Hinduisms', 575–83. • 154. Robert E. Frykenberg, 'Hindu Fundamentalism and the Structural Stability of India', in Marty and Appleby, eds., *Fundamentalisms and the State*, 239. • 155. Kopf. • 156. Rai, 103–05. • 157. Brian K. Smith, 20. • 158. Jordens, 35–39. • 159. Gold, 'Organized

Hinduisms', 544–46. • 160. Ibid., 585, note 46. • 161. Jordens, 271. • 162. Dr Chiranjiva Bhara Awaja, trans., *Swami Dayananda Saraswati, Light of Truth, or an English Translation of the Satyarthi Prakas* (New Delhi, 1975), 332. • 163. Ibid., 733. • 164. Jordens, 271. • 165. N. Gould Barrier, 'Sikhs and Punjab Politics', in Joseph T. O'Connell, ed., *Sikh History and Religion in the Twentieth Century* (Toronto, 1988). • 166. T. N. Madan, 'The Double-Edged Sword: Fundamentalism and the Sikh Religious Tradition', in Marty and Appleby, eds., *Fundamentalisms Observed*, 617. • 167. Armstrong, *Battle for God*. • 168. Oberoi, 'From Ritual to Counter-Ritual', 149. • 169. Oberoi, 'Sikh Fundamentalism', 258, 280. • 170. Ruthven, 29. • 171. Fay Weldon, *Sacred Cows* (London, 1989), 6, 12; Conor Cruise O'Brien, *The Times*, 11 May 1989. • 172. Gellner, 81. • 173. Shruti Kapila and Faisal Devji, 'Introduction', in Kapila and Devji, eds., xii–xiv. • 174. C. A. Bayly, 'India, the *Bhagavad Gita* and the World', in Kapila and Devji, eds., 1–7. • 175. Immanuel Kant, *Grounding for the Metaphysics of Morals*, trans. Christine M. Korsgaard (Cambridge, 1998), 34. • 176. Laurie E. Patton, 'The Failure of Allegory: Notes on Textual Violence in the *Bhagavad Gita*', in Renard, ed., 184–86. • 177. Ibid., 186–88; Robert Minor, *Modern Indian Interpreters of the Bhagavad Gita* (New York, 1986), 11–34; Annie Besant, *Hints on the Study of the Bhagavad Gita* (Benares, 1906). • 178. Ghose, *Essays on the Gita*, 39; Jeffrey D. Long, 'Religion and Violence in Hindu Traditions', in Murphy, ed., *Blackwell Companion*, 204–08. • 179. *Bhagavad Gita* 2.37; trans. Barbara Stoler Miller. • 180. Ibid., 2.64; trans. Barbara Stoler Miller. • 181. Patton, 'Failure of Allegory', 191–94. • 182. Ibid., 195–96. • 183. For a detailed account of this, see my *Muhammad: A Biography of the Prophet* (San Francisco, 1992), 22–44. • 184. Stefan Wild, 'Political Interpretation of the Qur'ān', in McAuliffe, ed., *Cambridge Companion to the Qur'an*, 276–79; Saeed, 180–82. • 185. Wilfred Cantwell Smith, *Islam in Modern History*, 95. • 186. Daniel Crecelius, 'Non-Ideological Responses of the *Ulema* to Modernisation', in Keddie, ed., *Scholars, Saints and Sufis*, 54–58. • 187. Afsaruddin, *Contemporary Issues in Islam*, 57. • 188. Fazlur Rahman, 'The Living Sunnah and the al-Sunnah wa'l Jama'ah', in P. K. Koga, ed., *Hadith and Sunnah: Ideals and Realities – Selected Essays* (Kuala Lumpur, 1996), 136. • 189. Fazlur Rahman, *Islam and Modernity: Transformation of an Intellectual Tradition* (Chicago, 1982), 147. • 190. Ibid., 6–7. • 191. Al-Shafii, *Al Risala fi usul al-fiqh* (Cairo, 1940), 110. • 192. Saeed, 78. • 193. Rahman, *Islam*, 66. • 194. Afsaruddin, *Contemporary Issues*, 47–50. • 195. For example, Robert Piggott, 'Turkey in Radical Revision of Islamic Texts', BBC News, 26 February 2008. • 196. Quran 4.2–3; trans. Abdel-Haleem. • 197. Fazlur Rahman, *Major Themes of the Qur'an*, 2nd edn (Chicago, 1980, 2009), 95. • 198. Quran 4:127; trans. Abdel-Haleem. • 199. Rahman, *Major Themes*, 47–48. • 200. Ibid., 47. • 201. Quran 2:256; trans. Muhammad Asad, *The Message of the Qur'ān* (Gibraltar, 1980). • 202. Quran 2:108, 217; 47:25; 16:109. It becomes a capital offence only if combined with other crimes, such as treason or sedition. • 203. Jamal al-Banna, *Al-Awda ila l-qur'ān* ('Return to the Quran') (Cairo, 1984); Afsaruddin, *Contemporary Issues*, 43–53. • 204. Quran 16:102; trans. Abdel-Haleem.

• 205. Abdulaziz Sachedina, *The Islamic Roots of Democratic Pluralism* (Oxford, 2001); 'The Qur'*an* and Other Religions', in McAuliffe ed., *Cambridge Companion to the Qur'an*. • 206. Quran 5:48; trans. Asad, *Message of the Qur'ān*. • 207. Quran 2:62; trans. Abdel-Haleem. The Sabians were a monotheistic group in pre-Islamic Arabia. • 208 Quran 33:35; trans. Abdel-Haleem. • 209. Fatima Mernissi, *Women and Islam: An Historical and Theological Enquiry,* trans. Mary Jo Lakeland (Oxford, 1991), 115–31; Asma Barlas, *'Believing Women' in Islam: Unreading Patriarchal Interpretations of the Qur'ān* (Austin, 2002), 20. • 210. L. Marlow, *Hierarchy and Egalitarianism in Islamic Thought* (Cambridge, 1977), 93, 66; Leila Ahmed, *Women and Gender in Islam* (New Haven, 1992), 102–23. • 211. Quran 7:10–14; trans. Abdel-Haleem; Aziza al-Hibri, 'An Introduction to Women's Rights', in G. Webb, ed., *Windows of Faith: Muslim Women Scholar-Activists in North America* (Syracuse, 2000), 52–54. • 212. Amina Wadud, *Qur'ān and Women: Rereading the Sacred Text from a Woman's Perspective* (Oxford, 1999). • 213. Quran 16:74; trans. Abdel-Haleem; Barlas, *'Believing Women'*, 11. • 214. Quran 4:37; trans. Abdel-Haleem. • 215. Quran 4:23; trans. Abdel-Haleem. • 216. Quran 2:225–40; 65:1–70; trans. Abdel-Haleem. • 217. Quran 4:19; trans. Abdel-Haleem; Tabari, *Tafsir*, 9.235; Mernissi, *Women and Islam*, 131–32; Ahmed, *Women and Gender*, 53. • 218. Quran 2:282; trans. Abdel-Haleem. • 219. In the Quran, hijab does not mean 'veil', it is rather a 'curtain' functioning as a room-divider (Quran 33:53). • 220. Quran 24:30–31; trans. Abdel-Haleem. • 221. Quran 33:59; trans. Abdel-Haleem. • 222. Wadud, *'Believing Women'*, 57; author's emphasis. • 223. Quran 4:34; trans. Abdel-Haleem. • 224. Quran 4:128; trans. Abdel-Haleem; Afsaruddin, *Contemporary Issues*, 103. • 225. Muhammad ibn Sad, *Kitab at-Tabaqat al Kabir*, 8.205, in Mernissi, *Women and Islam*, 156–57. • 226. Afsaruddin, *Contemporary Issues*, 104. • 227. Quran 33:28–29; trans. Abdel-Haleem. • 228. Khaled Abou El Fadl, *Speaking in God's Name: Islamic Law, Authority and Women* (Oxford, 2001), 264. • 229. Abou El Fadl, *The Great Theft*, 95. • 230. Ibid., 97. • 231. Rahman, *Major Themes*, 31. • 232. Ibid., 100. • 233. Abdulkarim Soroush, *The Expansion of Prophetic Experience: Essays on Historicity, Contingency and Plurality in Religion*, trans. Nilou Mobasser (Leiden, 2009), xxxvii. • 234. Ibid. • 235. Ibn Ishaq, *Sirah Rasul Allah*, 151, in A. Guillaume, ed. and trans., *The Life of Muhammad from the Earliest Sources* (London, 1955), 105. • 236. Jalal al-Din Suyuti, *al-itqan fi'ulum al-aqran*, in Maxime Rodinson, *Mohammed*, trans. Anne Carter (London, 1971), 74. • 237. Bukhari 1.3, in Martin Lings, *Muhammad: His Life Based on the Earliest Sources* (London, 1983), 44–45. • 238. Mohammed Arkoun, 'The Notion of Revelation: From Ahl al-Kitab to the Societies of the Book', *Die Welt des Islams*, 28 (1988). • 239. Ibid. • 240. Saeed, 53–61. • 241. Karen Armstrong, *Fields of Blood: Religion and the History of Violence* (London, 2014). • 242. Khurshid Ahmad and Zafar Ushaq Ansari, *Islamic Perspectives* (Leicester, 1979), 378–81. • 243. Qutb, *Milestones*, 81. • 244. Burke, 32–35. • 245. Quran 9:73–74, 63.1–3; trans. Abdel-Haleem; Firestone, *Jihad*, 42–45. • 246. Bonner, 99–106. • 247. 'The Covenant of the Islamic Resistance Movement, Section 1', in Esposito, *Unholy War*, 96; David

Cook, *Understanding Jihad* (Berkeley, 2005), 116. • 248. Beverly Milton-Edwards, *Islamic Politics in Palestine* (London, 1996), 73–116, 118. • 249. 'Final Instructions to the Hijackers of September 11', Appendix A in Lincoln, 97–102. • 250. Ibid., paragraph 2; 97. • 251. Quran 8:26; trans. Abdel-Haleem. • 252. Quran 9:38; trans. Abdel-Haleem. • 253. 'Final Instructions', Section 14, in Lincoln. • 254. Quran 3:173; trans. Abdel-Haleem. • 255. 'Final Instructions', Section 23, in Lincoln, 100. • 256. 'Final Instructions', Sections 16, 29, in Lincoln, 101. • 257. 'Final Instructions', Section 34, in Lincoln, 102. • 258. Quran 4:74–76; trans. Abdel-Haleem. • 259. Quran 49:13; trans. Abdel-Haleem.

Post-Scripture

1. Sayyed Muhammad Naquib al-Attas, *Islam, Secularism and the Philosophy of the Future* (London, 1985), 138. • 2. Tibi, 73–78. • 3. Iqbal, 1682. • 4. Quran 28:71–73; trans. Abdel-Haleem. • 5. Quran 28:77; trans. Abdel-Haleem. • 6. Quran 24:35; trans. Abdel-Haleem. • 7. Quran 21:30; trans. Abdel-Haleem. • 8. Iqbal, 1689, 1691. • 9. Keith Moore, *The Developing Human: Clinically Oriented Embryology, with Islamic Additions*, 3rd edn (Jeddah, 1983). • 10. Quran 23:12–14; trans. Abdel-Haleem. • 11. Nelson, 99. • 12. 1 Corinthians 13:2–3. • 13. Augustine, *On Christian Teaching*, 3.10.16; trans. Carruthers, *Craft of Thought*, 16. • 14. North, *In the Shadow of Plenty*, xiii; *Sinai Strategy*, 213–14. • 15. At the time of writing, there are signs of an incipient reform in Saudi Arabia. • 16. Twitchell, 282. • 17. Smith and Denton, 164–65. • 18. McGilchrist. • 19. Gregory, 235–39. • 20. Ford. • 21. Buber, *On Judaism; On the Bible*. • 22. Martin Buber, *Biblical Humanism* (London, 1968), 214. • 23. Aphorism recast by Michael Fishbane, 'Martin Buber's Moses', in Fishbane, *Garments of Torah*, 97–98. • 24. Frei, 8. • 25. George Lindbeck, 'Toward a Post-Liberal Theology', in Ochs, ed., 83–100. • 26. Aquinas, *Summa Theologiae*, 1.1.10. • 27. Lindbeck, 'Toward a Post-Liberal Theology', 100. • 28. Mann, 'The Joseph Novels', 218–19; Mann's emphasis. • 29. The biblical narrative of this incident is confusing; it seems to be an amalgamation of two separate traditions, and the sequence of events is not clear. • 30. Mann, 'The Joseph Novels', 221. • 31. Campbell. • 32. Thomas Mann, 'The Making of *The Magic Mountain*', 719–29. • 33. Mann, 'The Joseph Novels', 229. • 34. Maven Niehoff, *The Figure of Joseph in Post-Biblical Jewish Literature* (Leiden, 1992), 78–80; Nolte, 95–97. • 35. Mann, *Joseph and His Brothers*, 281. • 36. Hartwich, 154. • 37. Ibid., 161; Nolte, 116–19. • 38. Hartwich, 160–61. • 39. Nolte, 68–69. • 40. Mann, *Joseph and His Brothers*, 287. • 41. Ibid., 285. • 42. Hartwich, 153. • 43. Mann, *Joseph and His Brothers*, 285. • 44. Ibid., 284. • 45. Genesis 50:15. • 46. Mann, *Joseph and His Brothers*, 1195. • 47. Ibid., 29. • 48. Hartwich, 166. • 49. Mann, *Joseph and His Brothers*, 1207. • 50. Judges 15:30. • 51. Grossman, 31. • 52. Ibid., 113. • 53. Ibid., 101. • 54. Ibid., 87. • 55. Ibid. • 56. Ibid., 88. • 57. Ibid., 89. • 58. Ibid., 142–43. •

59. The Hebrew is ambiguous here; it has been translated as 'after a few days' but it could mean 'after a certain period': and commentators have noted that it would take at least a year for a lion to decompose completely. • 60. Grossman, 54–55; author's emphasis. • 61. Ibid., 55. • 62. Ibid. • 63. Ibid., 60. • 64. Judges 14:14. • 65. Judges, 15:3–5. • 66. Grossman, 84–85. • 67. Elvin, *Another History*. • 68. Tu, 'The Ecological Turn'. • 69. *Doctrine of the Mean*, 26.9; trans. Chan, *Source Book*. • 70. Cited in Tu, 'The Ecological Turn', 497. • 71. Hermès Trismégiste, *Corpus Hermeticum,* 4 vols., ed. A. D. Nock and A. J. Festugière (Paris, 1954); Vol. 2: *Asclepius*, 24–26; trans. in Jan Assmann, '*Officium Memoriae*: Ritual as the Medium of Thought', in Assmann, *Religion and Cultural Memory*, 153.

INDEX

penguin.co.uk/vintage